FLORIDA REAL PROPERTY PRACTICE III

SECOND EDITION
(Includes September 1983 Supplement)

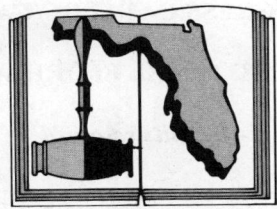

THE FLORIDA BAR
CONTINUING LEGAL EDUCATION

LIBRARY OF CONGRESS CATALOG CARD NO. 72-156745

©1976, 1983 by THE FLORIDA BAR

All rights reserved

Second Printing February 1979

Third Printing October 1983
(includes September 1983 Supplement)

CONTINUING LEGAL EDUCATION COMMITTEE
1975–1976

Thomas L. Wolfe, Chairman
Robin Gibson, Vice Chairman
A. Obie Stewart, Vice Chairman
Ruth Fleet Thurman, Vice Chairman

Robert P. Barnett
Robert B. Bratzel
Daniel N. Burton
Albert G. Caruana
Laurence I. Goodrich
William O. E. Henry
J. Reid Heuer
Carl M. Kuttler, Jr.
Parker Lee McDonald

David L. Middlebrooks
E. R. Mills, Jr.
H. Edward Moore, Jr.
Stephen A. Rappenecker
Christian D. Searcy
William E. Sherman
Larry S. Stewart
Sidney A. Stubbs, Jr.
Council Wooten, Jr.

Representative Members

Dean Richard T. Dillon
Dean Lawrence M. Hyde, Jr.
Dean Joseph R. Julin
Dean Soia Mentschikoff
Dean Joshua M. Morse III

STEERING COMMITTEE

Henry P. Trawick, Jr., Chairman
William C. Andrews
Robert Barnett
John H. Cotten
Edward J. Kohrs
Robert E. Livingston
Robert L. Rowe, Jr.
Edmund P. Russo

FORMS ADVISER

Henry P. Trawick, Jr.

CONTINUING LEGAL EDUCATION STAFF

Sylvan Strickland, Director
Preston W. DeMilly, Associate Director For Publications
John N. Hogenmuller, Associate Director For Programs

PREFACE

This is another in a continuing series of practice manuals designed to aid Florida lawyers to practice more efficiently and effectively.

This manual, like its predecessors, is the product of teamwork among the Continuing Legal Education Committee, the steering committee for the course, the authors and the editors. The Florida Bar is indebted to the authors and committee members for their donations of time and talent to the project. However, The Florida Bar does not have an official view of the contents of this manual. Like other legal publications, it is the work product of the individuals who contributed to it, and The Florida Bar joins them in the confident hope that it will fulfill its purpose of professional and public service.

        Sylvan Strickland
        Director of Continuing Legal Education
        February 1976

Through the efforts of the Continuing Legal Education Committee, the steering committee, the authors and editors this manual is supplemented to September 1983. The supplement updates and expands the 1976 edition.

        Preston W. DeMilly, Director
        Continuing Legal Education Publications
        September 1983

TABLE OF CONTENTS

CHAPTER	Page
1. **Quieting Title** S. Austin Peele and Rollin D. Davis, Jr.	1
2. **Boundary Litigation** Edward J. Kohrs and Robert G. Cochran	31
3. **Ejectment** Roger H. Staley	49
4. **Partition** W. J. Oven, Jr.	75
5. **Mortgage Foreclosures** James F. Durham II and Henry H. Fox	97
6. **Mechanic's Lien Foreclosures** Joseph B. Reisman	157
7. **Reformation, Rescission And Cancellation Of Instruments** Gene Essner and Lewis Kanner	191
8. **Reestablishing Lost Instruments** Robert P. Barnett	215
9. **Breach Of Sale Contract** Sheldon Rosenberg	231
10. **Breach Of Construction Contracts And Loan Agreements** William L. Stewart and Alan T. Dimond	249
11. **Removal Of Restrictive Covenants** Edward A. Linney and James I. Knudson	261
12. **Access To Property By Nonowner** A. Gordon Patton	291
13. **Zoning** H. David Faust	307
14. **Slander Of Title** J. Tracy Baxter, Jr.	337
15. **Landlord And Tenant** Winifred J. Sharp and Robert D. Gatton	349

INDEXES

Florida Statutes 351

Rules of Civil Procedure 358

Cases 359

Subjects 374

The September 1983 Supplement appears at the end of this volume.

S. AUSTIN PEELE*†
ROLLIN D. DAVIS, JR.**

1

QUIETING TITLE

I. PRELIMINARY CONSIDERATIONS

    A. [§1.1] Initial Contact With Client

    B. [§1.2] Investigation

    C. Alternatives In Determining The Type Of Action

        1. [§1.3] In General

        2. [§1.4] Comparison With Ejectment

        3. [§1.5] Comparison With Partition

        4. [§1.6] Declaratory Action Distinguished

        5. [§1.7] Nonjudicial Remedies

    D. Types Of Quieting Title Actions

        1. [§1.8] The Significance of *F.S.* 65.011 And 65.021−.051

---

*J.D., 1963, University of Florida. Mr. Peele is a member of the Lake City, Third Circuit and American bar associations and is a partner in the firm of Jopling, Darby, Peele & Page. He practices in Lake City.

**LL.B., 1956, University of Florida. Mr. Davis is a member of the American and Escambia-Santa Rosa bar associations and is a partner in the firm of Shell, Fleming, Davis & Menge. He practices in Pensacola.

†Mr. John W. Prunty and Mr. Michael C. Slotnick were the authors of this chapter in the first edition.

2. [§1.9] The 1925 Act As Amended; The Quasi In Rem Procedure

3. [§1.10] Inchoate Dower; Conveyance As A Single Man; 30-Year Separation

4. Tax Titles

    a. [§1.11] In General

    b. [§1.12] The Complaint

    c. [§1.13] Final Judgment

E. [§1.14] Determination Of Parties

II. JURISDICTION

A. [§1.15] In Rem Proceedings

B. Constructive Service Of Process

1. [§1.16] In General

2. [§1.17] Making Diligent Search And Inquiry

3. [§1.18] Sample Affidavit For Constructive Service

4. [§1.19] Service Under *F.S.* 48.193 And 48.194

III. THE COMPLAINT

A. [§1.20] In General

B. Drafting The Complaint

1. [§1.21] In General

2. [§1.22] Sample Complaint

IV. [§1.23] GUARDIAN AD LITEM

V. ATTORNEY AD LITEM

A. [§1.24] In General

B. [§1.25] Sample Motion To Appoint Attorney Ad Litem

  C. [§1.26] Sample Order Appointing Attorney Ad Litem

VI. PROOF

  A. [§1.27] In General

  B. [§1.28] Diligent Search And Inquiry

  C. [§1.29] Default Against Defendants

  D. [§1.30] Statutes Of Limitation And Curative Statutes

  E. [§1.31] Marketable Record Title Act

  F. [§1.32] Adverse Possession

VII. [§1.33] DEFENSES

VIII. [§1.34] SAMPLE FINAL JUDGMENT

I. PRELIMINARY CONSIDERATIONS

A. [§1.1] Initial Contact With Client

Often an attorney becomes involved with a serious title problem before the necessity of a quiet title action becomes apparent. Later he finds himself undertaking the matter, considering his employment as an unwelcome by-product of his otherwise not unenjoyable real property practice. Regardless of whether the attorney drifts into the litigation in that manner or the client has already received advice from another examiner and is certain of the need of a quiet title action at the time of first contact, it is extremely important that the attorney educate his client at an early time as to the possible extent and cost of his services.

If the action is against known living defendants upon whom process can be obtained easily, or the defendants are such that it is clear that there is no possibility of acquiring any information about them, the attorney is in a position to make as accurate an estimate of the time involved as he could in any other litigation. In the classic quiet title situation the attorney is not so fortunate and has no idea of how many leads he must exhaust before he can execute honestly the affidavit of diligent search and inquiry. The client should be made aware of this uncertainty, not only because of the cost factor involved but also because of the delay that may be necessary before consummation of the proceedings. It is well for the attorney to point out to the client that no corners should be cut because the work product of the attorney is almost certain to undergo the close scrutiny of future title examiners.

It is not unusual for the attorney for the proposed lender or buyer to receive a request to quiet the title of the problem that that attorney has raised. In addition to the ethical considerations involved, the attorney faces a possibility that his client will complain loudly for years of how the attorney raised a frivolous objection to title in order to extract a fee for his services in providing the cure of the alleged defect. Care should be taken to avoid such a situation, realizing that it is more likely to arise if the proposed client is unsophisticated in real property matters.

The scope of this chapter properly does not include a full discussion of the ethical considerations encountered by an attorney for the lender or buyer who is requested to conduct curative proceedings at the expense of the seller, but it is suggested that full disclosure to and consent by all affected parties should be obtained at the outset.

B. [§1.2] Investigation

It is important that an attorney involved in a quiet title action obtain complete title information concerning the history of the title in question. This advice would appear superfluous, but title examiners often find a fatal title defect existing before a quiet title final judgment that could have been solved in that action. The situation arises because the client has handed his attorney a title opinion or title binder pointing out a specific defect with the instructions that that defect be removed as expeditiously as possible. The dutiful attorney then suffers much embarrassment when a second quiet title action is commenced on the same property.

Depending upon the situation involved, a survey of the property and a personal view of the premises may be necessary. Some quiet title actions arise from survey problems and therefore the extent and accuracy of the survey information is most important.

While determining the defects that the quiet title action should cure, the attorney also should immediately ascertain the availability and strength of evidence of adverse possession by the current title claimant and his predecessors in title. Adverse possession is the ground upon which relief usually is based, and from the inception the attorney should be looking for proof of acts of possession.

Most of the time spent in preparation of the papers in a quiet title action is spent on the diligent search and inquiry. It will be fully discussed later in this chapter.

C. Alternatives In Determining The Type Of Action

1. [§1.3] In General

Actions to quiet title or remove clouds have as their purpose the curing and perfecting of legal title to real property. Quiet title actions have a statutory basis in *F.S.* Chapter 65 and actions within that chapter fall within two major classifications:

1. Quasi in rem actions to quiet title.

2. Actions to quiet tax titles.

An action to quiet title constitutes an equitable remedy and falls within the jurisdiction of the circuit courts. *F.S.* 26.012. There also is nonstatutory chancery jurisdiction. See §1.8. In addition there are alternative actions that similarly settle questions regarding title and possession of real property.

2. [§1.4] Comparison With Ejectment

At times, quiet title actions may be concurrent with the action of ejectment. This creates a certain problem, since the parties in an ejectment action are entitled to a trial by jury, while ordinarily jury trials are not available for equitable remedies. See FLORIDA CIVIL TRIAL PRACTICE §23.5 (CLE 2d ed. 1970). But see below.

Ejectment is a possessory action, and although it frequently becomes a means of trying title, the gravamen of the action is the recovery of *possession* of real property. Consequently, the plaintiff must be the party out of possession with an immediate right to possession and the defendant must be the party in possession. See *F.S.* Chapter 66.

If the defendant is not in possession of the premises, there is no conflict between the quiet title action and the action of ejectment. In such a situation a vital element of the ejectment action is missing; however, if a plaintiff desires to remove a cloud on title or to quiet title and the defendant *is* in possession, the requisites of a common-law action of ejectment are present. Indeed, the quiet title statutes provide that when it appears that the defendant is in actual possession, a jury trial may be demanded by either party and the court must cause an issue in ejectment to be made up and tried by a jury. See *F.S.* 65.061(1) and .081(2).

3. [§1.5] Comparison With Partition

Partition, as governed by *F.S.* Chapter 64, is an action by which co-owners of property either cause it to be divided in kind into as many shares as there are owners, according to their proportionate interests, or, if this cannot be equitably accomplished, to be sold for the best obtainable price and the proceeds from the sale distributed among the parties. Thus, although an action for partition may be quasi in rem in nature just as an action to quiet title may be, and a judgment in an action for partition necessarily settles who has legal title and the right of possession in property, the nature of the parties to an action for partition must be that of co-owners in order for partition to be the proper equitable remedy.

4. [§1.6] Declaratory Action Distinguished

The following excerpt from *Stark v. Frayer*, 67 So.2d 237 (Fla. 1953) distinguishes between an action under the declaratory judgment statutes, presently *F.S.* Chapter 86, and other types of civil procedure:

> The complaint shows that the subject matter of the suit is a claimed dispossession of a strip of land owned by the original plaintiffs occasioned by the possession of the strip by the original defendants. . . . Therefore, it is apparent that the real purpose of the complaint was an attempt to litigate a boundary line dispute under the declaratory judgment statute, F.S.A. §87.01 et seq., when a suit in ejectment was the appropriate remedy. This is not allowable. As the matter is stated in Bowden v. Seaboard Air Line R. Co., Fla., 47 So.2d 786, 787, a suit involving a similar issue, ". . . we cannot permit an unauthorized extension of the Declaratory Decree Statute to a point where it might be substituted for another normally appropriate action in the absence of a bona fide foundation for a declaratory decree as contemplated by Sec. 87, Florida Statutes, 1941, F.S.A. . . . Although our Declaratory Decree Act is broad in its scope and should be liberally construed in order to effectuate its purpose, it was never intended that it should supplant all other types of civil procedure known to our jurisprudence. . . ." See also Coral Gates Properties, Inc. v. Hodes, Fla., 59 So.2d 630, and compare Doggett v. Hart, 5 Fla. 215. This reasoning is not applicable, of course, when the facts are such that ejectment will not lie, as in the case of a suit by one occupying land under a purported agreement of "boundary by acquiescenc." Shaw v. Williams, Fla., 50 So.2d 125, 126.

For further discussion of a boundary dispute being properly settled by an ejectment action see Chapter 2 of this manual and *Giovannielli v. Lacedonia*, 177 So.2d 506 (3d D.C.A. Fla. 1965). See, however, *State Board of Trustees of Internal Improvement Trust Fund v. Pineta Company*, 287 So.2d 126 (3d D.C.A. Fla. 1973), which appears to recognize that an action for declaratory relief and quit title may be brought as between adjoining owners to determine the location of a common boundary line.

For a discussion of the problem of pursuing a declaratory judgment when there is no doubt as to the meaning of a written instrument, with the issue being one of fact as to whether one of the parties falls within the terms of the instrument, see *Lambert v. Justus*, 313 So.2d 140 (2d D.C.A. Fla. 1975).

5. [§1.7] Nonjudicial Remedies

Since quiet title actions are concerned with the curing or removing of defects or clouds on title, litigation can be avoided or reduced in many instances by negotiation. An attempt always should be made to obtain quitclaim deeds or releases from known parties who claim to have some adverse interest against the property. This applies also to those whom the record may indicate have such an interest. Even if there are a multitude of possible adverse claimants, it is desirable to obtain as many quitclaim deeds as possible in order to limit the number of named defendants who must be included and served in the quiet title action.

As a practical matter, there may be less opportunity for error in obtaining quitclaim deeds or releases from possible claimants than in bringing action against them. Many quiet title actions fail to achieve their purpose because of defects in the pleadings and procedure, such as insufficient service of process, improper entry of a default judgment, failure to name a claimant or error in drafting the allegations of the complaint or of the final judgment.

When considering nonjudicial remedies, the attorney should review the possibility of obtaining title insurance against certain defects and decide whether curative statutes may be relied upon to eliminate objections to title. In the usual situation in which a quiet title action is considered, the client is involved in either a sale or mortgage of the property and the buyer or mortgagee's attorney may agree to accept title insurance or rely upon the curative acts in lieu of a quiet title action. These possibilities should be fully investigated before determining that a quiet title action should be brought.

D. Types Of Quieting Title Actions

1. [§1.8] The Significance of *F.S.* 65.011 And 65.021–.051

F.S. 65.011, adopted in 1889, does little more than give statutory recognition to the power of a court of equity to entertain actions for the purpose of determining title, quieting it in the rightful owner and granting incidental relief.

F.S. 65.021–.051 provide for removing clouds from titles in proceedings that may be brought by any person or corporation, whether or not in actual possession, that claims legal or equitable title to real estate against any person or corporation not in actual possession that either has or appears to have or claim an adverse legal or equitable estate, interest or claim in that real estate. Relief may be granted even though the title has not been litigated at law or there is only one litigant to each side of the controversy. Relief also is provided when the adverse claim, estate or interest is void upon its face or, though not void on its face, requires evidence extrinsic of the claim itself to establish its validity. 65.021. An action could be brought in the name of the owner or of any prior owner who may have warranted the title involved. 65.031.

2. [§1.9] The 1925 Act As Amended; The Quasi In Rem Procedure

F.S. 65.061, adopted in 1925, provides for the quasi in rem procedure for quieting titles. The Florida Supreme Court in *McDaniel v. McElvy*, 91 Fla. 770, 108 So. 820 (1926), 51 A.L.R. 731 noted that this act enlarged and extended the equitable rights of persons claiming the title to real property and the procedure by which those rights might be adjudicated; however, the court said that neither the rights of parties nor the method of procedure was essentially changed in character and, in certain respects, the procedure afforded by the act did not depart from what legitimately belonged to the practice of a court of chancery.

The grounds for this additional remedy of quieting title are stated in *F.S.* 65.061(2):

> When a person or corporation not the rightful owner of land has any conveyance or other evidence of title thereto, or asserts any claim, or pretends to have any right or title thereto, which may cast a cloud on the title of the real owner, or when any person or corporation is the true and equitable owner of land the record title to which is not in the person or corporation because of the defective execution of any deed or mortgage because of the omission of a seal thereon, the lack of witnesses, or any defect or omission in the wording of the acknowledgment of a party or parties thereto, when the person or corporation claims title thereto by the defective instrument and the defective instrument was apparently made and delivered by the grantor to convey or mortgage

the real estate and was recorded in the county where the land lies, or when possession of the land has been held by any person or corporation adverse to the record owner thereof or his heirs and assigns until such adverse possession has ripened into a good title under the statutes of this state, such person or corporation may file complaint in any county in which any part of the land is situated to have the conveyance or other evidence of claim or title canceled and the cloud removed from the title and to have his title quieted, whether such real owner is in possession or not or is threatened to be disturbed in his possession or not, and whether defendant is a resident of this state or not, and whether the title has been litigated at law or not, and whether the adverse claim or title or interest is void on its face or not, or if not void on its face that it may require extrinsic evidence to establish its validity. A guardian ad litem shall not be appointed unless it shall affirmatively appear that the interest of minors, persons of unsound mind, or convicts are involved.

Unlike the earlier statutes pertaining to removing clouds, which, in effect, provide for ejectment when the defendant is in possession, under *F.S.* 65.061(1) it is not necessary that the defendants be out of possession. This statute, however, does provide for a jury trial on an issue in ejectment when the defendant is in the actual possession of any part of the land involved in the quiet title action.

In general, the statute provides for an action against known defendants to quiet title against a cloud of a known or an unknown nature, and against unknown defendants to quiet title against a cloud of a known nature. But it does not apply to remove a cloud, the nature and existence of which is wholly unknown, against defendants who also are wholly unknown. *Mainor v. Hobbie,* 218 So.2d 203 (1st D.C.A. Fla. 1969), *app. dism.* 225 So.2d 530.

This type of proceeding to quiet title will be discussed in more detail in §§1.20 and .21.

3. [§1.10] Inchoate Dower; Conveyance As
A Single Man; 30-Year Separation

In addition to the statutes mentioned above, *F.S.* 65.071 provides a method for quieting titles as to deeds made without the joinder of a wife if the husband and wife have been separated for 30 years or more. This would be a cloud only when the spouse died before October 1, 1973 because FLA. LAWS 1973, ch. 73-107 abolished the right of dower in property transferred before death, effective October 1, 1973.

4. Tax Titles

a. [§1.11] In General

F.S. 65.081 provides for the quieting of tax titles. It applies to any grantee under a tax deed issued by the state, a municipality or other political subdivision or any purchaser of land that had been acquired by the state, municipality or political subdivision through foreclosure for nonpayment of taxes or of a special assessment. It permits those persons to maintain an action for the purpose of quieting the title against the holders of the record title to the property. It also provides for those actions against any other person or corporation claiming any interest in or any lien or encumbrance on the land before the issuance of the tax deed or before the loss of title to the lands in any tax proceeding or foreclosure.

Actions to quiet tax titles may be maintained whether or not the plaintiff is in possession of the lands; however, when the defendant is in actual possession a jury trial may be had.

The statute providing for the quieting of tax titles was upheld as constitutional by the Florida Supreme Court in *Beebe v. Richardson*, 156 Fla. 559, 23 So.2d 718 (1945). Since tax deeds are not acceptabe universally to title examiners, the desirability of an action to quiet the tax title is apparent.

b. [§1.12] The Complaint

In an action to quiet a tax title, the complaint need not deraign title beyond the issuance of the tax deed or the conveyance by a governmental entity of land acquired by it through a foreclosure or other proceeding for the nonpayment of taxes. *F.S.* 65.081. "Beyond" as used in the statute may not be construed to require deraignment of title before issuance of the deed. *Markley v. Madill*, 259 So.2d 723 (2d D.C.A. Fla. 1972).

In *Suddath v. Hutchison*, 42 So.2d 355 (Fla. 1949), a complaint was held sufficient that set out the claim of the plaintiff and supported it by a copy of the tax deed that was in the required statutory form;

alleged the holder of the tax deed to be in the actual, open and exclusive possession of all of the property described in the deed; and asked that the title be quieted and confirmed against the defendants, whose claims or interests in the land appeared to have been acquired before the issuance of the tax deed. It should be noted, however, that it is not necessary that the plaintiff be in possession; the plaintiff may bring an action even though the defendant is in actual possession, although the defendant in such a case may demand a jury trial.

c. [§1.13] Final Judgment

The Florida Statutes do not provide specifically for the contents of a final judgment quieting a tax title. It appears that the final judgment quieting a tax title should be similar in language to that entered under the quasi in rem type of proceeding. See §1.34.

E. [§1.14] Determination Of Parties

Probably the most important caveat in an action to quiet title is to assure that all persons having any possible adverse claims whatsoever against the property are named as defendants. A quiet title action serves little purpose unless it actually does clear title. If the plaintiff omits a party, then he most likely will have to bring another quiet title action the next time the abstract of title is examined.

II. JURISDICTION

A. [§1.15] In Rem Proceedings

In *Key v. All Persons Claiming Any Estate, Etc.,* 160 Fla. 723, 36 So.2d 366 (1948), a decision based on a statute that was later repealed, it was held that former *F.S.* 66.28–.47 was unconstitutional in that an action against unknown defendants to remove unknown clouds is ineffective for lack of process.

B. Constructive Service Of Process

1. [§1.16] In General

Constructive service of process in Florida has its foundation in the provisions of *F.S.* Chapter 49. Constructive service provisions of Chapter 65 have been eliminated by amendment. Constructive service of process frequently is referred to as service by publication.

With respect to a quasi in rem action to quiet title or remove a cloud, the statutes authorize the use of the constructive service provisions in any proceeding brought: "[t]o quiet title or remove any encumbrance, lien or cloud on the title to any real or personal property within the jurisdiction of the court or any fund held or debt owing by any party on whom process can be served within this state." *F.S.* 49.011(2). Constructive service is authorized by 49.021 against any of the following persons:

(1) Any known or unknown natural person, and, when described as such, the unknown spouse, heirs, devisees, grantees, creditors or other parties claiming by, through, under or against any known or unknown person who is known to be dead or is not known to be either dead or alive;

(2) Any corporation or other legal entity, whether its domicile be foreign, domestic or unknown, and whether dissolved or existing, including corporations or other legal entities not known to be dissolved or existing, and, when described as such, the unknown assigns, successors in interest, trustees, or any other party claiming by, through, under or against any named corporation or legal entity;

(3) Any group, firm, entity or persons who operate or do business, or have operated or done business, in this state, under a name or title which includes the word "corporation," "company," "incorporated," "inc." or any combination thereof, or under a name or title which indicates, tends to indicate or leads one to think that the same may be a corporation or other legal entity; and,

(4) All claimants under any of such parties.

Unknown parties may be proceeded against exclusively or together with other parties.

A comprehensive discussion of Florida's body of law covering constructive service appears in Kooman, *Constructive Service in Florida,* 9 U.FLA.L.REV. 1 (1956). Constructive service of process is discussed also in FLORIDA CIVIL PRACTICE BEFORE TRIAL §§14.10–.19 (CLE 3d ed. 1975). Attention is directed to the discussion included in those publications relating to notice of action being directed to the defendant. See also *F.S.* 49.08–.12.

2. [§1.17] Making Diligent Search And Inquiry

As indicated in the affidavit set out in §1.18, a condition precedent to the use of constructive service is a diligent (but unsuccessful) search and inquiry to locate the defendant so that personal service might be achieved. See *F.S.* 48.041–.061.

The making of diligent search and inquiry as to the whereabouts of a defendant is a matter too often taken lightly. The wise attorney will not accept the client's statements to the effect that "I have not seen or heard from Aunt Mary for years," or "Cousin John and his wife separated years ago and she has not been heard from since." Rare is the individual who can lose himself without a trace, and a little pursuit of the matter by the attorney with the client as to the names and addresses of known relatives or parties often will produce much information about how to locate those supposed to be missing. Ordinarily it does not take the skill of a Pinkerton Agency man to accomplish the task.

When the legitimate purpose and nature of the inquiry are disclosed, much valuable information can be obtained through the bureaus of personnel of the various branches of the military service, the various bureaus of vital statistics of the departments of health of the several states, the Veterans Administration and through the Social Security Administration. In many instances, former employers know the present whereabouts of individuals. The tax receipt book maintained by the tax collector should be examined before resorting to constructive service by publication. *Gmaz v. King,* 238 So.2d 511 (2d D.C.A. Fla. 1970). At any rate, no statement of diligent search and inquiry should be made too casually, for the appearance of a defendant thought to be lost can be rather embarrassing, especially if his name and a complete listing for him appear in the local telephone or city directory. See *Sheffield v. Carter,* 141 So.2d 780 (2d D.C.A. Fla. 1962).

3. [§1.18] Sample Affidavit For Constructive Service

(Title of Court)

(Title of Cause)   **AFFIDAVIT**

Before me, the undersigned authority, personally appeared M. N., who was sworn and said:

1. He is attorney for the plaintiff, A. B., in this action.

2. Diligent search and inquiry have been made to discover the names and residences of defendants C. D. and E. F., and they are set forth as particularly as are known to the affiant; the age of each of them is over 21 years; and the residence of each of them is unknown.

3. The affiant does not know and has not been able to ascertain by diligent search and inquiry whether defendant E. F. is dead or alive.

4. The affiant believes that there are persons who are or may be interested in the subject matter of this action whose names and residences, after diligent search and inquiry, are unknown to the affiant, and who claim as spouses, heirs, devisees or grantees of or otherwise by, through, under or against E. F., who is not known to be dead or alive, and G. H., who is known to be dead, respectively.

M. N.

Sworn to and subscribed before me
this .... day of ....

Notary Public

COMMENT: Although the statute (F.S. 49.031) provides that the affidavit may be by the plaintiff, his agent or attorney, many attorneys prefer to have the affidavit signed by the plaintiff. F.S. 49.041 describes the contents of the above notice for a natural person. For corporations see 49.051 and for parties doing business under a corporate name see 49.061.

4. [§1.19] Service Under F.S. 48.193 And 48.194

F.S. 48.193 and .194 authorize service of process on persons outside the state in certain instances. Although 48.193(1)(c) authorizes this kind of service on a defendant who "owns, uses or possesses any real property" in Florida, it is not clear whether this would apply to an action to quiet title because it is alleged that the plaintiff is the true "owner" and that the defendant does not "own" the property; thus, the complaint would not be "for any cause of action arising from the doing of" the acts specified in 48.193(1)(c); 49.021, however, states that constructive service is available only if personal service cannot be obtained. Service under 48.193 and .194 should not be attempted. Service by publication should be used.

III. THE COMPLAINT

A. [§1.20] In General

The usual quiet title action is the one brought pursuant to *F.S.* 65.061. A very extensive treatment and analysis of that act is contained in *McDaniel v. McElvy,* 91 Fla. 770, 108 So. 820 (1926), 51 A.L.R. 731. In that decision the court characterized those proceedings as follows:

> . . . Suits of this nature are not technically suits in rem, nor are they strictly speaking in personam, but, being against the person in respect of the res, wherein the decree does not extend beyond the property in controversy, these proceedings acquire a status that may be characterized as suits quasi in rem. . . .

The complaint must state the names and places of residence of all persons interested in the land, as far as known to the complainant or he can ascertain by diligent search and inquiry. If the name of persons interested or the places of residences are unknown and have not been ascertained, after diligent inquiry, the complaint must so state and be sworn. Strict compliance with the constructive service statute, *F.S.* Chapter 49, is required. If the names and places of residence of persons in interest are given, they must be made parties defendant.

It might be well to emphasize at this point that in all cases when either the place of residence of a named defendant is unknown or it is unknown whether a named defendant is dead or alive, the verified complaint should state those facts and include allegations adding the heirs, devisees, legatees and grantees of the named defendants and also anyone claiming by, through and under the named defendants unless a separate affidavit is used. If an affidavit of diligent search and inquiry is used for the purpose of obtaining constructive service, the affidavit should specify such persons as the heirs or devisees of the named defendants. See §1.18. The plaintiff may not properly publish notice against the heirs and other persons claiming under the named defendant unless the sworn complaint or affidavit includes those persons. Further, if "address" is used instead of the statutory language "residence," no jurisdiction is obtained over a natural person and a judgment will be void. *Wilmott v. Wilmott,* 119 So.2d 54 (1st D.C.A. Fla. 1960). In addition, if the heirs or devisees are not mentioned and the places of residence of named defendants are unknown, or the named defendants are not known to be dead or alive, the quiet title action is defective and does not foreclose all known interests. Consequently, a new quiet title action against the heirs and persons claiming under the named defendant may be necessary.

The plaintiff's complaint must set forth his claim of title and under *F.S.* 65.061(3) the plaintiff must deraign his title from the original source or for a period of at least seven years prior to the filing of a complaint, unless the court directs otherwise or unless he claims from a common source with the defendant. The plaintiff also must set forth the book and page of those records when any instrument affecting the title is recorded.

The complaint also must show that the plaintiff seeks the relief embraced within one of the three general situations mentioned in this procedure. See *F.S.* 65.061(2). This necessitates an appropriate allegation pertaining to the title or claim of the defendant. In *McDaniel v. McElvy, supra,* the Florida Supreme Court discussed the necessary allegations under each one of the general situations as follows:

> . . . Thus, if the suit is brought to remove a particular cloud, the facts which show the existence — actual, apparent, or potential — of that cloud are essential parts of the complainant's cause of action, and must be alleged. . . . The same observation applies to a suit brought under this act to quiet a title against a defect in the execution of a deed or mortgage under which complainant claims. If the suit is to quiet and establish a title by adverse possession against the existing record title, the facts which show the existence of the record title must be alleged. If the suit is brought to quiet and establish a title as against an unknown cloud, as for instance where a deed under which the complainant claims was executed by a grantor without mention as to his or her celibacy, and there is no joinder of husband or wife, or where a deed in complainant's chain of title is executed by persons asserting themselves to be heirs of a former record owner out of whom there is no conveyance, and the complainant is uncertain whether the former owner is dead, and, if so, whether such grantors are in fact the heirs, or all the heirs, of such former owner of the record title, then the facts which show the apparent existence of a potential cloud should be alleged. . . .

A notice of lis pends should be filed at the time the complaint is filed. See *RCP* Form 1.918 for a form for a notice of lis pendens. See also *Stark v. Frayer,* 67 So.2d 237 (Fla. 1953); *Woodruff v. Taylor,* 118 So.2d 822 (2d D.C.A. Fla. 1960).

When the action to quiet title results from disapproval of the title by an attorney for a person with whom the plaintiff intends to deal, it is helpful to furnish copies of the complaint and other papers for that attorney's approval before filing them.

B. Drafting The Complaint

1. [§1.21] In General

The complaint should allege that the plaintiff is the owner of the land and describe it. The description need not be typed again in the complaint but can be referred to by paragraph number in other allegations if appropriate. It is unnecessary to type the description again in the demand for judgment. Greater particularity is required in the description of land in complaints and judgments than in deeds. See *Brown v. Sohn,* 276 So.2d 501 (1st D.C.A. Fla. 1973).

If one of the clouds is an error in the description in the plaintiff's deed, the drafter should allege the plaintiff's ownership by the accurate description and allege the defective description in a separate paragraph.

Efficiency suggests that deraignment not be carried back further than seven years or to the most recent deed concerning which there is no question or to the most recent unquestioned deed that was recorded before the oldest cloud, whichever is further back in time. Unless required by an issue or a cloud, deraigning title to the original source wastes the time of the secretary, the lawyer and the judge, and wastes paper as well. Many pleaders include an allegation as to the original patent or grant by the United States of America or the State of Florida to show affirmatively that the sovereign has divested the title. Also, if the plaintiff is relying partly upon the Marketable Records Title Act (*F.S.* Chapter 712) to establish clear title, or upon any other curative statute deraignment should be back at least as far as the instrument of record from which the particular curative statute will commence running.

It is suggested that the allegation of adverse possession in paragraph 7 of the sample complaint in §1.22 is sufficient, using the pertinent language of *F.S.* 95.16 together with the phrase "adverse to defendants" suggested by 65.061(2).

The requirement of former *F.S.* 66.18 that the complaint be sworn to is not contained in *F.S.* Chapter 65. The statement in the affidavit for constructive service may be alleged in the complaint instead, at the option of the plaintiff, and if that is done the complaint must be verified. 49.031(1).

In the complaint the category of defendants described as all parties having or "claiming to have any right, title or interest in the lands hereafter described" accomplishes the function of including as defendants the unknown heirs of an unknown party claiming under a known party or person (E. F. or G. H.) if an unknown heir has died; for example, if an unknown son of E. F., deceased, survived E. F. and died before the complaint was filed leaving several heirs, perhaps the quoted clause was intended to include the son's heirs as parties and to acquire jurisdiction over them. The quoted clause was based on *F.S.* 49.08(1). But the effect of the judgment cannot be broader than to remove the clouds alleged in the complaint because a judgment against unknown parties purporting to remove unknown clouds would be a denial of due process. See §1.15 for the holding in *Key v. All Persons Claiming Any Estate, Etc.,* 160 Fla. 723, 36 So.2d 366 (1948) based on a statute that was later repealed.

The quoted clause therefore should not be used if all parties are known, and are known to be alive. In an action against a known defendant who is known to be alive, including as defendants all parties having or "claiming to have any right, title or interest in the lands hereafter described" presumably would accomplish nothing since obviously an unrecorded nonpossessory cloud is not a cloud at all in that instance.

2. [§1.22] Sample Complaint

(Title of Court)

(Title of Cause)   COMPLAINT

Plaintiff, A. B., sues defendants, C. D.; E. F., if alive, and if dead his unknown spouse, heirs, devisees, grantees, creditors and all other parties claiming by, through, under or against him; the unknown spouse, heirs, devisees, grantees and creditors of G. H., deceased, and all other parties claiming by, through, under or against him; and all unknown natural persons if alive, and if dead or not known to be dead or alive, their several and respective unknown spouse, heirs, devisees, grantees and creditors, or other parties claiming by, through or under those unknown natural persons; and, the several and respective unknown assigns, successors in interest, trustees or any other person claiming by, through, under or against any corporation or other legal entity named as a defendant; and all claimants, persons or parties, natural or corporate, or whose exact legal status is unknown, claiming under any of the above named or described defendants or parties or claiming to have any right, title or interest in and to the lands hereafter described, and alleges:

1. This is an action to quiet and confirm title of plaintiff in and to lands located in Lemon County, Florida.

2. Plaintiff owns the following-described property in Lemon County, Florida:

[legal description]

3. Plaintiff deraigns his title as follows:

a. I. J. conveyed the land to defendant E. F. by warranty deed dated November 10, 1940, recorded December 15, 1940 in Deed Book JJ, page 384, of the public records of Lemon County.

b. Defendant E. F. conveyed or attempted to convey the land to G. H. by warranty deed dated January 16, 1943, recorded January 19, 1943 in Deed Book MM, page 146, of the public records of Lemon County.

c. G. H. conveyed or attempted to convey the land to defendant C. D. by warranty deed dated January 7, 1947, recorded January 8, 1947 in Deed Book VV, page 455, of the public records of Lemon County.

d. The State of Florida by tax deed dated March 31, 1952, recorded April 12, 1952 in Deed Book No. 1, page 187, of the public records of Lemon County, conveyed or attempted to convey the land to K. L.

e. K. L. conveyed the land to plaintiff by warranty deed dated March 22, 1956, recorded March 22, 1956 in Official Records Book 123, page 456, of the public records of Lemon County.

4. The property description in the deed executed by defendant E. F. is so uncertain that it is doubtful whether title passed to the grantee, thus casting a cloud on plaintiff's title.

5. The property description in the deed executed by G. H. is the same as that in the deed executed by defendant E. F., thus casting a cloud on plaintiff's title.

6. The property description in the tax deed is the same as that in the deed executed by defendant E. F., and it is doubtful that the tax deed extinguished the interests of G. H. and defendants.

7. In 1956 the plaintiff entered into possession of all of the land under a claim of title exclusive of any other right, founding his claim on the deed from K. L. and continuously maintained occupation and possession adverse to defendants for more than seven years and paid taxes.

WHEREFORE plaintiff demands judgment against the defendants removing the clouds from his title to the land and quieting the title in him.

Attorney

.................(address).................

COMMENT: The foregoing sample is less extensive in its allegations than most complaints filed in quiet title actions. Many pleaders include a more detailed description of the unknown parties, and also include allegations for constructive service within the body of the complaint. If they do, the complaint must be verified. *F.S.* 49.031(1).

IV. [§1.23] GUARDIAN AD LITEM

F.S. 65.061(2) provides: "A guardian ad litem shall not be appointed unless it shall affirmatively appear that the interest of minors, persons of unsound mind, or convicts are involved." *RCP* 1.210(b), however, provides: "The court shall appoint a guardian ad litem for an infant or incompetent person not otherwise represented in an action or shall make such other order as it deems proper for the protection of the infant or incompetent person." See also *RCP* 1.500. The Florida Supreme Court had held that if the court acquired jurisdiction of a minor, failure to appoint a guardian ad litem does not make the judgment absolutely void, but only voidable. *Sample v. Ward,* 156 Fla. 210, 23 So.2d 81 (1945). It should be noted that this case preceded the rule in its present form as well as *Fla.Const.* art. V, §2(a) and *RCP* 1.010. Thus, any action involving service by publication against either known persons of an unknown residence or against unknown persons should take into consideration that some of the defendants may be minors or otherwise incompetent, and, if so, the rules would prevent any valid judgment being entered against those defendants unless the guardian ad litem is appointed or the court specifically finds that a representative is not necessary. In a case under *F.S.* 65.061(2) a guardian ad litem should be appointed or the final judgment should contain a specific finding under *RCP* 1.210(b) that no guardian ad litem is required to protect the rights of those persons.

In practice, if a default is entered, the order appointing the guardian ad litem supersedes the effect of the default. A statement in the motion for appointment of guardian ad litem that no paper has been served or filed should make the record complete without entry of a default.

Service of process on a guardian ad litem is necessary unless he voluntarily appears. *F.S.* 48.041(1). The order appointing him should require appearance without process.

The guardian ad litem should not regard his duties as perfunctory. An example of extensive services is that in the case of *Key v. All Persons Claiming Any Estate, Etc.,* 160 Fla. 723, 36 So.2d 366 (1948) the guardian ad litem raised the issue of the constitutionality of former *F.S.* 66.28−.47 and the case was carried to the Supreme Court.

V. ATTORNEY AD LITEM

A. [§1.24] In General

Under 50 *U.S.C.App.* §520 if it cannot be determined whether a defendant is in the military service, a motion to appoint an attorney ad litem and a supportive affidavit should be filed. It is permissible to enter a default according to TRAWICK'S FLORIDA PRACTICE AND PROCEDURE §25-2 (1975). An allegation that it cannot be determined whether a defendant is in the military is premature in the complaint or the affidavit filed with the complaint. Under these circumstances an allegation should be included only with the motion filed after the answer is due.

Although the federal statute (50 *U.S.C.App.* §520) does not specifically so provide, it would appear that the order appointing the attorney ad litem may provide that service of process is not required, and provide a time within which he must file responsive pleadings. A question may exist as to whether the attorney ad litem may waive service by filing an answer in view of the language of §520(3), which provides that the attorney has no power to waive any right of the person for whom he is appointed. The order requiring the filing of responsive pleadings without service should eliminate the question.

As with the appointment of a guardian ad litem, the attorney ad litem should not regard his duties as perfunctory.

B. [§1.25] Sample Motion To Appoint Attorney Ad Litem

(Title of Court)

(Title of Cause)   PLAINTIFF'S MOTION TO
APPOINT ATTORNEY AD LITEM

Plaintiff moves for the appointment of an attorney ad litem for defendants because they are in default for failure to serve any paper on the undersigned or file any paper as required by law and plaintiff is not able to determine whether any of the defendants are in military service. The affidavit of the undersigned pursuant to 50 U.S.C.App. §520 appears below.

                                             Attorney

                                    ....(address)..................

STATE OF FLORIDA
COUNTY OF LEMON

Before me, the undersigned authority, personally appeared M. N., who after being sworn said that he is the attorney for plaintiff in this action and that plaintiff is not able to determine whether defendants are in military service.

                                             M. N.

(Jurat)

COMMENT: The affidavit may be on a separate paper. 50 *U.S.C.App.* §520 requires an affidavit "if there shall be a default of any appearance by the defendant." An affidavit executed on or before the return day apparently would be premature, especially if it states that the defendants are not in military service and no attorney ad litem is appointed. That might be the fact when the complaint is filed but not when a default is entered. No default should be entered if an attorney ad litem is to be appointed. This sample supposes that no guardian ad litem was appointed because it did not "affirmatively appear that the interest of minors, persons of unsound mind, or convicts are involved." See *F.S.* 65.061(2).

C. [§1.26] Sample Order Appointing Attorney Ad Litem

(Title of Court)

(Title of Cause)   **ORDER APPOINTING ATTORNEY AD LITEM**

This action was heard on plaintiff's motion for the appointment of an attorney ad litem for defendants.

IT IS ADJUDGED that

1. O. P. is appointed attorney ad litem for the defendants and he shall serve written defenses without service of process on him.

2. It shall not be necessary for the attorney ad litem to file an oath. The filing of an answer or other paper shall be an acceptance of this appointment and an undertaking on his part to discharge faithfully the duties of his office.

ORDERED at ...., Florida on ....(date)..........

_____
                                             Circuit Judge

Copies furnished to: ....

COMMENT: The provision of this order that the attorney shall represent the defendants and protect their interests is taken from the clause of 50 *U.S.C.App.* §520 that the court shall appoint "an attorney to represent defendant and protect his interest." Many attorneys obtain appointment of one person as both attorney and guardian ad litem. In most cases, it would appear to be advisable to appoint both since it is virtually impossible to determine if the interests of minors or persons in the military are involved when unknown defendants are joined as parties.

VI.   PROOF

A.   [§1.27] In General

The question of proving anything in a quit title trial causes confusion among some members of the bar who do not carefully analyze what happens. It is not necessary to have a verified complaint to bolster proof at trial. Under Florida procedure all allegations of a complaint to quiet title that are not denied are deemed admitted. Since the exception for damages does not apply, this means that a default entered against all of the defendants in a quiet title action admits all of the allegations of the complaint by operation of law. At this point the only thing remaining to be done is to enter final judgment. If a lawyer tries to prove his case, he is gilding the lily.

Of course, this does not apply to a contested quiet title action, in which the issues are handled just as they would be in any other trial.

B. [§1.28] Diligent Search And Inquiry

Assuming the allegations of a complaint (or separate affidavit) comply with the requirements of the constructive service statutes (*F.S.* Chapter 49), it is unlikely that an issue would be raised at trial that would require proof. A cautious attorney, however, will maintain complete and accurate records and proof of the steps taken to comply with the statutory and case law requirements. See §§1.16–.19. Those facts, submitted in affidavit form or by direct testimony, should be sufficient to establish proof of compliance, should the issue be raised at final hearing.

C. [§1.29] Default Against Defendants

Evidence on the merits is not required to be taken if default is entered against all defendants. *F.S.* 65.061(4). This is not applicable when a guardian or attorney ad litem is appointed, at least as to the defendants represented by him. See §1.20.

D. [§1.30] Statutes Of Limitation And Curative Statutes

In establishing proof that the various claims of defendants are barred or unenforceable clouds on the title, the plaintiff may rely upon the statutes of limitation and curative acts in effect in Florida, including:

1. *F.S.* 95.14, which bars claims of title to real property unless the claimant has been in possession within seven years. See also 95.12 which bars the plaintiff's claim if not in possession within the seven-year period.

2. *F.S.* 95.13, which raises a presumption of possession in favor of "the person establishing legal title."

3. *F.S.* 95.22, which bars claims of other heirs when a deed from persons purporting to be all the heirs of a decedent, when the deed has been of record for the required statutory period.

4. *F.S.* 95.231, which bars claims adverse to a deed or will that has been of record five years or more.

5. *F.S.* 95.231, which bars enforcement of mortgage liens after expiration or the statutory period.

6. *F.S.* 695.05, which purports to cure defects in acknowledgments and other defects in the execution of instruments.

7. *F.S.* 695.20, which bars claims of purchasers under unperformed contracts for purchase of real property.

8. *F.S.* Chapter 694, which purports to cure various defects in conveyances that have been of record for the required statutory period.

See Day, *Curative Acts and Limitations Acts Designed to Remedy Defects in Florida Land Title,* 8 U.FLA.L.REV. 365 (1955).

E. [§1.31] Marketable Record Titles Act

F.S. Chapter 712, known as the Marketable Record Titles Act, may be relied upon by the plaintiff to establish his paramount title to the property when its applicability is clearly shown. The plaintiff's attorney should review the statute carefully to determine if title can be established under it. The applicability of the act is somewhat limited and its validity and constitutionality has not yet been directly ruled upon by any Florida appellate court. The act has been applied upon the assumption that it is valid. See *Marshall v. Hollywood, Inc.,* 236 So.2d 114 (Fla. 1970).

F. [§1.32] Adverse Possession

The two basic statutes concerning adverse possession are adverse possession under color of title in *F.S.* 95.16 and adverse possession not under color of title in 95.18. Adverse possession with color of title is defined in 95.17 and adverse possession not under color of title is defined in 95.19. These statutes are analyzed in I FLORIDA REAL PROPERTY PRACTICE §§7.8–.10 (CLE 2d ed. 1971), and §7.11 emphasizes the primary differences between adverse possession with and adverse possession without color of title.

Some recent cases that construe the adverse possession statutes are:

Stephens v. Stephens, 94 So.2d 366 (Fla. 1957)

Levering v. City of Tarpon Springs, 92 So.2d 638 (Fla. 1957)

Van Meter v. Kelsey, 91 So.2d 327 (Fla. 1956)

Seaboard Air Line Ry. Co. v. Atlantic Coast Line R. Co., 117 Fla. 830, 158 So. 459 (1935)

Forman v. Ward, 219 So.2d 68 (1st D.C.A. Fla. 1969)

Chasteen v. Chasteen, 213 So.2d 509 (1st D.C.A. Fla. 1968)

Moore v. Musa, 198 So.2d 843 (3d D.C.A. Fla. 1967)

Seaside Properties, Inc. v. State Road Department, 190 So.2d 391 (3d D.C.A. Fla. 1966), *cert. den.* 201 So.2d 464, *app. dism.* 389 U.S. 569

Brooks v. Taylor, 190 So.2d 205 (1st D.C.A. Fla. 1966)

Cahill v. Chesley, 189 So.2d 818 (2d D.C.A. Fla. 1966)

Daniels v. Alico Land Development Company, 189 So.2d 540 (2d D.C.A. Fla. 1966)

Deverick v. Bailey, 174 So.2d 440 (2d D.C.A. Fla. 1965), *cert. den.* 183 So.2d 209

Stewart v. Gadarian, 141 So.2d 289 (1st D.C.A. Fla. 1962)

Culbertson v. Montanbault, 133 So.2d 772 (2d D.C.A. Fla. 1961)

Simpson v. Lindgren, 133 So.2d 439 (3d D.C.A. Fla. 1961)

Tampa Mortgage & Title Company v. Smythe, 109 So.2d 202 (2d D.C.A. Fla. 1959)

Lykes Bros. v. Brautcheck, 106 So.2d 582 (2d D.C.A. Fla. 1958)

VII. [§1.33] DEFENSES

Generally, if the complaint alleges and the plaintiff can prove proper grounds for the quieting of title, few, if any, defenses interposed will be successful. Certain defenses may be available, however, depending upon the facts of a given case.

Defenses relating to acquisition by the defendant of superior title by adverse possession or the failure to prove the plaintiff's adverse possession are factual matters that must be carefully considered and reviewed. In situations when the plaintiff and defendant were cotenants, and the plaintiff's possession was not adverse, or when the adverse possession of the plaintiff was not continuous for the required statutory period, proper defenses may be raised. Questions about minority, incompetence or other legal disability of a defendant also are factual questions that may give rise to defenses.

Defense counsel also should consider whether there are any procedural defects about the bringing of the action itself, particularly with respect to the allegations of the complaint or description of the defendants, which would give rise to defenses that could be asserted by motion to dismiss. The procedural defenses are unlikely to defeat the ultimate remedy requested by the plaintiff.

It has been recognized that under certain circumstances laches and estoppel may constitute proper defenses in a quiet title action. *Cook v. Katiba,* 190 So.2d 309 (Fla. 1966); *Norton v. Jones,* 83 Fla. 81, 90 So. 854 (1922). Again, the facts and circumstances that would give rise to the defenses should be thoroughly investigated by the defendant's attorney and can be determined only upon the particular facts of each case.

VIII. [§1.34] SAMPLE FINAL JUDGMENT

(Title of Court)

(Title of Cause)   **FINAL JUDGMENT**

This action was tried before the court. On the evidence presented,

IT IS ADJUDGED THAT:

1. The title of plaintiff, A. B., to the following-described real property in Lemon County, Florida:

[legal description]

is a good title against the claims or purported claims of defendants, E. F., G. H. and C.D., if alive, and if dead their unknown spouse, heirs, devisees, grantees and creditors and all other parties claiming by, through, under or against them; all parties having or claiming to have any right, title or interest in that property; and of all persons claiming by, through or under defendants since the filing of the notice of lis pendens; and those claims or purported claims are canceled; and the title to the property is forever quieted in plaintiff.

2. The sum of $.......... as compensation for the attorney ad litem is taxed as an item of costs. All costs are taxed against plaintiff.

ORDERED at ...., Florida on ....(date)..........

_____
Circuit Judge

Copies furnished to: ....

COMMENT: See *RCP* Form 1.993.

EDWARD J. KOHRS*
ROBERT G. COCHRAN†

2

BOUNDARY LITIGATION

I. [§2.1] INTRODUCTION

II. [§2.2] ROLE OF THE SURVEY

III. SETTLEMENT OF BOUNDARY DISPUTES UNDER DOCTRINES OF ADVERSE POSSESSION, BOUNDARY BY RECOGNITION AND ACQUIESCENCE OR BOUNDARY BY AGREEMENT

   A. [§2.3] In General

   B. Boundary By Adverse Possession

      1. [§2.4] In General

      2. Necessary Requirements

         a. Statutory Period

            (1) [§2.5] With Color Of Title

            (2) [§2.6] Without Color Of Title

         b. Actual, Open And Continuous Exclusive Possession

            (1) [§2.7] In General

---

*LL.B., 1957, Vanderbilt University. Mr. Kohrs is a member of the Hillsborough County and American bar associations and is a partner in the firm of Macfarlane, Ferguson, Allison & Kelly. He practices in Tampa.

†J.D., 1972, University of Florida. Mr. Cochran is a member of the American Bar Association and is an associate in the firm of Macfarlane, Ferguson, Allison & Kelly. He practices in Tampa.

        (2) [§2.8] With Color Of Title

        (3) [§2.9] Without Color Of Title

    c. [§2.10] Hostility Of Possession (Intent Of Possessor)

    d. Payment Of Taxes

        (1) [§2.11] With Color Of Title

        (2) [§2.12] Without Color Of Title

  C. [§2.13] Boundary By Recognition And Acquiescence

  D. [§2.14] Boundary By Agreement

IV. [§2.15] REMEDIES

I. [§2.1] INTRODUCTION

Boundary disputes, while not an everyday type of litigation, have become increasingly frequent in recent years. As land values have risen it has become more likely that practitioners who have not experienced this type of litigation previously will have occasion to do so. Unlike some types of litigation in which either fact situations or legal proceedings, or both, tend to follow a pattern from case to case, the lawyer who has occasion to handle several boundary disputes will find that no two are alike. Accordingly, this chapter cannot present a step-by-step formula for boundary litigation and emphasis primarily will be upon the legal doctrines that determine the ultimate outcome.

The client generally will not come to the lawyer with a request for assistance in determining a boundary. By the time the attorney is in the picture a dispute usually is under way. Those disputes often are occasioned by a change in ownership by sale or by inheritance and the new owner wants what his deed or other instrument purports to grant him, and has employed a surveyor to show him exactly where the boundary is. The lawyer may be confronted with a situation in which one party has attempted to employ self-help by tearing down or relocating a fence or hedge. Once adjacent property owners have become involved in a dispute the attorney may find it difficult to fashion a compromise for the purpose of settling the matter. Feelings in these cases tend to run high, even when the value of the strip of land in controversy may not appear to warrant the expense of the impending litigation.

II. [§2.2] ROLE OF THE SURVEY

In many parts of the state surveyors open their files to each other and make use of corner locations established by surveyors who have worked in an area previously. If the surveyors are in actual disagreement as to the location of the true property line, it may be due to inability to agree upon the location of a government corner from which to proceed, or it may arise from one surveyor placing more emphasis on "occupation" than the other.

The State of Florida was surveyed by the United States Government, for the most part during the latter part of the nineteenth century. This was done in accordance with the rules of survey now embodied in Title 43, Chapter 18, §751, United States Code, and subsequent sections. This act basically provides for division of land into townships of six miles square and for division of each township into sections of one mile square. Apportionment of excesses or deficiencies is covered by the act. The surveyor was required to make field notes and preserve these notes, as well as the map of his survey.

It now is very difficult, generally, to locate original government corners solely from the original field notes. These corners have been perpetuated or re-established by the work of subsequent surveyors.

Some boundary litigation is occasioned by inaccuracies in older plats. Both before and during the Florida land boom of the twenties there was no governmental control over the filing of plats. Many plats of subdivisions were prepared in the broker's office on the untrue assumption that every section was a standard one mile section. Upon completion of a plat of his land the property owner simply filed it with the clerk of the circuit court without any central control over the accuracy of the plat having been exercised. Shortages and excesses in sections have been discovered subsequently and have resulted in subdivisions being undersized or oversized.

Notwithstanding errors in old plats, it is well established that one who takes title to a subdivision lot by a recorded plat owns what the plat purports to give him to the extent the land was owned by the original subdivider at the time the plat was filed. In other words, within the subdivision itself the plat normally controls. See *Akin v. Godwin*, 49 So.2d 604 (Fla. 1951). Real problems can be caused, however, by using erroneous subdivision plats as a basis for surveying adjacent lands or nearby lands not within the subdivision. The parties owning lands outside the subdivision are not bound by the errors contained in a neighboring subdivision plat merely by virtue of the existence of the subdivision.

The first step in examining any boundary question is to obtain a copy of the survey upon which the client is relying and any conflicting survey, if available. Earlier surveys, whether of the particular parcel in question or of the adjoining parcels, should be searched out and examined. If the problem is to be analyzed logically it does no good to talk loosely in terms of adverse possession and acquiescence without having first determined what an accurate survey shows about the boundary in question. If the property is within a subdivision the survey must be reconcilable with the original plat of that subdivision, subject to proper apportionment of known overages or shortages in the plat, and should begin from some ascertainable corner shown on the plat. If the property is not subdivided (platted) land it should be determined whether the surveyor proceeded from a well-accepted government corner or himself established a corner, and if the latter, what he did. Clients often attach greater significance to the location of roads and utility poles than is warranted. Frequently, roads were built wherever a county commissioner desired, and utility poles are planted where it is most convenient for the utility.

When the attorney ascertains that the surveyor relied heavily upon "occupation" in establishing boundaries, inquiry should be made as to whether this occupation conflicts with the location of the boundary if it were established by reference to an accepted government corner. While a general trend as to occupation in an area is relied upon by surveyors to some extent, it is well for the attorney to ask himself at what point should the surveyor be considered to have usurped a judicial function and performed his work on the basis of a factual and legal analysis that may not be accurate. The better practice with surveyors if there is a difference between occupation and the location of the true land line is to show both. The lawyer should beware of any surveying map that indicates that it is an occupational survey. A proper certification over the surveyor's signature and a map bearing the surveyor's seal are an essential point of beginning, of course. Very often a client will bring a drawing to his attorney and indicate that it is a survey when actually it is an office drawing, possibly done by a developer who at that point did not wish to spend money on a true survey. The drawing, although having certain limited usefulness, clearly is not an actual survey of the property.

The grid system of surveying followed by government surveyors must be adapted to give consideration to the curvature of the earth. This is done by corrections that produce the phenomenon of double corners. When those corrections have been made, the northwest and northeast corners of two adjoining sections at the top of the township will not correspond to the southeast and southwest corners of two adjoining sections in the bottom tier of the township above. See Chapter 7 of CLARK ON SURVEYING AND BOUNDARIES (3d ed. 1959) for full explanation of this process. Needless to say, double corners can be confusing to a surveyor not familiar with the area in which he is working.

If investigation shows a genuine dispute between surveyors, the attorney should prepare for a battle of experts.

In Chapters 9 and 10 of I FLORIDA REAL PROPERTY PRACTICE (CLE 2d ed. 1971), these matters are treated in some detail.

III. SETTLEMENT OF BOUNDARY DISPUTES UNDER DOCTRINES OF ADVERSE POSSESSION, BOUNDARY BY RECOGNITION AND ACQUIESCENCE OR BOUNDARY BY AGREEMENT

A. [§2.3] In General

Whether there is an actual dispute between surveyors as to the location of the boundary or not, other questions involving certain legal doctrines for the settling of boundary disputes may arise. One or both parties, by mistake or design, may establish a boundary that in fact does not comport with the true land line. Under certain conditions the courts recognize erroneously located boundaries under three distinct legal doctrines, namely adverse possession, boundary by recognition and acquiescence and boundary by agreement.

Once the surveying question has been investigated and analyzed thoroughly (which definitely involves a detailed review of the matter with the surveyors who have surveyed the property in question and other lands in the area), there may be a question involving one of these legal doctrines that in effect would recognize a boundary other than the true land line as located by accurate survey.

In that case, the attorney rather early in the investigation should obtain and examine an abstract or chain of title to both parcels involved in the disputed boundary. Prior owners and witnesses who reside or have resided in the neighborhood must be located and interviewed. A fence or other artificial divider located off the true land line may have a very interesting history and sometimes older witnesses will be located who have very good memories concerning the circumstances involved in the construction of the fence.

Before gathering factual background on a disputed boundary, the attorney must be aware of the principles embodied in the three doctrines mentioned above so that he may determine as he proceeds with investigation which of these doctrines is available to him or to his adversary.

B. Boundary By Adverse Possession

1. [§2.4] In General

It has long been recognized in this state that possession of real property owned in fee by another may be acquired legally by means of adverse possession. *F.S.* 95.12 provides that:

No action to recover real property or its possession shall be maintained unless the person seeking recovery or his ancestor, predecessor, or grantor was seized or possessed of the property within seven years before commencement of the action.

In addition, *F.S.* 95.16 and .18 outline the requirements for the establishment of adverse possession with and without color of title. The principles of law applicable to establishing adverse possession in general also apply to the establishment of adverse possession up to erroneously located boundaries. Of course, all statutory and case law requirements for the establishment of adverse possession must be present. In addition, the party who seeks to assert adverse possession bears the burden of proving the facts necessary to constitute it by "clear and positive proof," and proof of adverse possession "cannot be established by loose, uncertain testimony which necessitates resort to mere conjecture." *Downing v. Bird,* 100 So.2d 57 (Fla. 1958).

2. Necessary Requirements

    a. Statutory Period

    (1) [§2.5] With Color Of Title

F.S. 95.16 provides that when the occupant, or those under whom he claims, entered into possession of property under a claim of title arising from a written instrument, such as a conveyance or final judgment, and his possession continued for a period of seven years, the premises are deemed to have been held adversely. The statute further provides that after December 31, 1945 the possession shall not be deemed to be adverse until the instrument serving as color of title has been recorded in the office of the clerk of the circuit court of the county in which the property is located.

Possession must be continuous for the statutory seven-year period, of course, and an abandonment of the property for any period, however short, without an intention to return by the possessor will serve to toll the running of the statutory period. *Doyle v. Wade,* 23 Fla. 90, 1 So. 516 (1887).

The possession may be accomplished by the occupant, or those under whom he claims, and periods of possession by predecessors in title may be tacked. The possession is deemed to be for the statutory period as long as the total time of possession meets the statutory requirements. See *Coogler v. Rogers,* 25 Fla. 853, 7 So. 391 (1889).

Color of title, as required by the statute, is defined as a "written instrument." In this regard, tax deeds, land patents, masters' deeds, sheriffs' deeds and trust deeds have all been held to qualify as instruments giving color of title. Even void deeds and wills have been held sufficient as color of title.

(2) [§2.6] Without Color Of Title

F.S. 95.18 provides that when there has been actual continued occupation for seven years of property *not* founded upon a written instrument or judgment, the premises occupied are deemed to have been held adversely. But the statute requires that the property be returned for taxes during the seven-year period by the possessor, which will be discussed in §2.11. The possession must be continuous and the running of the statutory period will be interrupted by abandonment at any time by the possessor with intent not to resume possession.

b. Actual, Open And Continuous Exclusive Possession

(1) [§2.7] In General

The possessory acts required for the establishment of adverse possession with and without color of title are prescribed by statute. See *F.S.* 95.16(2) and .18(2). These requirements are somewhat more stringent for adverse possession without color of title.

(2) [§2.8] With Color Of Title

F.S. 95.16(2) prescribes certain possessory acts that are to be deemed sufficient upon which to base a claim of adverse possession with color of title. These possessory acts are as follows:

    a.   When the property has been usually cultivated or improved.

    b.   When the property has been protected by a substantial enclosure.

    c.   When, although not enclosed, the property has been used for the supply of fuel, or fencing timber for the purpose of husbandry, or for the ordinary use of the occupant.

The above statute raises a presumption only in that the prescribed acts are to be deemed to be sufficient possessory acts, and what constitutes sufficient possession of the property is a fact question to be determined in each case as it arises. *Horton v. Smith-Richardson Inv. Co.,* 81 Fla. 255, 87 So. 905 (1921); *Doyle v. Wade,* 23 Fla. 90, 1 So. 516 (1887). The use to which the property is adapted, the circumstances and situation of the possessor and, to a certain extent, the possessor's intention must be considered in this connection. *Horton, supra; Doyle, supra.* The main test in Florida seems to be whether the acts of ownership manifested by the possessor were all that a true owner could reasonably be expected to exercise over land of the particular quality and quantity involved. If the possessory acts proved were acts that would be expected to be exercised by the true owner of the property in light of the nature of the property, then the possession probably will be deemed sufficient.

(3) [§2.9] Without Color Of Title

F.S. 95.18(2) provides that certain possessory acts shall be deemed sufficient to constitute adverse possession without color of title. These possessory acts are as follows:

a. When the property has been protected by substantial enclosure.

b. When the property has been usually cultivated or improved.

The statute further provides that *only* those specified acts constitute adverse possession. Thus in cases of adverse possession without color of title, the acts necessary to constitute adverse possession are stringent and prescribed by statute.

Several Florida cases have held that an enclosure is substantial if it is sufficient in strength and in permanency to turn cattle. See, *e.g., Adams v. Fryer,* 59 Fla. 112, 52 So. 611 (1910). It also has been held that whether a particular fence or enclosure is of a substantial nature is a matter for the jury to determine. *Wicker v. Williams,* 137 Fla. 752, 189 So. 30 (1939).

As to the statutory category of having been "usually cultivated or improved," the question whether a particular fact situation meets the statutory requirement calls for consideration of the property involved, the use made of it and the circumstances and situation of the possessor.

The possession of property, in order to constitute an adverse possession (with or without color of title), also must be open, exclusive and notorious. The requirement of open and notorious possession simply means that the adverse possessor's claim of ownership must be evidenced by acts and conduct sufficient to put a man of ordinary prudence on notice of the fact that the property is held by the claimant as his own. 1 AM.JUR.2d *Adverse Possession* §47. Actual knowledge by the owner of the adverse possession is unnecessary, the requirement being simply that the possession is of such a nature that a prudent owner of property would be made aware of the adverseness of the holding. See *Watrous v. Morrison,* 33 Fla. 261, 14 So. 805 (1894). It follows that a clandestine or secret possession is insufficient upon which to base a claim of adverse possession.

In addition, the possession must be exlucisve as to the possessor and his predecessors. It should be noted, however, that two or more individuals can constitute a single adverse possession of property, which, if proved, would give rise to co-ownership based upon the adverse possession.

c. [§2.10] Hostility Of Possession (Intent Of Possessor)

The intent necessary in order to establish adverse possession in boundary cases has been discussed frequently in Florida. A concise statement of the rule may be found in *Shaw v. Williams,* 50 So.2d 125 (Fla. 1951). In that case the Supreme Court concluded as follows:

> ... If the occupancy is by mistake, with no intention upon the part of the occupant to claim as his own, land which does not belong to him, but he intends to claim only to the true line, wherever it may be, the holding is not adverse. If however, the occupant takes possession, believing the land to be his own up to the mistaken line and claiming title to it and so holds, the holding is adverse. The intent to claim title up to the line is an indispensable element of adverse holding. The claim of right must be as broad as the possession. . . .

See also *Bossom v. Gillman,* 70 Fla. 310, 70 So. 364 (1915); *Watrous v. Morrison,* 33 Fla. 261, 14 So. 805 (1894).

Possession to an erroneously located boundary, therefore, is adverse as long as the possessor believes the boundary to be correct and intends to and does hold up to the mistaken line claiming title to it. If, however, the possessor is aware that the boundary may be mistaken, it would seem that he must have formulated an affirmative intention to hold to the boundary lines in spite of the possibility of error. If the possessor, at any time, expresses the intent to hold to the true boundary only, the possession would not be deemed to be adverse to the ownership of the property. See *Shaw v. Williams, supra.*

d. Payment Of Taxes

(1) [§2.11] With Color Of Title

In prescribing the requirements of adverse possession with color of title, *F.S.* 95.16 makes no requirement as to payment of taxes on the property by the possessor. Payment of taxes by the possessor, even in cases of adverse possession with color of title, nevertheless is an evidentiary factor to be considered in determining whether the possessor has evidenced the necessary possessory acts.

(2) [§2.12] Without Color Of Title

F.S. 95.18(1) provides that possession without color of title is not adverse unless the person claiming adverse possession made a return of the property by proper legal description to the tax assessor of the county where it is located within one year after entering into possession and subsequently has paid all taxes and matured installments of special improvements liens levied against it by the state, county or municipality. This requirement severely limits the doctrine of adverse possession in its application to boundary disputes. Inasmuch as the typical boundary dispute involves a possessor without color of title, and in view of the fact that typically the possessor will not return the property for taxes, the doctrine of adverse possession in boundary disputes quite frequently is unavailable to the possessor. In this regard, note should be taken of *F.S.* 95.16(2)(b) pertaining to requirements of adverse possession under color of title, in which the following language appears: "All contiguous land protected by the enclosure shall be property included within the written instrument, judgment or decree, within the purview of section 95.16(1)."

Accordingly, one might reason that if the possessor's property is surrounded by a substantial enclosure that also extends to the disputed boundary line and encloses the disputed strip of property as well as property owned of record by the possessor, the possessor may be deemed to be holding adversely with color of title as to the disputed strip of property. In this situation, it would not be necessary for the possessor to return the property for taxes as would be the case of possession without color of title. In this manner, the possessor may bring himself within the requirements of adverse possession with color of title.

The Supreme Court in *Meyer v. Law,* 287 So.2d 37 (Fla. 1973), however, refused to accept, over a strong dissent, this reading of the statute in question, and held that color of title only extended to lands described in the paper title regardless of enclosure. This decision would seem to put an end to attempted use of this statutory exception to the requirements of adverse possession without color of title in boundary dispute cases. See also *Peters v. Straley,* 306 So.2d 588 (Fla. 1975).

C. [§2.13] Boundary By Recognition And Acquiescence

Florida case law has recognized that title to another's property may be acquired by a possessor if it can be shown that both parties were in doubt as to the true boundary line between their respective parcels of property, and there has been a mutual continued recognition of a new boundary and continued occupation and acquiescence in it for a period of more than the statute of limitation. See *Shaw v. Williams,* 50 So.2d 125 (Fla. 1951); *Palm Orange Groves v. Yelvington,* 41 So.2d 883 (Fla. 1949); *King v. Carden,* 237 So.2d 26 (1st D.C.A. Fla. 1970).

Repeating, boundary by acquiescence involves at least three elements:

1. A dispute from which it can be implied that both parties are in doubt as to boundary.

2. *Mutual* recognition of the establishment of a new boundary regardless of the true boundary between properties.

3. Continued occupation and acquiescence in the new boundary for a period in excess of the statute of limitation.

Kerrigan v. Thomas, 281 So.2d 410 (1st D.C.A. Fla. 1973), *cert. den.* 287 So.2d 97. See also *Van Meter v. Kelsey,* 91 So.2d 327 (Fla. 1956).

The word "mutual" is emphasized inasmuch as the law seems settled that the establishment of a new boundary by one party acting independently of the other, or the action of one party in establishing a boundary line for convenience without the knowledge that it was intended to be a boundary having been brought home to the other party, will not be sufficient to give the possessor title to the disputed boundary line by reason of recognition and acquiescence. Evidence must be adduced that both parties recognized that some question as to the true location of the boundary existed or that there actually was a dispute between the parties as to the true location of the boundary.

Proof must consist of facts that show that a dispute as to the true boundary of the property existed between the parties, that a new boundary was established and that knowledge of the establishment of the new boundary was brought home to both parties, and thereafter both parties acquiesced in the new boundary for a period of time in excess of the statute of limitation. All three elements must be present and sufficiently proved in order to meet the requirements of recognition and acquiescence.

It should be pointed out that the return of the property and payment of taxes on it by the possessor is not necessary in order to establish recognition and acquiescence in the new boundary, nor is it necessary that the statutory requirements as to adverse possession be established. The doctrine of recognition and acquiescence therefore quite frequently is available to possessors of property when the facts fail to meet the requirements of adverse possession.

Boundary by recognition and acquiescence may be distinguished from boundary by mutual agreement (discussed in §2.14) in that establishment of a new boundary by recognition and acquiescence does not require proof of an agreement between the parties, either expressed or implied. Further, the acquiescence in the boundary must continue for a period of time at least equal to the statute of limitation in regard to real actions, while boundary by mutual agreement requires only that occupation by the parties up to the agreed upon boundary occur for a period of time sufficient to show a settled recognition of the line as the permanent boundary. Thus, boundary by recognition and acquiescence may be established when there has been no expressed or implied agreement between the parties but there has been recognition by one party of the establishment of a boundary by the other, and acquiescence in that boundary for the required period of time. In fact situations in which the establishment of either an expressed or an implied agreement between the parties presents an insurmountable obstacle, boundary by recognition and acquiescence may still be available to the possessor.

Finally, in regard to the requirement of occupation of the property up to the newly established boundary and acquiescence in the occupation, it should be noted that lying by without objection for the statutory period in cases of *adverse holding* will bind the party so lying by to the line, even though it is not the true boundary line. The reference to a party holding adversely may raise some question as to the facts that will show an occupation up to the newly established boundary sufficient to vest title in the disputed strip in the possessor. While the occupation of the disputed strip certainly need not meet the statutory requirements necessary for adverse possession, there must be some possessory acts by the possessor. The writers suggest that the necessary possessory acts would be manifested whenever the acts of the possessor were those that a true owner could reasonably be expected to exercise over land of the particular quality and quantity involved. Of course, the property need not be returned for taxes by the possessor and, further, the possessory acts necessary to establish occupation should not be controlled by the statutes relating to adverse possession. In other words, "occupation" is not as stringent a requirement as "adverse possession," and while several of the cases talk in terms of holding adversely, this requirement should not be equated with the requirements of adverse possession.

D. [§2.14] Boundary By Agreement

Boundaries between parcels of property may be established by the parties involved by agreement, provided occupation of the parcel pursuant to the agreement up to the newly established boundary line is undertaken by both parties. The essential requirements of boundary by agreement consist of the following:

1. Uncertainty or dispute as to the true boundary.

2. An agreement by both parties, either oral or implied, that a certain line will be treated by the parties as the true line.

3. Subsequent occupation by the parties in accordance with that agreement for a period of time sufficient to show a settled recognition of the line as the permanent boundary.

The above test as to boundary by agreement has been discussed in several Florida cases. See *Watrous v. Morrison,* 33 Fla. 261, 14 So. 805 (1894); *King v. Carden,* 237 So.2d 26 (1st D.C.A. Fla. 1970); *Reil v. Myers,* 222 So.2d 42 (4th D.C.A. Fla. 1969). The agreement between the parties may be oral or implied. See *Watrous v. Morrison, supra.* It is essential that the true boundary be in dispute or unknown at the time the oral agreement is entered into, however. If the true boundary is known, an oral agreement as to relocation of the boundary would fall within the statute of frauds and the conveyancing statute. *F.S.* 689.01.

Occupation up to the agreed upon boundary is essential in order to make the agreement binding upon the parties involved and their successors in title. The occupancy need not be for a time period equal to the statute of limitation, however. The time period required appears to be a fact question, the only test being whether occupancy was for a sufficient period of time to indicate a "settled recognition" of the agreed upon line as the permanent boundary.

This form of acquiring title in boundary situations may be distinguished from recognition and acquiescence in that an agreement, implied or oral, must be proved between the parties and be followed by actual occupancy by both parties to the agreed upon line. Proof of the agreement is essential.

IV. [§2.15] REMEDIES

The vehicle for determination of a boundary dispute when the defendant is claimed to be in possession of the plaintiff's land normally will be by an action in ejectment. *F.S.* Chapter 66, which is very brief, should be reviewed. Ejectment is the subject of Chapter 3 of this manual. The advantages and disadvantages of a jury trial in ejectment must be considered carefully. The issues frequently are complex even for a judge and more than likely will confuse a jury.

If the plaintiff is in possession of lands that are claimed in connection with a boundary dispute by the adjoining property owner, the proper remedy is an action to quiet title based upon adverse possession, boundary by agreement or acquiescence. Frequently all three doctrines will be invoked. *F.S.* 65.061, the so-called "additional remedy," provides the broadest relief for quieting title and sets forth fairly particular requirements. Chapter 1 of this manual discusses quieting title.

It has been held in Florida that declaratory relief may not be utilized to establish a boundary. See FLORIDA CIVIL PRACTICE BEFORE TRIAL §22.8 (CLE 3d ed. 1975).

The lawyer who is asked to defend a boundary dispute case should make the same investigation as described above for one representing the plaintiff. The complaint should be attacked by motion if adverse possession or agreement or acquiescence, or any combination of these doctrines, is relied upon and the facts needed to support that doctrine are not set forth. In answering, the defendant's attorney may wish to counterclaim for appropriate relief.

A boundary case does not lend itself to last-minute preparation. Early preparation, in addition to the obvious advantages, will disclose unusual questions of evidence that may arise with respect to documents, hearsay and expert opinion. The failure to prepare for these questions may result in loss of ability to introduce important evidence or to raise effective objections to the opponent's case.

Discovery may be a very significant part of a boundary action. Requests for admission of the genuineness of documents at a pretrial conference will save time at the trial. Witnesses who are aged and infirm should be deposed. Those witnesses frequently will recall facts best if deposed at home, and may remember events of years ago with amazing clarity. See Chapter 16, "Discovery," FLORIDA CIVIL PRACTICE BEFORE TRIAL (CLE 3d ed. 1975).

It frequently is helpful, particularly if the judge has not had considerable exposure to the case by arguments on motions, to submit at a pretrial conference a brief memorandum concerning the legal doctrines relied upon, with case citations. A busy judge who is thoroughly familiar with many other types of litigation may be on unfamiliar ground in a boundary case and will appreciate this assistance from the attorney.

ADDITIONAL REFERENCES:

1. 11 C.J.S. *Boundaries*

2. 12 AM.JUR.2d *Boundaries*

3. Day, *Validation of Erroneously Located Boundaries By Adverse Possession and Related Doctrines,* 10 U.FLA.L.REV. 245 (1957)

4. Comment, 4 U.FLA.L.REV. 262 (1951) (effect of tax deed upon boundary agreement)

5. 5 AM.JUR. PLEADING AND PRACTICE FORMS ANNOTATED *Boundaries,* 137

6. CLARK ON SURVEYING AND BOUNDARIES (3d ed. 1959)

7. A.L.R. Annotations:

   Adverse possession due to ignorance or mistake as to boundaries, 97 A.L.R. 14 (1935)

   Establishment of boundary line by oral agreement or acquiescence, 69 A.L.R. 1430 (1930); 113 A.L.R. 421 (1938)

   Fence as a factor in fixing location of boundary line, 170 A.L.R. 1144 (1947)

   Specific description with reference to water and conveyance of riparian land as marking the extent of grantee's ownership of the submerged land and the shore, 74 A.L.R. 597 (1932)

   Apportionment and division of area of river as between riparian tracts fronting on same bank in absence of agreement or specification, 65 A.L.R.2d 143 (1959)

   Reversion of title upon abandonment or vacation of public street or highway, 18 A.L.R. 1008 (1922); 70 A.L.R. 564 (1931)

   Description with reference to highway as carrying title to center or side of highway, 49 A.L.R.2d 982 (1956)

   Boundary under conveyance of land bordering on railroad right of way, 85 A.L.R. 404 (1933)

ROGER H. STALEY*

3

EJECTMENT

I. [§3.1] SCOPE OF CHAPTER

II. INTRODUCTION

    A. Purpose Of Action

        1. [§3.2] In General

        2. [§3.3] As Contrasted To Action To Quiet Title

        3. [§3.4] As Contrasted With Action For Forcible Entry And Unlawful Detainer

    B. [§3.5] Inapplicability To Easements

    C. [§3.6] Relationship To Chain Of Title

    D. Demand For Possession As Condition Precedent To Action Of Ejectment

        1. [§3.7] In General

        2. [§3.8] Form For Demand For Possession

III. THE COMPLAINT

    A. [§3.9] Determination Of Parties

    B. Chain Of Title

---

*J.D., 1956, University of Miami. Mr. Staley is a member of the Broward County and American bar associations and is a partner in the firm of Saunders, Curtis, Ginestra & Gore. He practices in Fort Lauderdale.

†Mr. John W. Prunty and Mr. Michael C. Slotnick were the authors of this chapter in the first edition.

1. [§3.10] In General

2. [§3.11] Form For Chain Of Title

C. [§3.12] Claim For Mesne Profits

D. [§3.13] Form For Averments And Demand In Complaint

IV. THE ANSWER AND COUNTERCLAIMS

A. The Answer

1. [§3.14] In General

2. [§3.15] Defenses Based On Statutes Of Limitation And Adverse Possession

3. [§3.16] Form For Answer

B. [§3.17] Counterclaims

V. CONDUCT OF THE TRIAL

A. [§3.18] In General

B. Clarifying The Issues Before Trial

1. [§3.19] In General

2. [§3.20] Form For Motion To Test Legal Sufficiency Of Instrument Or Court Proceedings

C. [§3.21] Burden Of Proof

D. Presentation Of Proof

1. [§3.22] In General

2. [§3.23] Proof Of Damages

VI. THE VERDICT

A. [§3.24] In General

B. [§3.25] Form For Verdict For Defendant

VII. THE JUDGMENT

      A. [§3.26] In General

      B. [§3.27] Taxing Of Costs

      C. [§3.28] Form For Judgment For Plaintiff

VIII. ENFORCING THE JUDGMENT AND TERMINATION PROCEDURES

      A. [§3.29] In General

      B. [§3.30] Form For Writ Of Possession And Execution

IX. [§3.31] ATTORNEYS' FEES IN ACTION OF EJECTMENT

X. BETTERMENT

      A. [§3.32] In General

      B. Petition

          1. [§3.33] In General

          2. [§3.34] Form For Petition For Compensation For Betterments

      C. [§3.35] Reply

      D. [§3.36] Trial

      E. [§3.37] The Verdict

      F. The Judgment

          1. [§3.38] In General

          2. [§3.39] For Plaintiff

          3. For Defendant

              a. [§3.40] In General

              b. [§3.41] The Vesting In Defendant Of Title To The Land Upon Plaintiff's Failure To Pay Betterment Judgment

I. [§3.1] SCOPE OF CHAPTER

This chapter deals with actions at law known as ejectment, including those proceedings for the benefit of defendants in ejectment actions known as betterment proceedings.

II. INTRODUCTION

A. Purpose Of Action

1. [§3.2] In General

Ejectment is an action at law for the recovery of possession of real property, for the recovery of any damage that may have accrued because of its withholding and for loss of mesne profits. Ejectment is strictly a statutory action and is contained in *F.S.* Chapter 66. It also abolishes common-law ejectment and includes the proceedings for betterment.

Although the action of ejectment may and frequently does become the means of trying title, it is a possessory action. The plaintiff must be a person out of possession of property who has an immediate right to possession. This right may emerge from a paramount record title to the property or from a possessory right not based upon record title.

The subject matter of an ejectment action is real property. It will not lie for the recovery of personal property but of course does lie for the recovery of a fixture since it has become realty by reason of annexation. Ejectment also lies for the recovery of standing timber, and submerged or tidal lands if the plaintiff has legal title to the land or the right to use it.

2. [§3.3] As Contrasted To Action To Quiet Title

Actions of ejectment vary substantially from actions to quiet title. Ejectment is an action at law to recover possession, while an action to quiet title is an equitable proceeding to determine title. Actions in ejectment are actions in personam, while actions to quiet title ordinarily are proceedings in rem or quasi in rem.

In ejectment the plaintiff is the party out of possession and the defendant must be the party in possession. On the other hand, the plaintiff in an action to quiet title may or may not be in possession. The defendants in a quiet title action who also may or may not be in possession usually are persons who have or may have some claim against the property, which claim the plaintiff alleges to be inferior to his title.

In summary, when a plaintiff is out of possession and desires to recover possession, his remedy is an action of ejectment; when he claims title to property and desires to remove adverse claims or clouds affecting that title, his remedy is an action to quiet title.

3. [§3.4] As Contrasted With Action For Forcible Entry And Unlawful Detainer

The difference between an action of ejectment and an action of forcible entry and unlawful detainer is much more subtle. Both actions are possessory and both are directed toward real property. Both are statutory actions (the action of forcible entry and unlawful detainer is set forth in *F.S.* Chapter 82.

Forcible entry and unlawful detainer is a summary proceeding to recover real property after the defendant has forced his way onto the plaintiff's property or, having entered it lawfully, continues to remain on it past the period of the plaintiff's consent. While the action of ejectment may and frequently does become a means of trying title, by statutory mandate (*F.S.* 82.05), no question of title may be tried in forcible entry and unlawful detainer.

To summarize, an action of ejectment is proper when:

1. the plaintiff does not have possession and the defendant is in possession;

2. the plaintiff seeks to recover possession; and

3. the plaintiff wants to try his right or title upon which his claim of possession is based.

The action of forcible entry and unlawful detainer should be brought when:

1. the plaintiff had prior possession;

2. the defendant has present possession;

3. the plaintiff desires to recover possession; and

4. the plaintiff desires a speedy remedy and is not interested in trying the right of title.

B. [§3.5] Inapplicability To Easements

As a general rule the action of ejectment will not lie for the recovery of a mere license, easement or right of use; however, when the easement includes a right of possession, ejectment may be a proper remedy. For example, a county having a right of possession of land constituting a county highway may bring an action in ejectment for the purpose of recovering possession of any part of the highway unlawfully taken or possessed by an adverse claimant, even though the legal title to the underlying land is not in the county.

C. [§3.6] Relationship To Chain Of Title

Although the action of ejectment is a possessory action, it very frequently is used as a means of trying title to the land. To recover possession of land in an action of ejectment, the plaintiff must be able to demonstrate title in himself with a paramount right to possession or prove that he has been in the actual bona fide possession of the land and was ousted by the defendant. Naturally, if the plaintiff is relying upon his legal title, rather than mere bona fide possession, it is essential that his chain of title be available for examination in the proceeding.

As will be discussed subsequently in §3.10, *F.S.* 66.021(4) requires that both the plaintiff and the defendant in their respective pleadings set forth chronologically the chain of title upon which they will rely at the trial. See also *RCP* Form 1.940.

D. Demand For Possession As Condition Precedent To Action Of Ejectment

1. [§3.7] In General

Florida court decisions are scarce on the necessity of a demand for possession as a condition to the use of ejectment. The general law reveals that a notice to quit or a demand for possession of unlawfully occupied land is *not* a condition precedent to an action of ejectment when there is no privity between the parties; however, the notice or demand usually *is* required when the one in possession has legally entered the land and is not a trespasser. Consequently, it has been held in Florida that ejectment lies by a vendor against a defaulted vendee in possession under an executory contract only after notice. *Wismer v. Alyea,* 103 Fla. 1102, 138 So. 763 (1932).

There is no Florida statute specifying how a demand for possession should be served. Personal service on the party in possession, with the person making the service issuing a certificate to that effect is always the safest method. If the party in possession cannot be found, posting a copy of the demand at the site of the property may suffice. The latter procedure should be accompanied by mailing a registered or certified letter of the demand to the last known residence of the party in possession. Since the action of ejectment seeks recovery of possession, personal service may be obtained in most instances.

2. [§3.8] Form For Demand For Possession

To: ....(party in possession)..........

...................(address).....................

YOU ARE NOTIFIED that you are in unlawful possession of the following-described premises:

[description of land]

The undersigned has the right of possession to the property and demands that you surrender it immediately.

..........(date)..........

(signature of party seeking possession)

III. THE COMPLAINT

A. [§3.9] Determination Of Parties

In drafting the complaint it is imperative to determine those persons who must be named as proper parties. *F.S.* 66.011 has eliminated the common-law need for fictitious parties in actions of ejectment. Generally, the plaintiff is the person who holds legal title, but as long as the party instituting the action is entitled to present possession, he is the proper party plaintiff; however, it has been established in Florida that when a conveyance is made of lands held adversely at that time by one not a party to the deed, the action of ejectment will not lie in the name of the grantee in the deed but lies only in the name of the grantor. *M. & M. Auto Parts Co. v. Riddle,* 102 Fla. 598, 136 So. 437 (1931); *Coogler v. Rogers,* 25 Fla. 853, 7 So. 391 (1889).

The defendant in an action for ejectment is the party in possession or the one claiming adversely to the plaintiff. Under *F.S.* 66.021(1) when a defendant is in possession as a tenant only, his landlord must be made an additional defendant, unless otherwise ordered by the court.

In *RCP* 1.260(a) provision is made for the continuation of the action when a party dies during the proceeding. Consequently, the legal representative and the heirs or devisees of the party may be substituted as the proper parties in an action of ejectment. This rule also provides that additional parties in interest or possession may be made parties.

B. Chain Of Title

   1. [§3.10] In General

F.S. 66.021(4) requires a statement of the chain of title to be attached to the complaint. See *RCP* Form 1.940. The statement should set forth chronologically the chain of title upon which the plaintiff will rely at trial. If any part of the chain of title is recorded, the statement should set forth the names of the grantors and the grantees and the book and page of the recording; if an unrecorded instrument is relied upon, a copy of it should be attached, and the court may require the original to be submitted to the opposite party for inspection. In any event, the instrument relied upon or the title deraigned by the plaintiff must be sufficiently valid and be paramount or superior to, or older or better than the defendant's.

When both the plaintiff and the defendant rely upon tax deeds, the holder of the subsequent deed, in the absence of any showing successfully impeaching it, exhibits a superior right to recovery. The doctrine of *idem sonans* would be applicable to admit an ancient deed when the name of the grantor differs from that of the actual name of the person who owns the land, if the deed otherwise is sufficient to establish chain of title. If a deed relied upon by the plaintiff contains an imperfect description so as not to be effectual to convey the land, it will not sustain an action of ejectment. An omission from a deed of a plat and the place of recordation, however, is considered so minor that it would not defeat the plaintiff's claim of title.

If a plaintiff relies upon prior possession to establish his right of possession, he must show prior possession by proper evidence. If he relies upon a claim or right without color of title, the statement should specify how and when the claim originated and the facts upon which it is based. If both the defendant and the plaintiff claim under a common source, the statement need not deraign title prior to the common source.

Probably the simplest method of treating the chain of title is to attach it to the complaint as an exhibit. Both the complaint and answer should contain an allegation that the chain of title is attached as an exhibit. See *RCP* Form 1.940.

2. [§3.11] Form For Chain Of Title

CHAIN OF TITLE

Plaintiff deraigns his title to

[legal description]

in the following manner:

1. Patent from the United States of America, to ...., dated ...., filed for record ...., and recorded in Deed Book ...., page ...., of the public records of .... County, Florida.

2. Warranty deed from .... to ...., dated ...., filed for record ...., and recorded in Deed Book ...., page ...., of the public records of .... County, Florida.

3. Quitclaim deed from .... to ...., dated ...., filed for record ...., and recorded in Official Records Book ...., page ...., of the public records of .... County, Florida.

C. [§3.12] Claim For Mesne Profits

Mesne profits must be considered in preparing a complaint in ejectment. They are defined as the value of the use and occupation of the land during the period the defendant is shown to have been wrongfully in possession. The mesne profits are recoverable from the initial date of the detention up to the time of trial.

In *Kester v. Bostwick,* 153 Fla. 437, 15 So.2d 201 (1943), the Florida Supreme Court held that the measure of mesne profits was the value of the use and occupation during the period of wrongful possession, which may be determined by the value of the net rents and profits. The court said that "net rents and profits has reference to a fair rental value less the cost of rental and collection but does not contemplate interest on the investment."

In addition, under proper allegations in the complaint the plaintiff also may recover damages for waste and dilapidation or injuries to the freehold, the measure of which is the diminished value of the land. This would include, for example, damages for the cutting and removal of timber or the destruction and removal of buildings from the premises.

The suggested form for the ejectment complaint in *RCP* Form 1.940 includes a demand for damages. For convenience, the form is set out below with some modification.

D. [§3.13] Form For Averments And Demand In Complaint

COMPLAINT

Plaintiff, A. B., sues defendant, C. D., and alleges:

1. This is an action to recover real property in .... County, Florida.

2. Defendant is in possession of the following real property in that county:

[legal description]

to which plaintiff claims title as shown by the attached statement of plaintiff's chain of title.

3. Defendant refuses to deliver possession of the property to plaintiff or pay him the profits from it.

WHEREFORE plaintiff demands judgment for possession of the property and damages against defendant.

COMMENT: This form is based on the one suggested in *RCP* Form 1.940. If trial by jury is desired, demand for it in writing must be made. *RCP* 1.430.

IV. THE ANSWER AND COUNTERCLAIMS

A. The Answer

1. [§3.14] In General

The defendant's answer in ejectment should specify those allegations of the complaint with which he takes issue, whether concerning plaintiff's title to the lands in controversy, defendant's possession or otherwise. See *RCP* 1.110(c). *F.S.* 66.021(4) requires that the defendant, as well as the plaintiff, file a statement setting forth chronologically the chain of title upon which he will rely at trial. As in the case of the complaint, the chain of title should be attached to the answer as an exhibit. See §3.10.

There are a multitude of defenses available in an ejectment action. Generally, anything that shows that the plaintiff is not entitled to immediate possession is a valid defense. This includes, among others, such matters as:

1. legal title not in the plaintiff at time of commencement of action;

2. adverse possession;

3. title in the defendant;

4. acquiescence by plaintiff in a boundary line;

5. the statutes of limitation;

6. laches; and

7. estoppel.

Defenses based on statutes of limitation and adverse possession will be discussed further in §3.15.

2. [§3.15] Defenses Based On Statutes Of Limitation And Adverse Possession

Defenses based on statutes of limitation and on adverse possession both involve a period of seven years. See *F.S.* 95.12, .16 and .18 and Chapter 7 FLORIDA REAL PROPERTY PRACTICE I (CLE 2d ed. 1971). Yet, they appear to constitute two distinct defenses.

When the defendant desires to establish his own title by adverse possession, proof is required of all the elements of adverse possession, such as continuity, openness, hostility, notoriety and exclusiveness. See §§5.14 and 7.8–.11 FLORIDA REAL PROPERTY PRACTICE I (CLE 2d ed. 1971).

If the defendant is concerned merely with an absolute defense to the ejectment action, the statutes of limitation should present a much more expeditious defense and reduce the extent of proof required. Under the statute of limitations, *F.S.* 95.12, the defendant should have to show only that the plaintiff was out of possession for a period in excess of seven years, or that the plaintiff had a cause of action that accrued more than seven years before the institution of the action.

Notwithstanding the above comments, *F.S.* 95.13 states in effect that in an ejectment action a person establishing a legal title will be presumed to have been possessed of that title within the time prescribed by law. It further states that the occupation of the property by any other person will be deemed to have been in subordination to the legal title, unless it appears that the property had been held and possessed adversely to that legal title for seven years before the commencement of the action. Consequently, in the early case of *Wade v. Doyle,* 17 Fla. 522 (1880), it was held that a defense to an ejectment action based upon the statutes of limitation, which simply denied the possession of the plaintiff within seven years before the commencement of the action, was insufficient and the defense of adverse possession should have been set forth instead.

3. [§3.16] Form For Answer

(Title of Court)

(Title of Cause)   ANSWER

Defendant, ..., answers the complaint and alleges:

1. Defendant admits paragraph 1.

2. Defendant denies paragraphs 2 and 3.

FIRST DEFENSE

3. Title to the lands described in the complaint is vested in defendant, as shown by the attached statement of the chain of title on which defendant will rely at trial.

SECOND DEFENSE

4. Defendant claims title by adverse possession, under color of title, to the lands described in the complaint.

THIRD DEFENSE

5. Plaintiff and his predecessors in title acquiesced in the boundary line as established between their property and the property of defendant on and after ....(date)..........

FOURTH DEFENSE

6. Plaintiff and his predecessors knew of the construction by defendant of valuable and extensive improvements on the lands described in the complaint, yet made no objection to that construction of improvements; all of the improvements were made by defendant on the assumption that he was the undisputed owner of the property on which they were made; and plaintiff now is estopped to claim title to the lands or assert a claim to possession of them.

FIFTH DEFENSE

7. Each cause of action, claim and item of damages did not accrue within the time prescribed by law for them before this action was brought.

WHEREFORE, defendant demands judgment against plaintiff, together with costs of this action.

```
                                              _____
                                              Attorney

                                              .................(address).................
(Certificate of Service)
```

COMMENT: All of the above defenses are not necessarily appropriate in every case. As indicated in paragraph 3 of the answer, the defendant should set out as an exhibit his chain of title, just as the plaintiff must with his complaint. See §§3.10 and .11.

B.   [§3.17] Counterclaims

Counterclaims are permissible in ejectment actions. Formerly counterclaims in ejectment actions were prohibited by the statutes.

Former *F.S.* 46.08 provided that replevin and ejectment could not be joined together or with other causes of action. The statute was repealed by FLA. LAWS 1967, ch. 67-254.

V. CONDUCT OF THE TRIAL

A. [§3.18] In General

In actions of ejectment the plaintiff must recover on the strength of his own title and not on the weakness of the title of the defendant. Indeed, the plaintiff cannot recover even as against one without title, unless he shows paramount title or prior possession. It has been stated also that a plaintiff cannot recover in an action in ejectment by showing title in a third party. See *Hogans v. Carruth,* 18 Fla. 587 (1882). Of course, when both parties claim title, the better title will determine the right to possession.

When the plaintiff is relying on legal title, he must show a regular and continuous chain of title from the government or from someone having possession and the right to convey title. A plaintiff relying upon a conveyance from a person who had no legal title and who was never in possession cannot recover in ejectment. When both parties assert title from a common source, the plaintiff need not go back behind the common source since neither party in ejectment can deny the earlier title under which he claims. See *F.S.* 66.021(4).

When the plaintiff relies upon legal title for recovery in ejectment, that title must exist in the plaintiff at the time he commences the action. The acquisition of a legal title subsequent to the action will not be sufficient.

B. Clarifying The Issues Before Trial

1. [§3.19] In General

The use of a pretrial conference is an invaluable asset in an ejectment action. At the pretrial conference all questions of law should be raised by the parties and settled by the court and all documents to be offered in evidence should be submitted to the court by the parties. Frequently, this procedure permits agreement on certain phases of the title that may be acceptable to both sides and thus diminishes the labor required in proof at the trial. It also frequently develops that the defendant may not be claiming the entire parcel of property and the areas not claimed by the defendant can be disposed of at that time.

The pretrial conference generally is discussed more fully in Chapter 17 of FLORIDA CIVIL PRACTICE BEFORE TRIAL (CLE 3d ed. 1975).

At the time of trial, any remaining legal questions, particularly questions that may have arisen since the time of the pretrial conference, should be resolved by the court before presentation of testimony and other evidence. It is also well to anticipate legal situations or questions that may arise during the course of the trial and attempt to obtain a ruling in respect to them before the commencement of the actual trial.

The burden of proving title in an ejectment action has been reduced. *F.S.* 66.021(5) provides that if either party desires to test the legal sufficiency of an instrument or court proceeding in the chain of title of the opposite party, he must do so before trial by a motion, with a copy of the instrument or court proceedings attached, setting up his objections. The motion must then be disposed of before trial. If either party then determines that he will be unable to maintain his cause by reason of that order, he may so state in the record and final judgment will be entered by the court for the opposite party.

2. [§3.20] Form For Motion To Test Legal Sufficiency Of Instrument Or Court Proceedings

(Title of Court)

(Title of Court)

PLAINTIFF'S MOTION TO TEST LEGAL SUFFICIENCY OF INSTRUMENT OR COURT PROCEEDINGS

Plaintiff moves to test the legal sufficiency of the instrument (or court proceeding) described in defendant's chain of title as ....(description of instrument or court proceeding).........., a copy being attached, on the following grounds:

[list grounds for objections]

Attorney for Plaintiff

..................(address)..................

(Certificate of Service)

COMMENT: See *F.S.* 66.021.

C. [§3.21] Burden Of Proof

A plaintiff who relies on possession alone must show a possession anterior in date to the possession of the defendant. When no legal title is shown in either party, the party showing prior possession in himself or those through whom he claims will be held to have the better right.

The burdens of the respective parties in an ejectment action have been expressed aptly by the Florida Supreme Court in a syllabus to *L'Engle v. Reed,* 27 Fla. 345, 9 So. 213 (1891) as follows:

> A plaintiff in ejectment must show a better title than that of defendant, or a prior actual possession to that of defendant, or a good conveyance to himself from one in actual possession and prior to that of defendant, in order to put the defendant to the necessity of supporting his possession by a title superior to one of naked possession.

See also *Tilman v. Niemira,* 99 Fla. 833, 127 So. 855 (1930).

It should be noted that the above principles do not require the plaintiff to exhibit a perfect chain of title from the original source, but the plaintiff only has to exhibit so much as will shift to the defendant the burden of proof as to the invalidity of the plaintiff's title or the burden of supporting his possession by proof of "a title superior to one of naked possession." See *L'Engle v. Reed, supra.*

D. Presentation Of Proof

1. [§3.22] In General

It is better practice for the plaintiff to present his case initially in a substantial manner. In other words, he should go beyond the presentation of a mere prima facie case. To limit the plaintiff's proof to a mere prima facie showing of a better title and right of possession than that of the defendant may place the plaintiff in a position of having to present a major part of his case in rebuttal with all of the restrictions applicable to rebuttal testimony.

The defendant should present all of his evidence in his case in chief.

2. [§3.23] Proof Of Damages

As noted in §3.12, damages in ejectment are the mesne profits. This is measured by the value of the rents and profits during the period the defendant was wrongfully in possession. It therefore is incumbent upon the plaintiff to establish the reasonable rental or use value of the property.

Customarily, expert witnesses are utilized on the issues of profits or damages. The names of those witnesses should be disclosed at the time of the pretrial conference. It is also good practice to have the court limit the number of experts to be used by the respective sides.

VI. THE VERDICT

A. [§3.24] In General

At a pretrial or other conference, jury instructions should be submitted to the court for consideration. See FLORIDA STANDARD JURY INSTRUCTIONS (Civil Cases). They should be prepared carefully and supported by adequate authority. Also, the forms of the verdicts should be drafted by the parties in advance and approved by the court. Care should be taken in drafting the verdict to provide for separate disposition of the issues of profits and damages.

F.S. 66.031(1) requires that a verdict for the plaintiff in ejectment state the quantity of the estate of the plaintiff and describe the land by its metes and bounds, the number of the lot or by other certain description. Although this statute does not so specify, a verdict for the plaintiff also must find the right of possession in him, and make appropriate findings as to mesne profits or damages, if sought by the plaintiff.

B. [§3.25] Form For Verdict For Defendant

(Title of Court)

(Title of Cause)   **VERDICT FOR DEFENDANT**

We, the jury, find for defendant, ..., and that he has the right of possession of the following-described property:

[legal description]

..........(date)..........

_____
as Foreman

Copies furnished to: ....

COMMENT: See also the forms set out in FLORIDA CIVIL TRIAL PRACTICE Chapter 18 (CLE 3d ed. 1975). A form for a verdict for the plaintiff, with damages, is in the form for judgment for a plaintiff set out in §3.28.

VII. THE JUDGMENT

A. [§3.26] In General

F.S. 66.031(2) requires that the judgment awarding possession, as in the verdict, state the quantity of the estate and give a description of the land recovered. Failure to include these renders the judgment fatally defective. Likewise, a judgment in ejectment should determine the right of possession and provide for recovery of possession and mesne profits or damages, if any.

The judgment does not create a new estate or vest a new title in the plaintiff, but rather establishes the plaintiff's right to possession.

B. [§3.27] Taxing Of Costs

Ejectment is an action at law and the usual rule relating to costs prevails, namely, that costs will be awarded to the prevailing party. Attorneys' fees are not taxable as costs. See §3.31.

C. [§3.28] Form For Judgment For Plaintiff

(Title of Court)

(Title of Cause) FINAL JUDGMENT FOR PLAINTIFF

Pursuant to the verdict rendered in this action,

IT IS ADJUDGED THAT:

1. Plaintiff is and was at the institution of this action the owner in fee simple and entitled to the possession of the following-described property:

[quantity and legal description]

2. Plaintiff recovers from defendant possession of the property described above, for which let writ of possession issue.

3. Plaintiff recovers from defendant the sum of $.........., as damages for mesne profits, and his costs now taxed at $.........., for which let execution issue.

ORDERED at ...., Florida on ....(date)..........

Copies furnished to: ....   Circuit Judge

COMMENT: See also the forms suggested in FLORIDA CIVIL TRIAL PRACTICE Chapter 22 (CLE 3d ed. 1975).

VIII. ENFORCING THE JUDGMENT AND TERMINATION PROCEDURES

A. [§3.29] In General

F.S. 66.021(3) deals with the enforcement of judgments in ejectments. This statute provides that when the plaintiff recovers in ejectment, he may have one writ for possession, damages and costs. In the alternative, a plaintiff may elect to have separate writs for possession and for his damages. Separate writs probably would be appropriate in actions in which the plaintiff may not desire to collect the damages at the same time as possession, or when a levy of execution for damages must be made in a county or place other than where the real property is located.

B. [§3.30] Form For Writ Of Possession And Execution

THE STATE OF FLORIDA:

To All and Singular the Sheriffs of the State:

YOU ARE COMMANDED to remove all persons from the following-described property in .... County, Florida:

[legal description]

and to put ....(plaintiff).......... into possession of it.

YOU ARE FURTHER COMMANDED to levy on the goods and chattels, lands and tenements of ....(defendant).......... in the sum of $.......... with legal interest thereon from ....(date).......... until paid and to have this writ before the court when satisfied.

WITNESS my hand and the seal of this court on ....(date)..........

....
As Clerk of the Court

By: _____
As Deputy Clerk

COMMENT: The above form is a combination of *RCP* Forms 1.914 and 1.915.

IX. [§3.31] ATTORNEYS' FEES IN ACTION OF EJECTMENT

Since ejectment involves real property, which may have little or great value, the attorney in fixing his fee for instituting or defending the action necessarily must take into account the value of the real property involved. He also must consider the complexity of the case.

There is no provision in the statutes for the recovery of attorneys' fees, and as the action is not based on contract between the parties, attorneys' fees are not recoverable from the opponent.

X. BETTERMENT

A. [§3.32] In General

The Florida ejectment statute offers relief to a defendant who is evicted from the property by the plaintiff after he has placed improvements upon the property. This relief is known as "betterment" and is provided for in *F.S.* 66.041–.101.

B. Petition

1. [§3.33] In General

Within 60 days after the rendition of a judgment of eviction or of its affirmance on appeal, against the defendant in an ejectment action, the defendant may file a betterment petition in the circuit court in which the judgment was rendered. The petition is filed in the ejectment action and does not necessitate the institution of a new lawsuit. *F.S.* 66.041 provides that the betterment petition must set forth:

(1) Defendant had been in possession and that he or those under whom he validly derived had permanently improved the value of the property in controversy before commencement of the action in which judgment was rendered.

(2) Defendant or those under whom he validly derives held the property at the time of such improvement under an apparently good legal or equitable title derived from the English, Spanish or United States governments or this state; or under a legal or equitable title plain and connected on the records of a public office or public offices; or under purchase at a regular sale made by an executor, administrator, guardian or other person by order of court; and

(3) When defendant made the improvements or purchased the property improved, he believed the title which he held or purchased to the land thus improved to be a good and valid title. The petition shall demand that the value of the improvements be assessed and compensation awarded to him therefor.

It should be observed that a successful defendant in a betterment action has a considerable burden of proof, going both to his title and his state of mind concerning that title, in addition to the facts of betterments.

 2. [§3.34] Form For Petition For Compensation For Betterments

(Title of Court)

(Title of Cause)   **DEFENDANT'S PETITION FOR COMPENSATION FOR BETTERMENTS**

The petition of defendant, ..., shows:

1. Defendant has been in possession of the following-described property:

[legal description]

until the entry of the judgment of ejectment in this action on ....(date)..........

2. The possession of the property by defendant, or those under whom he validly derived, was held under an apparently good legal or equitable title, plain and connected upon the public records of .... County, Florida.

3. Defendant, or those under whom he validly derived, during that possession, had reasonable grounds to believe defendant, or those under whom he validly derived, was the rightful owner and entitled to the sole and rightful possession of the property, and defendant, or those under whom he validly derived, during the period of his possession, had no knowledge of any claim to possession by plaintiff or any other party.

4. During the possession of the property by defendant, or those under whom he validly derived, defendant made certain permanent improvements to the property consisting of the following:

[describe, such as a garage, landscaping, driveways or fencing]

The improvements have permanently improved and increased the value of the property upon which the improvements have been erected. The improvements have been entirely paid for by defendant.

5. By reason of the judgment of ejectment entered in the above cause, plaintiff has taken possession of the property and the improvements located on it and plaintiff stands to gain and will be unjustly enriched by the acquisition of the improvements provided by defendant.

WHEREFORE, defendant demands compensation for the improvements placed upon the property.

Attorney for Defendant

.................(address).................

(Certificate of Service)

COMMENT: See *F.S.* 66.041.

C. [§3.35] Reply

The plaintiff has a period of 20 days after notice to him of the filing of the petition within which to reply to it. *F.S.* 66.051.

D. [§3.36] Trial

F.S. 66.061 provides that after the reply has been filed or, if no reply is filed (subsequent to the passing of 20 days from the time the petition was filed) the issues will be tried at a time set by the court. If no reply is filed, the trial proceeds ex parte, but the defendant still must prove every allegation of his betterment petition and a jury must try the issues, unless trial by jury is waived. See §3.33.

E. [§3.37] The Verdict

If the defendant successfully proves the allegations of the betterment petition, F.S. 66.061 requires the trier of fact to assess the following items:

(1) The value of the land at the time of the assessment, irrespective of the improvements put upon the land by defendant or those under whom he derives, and if any, the injury done to the land by defendant or those under whom he derives.

(2) The value of the permanent improvements at the time of the assessment.

(3) The injury, if any, done to the land by defendant or those under whom he derives.

(4) The value of the use of the land by defendant between the time of the judgment in ejectment and the time of the assessment or if defendant has been evicted from or has surrendered the premises, from the time of the judgment to the time of the surrender or eviction. The findings shall be specified separately on each of these matters.

F. The Judgment

1. [§3.38] In General

After the rendition of a verdict on the betterment petition, the court causes the clerk to ascertain whether the balance of the last three assessments listed in §3.37 are in favor of the plaintiff or the defendant who brought the betterment action, and to ascertain the amount of the balance. F.S. 66.071.

2. [§3.39] For Plaintiff

If the verdict on the defendant's betterment petition is in favor of the plaintiff, a judgment is rendered against the defendant for costs, whether the balance of the assessments was in the favor of the defendant or the plaintiff. In the latter event, the plaintiff also gets judgment for the balance. *F.S.* 66.071.

3. For Defendant

a. [§3.40] In General

If the verdict on the betterment petition is in favor of the defendant who brought it and the balance of assessments is also in his favor, a judgment for costs and the balance is entered against the plaintiff. Further, the defendant's judgment should require the plaintiff to pay the amount of the balance of the assessments previously mentioned within 20 days, and the plaintiff's failure to do so will have the consequence noted in §3.41. *F.S.* 66.081.

b. [§3.41] The Vesting In Defendant Of Title To The Land Upon Plaintiff's Failure To Pay Betterment Judgment

If the defendant's betterment judgment requires the plaintiff to pay a balance of the assessments to the defendant, the plaintiff then either may pay the balance in cash or execute and deliver to the defendant a bond conditioned to pay him the amount of the judgment. The bond must be with surety, to be approved by the clerk of the court, and the balance is to be paid in two equal annual installments, with interest at six per cent. *F.S.* 66.091. If the plaintiff does not pay or bond the judgment within 20 days after its rendition, or having bonded the judgment fails to pay it when due, the defendant has the right within 20 days to pay to the plaintiff the value of the land as assessed. 66.081 and .101. As an alternative, the defendant may give the plaintiff a bond conditioned to pay to the plaintiff the value of the land in two equal annual installments with interest at six per cent. This bond also must be with a surety, to be approved by the clerk of the court. See the statutory definition of "bond" in *F.S.* 45.011.

Upon the payment by the defendant of the value of the land to the plaintiff, the title to the land vests in the defendant. *F.S.* 66.101. The plaintiff, although previously having been successful in his action of ejectment against the defendant, then must give the defendant a deed to the property. He also must relinquish possession to the defendant if the defendant had been evicted or had surrendered possession to the plaintiff in accordance with the action of ejectment.

W. J. OVEN, JR.*

4

PARTITION

I. THE REMEDY

    A. [§4.1] Introduction

    B. Property And Estate Subject To Partition

        1. [§4.2] In General

        2. [§4.3] Oil And Mineral Rights

    C. [§4.4] Scope Of Remedy

    D. [§4.5] Incidental Relief

    E. [§4.6] Necessary Interest Of Plaintiff

    F. [§4.7] Waiver Of Right

    G. [§4.8] Discretion Of Court

    H. [§4.9] Partition In Part Only

II. PROCEDURE

    A. Complaint

        1. [§4.10] Necessary Title Information

        2. [§4.11] Statutory Requirements

---

*LL.B., 1933, University of Virginia. Mr. Oven is a member of the Second Circuit, Tallahassee and American bar associations and has been admitted to the practice of law in the State of Virginia. He is a sole practitioner in Tallahassee.

†Mr. W. G. Ward was the author of this chapter in the first edition.

3. [§4.12] Allegations Of Necessity Of Sale

4. [§4.13] Sample Complaint For Partition

B. [§4.14] Defenses And Counterclaims

C. Judgment For Partition

1. [§4.15] Parts To Be Divided

2. [§4.16] Accountings

3. [§4.17] Order Of Sale

4. [§4.18] Appointment Of Commissioners

5. [§4.19] Special Equities To Be Considered

D. Powers And Duties Of The Commissioners

1. [§4.20] Incidental Power

2. Reports

a. [§4.21] Contents

b. [§4.22] Number Required To Join In Report

c. [§4.23] Necessity For Notice

d. [§4.24] Objections

e. [§4.25] Property Not Divisible

E. Final Judgments

1. [§4.26] Taxation Of Costs

2. Attorneys' Fees

a. [§4.27] Persons Entitled

b. [§4.28] Factors Considered In Determining

c. [§4.29] Attorneys' Fees On Dismissal

3. [§4.30] Doctrine Of Owelty

      4. [§4.31] Protection Of Lienors

      5. [§4.32] Retention Of Jurisdiction

      6. [§4.33] Sample Judgment Of Partition

F. Sale Of Property

      1. [§4.34] Public Or Private

      2. [§4.35] By Whom Made

      3. [§4.36] Persons Entitled To Bid

      4. [§4.37] Approval Of Court And Distribution Of Proceeds

I. THE REMEDY

A. [§4.1] Introduction

Partition in Florida is more or less a statutory remedy, *Lovett v. Lovett,* 93 Fla. 611, 112 So. 768 (1927), the procedure for which is prescribed by *F.S.* Chapter 64. Other than in terminology, the procedure has been changed little since the original act of March 14, 1844. One significant change, however, is incorporated in *F.S.* 64.061(4), which provides that upon allegation and proof that the property is not subject to partition in kind without prejudice to the owners, the court may appoint a special master or the clerk to sell the property at public or private sale (otherwise, commissioners are appointed). Another significant change was the addition of *F.S.* 64.091, which makes personal as well as real property subject to partition.

B. Property And Estate Subject To Partition

1. [§4.2] In General

By statute, *F.S.* 64.091, personal as well as real property is subject to partition. In *Reed v. Fink,* 259 So.2d 729 (3d D.C.A. Fla. 1972), this remedy was applied to a stallion.

The following estates have been held subject to partition: joint tenancy; tenancy in common; tenancy as co-partners, *F.S.* 64.031; and land held in trust, when the trustee holds only a naked trust, *Elvins v. Seestedt,* 141 Fla. 266, 193 So. 54 (1940), 126 A.L.R. 1001. It also has been held applicable to homestead property upon death of the head of the family, *Donly v. Metropolitan Realty & Investment Co.,* 71 Fla. 644, 72 So. 178 (1916). It probably is not applicable if the homestead is subject to a life estate in the surviving widow, *Weed v. Knox,* 157 Fla. 896, 27 So.2d 419 (1946), in which case, of course, the remaindermen have no right of immediate possession. See also *Moore v. Price,* 98 Fla. 276, 123 So. 768 (1929), decided prior to the Probate Act of 1933. In each of the three cases cited above it was apparent that the court recognized that after the widow had elected to take a child's part, or after her dower had been assigned, dower being then a life estate only, the homestead character of the land was lost.

The fact that the property is subject to a leasehold estate in a person not otherwise interested in it does not prevent a partition. *Leonard v. Browne,* 134 So.2d 872 (1st D.C.A. Fla. 1961).

Property formerly held as an estate by the entirety may be partitioned after dissolution of the marriage, since upon dissolution the owners become tenants in common. *Kollar v. Kollar,* 155 Fla. 705, 21 So.2d 356 (1945). If properly plead, the property may be partitioned as a part of the dissolution proceedings. See *Rankin v. Rankin,* 258 So.2d 489 (2d D.C.A. Fla. 1972).

On the other hand, estates by the entireties are not subject to partition. See *Hunt v. Covington,* 145 Fla. 706, 200 So. 76 (1941). This is true even though the spouses may have separated. *Naurison v. Naurison,* 132 So.2d 623 (3d D.C.A. Fla. 1961). Nor may remaindermen obtain partition when there is a life estate outstanding, *Weed v. Knox, supra.* A trustee in bankruptcy cannot require partition, *Hobbs v. Frazier,* 56 Fla. 796, 47 So. 929 (1908), even though authorized to do so by the bankruptcy court, *Langford v. Brickell,* 103 Fla. 672, 138 So. 75 (1931), unless it is necessary to protect fully the rights of creditors. Further, an administrator may not demand partition, even though the action originally was instituted by his intestate, *Greeley v. Hendricks,* 23 Fla. 366, 2 So. 620 (1887). An executor may not seek partition unless it is shown by the will that he is invested with and authorized to represent the title. *Nelson v. Haisley,* 39 Fla. 145, 22 So. 265 (1897).

2. [§4.3] Oil And Mineral Rights

Mineral rights generally are subject to partition, even though held separately from surface rights. The fact that the surface rights are held entirely by a single party does not prevent a partition of the mineral rights held by more than one person. *Rudman v. Baine,* 133 So.2d 760 (1st D.C.A. Fla. 1961). In that case, the court expressly refrained from passing on the question as to whether a partition should be accomplished by a division in kind or by a sale of the rights and a division of the proceeds, or whether the sale should be public or private. Of course, if the instrument by which the mineral rights and surface rights were separated sets out a reasonable method of dividing the mineral rights, judicial partition will not be granted until that method has been applied. *Robinson v. Speer,* 185 So.2d 730 (1st D.C.A. Fla. 1966), *cert. den.* 192 So.2d 498. It has been suggested that with so much land in Florida subject to outstanding fractional mineral interests not held by the surface owners, an increase in the use of partition actions to get rid of these outstanding fractional interests may be seen.

C.   [§4.4] Scope Of Remedy

The courts have repeatedly held that an action for partition cannot be utilized as a substitute for an action in ejectment; for the sole purpose of testing the legal title, *Griffith v. Griffith,* 59 Fla. 512, 52 So. 609 (1910); nor for settling a disputed title, *Rountree v. Rountree,* 101 So.2d 43 (Fla. 1958).

On the other hand, the fact that one of the alleged owners claims adversely under a legal title or disputes the other's title or right to possession does not defeat the remedy. *Camp Phosphate Co. v. Anderson,* 48 Fla. 226, 37 So. 722 (1904). If a complaint for partition does not include all the lands of the cotenancy, any defendant may call the omission to the court's attention and insist upon the omitted lands being included in the action. See *Lovett v. Lovett,* 93 Fla. 611, 112 So. 768 (1927). In the event of a dispute as to ownership, the title is determined by the court, not by the commissioners, *Street v. Benner,* 20 Fla. 700 (1884), and all controversies as to legal title and right of possession should be so determined, *Camp Phosphate Co. v. Anderson, supra.* A defendant may be entitled to foreclose his mortgage on part of the land by filing a counterclaim. *Miles v. Miles,* 117 Fla. 884, 158 So. 520 (1935). Partition may be ordered as to some of the owners jointly rather than severally. *Shaffer v. Pickard,* 77 Fla. 697, 82 So. 232 (1919).

D.   [§4.5] Incidental Relief

When an action for partition is properly brought, all controversies about the title should be settled in that action. *Ellis v. Everett,* 79 Fla. 493, 84 So. 617 (1920). The court in one action can order partition of undivided estates, take an accounting, cancel fraudulent conveyances and determine antagonistic claims to the subject matter, if all of these forms of relief are necessary to the granting of complete relief. See *Williams v. Ricou,* 143 Fla. 360, 196 So. 667 (1940). Family relationships and the financial status of the parties are not properly considered as affecting the right to partition. *Keyes v. Rymer Realty Corporation,* 219 So.2d 711 (3d D.C.A. Fla. 1969). A mortgage held by one owner against part of the land may be foreclosed in the partition action, *Miles v. Miles,* 117 Fla. 884, 158 So. 520 (1935), and a judgment lien held by some of the owners against other owners likewise may be settled in the partition action. *Burney v. Dedge,* 56 So.2d 715 (Fla. 1952). The matter of an accounting on partition is discussed in §4.16.

E. [§4.6] Necessary Interest Of Plaintiff

Partition is available only when the plaintiff has possession or a right to immediate beneficial possession of the property. *Black v. Miller,* 219 So.2d 106 (3d D.C.A. Fla. 1969), *cert. den.* 225 So.2d 920. It cannot be enforced if there is a life estate outstanding. *Weed v. Knox,* 157 Fla. 896, 27 So.2d 419 (1946). Generally speaking, the action may be brought by any joint tenant, tenant in common or coparcener, even though one joint owner has ousted him, claims adversely under a legal title or disputes his right to possession. *Camp Phosphate Co. v. Anderson,* 48 Fla. 226, 37 So. 722 (1904). A complaint for partition must show title in the plaintiff. A mere equitable interest is not sufficient even though enforceable in a proper proceeding. *Williams v. City of St. Petersburg,* 57 Fla. 544, 48 So. 754 (1909). A legal title in the plaintiff is not necessary. A partition action may be maintained by a cestui que trust, when the trustee holds only a naked legal title. *Elvins v. Seestedt,* 141 Fla. 266, 193 So. 54 (1940), 126 A.L.R. 1001. The fact that the land is adversely claimed by a cotenant in possession does not defeat the plaintiff's right to partition. *Girtman v. Starbuck,* 48 Fla. 265, 37 So. 731 (1904).

F. [§4.7] Waiver Of Right

The right to partition may be waived, or one may be estopped from enforcing his remedy. An agreement not to partition, when reasonable, is enforceable. *Forehand v. Peacock,* 77 So.2d 625 (Fla. 1955). An agreement not to partition is not enforceable if it is so unreasonably restrictive as to be contrary to public policy, such as an agreement never to seek partition. An agreement, even though oral, never to seek partition during the life of any of the tenants in common has been held not to be valid. *Condrey v. Condrey,* 92 So.2d 423 (Fla. 1957).

G. [§4.8] Discretion Of Court

If the statute has given a person the right to partition, the court has no discretion in granting the remedy and cannot consider such matters as family relationships or the relative financial standing of the parties. *Keyes v. Rymer Realty Corporation,* 219 So.2d 711 (3d D.C.A. Fla. 1969).

H. [§4.9] Partition In Part Only

Ordinarily, a complaint for partition should include all of the lands of the cotenancy. A cotenant cannot enforce a partition of a part only of the common lands, leaving the rest undivided. If the complaint does not include all the lands of the cotenancy, any defendant can call that omission to the court's attention and insist upon its inclusion. See *Lovett v. Lovett,* 93 Fla. 611, 112 So. 768 (1927). On the other hand, on proper proceedings the court may deem that partition be made to some of the parties jointly instead of severally. *Shaffer v. Pickard,* 77 Fla. 697, 82 So. 232 (1919).

II. PROCEDURE

A. Complaint

1. [§4.10] Necessary Title Information

It is necessary that the attorney drafting a complaint for partition have complete title information. There may be mortgages outstanding against a fractional interest, or judgments of record against a co-owner, conveyances of fractional interests among the co-owners, or to outside persons, or wills of record that alter the normal descent of property. If all parties having interests in or liens upon the land in question are not properly brought into court, a second action may be necessary. If a mere partition among titleholders is desired, only they are necessary parties.

2. [§4.11] Statutory Requirements

F.S. 64.041 requires that the complaint allege:

1. A description of the lands of which partition is demanded;

2. The names and places of residence of the owners, joint tenants, tenants in common, coparceners or other persons interested in the lands;

3. The quantity held by each;

4. Any other matters necessary to enable the court to adjudicate the rights and interests of the parties.

If any of the names, residences or quantities of interest is unknown, that fact should be so stated. If the name is unknown, the action may proceed as though the unknown persons in fact were named.

If the complaint seeks other incidental relief, it should allege a proper predicate. Likewise, if the plaintiff seeks some particular equity, such as consideration for improvements placed by him on the common property, the circumstances entitling him to special treatment should be clearly stated.

The former requirement that the complaint be verified was eliminated by FLA. LAWS 1967, ch. 67-254, §19.

3. [§4.12] Allegations Of Necessity Of Sale

F.S. 64.061(4) provides that when a pleading alleges that the property sought to be partitioned is indivisible, and the allegation is not contested or, if contested, is satisfactorily proved, the court may appoint a special master or the clerk to make sale of the property either at private sale or public sale. If the plaintiff prefers to have a private sale made by a special master, it is most important that he make this allegation in the complaint; otherwise, the court must appoint the commissioners as prescribed in *F.S.* 64.061(1), even though it is obvious they will have to report back that partition cannot be made without prejudice to the owners.

See also §4.17.

4. [§4.13] Sample Complaint For Partition

(Title of Court)

(Title of Cause)   **COMPLAINT**

Plaintiff, Mary R. Doe, sues defendant, T. Richard Roe, and alleges:

1.   This is an action for partition of real property.

2.   The property sought to be partitioned is in .... County, Florida, and is described as:

[legal description]

3.   The property was acquired by Archibald Roe by deed dated May 23, 1905, and recorded at page 14 of Deed Book 50 of the records in the office of the clerk of this court. Archibald Roe died intestate on August 31, 1911, leaving surviving him a widow, since deceased, and three children: plaintiff, Mary R. Doe, Defendant, T. Richard Roe, and one Oscar K. Roe, since deceased. Oscar K. Roe

died leaving a last will and testament dated August 6, 1920, and recorded at page 35 of Will Book 27 of the records formerly in the office of the county judge of .... County, Florida. In and by his last will and testament, Oscar K. Roe devised all of his real estate in .... County, Florida, to his five children, the Defendants, Sally R. Roe, John K. Roe, Alexander M. Roe, Elsa R. Roe and Jessie J. Roe.

4. Archibald Roe and his descendants have possessed the property until the present time.

5. The following parties to this action are the owners of the property in the proportions set opposite their respective names. Their places of residence are set out opposite their respective names.

[set out names, residences and proportions]

6. The property is indivisible and is not subject to partition in kind without prejudice to its owners.

WHEREFORE, plaintiff respectfully demands that a partition of the property be ordered.

_____

Attorney for Plaintiff

..................(address)..................

(Acknowledgment)

B. [§4.14] Defenses And Counterclaims

The defense of laches is not available as a bar to an action for partition. *Thomas v. Greene,* 226 So.2d 143 (1st D.C.A. Fla. 1969), *cert. den.* 234 So.2d 117. The existence of a valid agreement not to partition is a good defense. *Forehand v. Peacock,* 77 So.2d 625 (Fla. 1955). If a defendant claims an accounting or an equitable right to have a particular portion of the premises set aside to him, the basis for that claim should be alleged in the defense or counterclaim. *Boley v. Skinner,* 38 Fla. 291, 20 So. 1017 (1896). Failure of the plaintiff to ask for partition of the entire tract held in cotenancy can be set up as a defense. See *Lovett v. Lovett,* 93 Fla. 611, 112 So. 768 (1927). Likewise, if some of the defendants want partition to be made to them jointly rather than severally, the basis for that relief must be alleged in the defense pleadings. *Shaffer v. Pickard,* 77 Fla. 697, 82 So. 232

(1919). If one of the owners has a lien or other claim against another's share, the facts giving rise to it should be alleged. *Miles v. Miles,* 117 Fla. 884, 158 So. 520 (1935). The court cannot require one cotenant to account for the other's share of the rental value of the property if no claim for it was made in the pleadings. See *Joyner v. Rogers,* 182 So.2d 628 (4th D.C.A. Fla. 1966).

C.   Judgment For Partition

   1. [§4.15]   Parts To Be Divided

The judgment should determine the respective rights and interests of the parties. *F.S.* 64.051. If the rights and interests of the plaintiffs are established or are undisputed, the statute provides that the court may order partition and order the interests of the plaintiffs and such of the defendants as have established their interest to be alloted to them, leaving for future adjustment in the same action the interest of any other defendants. It is error for the court to direct the commissioners to determine the respective rights of the parties and to make partition accordingly. *Street v. Benner,* 20 Fla. 700 (1884). Upon proper proceedings, the court may order that partition be made to some of the parties in severalty. *Shaffer v. Pickard,* 77 Fla. 697, 82 So. 232 (1919). All equities incidental to the main relief should be determined in the judgment. *Farrell v. Forest Inv. Co.,* 73 Fla. 191, 74 So. 216 (1917), 1 A.L.R. 25.

   2. [§4.16]   Accountings

Accountings between the parties frequently are sought and granted as incidental to the main relief. One tenant cannot charge another for use and occupation of the premises jointly held. *Bird v. Bird,* 15 Fla. 424 (1875). The courts make a distinction between one tenant receiving more than his share of the profits of the land, for which he is accountable to his cotenants, and the same tenant enjoying more of the benefit or making more by its occupation than the other, for which he is not accountable to the others. *Bird v. Bird, supra.* If the cotenant held exclusive possession of the premises adversely to the other owners, however, or as the result of ouster or its equivalent, he may be held accountable to the other owners for their shares of the fair rental value. *Coggan v. Coggan,* 230 So.2d 34 (2d D.C.A. Fla. 1969), *quashed* in part 239 So.2d 17. One cotenant may recover from the others their proportionate shares of money paid on principal and interest of an outstanding mortgage, for taxes and insurance and for other money spent on essential improvements to preserve the property.

Potter v. Garrett, 52 So.2d 115 (Fla. 1951). When such a claim is made, the reasonable value of the use and occupancy by that tenant can be set off against the amounts claimed for the advances. *Potter v. Garrett, supra.* Further, one cotenant cannot charge another for improvements made to the jointly-held premises. *Boley v. Skinner,* 38 Fla. 291, 20 So. 1017 (1896). He may have set off to him the portion so improved, however, leaving to the other tenants so much of the remaining land as would make its value equal to the portion given to him, without taking into account the value of the improvement. *Boley v. Skinner, supra.* An order granting a party the right to have an appraiser enter and inspect the property is not an abuse of discretion. *Coggan v. Coggan,* 213 So.2d 902 (2d D.C.A. Fla. 1968), *cert. den.* 222 So.2d 25. But a cotenant cannot charge another for his expenses in having the land surveyed during trial, in the absence of an order authorizing or requiring the survey or an expression of approval by the court. *Taylor v. Taylor,* 119 So.2d 811 (2d D.C.A. Fla. 1960).

3. [§4.17] Order Of Sale

On an uncontested allegation in a pleading that the property sought to be partitioned is indivisible and is not subject to partition without prejudice to the owners, or if a judgment of partition is entered and the court is satisfied that the allegation is correct, the court may appoint a special master or the clerk to make sale of the property. *F.S.* 64.061(4). The sale may be either public or private. If the sale is to be a private one, or if the owners do not intend to bid on the property, it is suggested that a sale by a special master might be more advantageous. It is to be noted that the appointment of commissioners cannot be bypassed without an allegation in "a pleading," not necessarily the complaint, that the property is indivisible and not subject to sale without prejudice to the owners. See §4.12.

The sale, if ordered, may be a private one or one as provided by *F.S.* 64.071 or 64.061(4). *F.S.* 64.071 provides for sale at public auction, but also contains the provision that for good cause shown the court may order the sale made on "reasonable credit," but at least one third of the purchase money must be paid in cash, unless all parties consent to credit otherwise. Any deferred payments must be secured by a mortgage on the land and such other security as the court directs. *F.S.* 64.071(2).

The sale must be reported to the court, unless sale is made by the clerk under *F.S.* 45.031. The proceeds are paid into the court and the sale must be approved by the court before any conveyance pursuant to the sale is made. 64.071(3). If sale is by the clerk under 45.031, the clerk issues a certificate of sale and, if no objections are filed within ten days, issues a certificate of title and disburses the proceeds as provided in the judgment. If the owners intend to bid on the property, it is suggested that 64.071(3) offers the most advantageous route.

Until it has been determined that the property cannot be partitioned in kind, it is error to order its sale. See *Hasle v. Maasbrock,* 120 So.2d 794 (3d D.C.A. Fla. 1960). In *Keyes v. Rymer Realty Corporation,* 219 So.2d 711 (3d D.C.A. Fla. 1969), the appellate court upheld a finding that a shopping center that had a common private roadway and was operated for the common good of all the tenants, and had many leases limiting the types of businesses that could be operated in it, was clearly indivisible.

4. [§4.18] Appointment Of Commissioners

Unless the property is found to be indivisible under *F.S.* 64.061(4), the court in a judgment of partition appoints three persons as commissioners to make the partition. They are selected by the court unless agreed on by the parties. For good cause, they may be removed by the court and others appointed in their places. *F.S.* 64.061(1).

5. [§4.19] Special Equities To Be Considered

In making partition, the court may order a part on which one cotenant has made improvements allotted to that cotenant without taking into consideration the value of the improvements. *Boley v. Skinner,* 38 Fla. 291, 20 So. 1017 (1896). See §4.14. It also may provide that a particular cotenant be allotted the part containing the homestead. *Bird v. Bird,* 15 Fla. 424 (1875).

If they so request, some cotenants may lump their parts and have them allotted to them as joint tenants, rather than receiving smaller portions in severalty. *Shaffer v. Pickard,* 77 Fla. 697, 82 So. 232 (1919). In *Bird v. Bird, supra,* the court stated:

> . . . Mr. Justice Story says: "The court should assign to the parties respectively such parts of the estate as would best accommodate them and be of most value to them with reference to their respective situations in relation to the property before partition." Nor will courts of equity, in making these adjustments, "confine themselves to the mere legal rights of the original tenants in common, but

will have regard to the legal and equitable rights of all other parties interested in the estate, which have been derived from any of the original tenants in common."

D. Powers And Duties Of The Commissioners

1. [§4.20] Incidental Power

Commissioners are specifically authorized to employ a surveyor. Reasonable compensation is allowed them by the statute. The commissioners must take an oath. *F.S.* 64.061(2).

2. Reports

    a. [§4.21] Contents

The commissioners should make partition of the lands in question according to the court's order and report their partition in writing "without delay." *F.S.* 64.061(2). The report should specify which owners are allotted each particular parcel, and should indicate that no part of the premises has been left in joint ownership unless specifically so ordered. If found to be the case, the commissioners may instead report that the lands involved are so situated that partition cannot be made without prejudice to the owners. 64.071(1).

    b. [§4.22] Number Required To Join In Report

Because of death, disability or disagreement among themselves, it may not be possible to have all three commissioners sign their report. In that event, a report signed by only two of the three is effective. 59 AM.JUR.2d *Partition* §114. It is suggested that if less than all three sign, however, the reasons be stated that prevent the third commissioner from signing.

    c. [§4.23] Necessity For Notice

Notice of filing the report of the commissioners must be served on all known parties, and any party may file objections to the report "within ten days after it is served." *F.S.* 64.061(3). It is error to enter a final judgment before the expiration of the statutory time for filing objections. *Munroe v. Birdsey,* 102 Fla. 544, 136 So. 886 (1931). Parties are entitled to notice even though a default has been entered against them, and the default goes only to the form and content of the complaint, not to the procedure for making division of the property. *Munroe v. Birdsey, supra.*

d. [§4.24] Objections

Upon hearing the objections, the court may overrule or sustain them, and in the latter event, may remand the matter to the commissioners or appoint new commissioners. *F.S.* 64.061(1). If the objections are overruled, a final judgment is entered vesting in the parties the title to the parcels of lands allotted to them respectively, and quieting title to their respective shares as against the other parties or those claiming under them. 64.061(3). In some jurisdictions it is customary also to direct the commissioners to execute and deliver deeds to the respective parcels.

e. [§4.25] Property Not Divisible

As noted previously, if the commissioners report that the lands are so situated that partition cannot be made without prejudice to the owners and the court is satisfied as to that finding, the court may order the land sold at public auction by the commissioners or clerk. *F.S.* 64.071(1). The proceeds are paid into court and divided among the parties in proportion to their interests. For good cause, the court may permit a sale on reasonable credit for part or all of the purchase money, but at least one third must be paid in cash, unless all parties consent otherwise. 64.071(2). The deferred payments are secured by a mortgage on the land "and such other security as the court directs." The sale is reported to the court (unless the route set up by *F.S.* 45.031 is followed) and the money paid into court. 64.071(3). Before any conveyance is made, the sale must be approved by the court and the conveyance be directed by the court.

E. Final Judgments

1. [§4.26] Taxation Of Costs

Each party is bound by the judgment to pay a share of the costs, including attorneys' fees (see §§4.27–.29), to be determined on equitable principles in proportion to his interest. *F.S.* 64.081. The judgment is "binding on all his goods and chattels, lands or tenements." In case of sale, the court may order costs and fees retained out of the sums arising from the sale. All taxes, including municipal taxes, due at the time of sale also are paid out of the purchase price. While the statute does not specifically so provide, the reasonable fees and expenses of the commissioners usually are taxed as an item of costs. It has been held error to require one coparcener to pay one third of the costs and attorneys' fees, but the estate of a deceased coparcener none, and make the plaintiff's one-third interest liable for the other two thirds of the costs and attorneys' fees. *McQueen v. Forsythe,* 55 So.2d 545 (Fla. 1951). Costs, including attorneys' fees, must be apportioned strictly on a mathematical basis; equitable principles cannot be taken into consideration. *Deltona Corporation v. Kipnis,* 194 So.2d 295 (2d D.C.A. Fla. 1967). Expenses of surveyors, when not ordered by the court or the commissioners, are not a proper element of costs. *Taylor v. Taylor,* 119 So.2d 811 (2d D.C.A. Fla. 1960).

2. Attorneys' Fees

a. [§4.27] Persons Entitled

Formerly, only the plaintiff in a partition suit was allowed attorneys' fees. This often resulted in a mad race for the courthouse to see who could file suit first. The statute now provides for attorneys' fees to "plaintiff's or defendant's attorneys or to each of them commensurate with their services rendered and of benefit to the partition, to be determined on equitable principals in proportion to his interest." *F.S.* 64.081. An attorney who represents himself in the partition proceedings is not entitled to an attorney's fee. *Girtman v. Starbuck,* 48 Fla. 265, 37 So. 731 (1904).

b. [§4.28] Factors Considered In Determining

The services performed, responsibility incurred, nature of the service, skill required, circumstances under which it was rendered, customary charge for the services involved and the ability of the litigants to respond are elements to be considered in fixing attorneys' fees. *Munroe v. Birdsey,* 102 Fla. 544, 136 So. 886 (1931). The value of the lands involved has "little or no place" in fixing fees, if the proceedings are routine and the title is not litigated. *Munroe v. Birdsey, supra.* A claim for legal services based upon an implied contract cannot be allowed in a partition action. *Lamoureux v. Lamoureux,* 59 So.2d 9 (Fla. 1952). The fixing of fees purely on the basis of a schedule of fees suggested by a local bar assocation is improper. *Adler v. Schekter,* 197 So.2d 46 (3d D.C.A. Fla. 1967). If the attorney representing a minority interest has performed services of greater value than those performed by the attorney representing the majority interest, the one representing the minority interest should receive the larger fee, but the burden of both fees is to be borne by the parties in proportion to their interests. *Adler v. Schekter, supra.* Fees may be allowed for services rendered incident to an appeal. *Hickman v. Hickman,* 147 So.2d 555 (2d D.C.A. Fla. 1962), *cert. den.* 155 So.2d 150.

c. [§4.29] Attorneys' Fees On Dismissal

When the action is dismissed prior to the judgment for partition, the plaintiff's attorney has no right against the defendants for attorneys' fees. *Glass v. Layton,* 140 Fla. 522, 192 So. 330 (1939). The court, however, may withhold dismissal until the persons properly liable have paid or secured the fees and, if the dismissal is collusive, the defendants may be held liable for their proportion of the fees. *Glass v. Layton, supra.*

3. [§4.30] Doctrine Of Owelty

Chancery courts in some jurisdictions require one party who has been allotted a share of greater value than another to pay the latter a sum that will equalize the respective shares. *Annot.,* 65 A.L.R. 352 (1930). Since partition in Florida is a statutory proceeding and the statute readily provides for a sale if the property is determined to be indivisible, the author doubts that this doctrine of owelty could be invoked.

4. [§4.31] Protection Of Lienors

Generally, a lien on an undivided interest of a cotenant will be considered as shifting to the whole interest of such part of the land as is allotted subsequently in partition proceedings to the person from whom the lien is derived, but the creditor cannot be deprived of his lien through fraud or an unfair division between cotenants designedly or inadvertantly entered into to the injury of the lien creditor. *Baltzell v. Daniel,* 111 Fla. 303, 149 So. 639 (1933), 93 A.L.R. 1259.

5. [§4.32] Retention Of Jurisdiction

A retention clause in the judgment reserving jurisdiction for the purpose of granting such further relief as shall be necessary is proper. *Foster v. Thomas,* 112 So.2d 33 (1st D.C.A. Fla. 1959).

6. [§4.33] Sample Judgment Of Partition

(Title of Court)

(Title of Cause)   **JUDGMENT OF PARTITION**

This action was heard before the court. On the evidence presented, the court finds that the property sought to be partitioned is indivisible and is not subject to partition in kind without prejudice to its owners, and it is

ADJUDGED that:

1. The following-named persons, in the respective proportions set opposite their names:

[set out names and proportions]

are the owners of real property in .... County, Florida, described:

[legal description]

2. The property is indivisible and none of it is subject to partition without prejudice to its owners.

3. ...., a practicing attorney of this court, is appointed special master to sell the premises in the manner provided for sales in such cases by F.S. 64.061(4) and 64.071(1); the sale, if public, shall be made within the legal hours of sale, at public auction, to the highest bidder, before the main west door of the .... County Courthouse, at ...., Florida, after publishing notice once each week for four consecutive weeks prior to the sale, in a newspaper regularly published and in general circulation in .... County, Florida. In the meantime, if the special master can secure an offer of a fair price for the premises at a private sale, he shall report that, with his recommendations, to this court.

4. This court retains jurisdiction of this action to enforce this judgment.

ORDERED at ...., Florida, on ....(date)..........

Circuit Judge

COMMENT: Most judicial sales in this state are made by the clerk of the court in accordance with the procedure set out in *F.S.* 45.031. The above suggests the alternative procedure. If the property is divisible, the following form is suggested:

It is accordingly **ADJUDGED** that:

1. The following-named persons, in the respective proportions set opposite their names:

[set out names and proportions]

are the owners of real property in .... County, Florida, described:

[legal description]

2. Partition shall be made between the plaintiff, Mary R. Doe, and the defendants, T. Richard Roe, et al., of all pieces and parcels of land described in this proceeding, so that plaintiff and defendants may respectively have and hold in severalty such parts and portions of the premises as shall be allotted and assigned to them respectively upon partition.

3. ...., ... and .... are appointed commissioners to make the partition. The commissioners shall severally be sworn faithfully and impartially to execute the trust imposed in them and to make partition as directed by this court, before proceeding to the execution of their duties.

4. The commissioners shall make a full and ample report of their proceedings to this court in writing, specifying the manner of discharging their duties, describing the land divided and the share allotted each party, and file their report with the clerk of this court without delay. The commissioners are authorized to employ a surveyor and to cause all necessary maps and surveys to be made.

5. In case partition cannot be made as above directed without manifest injury to the rights and interests of the respective parties, the commissioners shall so report back to this court.

F.   Sale Of Property

1. [§4.34]   Public Or Private

As discussed previously, on an uncontested allegation in a pleading that the property sought to be partitioned is indivisible and is not subject to partition without prejudice to the owners, or if a judgment of partition is entered and the court is satisfied that the allegation as to indivisibility is correct, the court may appoint a special master or the clerk to make sale of the property at private or public sale. *F.S.* 64.061(4). If there is no allegation in a pleading as to indivisibility, the matter must be referred to three commissioners. 64.061(1). If the commissioners in turn report the land is indivisible and the court sustains that report, the court must order the land to be sold at public auction by the commissioners or the clerk, with the proceeds to be paid into the court. 64.071(1). See §4.35.

2. [§4.35] By Whom Made

Upon an allegation in a pleading that the property is indivisible, the court may order sale by the clerk or by a special master. *F.S.* 64.061(4). Otherwise, the sale, if ordered, is made by the commissioners or by the clerk. 64.071(1). In this state, most judicial sales are made by the clerk under the procedure set out in *F.S.* 45.031.

3. [§4.36] Persons Entitled To Bid

There are no restrictions in the statute on who is entitled to bid on the property. Parties to the litigation more frequently than not bid against each other at the sale.

4. [§4.37] Approval Of Court And Distribution Of Proceeds

Unless the sale is made as provided under *F.S.* 45.031, the sale is reported to the court, and the money arising from it is paid into the court. 64.071(3). The sale, unless made under 45.031, must be approved by the court and a conveyance ordered by the court before title passes to the purchaser. 64.071(3).

JAMES F. DURHAM II*
HENRY H. FOX†

5

MORTGAGE FORECLOSURES

I. INTRODUCTION

    A. [§5.1] In General

    B. [§5.2] Foreclosure Of Government Insured Mortgages

II. PREPARATION BEFORE FILING COMPLAINT

    A. [§5.3] Letter Of Instruction

    B. [§5.4] Abstract Of Title

    C. Determination Of Parties Defendant

        1. [§5.5] Necessary And Proper Parties

        2. Compliance With Soldiers' And Sailors' Civil Relief Act

            a. [§5.6] In General

            b. [§5.7] Effect Of Act

            c. [§5.8] Necessity To Determine Military Status

            d. [§5.9] Procedure To Determine Military Status

---

*J.D., 1954, Vanderbilt University. Mr. Durham is a member of the Dade County, American and International bar associations and has been admitted to the practice of law in the Commonwealth of Kentucky. He is a partner in the firm of Shutts & Bowen and practices in Miami.

**J.D., 1966, Duke University. Mr. Fox is a member of the Broward County, Dade County and American bar associations and is an associate in the firm of English, McCaughan & O'Bryan. He practices in Fort Lauderdale.

†Mr. Durham and Mr. Robert E. Gunn were the authors of this chapter in the first edition.

  e. [§5.10] Form For Affidavit As To Military Service

  f. [§5.11] Procedure If Mortgagor Is In Military Service

III. THE COMPLAINT AND NOTICE OF LIS PENDENS

 A. [§5.12] Time For Filing Complaint

 B. Allegations Of Complaint

  1. [§5.13] In General

  2. [§5.14] United States As Defendant

  3. [§5.15] State Of Florida As Defendant

 C. [§5.16] Form For Complaint To Foreclose Mortgage

 D. Notice Of Lis Pendens

  1. [§5.17] In General

  2. [§5.18] Form For Notice Of Lis Pendens

IV. SERVICE OF PROCESS

 A. [§5.19] In General

 B. Personal Service

  1. [§5.20] In General

  2. Service On The United States

   a. [§5.21] In General

   b. [§5.22] Affidavit Of Compliance With 28 *U.S.C.* §2410

  3. [§5.23] Service On State Of Florida

 C. Constructive Service

  1. [§5.24] In General

  2. Requirement For Diligent Search And Inquiry

  a. [§5.25] In General

  b. [§5.26] Checklist Of Inquiries

  c. [§5.27] Additional Sources Of Information

  d. [§5.28] Form For Affidavit For Constructive Service

 3. Notice Of Action

  a. [§5.29] In General

  b. [§5.30] Form For Notice Of Action

V. [§5.31] DEFAULTS

VI. THE FINAL JUDGMENT

 A. [§5.32] In General

 B. [§5.33] Final Judgment After Default

 C. [§5.34] Final Judgment After Defendant Answers

 D. Forms Relating To Final Judgments

  1. [§5.35] Motion For Summary Final Judgment In Foreclosure

  2. [§5.36] Attorney's Affidavit As To Record Title

  3. [§5.37] Affidavit Of Amounts Due

  4. [§5.38] Affidavit Of Attorney As To Costs

  5. [§5.39] Affidavit As To Attorneys' Fees

  6. [§5.40] Final Judgment

VII. JUDICIAL SALE

 A. [§5.41] In General

 B. Notification Of FHA And VA

  1. [§5.42] In General

2. [§5.43] Form For Motion For Substitution Of Photostatic Copies And Order Allowing Substitution

C. Notice Of Sale

1. [§5.44] In General

2. [§5.45] Form For Notice Of Sale

D. [§5.46] Payment By Defendant Of Amount Due In Final Judgment Prior To Sale; Completion And Confirmation Of Sale

E. The Sale Procedure

1. [§5.47] In General

2. Bidding By The Mortgagee

    a. [§5.48] Amount Due Under Final Judgment Credited Against Amount Bid

    b. [§5.49] Bids Less Than Value Of Property

    c. [§5.50] Determination Of Amount Of Gain To Mortgagee For Income Taxation Purposes

    d. [§5.51] Bid In Accordance With Instructions From VA

VIII. POST SALE PROCEDURE

A. [§5.52] Certificates Of Sale, Title And Disbursements

B. Writ Of Assistance

1. [§5.53] In General

2. [§5.54] Form For Motion For Writ Of Assistance And Order

3. [§5.55] Form For Supporting Affidavit

C. Post Sale Procedure In Relation To FHA Mortgages When Mortgagee Is Successful Bidder At Sale

1. Execution Of Instruments By Mortgagee

    a. [§5.56] In General

    b. [§5.57] Form For Special Warranty Deed

2. [§5.58] Recording Of Deed

3. Evidence Of Title

    a. [§5.59] In General

    b. [§5.60] Form For Attorney's Certificate Of Title

4. [§5.61] Submission To FHA By Mortgagee Of Deed, Title Evidence, Fiscal Data And Supporting Documents

D. Post Sale Procedure In Relation To VA Mortgages When Mortgagee Is Successful Bidder At Sale

1. [§5.62] Mortgagee's Notice To VA And Execution Of Deed

2. [§5.63] Eviction Of Mortgagor

3. [§5.64] Forwarding Documents To VA

E. [§5.65] Deficiency Judgments

IX. DEED INSTEAD OF FORECLOSURE

A. [§5.66] In General

B. [§5.67] Form For Special Warranty Deed Instead Of Foreclosure

C. [§5.68] Form For Estoppel And Solvency Affidavit

D. [§5.69] Form For Lien Affidavit

X. THE MORTGAGE IN THE UNITED STATES DISTRICT COURT

A. [§5.70] Introduction

B. [§5.71] Final Judgment In United States District Court

    C. [§5.72] Form For Additional Paragraphs In Final Judgment In United States District Court

    D. Foreclosure Sale In United States District Court

        1. [§5.73] Statutory Requirements

        2. [§5.74] Form For Additional Terms For Notice Of Sale In United States District Court

        3. [§5.75] Conduct Of Sale And Confirmation

        4. [§5.76] Form For Motion For Order Confirming Sale And Disbursing Funds

        5. [§5.77] Form For Order Confirming Sale

XI. THE MORTGAGEE IN BANKRUPTCY PROCEEDINGS

    A. [§5.78] In General

    B. [§5.79] Stays Of Foreclosure Proceedings

    C. [§5.80] Dissolving Or Modifying Stay Order

    D. [§5.81] Action After Dissolving Stay

    E. [§5.82] Other Actions

XII. [§5.83] CONCLUSION

I. INTRODUCTION

A. [§5.1] In General

This chapter sets forth briefly a practical, step-by-step procedure that an attorney may use as a general guide in foreclosing either conventional or government insured mortgages. No attempt has been made to inquire extensively into many substantive points of Florida law that may arise in particular cases nor to present a detailed analysis of the complex statutory and regulatory provisions governing procedures of the Veterans Administration and Federal Housing Administration.

Mortgage liens were discussed briefly in I FLORIDA REAL PROPERTY PRACTICE §§8.2–.20 (CLE 2d ed. 1971).

In this chapter there will be only limited discussion relating to deficiency judgments. It should be pointed out, however, that the granting of a deficiency judgment lies almost wholly within the discretion of the trial judge, and there is no uniformity in the state as to the exercise of that discretion.

In conjunction with this chapter, reference should be made to Durham and Gunn, *Foreclosure of Conventional and Government Insured Mortgages in Florida,* 15 U.FLA.L.REV. 185 (1962).

B. [§5.2] Foreclosure Of Government Insured Mortgages

The basic provisions pertaining to the VA and FHA are to be found in 38 *U.S.C.* §§1801–1824, 12 *U.S.C.* §§1707–1715 and applicable regulations. Valuable information concerning FHA requirements is to be found in the FHA Mortgagee's Handbook, a copy of which may be obtained from the Superintendent of Documents, United States Government Printing Office, Washington, D.C. 20402.

In regard to VA procedure, the general policies and requirements are set forth in §§36.4319–.4320 of the Lenders Handbook, VA Pamphlet 26-7 (revised 1970). These regulations are too lengthy to be set forth in this article, but attention is called to the required notices that must be furnished the Administrator before any contemplated action to terminate the debtors' rights in property secured by a guaranteed loan are initiated and subsequent required notification.

II. PREPARATION BEFORE FILING COMPLAINT

A. [§5.3] Letter Of Instruction

The attorney's initial instructions to foreclose should come directly from the mortgagee or its local servicing agent. Since some judges require the attorney to prove that he has authority to foreclose, the instructions should be in the form of a letter. The letter also should give the date of default and state the remaining amount of unpaid principal, interest through a certain date with a per diem interest, whether the property is occupied and, if so, the names of the present occupants. Enclosed with the letter should be the original promissory note and mortgage with any assignment and the opinion of title or mortgagee title insurance policy, if any. If the mortgagee or its servicing agent has an abstract of title, or a receipt showing where the abstract is located, the abstract or receipt also should be enclosed.

When the papers are received, a letter should be written by the attorney to the sender acknowledging receipt of the foreclosure instrument and all enclosed original instruments.

B. [§5.4] Abstract Of Title

At the time the letter of acknowledgment is written, a partial abstract should be ordered covering the property in question commencing with the execution date of the mortgage being foreclosed, if the status of the title prior to that date is known through the examination of title opinion or title policy. If a prior abstract is available, it should be continued from the last continuation to date. If no opinion is available, the abstract should begin a reasonable period of time prior to the date of the mortgage to allow the attorney to determine if additional persons should be joined in the foreclosure action, or to allow their interest in the property to be determined or terminated. The VA requires an examination of at least 40 years prior to the mortgage either by the attorney foreclosing or the prior examiner on whom he depends in part.

C. Determination Of Parties Defendant

1. [§5.5] Necessary And Proper Parties

As soon as the partial abstract is received, it should be examined to determine who the defendants will be. In a foreclosure action the titleholder is an indispensable party. *Jordan v. Sayre,* 24 Fla. 1, 3 So.

329 (1888); *Pan American Bank of Miami v. City of Miami Beach,* 198 So.2d 45 (3d D.C.A. Fla. 1967). If the titleholder is not joined in the action, he will retain his interest in the property after the action is completed.

Since an interest superior to the mortgage being foreclosed cannot be affected in any way by the foreclosure of a junior interest, a prior mortgagee, lienholder or other claimant is neither a *necessary* nor a proper party. See *Cone Bros. Constr. Co. v. Moore,* 141 Fla. 420, 193 So. 288 (1940).

All subsequent mortgagees, judgment creditors, junior lienholders, parties in possession, with or without a lease, and other persons who appear to have an inferior interest in the property should be joined. A personal inspection of the property may disclose an advertising sign, driveway or road across the property, or similar situation that would give notice of an express or implied easement that should be determined. The holder of that interest should be joined as a party defendant. If it is uncertain whether a person's interest is prior or subsequent to that of the plaintiff, the best practice is to join that person as a defendant and determine the priority of his interest during the foreclosure action.

2. Compliance With Soldiers' And Sailors' Civil Relief Act

a. [§5.6] In General

Once the defendants are identified, a determination should be made as to whether any of them are members of the armed forces (which includes the Coast Guard and some members of the United States Public Health Service) and thus are entitled to the protections afforded by the Soldiers' and Sailors' Civil Relief Act of 1940 as amended, 50 *U.S.C.App.* §§501–591. Principally, the act provides a method of suspension of proceedings and transactions involving members of the armed forces and its allies.

The provisions of the act most likely to be encountered are found in 50 *U.S.C.App.* §520; they establish the procedure to be followed after default of appearance of the defendant and generally require the affidavit of the plaintiff that the defendant is not in the military service before entering judgment. The permitted procedure with respect to and the form of the affidavit necessary to support the judgment will vary from one circuit to the next.

b. [§5.7] Effect Of Act

The act provides that no foreclosure of property for the nonpayment of any sum due under any mortgage obligation will be valid if made during the period of military service of the obligor or within three months after completion of military service. 50 *U.S.C.* §532. The act makes this apply only if the obligation was incurred *before* the debtor entered military service. The purpose of the act is to protect the serviceman who, upon entering military service, suffers a reduction in income and is unable to keep up with his monthly obligations.

No protection is afforded by the act from the modification, termination, cancellation or foreclosure of any lien or possessory or foreclosure right based upon a written agreement executed during or after the period of military service. 50 *U.S.C.App.* §517; *Whitaker v. Hearnsberger,* 233 P.2d 389 (Colo. 1951).

c. [§5.8] Necessity To Determine Military Status

If it becomes necessary to seek a default against any defendant for his failure to file an appearance, the plaintiff's attorney next must consider the effect of 50 *U.S.C.* §520. Before a default judgment may be entered in any action, the plaintiff under this section should file an affidavit that the defendant is not in the military service. A form for the affidavit appears in §5.10. If the plaintiff is unable to do this, he should file an affidavit stating that the defendant is in the military service or that the plaintiff is without knowledge as to whether the defendant is or is not in the military service. If the plaintiff cannot do this, an attorney ad litem should be appointed to protect the defendant's interest. Failure to comply can result in the serviceman's setting aside the judgment if he can show he was prejudiced by it.

The attorney so appointed should not be expected to serve without compensation and a fee may be provided him, to be taxed as a cost in the proceeding. The appointed attorney should make every reasonable effort to contact or correspond with the defendant to determine what defense or rights, if any, should be asserted. Under the act, he cannot waive anything or bind his client.

d. [§5.9] Procedure To Determine Military Status

The military status of a defendant may be determined in a number of ways. If he can be located, the defendant himself may provide the information. If any of his friends or relatives can be located, they may be of some assistance. Some of the procedures set forth in §§5.25—.27 for diligent search and inquiry with respect to constructive service may be useful in determining the military status of the defendant. The most reliable procedure is to write letters to each of the five armed services and the Public Health Service. The drawback to this latter method is the fee charged by each public officer providing the information, unless the foreclosure is of an FHA or VA loan, in which case the information will be provided without cost.

The letters should be sent to:

1. The Adjutant General, Department of the Army

2. The Air Adjutant General, Department of the Air Force

3. The Bureau of Naval Personnel, Department of the Navy

4. Headquarters, United States Marine Corps, Department of the Navy

5. Headquarters, United States Coast Guard, United States Treasury

6. The Surgeon General, United States Public Health Service, Department of Health, Education and Welfare, Attention: Division of Commissioned Officers

The request should show the borrower's full name, last known address, social security if known and date of birth. In FHA or VA foreclosures, the information is furnished without cost by the military services, but in order to assure the avoidance of a fee or service charge for the certificate it is important that the request include the following statement or words of similar import:

> This request is made in connection with a loan guaranteed (or insured) under [Title 28 U.S.C. Chapter 37, formerly the Servicemen's Readjustment Act of 1944, as amended] [the National Housing Act]. Any fee imposed and paid for this service will be charged ultimately to [the Veterans Administration] [the Department of Housing and Urban Development], an agency of the federal government.

In most instances, information can be obtained concerning the defendant from local sources. If the information is obtained from the defendant or his relatives or friends, the source of the information should be set forth in the affidavit. A suggested form for an affidavit is set out below.

e. [§5.10] Form For Affidavit As To Military Service

(Title of Court)

(Title of Cause)   AFFIDAVIT AS TO MILITARY SERVICE

STATE OF FLORIDA
COUNTY OF ....

Before me, the undersigned authority, personally appeared ...., who was sworn and says:

1. He is the ....plaintiff/defendant.......... in this action.

2. None of the defendants in this action are on active duty with the military services of the United States, nor have served in that capacity since the institution of this action.

_____
Affiant

(Jurat)

f. [§5.11] Procedure If Mortgagor Is In Military Service

If the mortgagor is in the military service, the court first must ascertain whether the obligation under the mortgage was incurred by the mortgagor before or after entering that service. In the latter event, the foreclosure may proceed, but in the former the court must determine whether the mortgagor's ability to pay was affected materially by his induction into the armed service; if so, the proceedings must be stayed, or the court may "make such other disposition of the case as may be equitable to conserve the interests of all parties." 50 *U.S.C.App.* §532(2)b.

III. THE COMPLAINT AND NOTICE OF LIS PENDENS

A. [§5.12] Time For Filing Complaint

The complaint should be filed immediately after the determination of the parties defendant. The longer the delay in filing the complaint, the greater will be the chance that someone may record an instrument before the notice of lis pendens is filed and thus necessitate amending the complaint to join him as a new defendant. See §5.18.

There is an additional incentive in FHA and VA cases to file the complaint promptly. When the action is concluded and the property is conveyed to the FHA or VA, the debentures given to the mortgagee in exchange for the property accumulate interest from the date foreclosure proceedings were instituted. See 12 *U.S.C.* §1710(d).

B. Allegations Of Complaint

1. [§5.13] In General

The foreclosure complaint should allege the execution and delivery of the promissory note and mortgage, the present ownership in the plaintiff, the description of the real property, the names of the present titleholders, the default and the amount remaining due on the debt. In addition, the original note and mortgage, or copies, must be attached to the complaint. *RCP* 1.130. It is not necessary to attach copies of assignments. *Powell v. New York Life Ins. Co.*, 141 Fla. 758, 194 So. 232 (1940).

Under prevailing case law it is not necessary to allege specifically the interest of each defendant. It is sufficient to state that whatever the defendant's interest may be, it is subordinate and inferior to the mortgage being foreclosed. *International Kaolin Co. v. Vause*, 55 Fla. 641, 46 So. 3 (1908).

2. [§5.14] United States As Defendant

If the United States or any of its agencies or departments is a defendant, care must be taken to comply with the requirements of 28 *U.S.C.* §2410. Initially, it must be remembered that the defendant is "The United States of America," not the Director of Internal Revenue or the United States Department of Agriculture, for example. Secondly, the United States has 60 days in which to serve a responsive pleading instead of 20, and the regular summons form issued by the court must be altered to reflect this longer period.

When the interest of the United States being foreclosed is a tax lien, the complaint must contain the name and address of the taxpayer whose liability created the lien. If a notice of tax lien was filed, the date and place filed and the identity of the office filing the notice must be alleged and a copy of the tax lien notice must be attached as an exhibit to the complaint.

Of particular interest is the right of redemption given the United States by 28 *U.S.C.* §2410(c). The right of redemption lasts for 120 days from the date of sale if the interest of the United States arose under the tax laws, and one year from the date of sale if the lien arose otherwise. This right, especially if it is for a year, can have a chilling effect on bids at a foreclosure sale, if the interest of the United States is at all substantial. Consideration should be given immediately to a request for release or waiver of the lien, or the right of redemption should be initiated. Although the United States as a matter of course does not remove actions from a state court to a federal court, this may occur. See §5.70.

The United States may waive and release its lien or right of redemption under 28 *U.S.C.* §2410(e) when the appropriate officer charged with the administration of the laws in respect of which the lien of the United States arises investigates and finds that: the proceeds from the sale of the property would be insufficient to satisfy the lien of the United States wholly or partly; the claim of the United States has been satisfied; or, by lapse of time, or otherwise, the lien has become unenforceable. In those circumstances, the officer reports the fact to the Comptroller General, who *may* issue a certificate releasing the property from the lien. When it appears that the United States is a probable defendant and the provisions of 28 *U.S.C.* §2410(e) are applicable, the attorney should determine immediately whether to initiate the actions necessary to request a ruling by the appropriate officer. In most cases, the interest of the United States will be a tax lien and application should be made to the District Director, Internal Revenue Service, for release or discharge of the tax lien. The director has discretionary power to discharge or release tax liens under certain I.R.S. regulations implementing the Internal Revenue Code. See the current regulations supplementing *IRC* §§6325 and 7425 specifically, and other sections as may be appropriate. It should be noted that after the United States has been joined as a party to a judicial proceeding, some discretion of the district director is revoked. Therefore, the lawyer may determine that it is in his client's best interest to request a release of the tax lien prior to joining the United States as a defendant, especially if there is little or no equity in the property being sold.

3. [§5.15] State Of Florida As Defendant

If the state or one of its instrumentalities has an interest or lien in the subject property that requires its joinder as a defendant, that interest or lien must be set forth with particularity. *F.S.* 69.041(2). See §5.23.

C. [§5.16] Form For Complaint To Foreclose Mortgage

(Title of Court)

(Title of Cause)   **COMPLAINT**

Plaintiff, ..., sues defendants, ... and ...., and alleges:

1. This is an action to foreclose a mortgage on real property in .... County, Florida.

2. On ....(date).........., defendant executed and delivered a promissory note and a mortgage securing payment of it to plaintiff; the mortgage was recorded on ....(date).......... in Official Records Book .... at page .... of the public records of .... County, Florida, and mortgaged the property described in it, then owned by and in possession of the mortgagor, a copy of the mortgage containing a copy of the note being attached.

3. .... assigned the promissory note and mortgage to plaintiff.

4. Plaintiff owns and holds the note and mortgage.

5. Defendants have defaulted under the note and mortgage [by failing to make the payment due ....(date).........., and all subsequent payments] [by failing to pay the taxes in the sum of $.........., which were due and payable on or before ....(date)..........] [by failing to keep the mortgaged property insured as required by the terms of the mortgage].

6. Plaintiff declares the full amount payable under the note and mortgage to be due.

7. Defendant owes plaintiff $.......... that is due on principal on the note and mortgage, interest from ....(date).........., and title search expense for ascertaining necessary parties to this action.

8. Defendant, ..., claims some interest in the property by virtue of a claim of lien recorded on ....(date).......... in Official Records Book .... at page .... of the public records of .... County, Florida, but that interest is inferior to that of plaintiff.

9. Plaintiff is obligated to pay his attorneys a reasonable fee for their services.

WHEREFORE, plainfiff demands an accounting of the sum due to plaintiff under the note and mortgage and if the sum is not paid within the time set by this court, that the property be sold to satisfy plaintiff's claim and if the proceeds of the sale are insufficient to pay plaintiff's claim, that a deficiency judgment be entered for the sum remaining unpaid against the defendant and that the estate of defendant and all persons claiming under or against defendant since the filing of the notice of lis pendens be foreclosed.

Attorney

..................(address)................

COMMENT: This form is based on *RCP* Form 1.944.

D.   Notice Of Lis Pendens

1. [§5.17] In General

The plaintiff should file a notice of lis pendens with the complaint. *F.S.* 48.23. The notice cuts off the rights of any person whose interest arises after its filing. There is considerable confusion in the case law as to whether a notice of lis pendens cuts off an interest that arises before the filing of the notice but that is not recorded until after that filing. *O'Bryan v. Dr. P. Phillips & Sons,* 123 Fla. 302, 166 So. 820 (1936); *Bowers v. Pearson,* 101 Fla. 714, 135 So. 562 (1931); *Freligh v. Maurer,* 111 So.2d 712 (2d D.C.A. Fla. 1959). For an interesting discussion of these cases, see 15 U.FLA.L.REV. 580 (1963). In order to avoid the possibility of having a clouded title when the foreclosure is complete, it is best to amend the complaint to join as a defendant any person who records an interest after the filing of the lis pendens that actually arose before its filing.

As soon as the complaint has been filed and the notice of lis pendens recorded, the abstract should be continued to show the lis pendens and determine if any other persons should be joined as defendants.

See also I FLORIDA REAL PROPERTY PRACTICE §9.33 (CLE 2d ed. 1971) and FLORIDA CIVIL PRACTICE BEFORE TRIAL §§9.2–.8 (CLE 3d ed. 1975).

2. [§5.18] Form For Notice Of Lis Pendens

(Title of Court)

(Title of Cause)   NOTICE OF LIS PENDENS

TO DEFENDANT ...., AND ALL OTHERS WHOM IT MAY CONCERN:

YOU ARE NOTIFIED of the institution of this action by plaintiff against you seeking to foreclose a mortgage on the following property in .... County, Florida:

[legal description]

DATED ....

_____
Attorney

COMMENT: This is based on *RCP* Form 1.918.

IV. SERVICE OF PROCESS

A. [§5.19] In General

Although an extensive discussion of service of process is beyond the scope of this chapter, recurrent problems peculiar to foreclosures warrant some discussion, set out below.

B. Personal Service

1. [§5.20] In General

When it is possible to achieve personal service, there usually is no particular problem for the plaintiff's attorney. The statutes in this area are virtually self-explanatory. See *F.S.* Chapter 48 and *RCP* 1.070.

2. Service On The United States

a. [§5.21] In General

When the United States is made a party, it is important to note carefully 28 *U.S.C.* §2410(b), mentioned previously in §5.14. Service on the United States is accomplished by serving the process and a copy of the complaint upon the United States attorney, or his designee, for the district in which the property is located. A copy of the process and the complaint also must be mailed by certified or registered mail to the Attorney General of the United States, Washington, D.C. Since compliance with this statute is jurisdictional, it is suggested that a return receipt be requested and that the receipt be attached to an affidavit of compliance, which should be filed with the court.

b. [§5.22] Affidavit Of Compliance With 28 *U.S.C.* §2410

(Title of Court)

(Title of Cause)   AFFIDAVIT OF COMPLIANCE
WITH 28 U.S.C. §2410

Before me, the undersigned authority, personally appeared ...., who was sworn and says:

1. He is the attorney for the plaintiff in the above cause.

2. A copy of the summons and complaint in this action was mailed by certified mail, return receipt requested, to the Attorney General of the United States, Washington, D.C. on ....(date).......... The receipt of the Attorney General of the United States is attached as Exhibit A.

_____

Affiant

(Jurat)

3. [§5.23] Service On State Of Florida

When the State of Florida is a party because of a tax lien, service is made on the Department of Revenue under *F.S.* 48.111. If the state's interest is other than a tax lien, service is accomplished by serving the state attorney for the circuit in which the action is brought and by mailing two copies of the process and complaint to the Attorney General of Florida by certified or registered mail. 48.121. The state has

40 days in which to file a responsive pleading and the printed summons form should be modified to reflect this. The filing of an affidavit of compliance as discussed relative to the United States in §5.21 is recommended. Service on cities, counties or other governmental bodies should be made in compliance with 48.111.

C. Constructive Service

1. [§5.24] In General

In those cases in which personal service of process cannot be made, the plaintiff of course must resort to constructive service of process. Provision for constructive service of process is made in *F.S.* Chapter 49 and *RCP* 1.070(e).

2. Requirement For Diligent Search And Inquiry

a. [§5.25] In General

In the area of constructive service of process, the most common problems are those arising in the interpretation and application of the phrase "diligent search and inquiry" appearing in *F.S.* 49.041 and other statutes. In many cases, the property owner deserts his home and leaves no trace of his whereabouts. In such a situation, the statute allows service by publication only upon affidavit that the plaintiff, or someone acting in his behalf, has made a diligent search and inquiry to locate the defendant, but is unable to do so. A form for that affidavit is suggested in §5.28.

The Florida Supreme Court, in construing diligent search and inquiry, has held that extraordinary steps to ascertain the whereabouts of the parties are not required. It is only necessary that the complainant reasonably employ knowledge at his command, make diligent inquiry and exert an honest and conscientious effort appropriate to the circumstances of each case to acquire the information necessary to enable him to effect personal service on the defendant. *McDaniel v. McElvy*, 91 Fla. 770, 108 So. 820 (1926), 51 A.L.R. 731.

b. [§5.26] Checklist Of Inquiries

In specific cases, the Florida courts have indicated that a diligent search and inquiry should include the following:

1. An inquiry of tenants in possession of the property. *MacKay v. Bacon*, 155 Fla. 577, 20 So.2d 904 (1945).

2. A check of the records of the clerk of the circuit court with respect to any transaction to which the defendants were parties, as indicated in the partial abstract obtained before the filing of the foreclosure action. *Adams v. Fielding*, 148 Fla. 552, 4 So.2d 678 (1941); *Klinger v. Milton Holding Co.*, 136 Fla. 50, 186 So. 526 (1939); *Eldridge v. E. C. Fitz & Co.*, 126 Fla. 548, 171 So. 509 (1936).

3. If the defendant is known to be an officer, resident agent or director of a corporation, an inquiry of the Florida Secretary of State. *Adams v. Fielding, supra.*

4. A check of the phone book and city directory. *Adams v. Fielding, supra.*

5. A telephone call to the grantor of the deed to the defendant. *Klinger v. Milton Holding Co., supra.*

6. An inquiry of any agent whose sign appears on the property advertising it for sale. *Smetal Corporation v. West Lake Inv. Co.*, 126 Fla. 595, 172 So. 58 (1937).

7. A search of the tax collector's receipt book. *Gmaz v. King*, 238 So.2d 511 (2d D.C.A. Fla. 1970).

c. [§5.27] Additional Sources Of Information

In addition to the above, the following sources of information have been found to be fruitful:

1. Neighbors, relatives or friends of the defendants.

2. The post office (the inquirer should send a certified or registered letter to the person at the property address, requesting a return receipt indicating where delivered).

3. If the mortgage being foreclosed is guaranteed by the VA, an inquiry should be made of the local VA office.

4. Present or last known employer.

5. The Director, Department of Motor Vehicles.

6. If the defendants are known to have children, the local school board.

7. The telephone information operator.

8. Local utility companies. See *Naples Park-Vanderbilt Beach Water District v. Downing,* 244 So.2d 464 (2d D.C.A. Fla. 1971), *cert. den.* 245 So.2d 257.

9. Supervisor of voter registration.

For a good discussion, see Kooman, *Constructive Service in Florida,* 9 U.FLA.L.REV. 1 (1956); for a later commentary, see Rose and Schmuckler, *Civil Procedure,* 24 U. MIAMI L. REV. 534 (1970).

d. [§5.28] Form For Affidavit For Constructive Service

(Title of Court)

(Title of Cause)   **AFFIDAVIT FOR CONSTRUCTIVE SERVICE**

Before me, the undersigned authority, personally appeared ...., who was sworn and says:

1. He is the plaintiff in this action.

2. Diligent search and inquiry have been made to discover the residence of the defendants listed below.

The residence of each of the following defendants is as follows:

[list name of each defendant whose *residence* is known, but who is not in Florida, and set out his residence]

3. Affiant has been unable to determine the residence of each of the following defendants, whose last mailing address, if known, is as follows:

[list]

4. Each of the persons listed in the preceding paragraph is over the age of 18 years, unless otherwise expressly noted in this affidavit.

5. Affiant believes that there is no person in the State of Florida upon whom service of process would bind the absent defendants.

                                                      Affiant

(Jurat)

COMMENT: If the action also is against unknown parties, the following paragraph should be added to the affidavit:

Affiant believes that there are unknown parties who are or may be interested in the subject matter of this cause and who may claim by, through or under the defendant, ..., if dead, and that after diligent search and inquiry are unknown to affiant.

The statute requires that the *residence*, not the *address*, of the defendant be stated if known.

3. Notice Of Action

    a. [§5.29] In General

Upon the filing of the affidavit for service by publication, the plaintiff is entitled to have the clerk or the judge issue a notice of action. A form for the notice of action is set out below in §5.20. The return date set forth in the notice must be not less than 28 nor more than 60 days after the first publication. The notice must be published once each week for four consecutive weeks and a proof of publication must be filed after the last publication. *F.S.* 49.09 and .10.

    b. [§5.30] Form For Notice Of Action

(Title of Court)

(Title of Cause)   **NOTICE OF ACTION**

TO: ....

    YOU ARE NOTIFIED that an action to foreclose a mortgage on the following property in .... County, Florida:

[legal description]

has been filed against you and you are required to serve a copy of your written defenses, if any, to it on ...., plaintiff's attorney, whose address is ...., on or before ....(date).........., and file the original with the clerk of this court either before service on plaintiff's attorney or immediately thereafter; otherwise a default will be entered against you for the relief demanded in the complaint or petition.

      WITNESS my hand and the seal of this court on ....(date)..........

....
As Clerk of the Court

By _____
As Deputy Clerk

COMMENT: This form is substantially similar to *RCP* Form 1.920. It must be published once each week for four consecutive weeks. *F.S.* 49.10.

V.   [§5.31] DEFAULTS

In the majority of the foreclosure actions the titleholders do not file an answer. It usually is necessary to obtain a default against those defendants. *RCP* 1.500. A default in a foreclosure action is the same as in any other civil action. For a full discussion of defaults, see Chapter 18, FLORIDA CIVIL PRACTICE BEFORE TRIAL (CLE 3d ed. 1975). A form for the motion for default is found at §18.17 of that manual. As discussed in §5.8, a nonmilitary affidavit may have been filed along with the motion for default. Ordinarily, the clerk will enter the default, *RCP* 1.500(a), unless the defendant has filed some response, such as a letter to the judge, in which event the court must enter the default with proper notice to the defendant, *RCP* 1.500(b).

VI.   THE FINAL JUDGMENT

A.   [§5.32] In General

A final judgment will be entered in one of two circumstances, the first being when a default is entered against all defendants (see §5.33) and the second being after one or more defendants files an answer (that is, after trial or upon summary judgment – see §5.34). Depending on the response received from the defendants, the two situations must be treated procedurally in a different manner.

B. [§5.33] Final Judgment After Default

If all defendants default, a final judgment should be obtained immediately following the entry of the default. This is an ex parte proceeding, but should not be confused with a motion for summary judgment under *RCP* 1.510. Affidavits establishing the amounts due the plaintiff, the costs incurred in the action and a reasonable attorney's fee must be filed. See the forms set out in §§5.36—.39.

C. [§5.34] Final Judgment After Defendant Answers

In some cases the defendant will serve an answer denying all of the allegations, or will write a letter to the court that must be construed as an answer. In other cases answers will be served by one or more of the defendants who were joined because they are subordinate lienholders. Their answers usually state in essence that they are without knowledge as to most of the allegations of the complaint, with the exception of the paragraph setting forth their own interest, which they admit, and with the additional exception of the paragraph stating that the interest of the plaintiff is superior to the interest of the defendant, which usually is denied. In many of these cases the answer will close with the demand that if the plaintiff's mortgage is found to be superior and a foreclosure sale is held, the proceeds of the sale, to the extent that they exceed the amount due the plaintiff under the final judgment, will be held for the benefit of the answering defendant. It is improper for a defendant to deny what is shown by the public records of the county.

If a sole defendant answers and admits all of the allegations of the complaint, a motion for judgment on the pleadings, *RCP* 1.140(c), may be made as to that defendant. See FLORIDA CIVIL PRACTICE BEFORE TRIAL §13.14 (CLE 3d ed. 1975). If any allegations are denied or other affirmative averments are made in the answer, the plaintiff must serve a motion for summary judgment or set the matter for trial, if necessary.

When a motion for summary judgment is served, an appointment for the hearing should be scheduled as soon as possible. The motion for summary judgment, supporting affidavits and the notice of hearing are served upon the answering defendants. *RCP* 1.510(c) requires that the motion be served at least 20 days prior to the hearing, unless the defendant has waived any further notice of hearing.

A form for the motion for summary judgment is found at FLORIDA CIVIL PRACTICE BEFORE TRIAL §19.25 (CLE 3d ed. 1975), or the form set out below in §5.35 may be utilized. The affidavits set out in §§5.36–.39 should accompany the motion for summary judgment, with any other affidavits needed to disprove allegations raised by the defendants. The form for the final judgment in §5.40 can be prepared beforehand for presentation to the court, assuming the mortgagee prevails. While some may argue that sending copies of the proposed final judgment is not required by *RCP* 1.080, it is a courtesy to the other attorney and parties to send these copies before the hearing. This practice also may prevent last-minute haggling over the wording of the judgment.

If a motion for summary judgment is inappropriate or unsuccessful, the foreclosure action must proceed to trial on the contested issues as in other civil cases.

D.   Forms Relating To Final Judgments

   1. [§5.35] Motion For Summary Final Judgment in Foreclosure

(Title of Court)

(Title of Cause)

PLAINTIFF'S MOTION FOR SUMMARY FINAL JUDGMENT IN FORECLOSURE

Plaintiff, ..., shows unto this court that there is no genuine issue as to any material fact in the above-entitled cause and that plaintiff is entitled to judgment as a matter of law, and, therefore, moves for summary final judgment in foreclosure in its favor for the amount found by the court to be due plaintiff from defendant under the promissory note secured by the mortgage being foreclosed in this cause, and further adjudging that in default of the payment of that amount by the defendant, the mortgaged property be sold in the interest of all parties. Plaintiff attaches to this motion affidavits as to indebtedness setting forth the amount due plaintiff by defendant and other affidavits in support of this motion.

Attorney

..................(address)..................

(Certificate of Service)

COMMENT: This form is permissible, but not mandatory. It is not necessary to move for a final judgment to which one is entitled by law.

2. [§5.36] Attorney's Affidavit As To Record Title

(Title of Court)

(Title of Cause)   AFFIDAVIT

Before me, the undersigned authority, personally appeared ...., who was sworn and says:

1. I am a practicing attorney in ...., ... County, Florida, and as such I have examined a policy of title insurance and partial abstract of title in connection with the following-described property:

[legal description]

2. The title to this property is presently vested in ...., subject to that certain first mortgage held by ...., dated .... and recorded in Official Records Book .... at page .... of the public records of .... County, Florida. The mortgage that is the subject matter of this cause is a valid existing mortgage on the above-described property and the plaintiff, ..., is the holder of that mortgage, and the mortgage constitutes a lien on the above-described property that is superior in dignity to all liens of the defendants.

                                                                      Affiant

(Jurat)

COMMENT: The purpose of this affidavit is merely to establish the name of the record titleholder and the fact that, according to the public records, the mortgage is a first lien on the property. The affidavit is not essential and of course one cannot create title by affidavit.

3. [§5.37] Affidavit Of Amounts Due

(Title of Court)

(Title of Cause)   AFFIDAVIT

Before me, the undersigned authority, personally appeared ...., who was sworn and says:

Affiant's name is .... and he is ....(title).......... of .... Company, with offices located at ...., Florida, which is a local servicing contractor for the plaintiff, ..., the owner and holder of a mortgage and note that is in default by reason of [the failure to make the payment due ...., which sum has not been paid as of the date of this affidavit] [failure to pay the taxes due on ....]; the plaintiff has agreed to pay its attorneys the sum of $.......... for services rendered in these proceedings; and the amount due upon the mortgage as of ....(date).......... is as follows:

    Principal due on the note and mortgage
    ....(date).......... to ....(date).......... $....................

    Interest from ....(date).......... to ....(date)..........
    at the rate of .... per cent per annum   ....

    Interest from ....(date).......... to ....(date)..........
    at the rate of .... per cent per annum (default rate)   ....

    Late charges   ....

    Taxes paid by plaintiff   ....

    Less escrow balance (if any)   (....................)
    TOTAL $....................

    Plus interest at the rate of $..........
    per day from ....(date)............

                                                                          Affiant

(Jurat)

COMMENT: The affidavits for amounts due and costs (§5.38) can be combined if the plaintiff or his agent are available and familiar with the costs.

4. [§5.38] Affidavit Of Attorney As To Costs

(Title of Court)

(Title of Cause)   **AFFIDAVIT**

    Before me, the undersigned authority, personally appeared ...., who was sworn and says that he is a member of the law firm of ...., the attorneys for the plaintiff in this action, that he knows the costs advanced by plaintiff or on his behalf in connection with the foreclosure, which are as follows:

Partial abstract of title $....................

Clerk of circuit court .... costs   ....

Sheriff of .... County .... costs   ....

Publication costs (if not included in clerk's costs)   ....

Photostats   ....

Total advanced on expenses $....................

_____
                                                    Affiant
(Jurat)

COMMENT: Authority for each of the cost items included in the affidavit and for the charging of a reasonable attorney's fee normally is found in the mortgage instrument itself. The mortgage usually provides that if the mortgagor fails to comply with any of the agreements and covenants of the note and mortgage, the mortgagor must pay all the costs, charges and expenses, including reasonable attorneys' fees and costs of abstracts of title.

5. [§5.39] Affidavit As To Attorneys' Fees

(Title of Court)

(Title of Cause)   AFFIDAVIT

On this day personally appeared ...., who was sworn and says that he is a practicing attorney in .... County, Florida, and as such he has had experience in the foreclosure of mortgages. He is familiar with the amount customarily charged by attorneys and allowed by this court for attorneys' fees for foreclosing mortgages. He knows the reasonable value of those services and he has been advised as to the amount due on the mortgage sought to be foreclosed in this action and the extent of the services rendered by the plaintiff's attorneys. In his opinion the sum of $.......... would be a reasonable attorney's fee to be allowed the plaintiff's attorneys for their services.

_____
                                                    Affiant
(Jurat)

COMMENT: See FLORIDA CIVIL TRIAL PRACTICE §§21.19–.21 (CLE 2d ed. 1970). Formerly, in many areas of the state, attorneys' fees for foreclosing a mortgage were regulated by a minimum fee schedule. Today, some law offices may maintain their own suggested minimum fee schedules for those actions, which may be useful in obtaining affidavits concerning a reasonable fee. Accurate time records should be kept in all cases, especially in any case with unusual difficulties, as they are extremely persuasive in justifying an adequate fee. In foreclosure of government insured loans, a low maximum fee is set in the appropriate regulations. See §5.2 for references to VA and FHA regulations regarding this subject.

6. [§5.40] Final Judgment

(Title of Court)

(Title of Cause)

SUMMARY FINAL JUDGMENT
IN FORECLOSURE

This action was heard on plaintiff's motion for summary final judgment, and it is

ADJUDGED that:

1. Plaintiff, ..., is due $.......... as principal, $.......... as interest to date of this judgment, $.......... for title search expense, $.......... for taxes, $.......... for insurance premiums and $.......... for attorneys' fees with $.......... court costs now taxed, less $.......... for undisbursed escrow funds, and less $.......... for unearned insurance premiums, under the note and mortgage sued on in this action making a total sum of $..........

2. Plaintiff holds a lien for the total sum superior to any claim or estate of defendant, ..., on the following-described property in .... County, Florida:

[legal description]

3. If the total sum with interest at the rate prescribed by law and all costs of this action accruing subsequent to this judgment are not paid within three days from this date, the clerk of this court shall sell the property at public sale on ....(date).........., between ....(times).........., to the highest bidder for cash, except as set forth below, at the .... door of the courthouse in .... County in ...., Florida, in accordance with F.S. 45.031.

4. Plaintiff shall advance all subsequent costs of this action and shall be reimbursed for them by the clerk if plaintiff is not the purchaser of the property at the sale. If plaintiff is the purchaser, the clerk shall credit plaintiff's bid with the total sum with interest and costs accruing subsequent to this judgment or such part of it as is necessary to pay the bid in full.

5. On filing the certificiate of title the clerk shall distribute the proceeds of the sale, as far as they are sufficient, by paying: first, all of plaintiff's costs; second, documentary stamps affixed to the certificate; third, plaintiff's attorneys' fees; fourth, the total sum due to plaintiff less the items paid plus interest at the rate prescribed by law from this date to the date of the sale; and by retaining any amount remaining pending the further order of this court.

6. On filing the certificate of title defendant and all persons claiming under or against him since the filing of the notice of lis pendens are foreclosed of all estate or claim in the property and the purchaser at the sale shall be let into possession of the property.

7. Jurisdiction of this action is retained to enter further orders as are proper including, without limitation, writs of assistance and deficiency judgments.

ORDERED at ...., Florida on ....(date)..........

Copies furnished to: ....

_____
Judge

COMMENT: The above form in substance is *RCP* Form 1.996. It should be noted that provision can be made for the assignment of the plaintiff's right to bid. This may be utilized as a device to save documentary stamps and surtaxes on a transaction in which the plaintiff already has made plans to re-sell or assign the property, such as in a VA or FHA foreclosure.

VII. JUDICIAL SALE

A. [§5.41] In General

The court under its inherent equitable powers may order the sale of the property under any terms and conditions it may set, such as for notice and time of sale. Upon the completion of the sale, the court then must confirm the sale. *F.S.* 45.031 provides for an alternative procedure, which as a practical matter almost always is utilized and is recommended except in unusual cases.

Under the statutory sale procedure, *F.S.* 45.031, when the judge signs the final judgment, the clerk will record the judgment. The sale must be at least ten days after the date of the judgment and must be advertised at least once seven days prior to sale and be held at the appointed time. Immediately after the sale, the clerk will issue and file a certificate of sale. Objections to the sale may be made within ten days from the date the clerk issues his certificate of sale. If no objections are made after ten days has elapsed, the clerk issues a certificate of title to the purchaser and disburses the sale proceeds in accordance with the instructions of the final judgment. The statute provides that the sale is confirmed upon the issuance of the certificate of title.

The statute, *F.S.* 45.031, sets out forms for the certificate of sale, the certificate of title and the certificate of disbursements.

B. Notification Of FHA And VA

1. [§5.42] In General

The FHA and VA require that they be notified of the date of the foreclosure sale as soon as it is set. The FHA usually is notified by the servicing agent upon receipt from the attorney of a conformed copy of the final judgment. The VA must be notified directly and a conformed copy of the final judgment will suffice. The VA requires copies of the complaint, the final judgment and the certificates of sale, title and disbursements. The FHA does not require copies of any of those instruments.

Since both the FHA and the VA require that the original note and mortgage be surrendered to them at the completion of the foreclosure, it is necessary in those cases to prepare a motion and order allowing the substitution of copies for the originals. The motion and order usually may be submitted with the final judgment, although some judges prefer not to sign the order until after the sale.

2. [§5.43] Form For Motion For Substitution Of Photostatic Copies And Order Allowing Substitution

(Title of Court)

(Title of Cause)

PLAINTIFF'S MOTION FOR SUBSTITUTION OF PHOTOSTATIC COPIES

Plaintiff moves to allow the substitution of photostatic copies of the original promissory note and mortgage filed in this action.

Attorney

.................(address).................

(Certificate of Service)

ORDER

This action was heard on the foregoing matter, and it is

ADJUDGED that plaintiff may substitute photostatic copies of the original promissory note and mortgage and the clerk of this court is directed then to deliver the original promissory note and mortgage to plaintiff's attorneys.

ORDERED at ...., Florida on ....(date).........

_____
Circuit Judge

Copies furnished to: ....

COMMENT: The above can be accomplished by oral motion and incorporation in the final judgment.

C. Notice Of Sale

1. [§5.44] In General

As mentioned in §5.41, at least seven days before the sale a notice of foreclosure sale must be published in a local newspaper. *F.S.* 45.031(1). In some counties this is done by the clerk. In others, however, the attorney must prepare the notice and send it to the clerk, who then has it published. A form for the notice is set out below. It should be remembered that VA regulations require a copy of the notice of sale to be sent to the VA at least ten days before the sale.

2. [§5.45] Form For Notice Of Sale

(Title of Court)

(Title of Cause)

NOTICE OF SALE
PURSUANT TO CHAPTER 45

Notice is given that pursuant to a final judgment dated .... in Case No. .... of the Circuit Court of the .... Judicial Circuit in and for .... County, Florida, in which .... is the plaintiff and .... and .... are the defendants, I will sell to the highest and best bidder for cash in the lobby at the .... door of the .... County Courthouse in ...., ... County, Florida, at ....(time).......... on ....(date).........., the following-described property set forth in the order of final judgment:

[legal description]

Dated ....

....
Clerk of Circuit Court

By _____
Deputy Clerk

Publication of this notice on ....(date).......... in the ....(name of newspaper)..........

D. [§5.46] Payment By Defendant Of Amount Due In Final Judgment Prior To Sale; Completion And Confirmation Of Sale

F.S. 45.031(1) allows the defendant to redeem the property at any time before sale. This has been held to mean that a defendant may redeem the property any time prior to the confirmation of the sale, which occurs upon the issuance of the certificate of title by the clerk under 45.031(3). *Allstate Mortgage Corporation of Florida v. Strasser,* 277 So.2d 843 (3d D.C.A. Fla. 1973), *aff'd* 286 So.2d 201. Presumably, after the issuance of a certificate of title by the clerk the sale is confirmed and no further objection to the sale or redemption can be made, as 45.031(4) provides that the sale will be confirmed and title will pass to the purchaser named in the certificate of title upon its filing by the clerk. See also *R. K. Cooper Construction Company v. Fulton,* 216 So.2d 11 (Fla. 1968); *Confederate Point Partnership, Ltd. v. Schatten,* 278 So.2d 661 (1st D.C.A. Fla. 1973).

E. The Sale Procedure

1. [§5.47] In General

The foreclosure sale normally is conducted by the clerk of the circuit court pursuant to *F.S.* 45.031. The plaintiff or his representative should attend the sale to preclude a third party from obtaining the property for an inadequate consideration. Most clerks will not hold the sale if the plaintiff is not represented. If the sale is not held, the plaintiff must seek an order setting a new sale date and again publish a notice of sale.

2. Bidding By The Mortgagee

a. [§5.48] Amount Due Under Final Judgment Credited Against Amount Bid

The amount that the plaintiff should bid at the sale is determined by a number of considerations. Of prime importance is the fact that the plaintiff is allowed to credit against the amount of his bid the amount due him under the final judgment, plus interest and costs through the date of the sale. The plaintiff's bid should not exceed this total amount unless the property is commensurately valuable to him and he is prepared to pay cash for the excess.

b. [§5.49] Bids Less Than Value Of Property

F.S. 45.031(7) provides that the amount bid for the property at sale shall be conclusively presumed to be sufficient consideration for the sale, but allows any party to object to the sale within ten days. This statute also provides that, if there is a deficiency and application is made for a deficiency judgment, the amount bid at sale is one factor that may be considered by the court in its determination as to whether a deficiency should be entered. Thus, the mortgagee who bids an artificially low price at the foreclosure sale and buys the property at that price may find that although the mortgagor cannot have the sale set aside, the mortgagor may be able to defeat the attempt of the mortgagee to obtain and enforce a deficiency by showing that the value of the property was in excess of the amount the mortgagee paid. In *R. K. Cooper Construction Co. v. Fulton,* 216 So.2d 11 (Fla. 1968), in a subsequent action on the note to collect the deficiency after the sale the court held that the amount of the prior sale does not conclusively bind the court in the second action in determining whether a deficiency should be allowed and enforced.

Another matter to be considered when the United States has an interest in the property is the effect of 28 *U.S.C.* §§2410(c) and (d), which give the United States a right of redemption. By its terms, the amount to be paid by the United States is the amount of the sale plus the interest. Thus, if the sale bid is artificially low and the United States redeems at the low price, the mortgagee may be without the property and unable to obtain a deficiency, although normally this will not be done.

Actions for deficiency judgment are discussed further in §5.65.

c. [§5.50] Determination Of Amount Of Gain To
Mortgagee For Income Taxation Purposes

Consideration should be given by the mortgagee to the possible income tax effects of the foreclosure and the amount of the bid. Discussion of these aspects is beyond the scope of this chapter.

d. [§5.51] Bid In Accordance With Instructions From VA

In VA cases the attorney will receive a letter from the regional VA office giving bidding instructions. In these cases the bids for the property should be in accordance with the instructions.

VIII. POST SALE PROCEDURE

A. [§5.52] Certificates Of Sale, Title And Disbursements

After the sale the clerk will issue the certificates of sale, title and disbursements in accordance with *F.S.* 45.031(2)–(6). See §5.41. Forms for these certificates are set out in that statute and, therefore, are not reprinted here. In most circuits the clerk will issue these automatically, but in others the attorney must prepare the certificates and present them to the clerk for his signature.

B. Writ Of Assistance

1. [§5.53] In General

In the foreclosure of a conventional mortgage, the duties of the attorney are concluded upon receipt of the certificate of title, unless it is necessary to seek a writ of assistance to evict the former mortgagors or other parties in possession. The issuance of the writ of assistance is covered by *RCP* 1.580. The rule requires only an affidavit stating that demand for possession has been made by the plaintiff or his representative as a prerequisite for the issuance of the writ.

In some circuits there is a practice of issuing writs ex parte upon proper motion. In other circuits or when there has been a contested case, the judge may require a hearing on the motion. In practice, the motion and affidavit should be secured and a hearing scheduled. These matters should be set for hearing rapidly by the judge, as they constitute a potential irreparable harm to plaintiff. A foreclosed mortgagor in possession can do an inordinate amount of damage in a short period of time. Notice of the hearing and copies of the motion and affidavit should be served in accordance with the rules. If the defendant is not represented by an attorney and difficulties can be anticipated, consideration should be given to having the notice served by a process server or the sheriff.

At the hearing or, if ex parte, accompanying the motion, the lawyer should send the appropriate order directing the clerk to issue the writ. See §5.54 for a combination motion and order. *RCP* Form 1.916 is a form for the writ of assistance. Upon presentation of the order to the clerk, the clerk will issue the writ. The sheriff usually requires copies for each person to be served with the original along with his usual fee.

There is some question whether a writ of assistance may be directed against personal property (not covered by the mortgage) that has been left on the premises after the mortgagor has vacated. If the problem arises, the mortgagee's remedy may lie in the provisions of *F.S.* Chapter 717, "Disposition of Unclaimed Property."

2. [§5.54] Form For Motion For Writ Of Assistance And Order

(Title of Court)

(Title of Cause)　　　　　　　　　　**PLAINTIFF'S MOTION FOR
WRIT OF ASSISTANCE**

Plaintiff, ..., moves for an order directing the clerk of this court to issue a writ of assistance directing that defendant, ..., be removed from possession of the following-described property:

[legal description]

and attaches affidavits in support of this motion.

　　　　　　　　　　　　　　　　　　　　　　　————————————
　　　　　　　　　　　　　　　　　　　　　　　　　　　　Attorney

　　　　　　　　　　　　　　　　　　　　　　　..................(address)..................

(Certificate of Service)

ORDER

This action was heard on motion for writ of assistance, and it is

ADJUDGED that the clerk of this court issue a writ of assistance directing that defendant, ..., be removed from the property described in the motion.

ORDERED at ...., Florida on ....(date)..........

_____
Circuit Judge

Copies furnished to: ....

3. [§5.55] Form For Supporting Affidavit

(Title of Court)

(Title of Cause)   AFFIDAVIT

Before me, the undersigned authority, personally appeared ...., who was sworn and says:

1. Affiant is a member of the law firm of ...., attorneys for the plaintiff, ...

2. A final judgment in foreclosure was entered in the above-named cause on ....(date).........., requiring defendant, ..., to deliver to plaintiff possession of the following-described property:

[legal description]

3. Demand was made by affiant upon defendant for delivery of the property on ....(date).......... at ...., Florida, by certified mail, but defendant has wholly refused to deliver possession and still refuses to do so.

_____
Affiant

(Jurat)

C.   Post Sale Procedure In Relation To FHA Mortgages When Mortgagee Is Successful Bidder At Sale

    1. Execution Of Instruments By Mortgagee

        a. [§5.56] In General

When the foreclosed property is subject to FHA regulations and the mortgagee is the successful bidder at the sale and desires to convey the property to the FHA, the mortgagee's servicing agent should be notified to this effect immediately after the sale and be given the amount of the bid. Normally, the mortgagee will elect to convey to the FHA, for quite probably there will be little equity in the home in the case of FHA and VA mortgages. Next, a special warranty deed from the plaintiff-mortgagee to the Secretary of Housing and Urban Development should be prepared by the attorney handling the foreclosure and sent to the mortgagee, with the original promissory note, which should have been withdrawn from the court file by this time. See the form for a special warranty deed set out in §5.57. The mortgagee should execute the deed, endorse the note over to the Secretary of Housing and Urban Development, his successors and assigns, and return them to the servicing agent. Some larger banks and insurance companies prepare these instruments themselves and will want everything sent directly to them.

b. [§5.57] Form For Special Warranty Deed

SPECIAL WARRANTY DEED

BY THIS SPECIAL WARRANTY DEED, grantor, in consideration of ten dollars paid by the Secretary of Housing and Urban Development, Washington, D.C. 20412, his successors and assigns, grantee, conveys to grantee the following-described real property in .... County, Florida:

[legal description]

Grantor covenants with grantee that grantor is lawfully seized of the property in fee simple; that grantor has good right and lawful authority to sell and convey the property; that grantor warrants the title to the property for any acts of grantor and will defend it against the lawful claims of all persons claiming by, through or under grantor.

DATED on ....

Signed in the presence of:

_____

_____

_____

(Acknowledgment)

2. [§5.58] Recording Of Deed

Once the executed deed is received by the servicing agent from the mortgagee, the deed should be recorded. The FHA requires that the deed be recorded within 30 days after the sale. If unavoidable delays are encountered, extensions of this deadline may be granted. The attorney must affix the proper documentary stamps and record the deed.

3. Evidence Of Title

a. [§5.59] In General

The FHA requires title evidence. This evidence may consist of any one of the following:

1. Fee owner's title policy issued by a title company duly authorized by law and qualified by experience to issue such a policy;

2. An abstract of title accompanied by a legal opinion of the quality of the title signed by an attorney experienced in examination of titles covering a period of time at least 40 years prior to the date of the certificate to a well-recognized source of good title; or

3. The mortgagee's policy of title insurance supplemented by a partial abstract and an attorney's certificate of title. The partial abstract must cover the period of time beginning with the date of the mortgage and running through the recorded deed to the Secretary of Housing and Urban Development. The terms of the policy must be such that the liability of the title company continues in favor of the Secretary after title is conveyed to him.

The latter of the three types of title evidence is the one most commonly used. It requires the attorney to prepare a certificate of title covering only that period of time from the date of the mortgage through the date of the recording of the deed to the Secretary. FHA Form 2319, "Attorney's Certificate of Title," is set out below.

b. [§5.60] Form For Attorney's Certificate Of Title

FHA FORM NO. 2319 DEPARTMENT OF HOUSING AND URBAN DEVELOPMENT
FEDERAL HOUSING ADMINISTRATION

MORTGAGEE OR SERVICER PLEASE NOTE: PLEASE FORWARD THE THREE (3) FHA FORMS 2319 OF THIS PACKET TO YOUR ATTORNEY IMMEDIATELY FOR HIS PROMPT COMPLETION.

ATTORNEY'S CERTIFICATE OF TITLE

IN CONNECTION WITH MORTGAGE INSURED BY SECRETARY OF HOUSING AND URBAN DEVELOPMENT
(SEE NOTE BELOW)

TO: SECRETARY OF HOUSING AND URBAN DEVELOPMENT   FHA Case No. _____

THIS CERTIFIES that the undersigned has examined all of the public records relative to real estate titles of the county and State in which the land described in schedule A below is situated, or has examined abstracts of title purporting to reflect the contents of such records relative to said land, which abstracts are deemed sufficiently complete and worthy of confidence, and that said examination began with a well recognized source of good title and covered a period which, in the opinion of the undersigned and in accordance with the practice of competent local title attorneys, is deemed sufficient to establish good title. After such examination it is the opinion of the undersigned that, subject only to the matter shown under schedule B hereof, a good and merchantable fee-simple title to the premises described in schedule A hereof was, at the date of this certificate, indefeasibly vested in:

_____

by _____ deed from _____

dated _____, 19___ Recorded _____, 19___

in book _____ page _____ of the county records.

SCHEDULE A

Accurate description of the property:

ALL THAT CERTAIN tract or parcel of land, situate, lying, and being in the _____
of _____, county of _____, State of _____

A SKETCH OR DIAGRAM should be attached to this Certificate showing location of the property with respect to streets on which the property fronts and nearest adjoining streets, if no survey is available.

NOTE. - This certificate may be executed upon recordation of the mortgage to be insured and should be in addition to the form required by the mortgagee. It should not be sent to the Secretary unless or until claim is filed, but should be attached to the abstract and is intended to eliminate reexamination of the back title by the attorney who may subsequently certify title in the event of claim under the insurance contract. In such event the subsequent attorney may execute a similar form amended to cover the continuation only.

(Over)
FHA FORM NO. 2319 Rev. 6/66

SCHEDULE B

If there are no liens, encumbrances, or objections of the type described, circle the word "NONE" as it appears before each item. If objections are noted, they should be set forth in full after the applicable item. (Attach riders if necessary)

NONE   1. MORTGAGES:

NONE   2. MECHANICS' LIENS:

NONE   3. JUDGMENTS: (State and Federal, including fines and penalties in criminal proceedings.)

NONE   4. ATTACHMENTS:

NONE   5. SUITS PENDING OR LIS PENDENS AFFECTING TITLE:

NONE   6. BANKRUPTCY PROCEEDINGS: (By or against all parties in chain of title within 10 years last past.)

NONE   7. LEASES OR LAND CONTRACTS: (Recorded or known.)

NONE   8. PARTY WALL AGREEMENTS, ENCROACHMENTS, AND EASEMENTS (Recorded or known.)

NONE   9. RESTRICTIVE COVENANTS AND ZONING ORDINANCES: (Show record reference, and indicate any known violation.)

Do they contain reversionary, forfeiture clause, or right of reentry to abate nuisance? _____ If so, has such clause or right been waived or subordinated in favor of mortgagee? _____ Does recorded plat show building-restriction line? _____ If so give details.

NONE   10. OIL OR MINERAL RIGHTS:

Do such rights permit injury to surface without payment of adequate damages? _____

NONE   11. Estate and Income Taxes: (Federal and State.)

NONE   12. Water and Sewer Charges: (Give amounts and due date.)

NONE   13. Taxes: (Including outstanding tax certificates, unredeemed tax sales, estate, income, corporation, franchise, unemployment, old-age, and personal-property taxes where liens. Give year, amount, and due date.)

NONE   14. Special Assessments: (Show character of improvement, amount, and due dates. If payable in future installments, show amounts and due dates of each installment. Also the date the assessment became a lien.)

NONE   15. OTHER LIENS, OBJECTIONS, AND DEFECTS:

This certificate is dated the _____ day of _____, 19____, and my title examination covered the preceding period beginning on _____, 19____, and
                                                                              (Month)   (Day)
continued to the certification date above set forth.

Name and address of attorney (type):

_____   _____
                                                                                                                 Attorney

_____

4. [§5.61] Submission To FHA By Mortgagee Of Deed, Title Evidence, Fiscal Data And Supporting Documents

On the date the deed is filed for record, the mortgagee must submit to the FHA Assistant Commissioner Comptroller, through the servicing agent, FHA Form No. 1025, "Notice of Property Transfer and Application for Debentures."

The FHA requires that all title evidence, fiscal data, the special warranty deed and other supporting documents be forwarded through the mortgagee's servicing agent within 30 days after the recording of the special warranty deed.

It is still necessary for the mortgagee or its servicing agent to prepare numerous forms including fiscal data and a claim for debentures. Some of the information for these forms is furnished by the attorney. All original instruments and the special warranty deed, attorney's certificate of title, abstract and the various receipts should be sent by the attorney to the servicing agent within approximately two weeks following the recording of the special warranty deed.

After all these steps are completed, the mortgagee is reimbursed for its loan through the debentures of the FHA.

D. Post Sale Procedure In Relation To VA Mortgages When Mortgagee Is Successful Bidder At Sale

1. [§5.62] Mortgagee's Notice To VA And Execution Of Deed

If the plaintiff-mortgagee is the successful bidder at the foreclosure sale of property subject to VA regulations and he wishes to convey the property to the VA, his attorney must notify the VA Regional Office directly by mail that the plaintiff was the successful bidder at the sale. The attorney should inform the VA of the amount of the bid and state that the plaintiff has elected to convey the property to the VA, unless the mortgagee directs otherwise. Upon receiving this notice, the VA sends its own special warranty deed form to the mortgagee, who executes it and transmits it to the attorneys handling the foreclosure.

2. [§5.63] Eviction Of Mortgagor

The VA also requires the property to be vacant when it receives title. If the mortgagors are still living on the property, eviction proceedings should be instituted. See §5.53.

3. [§5.64] Forwarding Documents To VA

When the deed is received from the mortgagee and the mortgagor is removed from the premises, the original instruments and the unrecorded special warranty deed, partial abstract and various receipts should be forwarded to the servicing agent. The VA does not require a certificate of title. It normally obtains its own title insurance.

E. [§5.65] Deficiency Judgments

In an action to foreclose a mortgage, the right to sue for a deficiency is specifically protected by *F.S.* 702.06. That statute leaves the award of a deficiency judgment to the "sound judicial discretion" of the court. This doctrine has been repeatedly endorsed by Florida courts. See, *e.g., Maudo, Inc. v. Stein,* 201 So.2d 821 (3d D.C.A. Fla. 1967). It also has been pointed out that this discretion is not absolute and unbridled, but must be supported by established equitable principles as applied to the facts of the case. *Sohn v. Cominole,* 253 So.2d 898 (1st D.C.A. Fla. 1971).

Deficiency judgments were mentioned also in §5.49, and that section should be read in conjunction with this one. See also §5.75 (concerning a motion for a deficiency judgment when the foreclosure is in a federal district court) and §5.77 (concerning provision for assessing a deficiency judgment in the order confirming sale).

As of this writing, since 1962 the district courts of appeal have reviewed the award of deficiency judgments in at least 14 cases. In six of those cases, the appellate court affirmed the grant of deficiency judgments, ranging from two to 28 million dollars. In three cases the court affirmed the denial of a deficiency judgment. In each case the court was careful to indicate that the mortgagee had already received equitable payment. In five cases the court reversed denial of a deficiency judgment. In each case the court cited the absence of equitable principles to support the trial court's denial.

The decisions are listed below:

Deficiency grant affirmed:

Boyles v. Atlantic Federal Savings & Loan Ass'n, 201 So.2d 909 (4th D.C.A. Fla. 1967)

Maudo v. Stein, 201 So.2d 821 (3d D.C.A. Fla. 1967)

Diversified Enterprises of Florida, Inc. v. Holt, 188 So.2d 693 (2d D.C.A. Fla. 1966)

Matlack v. Owen, 181 So.2d 602 (2d D.C.A. Fla. 1966)

Builders Finance Co., Inc. v. Ridgewood Homesites, Inc., 157 So.2d 551 (2d D.C.A. Fla. 1963)

Denial affirmed:

Jonas v. Bar-Jam Corp., 170 So.2d 479 (3d D.C.A. Fla. 1965)

Alkow v. Blocker, 168 So.2d 340 (3d D.C.A. Fla. 1964)

Kennedy v. Kay, 154 So.2d 345 (3d D.C.A. Fla. 1963)

Denial reversed:

Larsen v. Allocca, 187 So.2d 903 (3d D.C.A. Fla. 1966), cert. den. 195 So.2d 566

Weinstein v. Park Manor Construction Company, 166 So.2d 842 (2d D.C.A. Fla. 1964)

Nathanson v. Weston, 163 So.2d 41 (3d D.C.A. Fla. 1964), cert. disch. 173 So.2d 451

Colmes v. Hoco, Inc. of Dade County, 152 So.2d 524 (3d D.C.A. Fla. 1963)

Kurkjian v. Fish Carburetor Corporation, 145 So.2d 523 (1st D.C.A. Fla. 1962)

Sohn v. Cominole, 253 So.2d 898 (1st D.C.A. Fla. 1971)

IX. DEED INSTEAD OF FORECLOSURE

A. [§5.66] In General

Occasionally, the circumstances of the titleholder will be such that the mortgagee will be willing to accept a deed from him rather than foreclose against him in the circuit court. If the mortgagee does indicate that he will accept a deed, his attorney must examine the abstract since the date of the mortgage to determine whether there are any junior encumbrances. If so, they will have to be satisfied. If it is not possible to get them satisfied, the mortgagee will have no choice but to foreclose in order that he may acquire a clear title.

Assuming that the mortgagee is willing to accept a deed instead of foreclosure and that the title examination reveals that there are no junior liens, the attorney should prepare certain instruments, including a special warranty deed, an estoppel and solvency affidavit, a lien affidavit and a standard satisfaction of mortgage. The VA has its own forms for a deed instead of foreclosure and therefore the attorney need not prepare a deed in the case of a VA mortgage.

B. [§5.67] Form For Special Warranty Deed Instead Of Foreclosure

WARRANTY DEED

BY THIS SPECIAL WARRANTY DEED, ..., grantor, in consideration of ten dollars paid by the Secretary of Housing and Urban Development, Washington, D.C. 20412, his successors and assigns, grantee, conveys to grantee the following-described real property in .... County, Florida:

[legal description]

Grantor certifies that he does not own any other property subject to a mortgage insured or held by the Federal Housing Administration.

This deed is an absolute conveyance in satisfaction of that certain mortgage dated ...., filed ....(date).......... and recorded in Official Records Book ..... at page ..... of the public records of .... County, Florida, given by .... and ...., his wife, to ...., which mortgage has been assigned subsequently to ....

Grantor covenants with grantee that grantor is lawfully seized of the property in fee simple; that grantor has good right and lawful authority to sell and convey the property; that grantor warrants the title to the property for any acts of grantor and will defend it against the lawful claims of all persons claiming by, through or under grantor.

DATED on ....

Signed in the presence of:

(Acknowledgment)

COMMENT: Notice should be made of the provision in the special warranty deed that says that the grantors do not own any other property subject to a mortgage insured or held by the FHA. The FHA requires this affirmation in every such deed. FHA Mortgagee's Handbook §1410. If the grantors cannot make this statement, special permission to accept the deed must be obtained from the FHA.

C.   [§5.68]   Form For Estoppel And Solvency Affidavit

ESTOPPEL AND SOLVENCY AFFIDAVIT

STATE OF ....
COUNTY OF ....

Before me, the undersigned authority, personally appeared .... and ...., his wife, who were separately sworn and say:

They are the parties who made, executed and delivered that certain deed to ....(grantee).........., his successors and assigns, dated .... conveying the following-described property:

[legal description]

The deed was an absolute conveyance of the title to the property to the grantee named in it in effect as well as in form, and was and is not intended as a mortgage, trust conveyance or security of any kind, and possession of the premises has been surrendered to the grantee; the consideration in the deed was and is the full cancellation of all debts, obligations, costs and charges previously existing under and by virtue of the terms of a certain mortgage previously existing on the property described in that mortgage and in this instrument, executed by .... and ...., his wife, as mortgagors, to ...., as mortgagee, dated .... and recorded in Official Records Book .... at page .... of the public records of .... County, Florida, and the cancellation of record of the mortgage by its holder.

The deed and conveyance were made by these deponents as the result of their request that the grantee accept the deed and was their free and voluntary act; at the time of making the deed these deponents felt and still feel that the mortgage indebtedness above mentioned represented a fair value of the property so deeded; the deed was not given as a preference against any other creditors of the deponents or either of them; at the time it was given there was no other person or persons, firms or corporations, other than the grantee named in the deed, interested, either directly or indirectly, in the property; these deponents are solvent and have no other creditors whose rights would be prejudiced by the conveyance; deponents are not obligated upon any bond or other mortgage by which any lien has been created or exists against the property described in the deed; deponents in offering to execute the deed to the grantee and in executing the deed were not acting under any duress, undue influence, misapprehension or misrepresentation by the grantee in the deed, or the agent or attorney or any other representative of the grantee in the deed; and it was the intention of these deponents as grantors in the deed to convey and by the deed these deponents do convey to the grantee all their right, title and interest absolute in and to the property described in the deed.

This affidavit is made for the protection and benefit of the grantee in the deed, his successors and assigns, and all other parties hereafter dealing with or who may acquire any interest in the property described in the deed, and shall bind the respective heirs, executors, administrators and assigns of the undersigned.

                                                         Husband

                                                         Wife

(Jurat)

COMMENT: The attorney should note the provision in the estoppel and solvency affidavit that says that the deed is given as an absolute conveyance in return for the satisfaction of a mortgage and is not intended as additional security. This is a very important provision in light of *Stovall v. Stokes,* 94 Fla. 717, 115 So. 828 (1928), in which the court found that a deed given to a mortgagee was intended by the parties only as additional security and not as an absolute conveyance.

D.   [§5.69] Form For Lien Affidavit

LIEN AFFIDAVIT

STATE OF ....
COUNTY OF ....

    Before me, the undersigned authority, personally appeared .... and ...., his wife, who were sworn and say:

    1. They are the owners of the following-described property:

[legal description]

    2. There are no mechanics' liens against the premises, and no claims for labor, services or materials furnished for improving the premises that remain unpaid

to date, and no work has been done nor materials furnished, bills for which remain unpaid.

3. The property is unencumbered by the lien of any judgment, writ or attachment, income tax or intangible property tax made or suffered by the affiants.

4. There are no violations of zoning ordinances affecting the above-described property and affiants are in possession of the property.

5. Affiants make this affidavit well knowing that it is being relied upon, and that any false statement contained in it would subject affiants to all penalties imposed by law.

This affidavit is made as an inducement for the Secretary of Housing and Urban Development to accept a conveyance from affiants.

_____
Husband

_____
Wife

(Jurat)

COMMENT: See also the form in I FLORIDA REAL PROPERTY PRACTICE §14.32 (CLE 2d ed. 1971).

X. THE MORTGAGE IN THE UNITED STATES DISTRICT COURT

A. [§5.70] Introduction

The mortgagee may find that the foreclosure action that he filed in the circuit court must be removed to the United States district court if the United States is a party defendant, or conceivably for diversity of citizenship of the defendants. Fortunately, the United States normally does not remove cases from the state court to the United States district court unless a substantial federal issue is involved or is apt to be raised in the action by a party, or there are other unusual circumstances. 28 U.S.C. §1444 provides that when an action is brought against the United States, under 28 U.S.C. §2410, the cause may be removed to the United States district court for the district and division in which the action is pending. See 28 U.S.C. §§1446–1449 and Rule 81, Federal Rules of Civil Procedure for the procedure involved in removal.

The removal to the federal court may prove burdensome and timeconsuming to the plaintiff's attorney, especially if the court does not sit regularly in his locale. While the actual progress of the action after it is at issue may not take any longer with the federal court than with the circuit court, the additional requirements imposed by federal rules and statutes may make the action take considerably longer when compared to the average foreclosure in the state court, especially if the United States is a party.

Initially the United States has 60 days in which to file a responsive pleading. After the action is at issue, it will proceed to judgment as rapidly as the calendar of the judge permits in the same manner as other civil cases in the United States district court. The local rules of all Florida districts require that a memorandum of law accompany the motion. The memorandum need not be lengthy, but should contain basic citations of law to support the position taken and a brief recitation of the facts, when necessary.

B.   [§5.71]   Final Judgment In United States District Court

It is only after the motion for summary judgment has been granted or final hearing has been held with the ruling in favor of the mortgagee, and a final judgment has been entered, that the practice varies from cases in the state court. The method of sale in the federal court is different and considerably longer. The form of the final judgment entered in the federal court will be similar in many respects to the final judgment form set out in §5.40, but there are some distinct differences. The basis of the jurisdiction of the court should be specifically recited and the method of sale specified more distinctly. If the United States is a party defendant, the final judgment and all notices of sale should contain a specific reference to the right of redemption of the United States under 28 *U.S.C.* §2410. See §5.14. Forms for modifying the from at §5.40 are set out below.

C.   [§5.72]   Form For Additional Paragraphs In Final
                Judgment In United States District Court

COMMENT: After the recitations of jurisdiction, the finding of fact and the amounts due and other matters as set forth in the final judgment form in §5.40, the following language is suggested:

8. Unless defendants shall pay the sums above specified, the real property encumbered by the mortgage and more fully described as:

[legal description]

shall be sold at public auction to the highest bidder for cash. The sale shall be held at a time and place set by the special master appointed in this judgment, according to law. The sale shall be free and clear of all right, title and interest of defendants or any persons, firms or corporations claiming by, through, under or against defendants, but subject to any taxes levied by the State of Florida, ... County, or the City of .... The special master shall sell the real property, stating at the time that it is subject to the taxes mentioned above and the right of redemption of the United States as set forth below. The special master is directed to publish a notice of sale, describing the property to be sold, once a week, for four consecutive weeks prior to the sale, in a newspaper of general circulation in .... County, Florida. Plaintiff may bid at that sale and shall be entitled to a credit against its bid up to the amount due it under this judgment, and plaintiff is granted the authority to assign its bidding rights and in the event it does so, the assignee shall be entitled to credit against his bid for the full amount of this judgment. All other bids shall be paid 10% at the time of sale and the remainder within 24 hours, except in the event the United States of America is the successful bidder at the foreclosure sale, it shall be allowed 15 days in which to deliver a United States Treasury check in the amount of its bid.

9. .... is appointed as special master for the purpose of conducting the foreclosure sale called for in the preceding paragraph. He is directed to publish a notice of this sale in accordance with the directions set forth above, and that notice shall contain a reference to this judgment, a description of the property to be sold and the time, place and terms of the sale, including a specific reference to the right of redemption of the United States. Upon the sale, the special master shall receive proceeds from it and shall file his report of the sale, along with proof of the publication of the notice of sale.

10. Upon confirmation by the court of any sale, the proceeds of the sale shall be distributed as directed in an order confirming the sale.

11. Upon confirmation by the court of any sale under this judgment, the purchaser at the sale shall be entitled to conveyance by special master's deed, free and clear of all rights of defendants, and all persons claiming by, through, under or against defendants shall stand forever barred and foreclosed of all right, title and interest of whatever kind or nature in and to the property, and the purchaser shall be entitled to the immediate possession of the property, but subject to taxes and the right of redemption of the United States of America as set forth in this judgment. The purchaser will pay for and affix any documentary stamps or taxes required for the recordation of the special master's deed.

12. The United States of America shall have the right of redemption afforded it by 28 U.S.C. §2410 for ....120 days/one year.......... from the date of

foreclosure sale of the property described above. If the United States of America or its assignee exercises the right of redemption, it shall do so by tendering to the purchaser at the foreclosure sale the amount of the purchaser's bid at the sale, with interest on that amount at ....(per cent).......... a year from the date of the sale and the amount, if any, equal to the excess of the expenses necessarily incurred in connection with the property, over the income from the property, plus (to the extent the property is used by the purchaser) the reasonable rental value of the property.

COMMENT: The United States has 120 days to exercise its right of redemption if its interest arose under tax laws; it has one year if its interest arose otherwise. §5.14.

This court retains jurisdiction of this action to make further orders that are proper, including an order confirming sale and establishing a deficiency judgment.

ORDERED at ...., in the .... District of Florida on ....(date)..........

United States District Judge

Copies furnished to: ....

D. Foreclosure Sale In United States District Court

1. [§5.73] Statutory Requirements

The attorney who is accustomed to the rapid processing of a judicial sale in the circuit court under *F.S.* Chapter 45 is in for a surprise when he attempts to have a sale in a United States district court. 28 *U.S.C.* §§2001–2003 are the applicable statutes. §2001(a) requires that a public sale be held at the courthouse in the county or city in which the property is located, unless a private sale is authorized under §2001(b) after notice and appropriate advertisement. Private sales rarely will be conducted. For a public sale, §2002 requires that before the sale the notice of sale be published once a week for four weeks in a newspaper of general jurisdiction in the county or district where the property is located. This is an unwelcome delay to the mortgagee attempting to sell the property rapidly.

The notice of sale used is similar to the form set out in §5.45 for the state court, except that the language advising of any prior liens to which any sale is subject, the right of redemption of the United States (if applicable) and the terms of the sale should be set out. Additional language to be added to the form in §5.45 is set out below.

2. [§5.74] Form For Additional Terms For Notice of Sale In United States District Court

Terms of the sale shall be 10% of the bid price in cash or by certified check at the time of sale with the balance to be paid in cash or by certified check to the special master within 24 hours thereafter, except that if the United States of America is the successful bidder at the foreclosure sale, it shall be allowed 15 days in which to deliver a United States Treasury check in payment of the amount of its bid.

This property will be sold free and clear of all right, title and interest of defendants or any persons, firms or corporations claiming by, through or against defendants in this cause, but subject to any taxes levied by the State of Florida, ... County or the City of ....

The purchaser at the sale shall pay for and be responsible for the affixing to the special master's deed any documentary stamps or taxes imposed upon the recordation of the deed.

The United States of America shall have the right of redemption afforded it by 28 U.S.C. §2410 for one year from the date of sale.

3. [§5.75] Conduct Of Sale And Confirmation

The next question is who shall sell the property. The United States marshal can and will sell the property, but strong consideration should be given to the appointment of a special master for the sale. Frequently, the cost of paying a special master a reasonable fee will be considerably less than the statutory fees of the United States marshal. 28 *U.S.C.* §1921 sets the amount of the marshal's fees for seizing and selling the property. As of this writing, they are 3% on the first $1,000 and 1½% on any sum over $1,000. Additionally, if the property is located in an outlying county, the travel expenses of the deputy going to conduct the sale will be added. Thus, the marshal's fee on a $41,000 residence would be $630 plus costs. Also, another attorney appointed as a special master can be expected to prepare his own reports and documents expeditiously. If the United States marshal sells the property, the plaintiff's attorney must prepare all documents, and processing in the marshal's office can cause additional delays.

After the sale the marshal, or the special master will make and file a report of sale. A motion for confirmation of sale and disbursal of funds with supporting memoranda should be made with the appropriate service of copies, pursuant to the rules. See §5.76 for a form for a motion for confirmation. Unless oral argument is requested by opposing parties or the court so directs, the sale will be confirmed ex parte by written order. Although the practice varies with different judges, a proposed order normally should be submitted with the motion for confirmation. See the form in §5.77. Upon the order confirming the sale, the marshal or special master will execute and deliver a United States marshal's or special master's deed. It should be noted here that unlike the circuit court, in which the clerk affixes the necessary documentary stamps to the deed, the United States marshal and special master do not, although the purchaser at the sale must affix the stamps prior to its recordation. A recitation to this effect in the final judgment and notice of sale will save argument with the purchaser's attorney.

Disbursement of the funds held by the marshal or the special master will be made in accordance with the order confirming the sale. Surplus funds, if any, are available to other parties. If a deficiency is sought, a separate motion may be made, or the plaintiff may include a demand for establishing a deficiency in its motion for confirmation. If oppostion is expected to the attempt to establish a deficiency, but not to the confirmation of sale and disbursement, the two motions should be made separately so as not to delay confirmation of the sale and disbursement of the funds.

4. [§5.76] Form For Motion For Order Confirming Sale And Disbursing Funds

(Title of Court)

(Title of Cause) **PLAINTIFF'S MOTION FOR ORDER CONFIRMING SALE AND DISBURSAL OF FUNDS**

Plaintiff, ..., moves to confirm the sale and direct disbursement of funds from the sale because:

1. Pursuant to the court's order of ....(date).........., the real property, described below as:

[legal description]

was sold by ...., as special master, to the highest and best bidder for cash on ....(date)..........

2. The special master's report of sale has been filed in this action.

3. The highest bid offered for the real property was $.........., offered by ....

_____

Attorney

..................(address)..................

(Certificate of Service)

5. [§5.77] Form For Order Confirming Sale

(Title of Court)

(Title of Cause)   ORDER CONFIRMING SALE

This action was heard on the motion to confirm the sale and direct disbursement of funds.

ADJUDGED that:

1. The sale is confirmed and that the special master shall make, execute and deliver his special master's deed conveying the real property described in the final judgment to .... The deed shall be subject to any taxes imposed by the State of Florida, ... County or the City of ...., and to the right of redemption to the United States.

2. The special master shall pay to himself the sum of $.......... as a reasonable fee for his services, and the sum of $.......... as his costs in this action.

3. The special master shall pay to plaintiff the sum of $.......... with interest from ....(date).......... at ....%.

4. This court shall retain jurisdiction of this action for the purpose of making such further orders [as are necessary to disburse the remaining funds held by the special master to the parties entitled] [to assess a deficiency judgment against the defendant, ..., if appropriate].

ORDERED at ...., Florida, on ....(date)..........

_____

United States District Judge

Copies furnished to: ....

XI. THE MORTGAGEE IN BANKRUPTCY PROCEEDINGS

A. [§5.78] In General

Perhaps one of the more perplexing problems to face the average practitioner representing the mortgage holder is when the mortgagor and his property become involved in bankruptcy proceedings. A thorough discussion of the bankruptcy rules is beyond the scope of this chapter, but some salient points are set out below. See BANKRUPTCY RULES AND PRACTICE IN FLORIDA (CLE 1973).

Initially, the attorney must know that normally there are four different types of bankruptcy proceedings: (1) a normal bankruptcy (Chapters I through VII of the Bankruptcy Act); (2) a wage earner's bankruptcy (Chapter XIII); (3) a corporate reorganization (Chapter X); and (4) an arrangement of creditors (Chapter XI). Recently, the rules relating to regular bankruptcy and wage earners' bankruptcy were completely revised and as of the time of this writing revisions are being made to the rules relating to the other types of bankruptcy proceedings. Care thus should be taken to ensure that references made in this chapter have not been superseded or amended. Because of those presently pending changes in the rules relating to Chapter X and Chapter XI proceedings, only passing reference will be made to the rules relating to those areas.

Chapter XII of the Bankruptcy Act also should be mentioned. Its purpose primarily is the alteration or modification of the rights of creditors, or of any class of them, holding debts secured by real property or a chattle real of which the debtor is the legal or equitable owner. This is accomplished, as in Chapter XI proceedings, by acceptance of a plan called an "arrangement." The rules for Chapter XII currently are being revised also.

B. [§5.79] Stays Of Foreclosure Proceedings

In a straight bankruptcy *Rule* 601 of the Bankruptcy Rules provides an automatic stay of the commencement or continuation of actions to foreclose a mortgage on the property of the bankrupt upon the filing of a petition in bankruptcy. A similar automatic stay is provided for in a Chapter XIII bankruptcy by *Rule* 13-401(a). Thus, if the client advises that the mortgagee is about to file or has filed bankruptcy, the attorney should check to see if in fact a petition for bankruptcy has been filed, as this would prohibit initiation or continuance of foreclosure proceedings. Both Chapter X and Chapter

XI provide for the issuance of a stay order. §113 of that act allows the issuance of a stay "upon cause shown" in Chapter X proceedings and §314 allows a stay "upon notice and for cause shown" in Chapter XI proceedings. Thus, if proceedings have been instituted under either Chapter X or Chapter XI, the court file must be examined to determine whether a stay has been entered, unless notice of a stay has been delivered to the client. It should be noted that often a notice of a meeting of creditors or similar notice will contain language setting out the entry of a stay order.

Chapter X, reorganizations, and Chapter XI, arrangements, are somewhat more complicated, but have a basic important difference. Hypothetically, the Chapter XI proceeding cannot permanently affect the rights of the secured creditor, but only delays them temporarily, but the Chapter X proceeding can hold off the secured creditor indefinitely. Unfortunately, the delay in enforcement of the creditors' rights sometimes permanently and adversely affects the creditor. Fortunately, Chapter X proceedings are limited to corporations with substantial assets, and the average practitioner will not become involved in representing a mortgagee in those proceedings.

The big difference between proceedings under these two chapters and those previously discussed is that the filing of a petition under these two chapters does not result in an automatic stay at foreclosure proceedings. A stay order may be issued by the bankruptcy court under §113 of Chapter X and §314 of Chapter XI. But a stay entered under either section must be for cause shown and under Chapter XI the stay can be issued only upon notice, as well as for cause shown. In some instances, however, restraining orders are entered ex parte in Chapter XI proceedings despite the language of the act. See *In re Haines Lumber & Millwork Co.*, 144 F.Supp. 108 (E.D. Pa. 1956). The onus is then put on the mortgagee's attorney to have the stay modified or annulled. Frequently, the only effective relief is an appeal of the stay order to the district judge. For a discussion of the effect of §314, see Yacos, *Secured Creditors and Chapter XI of the Bankruptcy Act*, JOURNAL OF THE NATIONAL CONFERENCE OF REFEREES IN BANKRUPTCY (January and April, 1970).

C. [§5.80] Dissolving Or Modifying Stay Order

If a stay is in effect, the attorney must determine whether it is in his client's best interest to attempt to have it dissolved. He must consider whether the stay is likely to be dissolved or whether there is a certainty that his efforts will be denied. When there is little or no equity in the property the client seeks to reach, the chances of success are reasonable. When there is equity in the property that would be lost to the estate or the foreclosure would have other similar adverse effect on the bankrupt's over-all estate, then the likelihood of having the stay dissolved probably is not good, unless the stay has been in existence for some time. The best practice is to approach the trustee or his attorney to see what their position is. In some instances, the trustee may abandon the property, thus obviating the need for an adversary proceeding.

In any event before proceeding the attorney should advise the client of the potential of success and make sure that his fee arrangement with the client will be sufficient to compensate the attorney adequately for his time and effort if he is unsuccessful in getting the stay dissolved. If the stay is dissolved and the foreclosure takes place, then the attorney's reasonable fee is determined in the foreclosure action. If the property ultimately is sold by the bankruptcy trustee, then the attorney's fee must come out of the bankrupt's estate as a part of the secured claim. If this is the case, the fee, if one is awarded, usually will not compensate the attorney adequately for his effort and time, and in some instances the courts have held that no attorneys' fees are to be awarded to the creditor. See *In re Essential Industries Corporation,* 150 F.2d 326 (2d Cir. 1945), 161 A.L.R. 968 and the cases annotated there. But also see *In re Advance Printing and Litho Company,* 277 F.Supp. 101 (W.D. Pa. 1967), *aff'd* 387 F.2d 952. See *Rule* 219 for procedures and factors considered in applying for a fee in ordinary bankruptcy. The prudent attorney will come to a clear understanding with his client that he is to be compensated based on his efforts and time, and not on the amount awarded by the bankruptcy court.

If the determination is made to attempt to modify an existing stay order in a Chapter VII or Chapter XIII proceeding, what is involved is an adversary proceeding under Part VII of the new rules. A complaint must be filed with the appropriate summons and notice under *Rule* 705. Although the schedule of the bankruptcy courts is often crowded, attention is called to *Rule* 601(c), "Relief from Stay," which provides that when a complaint seeking relief from a stay is filed, it shall be set for trial at the earliest possible date, and it shall take precedence over all matters except older matters of the same nature. Consideration likewise should be given to *Rule* 601(d), "Ex Parte Relief from Stay."

In a proceeding under Chapter X or XI, the existing general orders in bankruptcy and the local bankruptcy rules are applicable with respect to the procedure for dissolving a stay until the adoption of new rules relating to these chapters (not yet adopted as of the time of this writing).

D.   [§5.81]   Action After Dissolving Stay

If the stay is dissolved and permission is granted to foreclose, the trustee in bankruptcy should be joined as a party defendant, and the order dissolving the stay should be set forth in the complaint and a certified copy of the order attached as an exhibit. If the trustee abandons the property, that action should be documented by appropriate written document filed and approved in the bankruptcy court. If the trustee has abandoned the property, he is not a necessary party to the foreclosure action, although the bankrupt as the fee owner still must be joined. See FLA. UNIFORM TITLE STANDARD §2.4, 20 F.S.A. 225.

E.   [§5.82]   Other Actions

If the decision is made not to attempt to modify the stay order, or the petition to dissolve is denied, the attorney must determine what action to take. The filing of claims in bankruptcy is beyond this chapter. There is one pitfall that the mortgagee's attorney in a Chapter XI proceeding should be aware of, however — the estoppel doctrine set forth in *Famers Bros. Co. v. Huddle Enterprises, Inc.,* 366 F.2d 143 (9th Cir. 1966). If a mortgagee is too agreeable and becomes too involved in the proposed arrangement, he may find himself estopped to foreclose his mortgage under the doctrine set forth in that case. Although the secured creditor may appear to be fully protected, its agreement or approval of any plan should be conditioned on no waiver of its right to foreclose upon any subsequent default, and this statement should be made a matter of record in the proceedings.

XII.   [§5.83]   CONCLUSION

Although at the time of this writing the rate of foreclosures is low, it is certain that almost every attorney sooner or later will encounter a foreclosure action either as the representative of a plaintiff or a defendant. The action will occupy the attorney's time for a period that varies from three to six months, depending upon any number of factors that cannot be fully anticipated before the action is filed.

Consideration should be given at the outset as to whether the defense of usury might be raised by the mortgagor, particularly in view of the high interest rates being charged at this time by lenders. For a thorough study of this subject matter, see Anderson, *Tight-Money Real Estate Financing and the Florida Usury Statute,* 24 U. MIAMI L. REV. 642 (1970).

As a concluding suggestion, the attorney representing the plaintiff in any foreclosure action is urged to maintain a close liaison with the mortgagee or its servicing agent, for they can be most helpful in assisting him in processing the matter and in the making of a diligent search for any defendant whose residence is not readily ascertainable.

JOSEPH B. REISMAN*†

6

MECHANIC'S LIEN FORECLOSURES

I. [§6.1] INTRODUCTION AND SCOPE

II. PREPARATION PRIOR TO ACTION

    A. [§6.2] Determination Of Existence Of Claim Of Lien

    B. Perfection Of Claim Of Lien

        1. [§6.3] In General

        2. [§6.4] The Contractor

        3. [§6.5] Form For Contractor's Affidavit

        4. [§6.6] Parties In Privity Other Than The Contractor

        5. [§6.7] Parties Not In Privity

    C. [§6.8] Determination Of Property Covered

    D. [§6.9] Determination Of Parties

    E. [§6.10] Time For Bringing Action

III. THE COMPLAINT AND NOTICE OF LIS PENDENS — FORECLOSURE

    A. [§6.11] In General

---

*LL.B., 1951, University of Miami. Mr. Reisman is a member of the Dade County and American bar associations, and is a partner in the firm of Rosenberg, Rosenberg, Reisman & Glass. He practices in Miami.

†Mr. Richard E. Cours was the author of this chapter in the first edition.

    B. [§6.12] Jurisdiction And Venue

    C. [§6.13] Notice Of Lis Pendens

    D. [§6.14] Attorneys' Fees

    E. Forms For Complaint

        1. [§6.15] For Contractor

        2. [§6.16] For Materialman In Privity

        3. [§6.17] For Subcontractor (Or Materialman) Not In Privity

        4. [§6.18] For Laborer's Summary Action

    F. [§6.19] Form For Summons — Summary Procedure

    G. [§6.20] Form For Notice Of Lis Pendens

IV. THE COMPLAINT — ACTION ON BOND

    A. [§6.21] In General

    B. Forms For Complaints On Bonds

        1. [§6.22] On Payment Bond — Materialman To Subcontractor

        2. [§6.23] Subcontractor's Lien Transferred To Bond

V. [§6.24] JOINDER, CONSOLIDATION AND INTERVENTION

VI. ANSWER AND CROSS-CLAIM

    A. [§6.25] In General

    B. [§6.26] Form For Answer And Cross-Claim — Materialman Not In Privity

VII. INTERPLEADER

    A. [§6.27] In General

    B. [§6.28] Form For Complaint To Interplead Contractor And Subcontractor

VIII. [§6.29] TERMINATION OF JOB BEFORE COMPLETION

IX. [§6.30] PRIORITY OF LIENS

X. PROOF AT TRIAL

    A. [§6.31] In General

    B. [§6.32] Existence And Validity Of Lien

    C. [§6.33] Amount Of Claim

    D. [§6.34] Priority

XI. THE JUDGMENT

    A. [§6.35] In General

    B. [§6.36] Form For Judgment In Lien Foreclosure Action

XII. OTHER REMEDIES

    A. [§6.37] Repossession

    B. [§6.38] Liens Upon And Removal Of Improvements

    C. [§6.39] Other Actions Not Barred

XIII. [§6.40] SPECIAL PROBLEM – THE LONG JOB AND THE EARLY COMPLETING LIENOR

I. [§6.1] INTRODUCTION AND SCOPE

This chapter discusses the litigation of statutory claims of lien upon real property for the improvement of the property. *F.S.* Chapter 713, Part I (713.01–.36), entitled "Mechanics' Lien Law," defines the parties entitled to these liens, the services rendered or materials furnished for which liens may be asserted and the interests subject to them. *F.S.* 85.011 and .021 provide the methods of enforcement of these liens.

The Supreme Court of Florida has stated that the fundamental purpose of the mechanics' lien law is:

> ... to protect those whose materials, labor and skills improve the land of others by providing a plan by which such persons or firms may receive their fair share of the moneys payable by the owner to the general contractor under the direct contract — or, in circumstances specified by the statute, may record and foreclose a Claim of Lien against the property so improved. *Crane Co. v. Fine,* 221 So.2d 145 (Fla. 1969).

Although not strictly lien litigation, actions involving claims against bonds furnished to obtain exemption from the mechanics' lien law or to transfer liens to security and repossession of materials are considered in this chapter because these remedies form an integral part of the scheme of the mechanics' lien law.

In this chapter all liens under the mechanics' lien law are referred to as mechanics' liens regardless of whether the lien arises for labor, professional services or materials, and the mechanics' lien law is referred to as the "act." Mechanics' liens are discussed generally in I FLORIDA REAL PROPERTY PRACTICE §§8.30–.44 (CLE 2d ed. 1971).

II. PREPARATION PRIOR TO ACTION

A. [§6.2] Determination Of Existence Of Claim Of Lien

F.S. 713.02 through .06 describe the parties entitled to liens under the act. Generally, these are parties who contribute to the permanent improvement of the realty. By specific provision, architects, landscape architects, engineers and land surveyors performing services in the preparation of plans, specifications or drawings are included and their liens extend to the property in connection with which their services are performed regardless of whether the planned improvements actually are constructed. 713.03. Parties furnishing plants that are planted on the property [713.02(7)] and those furnishing carpets or rugs that are permanently affixed [713.02(8)] also are specifically given liens.

Various property is exempt or may be exempted from liens. Except for a party in privity with the owner, the act exempts any improvement to an existing improvement for which the contract price is no more than $500 and that is completed within six months from actual commencement. *F.S.* 713.02(5). An owner who requires the contractor to furnish a payment bond as provided in 713.23 exempts his property from liens under the act, except for the lien of the contractor furnishing the bond. 713.02(6). To protect public works against liens and as a substitute for the mechanic's lien, *F.S.* 255.05 requires bond of any party contracting "with the state or any county, city, or political subdivision thereof, or other public authority." Any party having an interest in the real property may relieve the property of a claim of lien filed against it by transferring that lien to a cash deposit or surety bond. 713.24(1).

B. Perfection Of Claim Of Lien

1. [§6.3] In General

If the claimant is within the class entitled to liens under the act and the property is not exempt, it is necessary that the lien be perfected and the conditions precedent to action met. The requisities depend upon whether the claimant is in privity with the owner and whether the claimant is a contractor, subcontractor, laborer or materialman as defined in *F.S.* 713.01.

2. [§6.4] The Contractor

A contractor, being one other than a materialman or laborer who enters into a contract with the owner, acquires no lien until a claim of lien is recorded, but is not required to serve a notice to the owner under *F.S.* 713.06(2). In 713.06(3)(d)1 it is provided that the contractor has "no lien or right of action" while in default by not having given to the owner the affidavit required by that statute. The affidavit should state either that all lienors have been paid or, if the fact is otherwise, give the name of each lienor who has not been paid in full and the amount due that lienor. The affidavit must be delivered to the owner at least five days before instituting an action to enforce the lien.

The claim of lien is required to be filed not later than 90 days after the final furnishing of the labor or services or materials by the lienor. *F.S.* 713.08(5). Failure to serve a copy of the claim of lien within ten days after recording renders the claim of lien voidable to the extent that the failure or delay prejudices any party entitled to rely on receipt of the claim of lien. 713.08(4)(c). The parties so entitled are the owner and his designees in the notice of commencement filed under 713.13. Although the act provides that the contractor has no lien before the delivery of the contractor's affidavit, in *Stenholm v. Calbeck*, 265 So.2d 531 (2d D.C.A. Fla. 1972) it was held that a contractor's claim of lien filed within the 90-day period was not invalidated by the failure to serve the contractor's affidavit within the prescribed period. Rather, the court held the right to enforce the lien was suspended while the lienor was in default for failure to serve the affidavit and that five days after serving it the lienor could file a foreclosure action if that date occurred within one year [713.22(1)] after the filing of the claim of lien.

A form for a claim of lien is provided by *F.S.* 713.08(3) and a suggested form for the contractor's affidavit is set out below in §6.5.

In summary, the following should be timely accomplished in the perfection of the contractor's lien before institution of an action to foreclose:

    a.   Service of contractor's affidavit. *F.S.* 713.06(3)(d)1.

    b.   Filing of claim of lien. 713.08.

    c.   Service of copy of claim of lien. 713.08.

3. [§6.5] Form For Contractor's Affidavit

STATE OF ....
COUNTY OF ....

Before me, the undersigned authority, personally appeared ...., who was sworn and says:

1. Affiant is treasurer of ...., the contractor on the construction job at ...., under a direct contract with ....

2. **Final payment under the direct contract is now due the contractor.**

3. All lienors furnishing labor, services or materials in the performance of the job under the direct contract have been paid in full, except: [here list the name of each lienor who has not been paid in full and the amount due or to become due].

_____(SEAL)
Affiant

(Jurat)

4. [§6.6] Parties In Privity Other Than The Contractor

Other parties than a contractor may be in privity with the owner, such as materialmen and laborers and those performing services in the preparation of plans. These parties acquire no liens until claims of lien are filed, but they are not required to give notices to the owner under F.S. 713.06(2)(a). A lienor of this type, not being a "contractor" under the act, is not required to furnish a contractor's affidavit before filing an action to foreclose his liens. By definition, however, one who contracts with the owner and who furnishes both labor and materials would appear to be a contractor and, consequently, bound to furnish the contractor's affidavit. See 713.01(2), (9) and (11).

5. [§6.7] Parties Not In Privity

By definition a lienor not in privity with the owner cannot be a contractor but must be a subcontractor, materialman or laborer. Such a lienor, except for a laborer, in addition to filing and serving his claim of lien also must serve upon the owner a notice stating the lienor's name and address, a description sufficient for identification of the real property and the nature of the services furnished or to be furnished. F.S. 713.06(2)(a). A copy of the notice also must be mailed to whatever party, if any, the owner designates in his notice of commencement, but failure to do so does not invalidate an otherwise valid lien. 713.06(2)(b). The form of the notice to owner is set out in 713.06(2)(c). The notice usually is served upon the owner by certified mail, but may be served in any manner provided in 713.18.

The notice to owner is required to be served upon the owner not later than 45 days after commencement of the furnishing of services or materials, but in any event before the furnishing of the contractor's affidavit, and may be served before that commencement. F.S. 713.06(2)(a).

Notwithstanding the provision that service on the owner of the notice to owner is a "prerequisite to perfecting a lien," F.S.

713.06(2)(a), failure to serve it timely may not defeat the lien totally, but rather may affect the priority of the lien and limit the amount recoverable from the owner and secured by the lien. See *Trowbridge, Inc. v. Hathaway,* 233 So.2d 129 (Fla. 1970); *Crane Co. v. Fine,* 221 So.2d 145 (Fla. 1969).

In summary, the following should be accomplished timely in perfecting the lien of a lienor not in privity with the owner:

    a.   Service of notice to owner by lienor other than a laborer. F.S. 713.06(2)(a).

    b.   Filing of claim of lien. 713.08.

    c.   Service of claim of lien. 713.08(4)(c).

C.   [§6.8] Determination Of Property Covered

The lien provided by the act is a lien "on the real property improved." *F.S.* 713.03, .05 and .06. When the services or materials are furnished for subdivision improvements on land then or thereafter dedicated to the public use and are furnished under contract with the owner of abutting land, the lienor is entitled to a lien on the abutting land for the unpaid cost of the services or materials. 713.04.

A legal description of the property against which the lien is asserted sufficient to identify the property is required to be stated in the claim of lien and, of course, in the complaint filed to foreclose it. The description is obtainable from the recorded notice of commencement, but if the owner has failed to file, resort should be had to public records, plats and abstract company facilities.

D.   [§6.9] Determination Of Parties

F.S. 713.10 extends the lien "to, and only to, the right, title and interest of the person who contracts for the improvement as such right, title and interest exists at the commencement of the improvement or is thereafter acquired in the real property." This statute, however, does extend the lien to the interest of the lessor when the improvement is made by the lessee in accordance with an agreement between the lessor and lessee unless the lease expressly prohibits liability of the lessor's interest for liens for improvements by the lessee and the lease is recorded.

The owner of the interest against which the lien is claimed is a necessary party to the foreclosure action and all other holders of interests or liens subject or subordinate to the lien being foreclosed are proper parties and ordinarily should be joined. Holders of liens of equal priority are proper parties.

In an action by a lienor not in privity with the owner, the party with whom the lienor contracted is a proper party and should be joined in order to subject him to personal judgment for the debt owed under the lienor's contract as contemplated by *F.S.* 713.28.

The identity of the interested parties and lienors who are to be joined should be determined from the public records by abstract or title search. The notice of commencement is required to identify the owner, who is defined in *F.S.* 713.01(12) to be the owner of any interest in the realty that can be reached and sold by any legal process, and who contracts for the improvement of the real property. The notice must state his interest in the site of the improvement and give the identity of the fee simple titleholder, if other than that owner. 713.13. The notice of commencement accordingly is a valuable starting point as to identity of parties in interest, but its contents should be brought up to date by title search.

E. [§6.10] Time For Bringing Action

The life of a lien under the act is limited to one year after the claim of lien has been recorded, unless within that time an action to enforce it is commenced in a court of competent jurisdiction. *F.S.* 713.22(1). The one-year period may be reduced by the owner recording a notice of contest of lien in the office of the clerk of the circuit court and having a copy of the notice served on the lienor by the clerk's mailing of the copy to the lienor at the address shown in the recorded claim of lien, or its most recent amendment. 713.22(2). The statute contains the prescribed form for the notice. This procedure reduces the life of the lien to 60 days after service of the copy of the notice, unless action is instituted to enforce the lien within the 60-day period. The 60-day period is not extended by the filing of an amended claim of lien subsequent to the mailing of the notice. *Jack Stilson & Co. v. Caloosa Bayview Corporation,* 278 So.2d 282 (Fla. 1973).

Any interested party, upon filing a complaint for that purpose, may have the clerk of the circuit court issue a summons to the lienor to show cause why his lien should not be enforced by action or canceled of record. Upon failure of the lienor either to show cause or to commence an action before the return date, the act requires the court forthwith to order cancellation of the lien. *F.S.* 713.21(4). The required action by the lienor may be commenced by filing a counterclaim for the enforcement of the lien in the action in which the summons to show cause was issued. *Wesley Construction Company v. Yarnell,* 268 So.2d 454 (4th D.C.A. Fla. 1972).

III. THE COMPLAINT AND NOTICE OF LIS PENDENS — FORECLOSURE

A. [§6.11] In General

The allegations of the complaint will vary depending upon whether the lienor is or is not in privity with the owner and, within those categories, upon the class of the lienor, *i.e.,* contractor, subcontractor, materialman, laborer or professional. Generally, the action should be for the foreclosure of the lien and personal judgment for any deficiency against any party personally liable. *F.S.* 85.011(4) provides a form of action for lienors in privity with the owner intended to result in a personal judgment that is a lien on the property improved and that directs execution against that property as well as other property of the defendant. But that procedure has no advantage over the customary foreclosure in which a personal deficiency judgment may be obtained against all parties personally liable and a sale is conducted by the clerk of the circuit court rather than by the sheriff under levy and execution. The forms for complaints set out in §§6.15—.17 are for customary foreclosure actions.

A summary form of action is provided for laborers, regardless of privity, in *F.S.* 85.011 and .021. A form for that complaint is suggested in §6.18.

As noted in §6.1, actions on bonds furnished to exempt or relieve real property of liens may not be lien litigation in a strict sense but since those actions arise under the mechanics' lien law and the relative rights of the parties depend in significant aspects on provisions of that law, those actions are treated in §§6.21—.23.

B. [§6.12] Jurisdiction And Venue

Jurisdiction of actions to foreclose mechanics' liens (other than summary actions to enforce liens for labor) is vested exclusively in the circuit court. See *Mills v. Robert W. Gottfried, Inc.,* 272 So.2d 837 (4th

D.C.A. Fla. 1973). Jurisdiction of the summary actions concerning labor liens is in the court having jurisdiction of the amount of the lien claimed. *F.S.* 85.011(5)(a). Jurisdiction of actions under 85.011(4), in which the lien must be enforced by issue of execution and levy rather than by foreclosure sale by the clerk, also lies in the court having jurisdiction of the amount of the claim.

Venue of an action to enforce a mechanic's lien against the property improved lies in the county in which the property lies. *Georgia Casualty Co. v. O'Donnell,* 109 Fla. 290, 147 So. 267 (1933).

C. [§6.13] Notice Of Lis Pendens

A notice of lis pendens should be filed at the time the complaint is filed in order to foreclose interests that arise subsequently and liens that accrue subsequently. *F.S.* 48.23 requires that the notice be recorded in the office of the clerk of the circuit court to be effective. It requires that the notice state the names of the parties, the time of institution of the action, the name of the court in which the action is pending, a description of the property involved and a statement of the relief sought as to the property. A suggested form for the notice of lis pendens is included at §6.20.

D. [§6.14] Attorneys' Fees

The mechanics' lien law provides that the prevailing party in an action to enforce a mechanic's lien is entitled to recover a reasonable fee for the services of his attorney. *F.S.* 713.29. The complaint should allege the employment of the attorneys and the agreement to pay a reasonable fee.

The prevailing party was held to be "that party who has affirmative judgment rendered in his favor at the conclusion of the entire case" in *Sharpe v. Ceco Corporation,* 242 So.2d 464 (3d D.C.A. Fla. 1971), *cert. den.* 247 So.2d 324. Another court, however, has ruled that when the lienor recovers no more than the amount tendered by the owner from the outset, the owner is the prevailing party. *Potter v. Rowan,* 266 So.2d 121 (2d D.C.A. Fla. 1972), *cert. den.* 271 So.2d 143.

The mechanics' lien law has been interpreted to permit the award of attorneys' fees only to the party prevailing in the action on the limited issue of the enforcement of the lien. *Houdaille-Duval-Wright Co. v. Charldon Const. Co.,* 266 So.2d 106 (3d D.C.A. Fla. 1972). In that case attorneys' fees were denied the contractor joined by the subcontractor-lienor as a defendant with the owner, although the lien was defeated by virtue of the contractor prevailing on a counterclaim for damages exceeding the amount of the lien claim. The court held that the contractor was not a prevailing party "in the cause of action presented to enforce the lien."

On the question of whether attorneys' fees are recoverable for services on appeal there is conflict among the decisions of the district courts of appeal. Recovery was denied in *John T. Wood Homes, Inc. v. Air Control Products, Inc.*, 177 So.2d 709 (1st D.C.A. Fla. 1965) and in *Babe's Plumbing, Inc. v. Maier*, 194 So.2d 666 (2d D.C.A. Fla. 1967), but was allowed in *Foxbilt Electric, Inc. v. Belefant*, 280 So.2d 28 (4th D.C.A. Fla. 1973).

E. Forms For Complaint

1. [§6.15] For Contractor

(Title of Court)

(Title of Cause)   COMPLAINT

Plaintiff, ..., hereafter called "contractor," sues defendants, ..., hereafter called "owner," and ...., hereafter called "mortgagee," and alleges:

1. This is an action to foreclose a mechanic's lien.

2. On ....(date).........., contractor and owner executed and delivered a written contract to each other to construct improvements upon real property owned by owner, located in .... County, Florida, described as follows:

[legal description]

A copy of the contract is attached as Exhibit "A".

3. On ....(date).......... owner filed in the office of the Clerk of the Circuit Court, ... County, Florida, a notice of commencement, which was recorded in Official Records Book ...., at page ...., of the public records of that county.

4. The contract was fully performed by contractor and the last item of labor, services and materials required in the construction of the improvements was furnished on ....(date)..........

5. There is due to contractor under the contract $.........., which remains unpaid. A statement of account is attached as Exhibit "B".

COMMENT: It is necessary either to allege that the owner has retained funds in his hands or made improper payments. *Roberts v. Lesser,* 96 So.2d 222 (Fla. 1957).

6. On ....(date).......... contractor delivered to owner contractor's affidavit, showing no unpaid lienors.

7. Contractor filed a claim of lien on ....(date).......... in the office of the Clerk of the Circuit Court, ... County, Florida, which was recorded in Official Records Book ...., at page ...., of the public records of that county. Contractor served a copy of the claim of lien on owner on ....(date)..........

8. Mortgagee claims a lien on the property under a mortgage filed for record on ....(date).......... in the office of the clerk and recorded in Official Records Book ...., at page ...., of the public records of the county. The mortgage is subordinate and inferior to contractor's lien.

9. Contractor has complied with all requirements of Chapter 713, Florida Statutes.

10. Contractor is obligated to pay his attorneys employed to prosecute this action a reasonable fee for their services.

WHEREFORE, contractor demands an accounting of the sum due contractor under the contract and judgment that contractor has a lien upon the property and that if that amount shall not be paid within the time set by this court, the property be sold to satisfy the amount due contractor and the right, title, interest and lien of defendants and all parties claiming by, through, under or against them since the filing of the notice of lis pendens be foreclosed. If the proceeds of sale shall be insufficient to pay the sums due contractor, contractor demands a deficiency judgment against owner.

                                                                                          Attorney

                                                                              ....(address)..................

2. [§6.16] For Materialman In Privity

(Title of Court)

(Title of Cause)   COMPLAINT

Plaintiff, ..., hereafter called "materialman," sues defendants, ..., hereafter called "owner," and ...., hereafter called "mortgagee," and alleges:

1. This is an action to foreclose a mechanic's lien.

2. On ....(date).........., materialman and owner executed and delivered a written contract to each other to supply electrical materials for use in construction of improvements upon real property owned by owner, located in .... County, Florida, described as follows:

[legal description]

A copy of the contract is attached as Exhibit "A".

3. On ....(date).......... owner filed in the office of the Clerk of the Circuit Court, ... County, Florida, a notice of commencement, which was recorded in Official Records Book ...., at page ...., of the public records of that county.

4. The contract was fully performed by materialman and the last item of material required was furnished on ....(date)..........

5. There is due to materialman under the contract the sum of $.........., which remains unpaid. A statement of account is attached as Exhibit "B".

COMMENT: See the comment following paragraph 5 in §6.15. Sometimes the statement of account is so bulky that it becomes an encumbrance rather than an aid, in which case it can be omitted.

6. Materialman filed a claim of lien on ....(date).......... in the office of the clerk, which was recorded in Official Records Book ...., at page ...., of the public records of the county. Materialman served a copy of the claim of lien on owner on ....(date)..........

7. Mortgagee claims a lien on the property under a mortgage filed for record on ....(date).......... in the office of the clerk and recorded in Official Records Book ...., at page ...., of the public records of the county. The mortgage is subordinate and inferior to materialman's claim of lien.

8. Materialman has complied with all requirements of Chapter 713, Florida Statutes.

9. Materialman is obligated to pay his attorneys a reasonable fee for their services in this action.

WHEREFORE, materialman demands an accounting of the sum due materialman under the contract and judgment that materialman has a lien on the property and that if that amount shall not be paid within the time set by this court, the property be sold to satisfy the amount due materialman and the right, title, interest and lien of defendants and all parties claiming by, through, under or against them since the filing of the notice of lis pendens be foreclosed. If the proceeds of sale shall be insufficient to pay the sums due materialman, materialman demands a deficiency judgment against owner.

Attorney

.................(address)..................

3. [§6.17] For Subcontractor (Or Materialman) Not In Privity

(Title of Court)

(Title of Cause)   COMPLAINT

Plaintiff, ..., hereafter called "subcontractor," sues defendants, ..., hereafter called "contractor," and ...., hereafter called "owner," and alleges:

1. This is an action to foreclose a mechanic's lien.

2. On or before ....(date).......... owner and contractor executed and delivered a contract for the construction of improvements by contractor upon the property of owner in .... County, Florida, described as follows:

[legal description]

3. On ....(date).......... owner filed in the office of the Clerk of the Circuit Court, ... County, Florida, a notice of commencement, which was recorded in Official Records Book ...., at page ...., of the public records of that county.

4. On ....(date).......... contractor executed and delivered a subcontract with subcontractor for the furnishing of the materials and labor necessary for the erection of the structural elements of the improvements, a copy being attached as Exhibit "A".

5. Subcontractor furnished labor and materials under the subcontract and furnished the last of them on ....(date)..........

6. Subcontractor on ....(date).......... served on owner a notice to owner.

7. The subcontract was fully performed by subcontractor.

8. There is due to subcontractor under the subcontract $.........., which remains unpaid. A statement of account is attached as Exhibit "B".

COMMENT: See the comment following paragraph 5 in §6.15.

9. Subcontractor filed a claim of lien on ....(date).......... in the office of the clerk, which was recorded in Official Records Book ...., at page ...., of the public records of the county. Subcontractor served a copy of the claim of lien on owner on ....(date)..........

10. Subcontractor has complied with all requirements of Chapter 713, Florida Statutes.

11. Subcontractor is obligated to pay his attorneys a reasonable fee for their services in this action.

WHEREFORE, subcontractor demands an accounting of the sum due subcontractor under the subcontract and judgment against contractor for the sums determined to be due to subcontractor declaring subcontractor has a lien on the property for all sums due subcontractor, including attorneys' fees, superior to any interest or lien of defendants and ordering a sale of the property to satisfy the lien if the sums shall not be paid within the time set by this court, and that the right, title, interest and lien of defendants and all parties claiming by, through, under or against them since the filing of the notice of lis pendens be foreclosed.

Attorney

..................(address)..................

4. [§6.18] For Laborer's Summary Action

(Title of Court)

(Title of Cause)   **COMPLAINT**

Plaintiff, ..., hereafter called "laborer," sues defendants, ..., hereafter called "contractor," and ...., hereafter called "owner," and alleges:

1. This is an action to foreclose a mechanic's lien that does not exceed $2500 exclusive of interest and costs.

2. On or before ....(date).......... owner and contractor executed and delivered a contract for the construction of improvements by contractor upon the property of owner in .... County, Florida, described as follows:

[legal description]

3. On ....(date).......... owner filed in the office of the Clerk of the Circuit Court in .... County, Florida, a notice of commencement, which was recorded in Official Records Book ...., at page ...., of the public records of that county.

4. On ....(date).......... contractor employed laborer to perform labor in the construction of the improvements, agreeing to pay laborer wages of $.......... an hour.

5. Laborer performed the last labor on ....(date)..........

6. There is due to laborer for the labor $.........., which remains unpaid.

COMMENT: See the comment following paragraph 5 in §6.15.

7. Laborer filed a claim of lien on ....(date).......... in the office of the clerk, which was recorded in Official Records Book ...., at page ...., of the public records of the county. Laborer served a copy of the claim of lien on owner on ....(date)..........

8. Laborer has complied with all requirements of Chapter 713, Florida Statutes.

9. Laborer is entitled to recover the statutory attorney's fee and costs as prescribed by Chapter 85, Florida Statutes.

WHEREFORE, laborer demands judgment against contractor for damages declaring laborer has a lien on the property for all sums due laborer superior to any interest or lien of defendants and ordering a sale of the property to satisfy the lien if the sums shall not be paid within the time set by this court, and that the right, title, interest and lien of defendants and all parties claiming by, through, under or against them since the filing of the notice of lis pendens be foreclosed.

Attorney

..................(address)..................

F.　[§6.19]　Form For Summons — Summary Procedure

(Title of Court)

(Title of Cause)   SUMMONS

THE STATE OF FLORIDA:

To All and Singular the Sheriffs of the State:

    YOU ARE COMMANDED to serve this summons and a copy of the complaint in this action on defendants .... and .... Each defendant is required to serve written defenses to the complaint on ...., plaintiff's attorney, whose address is ...., within five days after service of this summons on that defendant, exclusive of the day of service, and to file the original of the defenses with the clerk of this court either before service on plaintiff's attorney or immediately thereafter. If a defendant fails to do so, a default will be entered against that defendant for the relief demanded in the complaint.

    WITNESS my hand and the seal of this court on ....(date)..........

(SEAL)   ....
                                                           As Clerk of the Court

                                                      By: _____
                                                                As Deputy Clerk

G.　[§6.20]　Form For Notice Of Lis Pendens

(Title of Court)

(Title of Cause)   NOTICE OF LIS PENDENS

TO DEFENDANT ...., AND ALL OTHERS WHOM IT MAY CONCERN:

    YOU ARE NOTIFIED of the institution of this action by plaintiff against you seeking to foreclose a lien on the following property in .... County, Florida:

[legal description of property]

    DATED ....

                                                             _____

                                                              (Attorney's signature)

COMMENT: The above form is *RCP* Form 1.918.

IV. THE COMPLAINT – ACTION ON BOND

A. [§6.21] In General

An action by the lienor will lie against a bond rather than the property improved when the owner has exempted himself from the provisions of *F.S.* Chapters 85 and 713 (except 713.23), by requiring a payment bond of the contractor in the direct contract as permitted by 713.02(6). This also is the result when the lienor's claim of lien has been transferred specifically to cash or a surety bond under 713.24.

If the job has been bonded under *F.S.* 713.23, the owner is not a necessary party to the action. The contractor and the surety are necessary parties. If the lien has been transferred to cash or a surety bond, the depositor of the cash or the principal and surety on the surety bond should be parties to the action.

Copies of the payment bond under *F.S.* 713.23 are required to be furnished at cost of reproduction to lienors on their demand by the owner, contractor or surety. The notice of commencement is required to state the amount of the bond and the name and address of the surety.

F.S. 713.23 requires the delivery of written notice to the contractor by any party supplying labor or materials to a subcontractor of the furnishing of that labor or material within 90 days after performance of the labor or complete delivery of materials. No action can be brought against the contractor for that labor or materials unless that notice has been given. The statute also provides that except for laborers and for persons in privity with the *contractor,* no claimant may recover on a bond or from the contractor unless he shall have given notice to the *owner* under 713.06(2).

An action on a payment bond under *F.S.* 713.23 must be brought within one year from the performance of labor or completion of delivery of materials. Action on cash deposits or surety bonds furnished to transfer a claim of lien must be brought within one year after the recording of the claim of lien. See 713.24(4) and .22(1). Jurisdiction lies in the court having jurisdiction of the amount claimed.

Suggested forms for complaints in actions on the two types of bonds follow at §§6.22 and .23.

B. Forms For Complaints On Bonds

1. [§6.22] On Payment Bond — Materialman To Subcontractor

(Title of Court)

(Title of Cause)   COMPLAINT

Plaintiff, ..., hereafter called "materialman," sues defendants, ..., hereafter called "subcontractor," ...., hereafter called "contractor" and ...., hereafter called "surety," and alleges:

1. This is an action for damages exceeding $2500.

2. On or before ....(date).........., ... hereafter called "owner," and contractor executed and delivered a contract for the construction of improvements by contractor upon the property of owner in .... County, Florida, described as follows:

[legal description]

3. On ....(date).........., contractor and surety executed and delivered a bond to owner, a copy being attached as Exhibit "A".

COMMENT: A breach of the bond condition must be alleged (such as failure of the principal to pay) in order to allege a cause of action in covenant.

4. On ....(date).......... contractor executed and delivered a subcontract with subcontractor to furnish the materials and labor necessary for the erection of the structural elements of the improvements.

5. On ....(date).......... materialman executed and delivered a written agreement to supply [describe materials] for use in the erection of the structural elements of the improvements, a copy being attached as Exhibit "B".

6. Materialman has fully performed its obligations under the agreement and the last material required under the agreement was furnished on ....(date)..........

7. There is now due to materialman $..........

8. On ....(date).......... materialman served a notice to owner.

9. Within 90 days after completion of the performance required of materialman in the agreement, materialman delivered to contractor written notice of the delivery of materials under the agreement and their nonpayment.

10. Materialman is obligated to pay his attorneys a reasonable fee for their services.

WHEREFORE, materialman demands judgment against defendants for damages.

_____
Attorney

................(address)..................

2. [§6.23] Subcontractor's Lien Transferred To Bond

(Title of Court)

(Title of Cause)   **COMPLAINT**

Plaintiff, ..., hereafter called "subcontractor," sues defendants ...., hereafter called "contractor," ...., hereafter called "owner," and ...., hereafter called "surety" and alleges:

1. This is an action for damages that exceed $2500.

2. On or before ....(date).......... owner and contractor executed and delivered a contract agreement for the construction of improvements by contractor upon the property of owner in .... County, Florida, described as follows:

[legal description]

3. On ....(date).......... contractor executed and delivered a subcontract with subcontractor to furnish the materials and labor necessary to erect the structural elements of the improvements, a copy being attached as Exhibit "A".

4. Subcontractor furnished the labor and materials under the subcontract and furnished the last on ....(date)..........

5. Subcontractor, on ....(date).......... served on owner a notice to owner.

6. There is due to subcontractor under the subcontract $.........., which remains unpaid. A statement of account is attached as Exhibit "B".

7. Subsequent to subcontractor's filing its claim of lien and before institution of this action, owner transferred subcontractor's claim of lien to a bond executed by owner as principal and by surety.

COMMENT: See the comment to paragraph 3 in §6.22. In this form, the allegation of a breach of the bond condition should be phrased for the future.

      8. Subcontractor is obligated to pay his attorneys a reasonable fee for their services.

      WHEREFORE, subcontractor demands judgment against contractor, owner and surety for damages.

                                                      Attorney

                                    ....(address)..................

V.   [§6.24] JOINDER, CONSOLIDATION AND INTERVENTION

A party may set up in the same action as many causes of action or defenses in the same right as he has. *RCP* 1.110(g). The actions to enforce mechanics' liens may be joined with other causes of action. Joinder of causes of action is discussed in FLORIDA CIVIL PRACTICE BEFORE TRIAL §§11.13–.16 (CLE 3d ed. 1975).

F.S. 85.041 authorizes all persons having liens under Chapter 713 to join to enforce their respective liens. Accordingly, a single action may be brought by multiple plaintiffs to foreclose their respective liens on the property improved.

Intervention by a lienor in a pending lien enforcement action may be permitted under *RCP* 1.230. The intervention is in subordination to, and in recognition of, the propriety of the main proceeding, unless ordered otherwise by the court. See FLORIDA CIVIL PRACTICE BEFORE TRIAL §§11.9–.12 (CLE 3d ed. 1975).

VI.   ANSWER AND CROSS-CLAIM

A. [§6.25] In General

The defendant in an action to enforce a claim of lien should deny all allegations to be contested and set up as affirmative defenses matters such as proper payment, default in performance of the contract or undertaking upon which the claim of lien is asserted and failure of compliance by the plaintiff with any of the requisites to his having a claim of lien or right to enforce it.

Any claim of lien in which the amount is willfully exaggerated or in which work not performed or materials not furnished are willfully included is deemed a fraudulent lien. *F.S.* 713.31(2)(b). A lien compiled with such "willful and gross negligence" as to amount to willful exaggeration is also deemed fraudulent under the act. An owner against whose interest a fraudulent lien is filed is entitled to actual and punitive damages recoverable in an independent action or in a counterclaim or cross-claim. 713.31(2)(c).

A lienor who is joined as a defendant in an action by another lienor in order to lay the predicate for obtaining full relief in the action should file an answer and a cross-claim. The answer essentially will deny any unadmitted priority of the plaintiff's claim of lien over that of the defendant lienor. The cross-claim will set out the basis of the defendant lienor's claim of lien, its priority over the interests of the owner and any other subordinate parties and its parity with any liens of admitted equality. The relief sought by the cross-claim should be for determination of amount due, priority and for foreclosure.

A sample answer and cross-claim is shown in §6.16.

B. [§6.26] Form For Answer And Cross-Claim —
Materialman Not In Privity

(Title of Court)

(Title of Cause)   **ANSWER AND CROSS-CLAIM**

Defendant, ..., a Florida corporation, answers the complaint and alleges:

    1. Defendant is without knowledge of paragraph ...., ..., ... and ....

    2. Defendant admits paragraphs ...., ... and ....

COMMENT: The admitted allegations relate to such matters as ownership of the property improved, the prime contract and filing of notice of commencement.

    3. Defendant denies paragraph ....

CROSS-CLAIM

Defendant, ..., sues defendant, ..., contractor, and ...., owner, and alleges:

4. This is an action to foreclose a mechanic's lien.

5. On or about ....(date).......... this defendant executed and delivered a contract to defendant, ...contractor/subcontractor.........., for the furnishing of steel doors and frames for the improvement of the property in .... County, Florida, and described in paragraph .... of the complaint owned by defendant, ... A copy of the contract is attached as Exhibit "A". Subsequently, additions were made to the contract as extras, as represented by Exhibits "A-1", "A-2", "A-3", "A-4" and "A-5".

6. This defendant performed its contract by delivering the material covered by the contract to the property.

7. The last of the materials was furnished on or about ....(date)..........

8. The total contract price was $.........., of which $......... remains unpaid to this defendant from ....contractor/subcontractor.......... A statement of account is attached as Exhibit "B".

COMMENT: See the comment following paragraph 5 in §6.15.

9. This defendant served its notice to owner on ....(date)..........

10. This defendant filed its claim of lien on ....(date).......... in the office of the Clerk of the Circuit Court of .... County, Florida, which was recorded in Official Records Book ...., at page ...., of the public records of that county and on ....(date).......... served a copy of its claim of lien on the owner.

11. Plaintiff claims ownership of record of the real property and defendants, ...(lienors).........., each claim a lien on it by virtue of claims of lien recorded in the public records of the county, in Official Records Book ...., at page ...., and Official Records Book ...., at page ...., respectively. Any right, title, interest or lien held or claimed by plaintiff and those defendants is subordinate and inferior to the lien of this defendant described in this action.

12. This defendant has complied with *F.S.* Chapter 713.

13. This defendant is obligated to pay his attorneys a reasonable fee for their services.

WHEREFORE, this defendant demands an accounting of the sum due this defendant and judgment against ....contractor/subcontractor.......... for the sums determined to be due to this defendant and declaring this defendant has a lien on the property for all sums due this defendant superior to any interest or lien of plaintiff and all other defendants and ordering a sale of the property to satisfy the lien if those sums shall not be paid within the time set by this court, and that the right, title, interest and liens of plaintiff and all other defendants and all parties claiming by, through, under or against them since the filing of the notice of lis pendens be foreclosed.

_____
Attorney

..................(address)..................

(Certificate of Service)

VII. INTERPLEADER

A. [§6.27] In General

An owner or other person holding a fund for disbursement on an improvement has the right to interplead lienors disputing the amounts due them from the fund and obtain the transfer of all claims to the fund. The action is instituted by a complaint in the circuit court naming the claimants as defendants and seeking an order transferring their claims to the fund that the plaintiff tenders to the court. Upon the granting of the interpleader, the fund is deposited in the registry of the court and the property improved is discharged by order of the court of all claims of lien of the interpleaded parties. *F.S.* 713.27.

Interpleader in general is discussed in Chapter 23 of FLORIDA CIVIL PRACTICE BEFORE TRIAL (CLE 3d ed. 1975). A sample form for a complaint to interplead follows.

B. [§6.28] Form For Complaint To Interplead Contractor And Subcontractor

(Title of Court)

(Title of Cause)   **COMPLAINT**

Plaintiff, ..., hereafter called "owner," sues defendants, ..., "contractor" and ...., "subcontractor," and alleges:

1. This is an action of interpleader under §713.27, Florida Statutes.

2. Owner, on ....(date).........., executed and delivered a contract to contractor for the construction of a dwelling to be erected on the property of owner in .... County, Florida, described as follows:

[legal description]

A copy of the contract is attached as Exhibit "A".

3. The construction of the dwelling has been completed owner retains $.......... as the final payment due under the contract.

4. Subsequent to the execution of the contract between owner and contractor, a subcontract was entered into between the contractor and subcontractor to paint the dwelling under the contract.

5. Subcontractor, on ....(date).......... served on owner a notice to owner.

6. Contractor and subcontractor are in dispute about the sum due from contractor to subcontractor under the subcontract. Contractor has told owner that the amount due to subcontractor is $........... Subcontractor has notified owner in writing that the amount due to subcontractor if $........... Contractor has notified owner, in writing, that contractor disputes the amount claimed to be due by subcontractor.

7. Contractor and subcontractor have each filed claims of lien against the property of owner and each has served a copy upon owner. The total amount of the two claims of lien exceeds the amount remaining to be paid by owner under the contract and each is a claim against that fund. Plaintiff has no interest in the apportionment between the contractor and subcontractor of the retainage that owner admits is due on the prime contract and has no other interest in the retainage other than that it be properly applied between the claimants.

8. Owner will immediately deposit the retainage in the registry of the court upon the court ordering contractor and subcontractor to interplead in this action.

9. Owner is obligated to pay his attorneys a reasonable fee for their services.

WHEREFORE, owner demands that contractor and subcontractor be required to interplead in this action and upon deposit of the funds held by plaintiff that property described in this complaint be discharged of all liens and claims of lien of contractor and subcontractor and judgment for its costs and attorneys' fees payable out of the fund to be deposited.

Attorney

.................(address)..................

VIII. [§6.29] TERMINATION OF JOB BEFORE COMPLETION

When the job is terminated or abandoned before completion without fault of the lienor, he is entitled, assuming compliance with the act, to a lien for services and materials furnished. But if the termination does not result from default of the owner, the total of all liens for which the property of the owner is chargeable is limited to the contract price, less amounts properly paid by the owner to date and less the reasonable cost of completing the prime contract. See *Melnick v. Reynolds Metals Company,* 230 So.2d 490 (4th D.C.A. Fla. 1970). In these circumstances *F.S.* 713.06(3)(e) requires the owner to determine the amount due each lienor and to pay those amounts in full or pro rata as provided in 713.06(4), which establishes the order of payment of liens.

If the owner desires to recommence construction, *F.S.* 713.07(4) provides that if he pays all lienors in full or pro rata in accordance with 713.06(4) before recommencement, all liens for the recommenced construction take priority from the recommencement. This statute further provides that if the owner records an affidavit in the clerk's office stating his intention to recommence construction and that all lienors giving notice have been paid in full, except those listed, then the rights of any person acquiring any interest, lien or encumbrance on the improved property, including lienors on the recommenced construction, are superior to the rights of all lienors arising from the prior construction. Excepted are lienors claiming for services or materials provided to the prior construction who record claims of lien within 30 days after the recording of the affidavit. The act requires service of a copy of the affidavit on each lienor named in the affidavit and the recording and posting on the site of the improvement of a notice of commencement for the recommenced construction. These provisions are of obvious value and assistance in the case of a project required to be refinanced during construction.

IX. [§6.30] PRIORITY OF LIENS

F.S. 713.07 deals with the priority of liens under the act. It provides that liens for professional services and subdivision improvements attach as of the time of recordation of the claim of lien and take priority as of that time. All other liens attach and take priority as of the time of recordation of the notice of commencement if one has been filed and, if not, as of the time of the recording of the claim of lien.

X. PROOF AT TRIAL

A. [§6.31] In General

The party seeking to enforce a claim of lien must prove the existence and validity of the lien, its amount and its priority. The pleadings and pretrial procedures may limit the issues, of course. Discovery techniques for requests for admissions and for production of documents are particularly useful in lien enforcement cases.

The proof required in an action on a lien transfer bond ordinarily will be basically the same as in the trial of an action in which the lien is sought to be enforced against the property improved. In payment bond actions, although filing of the claim of lien is irrelevant, claimants other than laborers and those in privity with the contractor are required to establish compliance with *F.S.* 713.06(2), which requires service of the notice to owner.

B. [§6.32] Existence And Validity Of Lien

The existence and validity of the lien sought to be enforced should be proved by introduction in evidence of the documents required to establish the lien. These include the notice to the owner in cases in which the lienor is not in privity with the owner and is not a laborer; the recorded claim of lien; and evidence of the service of the notice to owner, when required, and the service of the claim of lien. In actions on payment bonds parties not in privity with the contractor will be required to prove service upon the contractor of written notice of the performance of the labor or furnishing of the materials and nonpayment.

C. [§6.33] Amount Of Claim

Proof of the amount of the lien or bond claim to which the claimant is entitled frequently is the most difficult aspect of proof, particularly for materialmen and subcontractors who furnish materials. Obviously, the records of the claimant ordinarily will be the source of this proof. If delivery receipts are being relied upon as the primary source of proof, the claimant's attorney should be prepared to prove the receipt of the material at the job site or the place of delivery designated by the purchaser and the identity and authority, apparent or real, of the party receipting for the delivery.

D.   [§6.34] Priority

The question of priority essentially is a question of law. While it may seem inconceivable that a case could arise in which the record notice provisions of the statutes would not apply, the question of priority possibly could depend upon proof of the date of the recording of the notice of commencement, the service of notice to the owner and the date of the filing of the claim of lien. These are matters of documentary proof.

XI.   THE JUDGMENT

A.   [§6.35] In General

The judgment in an action on a payment or lien transfer bond should be a money judgment against the principal and surety. The judgment in an action to foreclose a lien against the property improved should establish the amount of the lien, attorneys' fees, costs and interest as a charge upon the property, direct its sale to satisfy the amount of the judgment and provide for a deficiency judgment against the parties liable. A suggested form for a judgment follows.

B.   [§6.36] Form For Judgment In Lien Foreclosure Action

(Title of Court)

(Title of Cause)   FINAL JUDGMENT

This action was tried before the court. On the evidence presented

IT IS ADJUDGED that:

1. Plaintiff, ..., is due $.......... for services and materials furnished to the property hereafter described, $.......... as interest to the date of this judgment, $.......... for title evidence expense, $.......... for attorneys' fees and

$.......... court costs now taxed, making a total sum of $.......... due under the claim of lien sued upon in this action.

2. Plaintiff holds a lien for the total sum superior to any claim or estate of defendant, ..., on the following-described property in .... County, Florida:

[legal description]

3. If the total sum with interest at the rate prescribed by law and all costs of this action accruing subsequent to this judgment are not paid within three days from this date, the clerk of this court shall sell the property at public sale on ....(date).......... between 11:00 o'clock A.M. and 2:00 o'clock P.M. to the highest bidder for cash, except as set forth hereafter, at the .... door of the courthouse in .... County, in .... Florida, in accordance with §45.031, Florida Statutes.

4. Plaintiff shall advance all subsequent costs of this action and shall be reimbursed for them by the clerk, if plaintiff is not the purchaser of the property at the sale. If plaintiff is the purchaser, the clerk shall credit plaintiff's bid with the total sum with interest and costs accruing subsequent to this judgment or such part of it as is necessary to pay the bid in full.

5. On filing the certificate of title the clerk shall distribute the proceeds of the sale, as far as they are sufficient, by paying: first, all of plaintiff's costs; second, documentary stamps affixed to the certificate; third, plaintiff's attorneys' fees; fourth, the total sum due the plaintiff less the items paid plus interest at the rate prescribed by law from this date to the date of sale; and by retaining any amount remaining pending further order of this court.

6. On filing the certificate of title defendant and all persons claiming under or against him since the filing of the notice of lis pendens are foreclosed of all estate or claim in the property and the purchaser at the sale shall be let into possession of the property.

7. Jurisdiction of this action is retained to enter further orders as are proper, including, without limitation, writs of assistance and deficiency judgment.

ORDERED at ...., Florida, on ....(date)..........

Copies furnished to: ....

Judge

XII. OTHER REMEDIES

A. [§6.37] Repossession

Under F.S. 713.15, if for any reason the completion of an improvement is abandoned or, though completed, materials delivered are not used, the party delivering the materials that have not been incorporated in the improvement and for which he has not received payment may peaceably repossess or replevy the unused materials. The right of repossession extends only to materials for which the purchase price does not exceed the amount remaining due, but when part payment has been made, the vendor of the materials may repossess them by refunding the partial payment. Upon repossession, the lienor ceases to have a lien for the price of the materials and has no right against any person for the purchase price. The rights of the vendor in repossessed materials is the same as if he had never parted with possession.

Materials furnished to improve real property for which payment has not been made or waived are not subject to attachment, execution or other legal process to enforce any debt due by the purchaser, except a debt for the purchase price of the materials, "so long as in good faith the same are about to be applied to improve the real property." But if the owner has paid the contractor or subcontractor for the materials, those materials are not subject to legal process to enforce the debt for the purchase price. F.S. 713.17.

B. [§6.38] Liens Upon And Removal Of Improvements

Under F.S. 713.11 when the person contracting for the improvement has no interest as owner in the land, no lien attaches to the land. An exception applies when the contracting party is the spouse of the owner and is not separated and living apart. 713.12. If removal of the improvement from the land is practicable, the lien of the lienor attaches to the improvement on which he has performed services or for which he has furnished materials. The lien may be foreclosed and the improvement sold separately from the land, the purchaser being entitled to remove it within such time as the court may fix. The owner has the right to require the restoration of the land substantially to its condition before the improvement was commenced, and that cost is made a first charge on the deposited purchase price.

C. [§6.39] Other Actions Not Barred

The mechanics' lien law is cumulative to other remedies and is not to be construed to prevent any lienor from maintaining an action at law as though he had no lien. The bringing of that action does not prejudice the lienor's rights under the act. *F.S.* 713.30.

XIII. [§6.40] SPECIAL PROBLEM – THE LONG JOB AND THE EARLY COMPLETING LIENOR

The typical contract provides for the retention of a percentage of each progress payment becoming due. In fact, *F.S.* 713.06(3)(d)5 requires the owner to retain the last payment due under the contract or at least 10% of the original contract price, whichever is larger, until the contractor's affidavit for final payment has been delivered. Subcontracts, likewise, typically call for corresponding retainages from payments due the subcontractor. As noted previously, the act requires the subcontractor's claim of lien to be filed within 90 days after he has completed his subcontract and any action on his claim of lien to be instituted within one year after its recording.

Certain subcontractors, particularly those involved in the erection of structural elements in large projects, finish their subcontracts long before the project is completed and final payment due. For example, completion of the project and the due date for payment of retainage on a large office building ordinarily will occur much later than 15 months after completion of the subcontract for the steel or pre-cast erection. In order to preserve their claims of lien under the act these subcontractors must "lien" the job before the retainage is actually due under the contract and the subcontract, a practice not likely to gain friends. Moreover, these lienors are then faced with the problem of instituting an action to foreclose the lien before the final payment of the retainage is due. Agreements with the contractor and owner to extend the time periods provided by the statute are unavailing because those agreements may not preserve the priority or parity of the lien of the subcontractor in relation to the liens of other lienors on the job.

In the present state of the legislation, there appears to be no other course for the early completing subcontractor than to file his claim of lien within the 90-day period and institute an action within the one-year period in the expectation that the action will be stayed until the retainage becomes due. In the case of bonded jobs the situation is little different, because *F.S.* 713.23 requires the institution of the action on the bond within one year from completion of the subcontract. It appears that the early completing subcontractor is best advised to file his claim of lien on unbonded jobs. The claim of lien may then be transferred to the bond and the necessity of instituting an action within one year from the date of the filing of the claim of lien may be obviated by agreement between the claimant, the principal and the surety. Likewise, in the case of bonded jobs, it would appear that the alternative to institution of action within the one-year period from completion of the subcontract is an agreement extending that time between the claimant, the principal and the surety.

It is suggested that the problem of the early completing subcontractor is one that should be dealt with legislatively by inclusion in the mechanics' lien law of means for the extension at least of the period for instituting an action.

GENE ESSNER*†
LEWIS KANNER**

7

REFORMATION, RESCISSION AND CANCELLATION OF INSTRUMENTS

I. INTRODUCTION

    A. [§7.1] In General

    B. [§7.2] Reformation

    C. [§7.3] Rescission

    D. [§7.4] Cancellation

II. GROUNDS FOR RELIEF

    A. [§7.5] Reformation

    B. [§7.6] Rescission

    C. [§7.7] Cancellation

III. THE COMPLAINT

    A. [§7.8] In General

    B. [§7.9] Negating Possibility Of Other Relief

    C. [§7.10] Determining Necessary Parties

---

*J.D., 1951, University of Miami. Mr. Essner is a member of the Dade County Bar Association and is a partner in the firm of Blackwell, Walker, Gray, Powers, Flick and Hoehl. He practices in Miami.

**J.D., 1958, University of Florida. Mr. Kanner is a member of the American Bar Association and is a partner in the firm of Williams, Salomon, Kanner & Damian. He practices in Miami.

†Mr. James C. Truett was the author of this chapter in the first edition.

      D. [§7.11] Pitfalls

      E. Sample Complaints

          1. [§7.12] Sample Complaint For Reformation

          2. [§7.13] Sample Complaint For Rescission

          3. [§7.14] Sample Complaint For Cancellation

IV. THE ANSWER

      A. [§7.15] In General

      B. [§7.16] Sample Answer In Action For Rescission

V. [§7.17] BURDEN OF PROOF

VI. THE FINAL JUDGMENT

      A. [§7.18] In General

      B. [§7.19] Taxing Of Costs

      C. Sample Final Judgments

          1. [§7.20] Sample Final Judgment In Reformation

          2. [§7.21] Sample Final Judgment In Action For Rescission

          3. [§7.22] Sample Final Judgment In Action For Cancellation

I. INTRODUCTION

A. [§7.1] In General

This chapter is concerned with reformation, rescission and cancellation of instruments insofar as they apply in real property practice. Contracts of sale, options, deeds, mortgages, leases and building and construction contracts are but a few of the instruments that affect title to real estate and are commonly the subject of remedial proceedings described in this chapter.

The remedies described here are equitable in nature and relief is discretionary. See *International Realty Associates v. McAdoo*, 87 Fla. 1, 99 So. 117 (1924). Although the distinction between law and equity is being lessened constantly, the classical maxims and principles of equity are followed rather carefully by the courts in these proceedings.

B. [§7.2] Reformation

In reformation proceedings the plaintiff seeks to have a written instrument rewritten to speak the truth in some material respect. For example, intervention of the court may be necessary to correct a legal description or other language of an instrument so that it conforms with the intention of the parties at the time they executed the writing.

C. [§7.3] Rescission

In rescission proceedings, the plaintiff seeks to have a written instrument abrogated in its entirety. For example, in a proper case an agreement induced by fraud may be declared a nullity, or a party protected by statute may be entitled to rescission simply because the law confers that privilege upon him, or because the other has failed to make some disclosure or take some action required of him.

D. [§7.4] Cancellation

Cancellation, in the context of this chapter, is a proceeding to have stricken from the public records some instrument that is or appears to be a burden upon the title to land. In its proper sense cancellation is the physical effacement or destruction of an instrument, but in most real property litigation (in which the instruments have no negotiable character) an adjudication that an instrument is terminated generally will suffice as a cancellation without a directive that the document itself be physically destroyed. For example, cancellation may be sought to relieve the title to land from an unperformed option, lease or agreement for deed.

II. GROUNDS FOR RELIEF

A. [§7.5] Reformation

The grounds for reformation of instruments most often encountered are accident, mistake and fraud. The plaintiff must plead the:

1. existence of the instrument;

2. manner in which the document fails to speak the truth or is not in conformity with the intention and agreement of the parties;

3. time and manner in which the error was discovered;

4. damage to the plaintiff;

5. demand upon the defendant to correct the mistake and his refusal to comply with the demand; and

6. inadequacy or want of an adequate remedy at law.

The plaintiff should be prepared to show in his proof that he has acted in good faith and has been diligent in protection of his rights. He may show that an error grew out of simple negligence, but he must not have been guilty of gross negligence. Upon a clear and convincing presentation of the evidence in support of his position, the court may order reformation to the extent that makes the instrument speak in the manner the parties intended. But the court will not recast the instrument to create an entirely different transaction or one that the parties could not have made for themselves at the inception. Neither will the court relieve against an improvident business transaction, and although the plaintiff demonstrates equity in himself, this equity must be superior to that of the defendant.

B. [§7.6] Rescission

The grounds for rescission of agreements usually are fraud and mistake, although undue influence, duress, incompetency, failure or inadequacy of consideration and illegality also may be grounds upon which rescission is sought. The plaintiff must plead the:

1. existence of the agreement;

2. factual circumstances that constitute the ground for rescission;

3. damage to the plaintiff;

4. plaintiff's offer to restore to the defendant any benefits plaintiff has received;

5. plaintiff's demand upon the defendant for rescission and defendant's refusal to comply with the demand; and

6. inadequacy or want of an adequate remedy at law.

The demonstration of equitable conduct and diligent protection of rights required of a plaintiff in reformation proceedings also apply in rescission. See §7.5.

Of the remedies discussed in this chapter, *common-law rescission* is by far the most difficult to obtain. The fact that the plaintiff can be compensated adequately in damages is the most prevalent reason for denying this relief. The difficulty or impossibility of restoring the parties to their former status is another reason it is often denied. Perhaps for these reasons, there has been a great burst of consumer-oriented legislation that has created a class of *statutory rescission* that may require nothing more than a change of mind by a protected party (see, for example, the Truth in Lending Act, 15 *U.S.C.A.* §§1601 *et seq.*) or a failure of a vendor to make full disclosure or to take some action required, such as registration (see, for example, the Interstate Land Sales Full Disclosure Act, 15 *U.S.C.* §§1701, *et seq.* or any securities law).

C. [§7.7] Cancellation

The term "cancellation of instruments" when taken in its proper sense of the physical effacement or destruction of an instrument is not descriptive of a particular class of proceedings. Conceivably, cancellation may be ordered in a declaratory judgment proceeding, an action to quiet title and in an accounting. Further, it may be ordered in virtually any action based on equitable grounds. To add to the confusion, some text writers and classifiers in the law employ the terms "rescission" and "cancellation" as though the words were synonyms. Clearly they are not.

Rescission deals with the judicial annulment of rights and liabilities under an agreement, while cancellation deals with the literal or figurative destruction of a writing. Rescission may be granted without cancellation of the writing. For example, rescission without cancellation may be in order when an agreement is held invalid as to one party but effective as to others. Conversely, cancellation may be ordered without rescission. In a typical situation cancellation might be sought of an unexpired lease that has been terminated through the tenant's nonpayment of rent. Rescission would not be a factor, since the validity of the lease is recognized at least to the time of the breach.

In real property practice the two most important types of litigation that result in cancellation of instruments are actions for rescission of agreements and actions to remove clouds on title.

In further discussion in this chapter, attention is directed largely to proceedings in reformation and rescission. Cancellation is not treated at length for the reason that in its principal applications it is an incident to rescission or is properly an action to remove clouds from title. See also *F.S.* Chapter 65.

III. THE COMPLAINT

A. [§7.8] In General

In drafting the complaint, after the necessary allegations as to residence and the basic items, unnecessary to outline here, the essential facts outlined in §§7.5–.7 must be alleged to make a showing that entitles a party to relief. See Chapter 12, "Pleadings," FLORIDA CIVIL PRACTICE BEFORE TRIAL (CLE 3d ed. 1975).

The Supreme Court of Florida in *Willis v. Fowler,* 102 Fla. 35, 136 So. 358 (1931) said:

> ... But we must agree with the prevailing rule in other jurisdictions that good pleading requires that a bill to rescind a contract should set out the agreement, the parties thereto, and the time, place, and circumstances of its execution; that at least the substance of the contract

should be alleged in the bill, and, if it was a written contract, a copy thereof should either be incorporated in the bill or attached as an exhibit thereto, and the bill should also show with reasonable certainty what complainant received under the contract, and that he had seasonably returned or offered to return the same after discovering the fraud.

This language has been quoted many times as the guideline setting forth what must be shown in a complaint. Although brief, this statement is one that may be used as a guide in all instances.

The above-cited case relates to relief in which fraud is alleged. In those instances in which undue influence, mistake, accident or error is the basis for the relief sought, the factual matters that show these grounds should be set forth in detail.

It also must be alleged that demand has been made on the party from whom relief is sought before institution of the action. Adequate time must have been allowed for that party to correct the situation for which relief is desired.

The contract, deed or other instrument that is the subject matter of the action should be attached to the complaint. Of course, all other documents that relate to the transaction may be necessary exhibits to a complete understanding of the transaction. See Chapter 12, "Demonstrative Evidence," FLORIDA CIVIL TRIAL PRACTICE (CLE 2d ed. 1970).

B. [§7.9] Negating Possibility Of Other Relief

In §§7.5 and .6 it was pointed out that it must be shown in a complaint for reformation or rescission that no adequate remedy at law exists. It would be well to state again that when considering the filing of a complaint for reformation or rescission, the lawyer first must consider the possibilities of securing relief through a law action, whether the action is for damages or other relief. He must bear in mind that cancellation of an instrument, although only incidental to the main relief sought, may be an important basis upon which to predicate equitable jurisdiction.

In instances in which improper language or description has been used, no relief by any remedy other than reformation seems to be available.

C. [§7.10] Determining Necessary Parties

The general rule in equity that provides that all persons interested in the subject matter of the litigation should be named as parties to the action holds especially true in these proceedings. In determining the parties to be named in the complaint, any person whose rights might be affected by the final judgment being sought should be joined. Generally, it is good practice to obtain a title search or abstract in order to determine what persons should be made a party defendant. The search may not disclose all of the essential parties, but at least it will reveal the names of those whose participation is necessary to effect a complete adjudication with respect to record title. Once this has been done, an action ought to be commenced and notice of lis pendens filed promptly to prevent third parties who may not be bound by the judgment or who may be able to assert a superior equity as innocent purchasers from becoming involved in the transaction. It generally is a good idea to examine title after the notice of lis pendens has been filed to ensure that any parties whose interests appear since the previous examination are made parties to the action.

D. [§7.11] Pitfalls

As pointed out before, the courts are reluctant to grant reformation or rescission. The greatest pitfall that occurs in this area of practice is the filing of a complaint seeking reformation or rescission when no thorough analysis of the problem has been made, particularly with regard to the adequacy of damages.

E. Sample Complaints

1. [§7.12] Sample Complaint For Reformation

**IN THE CIRCUIT COURT
FOR SQUARE COUNTY, FLORIDA**

I. R. PITTSBORO, as Trustee for
ABLE HARDWARE, INC., Bankrupt,

                Plaintiff

      vs.

JOHN DOE and LENDERS, INC.,

              Defendants : **COMPLAINT FOR REFORMATION**

Plaintiff, ..., sues defendants, **JOHN DOE and LENDERS, INC.**, a Florida corporation, and alleges:

§7.12   REFORMATION, RESCISSION AND CANCELLATION OF INSTRUMENTS   §7.12

1. This is an action to reform a deed and a mortgage.

2. Plaintiff is the duly appointed trustee in bankruptcy for ABLE HARDWARE, INC.

3. On or about the 13th of September, 1967, and for some time before that date, ABLE HARDWARE, INC. was the owner in fee of the following-described property in Square County, Florida:

[legal description]

4. On or about July 14, 1967, ABLE HARDWARE, INC., conveyed to John Snow by warranty deed, recorded in Official Record Book 125, page 429, of the public records of Square County, Florida, the following-described property:

[legal description]

A copy of this deed is attached as Exhibit 1.

5. Thereafter, John Snow conveyed the property described in paragraph 4 to Jerry Olden, by deed recorded in Official Record Book 134, page 299, of the public records of Square County, Florida, a copy being attached as Exhibit 2.

6. Thereafter, Jerry Olden conveyed the property to defendant JOHN DOE by deed recorded in Official Record Book 134, page 300, of the public records of Square County, Florida, a copy being attached as Exhibit 3. JOHN DOE subsequently mortgaged the property to LENDERS, INC., by mortgage recorded in Official Record Book 134, page 301 of the public records of Square County, Florida, a copy being attached as Exhibit 4.

7. After ABLE HARDWARE, INC. went into bankruptcy and plaintiff was appointed trustee, the property described in paragraph 3 of this complaint was sold and at the time of the sale plaintiff had a survey prepared by Arthur Greenboy, which shows that the description of the property initially conveyed to ABLE HARDWARE, INC. was incorrectly described and the incorrect description has followed in the other instruments recited in paragraph 6 above. A copy of the survey is attached as Exhibit 5.

8. Plaintiff has requested defendant, JOHN DOE, to execute a quitclaim deed to plaintiff in return for which plaintiff would execute and deliver to defendant, JOHN DOE, a corrective deed describing that tract of land actually intended to be conveyed to defendant JOHN DOE'S predecessor in title. Defendant, JOHN DOE, has refused to execute that quitclaim deed and it has become necessary for plaintiff to file this complaint for reformation in order to clear the title to the property described in Paragraph 3.

9. Plaintiff has joined LENDERS, INC., as a defendant because it is also necessary to reform the description in the mortgage now held by LENDERS, INC., and although LENDERS, INC. has not been made aware of the errors in description, the description in the mortgage cannot be corrected until the description in the conveyance to JOHN DOE is also corrected, and by joining LENDERS, INC., the court will be able to grant complete relief to all of the parties.

WHEREFORE, plaintiff demands a judgment reforming the deeds and mortgage described in this complaint.

/s/ Horace E. Smith
Horace E. Smith
1410 Art Street
Flowertown, Florida
Attorney for Plaintiff

COMMENT: The sample final judgment in §7.20 is based upon the same hypothetical facts as are the basis of the above complaint.

2. [§7.13] Sample Complaint For Rescission

IN THE CIRCUIT COURT
FOR ROLLING COUNTY, FLORIDA

JOHN DOE and MARY DOE, his wife,

Plaintiffs

vs.

BILL BILDER,

Defendant : COMPLAINT FOR RESCISSION

Plaintiffs, JOHN DOE and MARY DOE, his wife, sue defendant, BILL BILDER, and allege:

1. This is an action to rescind a contract.

2. Defendant, BILL BILDER, is engaged in the building construction business and does business under the name of BILL BILDER, Contractor.

3. During the year 1965 defendant constructed a residence for resale on the property in Rolling County, Florida described as follows:

Lot 2, Block F, of Courtview as recorded in Plat Book 8, page 7, of the public records of Rolling County, Florida.

4. The property was conveyed to plaintiffs by defendant by warranty deed dated September 10, 1965, recorded in the public records of Rolling County, Florida, Official Record Book 256, at page 55, a copy of the deed being attached as Exhibit 1.

5. In the course of constructing the residence, defendant built it over a deposit of pipe clay and in such close proximity to it as to require special construction of the foundation, including additional footings not required in ordinary construction, in order to ensure a solid and firm foundation for the residence. Defendant did not construct the additional footings and foundation reasonably required by the character of the soil upon which the residence was erected.

6. During the course of constructing the residence defendant learned of the presence of pipe clay under the lot upon which the residence was being built and knew, or should have known, that the pipe clay deposits were close enough to the residence to require special construction of the type above described.

7. At or about the time the construction of the residence was completed by defendant, he listed it for sale and exhibited it to plaintiffs. Plaintiffs then began negotiations for the purchase of the residence. Defendant represented to plaintiffs that the residence was soundly constructed on a proper foundation and was suitable for use by plaintiffs as a residence, when in fact defendant knew those representations to be untrue. At the time the representations were made to plaintiffs, defendant knew that pipe clay deposits existed in close proximity to the foundations of the residence, and knew, or should have known, that the pipe clay deposits required a special construction in the foundations of the residence, which had not been incorporated in the foundations.

8. The negotiations between plaintiffs and defendant took place almost immediately after the residence was completed, and when the residence was exhibited to plaintiffs by defendant the physical signs now existing in the structure had not developed or become visible. Plaintiffs, being totally ignorant of the nature, character or attributes of pipe clay, did not know and could not have known that a deposit of pipe clay was in close proximity to the foundation or that the presence of pipe clay in close proximity to the foundation of the residence would or could cause the damage that has resulted from its presence.

9. Defendant fraudulently concealed the presence of the pipe clay deposits from plaintiffs and plaintiffs relied on defendant's representation as to the soundness and good quality of the residence.

10. Plaintiffs moved into the residence on or about September 10, 1965, and have made it their home since that time. Shortly thereafter small cracks appeared in the concrete blocks of the outside walls that have grown larger and now measure approximately one inch or more at the top of the wall and one fourth to one half of an inch at the bottom of the wall. The inside walls have split in the same manner. The tile and walls in the bathrooms have developed abnormal cracks. The window sills have separated from the walls. The baseboards have split or have torn away from the walls and the quarter round and other molding have either separated from their bases or have split asunder. The door openings are warped out of shape requiring physical force to close the doors set within them. The glass sliding doors leading to a patio have separated from the facings leaving space between the doors and the facings large enough to admit the entry of insects, some reptiles and other crawling creatures. This cracking, splitting and tearing of the walls, ceilings and floors is continuing and will continue. It is caused by and is the direct result of the footings or foundation of the residence being in close proximity to pipe clay deposits without proper allowance or provision being made for the pipe clay in the construction of the footings or foundations.

11. Plaintiffs learned since they purchased the residence that pipe clay deposits exist immediately under the foundations. They have made this condition known to defendant and have requested him to repair the existing damage and take the necessary steps to prevent the recurrence of this damage in the future, but he has failed and refused to do so.

12. Plaintiffs paid defendant the purchase price of $20,300 for the lot and residence and $1,575 in permanent improvements to the lot and residence by the addition of a central air-conditioning system and by sodding the part of the property left unsodded by defendant.

13. Plaintiffs are financially unable to expend the sums required to repair the existing damage to the residence or the sums required to reconstruct the foundation and footings of the residence to prevent a recurrence of the above-mentioned damage. Defendant has allowed the damage to the residence to progress to such a degree that the residence at this time can not be repaired and put in the condition that it would have been had defendant constructed the foundation for the residence as it should have been constructed.

14. Plaintiffs offer to restore to defendant everything of value received by them from defendant and to do all acts and things that may be necessary or proper to restore the parties to the position they occupied before the above-described conveyance.

WHEREFORE plaintiffs demand that the conveyance from defendant to plaintiffs be rescinded and defendant be required to refund the purchse price paid to him by plaintiffs plus the cost of the permanent improvements placed on the property.

/s/ P. R. Sackford

P. R. Sackford
First Bank Building
Blackville, Florida
Attorney for Plaintiffs

COMMENT: In §7.16 the sample answer in an action for rescission is based upon the same facts that are the basis of the above complaint. In §7.21 the same facts are the subject of the sample final judgment in an act for rescission.

3. [§7.14] Sample Complaint For Cancellation

IN THE CIRCUIT COURT
FOR LEMON COUNTY, FLORIDA

JOHN DOE and ELLEN DOE, his wife,

    Plaintiffs

  vs.

BIGG MORTGAGES, INC.,
 a Florida Corporation,

    Defendant

COMPLAINT FOR CANCELLATION OF MORTGAGE

Plaintiffs, JOHN DOE and ELLEN DOE, his wife, sue defendant, BIGG MORTGAGES, INC., a Florida corporation, and allege:

1. This is an action to cancel a mortgage on property in Lemon County, Florida.

2. Prior to November 10, 1965 plaintiffs made application for a loan from defendant. On November 10, 1965 plaintiffs signed a real estate mortgage and note in which defendant was mortgagee that was recorded in the public records of Lemon County, Florida, in Official Record Book 103, page 104 on November 18, 1965, a copy of the mortgage and note being attached.

3. Plaintiffs made fourteen payments of $60.00 each to defendant. On March 7, 1967 plaintiffs made payment of the balance due of $6,100 pursuant to a statement submitted by defendant dated March 2, 1967, a copy being attached.

4. Plaintiffs have fully performed under the terms of the mortgage and note but defendant has failed and refused to execute and deliver to plaintiffs a satisfaction of the mortgage.

5. Defendant appears to claim some interest in the property described in the mortgage that is a cloud on the title of plaintiffs.

WHEREFORE plaintiffs demand that the mortgage and note be canceled.

/s/ Arnold L. Fanbelt
Arnold L. Fanbelt
P. O. Box 91
Centertown, Florida
Attorney for Plaintiff

COMMENT: In §7.22 a form for an order in an action for cancellation is set out; it is based on the same hypothetical facts used above.

IV. THE ANSWER

A. [§7.15] In General

In the preparation of the answer all of the allegations of the plaintiff in the complaint should be given careful consideration by the defendant. Possible defenses to an action for reformation include that it would constitute an unnecessary or vain act; that it is precluded by a prior action or judgment at law; there is no agreement between the parties; or there is no mistake in the agreement. In an action for rescission, or cancellation, possible defenses include ratification or acquiescence and estoppel. Other general equitable defenses, such as the plaintiff's want of diligence or his own neglect, should be asserted when appropriate.

If there are any affirmative defenses that may be raised appropriately, they must not be overlooked, since failure to file an affirmative defense is a waiver of it. Important factual issues may be raised by general denials of the answer, but important differences as to how and when events occurred that may tend to raise the defenses of estoppel, waiver and laches should be plead with particularity. See

Chapter 12, "Pleadings," FLORIDA CIVIL PRACTICE BEFORE TRIAL (CLE 3d ed. 1975).

It is appropriate to point out here that one may find instances in which a defendant in some types of litigation other than for reformation or rescission may wish to file a counterclaim or a cross-claim to set up rescission or reformation of some instrument. In those instances the defendant occupies the position of plaintiff with respect to his claim and has the burden of proving his case as a party plaintiff. See §7.17.

B. [§7.16] Sample Answer In Action For Rescission

IN THE CIRCUIT COURT
FOR ROLLING COUNTY, FLORIDA

JOHN DOE and MARY DOE, his wife,

          Plaintiffs

vs.

BILL BILDER,

          Defendant   ANSWER

Defendant, BILL BILDER, answers the complaint and alleges:

1. Defendant admits paragraphs 1, 2, 3 and 4.

2. Defendant admits that there was pipe clay present on the lot upon which the residence was constructed but denies the other allegations of paragraph 5.

3. Defendant admits that there were pipe clay deposits on the land upon which the residence was built but denies the other allegations of paragraph 6.

4. Defendant denies paragraph 7 and affirmatively states that the dwelling was constructed in accordance with the plans and specifications as submitted to the Federal Housing Administration. Defendant in further answer to paragraph 7 states affirmatively that extra footings and special construction in the foundation were incorporated into the dwelling in order to compensate for the condition of the soil as found by defendant during the course of construction.

5. Defendant denies paragraphs 8 and 9.

6. Defendant admits the first sentence of paragraph 10 but is without knowledge of the remainder of the paragraph.

7. Defendant admits he has received requests from plaintiffs to repair certain items and at all times has made known to plaintiffs that defendant would make such repairs as would be necessary as alleged in paragraph 11, but plaintiffs have failed and refused to allow defendant to make those repairs.

8. Defendant admits that the purchase price of the property of plaintiffs was $20,300 as alleged in paragraph 12 but is without knowledge of the amounts of money expended on permanent improvements by plaintiffs.

9. Defendant is without knowledge of paragraphs 13 and 14.

FIRST DEFENSE

10. The time that has elapsed since plaintiffs took possession of the property on the 10th day of September, 1965 is an unreasonable length of time before filing of their complaint. The incorporation in the property of an air-conditioning unit and other permanent improvements at an alleged cost of $1,575 shows that plaintiffs were satisfied with the condition of the property. Plaintiffs' conduct in refusing to allow defendant to make repairs to correct the condition of the property shows that plaintiffs do not desire to have the property repaired but merely wish to be able to withdraw from the purchase of the property. All of these matters have prejudiced defendant and the conduct of plaintiffs should bar plaintiffs from relief.

SECOND DEFENSE

11. The residence of plaintiffs was constructed in exact accordance with the plans and specifications submitted to the Federal Housing Administration with the exception of the construction of additional footings and heavier footings with more reinforcement than was called for in the plans and specifications. The Federal Housing Administration inspections were made during the course of construction and the Federal Housing Administration found defendant had complied with and constructed the dwelling in accordance with the plans and specifications and issued it final compliance inspection report, upon which the Federal Housing Administration insured loan to plaintiffs was closed.

/s/ Billy Q. Raddman

Billy Q. Raddman
92½ Moss Street
Blackville, Florida
Attorney for Defendant

(Certificate of Service)

COMMENT: This sample answer is based upon the same hypothetical facts that are the subject of the complaint for rescission set out in §7.13 and of the final judgment appearing in §7.21.

V. [§7.17] BURDEN OF PROOF

The burden of proof in proceedings for reformation and rescission of instruments is the same as in any type of litigation. The burden of proving by a preponderance of the evidence is always upon the plaintiff to establish the cause of action alleged by him. Once a prima facie case is made, the burden of going forward with the evidence shifts to the defendant, who must present evidence of the facts that would establish the defendant's position and justify the denial of any relief by the court.

In actions for reformation of an instrument, the evidence presented on behalf of the plaintiff must show not merely that there is equity in his position but that he has an equity that is superior to the defendant's. The language of the courts in establishing what degree of proof must be met by the complainant seeking reformation has been set forth in a number of cases. See *Sobel v. Lobel,* 168 So.2d 195 (3d D.C.A. Fla. 1964). Perhaps it is best expressed that the proof must be clear, unequivocal and convincing. A mere preponderance of evidence is insufficient. *Watkins v. DeAdamich,* 187 So.2d 369 (2d D.C.A. Fla. 1966). The lawyer must keep in mind that in the event the evidence presented to the court can be considered in any way as weak or contradictory, the court may deny the relief that is sought.

The remedy of rescission, because of the harshness of its nature, is one that courts are reluctant to grant. Before granting that relief it must appear that the remedy of damages is inadequate and that the equitable relief will be appropriate and one that will more fairly place the parties back in the position they held or occupied before entering into the agreement.

VI. THE FINAL JUDGMENT

A. [§7.18] In General

In most instances the successful party in the litigation will be the one to prepare the final judgment. The judgment should be drawn carefully. The attorney must be certain that it embodies all of the relief sought that the court has granted.

If cancellation of an instrument is ordered, the instrument to be canceled should be set forth with particularity. The method by which the cancellation will be effected should be set out also and the method of effecting the cancellation should be specified. *RCP* 1.570.

If rescission is granted, the instrument to be rescinded should be set forth with particularity and any other instruments or acts that may be affected also should be specified.

If reformation is granted, the instrument should be set out and the manner by which the reformation is to be accomplished should be specified. In most instances it will be proper to direct the clerk of the court to enter an appropriate notation on the margin of the instrument to be reformed showing that the instrument has been reformed by order of court entered on a certain date and on a certain page of the public records.

Once the final judgment has been secured, the successful litigant should determine that it is carried into effect. If rescission has been granted, the exchange of instruments or moneys should be effected as soon as the appeal period has expired. This of course would hold true also insofar as cancellation and reformation of instruments are concerned.

B.   [§7.19]   Taxing Of Costs

Once the court has indicated its ruling, the question of costs should be brought up immediately and the court requested to tax the costs that have been incurred. The taxation of costs is in the discretion of the court. Generally, the court will tax costs in favor of the prevailing party. The matter of taxing of costs of course should be covered in the final judgment. It therefore is proper to have available at the time of the trial all evidence on costs sought to be taxed.

See Chapter 21, "Costs, Fees and Interest," FLORIDA CIVIL TRAIL PRACTICE (CLE 2d ed. 1970).

C.   Sample Final Judgments

     1. [§7.20]   Sample Final Judgment In Reformation

IN THE CIRCUIT COURT
FOR SQUARE COUNTY, FLORIDA

I. R. PITTSBORO, As Trustee for   :
ABLE HARDWARE, INC., Bankrupt   :
                                    :
           Plaintiff   :
                                    :
   vs.   :
                                    :
JOHN DOE and LENDERS, INC.,   :
                                    :
           Defendants   :   FINAL JUDGMENT

This action was heard on plaintiff's request for judgment and it is

ADJUDGED that:

1. The descriptions in the deeds recorded in Official Record Book 125, at page 429, Official Record Book 134, at page 299 and Official Record Book 134, at page 300, all of the public records of Square County, Florida, are reformed so that the descriptions contained in each of them shall read as follows:

[legal descriptions]

2. The description in the mortgage recorded in Official Record Book 134, page 301, of the public records of Square County, Florida, is reformed to read as follows:

[legal description]

3. The clerk of this court is directed to make proper marginal notations in the margin of the deeds and mortgage reciting that the descriptions contained in those instruments have been reformed by the final judgment.

ORDERED at Flowertown, Florida on July 6, 1971.

                                        /s/ J. Reynolds Holster
                                              Circuit Judge

Copies furnished to: ....

COMMENT: The hypothetical facts in the above sample judgment are based upon those utilized for the sample complaint for reformation in §7.12.

2. [§7.21] Sample Final Judgment In Action For Rescission

IN THE CIRCUIT COURT
FOR ROLLING COUNTY, FLORIDA

JOHN DOE and MARY DOE, his wife, :
                                  :
                Plaintiffs   :
                                  :
vs.   :
                                  :
BILL BILDER,   :
                                  :
                Defendant   :   FINAL JUDGMENT

This action was tried before the court on the evidence presented and it is

ADJUDGED that:

FINDINGS OF FACT

1. It is alleged in the complaint and admitted in the answer that defendant, BILL BILDER, is engaged in the construction business as a building contractor under the name of BILL BILDER, Contractor. During the year 1965 defendant constructed for the purpose of resale a residence located upon the real property that is described in paragraph 3 of the complaint. On September 10, 1965, defendant conveyed the property to plaintiffs, JOHN DOE and MARY DOE, his wife, for a purchase price of $20,300 by a warranty deed recorded in Official Record Book 256 at page 55 of the public records of Rolling County, Florida.

2. It is also alleged and shown by the evidence that in the course of constructing this residence defendant laid the foundations partly in or over deposits of pipe clay. Pipe clay is a plastic soil that makes its appearance in various places in the Blackville area. It has the quality of expanding when it becomes wet and as it dries it contracts. If the foundation of a building rests upon the pipe clay, a common experience is a marked settling of the foundation in periods of drought and a contrasting elevating or lateral course when there is a period of considerable rainfall. The action of the clay in these alternating conditions of moisture is capable of giving sufficient movement to the foundation so as to produce cracks up to one half of one inch width in both external and internal walls. It also is capable of causing the separation of joints and general warping and misalignment of other portions of the building.

3. This clay occurs in pockets and pools usually several feet under another type of soil and its presence can be ascertained only by borings. Extensive and costly experiences to builders in the general area where defendant constructed the above-mentioned residence have rendered it necessary, as a sound building process, to make tests of the subsoil down to a depth of eight feet. If there are eight feet of nonplastic firm soil between the foundation and the pipe clay, it is considered safe for the foundation to rest on soil with that much overburden; however, if the clay is found within the eight feet there are a variety of building practices that are pursued to overcome the handicap of the presence of the clay. It will not be necessary in this case to make a determination as to whether defendant pursued an accepted or common building practice. The point for determination will not be dependent upon that factor. It may be merely mentioned here that what was done ultimately proved to be inadequate to prevent substantial damage to the house because of the presence of pipe clay.

4. It was further shown that at the time the house was being constructed defendant discovered that pipe clay was present in some of the areas in which the foundations were to rest. He undertook to compensate for its presence and in building he pursued procedures that he deemed to be adequate and sound.

5. At the time plaintiffs and defendant were negotiating for the sale and purchase of the house, defendant stated that the house had met Federal Housing Administration inspection, but further than that he does not appear to have made any express representations as to construction. Defendant did not reveal to plaintiffs that pipe clay had been found on the lot or that it had existed in the area where the foundations were laid. Nothing at all was said about pipe clay in connection with the negotiations.

6. At the time of the negotiations and immediately after the purchase there were no cracks or other noticeable defects in the house. Plaintiffs moved in shortly after the purchase and have since that time made this their home. In the spring of 1966 some cracks began to develop that first were thought to be merely settlement cracks, but they got larger and larger, which brought on a suspicion of pipe clay. Warping and joint separations appeared. Plaintiffs had a soil test made by Mr. Eugene Fass, who is an expert on the subject, and it was found that pipe clay was within five feet of the surface at three of the four corners of the house. This information and complaints of the defects that had appeared were taken to defendant.

7. It will not be necessary to go into any detail as to the negotiations between the parties at this point. It will be sufficient to state that defendant expressed a willingness to make repairs but was not willing to pursue all the procedures that plaintiffs demanded.

8. The damage to the house caused by the expansion and contraction of the pipe clay consists of the following principal features [omitted from this sample]. These defects have not rendered the house dangerous to live in but they have impaired its comfort and utility very materially. Many of these defects are more of an aggravating nuisance than structural deficiencies; however, they do markedly reduce the attractiveness and the comfort that a house of that type and price should reasonably provide. In addition, the presence of these defects and the exposure of the presence of pipe clay are shown to have depreciated the market value of the property materially.

9. In April, 1966 plaintiffs installed air-conditioning equipment in the house at a cost of $1,575.

10. In accordance with certain provisions of the Housing Act of 1954 and Public Law 85-857 (38 U.S.C. §1805), defendant executed a written warranty that the dwelling involved in this case was constructed in substantial conformity to the plans and specifications that have been approved by the Federal Housing Commissioner. It does not appear that this particular warranty has been breached and its existence is not significant in the problems involved in this case.

CONCLUSIONS OF LAW

A. Plaintiffs seek a rescission and restoration to status quo of the parties on the ground that there have been misrepresentations, nondisclosures and breaches of warranty to them by defendant.

B. A preponderance of the evidence does not establish facts from which it can be found that defendant made any express representations as to the quality of construction or any other positive representations except what would be implicit in a statement that the house was constructed in accordance with F.H.A. requirements. The court will take judicial notice that F.H.A. requirements generally are regarded as reasonably high standards, which if followed would produce a dwelling house containing suitable and adequate materials with good workmanship resulting in a sound structure. It may be assumed that defendant was fully conscientious in any statement that he made or implied as to the quality of the materials and workmanship that went into the house; however, it appears that defendant was under a positive duty to tell plaintiffs before the sale that pipe clay existed at the places where it had been found by him. This he did not do.

C. ***

D. ***

E. ***

F. Thus, the liability of defendant to plaintiffs has been established. This does not resolve the problem fully as the nature of the relief that may be granted must be determined. Plaintiffs seek not only rescission but also to be compensated for air-conditioning improvements made since the purchase.

G.   * * *

H.   * * *

I. In the case at bar there are several elements that render substantial restoration to the status quo difficult and uncertain. The claim for compensation for the air-conditioning would require a rather detailed consideration of depreciation, use and present value. A reasonable value for the use of the premises by plaintiffs up to the present would be an important element. It does not appear that there is evidence before the court from which these equities may be assessed reasonably and safely. The remedy of damages is deemed to be adequate to render justice to the parties.

It is ADJUDGED that:

1. Rescission of the agreement between plaintiffs, JOHN DOE and MARY DOE, and defendant, BILL BILDER, is denied.

2. Plaintiffs, JOHN DOE and MARY DOE, his wife, shall recover $.......... from the defendant, BILL BILDER, for which let execution issue.

ORDERED at Blackville, Florida on November 17, 1968.

/s/ Morris E. Slinder
Circuit Judge

Copies furnished to: ....

COMMENT: In the above judgment portions of the opinion setting out the pertinent law are omitted, as were some of the findings of fact. The facts utilized are the same as those that form the basis of the complaint in §7.13 and the answer in §7.16.

3. [§7.22] Sample Final Judgment Action For Cancellation

IN THE CIRCUIT COURT
FOR LEMON COUNTY, FLORIDA

JOHN DOE and ELLEN DOE, his wife,

     Plaintiffs

vs.

BIGG MORTGAGES, INC.,
 A Florida Corporation,

     Defendant   FINAL JUDGMENT

  This action was heard on a stipulated statement of facts and instruments in writing, and it is

  ADJUDGED that the mortgage in which plaintiffs, JOHN DOE and ELLEN DOE, were mortgagors and BIGG MORTGAGES, INC. was mortgagee, dated November 10, 1965 and recorded in Official Record Book 103, page 104, of the public records of Lemon County, Florida be canceled and the clerk of this court shall execute and record a satisfaction of the mortgage.

  ORDERED at Centertown, Florida on May 10, 1968.

                 /s/ **Samuel S. Todt**
                     Circuit Judge

Copies furnished to: ....

COMMENT: The order is based upon the same hypothetical facts that are the basis of the complaint set out in §7.14.

ROBERT P. BARNETT*

8

REESTABLISHING LOST INSTRUMENTS

I. [§8.1] SCOPE

II. INTRODUCTION

    A. [§8.2] Definition

    B. [§8.3] In General

III. [§8.4] WHO MAY REESTABLISH

IV. INITIAL CLIENT INTERVIEW

    A. [§8.5] In General

    B. [§8.6] Obtaining Proof

    C. [§8.7] Fees And Costs

V. [§8.8] STATUTES OF LIMITATION AND LACHES

VI. BEGINNING THE ACTION

    A. [§8.9] Jurisdiction

    B. [§8.10] Venue

    C. [§8.11] Parties

    D. The Complaint

---

*J.D., 1969, University of Florida. Mr. Barnett is a member of the Dade County and the American bar associations. He is an associate in the firm of Salley, Barns, Pajon & Primm and practices in Miami.

        1. [§8.12] Allegation Of Facts

        2. [§8.13] Relief Requested

    E. [§8.14] Notice Of Lis Pendens

    F. [§8.15] Process

VII. [§8.16] DRAFTING THE ANSWER

VIII. PREPARATION FOR TRIAL

    A. [§8.17] The Trial Brief

    B. [§8.18] Stipulations, Admissions And Interrogatories

IX. TRIAL

    A. Order Of Proof

        1. [§8.19] Proof Of Execution

        2. [§8.20] Proof Of Reason For Nonproduction Of Original

        3. [§8.21] Proof Of Contents

    B. [§8.22] The Judgment And Its Effect

X. [§8.23] REESTABLISHING LAND TITLES DESTROYED BY FIRE

XI. FORMS

    A. [§8.24] Complaint For Reestablishment Of A Lost Promissory Note

    B. [§8.25] Notice Of Action

    C. [§8.26] Final Judgment Reestablishing Lost Promissory Note

    D. [§8.27] Complaint To Reestablish Land Title Destroyed by Fire

I. [§8.1] SCOPE

This chapter deals with the necessity for and the method of reestablishing lost or destroyed instruments relating to rights in real property.

Reestablishment of judicial records, such as pleadings and process in pending actions or writs of fieri facias, is not within the scope of this chapter. The practitioner confronted with those problems should consult *F.S.* 71.031 or 56.021, respectively. Neither is an attempt made to discuss here the reestablishment of marks and brands, as provided for in 71.021. While the reestablishment of a lost or destroyed will certainly may affect rights in real property, discussion of such a proceeding is outside the scope of this chapter and the reader is referred to FLORIDA PROBATE PRACTICE §§5.60−.62 (CLE 1973 ed.).

Although, strictly speaking, reestablishment of land titles destroyed by fire does not come within the scope of this chapter, it is considered important enough to warrant a brief discussion in §8.23, and a form for a complaint is set forth in §8.27.

II. INTRODUCTION

A. [§8.2] Definition

As used in this chapter, the term "lost instrument" refers to a document that cannot be found after a diligent search. Included are those that have been lost, stolen or destroyed.

B. [§8.3] In General

The right to reestablish lost instruments was recognized both in common-law courts and courts of equity. By statute, Florida has provided for the reestablishment of lost instruments and has made the statutory remedy concurrent with, not exclusive of, the common-law and equitable remedies. *F.S.* 71.011(3). Although the statutory remedy should cover the vast majority of cases and is the remedy dealt with in this chapter, the attorney should be aware that he may resort to a common-law or equitable action in exceptional circumstances in which the statutory remedy is inadequate.

Generally, the destruction, theft or unintentional loss of an instrument does not change the rights or obligations of the parties to the instrument. The writing itself is not the source of the rights and obligations, but merely evidence of them. When the owner of an instrument intentionally destroys it, however, he may have relinquished his rights evidenced by the writing and may be precluded from asserting them. 52 AM.JUR.2d *Lost And Destroyed Instruments* §§2 and 4.

III.   [§8.4]   WHO MAY REESTABLISH

F.S. 71.011(1) provides that "Any person interested in the paper, file or record to be re-established may re-establish it." Typically, this might include, among others, grantors and grantees, mortgagors and mortgagees, lessors and lessees, parties to a contract for sale and purchase, optionors and optionees, lienors and payors and payees of notes.

IV.   INITIAL CLIENT INTERVIEW

A.   [§8.5]   In General

Occasionally, a client may seek legal advice on how to reestablish an instrument without first considering the most obvious solution — that of having the instrument re-executed. This cannot always be done. Many times the parties necessary for re-execution are either unavailable or unwilling to cooperate. When possible re-execution usually is the quickest and most economical way to reestablish the instrument. The re-executed instrument is not considered to be a new instrument and need not be supported by new consideration. The original consideration will support the re-execution if it was sufficient for the original. 52 AM.JUR.2d *Lost And Destroyed Instruments* §9.

The necessity, or lack of necessity, for reestablishment should be made clear to the client initially. A lost mortgage may not be foreclosed until it and the note have been reestablished. *Harper v. Green,* 99 Fla. 1309, 128 So. 827 (1930). Although the usual practice is to obtain an indemnification agreement from the mortgagee, the maker of a mortgage note may wish to have the note reestablished so that it may be canceled properly after payment — especially if the original has been lost rather than destroyed. Since "lost" documents have a way of turning up unexpectedly and can cause problems, it is a good idea to have a copy of a lost note reestablished as the original and properly canceled. This seems especially wise when one considers that possession of an uncanceled note creates a presumption of nonpayment. *Speier v. Lane,* 254 So.2d 823 (3d D.C.A. Fla. 1971).

When the public record of a deed has been destroyed or lost, the present owner of realty may find it necessary to reestablish his deed or that of a predecessor in title, or both, in order to convey marketable title. If the reestablishment does not come within the scope of *F.S.* 71.041, relief may be obtained under 71.011.

Instruments that may be reestablished include, among others, the following: notes secured by mortgages, *Lovingood v. Butler Const. Co.,* 100 Fla. 1252, 131 So. 126 (1930), 74 A.L.R. 513; deeds, *Jones v. Escambia Land & Mfg. Co.,* 55 Fla. 783, 46 So. 290 (1908); certificates of practice, *York v. Pridgen,* 141 Fla. 439, 193 So. 433 (1940); and promissory notes, *Bigelow v. Summers,* 28 Fla. 759, 9 So. 690 (1891).

B. [§8.6] Obtaining Proof

The attorney should use the initial interview with his client to explore the possible sources of proof for the reestablishment action. Often, the best source may be the attorney's own file — or the file of the attorney who prepared the original document. Most attorneys keep file copies of documents they prepare for clients and these copies usually are more accessible than the client's copy. If neither the attorney nor the client has a copy of the document, it may be possible to obtain one from a bank or other lender. If the document is a mortgage note, a photostatic copy may have been attached to the recorded mortgage and can be obtained from the public records.

Even when an exact copy cannot be obtained, all available files should be checked for correspondence or other references to the document to be reestablished, which may help to verify its terms and contents.

C. [§8.7] Fees And Costs

At the initial interview the client should be informed that unlike the usual situation in which the prevailing party is entitled to recover his costs in full or in part, the plaintiff in the typical reestablishment action normally will have to pay his own costs. Usually, this will be only the filing fee and perhaps charges for certified copies and recording, but occasionally deposition expense and other costs will be incurred. There is no statutory provision for the payment of attorneys' fees and, since it is not anticipated that a document will be lost or destroyed, none will be provided for by contract. It is not unreasonable that the reestablishing party bear the burden of costs and attorneys' fees since the original document usually has been lost or destroyed through his fault or negligence.

V. [§8.8] STATUTES OF LIMITATION AND LACHES

Statutes of limitation generally are applicable to actions at law. *F.S.* 71.011(5) provides that the complaint to reestablish a document shall be filed "in chancery," thus making it clear that the action is equitable in nature. The defense of laches may apply to an action to reestablish an instrument if all of its elements are present. The elements are discussed in FLORIDA CIVIL PRACTICE BEFORE TRIAL §10.26 (CLE 3d ed. 1975).

F.S. 95.11(6) provides that laches shall bar any action unless it is commenced within the time provided for legal actions concerning the same subject matter. Thus, it appears that a reestablishment action may be limited by the time periods in 95.11(2)(b) or 95.11(3)(p).

The reestablished instrument has the effect of the original, *F.S.* 71.011(4)(a), and the court may refuse to reestablish an instrument when it is clear that it would be unenforceable because the statute of limitation has run and no other good reason for reestablishment is shown.

Laches, however, will not be imputed to an infant who seeks to reestablish an instrument. See *Watkins v. Watkins,* 123 Fla. 267, 166 So. 577 (1936).

VI. BEGINNING THE ACTION

A. [§8.9] Jurisdiction

As mentioned in §8.8, *F.S.* 71.011(5) requires the complaint to be filed "in chancery." Thus, jurisdiction of the action is placed in the circuit courts. See also *F.S.* 26.012.

B. [§8.10] Venue

F.S. 71.011(2) provides:

> If reestablishment is sought of a record or file, venue is in the county where the record or file existed before its loss or destruction. If it is a private paper, venue is in the county where any person affected thereby lives or if such persons are nonresidents of the state, then in any county in which the person seeking the reestablishment desires.

C. [§8.11] Parties

Any person who is interested in the document to be reestablished may institute the action as plaintiff by filing a complaint. *F.S.* 71.011(1) and (5). All known interested parties who do not wish to join as plaintiffs should be named as defendants and served. This might include, for example, a guarantor on a note or an inferior mortgagee. When in doubt whether to join a defendant, the better practice is to join him, and if the facts later warrant it, to drop him as a party. Persons entitled to be made parties, but who are not joined in the reestablishment proceeding, are not bound by a judgment in favor of the plaintiff. See 52 AM.JUR.2d *Lost And Destroyed Instruments* §27.

D. The Complaint

1. [§8.12] Allegation Of Facts

Factual allegations will vary with the nature of the instrument being reestablished. The following should be included in each complaint.

1. That the action is one to reestablish a document under *F.S.* 71.011.

2. An allegation of execution of the original document, including date, place and parties to the execution.

3. That the document in question has been lost or destroyed and is not within the custody or control of the plaintiff.

4. The time and manner of the loss or destruction.

5. That the attached exhibit (if such is the case) is a substantial copy of the original.

6. The nature of the interest of each of the parties to the action, and that the plaintiff knows of no other person interested in the reestablishment.

If a copy of the instrument is attached to the complaint, it is considered part of the complaint for all purposes. *RCP* 1.130(b). When that is the case, it is not necessary to allege the requisite formalities of execution if they appear on the face of the copy. If a copy is not attached the complaint should allege that the document was executed as required to be valid.

Many attorneys also include an allegation that diligent search for the instrument has been made but that it cannot be found. The statute does not require this, but it may be implied and probably should be included.

A form for a complaint for the reestablishment of a promissory note is set out in §8.24.

2. [§8.13] Relief Requested

The demand for relief should request that the court enter its order establishing the copy in place of the lost or destroyed original.

A request for a jury trial in a reestablishment action generally is futile and ill-advised since the action is equitable in nature. If the complaint seeks to reestablish the instrument *and* to enforce it in the same action, however, a demand for a jury trial may be in order, at least as to the enforcement once the instrument is reestablished if enforcement at law is proper.

As suggested in §8.7, a plaintiff generally cannot recover costs or attorneys' fees in a reestablishment action. Nevertheless, if the plaintiff feels he can establish a right to recover costs or fees, he should request them in his complaint.

E. [§8.14] Notice Of Lis Pendens

Although not required by *F.S.* 71.011, it is good practice for the plaintiff to record a notice of lis pendens with the clerk of the circuit court when the action is filed in order to protect his rights in the property pending the outcome of the reestablishment action. See *F.S.* 48.23. Lis Pendens is discussed in detail in FLORIDA CIVIL PRACTICE BEFORE TRIAL §§9.2−.8 (CLE 3d ed. 1975).

F. [§8.15] Process

In most reestablishment cases, personal service of process may be effected. If a defendant is one against which substituted service is authorized, that method may be utilized. See FLORIDA CIVIL PRACTICE BEFORE TRIAL §14.6 (CLE 3d ed. 1975). *F.S.* 49.011(6) permits constructive service by publication to reestablish "lost instruments or records which have or should have their situs within the jurisdiction of the court."

A plaintiff desiring to use constructive service must provide the clerk with sufficient copies of the complaint to be mailed to the defendants. *RCP* 1.070(f). All three types of service are discussed at length in Chapter 14 FLORIDA CIVIL PRACTICE BEFORE TRIAL (CLE 3d ed. 1975). A form for service by publication in the reestablishment of a promissory note is found in §8.25.

VII. [§8.16] DRAFTING THE ANSWER

In drafting an answer to a complaint to reestablish an instrument, the attorney must keep in mind the distinction between reestablishing the instrument and enforcing it. Defenses such as want of consideration, fraud or absence of delivery are matters to be raised in a proceeding to enforce the instrument rather than in the reestablishment action. See *Commissioners of Suwanee County v. Commissioners of Columbia County,* 18 Fla. 78 (Fla. 1881).

The answer may show that the instrument sought to be reestablished is not complete. If so, the answer should make the proper allegations and present to the court the missing parts for reestablishment. *Florida Cent. & W. R. Co. v. Bostwick,* 55 Fla. 665, 45 So. 1033 (1908).

When the facts warrant the defendant may deny one or more of the essential elements of the complaint. As in other actions allegations well plead and not denied are taken as true.

If the instrument has been lost rather than destroyed, or the defendant's attorney is not certain that in fact the instrument has been destroyed although the plaintiff alleged destruction, it is good practice to include in the answer a request that the plaintiff be required to post a bond in favor of the defendant sufficient to reimburse the defendant should he later be required to pay an innocent third party on the original instrument. See *Lovingood v. Butler Const. Co.,* 100 Fla. 1252, 131 So. 126 (1930), 74 A.L.R. 513.

VIII. PREPARATION FOR TRIAL

A. [§8.17] The Trial Brief

While perhaps not as important as in other types of cases, it may be wise for the attorney seeking to reestablish an instrument to prepare a trial brief as an aid to preparing and trying his case. See Chapter 1 of FLORIDA CIVIL TRIAL PRACTICE (CLE 3d ed. 1975). In doing so, he will satisfy himself that he has not omitted any essential elements of his case and he will have supporting citations readily at hand. The trial brief also serves as a checklist during the trial. Thus, the attorney defending against a reestablishment also can benefit from the opponent's trial brief in that it will enable him to tell at a glance if the opponent has failed to prove an element essential to his case.

B. [§8.18] Stipulations, Admissions And Interrogatories

The plaintiff's attorney should not overlook the opportunity of establishing at least part of his case without formal proof. Although the defendant's attorney may have denied one or more of the plaintiff's allegations in his answer, he may be willing to stipulate to it after having an opportunity to investigate the facts more fully.

Another method of obtaining proof is by serving requests for admissions under *RCP* 1.370 on the defendants. If a photocopy of the instrument is available, it can be attached and the defendant asked to admit that it is a true and correct copy of the instrument to be reestablished. If that admission is made, the plaintiff's attorney has gone a long way in establishing his case.

Written interrogatories also can be useful in preparing the case. For example, if the defendant has denied the authenticity of the instrument, he can be pinned down to specifics by written interrogatories. If the plaintiff does not have access to a copy of the instrument, he should include an interrogatory requiring the defendant to disclose whether he has a copy or knows where one may be obtained. If he does, a request for its production under *RCP* 1.350, may be in order.

IX. TRIAL

A. Order Of Proof

1. [§8.19] Proof Of Execution

Instruments regular on their face are presumed to have been executed properly and to have had all the formalities essential to their validity. 13 FLA.JUR. *Evidence* §106; see also *Christy v. Burch,* 25 Fla. 942, 2 So. 258 (1887). Thus, if a copy of the instrument is admitted into evidence, it will be presumed that the instrument complies with the formalities. The presumption is a rebuttable one and may be overcome by testimony to the contrary. See *Heath v. First National Bank in Milton,* 213 So.2d 883 (1st D.C.A. Fla. 1968). If the copy is not admitted, proper execution will have to be established by parol evidence.

2. [§8.20] Proof Of Reason For Nonproduction Of Original

If the instrument is known to have been destroyed, a person with firsthand knowledge of the destruction should be called to testify as to the time and manner of loss, if known, and if not known, then to the time and circumstances when he last had the instrument.

3. [§8.21] Proof Of Contents

Before an instrument is reestablished, the proof of its contents must be clear and satisfactory. *Selph v. Purvis,* 57 Fla. 188, 49 So. 289 (1909). Secondary evidence is admissible. See *Campbell v. Skinner Mfg. Co.,* 53 Fla. 632, 43 So. 874 (1907); EVIDENCE IN FLORIDA §13.3 (CLE 1971). A predicate must be laid, however, *Nahmod v. Nelson,* 147 Fla. 564, 3 So.2d 162 (1941).

The rules of evidence need not be applied too strictly, *Campbell v. Skinner Mfg. Co., supra.* If a witness cannot testify with certainty that he has seen the instrument to be reestablished, however, he should not be permitted merely to give his impression of its contents. *Cross v. Aby,* 55 Fla. 311, 45 So. 820 (1908).

There are several statutes that may aid the attorney in proving the contents of the document to be reestablished. *F.S.* 92.25−.27 deal with the admissibility and effect of abstracts, or copies of abstracts, to prove a document when the original document has been lost or destroyed by fire. Although these statutes probably are more useful as to actions under 71.041, they may apply also to actions under 71.011.

F.S. 92.29 provides that photocopies made in the regular course of business by any federal, state, county or municipal board, department or agency are admissible, whether the original is in existence or not, if that governmental body was required or authorized to make, file or record the copy.

F.S. 92.35 makes certain photographic copies of business and public records admissible into evidence.

B. [§8.22] The Judgment And Its Effect

F.S. 71.011(4)(a) provides:

> Any paper, record or file reestablished has the effect of the original. A private paper has such effect immediately on recording the judgment reestablishing it, but a reestablished record does not have that effect until recorded and a reestablished paper or file of any official, court or public officer does not have that effect until a certified copy is filed with the official or in the court or public office where the original belonged. A certified copy of any reestablished paper, the original of which is required or authorized by law to be recorded, may be recorded.

Thus, the plaintiff's attorney should record the judgment reestablishing the instrument immediately. Once recorded, it may be enforced as the original but subject also to the same defenses as the original. See *Prescott v. Johnson,* 8 Fla. 391 (1859), decided under an earlier statute.

The judgment granting or denying reestablishment also should dissolve the notice of lis pendens if a notice was filed.

A form for a final judgment granting reestablishment is found in §8.26.

X. [§8.23] REESTABLISHING LAND TITLES DESTROYED BY FIRE

The legislature has provided a specific statutory remedy for reestablishing land titles when the county records have been destroyed by fire to such an extent that a connected chain of title cannot be traced. *F.S.* 71.041. Presumably, if the records are destroyed by means other than fire — wind or water for example — reestablishment must be had under 71.011. Because the remedy under 71.041 is so limited, that statute is discussed only briefly.

An action under *F.S.* 71.041 is brought by the filing of a complaint in the circuit court of the county where the original records were destroyed. The plaintiff may be "any person claiming a freehold estate in any land in the county who, or whose grantors, were in the actual possession of the land at the time of destruction of the records and who is in possession thereof at the time of filing the complaint." Tenants in common or persons owning undivided interests may join as parties.

The requisites of the complaint are set out in *F.S.* 71.041(3). A form for the complaint is set forth in §8.27 of this manual.

If no one contests the complaint, the plaintiff is entitled to a judgment reestablishing his title. If the complaint is contested and a summary judgment is not in order, the plaintiff will have to prepare for an evidentiary hearing and prove his right to the relief requested.

As of this writing, there were no reported appellate decisions concerning *F.S.* 71.041.

XI. FORMS

A. [§8.24] Complaint For Reestablishment Of A Lost Promissory Note

(Title of Court)

(Title of Cause)   **COMPLAINT TO REESTABLISH LOST PROMISSORY NOTE**

Plaintiff, ..., sues defendant, ..., and alleges:

1. This is an action to reestablish a promissory note under F.S. 71.011.

2. On ......(date)......, at ......(place)......, defendant executed and delivered to plaintiff a promissory note in favor of plaintiff, in the principal amount of $....................., a substantial copy being attached.

3. The original promissory note was lost on or about ......(date)...... [or, if destroyed, allege time and manner of destruction] and is not within the custody or control of plaintiff.

4. Plaintiff knows of no parties except defendant who are interested in the reestablishment of the promissory note.

WHEREFORE plaintiff demands that this court reestablish the attached exhibit.

                                        Attorney for Plaintiff

                                        ....(address)................

B.   [§8.25]   Notice Of Action

(Title of Court)

(Title of Cause)   NOTICE OF ACTION

TO: ....

YOU ARE NOTIFIED that an action to reestablish a lost promissory note dated ...., in the original sum of $.................... has been filed against you and you are required to serve a copy of your written defenses, if any, on ...., plaintiff's attorney, whose address is ...., on or before ....(date).........., and file the original with the clerk of this court either before service on plaintiff's attorney or immediately thereafter; otherwise a default will be entered against you for the relief demanded in the complaint.

WITNESS my hand and seal of this court on ....(date)..........

(Name of Clerk)

As Clerk of the Court

By: _____
As Deputy Clerk

COMMENT: See *RCP* Form 1.920.

C.   [§8.26]   Final Judgment Reestablishing Lost Promissory Note

(Title of Court)

(Title of Cause)   FINAL JUDGMENT

This action was tried before the court. On the evidence presented, it is **ADJUDGED** that:

1. On ......(date)......, defendant executed and delivered to plaintiff a promissory note in the amount of $...................., payable to plaintiff, a substantial copy being attached to and made a part of this judgment.

2. The original promissory note has been lost.

3. The attached copy is reestablished as the original promissory note with all of the rights and privileges incident to it and subject to all of the obligations, duties, defenses or claims in relation to it.

ORDERED in ...., Florida on ......(date)......

Copies furnished to: ....

_____
Circuit Judge

COMMENT: The judgment also should dissolve the notice of lis pendens if a notice was filed. §8.22.

D. [§8.27] Complaint To Reestablish Land Title Destroyed By Fire

(Title of Court)

(Title of Cause)   COMPLAINT

Plaintiff, ..., sues defendant, ..., and alleges:

1. This is an action to reestablish a title to real property in .... County, Florida.

2. Plaintiff is the fee simple [or other freehold estate] owner of the real property in .... County, Florida, described as:

[legal description]

3. On ....(date).......... the public record of a warranty deed dated from .... [or other document granting freehold estate] conveying fee simple title of the property described in paragraph 1 to plaintiff, previously recorded in .... Book ...., at page ...., of the public records of .... County, Florida, was destroyed by fire so that a complete chain of title of the property cannot be traced to plaintiff.

4. Plaintiff now is, and was on ....(date).........., in actual possession of the property described in paragraph 1. [If the plaintiff was not in possession on the date the record was destroyed, allege that his grantors were in actual possession.]

5. Plaintiff knows of no persons other than defendants who claim an interest in the above-described lands. [If there are such persons, allege their names and the interest claimed.]

6. At no time between the destruction of the record and the filing of this complaint did plaintiff convey any interest whatsoever in the realty described in paragraph 1 to any other person or entity.

WHEREFORE, plaintiff demands that this court reestablish plaintiff's title of record.

_____
Attorney for Plaintiff

.................(address).................

SHELDON ROSENBERG*

9

BREACH OF SALE CONTRACT

I. [§9.1] ALTERNATIVE REMEDIES AVAILABLE

II. ACTIONS BY SELLER FOR BUYER'S BREACH

    A. [§9.2] In General

    B. [§9.3] Form For Complaint For Damages

    C. [§9.4] Buyer's Answer And Defenses

III. ACTIONS BY BUYER FOR SELLER'S BREACH

    A. Action For Damages When No Conveyance

        1. [§9.5] In General

        2. [§9.6] Measure Of Damages

    B. [§9.7] Form For Complaint

    C. Action For Damages When Purchase Fraudulently Induced

        1. [§9.8] In General

        2. [§9.9] Form For Complaint

IV. ACTION BY SELLER OR BUYER FOR SPECIFIC PERFORMANCE

    A. [§9.10] In General

---

*J.D., 1964, Harvard Law School. Mr. Rosenberg is a member of the North Dade and the American bar associations. He is a partner in the firm of Kates, Ress, Gomeg and Rosenberg and practices in North Miami.

  B. [§9.11] Form For Complaint For Specific Performance

V. ACTIONS ARISING OUT OF BREACH OF INSTALLMENT LAND SALE CONTRACT

  A. The Installment Land Sale Contract

    1. [§9.12] In General

    2. [§9.13] Time Of The Essence

    3. [§9.14] Acceleration

    4. [§9.15] Conveyance On Payment

    5. [§9.16] Forfeiture

    6. [§9.17] Repossession By Seller

  B. [§9.18] Specific Performance Of Land Sale Contract

VI. ACTIONS BY REAL ESTATE BROKERS

  A. [§9.19] In General

  B. [§9.20] Causes Of Action Available

  C. The Complaint

    1. [§9.21] In General

    2. [§9.22] Sample Complaint

VII. [§9.23] CONCLUSION

I. [§9.1] ALTERNATIVE REMEDIES AVAILABLE

If a contract for the sale and purchase of land is breached, the seller and buyer under the contract have certain alternative legal and equitable remedies available to them.

When it is the buyer who has breached the contract, the seller, in the case of an executory contract, may sue for specific performance or for damages arising out of the buyer's breach. If the contract has been executed, the seller may bring an action to rescind the contract or seek to recover the remaining balance on the contract price.

Corresponding remedies are available to the buyer when it is the seller who has failed to perform under the contract. If the seller is unable to convey the real estate, or fails or refuses to do so without legal justification, the buyer ordinarily will seek specific performance, since money damages often are insufficient with respect to land contracts. As an alternative, he may elect to recover damages. An action for damages also may be available to him when the seller is in a position to convey or has conveyed the land but its title is deficient. In this instance, the buyer may undertake to accept the conveyance and seek a reduction in the purchase price because of the title deficiency. There also is available to the buyer who has purchased land in reliance upon a seller's misrepresentation the remedies of an action for damages arising out of the seller's fraud or an action for rescission of the contract.

Election by the seller or the buyer of one avenue of relief ordinarily constitutes a waiver of the alternative remedies, and the parties themselves may limit the relief otherwise available to them by incorporating that limitation in the sales contract.

This chapter will not undertake to discuss rescission, reformation or cancellation of contracts for the sale of land since these subjects are covered in Chapter 7 of this manual. Instead, the chapter will concern actions for specific performance or for damages upon breach of the sales contract. In addition, actions arising out of the breach of installment land sale contracts will be considered. Actions by real estate brokers to recover for services rendered also will be discussed in view of the fact that attorneys involved in real property litigation most probably will be involved in this type of litigation.

II. ACTIONS BY SELLER FOR BUYER'S BREACH

A. [§9.2] In General

A seller's complaint to recover damages arising out of the buyer's default under a land sales contract should contain allegations setting forth the following:

1. Jurisdictional facts.

2. Execution of a land sales contract between the plaintiff seller and defendant purchaser.

3. Terms of the contract (by summary or by attachment of a copy as an exhibit).

4. Plaintiff's performance or readiness and ability to perform as seller.

5. Buyer's default.

6. Nature and extent of the damages sustained by the seller and a demand for judgment for those damages.

B. [§9.3] Form For Complaint For Damages

(Title of Court)

(Title of Cause)   COMPLAINT

Plaintiff, ...(seller).........., sues defendant, ...(buyer).........., and alleges:

1. This is an action for damages that exceed $..........

2. On or about ....(date).......... plaintiff and defendant entered into a written agreement, a copy being attached.

3. Plaintiff performed all conditions to be performed by him, or they have occurred.

4. Thereafter on ....(date).......... plaintiff tendered a deed to the property to defendant and called on defendant to make the payment agreed upon, but defendant breached the agreement by failing to make the payment and refusing to accept the deed. Plaintiff accordingly has rescinded the contract.

5. As a result of defendant's breach, plaintiff has been damaged in the sum of $..........

WHEREFORE plaintiff demands judgment for damages against defendant.

                                                    Attorney

                                       ....(address)..................

C.   [§9.4] Buyer's Answer And Defenses

When the contract is executory and the seller's title is defective, the buyer is under no obligation to pay the purchase price and the defense of failure of consideration is available to him. See *White v. Crandall,* 105 Fla. 70, 143 So. 871 (1932); *Morganthaler v. Holl,* 101 Fla. 452, 134 So. 223 (1931). If he has accepted the seller's deed, however, the rights of the parties are governed by the covenants of title contained in the deed, in the absence of mistake, fraud or a complete failure of title. *Mickler v. Reddick,* 38 Fla. 341, 21 So. 286 (1896).

III.   ACTIONS BY BUYER FOR SELLER'S BREACH

A.   Action For Damages When No Conveyance

    1. [§9.5] In General

A buyer's complaint for damages arising out of the seller's breach of the contract to sell real property should contain allegations setting forth the following:

1.   Jurisdictional facts.

2.   Execution of the sales contract.

3.   Relevant terms of the sales contract (by summary or by the attachment of a copy of the contract as an exhibit).

4.   The circumstances or the seller's acts or refusal to act that constitute the seller's breach of the contract.

5.   Buyer's compliance or ability and willingness to comply with all of the conditions of the sales contract.

6. Nature and extent of buyer's damages and a demand for judgment for those damages.

2. [§9.6] Measure Of Damages

Under an executory contract for the sale and purchase of real property, the buyer suing for damages is entitled to recover from the defaulting seller the purchase money he has paid, his out-of-pocket costs in examining title and interest on the money recovered. *Horton v. O'Rourke,* 321 So.2d 612 (2d D.C.A. Fla. 1975). He also may recover damages for his loss of bargain if there is a breach of a *continuing* obligation. *Southern Realty and Utilities Corp. v. Gettleman,* 197 So.2d 30 (3d D.C.A. Fla. 1967), *cert. den.* 201 So.2d 560. Furthermore, if there is a willful conversion, punitive damages may be in order. *Hanna v. American International Land Corporation,* 289 So.2d 756 (2d D.C.A. Fla. 1974).

B. [§9.7] Form For Complaint

(Title of Court)

(Title of Case)   COMPLAINT

Plaintiff, ...(buyer).........., sues defendant, ...(seller).........., and alleges:

1. This is an action for damages that exceed $..........

2. On or about ....(date).......... defendant as seller and plaintiff as buyer executed a written contract, a copy being attached.

3. Plaintiff has paid to defendant the down payment called for in the contract .... and has been ready, willing and able to perform under the contract, and on ....(date).......... offered to pay defendant the balance due of $..........

4. Notwithstanding this, defendant has refused and continues to refuse to perform his obligation to convey the real property to plaintiff.

5. As a result of this breach plaintiff has been damaged in the sum of $..........

WHEREFORE plaintiff demands judgment for damages against defendant.

                                                                            Attorney

                                                               ....(address)..................

C. Action For Damages When Purchase Fraudulently Induced

1. [§9.8] In General

The buyer may elect to rescind a fraudulently induced sale of real property and sue for recovery of the purchase price paid. See *Norris v. Eikenberry,* 103 Fla. 104, 137 So. 128 (1931); *Nixon v. Temple Terrace Estates,* 97 Fla. 392, 121 So. 475 (1929). Instead, the buyer may continue to hold title to the property and bring an action against the seller or his agent or representative who has induced the fraudulent purchase with the object of recovering the damages he has suffered as a consequence of the fraud. Those damages are the difference between the actual value of the property at the time of the contract and the value it would have had if the facts and representations of the seller had been accurate.

The buyer's complaint in an action to recover damages arising out of the seller's fraud should contain allegations of sufficient specificity to establish false and material representations and the buyer's reliance on them to his detriment. See *Norris v. Eikenberry, supra; Firstbrook v. Buzbee,* 101 Fla. 876, 132 So. 673 (1931); *Williams v. McFadden,* 23 Fla. 143, 1 So. 618 (1887).

2. [§9.9] Form For Complaint

(Title of Court)

(Title of Cause)   COMPLAINT

Plaintiff, ...(buyer).........., sues defendant, ...(seller).........., and alleges:

1. This is an action for damages that exceed $...........

2. On ....(date).......... defendant was the owner of the following-described real estate:

[legal description]

3. Defendant was engaged in constructing a residence.

4. Plaintiff and defendant entered into negotiations for the sale of the property and a structure on it under which plaintiff agreed to pay to defendant the

sum of $.......... During the negotiations that resulted in the sale to plaintiff, defendant represented to plaintiff that [set out fraudulent representations].

5. The representations were made by defendant with the intention that the plaintiff rely on them.

6. Each of the representations relates to an existing, material fact.

7. Defendant knew the representations were false.

8. Plaintiff, believing defendant's representations to be true, relied on them and as a result entered into the contract with defendant on ....(date).........., and thereafter concluded the sale by payment to defendant of the purchase price of $.......... Defendant then conveyed the property to plaintiff.

9. Defendant's fraudulent representations became known to plaintiff when [insert the facts and circumstances that brought the fraudulent representations to the buyer's attention].

10. As a result of being fraudulently induced to purchase the real property from defendant, plaintiff has suffered damages in the sum of $..........

WHEREFORE plaintiff demands judgment for damages against defendant.

                                                    _____
                                                           Attorney

                                                    ....(address)..................

IV. ACTION BY SELLER OR BUYER FOR SPECIFIC PERFORMANCE

A. [§9.10] In General

Either the seller or the buyer may bring an action for the specific enforcement of a contract for the sale of real property. See *Clements v. Leonard,* 70 So.2d 840 (Fla. 1954). The terms of the contract must be clearly set forth so that the court may determine the duties of each party. Unless the obligations of both seller and buyer and the time and method for performance are set forth specifically in the contract so as to be clear, definite and certain, a contract will not be specifically enforced by the court. This clearly extends to a description of the real property involved, which description must be sufficient to allow for the identification of the real property with reasonable certainty. *Cox v. La Pota,* 76 So.2d 662 (Fla. 1955).

The obligations of buyer or seller with respect to conditions of the contract and the actions to be taken by them must be specifically plead in any complaint for specific performance. Thus, if a purchaser seeks specific performance of a contract for the sale of real property he must allege in his complaint that payment under the contract has been made or tendered by him or that he has been ready, willing and able to pay, or has been excused from performance.

In addition, a contract for the sale of realty will not be specifically enforced unless it satisfies all of the formal requirements of those contracts as, for example, the requirement that there be two subscribing witnesses to the execution of the contract. Specific performance has been granted even under an oral contract for the sale of real property, however, but only when the purchaser at the time of the commencement of the action was in possession of the real property. See *Avery v. Marine Bank & Trust Company,* 216 So.2d 251 (2d D.C.A. Fla. 1968). Since an allowance of specific performance by the court is discretionary with the court, however, and not a matter of right possessed by the seller or buyer, the court may deny specific performance even when the terms of the contract are unambiguous. See *Mann v. Thompson,* 100 So.2d 634 (1st D.C.A. Fla. 1958).

A complaint for specific performance of a contract for the sale of real property should contain allegations setting forth the following:

1. Jurisdictional facts.

2. Allegations pertaining to the parties.

3. Allegations setting forth the ownership of the property.

4. The making of the contract and its provisions (most effectively set forth by attachment of a copy of the contract).

5. Allegations establishing performance, tender of performance together with readiness, willingness and ability to perform, and, when applicable, facts establishing prevention of performance.

6. Damages sustained by the plaintiff.

7. Relief demanded.

8. Endorsement of the complaint by the party or his attorney.

As a defensive matter, the defendant in an action for specific performance, in addition to attacking the validity of the contract being sued upon may raise the doctrine of laches. Whether or not such a defense will be sustained in any case will depend upon all of the relevant circumstances surrounding the contract and the period between the making of the contract and the filing of the action for specific performance. It should be noted, however, that when property valuation is subject to substantial fluctuation the failure to seek specific performance promptly may be prejudicial to seeking that relief at a later date. *Matousek v. Cooper,* 111 So.2d 65 (2d D.C.A. Fla. 1959).

Specific performance of a land sale contract is discussed in §9.18.

B. [§9.11] Form For Complaint For Specific Performance

(Title of Court)

(Title of Cause)   COMPLAINT

Plaintiff, ...(seller).........., sues defendant, ...(buyer).........., and alleges:

1. This is an action for specific performance of a contract for the sale of real estate in .... County, Florida.

2. At all times set forth in this complaint, plaintiff was and is now the owner of the following-described real property:

[legal description]

3. On or about ....(date).........., plaintiff as seller and defendant as buyer executed a written contract, a copy being attached.

4. Plaintiff has been and now is ready, willing and able to comply with the terms of the agreement by conveying the property to defendant.

5. Notwithstanding this, defendant has failed and refused to perform defendant's part of the contract of sale.

WHEREFORE plaintiff demands judgment requiring defendant to specifically perform the defendants obligations under the terms and conditions of the contract.

_____

Attorney

.................(address).................

COMMENT: See also *RCP* Form 1.941, which is a form for a complaint for specific performance by a plaintiff-buyer.

V. ACTIONS ARISING OUT OF BREACH OF INSTALLMENT LAND SALE CONTRACT

A. The Installment Land Sale Contract

1. [§9.12] In General

The installment land sale contract is, in effect, a security agreement by which the seller retains legal title as security for the payment of the purchase price, typically paid in installments, during the life of the debt. Under *F.S.* 697.01, the installment land sale contract in essence is a mortgage. For this reason, and pursuant to this statute governing instruments deemed to be mortgages, the seller and buyer respectively are afforded the same remedies as the creditor and debtor in a mortgage transaction. *H & L Land Company v. Warner*, 258 So.2d 293 (2d D.C.A. Fla. 1972).

Since Chapter 5 deals with mortgage foreclosures and the considerations and forms in mortgage foreclosures may be used as a guide to the foreclosure of the purchaser's interest under a conditional land sale contract, there will be no attempt in this chapter to cover in full the foreclosure of a conditional land sales contract.

2. [§9.13] Time Of The Essence

Most contracts for the sale of real property contain the clause: "Time is of the essence of this contract." Despite this, time normally is not of the essence of a land sale contract and the purchaser can obtain specific performance despite his delay in payments, compensating the seller in money for the damage caused by the delay. In any event, since the position of a prospective purchaser under a land sales contract is essentially that of a mortgagor under *F.S.* 697.01, until foreclosure he would have an equity of redemption conditioned upon his tender of the unpaid principal balance, interest and costs.

3. [§9.14] Acceleration

A common clause in the installment land sale contract is the provision that should the purchaser fail to make the payments as required or fail to keep any agreement under the contract, the seller at his option may "declare the whole unpaid principal balance of the purchase price with interest at once due and payable." Acceleration of future installment payments by the seller serves as the basis for an action for specific performance for the price or one for foreclosure in which the seller demands that the remaining purchase price be paid or, if not, that the purchaser's equities be foreclosed. Without acceleration, the amount ordered to be paid may be only the accrued installments and payment by the purchaser then merely rehabilitates his position under the contract. Since further dealings with a troublesome purchaser is not what the seller usually desires, this result should and can be avoided by his election to accelerate the debt.

4. [§9.15] Conveyance On Payment

The seller retains legal title in the conditional sales contract. Payment of the entire price (or payment of all but the last installment, depending upon the wording of the contract) is typically made an express condition precedent to the seller's obligation to convey title.

5. [§9.16] Forfeiture

The conditional land sales contract typically provides that in case of the purchaser's default, the seller at his option may seek foreclosure or may call the contract null and void, terminating all rights and interests of the purchaser. This is covered with a liquidated damages clause that provides that the seller may retain all payments as liquidated damages. But a provision terminating all rights and interests of the purchaser was held prohibited in *Mid-State Investment Corporation v. O'Steen,* 133 So.2d 455 (1st D.C.A. Fla. 1961), *cert. den.* 136 So.2d 349. The court asserted that the contract for deed was a mortgage subject to the rules of mortgage foreclosures, and upon default there was no automatic right in the seller to repossess the real property.

6. [§9.17] Repossession By Seller

The contract typically provides that the seller upon the purchaser's default may enter upon the land without process of law and take possession. This "self-help" is risky not only because it may involve a breach of the peace but also because it may be construed as a wrongful repudiation of the contract, entitling the purchaser to rescission and restitution, and likewise may be considered a wrongful conversion of the property. If the buyer does not assert his equity of redemption, however, it may be deemed waived by the court, which can then enter a judgment of cancellation. *Huguley v. Hall,* 157 So.2d 417 (Fla. 1963). Apart from the remedy of foreclosure, the seller may select from a variety of other remedies, including specific performance, rescission, an action at law for past due installments and forfeiture. Relying upon the most appropriate remedy, the lawyer must analyze (1) the facts and circumstances of the case; (2) the terms of the contract; (3) the solvency of the purchaser; (4) the ability to collect a money judgment; (5) changes of the market value of the land; and (6) the need to clear the record title of the purchaser's equity.

B. [§9.18] Specific Performance Of Land Sale Contract

Specific performance is an equitable remedy that may be available to the seller whether or not it is specifically mentioned in the contract. Although it also results in a money judgment for the unpaid balance of the contract, it is a remedy that is equitable in nature, the remedy of damages at law being inadequate. If the acceleration clause is exercised and full payment and conveyance are mutually dependent covenants, the seller's claim for money lies in the equitable proceedings. The technical reason is that historically only a court of equity could protect the purchaser by requiring that a deed be deposited in court or by conditioning payment upon the seller's conveyance. In such an action, the judgment unconditionally requires the purchaser to pay the balance of the contract price. Ability to enforce the judgment obviously is of practical importance.

RCP Form 1.941 is a form for a complaint for specific performance.

VI. ACTIONS BY REAL ESTATE BROKERS

A. [§9.19] In General

While not strictly a matter of real property litigation, an action by a real estate broker to recover commissions earned will stem from the breach of a sale contract. It may result from the breach of the seller or the buyer to conclude his obligation under a contract for the sale of real property. If the sale transaction has been closed, it may stem from failure of the person responsibile for the payment of brokerage commission to honor that responsibility. In any event, a real estate broker's action for his commission is closely related to contracts for the sale of real estate and for this reason it will be discussed in this chapter.

B. [§9.20] Causes Of Action Available

An attorney representing a real estate broker must ascertain from the facts recited by his client what cause of action or combination of causes of action is available to the broker. These might include an action against:

1. the person who has employed the broker and has agreed to pay his commission when (a) the transaction has not been consummated, due to the employer's fault, although the broker has found a purchaser ready, willing and able to buy or (b) the transaction has been consummated;

2. the buyer who has employed the broker and agreed to pay the commission when (a) the transaction has not been consummated, due to the fault of the employer, although the broker has produced a ready, willing and able seller or (b) the transaction has been consummated;

3. the seller who has employed the broker as the exclusive agent or granted the broker the exclusive right to sell the property, when the property has been sold;

4. the buyer who has agreed to make the purchase through the broker with the commission prepaid by the seller;

5. the buyer who by fraudulent representations induced the seller who employed the broker to breach the contract of employment; or

6. the buyer for conspiring to deprive the broker of the commission that would have been received but for the conspiracy.

C. The Complaint

1. [§9.21] In General

In drafting a complaint in a real estate brokerage action, consideration must be given not only to the causes of action available but to other significant matters, such as licensing, parties plaintiff and defendant, employment, compensation, performance, breach and damages.

An action for the commission against the person employing the broker is in personam and not in rem. The broker has no right to assert a lien against the property nor to file a lis pendens. *F.S.* 475.41 requires that a broker must allege and prove his licensing under the laws of the State of Florida, for it specifies that no contract for a commission "shall be valid" unless there has been compliance with the registration requirements of *F.S.* Chapter 475. The complaint must allege the precise nature of the specific employment involved in the given matter.

In addition to designating the proper defendant who employed the broker, the nature of the employment as alleged in the complaint must take into consideration whether such employment was:

a. by the owner or the prospect;

b. oral or written;

c. exclusive or general;

d. to procure a prospect on terms subject to negotiation or in terms specifically prescribed by the employer; or

e. restricted by written agreement conditioning the payment of commission on the consummation of the transaction.

It is essential when an agent is involved that the complaint be drawn properly to reflect (a) the liability of the person who employed the broker, (b) the authority of an agent acting on behalf of the employer and (c) the possible liability of the agent, even though acting for an undisclosed principal.

If the employer has acted through an agent, as in the case of a corporate employer, the complaint should specifically allege the relationship of the agent to the employer, *i.e.*, that the agent is an officer, stockholder or director of the employer. It also should specify the authority of the agent to act for the principal, *e.g.*, that the agent at all times mentioned was duly authorized to act for the principal and employ real estate brokers (including the plaintiff) to procure a purchaser for the property; to agree to the compensation of the broker; and to agree to the terms and conditions on which the property was to be sold.

Having duly alleged licensing, the relationship of the parties to the transaction, the employment of the broker and the agreement as to compensation, consideration next must be given to allegations of performance.

Because performance by the broker constitutes the consideration for his employment, allegations of performance are essential to a brokerage action. Unless the performance or excuse for nonperformance is alleged, the broker cannot be said to have fulfilled the basic condition of his contract. When a broker is employed to find a purchaser ready, willing and able to purchase, he need merely allege that he did so and need not allege completion of the transaction. If the broker is employed to procure a purchaser on specific non-negotiable terms designated by the employer, the complaint must allege procurement on those precise terms. Customarily, however, terms are given to the broker to induce and to obtain offers and in that case the complaint need allege only the procurement of a ready, willing and able buyer on terms and conditions agreeable between buyer and seller.

2. [§9.22] Sample Complaint

(Title of Court)

(Title of Cause)   **COMPLAINT**

      Plaintiff, ...(broker)..........., sues defendant, ...(employer).........., and alleges:

    1. This is an action for damages that exceed $..........

    2. At all times hereafter mentioned plaintiff was and still is a duly licensed real estate broker under the laws of the State of Florida.

    3. At all times hereafter mentioned defendant was and still is a domestic corporation duly organized and existing under the laws of the State of Florida.

4. At all times hereafter mentioned defendant was and still is the owner of a parcel of property described as:

[legal description]

5. At all times hereafter mentioned ....(name).......... was an officer, stockholder and director of defendant and was authorized to (a) act for and on behalf of defendant, (b) employ real estate brokers to procure a purchaser for the property and (c) agree to the terms and conditions upon which the property was to be sold.

6. On or about ....(date).......... defendant, acting by or through the duly authorized agent named above, employed plaintiff to procure a buyer for the property upon the terms and conditions set forth in a listing agreement, a copy being attached, or upon such other terms and conditions as might thereafter be agreed upon by defendant and the buyer to be procured by plaintiff.

7. Defendant agreed to pay to plaintiff the sum of $.......... as and for its commission.

8. Thereafter plaintiff procured a buyer, ..., ready, willing and able to purchase the property at a price and on terms and conditions satisfactory to defendant and defendant agreed to enter into a formal written contract of sale of the property to that buyer on those terms and conditions.

9. Defendant thereafter wrongfully and without justification failed and refused to enter into the formal written contract and failed and refused to sell the property to the buyer procured by plaintiff.

10. Plaintiff has duly performed all of the terms and conditions to be performed by plaintiff under plaintiff's agreement with defendant.

11. There is now due and owing from defendant to plaintiff the sum of $.......... with interest from ....(date).........., no part of which has been paid, although payment has been demanded.

WHEREFORE plaintiff demands judgment for damages against defendant.

Attorney

.................(address)..................

VII. [§9.23] CONCLUSION

While the avenues of relief available to the parties in a real property transaction have been well established by law and the forms of pleading requesting that relief increasingly simplified, the effective attorney must realize that the law in this area is not static. He will wish to think creatively both as to form and substance in representing his client in real property litigation.

WILLIAM L. STEWART*
ALAN T. DIMOND**

10

BREACHES OF CONSTRUCTION CONTRACTS AND CONSTRUCTION LOAN AGREEMENTS

I. [§10.1] INTRODUCTION

II. BREACH OF A CONSTRUCTION CONTRACT

    A. Remedies Available

        1. [§10.2] Remedies Of Owner Against The Contractor

        2. [§10.3] Remedies Of Contractor Against Owner Who Refuses To Pay

        3. [§10.4] Arbitration

    B. Action By Owner When Contractor Fails To Perform

        1. [§10.5] Investigation And Preparation

        2. [§10.6] Damages

        3. [§10.7] Conditions Precedent

        4. [§10.8] Penalty Provision

---

*LL.B., 1948, University of Florida. Mr. Stewart is a member of the Lee County and the American bar associations. He is a partner in the firm of Stewart, Stewart, Jackson & Keyes and practices in Fort Myers.

**J.D., 1968, George Washington University. Mr. Dimond is a member of the Dade County and the American bar associations and has been admitted to the practice of law in the State of Virginia and the District of Columbia. He is a partner in the firm of Greenberg, Traurig, Hoffman, Lipoff, Quentel & Wright and practices in Miami.

  5. [§10.9] Mitigation Of Damages

  6. [§10.10] Statute Of Limitations

  7. [§10.11] Sample Complaint

III. REMEDIES FOR BREACH OF CONSTRUCTION LOAN AGREEMENT

 A. [§10.12] In General

 B. [§10.13] Remedies For Breach By Borrower

 C. [§10.14] Remedies For Breach By Lender

I. [§10.1] INTRODUCTION

Remedies for breaches of construction contracts are treated separately from remedies for breaches of construction loans in this chapter. The former subject is treated in §§10.2–.11 and the latter, in §§10.12–.14.

Since the remedy of foreclosure of a mechanic's lien is treated in Chapter 6 of this manual, it will not be discussed in this chapter.

Another possible remedy relates to usury, which will be the subject of a future manual.

II. BREACH OF A CONSTRUCTION CONTRACT

A. Remedies Available

1. [§10.2] Remedies Of Owner Against The Contractor

In most cases the remedy for the builder's breach of a construction contract is an action for damages. When the facts are unusual so that a judgment for damages is inadequate, however, specific performance of the contract may be ordered. See *Connell v. Mittendorf*, 147 So.2d 169 (2d D.C.A. Fla. 1962). See §§10.5–.11 for a further discussion of the owner's remedies.

2. [§10.3] Remedies Of Contractor Against Owner Who Refuses To Pay

13 AM.JUR.2d *Building and Construction Contracts* §110 states:

> Upon the breach of a building or construction contract by the owner, the contractor has an election to pursue one of three remedies: (1) he may acquiesce in the breach, treat the contract as rescinded and recover upon quantum meruit so far as he has performed; (2) he may refuse to acquiesce in the breach, keep the contract alive for the benefit of both parties, being at all times ready and able to perform, and at the end of the time specified in the contract for performance sue under the contract; or (3) he may treat the breach or repudiation as terminating the contract and sue for the profits he would have realized if he had not been prevented from performing.

3. [§10.4] Arbitration

Many construction contracts contain a provision for compulsory arbitration. Unless waived, that provision is valid and binding. See *F.S.* Chapter 682 and *Mills v. Robert W. Gottfried, Inc.,* 272 So.2d 837 (4th D.C.A. Fla. 1973). If the contract does contain an arbitration provision, the issues must be settled by arbitration rather than by a court action. Once settled, the arbitration award can be made a rule of court.

B. Action By Owner When Contractor Fails To Perform

1. [§10.5] Investigation And Preparation

An action by the owner against the contractor invariably involves disputes regarding (1) performance by the contractor according to the requirements of the plans and specifications, (2) changes in the plans and specifications, (3) failure of the owner or his agent (an architect or engineer) to provide something upon which the contractor's performance depends or (4) time of completion. In any event, it is essential to determine what the plans and specifications called for, what changes have been agreed upon or are claimed to have been agreed upon and the specific failures of performance that are claimed by each party.

The investigation of the case cannot be stressed too strongly. It is the heart of this type of litigation. The help of a construction consultant or of the architect or engineer who prepared the plans and the architect or engineer who supervised the construction is invaluable. Written analysis of the defects or shortcomings should be made by the lawyer and reinforced by reports from the architect, the engineer and other witnesses.

2. [§10.6] Damages

After gathering the factual material on the various claims, the lawyer must determine the damages available on both sides. In the case of the owner, his usual measure of damages is "the difference between the contract price and the reasonable cost to the owner to complete the improvement in accordance with the contract." *Sea Ledge Properties, Inc. v. Dodge,* 283 So.2d 55 (4th D.C.A. Fla. 1973), *cert. dism.* 285 So.2d 618. To make this determination the lawyer needs the advice of architects, engineers and other contractors. After examining the plans and specifications and the work completed, they can submit plans to correct faulty construction or to complete the contract together with their estimates of the cost.

If the project has been completed but is not in substantial compliance with the specifications, the owner may wish to have demolition of the building and a rebuilding. The difference in value between the building as designed and as built may be a proper measure of damages.

Other items of damages in a completed structure because of improper construction may include additional maintenance costs. The building may have a lessened useful life. There also may be loss of income because of the improper construction.

3. [§10.7] Conditions Precedent

Before entering an action for breach of a construction contract, the contract must be examined for any conditions precedent to bring the action. This applies to an action either by the owner or the contractor. In the case of the owner, if there is a performance bond it is probable that the bond will require notice to the surety and an opportunity for the surety to correct the default or to finish the construction. A failure to supply that notice or opportunity may release the surety. In the case of the contractor, the contract may require an architect's certificate and the failure to have it may be a defense to the action.

4. [§10.8] Penalty Provision

The construction contract may contain provisions for liquidated damages for those elements that are difficult to estimate. *Hillsborough City Aviation A. v. Cone Bros. Contr. Co.,* 285 So.2d 619 (2d D.C.A. Fla. 1973). Those provisions will be enforceable unless the court determines that they constitute a penalty in addition to actual damages.

5. [§10.9] Mitigation Of Damages

If the contractor has failed to complete the construction, the owner has a duty to mitigate his damages. Unnecessary expenses are to be excluded from the damages. See *Bayshore Development Co. v. Bonfoey,* 75 Fla. 455, 78 So. 507 (1918).

6. [§10.10] Statute Of Limitations

Although the statutes cited below may be applied by the courts to disputes between owners and contractors, it is likely that *F.S.* 95.11(3)(c) is controlling whether the action is based on the contract or on negligence. That law produced by the 1974 legislature provides a four-year period that begins on the date the owner takes possession of the improvement or the date the contractor abandons the construction. Exceptions are provided for cases involving latent defects, products liability and fraud. 95.031(2) and .11(3)(c). In those cases the causes of action accrue when the defects or other facts giving rise to the cause of action are discovered or should be discovered.

An action on a written contract not under seal must be brought within five years of the time the cause of action accrues. *F.S.* 95.031 and .11(2)(b). It has been held that the cause of action accrues at the time the work is completed unless fraudulent concealment of the breach can be shown. *2765 South Bayshore Drive Corp. v. Fred Howland, Inc.,* 212 So.2d 911 (3d D.C.A. Fla. 1968).

If a negligence action is available, the limitations period is four years. *F.S.* 95.11(3)(a). Apparently, however, that cause of action accrues when the plaintiff discovers or should have discovered his right of action. *Smith v. Continental Insurance Company,* 326 So.2d 189 (2d D.C.A. Fla. 1976).

Appellate opinions will be required to resolve many questions as to which of the limitation provisions will apply as to the various types of cases. Obviously, however, the lawyer should make every effort to bring the action within four years of the date the construction is completed or abandoned.

7. [§10.11] Sample Complaint

(Title of Court)

(Title of Cause)   COMPLAINT

Plaintiff, John Owner, sues defendent, Sam Contractor, and alleges:

1. This is an action for damages that exceed $2,500.

2. On January 10, 1976 the plaintiff and defendant entered into a contract in which the defendant agreed to construct a residence for plaintiff. A copy of the contract and of the plans and specifications referred to in the contract are attached.

3. Although time was of the essence in the contract, the defendant failed to complete the work until June 1, 1976, 31 days after the date specified in the contract. The contract provided a liquidated damage of $100 per day for each day that completion was delayed beyond May 1, 1976.

4. The defendant breached the contract in the construction of the residence in the following particulars:

[set out the nonconformities with the plans and specifications]

5. Plaintiff has paid defendant the sum of $70,000 toward the contract price.

6. All conditions precedent to the bringing of this action have occurred.

WHEREFORE plaintiff demands damages from the defendant. Plaintiff demands trial by jury of all issues.

_____
Plaintiff

_____
Attorney

........(address and phone number)........

III. REMEDIES FOR BREACH OF CONSTRUCTION LOAN AGREEMENT

A. [§10.12] In General

In recent years many construction projects in Florida became embroiled in litigation as an outgrowth of the collapse of large parts of the real estate based economy. Many of these controversies revolved around the construction loan agreements that financed the projects. This section deals with litigation issues raised in that context.

As in the case of a breach of a construction contract (see §10.2) the usual remedy for breach of a construction loan agreement is an action for damages. Typically a construction loan agreement provides for periodic payments in accordance with a previously agreed upon construction budget. The breach may occur either by a lender's complete failure to fund, or by a lender's wrongful reduction of, or slow funding of, a periodic request for funding. The lender's breach may be wholly unrelated to the contractor's performance under his construction contract, but the breach, even if in the nature of a reduction of funding requests, may cause the contractor to be unable to meet his contractual commitments.

In Florida, uncertainty as to the cause of damages, as contrasted with the amount, will defeat recovery in an action for breach of contract. *Twyman v. Roell,* 123 Fla. 2, 166 So. 215 (1936). Essential to recovery is proof that damages are reasonably certain and not based solely upon speculation. *Asgrow-Kilgore Co. v. Mulford Hickerson Corp.,* 301 So.2d 441 (Fla. 1974). This is a difficult standard to meet in those cases in which slow funding is alleged.

Specific performance of a contract to lend money is rarely available. *Southampton Wholesale Food Terminal v. Providence Produce Warehouse Co.,* 129 F.Supp. 663 (D. Mass. 1955). The law presumes that money always is available in the money market, at the lawful rate of interest. 22 AM.JUR.2d *Damages* §68. Money damages, therefore, usually are appropriate to provide an adequate legal remedy. The presumption that money always is available may be rebutted with evidence to the contrary. It is irrelevant that the prospective borrower, because of its individual financial circumstances, was unable to procure an alternate loan. *Lowe v. Turpie,* 44 N.E. 25 (Ind. 1896). Nevertheless, some courts seem to be leaning toward specific performance as a more realistic remedy due to the difficulties of proving damages. *Vandeventer v. Dale Construction Company,* 534 P.2d 183 (Ore. 1975); *Selective Builders, Inc. v. Hudson City Savings Bank,* 349 A.2d 564 (N.J. 1975).

Moreover, Florida courts strictly construe a lender's obligation to fund as set forth in the construction loan agreement. Before commencing an action, the complete agreement must be read carefully as these agreements often provide escape provisions. *Sterritt v. Baher,* 333 So.2d 523 (1st D.C.A. Fla. 1976).

A general contractor's remedy may be to obtain an equitable lien against undisbursed construction loan funds. *Morgen-Oswood & Associates, Inc. of Florida v. Continental Mortgage Investors,* 323 So.2d 684 (4th D.C.A. Fla. 1976). An equitable lien, however, may not be imposed unless the court finds fraud, material misrepresentation or affirmative deception. *Merritt v. Unkefer,* 223 So.2d 723 (Fla. 1969); *Gancedo Lumber Company, Inc. v. Flagship First National Bank of Miami Beach,* 340 So.2d 486 (3d D.C.A. Fla. 1976); *J. G. Plumbing Service, Inc. v. Coastal Mortgage Company,* 329 So.2d 393 (2d D.C.A. Fla. 1976), *cert. dism.* 339 So.2d 1169; *Schraub v. Charest,* 277 So.2d 814 (3d D.C.A. Fla. 1973). See also *Marshall v. Scott,* 277 So.2d 546 (2d D.C.A. Fla. 1973); *Phillips Petroleum v. Schun Co.,* 222 So.2d 491 (4th D.C.A. Fla. 1969).

B. [§10.13] Remedies For Breach By Borrower

Most construction loan agreements are secured by mortgages on specific property — usually the property on which the improvement is to be constructed. Often the loan is further secured by personal guaranties, future rents and other assets. The traditional lender's remedy for a breach by the borrower is foreclosure. At times the lender may opt to sue on the guaranty rather than on the mortgage. Florida law allows the lender to bring a foreclosure action and then elect to recover any deficiency either in the form of a deficiency judgment in the foreclosure proceedings or in an action on the note. The lender may opt to sue on the note either by expressing his desire not to have the question of a deficiency considered in the foreclosure proceedings or merely by refraining from submitting the adjudication of that question to the court during the foreclosure proceedings. See *Coffrin v. Sayles,* 128 Fla. 622, 175 So. 236 (1937); *Coe-Mortimer Co. v. Dusendschon,* 113 Fla. 818, 152 So. 729 (1934). If the court declines to grant a deficiency judgment the lender may not then recover on the note. See *First Federal Savings and Loan Association of Broward County v. Consolidated Development Corporation,* 195 So.2d 856 (Fla. 1967).

Another type of a borrower's breach arises as a result of a construction cost overrun. Construction loan agreements often require the borrower to deposit with the lender funds necessary to complete construction that exceed the amount of the loan. The borrower's failure to make the required deposit may be a default under the mortgage and thus provide sufficient grounds for a foreclosure. The lender's other options include increasing the loan or, depending on the agreement, funding the cost overrun and thereafter seeking a judgment from the borrower for the extra amount funded.

Specific performance usually is not available to force a borrower to finish construction. See *Levene v. Enchanted Lake Homes, Inc.,* 115 So.2d 89 (3d D.C.A. Fla. 1959).

An action for damages may be maintained when the breach by the borrower is his failure to perform the construction work in accordance with the construction loan agreement. The measure of damages is the lender's additional cost caused by the necessity of obtaining a new contractor to complete the project. See *Sea Ledge Properties, Inc. v. Dodge,* 283 So.2d 55 (4th D.C.A. Fla. 1973), *cert. dism.* 285 So.2d 618.

This cause also may proceed along the lines suggested for a breach of a construction contract. See §§10.5–.11.

If the borrower fails to accept the loan after executing the loan documents the lender may have an action for damages. If the loan funds are not disbursed, however, the lender would be required to mitigate damages by attempting to lend money elsewhere. To the extent of its success, its damages would be limited to the difference in the rate of return on the loan. If a large institutional lender that constantly loans money is involved, it would be difficult to prove a failure to mitigate.

C. [§10.14] Remedies For Breach By Lender

If a lender fails to fund pursuant to a construction loan agreement, an action for breach of a contract to loan money may be commenced. The complaint should be similar to the sample complaint set forth in §10.11. But the available remedy, *i.e.,* the appropriate measure of damages, is different. Traditionally, only nominal damages may be recovered for breach of a contract to loan money. *Lowe v. Turpie,* 44 N.E. 25 (Ind. 1896). If the breach occurred at such a time as to deprive the borrower of the opportunity to procure the money elsewhere, however, more than nominal damages can be recovered.

In the absence of special circumstances reasonably within the contemplation of the parties when the contract was made, the measure of damages for breach of an agreement to loan money is the difference between the amount of interest that the borrower contracted to pay and what it was compelled to pay to procure the money. *Doddridge v. American Trust & Savings Bank,* 189 N.E. 165 (Ind. 1934); *Weissenberger v. Central Acceptance Corp.,* 28 N.E.2d 794 (Ohio App., 1940); *Bank of New Mexico v. Rico,* 429 P.2d 368 (N.M. 1967); 22 AM.JUR.2d *Damages* §68. In 22 AM.JUR.2d *Damages* §69, however, it is said:

> On breach of a contract to loan money where special circumstances were known to both parties from which it must have been apparent that special damages would be suffered from a failure to fulfill the obligation, such special damages as may appear to have been reasonably contemplated by the parties are recoverable. Thus, special damages may be recovered where the money is to be used for a particular purpose which is known at the time to the party agreeing to make the loan, provided, of course, that such damages are not speculative or remote. . . .

Often a breach of a construction loan agreement by either party is followed by a lender's foreclosure of the property that secured the construction loan. Since a lender is always entitled to credit for money loaned, whether by way of a judgment, credit or setoff, a borrower must prove its losses separately. *St. Paul at Chase Corp. v. Manufacturer's Life Ins. Co.*, 278 A.2d 12 (Md.App. 1971), *cert. den.* 404 U.S. 857.

There are several avenues to establishing a borrower's loss.

First, courts in other jurisdictions have held that the measure of damages in these cases is the difference between the value of the property at the date of loss and the amount of the liens and encumbrances upon it. Under those holdings, the borrower can recover only its equity in property that is lost as a result of breach of a contract to loan money. *St. Paul at Chase Corp. v. Manufactuer's Life Ins. Co., supra; Doushkess v. Burger Brewing Co.*, 47 N.Y.S. 312 (1897); *Hopewell Building Co. v. Callan*, 193 N.Y.S. 504 (1922); *F. B. Collins Inv. Co. v. Sallas*, 260 S.W. 261 (Tex. 1924). In this situation a borrower's equity is the difference between the market value of the property on the date it is lost and the amount of liens and encumbrances on it. *St. Paul at Chase Corp. v. Manufacturer's Life Ins. Co., supra; F. B. Collins Inv. Co. v. Sallas, supra.* The measure of loss in these cases clearly is not the purchase price of the land or total investment paid by the borrower. The thrust of the case law is against allowance of existing mortgage indebtedness as an element of damage.

A second measure of recovery is loss of anticipated profits. The general rule is that the profits are allowed only to the extent that the evidence affords a reasonable basis for estimating their amount with reasonable certainty. Moreover, profits that are remote, speculative, contingent or uncertain are not recoverable. *John W. Johnson, Inc. v. J. A. Jones Construction Co.*, 369 F.Supp. 484 (E.D. Va. 1973).

If a new business venture or evidence of enterprise is involved, evidence of past business records of other businesses is not admissible in fixing the measure of damages since a new business is a speculative venture. Likewise, projections of future profits, which depend on future bargains, the status of the market and other contingencies, will not provide evidence sufficient to avoid this safeguard imposed in fixing damages. *John W. Johnson, Inc. v. J. A. Jones Construction Co., supra.*

Finally, there may be a number of special circumstances known to both parties that may form an appropriate basis for recovery. For example, the lender may know that the money loaned was to be used by the borrower to pay a debt not related directly to the construction project. The known consequences or the failure to satisfy the unrelated debt may be visited upon the defaulting lender.

Today, with literally hundreds of construction projects stalled, the creative attorney may well provide the case law that will form the basis of the next modification of this chapter.

EDWARD A. LINNEY*
JAMES I. KNUDSON**

11

REMOVAL OF RESTRICTIVE COVENANTS

I. [§11.1] INTRODUCTION

II. PRELIMINARY CONSIDERATIONS

    A. Identifying The Restrictive Covenant

        1. [§11.2] In General

        2. [§11.3] Nature Of Restrictive Covenant

        3. [§11.4] Types Of Restrictive Covenants

        4. [§11.5] Personal Covenant Distinguished

        5. [§11.6] Easement Distinguished

        6. [§11.7] Fee Simple Determinable And Fee Simple Upon A Condition Subsequent Distinguished

    B. Determining If Restriction Is Applicable To Plaintiff's Land

        1. [§11.8] In General

---

*LL.B., 1949, Stetson University. Mr. Linney is a member of the St. Petersburg Bar Association. He is a sole practitioner in St. Petersburg.

†J.D., 1973, Tulane University. Mr. Knudson is a member of the American Bar Association. He is a sole practitioner in St. Petersburg.

        2. [§11.9] Constructive Notice And Implied Actual Notice

        3. [§11.10] Visual And Oral Notice

   C. [§11.11] Available Remedies

   D. Grounds For Removal

        1. [§11.12] Change Of Conditions

        2. [§11.13] Abandonment

        3. [§11.14] Ambiguity

        4. [§11.15] Contrary To Lawful Purpose, Public Policy, Statute Or Constitution

   E. Facts Insufficient To Justify Removal

        1. [§11.16] In General

        2. [§11.17] Zoning Changes

        3. [§11.18] Decrease In Value

        4. [§11.19] Release Of Retained Rights By Common Grantor Or Developer

        5. [§11.20] Release By Owner Of Parcels Subject To Restrictive Covenant

III. RELEASE OF COVENANT

   A. [§11.21] Release By All Parties Having Right To Enforce

   B. [§11.22] Reserved Right To Amend, Modify, Repeal Or Alter Restrictive Covenant

   C. [§11.23] Release By Less Than All Parties Possessing Right Of Enforcement

   D. [§11.24] Sample Release

IV. BEGINNING THE ACTION

   A. [§11.25] Jurisdiction And Venue

   B. Party Defendants

1. [§11.26] In General

2. [§11.27] When There Is No Plan Of Development

3. [§11.28] When There Is A Uniform Plan Of Development

4. [§11.29] Common Grantor

5. [§11.30] Defendants Revealed By Title Search

6. [§11.31] Use Of Class Actions

C. The Complaint

1. [§11.32] In General

2. [§11.33] Sample Allegations

3. [§11.34] Sample Complaint

D. [§11.35] Sample Allegations For Answer

E. Pretrial Proceedings

1. [§11.36] Pretrial Conference

2. [§11.37] Default Judgments

V. THE TRIAL

A. [§11.38] In General

B. [§11.39] View By Court

C. [§11.40] Visual Aids

D. Witnesses

1. [§11.41] Lay Witnesses

2. [§11.42] Expert Witnesses

VI. [§11.43] CHECKLIST

I. [§11.1] INTRODUCTION

This chapter treats the procedure for actions involving the removal of covenants running with the land, but is restricted to that category best described as "restrictive covenants." It includes some suggested forms for an affirmative action in quiet title to cause their removal. Suggested defenses also are included. Removal of restrictive covenants by means short of litigation (by waiver) is discussed and there is a brief discussion of those restrictions imposed by governmental authority as opposed to the actions of those privy to the title. A final checklist is proposed in §11.43.

It is not the purpose of this chapter to duplicate Chapter 12 of I FLORIDA REAL PROPERTY PRACTICE (CLE 2d ed. 1971), in which restrictive covenants are treated substantively.

II. PRELIMINARY CONSIDERATIONS

A. Identifying The Restrictive Covenant

1. [§11.2] In General

Because of the question of who are necessary parties in an action for removal of a restrictive covenant and the fact that certain restrictions on land have inherent forfeiture aspects, it is essential that the attorney be able to distinguish a restrictive covenant from other restrictions on land. He must be aware of the nature of the restrictive covenant and be familiar with at least some of the types of those covenants.

2. [§11.3] Nature Of Restrictive Covenant

In Florida, a restrictive covenant is a contractual right arising out of an agreement between a common grantor and one or more grantees by which the grantor imposes a common restriction on each grantee's ability to deal with his land by placing the restriction in a plat, declaration of restrictions, deed or some other written instrument that is duly recorded. It is a creature of equity, is often referred to as a negative easement or an equitable servitude and is enforceable by the successors in interest to the original parties when the restrictions are universal and reciprocal.

Although some jurisdictions treat restrictive covenants as servitudes or easements imposed on land, in Florida, as noted above, the theory is that they are contractual covenants created by the instrument in which they are embodied and that they can

> ... be enforced against both the promisor and those who take from him with notice, thereby including amongst those who may enforce the obligation not only the promisee, but those who take from him and those in the neighborhood who may be considered as beneficiaries of the contract.... *Osius v. Barton,* 109 Fla. 556, 147 So. 862 (1933), 88 A.L.R. 394.

Thus, if a restrictive covenant is imposed with intent to benefit persons other than the grantor, those persons may enforce the covenant as third party beneficiaries even though the covenant does not restrict their land, or restricts it in a different manner. A common example is a subdivision in which certain lots are restricted to residential use and others are restricted to commercial use. See *Vetzel v. Brown,* 86 So.2d 138 (Fla. 1956).

3. [§11.4] Types Of Restrictive Covenants

Generally, restrictive covenants are employed when land is being subdivided for sale by a common grantor-developer who desires to implement a uniform plan of development by imposing restrictions on the purposes for which the grantees' lots can be used or on the character of the buildings that can be erected on the subdivided lots. As long as they are for a lawful purpose, not contrary to public policy, and within reasonable bounds, *Moore v. Stevens,* 90 Fla. 879, 106 So. 901 (1925), 43 A.L.R. 1127, the types of restrictive covenants are restricted only by the imagination. Examples of modern legal ingenuity in this area are restrictions:

a. on who can provide essential services such as garbage collection to subdivision lot owners, *Sloane v. Dixie Gardens, Inc.,* 278 So.2d 309 (2d D.C.A. Fla. 1973);

b. requiring subdivision lot owners to pay yearly charges for maintenance of recreational facilities, *Henthorn v. Tri Par Land Development Corporation,* 221 So.2d 465 (2d D.C.A. Fla. 1969), *aff'd* on other grounds 241 So.2d 429; and

c. allowing only the developer to rent lots in a "trailer park condominium" to third parties, *Holiday Out In America At St. Lucie, Inc. v. Bowes*, 285 So.2d 63 (4th D.C.A. Fla. 1973).

4. [§11.5] Personal Covenant Distinguished

A restrictive covenant concerns the property conveyed and its occupation and enjoyment. It runs with the land because performance of the restrictive covenant touches and concerns the land. Further, it tends to either enhance the value of the property or render it more convenient and beneficial to the owner. In contrast, a personal covenant merely confers a benefit on the parties to the contract that does not pass to subsequent grantees. *Maule Industries v. Sheffield Steel Products*, 105 So.2d 798 (3d D.C.A. Fla. 1958), *cert. den.* 111 So.2d 41.

5. [§11.6] Easement Distinguished

An easement has been recognized by the Florida Supreme Court as being a privilege without profit that the owner of one tenement has the right to enjoy in or over the tenement of another. *Burdine v. Sewell*, 92 Fla. 375, 109 So. 648 (1926). It is a legal interest in land in contrast to a restrictive covenant, which, although sometimes called a negative easement, is a right arising out of contract. *Homer v. Dadeland Shopping Center, Inc.*, 229 So.2d 834 (Fla. 1970); *Board of Public Instruction v. Town of Bay Harbor Islands*, 81 So.2d 637 (Fla. 1955).

6. [§11.7] Fee Simple Determinable And
Fee Simple Upon A Condition
Subsequent Distinguished

A restrictive covenant is distinguished from a fee simple determinable and fee simple upon a condition subsequent in that the restrictive covenant does not provide for a form of reverter to the grantor or his successor in interest in the event of breach, either automatically as with a fee simple determinable or at the discretion of the grantor or his successor in interest as with a fee simple upon a condition subsequent. *Richardson v. Holman*, 160 Fla. 65, 33 So.2d 641 (1948). The difficulty arises when the grantor attempts to couple a reverter to an otherwise obvious restrictive covenant. The intent of the parties controls and the instrument containing the provision will be construed most favorably to the grantee to avoid the disfavored forfeiture. *Silver Springs, O. & G. R. Co. v. Van Ness*, 45 Fla. 559, 34

So. 884 (1903). Great care must be taken if the grantor has retained a form of reverter. Logically, the coupling of a reverter to a restriction would change the character of a restrictive covenant to a fee simple upon a condition subsequent, as was held in *Finchum v. Vogel,* 194 So.2d 49 (4th D.C.A. Fla. 1967). That the converse is also true is indicated by *Tolar v. Meyer,* 96 So.2d 554 (3d D.C.A. Fla. 1957), in which the common grantor waived his reverter right and the court treated the provision in question as a restrictive covenant. Because of the drastic difference in remedies upon breach (money damages or an injunction as contrasted to forfeiture), when the nature of the provision is not clear one seeking to avoid the constraining provision should bring an action in two counts; the first count should seek a declaratory judgment as to the nature of the provision and the second should seek removal, if the provision is determined by the court to be a restrictive covenant.

B. Determining If Restriction Is Applicable To Plaintiff's Land

1. [§11.8] In General

The party desiring not to be bound by a restrictive covenant must first determine whether the covenant actually is applicable to his land. Since he may not be bound by it if there is no record notice, he always should have a thorough title search on his parcel. See *Volunteer Security Co. v. Dowl,* 159 Fla. 767, 33 So.2d 150 (1948); *Hall v. Snavely,* 93 Fla. 664, 112 So. 551 (1927); but see *Silver Blue Lake Apts. v. Silver Blue Lake H. O. Ass'n,* 245 So.2d 609 (Fla. 1971) and *Hagan v. Sabal Palms, Inc.,* 186 So.2d 302 (2d D.C.A. Fla. 1966), *cert. den.* 192 So.2d 489, which indicate that actual non-record notice in certain circumstances may be sufficient for one's land to be subject to a restrictive covenant.

2. [§11.9] Constructive Notice And Implied Actual Notice

While the restrictive covenant need not be referred to in the deed of a grantee desiring removal for him to have notice, it must appear in his chain of title, in the subdivision plat or other instrument such as a subdivision declaration of restrictions evidencing a general plan of development. See *Batman v. Creighton,* 101 So.2d 587 (2d D.C.A. Fla. 1958), *cert. den.* 106 So.2d 199.

The owner has constructive notice of a restrictive covenant if it appears in such an instrument even though the instrument creating the restriction is not referred to in the current owner's deed. This constructive notice is in contrast to implied actual notice, which arises when the current owner's deed states that it is subject to restrictions of record or contained in a particular instrument. See *Tolar v. Meyer,* 96 So.2d 554 (3d D.C.A. Fla. 1957). Reference in a grantee's deed to a deed containing a restrictive covenant imposing a restriction on another subdivision lot, which therefore is not in the grantee's chain of title, may not give notice or otherwise affect the grantee's parcel, however. See *Mundy v. Carter,* 311 So.2d 773 (1st D.C.A. Fla. 1975).

3. [§11.10] Visual And Oral Notice

The rule in Florida has required some form of *record* notice for an owner to be bound by a restrictive covenant as noted in *Hall v. Snavely,* 93 Fla. 664, 112 So. 551 (1927). But the opinion in *Hagan v. Sabal Palms, Inc.,* 186 So.2d 302 (2d D.C.A. Fla. 1966), *cert. den.* 192 So.2d 489 suggests that the modern trend is to charge an owner with implied actual notice of unrecorded restrictive covenants not in his chain of title if he can observe a general plan of development resulting in uniform appearance of the area in which his lot is located, or if other owners have advised him of the existence of the restrictive covenant.

When the owner only has visual or oral notice of restrictive covenants not of record as to his parcel, it is suggested that he take great care because of the apparent conflict between *Hall* and *Hagan.*

C. [§11.11] Available Remedies

If the landowner finds that an objectionable covenant is applicable, he should consider the options available to him to be released from its limitations.

First, he should pursue obtaining a release from the restriction from the common grantor or developer and from all persons possessing the right to enforce the restriction. See §§11.21–.24. If this presents difficulties, he may seek relief through the courts. The following are the most common actions utilized to remove a restrictive covenant:

1. An action to quiet title under *F.S.* Chapter 65, which would remove the cloud on the title caused by the restrictive covenant.

2. A declaratory judgment action under *F.S.* Chapter 86 requesting that the restrictive covenant be declared null

and void and that all other subdivision lot owners be permanently enjoined from attempting to enforce it in the future.

3. If another subdivision lot owner has brought an action to enforce the restrictive covenant or to receive money damages at law for its breach, a counterclaim to quiet title or for declaratory judgment.

D. Grounds For Removal

1. [§11.12] Change Of Conditions

The most common ground for removal of a restrictive covenant is that the original purpose and intention of the original parties to the restrictive covenant have been frustrated and cannot reasonably be carried out without fault or neglect on the part of the landowner seeking removal because of material changes of condition in the neighborhood of the parcel sought to be relieved of the restrictive covenant. See *Barton v. Moline Properties,* 121 Fla. 683, 164 So. 551 (1935). The legal maxim allowing the removal is "lex no cogit ad impossibilia" and the legal theory justifying removal is the contract principal commonly described as discharge of contractual obligation by frustration of contractual object. *Osius v. Barton,* 109 Fla. 556, 147 So. 862 (1933), 88 A.L.R. 394.

Whether there has been a sufficient change of conditions to warrant nullification of a restrictive covenant is a question of fact to be determined by the trial judge on the basis of the peculiar circumstances of each given case. *Wilkes v. Kreutler,* 157 So.2d 194 (2d D.C.A. Fla. 1963). The trial judge is not limited to consideration of physical changes in the relevant neighborhood lands but, apparently, also can consider a decrease in the number of owners of parcels in the neighborhood who desire to have the restrictive covenant enforced. *Dade County v. Thompson,* 146 Fla. 66, 200 So. 212 (1941).

Inherent considerations in determining whether change of conditions has occurred are the time the restrictive covenant was placed on the land in relation to the date on which the party seeking removal obtained his title, and the time period the land in question has been subject to the restrictive covenant. Change occurring before the imposition of the restrictive covenant cannot be relied upon to warrant removal. See *Hall v. Briny Breezes Club,* 179 So.2d 128 (2d D.C.A. Fla. 1965). Similarly, courts have denied the relief of removal when the conditions changed subsequent to the imposition of the restrictive covenant and before the date the owner seeking removal obtained title to his land. *Allen v. Avondale Co.,* 135 Fla. 6, 185 So. 137 (1938); *Baker v. Field,* 163 So.2d 42 (2d D.C.A. Fla. 1964). The logic of these two cases is questionable. The focal point in the determination should be whether the intent of the original parties and their purpose in restricting the land have been frustrated by a change in conditions, not who owns the parcel sought to be relieved of the restriction at the time the action for removal is filed. Because of the thrust of these cases, however, it is wise for a purchaser desiring removal of the restriction to require the seller to institute an action for removal and obtain that relief before closing the transaction. If a restrictive covenant does not provide for its duration, the court will imply a reasonable period extending no longer than the intent and purpose can be reasonably carried out by the parties. *Barton v. Moline Properties, supra.*

2. [§11.13] Abandonment

If there have been such repeated breaches of a universal and reciprocal restrictive covenant as to constitute acquiescence and a waiver of its benefits, a court may hold that it has been abandoned by those who otherwise would have a right to enforce it. *Stephl v. Moore,* 94 Fla. 313, 114 So. 455 (1927). See also *Edgewater Beach Hotel Corporation v. Bishop,* 120 Fla. 623, 163 So. 214 (1935).

3. [§11.14] Ambiguity

When the terms of a restrictive covenant are ambiguous, the ambiguity is resolved against the party claiming the right to enforce the restrictive covenant. See *Moore v. Stevens,* 90 Fla. 879, 106 Fla. 901 (1925), 43 S.L.R. 1127. Failure to clearly set forth the intent of the parties imposing the alleged deed restriction indicates an intent that there be no such restriction. *Voight v. Harbour Heights Improvement Association,* 218 So.2d 803 (4th D.C.A. Fla. 1969).

4. [§11.15] Contrary To Lawful Purpose, Public Policy, Statute Or Constitution

To be enforceable, a restrictive covenant must have a lawful purpose and be within reasonable bounds. *Moore v. Stevens,* 90 Fla. 879, 106 So. 901 (1925), 43 A.L.R. 1127. If it is not lawful, it in effect can be removed.

A common ground alleged as a basis for removal has been that a restrictive covenant is void as constituting an unlawful restraint on alienation of real property, such as is proscribed by *F.S.* 689.18. If the restrictive covenant merely makes the property less desirable, however, it is not an unreasonable restraint on alienation. *Holiday Out In America At St. Lucie, Inc. v. Bowes,* 285 So.2d 63 (4th D.C.A. Fla. 1973).

Many pre-desegregation plats, declarations of restrictions and deeds contain restrictive covenants prohibiting the sale of lots in a subdivision to people of a particular race or creed. These covenants are not inherently void in the sense that they cannot be respected by the various lot owners between themselves. Nevertheless, a judgment attempting enforcement would be in violation of the privilege to own, use, occupy and dispose of property guaranteed to a citizen by the Fourteenth Amendment of The United States Constitution and would constitute state action in violation of the equal protection clause of that amendment. As a practical matter race restrictions can be ignored with impunity without the necessity of filing an action for removal. *Harris v. Sunset Islands Property Owners, Inc.,* 116 So.2d 622 (Fla. 1959); *Steuer v. Glevis,* 243 So.2d 453 (4th D.C.A. Fla. 1971); see *Shelley v. Kraemer,* 334 U.S. 1, 68 S.Ct. 836, 92 L.Ed. 1161 (1948).

Other restrictions might not be so clearly defined. The property owner who seeks to be relieved of its restriction should explore seeking a determination, perhaps by means of a declaratory judgment, of its legality.

E.   Facts Insufficient To Justify Removal

1. [§11.16]   In General

An understanding of the grounds and supporting facts that will justify removal of a restrictive covenant discussed above will result in an awareness of what facts are not sufficient to warrant removal. Again, it must be emphasized that the attorney must marshal all facts to preclude filing a lawsuit that in reality would be a futile and expensive act.

2. [§11.17]   Zoning Changes

The most common erroneous ground alleged for removal is that a governmental body has rezoned the petitioner's parcel to permit it to be used as the petitioner desires. Care must be taken not to make this mistaken assumption that a zoning ordinance controls when it conflicts with a restrictive covenant. The law in Florida is clear that the zoning or rezoning of real property in no way can abolish, abrogate or enlarge lawful, contractually created restrictive covenants. *Staninger v. Jacksonville Expressway Authority,* 182 So.2d 483 (1st D.C.A. Fla. 1966), 22 A.L.R.3d 950. A zoning change is merely a fact that can be admitted into evidence to be considered with all other evidence pointing to a change of conditions and is not conclusive in and of itself. *Wahrendorff v. Moore,* 93 So.2d 720 (Fla. 1957); see also *Roark v. Weldon,* 232 So.2d 216 (2d D.C.A. Fla. 1970). If there is a zoning change, however, the attorney should be sure to get that fact admitted into evidence and arrange for a zoning expert to testify regarding it.

3. [§11.18] Decrease In Value

The mere fact that a restrictive covenant makes a parcel less desirable for purchase does not constitute an illegal restraint on alienation, and is not a ground for removal.

4. [§11.19] Release Of Retained Rights By Common Grantor Or Developer

The mere fact that the common grantor-developer has released his right to enforce a restrictive covenant is not a sufficient ground to warrant removal unless the restriction was imposed for his sole benefit. He cannot bind or waive the right of enforcement held by other parties when restrictions have been imposed pursuant to a general plan of development. See *Tolar v. Meyer,* 96 So.2d 554 (3d D.C.A. Fla. 1957). This situation should be contrasted to the situation in which the common grantor reserves a right to amend, modify, repeal or alter a restrictive covenant, discussed in §11.22.

5. [§11.20] Release By Owner Of Parcels Subject To Restrictive Covenant

A release executed only by the owners of parcels subject to a particular restrictive covenant is a nullity and not a ground for removal. See *Gercas v. Davis,* 188 So.2d 9 (2d D.C.A. Fla. 1966); *Harwick v. Indian Creek Country Club,* 142 So.2d 128 (3d D.C.A. Fla. 1962).

III. RELEASE OF COVENANT

A. [§11.21] Release By All Parties Having Right To Enforce

Because restrictive covenants are contractual in nature, and not controlled by zoning, it is understandable that all parties having the right to enforce the restriction and who would be proper party defendants in an action for removal can abolish the covenant by executing a release document with all the formalities of a deed and recording it in the official public records of the county where the parcel is located.

The party desiring removal always should consider whether it is preferable to procure a voluntary release from all persons the title search on the subdivision parcels reveals have the right of enforcement before instituting an action for removal. The whole key to a voluntary relinquishment is that it must be joined by every person affected, just as the whole key to a successful quiet title action presupposes that everyone adversely affected is joined.

B. [§11.22] Reserved Right To Amend, Modify, Repeal Or Alter Restrictive Covenant

It is well settled that a common grantor-developer can reserve the right to alter, modify, repeal or amend restrictive covenants in his sole discretion without the consent of those grantees having the right of enforcement, and he can utilize that reservation to make the restrictive covenant either more or less restrictive. See *Johnson v. Three Bays Properties #2, Inc.,* 159 So.2d 924 (3d D.C.A. Fla. 1964), 4 A.L.R.3d 565. Such a clause is valid only as long as it is exercised in a reasonable manner that will not destroy the general scheme or plan of development. *Flamingo Ranch Estates, Inc. v. Sunshine Ranches Homeowners, Inc.,* 303 So.2d 665 (4th D.C.A. Fla. 1974). In *Flamingo,* there had been no breaches of the restrictive covenant or changes of condition, but in a fact situation in which there have been breaches and substantial changes it is logical for the common grantor-developer to exercise his reservation to abolish the general plan of development in order to clear the clouds on the title to the subdivision parcels.

C. [§11.23] Release By Less Than All Parties Possessing Right Of Enforcement

When the common grantor-developer has released all of his rights to enforce the restrictive covenant but has not specifically reserved a right to amend, modify, repeal or alter the covenant and exercised that right to remove the restriction, his release or waiver of enforcement rights has no effect on the right of enforcement possessed by others. See *Tolar v. Meyer,* 96 So.2d 554 (3d D.C.A. Fla. 1957). Likewise, a release executed by less than all of the property owners having the right to enforce the restrictive covenant is void and without effect. *Harwick v. Indian Creek Country Club,* 142 So.2d 128 (3d D.C.A. Fla. 1962). See also *Gercas v. Davis,* 188 So.2d 9 (2d D.C.A. Fla. 1966).

D.   [§11.24]   Sample Release

We, the undersigned, being the owners of all of the lots in all of the blocks of Black Acre Subdivision, as recorded in Plat Book 5, page 5 of the Public Records of Pinellas County, in consideration of the mutual benefits accruing to each of us, do nullify and remove the following restrictive covenant as it was originally set forth in the above-described plat as follows:

This subdivision is restricted to single family residences only.

WITNESSES

_____   _____

_____   _____

_____   _____

_____   _____

_____   _____

(Acknowledgements)

COMMENT: Two witnesses are required to every signature. Spouses should join in the execution to avoid the question of homestead, and each party must appear and acknowledge that the execution of the document was his free act and deed, all with the total formality of a deed.

IV.   BEGINNING THE ACTION

A.   [§11.25]   Jurisdiction And Venue

An action for removal of a restrictive covenant should be brought in the circuit court. See *F.S.* 26.012. The action may be brought in the county where the real property subject to the restrictive covenant is located or in which any defendant resides. 47.011 and 47.021. It is best brought in the county where the real property is located, however. It can be transferred to another county for the convenience of the parties if that county is one in which the action could have been filed. *F.S.* 47.122.

B.   Party Defendants

1. [§11.26]   In General

In bringing an action for removal of a restrictive covenant, it is essential that all beneficiaries of the covenant who would have standing to bring an action to enforce the restrictive covenant be joined as party defendants. Those not joined will not be bound by a final judgment removing the restrictive covenant. See *Tamiami Abstract And Title Company v. Malanka,* 185 So.2d 493 (2d D.C.A. Fla. 1966).

2. [§11.27]   When There Is No Plan Of Development

When there is no uniformity and reciprocity of restrictive covenants pursuant to a general plan of development and the restrictive covenant sought to be removed was imposed only for the benefit of the plaintiff's grantor and his successors in interest, only the grantor or his successor in interest need be joined as a defendant. See *Edgewater Beach Hotel Corporation v. Bishop,* 120 Fla. 623, 163 So. 214 (1935).

3. [§11.28]   When There Is A Uniform Plan of Development

If pursuant to a general plan of development the source of title subjects one parcel of land to a restrictive covenant with the intent to benefit one or more parcels constituting a portion of the original whole, all owners of the benefited parcels must be joined as defendants. See *Osius v. Barton,* 109 Fla. 556, 147 So. 862 (1933), 88 A.L.R. 394.

4. [§11.29]   Common Grantor

A good rule of thumb is to join the common grantor or his successor in interest in every case. If he retains no interest relating to the right to enforce the restrictive covenant he may allow a default to be entered against him or move to be dismissed as a party. If, however, through error, he is not joined but does hold a right relating to enforcement, a final judgment of removal will not bind him.

5. [§11.30] Defendants Revealed By Title Search

Although it may constitute a burdensome expense, it will be necessary at least to obtain an ownership and encumbrance report on the title to all parcels of land in the subdivision to ensure that the true owner of each parcel is joined as a party defendant.

Additionally, all co-tenants discovered by the title search must be joined as defendants, whether they derive their interest from a joint tenancy, tenancy by the entirety or a tenancy in common.

When the title search shows that real property is held in trust and it appears to be a naked trust, the trustee need only be joined as a party defendant, as he is deemed to have fee simple title. *F.S.* 689.07 and .071.

Often the title search will show that title is vested in a minor or other incompetent as defined in *F.S.* 744.102 or in a surviving spouse of homestead real property as a life tenant pursuant to 732.401, or in the holder of a life estate created otherwise. In the first situation, the incompetent's guardian of the property must be joined as a defendant. If there is no guardian, a guardian ad litem should be appointed to represent the incompetent's interest. See 744.102(2). Similarly, when the title search does not reveal the identity of certain owners, a guardian ad litem should be appointed and joined to represent their interest. If the owner of the lot in question holds a life estate, the life tenant and the vested remaindermen, if any, should be joined as defendants.

6. [§11.31] Use Of Class Actions

Because of the difficulty and expense in obtaining personal jurisdiction over all owners of lots who are benefited are numerous, a class action is a practical procedural tool to be employed by the plaintiff. Likewise, the class action is most useful when numerous owners desire to join as class plaintiffs for removal of a restrictive covenant. For a thorough discussion of a class action, see *Paulino v. Hardister,* 306 So.2d 125 (2d D.C.A. Fla. 1975), *cert. den.* 319 So.2d 30.

C. The Complaint

1. [§11.32] In General

Generally, a change of conditions is the basis for removal of a restrictive covenant. The most common vehicle is an action to quiet the cloud on the petitioner's title caused by the contractual right of enforcement held by other lot owners when universal and reciprocal restrictions were imposed by a common source of title. Other grounds, including those mentioned above, also may be present in a single case.

The attorney should assimilate all pertinent factual data, identify all breaches of the restriction and enumerate all changes of condition, and should thoroughly review his title search before filing the action for removal. After that review, an attempt should be made first to obtain voluntary release of the restrictive covenant as noted previously. To do otherwise is foolhardy.

If it appears that no release can be obtained, the alternative of course is to proceed with the filing of the complaint.

An action for removal of a restrictive covenant is one instance in which the so-called notice pleading of *RCP* 1.110 can be disregarded with emphasis being placed on pleading the elements of the cause of action specifically. Care must be taken not to plead facts that cannot be proved.

The complaint should set forth the ultimate facts justifying the removal of restrictions complained of and care should be taken not to allege facts not susceptible of practical proof.

2. [§11.33] Sample Allegations

    a.   At the time the restrictive covenant was placed of record, there was no intent by the parties to the instrument imposing it to effectuate a general plan of development.

    b.   At the time the restrictive covenant was placed of record, there was no intent by the parties to the instrument imposing it to benefit owners of neighboring parcels having the same source of title as the plaintiff.

    c.   The original source of title did not impose a universal and reciprocal scheme of restrictions on similarly situated parcels in the subdivision in which plaintiff's parcel is located, and therefore there exists no owner having the right in equity to enforce the restrictive covenant sought to be removed.

    d.   The restrictive covenant was placed on plaintiff's parcel for the sole benefit of the grantor imposing it and was personal to the grantor.

e. The restrictive covenant is so ambiguous as to preclude an accurate establishment of the intent of the parties imposing it and therefore is unenforceable.

f. The restrictive covenant is unenforceable because it was originally imposed for the following unlawful purposes: [list]

g. The restrictive covenant is unenforceable because it violates the following state (or federal) statutes: [list the statutes and the facts constituting the violation]

h. The restrictive covenant is unenforceable because it violates the following provisions of the Florida (or United States) Constitution: [list the particular provisions and the facts constituting the violation]

i. Alternatively, although originally created pursuant to a general plan of development established by the imposition of universal and reciprocal covenants, the right to enforce the restriction burdening plaintiff's parcel has been abandoned by the acquiescence of the other owners of subdivision parcels in the following-described breaches of reciprocal restrictions: [list the violations and the legal description of the parcels on which they occurred]

j. There has been such a change in the physical character and nature of the neighborhood in which plaintiff's parcel is located that the original intent of the parties imposing the restrictive covenant and the object and purpose of the restriction have been frustrated by the following-described changes:

(1) The following commercial establishments have commenced operation in the neighborhood:

(a) Restaurant on Lot 1, Block A

(b) Motel on Lots 8, 9 and 10, Block A

(c) [List all other commercial establishments in the immediate vicinity whether or not in plaintiff's subdivision]

(2) A large shopping center complex has been developed on lands contiguous to the south boundary of plaintiff's parcel.

(3) The following streets have been widened, altered or dedicated to permit the establishment of a commercially oriented traffic pattern to facilitate access to and from the commercial establishments in the immediate vicinity of plaintiff's parcel: [list the streets, describe the changes and specify the proximity of these streets to plaintiff's parcel]

(4) The city has rezoned plaintiff's parcel to permit commercial use.

(5) The county has designated the area in which plaintiff's parcel is located for commercial development on its officially adopted comprehensive land use plan.

(6) The city has grown from a small town of 700 population at the time the restrictive covenant was imposed to a city having a population of 90,000.

(7) As a consequence of the population change and the physical changes described above, plaintiff's parcel has been impressed with the nature of the commercial parcels in the neighborhood and is virtually useless for residential purposes.

(8) With the exception of the owner of Lot 15, Block A, the desire of all other subdivision lot owners regarding enforcement of the restrictive covenant has changed to such a degree that no other owners now desire enforcement.

k. As a consequence of the above-described changes, the original intent of the parties imposing the restrictive covenant has been thwarted, the original purpose of the restrictive covenant is incapable of being accomplished and enforcement of the restrictive covenant would have no effect other than to harass the defendant unreasonably, and the terms of the restrictive covenant have become so unreasonable as to result in oppression and inequity if given effect.

l. As a consequence of the changes, the restrictive covenant has no continuing benefit to the parties to the original instrument imposing it or to their successors in interest.

m. All of the changes occurred after the plaintiff acquired title to his parcel and without any fault of the plaintiff.

n. As a consequence of the changes and the resultant thwarting of the original purpose of the restrictive covenant, the restriction must be construed to have extended beyond a reasonable period of time in that continued enforcement will result in undue and inequitable prejudice to the plaintiff's property rights.

    o.   Plaintiff's parcel as restricted has little fair market or income value and is practically useless for residential purposes although heavily assessed for burdensome real property taxes because of its location in the vicinity of commercial property, but would have great fair market and potential income value as useful commercial property in the absence of the restrictive covenant.

    p.   Plaintiff can realize a due return on his parcel only if it can be used as commercial property rather than residential property.

    q.   To require plaintiff to continue to use his property solely for residential purposes would result in a practical confiscation of his property contrary to the best interest of the growth and prosperity of the city.

    r.   Neither the former nature, state or characteristics of plaintiff's parcel nor former value for residential purposes can be restored and its sole value and adaptability for use at the present time is determined by the uses of the property in the vicinity of plaintiff's parcel, which has been impressed with the commercial nature and character of the neighboring parcels.

    s.   The encroachment of commercial enterprises into the neighborhood where plaintiff's parcel is located has severely disturbed the former peaceful residential character of the neighborhood because of increased noises of sufficient decibels to violate the city's noise ordinance (No. 74-12).

    t.   The apparent right of other subdivision parcel owners to enforce the restrictive covenant constitutes an unreasonable and inequitable cloud upon plaintiff's title, which should be forever quieted by this court.

    3. [§11.34] Sample Complaint

COMMENT: Set forth below are suggested paragraphs for a complaint to quiet title, which in effect treats the restrictions complained of as a cloud on the plaintiff's title and for which he seeks relief by asking a court of equity to remove that cloud. Quieting title is the subject of Chapter 1 of this manual.

(Title of Court)

(Title of Cause)   COMPLAINT

    1. Plaintiff, A. B., sues defendants [set out names], and alleges:

    2. Plaintiff is the owner in fee simple absolute of Lot 1, Block 1, Black Acre as per the plat recorded with the Clerk of the Circuit Court, Pinellas County, Florida, in Plat Book 5, page 5.

COMMENT: Since this action is the nature of one to quiet title, the plaintiff must deraign his title for at least seven years. *F.S.* 65.061(3).

    3. Defendants are the owners of all of the remaining lots in all of the blocks of Black Acre Subdivision as shown by the schedule attached as plaintiff's Schedule "No. 1."

COMMENT: The schedule should show the names of the various respondents and, next to their names, the lot and block in Black Acre of which they are shown to be the record owners at the time of the filing of the complaint.

    4. Black Acre is a subdivision of the N. E. 1/4 of the N. E. 1/4 of Section 31, Township 30 South, Range 16 East, the plat thereof having been placed of record August 1, 1925.

    5. The restriction complained of is contained in a deed from John Jones to Black Acre, Inc., a Florida corporation, dated January 2, 1925 in the Public Records of Pinellas County, Florida, in Deed Book 100, page 200 and reads: "The lands herein conveyed are and hereafter shall be restricted to residential purposes only." The restriction was placed on the plat of Black Acre, Inc. A copy of the deed to Black Acre, Inc. and a copy of the plat are attached as plaintiff's Exhibits "A" and "B," respectively.

    6. In the year 1925, when the restriction complained of was first set forth, Black Acre Subdivision was surrounded on all sides by nonplatted acreage zoned for agricultural purposes only and not subject to any restrictive covenants of any kind.

    7. Attached as plaintiff's Exhibit "C" is an aerial photograph taken at an altitude of approximately 10,000 feet and at a scale of approximately one acre to the square inch, on which Black Acre Subdivision is outlined in blue.

8. In 1937 the lands immediately west of Black Acre Subdivision were platted into Allen's Industrial Park, outlined in red on Exhibit C.

9. A tract lying immediately west of Black Acre Subdivision was rezoned commercial by the City of St. Petersburg by ordinance adopted November 3, 1947 and now contains the Ajax Shopping Center complex. Those lands are outlined in green on Exhibit C.

10. The lands lying to the east and to the south of Black Acre Subdivision are presently zoned multi-family residential and are outlined in brown on Exhibit C, with the exception of two tracts of approximately one acre each, one on the east side and one on the south side, which have been zoned commercial and are outlined in purple.

11. Black Acre Subdivision has been subjected to numerous and various spot zoning changes and changes of condition over the years as follows:

A. Lot 3, Block 1, owned by defendant John Brown, has been rezoned from single family residential to light commercial by the City of St. Petersburg and is presently the site of John Brown's Hair Dressing Salon.

B. [Set forth similar allegations as to other spot zoning changes and changes of condition within the subdivision].

12. Plaintiff has caused his lot to be rezoned light commercial for the specific purpose of a small convenience store, but is advised that this use is prohibited by the restrictive covenant.

13. The changes in the character of the immediate neighborhood of Black Acre Subdivision and within Black Acre Subdivision, and in particular to plaintiff's lot, have utterly destroyed any continuing benefit to plaintiff and to those similarly situated in Black Acre Subdivision intended to be benefitted by the original restriction complained of and have clouded plaintiff's title.

WHEREFORE, plaintiff demands the quieting of the title to his land by the removal of the restriction complained of as it applies not only to plaintiff's lands but also as to all lands affected lying within Black Acre Subdivision.

Attorney

................(address)................

D. [§11.35] Sample Allegations For Answer

COMMENT: It necessarily follows that one or more of the defendants will take issue with the plaintiff's ultimate conclusions by asserting that there is a continued benefit to himself and to others similarly situated and that the restrictions should not be removed but remain in full force and effect. The pleading of ultimate facts to justify this position might include the following, which only are indicative of the broad scope of defenses that might be available to a defendant in a quiet title action of this nature:

1. Plaintiff purchased his lot on December 13, 1973 with full knowledge of the restriction complained of and with full knowledge of the character of the neighborhood as it existed then, and continues to exist.

2. Plaintiff's deed contained the restriction complained of, clearly indicating the intent of the parties as late as 1973.

3. The original deed to Black Acre, Inc. and the original plat of Black Acre Subdivision gave constructive notice to plaintiff of the existence of the restriction, and the restatement of the restriction in the deed gave both constructive and actual notice to plaintiff of the existence of the restriction.

4. The spot zoning and changes of condition alleged by plaintiff constitute less than two per cent of the total lands lying within Black Acre Subdivision.

5. The shopping center and the industrial park complained of by plaintiff are separated from Black Acre not only by a primary road but by a bumper strip not less than 60 feet in width, and by a 50-foot private access road, all of which is well landscaped. As can be ascertained by reference to plaintiff's Exhibit C, the uses complained of by plaintiff are well screened from Black Acre Subdivision.

6. None of the spot zoning and changes of condition complained of by plaintiff took place after his acquisition of his lot.

7. The men's hairdressing salon complained of by plaintiff is operated in the owner's home with no outside evidence of the use to which the property has been put, in compliance with a prohibition by the City of St. Petersburg.

8. Defendant is advised and earnestly believes, and therefore alleges, that plaintiff has entered into a contract for the sale of his property that is contingent upon the removal of the restriction, and if the relief sought by plaintiff is granted, only plaintiff's pocketbook will be directly affected.

9. Defendant has expended large sums of money in constructing his residence, where he intends to spend his remaining years, and defendant would be adversely affected by any further change in the character of the neighborhood such as contemplated by plaintiff.

E.   Pretrial Proceedings

1. [§11.36] Pretrial Conference

At the pretrial conference there should be a determination of what facts and issues of law are not in dispute. If possible, the plaintiff's attorney should have all charts, maps, photographs and other visual aids he will use to paint a picture of change in the neighborhood of the plaintiff's parcel, so that they can be identified and their admissibility into evidence can be stipulated or otherwise resolved. As noted in §11.39, a view by the court perhaps also should be requested.

2. [§11.37] Default Judgments

The plaintiff always should take a default judgment against all defendants not filing a responsive pleading. In addition to obvious advantages, the obtaining of a number of defaults would be an indication that numerous parcel owners do not desire to have the restriction enforced.

V.   THE TRIAL

A.   [§11.38] In General

An action to remove a restrictive covenant is always cognizable in equity and therefore will not be tried by a jury. The goal is to present a chronology of events and changes in the neighborhood. The attorney should begin by presenting a clear picture of the circumstances existing at the time the restrictive covenant was imposed. Next, he should present each change occurring in the neighborhood in the sequence it occurred to show that all the changes ultimately merged in effect to frustrate the original intent of the parties to the instrument imposing the restriction and to frustrate as well the purpose of the restriction. Finally, the current nature and character of the neighborhood should be presented in detail to enable the court to visualize the degree of change occurring over the years.

The trial brief of course should clearly re-acquaint the court with the degree of change necessary for the court to order removal of the restrictive covenant and be consistent with and supported by the testimony of the witnesses.

B. [§11.39] View By Court

Unless the visual aids and the witnesses' testimony will clearly show the dramatic change in the neighborhood, it is wise to request a view by the court at the pretrial conference or at the beginning of the trial. See *RCP* 1.520. Although the granting of the request is discretionary, because the focal point in the trial is the readily observable physical changes, the court normally will desire to take a view. When the court can resolve a dispute in testimony by taking a view but refuses, the party requesting the view, if the judgment is adverse to him, should assign that refusal as error, alleging abuse of discretion. See *Stanley v. Powers,* 125 Fla. 322, 169 So. 861 (1936).

C. [§11.40] Visual Aids

Each party should make substantial utilization of visual aids to buttress the testimony of his witnesses. The attorney should ensure that copies of plats and other recorded documents sought to be admitted into evidence are duly certified and that the individual taking photographs sought to be admitted is present to testify if the other party will not stipulate to their admissibility. Naturally, the proper and effective utilization of photographs and other visual aids may obviate the necessity for a view by the court, as observed above.

Examples of visual aids that might be used are:

1. Plats

2. Charts

3. Zoning and other maps

4. Comprehensive land use plans

5. Aerial photographs

6. Terrestrial photographs, both before and after

7. Survey

D. Witnesses

1. [§11.41] Lay Witnesses

The most valuable lay witness is the long-time resident of the neighborhood in which the alleged changes have occurred. If none are available, the attorney should attempt to locate persons who resided in the neighborhood during various periods to testify to specific changes occurring during their residency.

2. [§11.42] Expert Witnesses

The trial of an action for removal of a restrictive covenant is one in which great use can be made of real property and population experts who are familiar with the neighborhood where the restricted parcel is located. They can testify concerning the changes in the neighborhood's nature and conditions and comment on the effect of those changes on the uses for which the parcel is suited.

Examples of expert witnesses one might use are:

1. Real estate appraisers

2. Realtors

3. Land use planners

4. Subdivision and commercial developers

5. Zoning experts

6. Engineer-surveyors

7. Demographers

VI. [§11.43] CHECKLIST

1. Does the party seeking removal have record notice of the restrictive covenant, either constructive, actual or implied notice?

2. Did the common grantor-developer reserve the right to amend, modify, repeal or otherwise alter the restrictive covenant, and if so, will he exercise it in favor of the party seeking removal?

3. Will the common-developer or his successor in interest and all subdivision parcel owners having the right of enforcement execute a release of the restrictive covenant?

4. Does the complaint allege the basic elements of a quiet title or declaratory judgment action?

5. Has the complaint been filed in the proper court and proper venue?

6. Has the plaintiff, by means of a title search or otherwise, learned of and properly joined all persons having an apparent right to enforce the restrictive covenant?

7. Has personal jurisdiction been obtained over all defendants?

8. Is service of process by publication necessary?

9. Has a guardian ad litem been appointed for all unrepresented minors and other incompetents and unknown persons?

10. Have all joint tenants, tenants in common and tenants by the entirety, and spouses, been joined as defendants?

11. Has the court file been reviewed to ensure that all defendants were properly served?

12. Does the complaint have a legal description of the parcel in question and is it accurate?

13. Did the plaintiff deraign his title for at least seven years (quiet title action only)?

14. Does the complaint allege all grounds justifying removal?

15. Does the complaint specifically plead all facts in support of each ground for removal?

16. Has a default judgment been taken against all defendants failing to prepare a responsive pleading?

17. Have the necessary lay witnesses and expert witnesses been contacted and engaged, respectively?

18. Have all exhibits been procured and prepared?

19. Were exhibits marked for identification and questions regarding their admissibility settled at the pretrial conference?

20. Has the trial brief been prepared?

21. Has a sequence of witnesses been established so that a chronology of change is presented?

22. Is a view necessary and, if so, has it been requested?

23. Have opening and closing statements been prepared?

24. Does the restrictive covenant violate any state or federal statutes or constitutional provisions?

25. Does the restrictive covenant have a lawful purpose?

A. GORDON PATTON*

12

ACCESS TO PROPERTY BY NONOWNER

I. INTRODUCTION

    A. [§12.1] In General

    B. [§12.2] Basic Concepts

    C. [§12.3] Florida Historical Background

II. ACCESS TO PROPERTY BASED ON POLICE POWER

    A. [§12.4] Public Rights In Private Property

    B. [§12.5] Remedies For Excesses In Use Of Public Power

III. ACCESS TO PROPERTY BASED ON PRIVATE RIGHTS

    A. [§12.6] In General

    B. [§12.7] Right Of Eminent Domain

    C. [§12.8] Mineral Rights

    D. [§12.9] Surveyors' Right Of Entry

    E. Rights-Of-Way

        1. [§12.10] In General

        2. [§12.11] Sample Complaint To Establish Common-Law Way Of Necessity

---

*J.D., 1950; LL.M., 1954, George Washington University. Mr. Patton is a consultant to corporations on legal management matters and also has been admitted to the practice of law in the District of Columbia. He resides in Tallahassee.

I. INTRODUCTION

A. [§12.1] In General

This chapter is concerned with rights of strangers and governmental agencies to one's real property, which rights are not based on specific written documentation or other agreements between the parties involved. In essence these rights are not based on deeds, mortgages, express contracts, written easements, leases or other formal methods of granting certain rights in real property to others. It also is not concerned with trespass, business guests and invitees, condemnation, landlord and tenant relationships or aircraft overflight. Instead, it addresses itself to a growing body of law relating to the public or governmental rights in private property, and private rights of strangers in real property owned by private citizens.

B. [§12.2] Basic Concepts

When a person "owns" a parcel of real property he instinctively believes that he is possessed of all rights and privileges of which the property is capable and to the extent that a free society permits a person to enjoy it. Most owners would like to regard their rights in property to be purely allodial. Law school students early learn, however, that an owner's title to real property consists of no more than a "bundle of sticks" or "privileges." The extent to which an owner may exercise his privileges is based on the political tone of the times. BALLENTINE'S LAW DICTIONARY (3d ed.) defines allodial as:

> The tenure of an estate by an owner in fee simple under the state as sovereign, as opposed to feudal tenure. The dominion is absolute and direct, subject only to escheat in the event of failure of successors in ownership. Allodial tenure is characteristic of the ownership of land in the United States. 28 AM.JUR.2d *Estates* §4.

The above definition might have been reasonably accurate at one stage of the political development of this country, but as a society progresses toward a socialistic state the government takes away from the owner more of his privileges. It also should be kept in mind that the sovereign always reserves at least three sticks out of the bundle, *i.e.*, the power to tax, to police and to condemn.

Although the law of real property generally gives to the owner its free use and the owner's rights are under the police powers of the state, land, having physical limitations and generally being incapable of increase (except through accretion and certain reclamation work involving dredging and filling) cannot be regarded as the perpetual subject of sole and exclusive appropriation to the owner.

For the most part, however, private property historically has been regarded as a monopoly. This is a waning doctrine in modern society. In the complexities of today's real world, individual rights are yielding increasingly to the alleged best interests of society. As changes in political thinking tend to increase the importance of the state over the individual, so are the restrictions on the use of his property tightened. Zoning is an example of how the interests of the sovereign people transcend private rights.

The principle has been stated that:

> Property in land must be considered, for many purposes, not as an absolute, unrestricted dominion, but an aggregation of qualified privileges, the limits of which are prescribed by the equality of rights and the correlation of rights and obligations necessary for the highest enjoyment of land by the entire community of proprietors. *Thompson v. Andros-coggin River Imp. Co.,* 54 N.H. 545 (1874).

C. [§12.3] Florida Historical Background

Upon discovery of the American continent the principle was asserted or acknowledged by all European nations that discovery followed by actual possession gave title to the government by whose subjects or by whose authority it was made, not only against other European governments, but against the native Indians themselves. While the different nations of Europe respected the rights of the natives as occupants, they all asserted the ultimate dominion and title to be in themselves.

Upon the cession of the Floridas to the United States by Spain, which became effective in July 1821, the lands within the territory of East and West Florida became subject to the laws of the United States. *Apalachicola Land & Development Co. v. McRae,* 86 Fla. 393, 98 So. 505 (1923), citing *State ex rel. Ellis v. Gerbing,* 56 Fla. 603, 47 So. 353 (1908).

In *Waller v. First Savings & Trust Co.*, 103 Fla. 1025, 138 So. 780 (1931) the Florida Supreme Court referred to §87, Comp. Gen. Laws, §71, Rev. Gen. St., which declared the common law of England to be in force in Florida, in the absence of contrary statutes expressly excepting from that adoption of the common law any rule of the old English common law that is inconsistent with the constitution and laws of Florida. See *F.S.* 2.01.

Carrying the philosophical discussion to its current logic, in *City of Miami Beach v. Ocean & Inland Co.*, 147 Fla. 480, 3 So.2d 364 (1941) the Supreme Court stated:

> [I]t is fundamental that one may not be deprived of his property without due process of law, but he may be restricted in the use thereof when such is necessary in the common good. In order not to constitute a deprivation of property without due process of law, restrictions upon the use of property must be predicated upon the safety, health, morals or general welfare of the community.

II. ACCESS TO PROPERTY BASED ON POLICE POWER

A. [§12.4] Public Rights In Private Property

This section discusses public rights in private property, or what generally is referred to as the police powers of the sovereign. The police power of the State of Florida is not absolute. It is subject to limitations imposed by the Constitution of the United States and the Constitution of Florida. *Whitaker v. Parsons,* 80 Fla. 352, 86 So. 247 (1920). Police regulations must be reasonable, not arbitrary or oppressive, and the means used to effect the purpose of the police power must be appropriate to the end in view. *Hill v. State ex rel. Watson,* 155 Fla. 245, 19 So.2d 857 (1944), *reversed* 325 U.S. 538.

The exercise of the police power is confined to those acts that have reference to the protection of the public safety, welfare, morals or health and any exercise of this power not so confined is an abuse of it. *Hill v. State ex rel. Watson, supra.*

To justify the exercise of the police power to the detriment of an individual or class, it must be clear that the purpose to be served is not merely desirable but one that will so benefit the public as to justify interference with or destruction of private rights. The police power may be used only against those individual rights that are reasonably related to the accomplishment of the desired end serving the public interest. *L. Maxcy, Inc. v. Mayo,* 103 Fla. 552, 139 So. 121 (1932). See also CONSTITUTIONAL LITIGATION IN FLORIDA §§1.4 and .5 (CLE 1973).

The following are examples by which police powers of the state have been validly exercised in granting public officials access to private property:

1. The tax assessor by *F.S.* 193.023(2) is required to inspect physically all real property in his county every three years.

2. If a peace officer fails to gain admittance after he has announced his authority and purpose in order to make an arrest, either by a warrant or when authorized to make an arrest for a felony without a warrant, he may use all necessary and reasonable force to enter any building or property where the person to be arrested is or is reasonably believed to be. *F.S.* 901.19(1); *Benefield v. State,* 160 So.2d 706 (Fla. 1964).

3. The state fire marshal and his agents, when they deem it necessary, may inspect at any reasonable hour any building, equipment and vehicular equipment on the premises within their jurisdiction. If it is found that any building or structure is in the need of repair, or lacks sufficient fire escapes or alarm apparatus, they may order it removed or remedied within a reasonable length of time. *F.S.* 633.081.

4. City ordinances and state statutes of other jurisdictions often require persons engaged in certain businesses to maintain their premises according to minimum standards in order to promote public health requirements. They also require that private properties be maintained in a minimum safe condition to protect both occupants and the public in general. Periodic inspections often are authorized for the enforcement of these legal requirements. Some examples follow:

    a. In *Frank v. Maryland,* 359 U.S. 360, 79 S.Ct. 804, 3 L.Ed.2d 877 (1959), *reh. den.* 360 U.S. 914, Frank had been arrested and prosecuted for refusing to permit health inspectors to enter his home after a complaint had been received that the building was rat-infested. A majority of the United States Supreme Court held that the ordinance in question was a limited and reasonable public health measure. The court did not worry over possible Fourth Amendment considerations as entry was not being sought to obtain evidence for use in a criminal matter. Moreover, demand for entry could not be made unless there were grounds to suspect a nuisance existed and the inspection had to be made during daylight hours. The inspector had no power under the ordinance to force his way into the premises. Thus, a fine could be imposed by the court for refusal by the owner to permit the entry for inspection.

    b.   A conviction for refusal to permit a plumbing inspector to enter the petitioner's home also was affirmed by an equally divided court in *Ohio ex rel. Eaton v. Price,* 364 U.S. 263, 80 S.Ct. 1463, 4 L.Ed.2d 1708 (1960), *reh. den.* 369 U.S. 855. The maximum penalty was a $200 fine, 300 days in jail or both.

    c.   At this writing no general Florida statute covers this type of situation, but presumably legislation could be drafted to satisfy the *Frank v. Maryland* test.

    d.   The Attorney General of Florida in a recent opinion (074-292, 23 September 1974) stated that the governing body of the City of Tamarac could not validly provide for the warrantless entry upon and inspection of private buildings and construction projects within that municipality for the purpose of investigating the city's building department or to ensure proper conduct of the city's building inspectors and officials in the enforcement of the South Florida Building Code as statutorily incorporated into Chapter 71-575, FLA. LAWS, and made applicable to all municipalities and unincorporated areas of Broward County, Florida.

5.   By *F.S.* 581.152 the Department of Agriculture and Consumer Services is authorized to destroy citrus trees

under certain circumstances and to fumigate the soil. Any grove owner objecting to the destruction of his trees, infested or otherwise, before any further action on the part of the department nevertheless has the right to judicial declaration as to the validity of any rule or order requiring that destruction by bringing an action for a declaratory judgment. Moreover, the law provides a method to ensure the owner obtains reasonable compensation based on fair market value before destruction of the trees.

B. [§12.5] Remedies For Excesses In Use Of Public Power

The preceeding text included some examples of how the police powers of the state can be exercised in furtherance of legitimate public policies relating to the safety, health, morals or general welfare of the community. For the most part application of these principles creates few legal problems unless the official or other agent concerned exercises improper conduct in executing his duties. Generally, the remedy for the property owner for these excesses would be administrative in nature by complaint to the senior official or department head, or perhaps even to the governor. If a crime were committed the remedy would be by complaint to law enforcement personnel or to the state attorney's office.

III. ACCESS TO PROPERTY BASED ON PRIVATE RIGHTS

A. [§12.6] In General

Problems of considerably more legal import than those mentioned above are those rights by private persons, or third parties, based either on the common law or as the law has been codified either in the Florida Constitution or the statutes. In the following sections are examples illustrating how these rights are manifested. It is specifically pointed out, however, that some of the examples cited are intended to be provocative and the alleged rights stated could vanish if held to certain constitutional tests.

B. [§12.7] Right Of Eminent Domain

Article X, §6 of the Constitution of the State of Florida relates to eminent domain. Subparagraph (b) states, "Provision may be made by law for the taking of easements by like proceedings, for the drainage of the land of one person on or through the land of another."

This subparagraph raises interesting questions. In a leading Florida case involving the previous Florida Constitution, *Wilton v. St. Johns County,* 98 Fla. 26, 123 So. 527 (1929), 65 A.L.R. 488, the court noted that in some jurisdictions there has been some conflict of opinions as to whether statutes that provide for compulsory drainage of comparatively small tracts of land, when the owners are few in number and a majority of them desire the drainage while a minority object, can be upheld either as a valid exercise of the police power or as an appropriate use of the power of eminent domain. The court stated that the trend of opinion appeared to be toward the position that private property cannot be taken and permanently devoted to a particular use, against the will of the owner, except by the exercise of the power of eminent domain, which makes it essential that the taking be for a public purpose.

The court referred to §28 of Article XVI of the then Florida Constitution, which stated: "The legislature may provide for the drainage of the land of one person on or through that of another, upon just compensation therefor to the owner of the land on which such drainage is had."

Although the court considered that this provision of the constitution had no bearing on the issues of the case, it did state that:

> . . . It is not necessary for us to discuss the rather interesting question whether legislative measures to carry this section of the constitution into effect could be validly framed under the police powers or the power of eminent domain in such a way as would avoid conflict with the Federal Constitution. . . .

The court also stated that the legislature, under the guise of the exercise of the vast public and sovereign power of eminent domain, which can be executed only for a public purpose, cannot take without his consent one citizen's property and give it to another for his mere private use, even though compensation is paid. To do so would come in conflict with the Fourteenth Amendment to the United States Constitution as a deprivation of property without due process of law.

In *Childs v. Dougherty,* 73 Fla. 72, 75 So. 783 (1917), the court early decided that if an assertion by county commissioners of the right of eminent domain is admitted or proved to be in fact for a private rather than a county purpose, there is no right to exercise the authority, and the action taken may be enjoined in appropriate proceedings by a proper complainant.

It thus appears that not only would legislation on this subject fly in the face of the Fourteenth Amendment, but the provision in the Florida Constitution also would be defective. It should be noted that the present provisions in the Florida Constitution on this subject do not mention "just compensation."

C. [§12.8] Mineral Rights

In *P & N Investment Corp. v. Florida Ranchettes, Inc.,* 220 So.2d 451 (1st D.C.A. Fla. 1969) the court in discussing rights of parties involving minerals in real property stated that it was convinced that the weight of authority in the United States is as follows:

> . . . When the surface estate is severed from the mineral estate, the mineral estate is the dominant estate and, therefore, the owner of the mineral estate has the right of ingress and egress to explore for, locate, and remove the minerals, but he cannot so [*sic*] abuse the surface estate so as unreasonably to injure or destroy its value and is answerable in damages to the owner of the surface estate for any unreasonable injuries done.

Noting that the law provides for damages in the above situation, the reader should compare *F.S.* 715.06, "Real Estate; exploration for minerals," which states:

> Where title to the surface of real property and title to the subsurface and minerals on or under such real property is divided into different ownerships, then the surface owner and his heirs, successors and assigns shall be entitled to explore, drill and prospect such real property, including the subsurface thereof, for all minerals except oil, gas and sulphur without being liable to the owners of the minerals, or any party or parties claiming under such owners, for any damages or for the value of such minerals, as it is usual by customary prospecting methods and procedures to take from such land for the purpose of analyzing and determining the kind and extent thereof.

Although there are no reported cases on interpretation of the above-cited statute, it is not unlikely that under certain circumstances it could be held unconstitutional under Article I, §9 of the Constitution of the State of Florida, as well as under the Fourteenth Amendment of the United States Constitution.

D. [§12.9] Surveyors' Right Of Entry

F.S. 472.14 states that:

> Registered engineers and registered land surveyors be and they are hereby granted permission and authority to go on, over and upon the lands of others when necessary so to do to make land surveys, and in so doing to carry with them their agents, servants and employees necessary for that purpose, and that such entry under the right hereby granted shall not constitute trespass, and that such registered engineers and registered land surveyors shall not nor shall their agents, servants or employees so entering under the right hereby granted be liable to arrest or a civil action by reason of such entry; provided, however, that nothing in this section shall be construed as giving the said registered engineers, registered land surveyors, their agents, servants or employees any right to destroy, injure, damage or move anything on said lands of another without the written permission of the landowner.

In *Ragland v. Clarson,* 259 So.2d 757 (1st D.C.A. Fla. 1972) the court stated that the statute is clear and unequivocal and grants a license to a surveyor or his agents to enter upon a landowner's property without his permission and without fear of criminal prosecution for trespass. The court said it does not permit him to "break and enter," that is, to remove barricades for the convenience of driving vehicles on the landowner's property, and does not permit him to "destroy, injure, damage, or move anything without the written permission of the landowner." The court also said if a surveyor has to cut growing plants in order to run a line, he must procure the written permission of the landowner, or in the alternative be prepared to respond in damages; to construe the statute otherwise might well activate the constitutional guarantee that a citizen shall not be deprived of his property without due process of law.

The full impact of this statute obviously has not been determined and it is conceivable that circumstances could arise that would place it in conflict with the Fourteenth Amendment to the United States Constitution, as well as Article I, §9 of the Florida Constitution. It may well be that this statute is not a valid exercise of the police power of the state and would fall lacking other constitutional support.

E. Rights-Of-Way

1. [§12.10] In General

A problem of early historical origin and of continuing legal significance today relates to rights-of-way.

Right-of-way is incorporeal property, a thing that cannot be apprehended by the material senses, but is a legal right merely as a chose in action. It is:

> . . . a legal right which one man has, not to the property of another, but in it. . . . This right may be created by agreement or . . . by operation of law, as when one sells a parcel of land in the center of his own premise, the buyer by operation of law acquires a right-of-way over the grantor's other land which surrounds his. It is a right issuing out of, or concerning, or annexed to or exerciseable within a thing corporeal. Hence, the right is not the thing corporate itself, but something collateral thereto. . . . It has no corporeal tangible substance.

Thus, it is an incorporeal hereditament, something that is known in law as a "servitude, imposed upon land for the benefit of the person or persons owning the right, irrespective of the ownership of the land." §6. I THOMPSON ON REAL PROPERTY.

The right-of-way problem, or way of necessity, apparently has not been fully laid to rest in Florida. This state recognizes two types. One is the codification of the "common-law way of necessity." This type, set forth in *F.S.* 704.01(1), is an easement based on an implied grant of way of necessity. The statute recognizes such an easement (1) when a grantor conveys land to another to which the only access is over the grantor's land, or (2) when the grantor retains land that is inaccessible except over the land he has conveyed. The easement, called a way of necessity, arises, but only if title was derived from a common source other than the original grant from the State of Florida or from the United States. The legal fiction is that a right-of-way is presumed to have been granted or reserved. The easement is discussed in *Hanna v. Means*, 319 So.2d 61 (2d D.C.A. Fla. 1975).

In *Reyes v. Perez*, 284 So.2d 493 (4th D.C.A. Fla. 1973) the court held that when grantors conveyed land that was inaccessible except over lands retained by the grantors or over land previously conveyed by the grantors, there was created by implication a common-law easement from the inaccessible parcel over the grantors' property to the roadway; thus, a party entitled to a common-law implied way of necessity could not qualify for a statutory easement as provided for in *F.S.* 704.01(2). The court reasoned that the two subsections of the statute must be construed serially and that the existence of a common-law easement as described in 704.01(1) bars the establishment of a statutory easement under 704.01(2). The fact that another shorter or better way may exist over the land of a stranger in order to reach a public road or street will not destroy the easement or require the person entitled to it to acquire a new way from the stranger by paying him compensation. This may arise from an implication of law from the principle that when anything is granted the means to attain it are granted.

A form for a complaint to establish a common-law way of necessity is suggested in §12.11. The second type is purely statutory. *F.S.* 704.01(2) recognizes a separate way of necessity exclusive of any common-law right. It provides that when any land outside of a municipality is used for residential or agricultural purposes or for timber raising or cutting or stock raising and it is enclosed by lands, fencing or improvements of others so that no practical route of ingress or egress is available to the nearest public or private road, the owner or tenant of the enclosed lands may use and maintain an easement or way of necessity for persons, vehicles, stock and electricity and telephone service over and on the lands separating his lands and the public or private road. This way of necessity must be the nearest practicable route.

This statute is based on public policy rather than an implied grant. In *South Dade Farms, Inc. v. B. & L. Farms Co.,* 62 So.2d 350 (Fla. 1952), *F.S.* 704.01, which was then essentially the same as 704.01(2) is now, was declared unconstitutional by the Supreme Court because it deprived the servient owner of property without due process of law and without just compensation. In 1953, the legislature re-enacted the statute as 704.01(2), and to overcome the court's objection, added a new section, 704.04, which provided a method under which the owner of the servient land could be compensated. See also §12.8 of I FLORIDA REAL PROPERTY PRACTICE (CLE 2d ed. 1971).

Notwithstanding the legislature's efforts to correct the constitutional deficiency, the matter may not yet be settled. See *Stein v. Darby,* 126 So.2d 313 (1st D.C.A. Fla. 1961), *cert. den.* 134 So.2d

232. In this case the court stated that Article XVI, §29 of the Florida Constitution clearly implies that an "individual" under the authority of the legislature may exercise the power of eminent domain for the purpose of acquiring a way of necessity to his landlocked property, conditioned on paying "full compensation" to the owner. The court also stated that it could find no logic in the argument that the statute in question was unconstitutional as serving something other than a *public purpose*.

Since that decision, however, the Florida Constitution has been changed drastically as it affects this subject matter. Article X, §6 as revised in 1968 and subsequently amended, states as follows:

> (a) No private property shall be taken except for a public purpose and with full compensation therefor paid to each owner or secured by deposit in the registry of the court and available to the owner.

> (b) Provision may be made by law for the taking of easements, by like proceedings, for the drainage of the land of one person over or through the land of another.

Thus, the constitutional basis for the legislation has been significantly eroded if not altogether eliminated.

2. [§12.11] Sample Complaint To Establish Common-Law Way Of Necessity

(Title of Court)

(Title of Cause)   COMPLAINT TO ESTABLISH
COMMON-LAW WAY OF NECESSITY

Plaintiff, John Doe, sues defendant, William Rho, and alleges:

1. This is an action to establish a way of necessity.

2. Plaintiff is the fee simple owner of the following-described property in Blank County, Florida.

[legal description]

3. Defendant conveyed the property to plaintiff.

4. Plaintiff's property is bounded as follows:

a. To the east, south and west by undeveloped pasture lands containing hundreds of yards of open property leading to no roadway or way of access by which plaintiff can obtain ingress and egress to and from his property.

b. To the north by property of defendant.

5. The nearest public access road to plaintiff's property is located north of his property, and only the property of defendant lies between plaintiff's property and the access road. A way of necessity over the property of defendant is the only method by which access may be had.

6. For six months after the purchase of the above-described property, plaintiff used a roadway on defendant's property with defendant's acquiesence, that roadway being the most direct route from plaintiff's property to the public road. Defendant now refuses to let plaintiff on the roadway, has set up roadblocks and threatens to have plaintiff arrested should he go on the roadway for purpose of gaining access to plaintiff's property.

WHEREFORE, Plaintiff demands a final judgment declaring a way of necessity over the lands of defendant and an injunction restraining defendant from interfering with plaintiff's use of the way of necessity.

Attorney for Plaintiff

.................(address).................

H. DAVID FAUST*

13

ZONING

I. [§13.1] INTRODUCTION AND SCOPE

II. ZONING AUTHORITY

   A. [§13.2] Source

   B. Limitations On Zoning Power

      1. [§13.3] Conformity To A Comprehensive Plan

      2. [§13.4] Notice And Hearing

      3. [§13.5] Implications Of Sunshine Law

      4. [§13.6] Contract Zoning And Floating Zones

   C. [§13.7] Zoning Moratoriums

   D. [§13.8] Pending Zoning

III. EVALUATION OF ZONING PROBLEM

   A. [§13.9] Testing Of Planning Conclusions

   B. [§13.10] Economic Factors

   C. [§13.11] Traffic Studies

   D. [§13.12] Changing Neighborhood Conditions

---

*J.D., 1963, University of Florida. Mr. Faust is a member of the Palm Beach County and American bar associations. He is a partner in the firm of Burns Middleton Farrell & Faust and practices in Palm Beach.

    E. [§13.13] Aesthetics

IV. PREPARATION OF ZONING CASES

    A. [§13.14] In General

    B. [§13.15] Choice Of Remedy

    C. [§13.16] Standing To Maintain Action

    D. [§13.17] Effect Of Presumptions Of Validity

    E. [§13.18] Fairly Debatable Rule

    F. [§13.19] Use Of Exhibits

    G. [§13.20] Expert Witnesses

V. [§13.21] CONCLUSION

I. [§13.1] INTRODUCTION AND SCOPE

Zoning regulations are one of several legal devices used to implement a community's comprehensive plan for the control of its growth and development. In their traditional form, zoning regulations divide land into districts and establish regulations to be applied in each of those districts for the purpose of controlling height and bulk of buildings, population densities, traffic circulation and related matters. As a legislative exercise of the state's police power, zoning regulations must be reasonably related to the preservation and promotion of the public health, safety and welfare. *Watson v. Mayflower Property, Inc.,* 223 So.2d 368 (4th D.C.A. Fla. 1969), *aff'd* 233 So.2d 390.

Although most zoning ordinances follow a stereotyped pattern, the goals and plans that they attempt to implement vary widely and often may be deficient when measured against constitutional standards. As a result, the validity of some zoning provisions may be deficient due to inadequate evaluation of the constitutional limitations upon the legislative power by which they were adopted.

This chapter considers only judicial review of planning and zoning decisions made by legislative bodies in the exercise of their police power. Administrative proceedings before legislative and quasi-judicial bodies seeking relief (through variances or special exceptions) from zoning ordinances are not within its scope. Judicial review by certiorari under *F.S.* 163.250 of administrative proceedings of boards of adjustment involving zoning decisions also is outside the scope of this chapter.

II. ZONING AUTHORITY

A. [§13.2] Source

The adoption of zoning regulations (whether by county or municipality) is a legislative exercise of the police power of the state. Traditionally, an examination of the sources of the legislative power that underlies all zoning regulations has been considered an essential first step in the determination of their validity. This is true because, until recently, local governments have had no power to regulate land use unless it was granted to them specifically by the state.

Prior to the adoption of the Municipal Home Rule Powers Act, *F.S.* Chapter 166, legislative grants of zoning power were found in

Chapter 176 (The Model Zoning Enabling Act), Chapter 163 or special acts of the legislature. The adoption of the Municipal Home Rule Powers Act, however, initiated a fundamnetal shift in the authority of municipal governments in Florida to adopt zoning regulations. That act specifically repealed Chapter 176 (The Model Zoning Enabling Act) as well as all special acts pertaining to the power of a municipality. Indeed, all municipal charters established by various special acts also have been repealed and now are deemed mere ordinances, subject to modification or repeal just as any other ordinances that from time to time may be enacted.

Under the Municipal Home Rule Powers Act, the legislature has expressly recognized the residual home rule powers vested in municipal governments by Article VIII, §2 of the Constitution of the State of Florida. In implementing this constitutional provision, the legislature has declared that municipalities now have all the governmental, corporate and proprietary powers necessary to enable them to conduct municipal government, and further have been authorized to "exercise any power for municipal purposes, except when expressly prohibited by law." *F.S.* 166.021.

How the new home rule act will be interpreted as it relates to the zoning authority of municipal governments cannot yet be determined. Considerations of due process remain, however, and must be observed for the zoning authority of the local government to be constitutionally exercised.

The source of zoning authority for counties is found in the home rule and charter provisions of the 1968 Constitution as implemented by legislation.

See also *F.S.* 163.160–.315.

B.   Limitations On Zoning Power

1. [§13.3] Conformity To A Comprehensive Plan

For zoning regulations to be valid, they must be adopted in accordance with a comprehensive plan. *State ex rel. Henry v. City of Miami,* 117 Fla. 594, 158 So. 82 (1934). The procedural step of adopting a plan in the form of a formal document, however, need not necessarily precede the adoption of a zoning map and corresponding zoning district regulations. Instead, the requirement that zoning regulations be in conformity with a comprehensive plan relates to the necessity that they be comprehensive in character and take into consideration the lessening of congestion in the streets, the promotion of the general health and welfare, the provisions of adequate light and air and the prevention of overcrowding of land in the area being zoned. As stated in former *F.S.* 176.04 (the Model Zoning Enabling Act, now repealed):

> Regulations shall be made with reasonable consideration . . . to the character of the district and its particular suitability for particular uses, and with a view to encouraging the value of buildings and encouraging the most appropriate use of land throughout said municipalities.

The requirement that zoning be in furtherance of a comprehensive plan thus means that a city must be zoned on a comprehensive basis and must take into consideration all portions of the planning area, formal adoption of a planning document not being an essential prerequisite to the enactment of valid zoning regulations. 1 ANDERSON, AMERICAN LAW OF ZONING §5.02; 1 YOKLEY, ZONING LAW AND PRACTICE §3-2.

Merely because zoning regulations are enacted following the adoption of a comprehensive planning report or subsequent to a comprehensive review of the community's needs and goals does not conclude the question of the validity of those zoning regulations. As an exercise of the police power, all zoning ordinances must be reasonable in their application. *Stone v. Maitland,* 446 F.2d 83 (5th Cir. 1971); *Watson v. Mayflower Property, Inc.,* 223 So.2d 368 (4th D.C.A. Fla. 1969), *aff'd* 233 So.2d 390. The argument occasionally is made, however, that if particular zoning regulations conform to and are consistent with a comprehensive plan, they therefore must be valid, for they are in furtherance of the plan. This argument is fallacious and begs the constitutional question of validity, for the planning itself may be unreasonable and capricious and may incorporate unrealistic and arbitrary community goals. As noted in *Town of Surfside v. Abelson,* 106 So.2d 108 (3d D.C.A. Fla. 1958), *cert. den.* 111 So.2d 40, the application of the general plan through the zoning regulations must not be unreasonable or arbitrary.

In determining the validity of a zoning ordinance, therefore, it must be reviewed in the context of whether it is comprehensive in scope and implements a general community plan. It also must be reviewed to determine whether the general plan that it seeks to implement is reasonable and related to a lawful exercise of the police power. *Watson v. Mayflower Property, Inc., supra; County of Brevard v. Woodham,* 223 So.2d 344 (4th D.C.A. Fla. 1969), *cert. den.* 229 So.2d 872.

2. [§13.4] Notice And Hearing

Under the provisions of the recently enacted Municipal Home Rule Powers Act, *F.S.* Chapter 166, published notice of the proposed enactment of any ordinance is required, and all persons must be given an opportunity to be heard before the adoption of any ordinance. Former Chapter 176 contained a similar requirement as to zoning ordinances, as does Chapter 163. Although the foregoing statutory provisions apply generally to the adoption of any ordinance, the enactment of zoning regulations, which by their very nature affect property rights, of necessity must be preceded by notice and an opportunity to be heard in order to meet the procedural requirements always present in zoning ordinances and statutes. *Ellison v. City of Fort Lauderdale,* 183 So.2d 193 (Fla. 1966); *City of Miami Beach v. State ex rel. Fontainebleau Hotel Corp.,* 108 So.2d 614 (3d D.C.A. Fla. 1959), *app. dism.* and *cert. den.* 111 So.2d 437; *Sikes v. Pierce,* 94 S.E.2d 427 (Ga. 1956).

The importance of complying with the requirements of notice and public hearing readily appears from *Bal Harbour Village v. State ex rel. Giblin,* 299 So.2d 611 (3d D.C.A. Fla. 1974), *cert. den.* 311 So.2d 670, in which a zoning ordinance was held to be invalid due to a failure to give notice of its proposed adoption and the absence of public hearings before its enactment. This decision was reached regardless of the fact the ordinance had been relied upon and enforced for a period of some 25 years when its validity was first questioned.

The difficult question is not whether notice must be given, but rather concerns the adequacy of the notice as it relates to the proposed zoning regulations. Illustrative of the problem is *McGee v. City of Cocoa,* 168 So.2d 766 (2d D.C.A. Fla. 1964). From the facts of that decision it appears that the City of Cocoa gave the requisite notice of a proposed zoning amendment that would rezone certain property included within a multiple family district into a wholesale commercial district. Instead, only a part of the property was rezoned so as to be included within the wholesale commercial district. The ordinance that was adopted included a portion of the property within a more restrictive commercial classification, the remainder of the property being placed within the less restrictive wholesale commercial district in accordance with the notice. In rejecting the argument of neighboring property owners opposing the inclusion of a portion of the property in a commercial district other than that set forth in the notice of the proposed amendment, the court concluded that some deviation may be permitted when the deviation is a liberalization of the proposed amendment.

Although the general rule is that the notice must apprise the public of the suggested changes and that the ordinance must conform substantially to the notice of proposed changes, a deviation from the proposed changes as noticed may be immaterial if the ordinance as adopted does not increase the restraint on the use of the property from that originally existing. If the ordinance that rezoned the land within a multi-family zoning district had instead placed it within a single family district rather than the less restrictive commercial district, the notice of the proposed zoning change clearly would have been deficient.

A further example of the application of this rule is found in *Williams v. City of North Miami*, 213 So.2d 5 (3d D.C.A. Fla. 1968). The notice in that case announced a proposed rezoning of land from a single family residential use into a parking district. At the time that the ordinance was adopted, however, the land was not included within the parking district and instead was rezoned from its single family category into a multi-family residential district. Under these circumstances the deviation between the zoning requested by the notice and the zoning actually granted was not regarded as inconsequential and was held to be outside of the position adopted in *McGee v. City of Cocoa, supra.*

In determining the validity of zoning regulations, the attorney not only must consider whether a notice and hearing was provided prior to their adoption as required by both statutory and constitutional provisions, but, additionally, should make an inquiry as to the adequacy of the notice to support the ordinance actually adopted. If the ordinance as adopted varies substantially from the notice given at the time that the ordinance was originally proposed for consideration, the validity of the ordinance is open to serious question and it may be set aside.

3. [§13.5] Implications Of Sunshine Law

Under *F.S.* 286.011, all governing bodies in considering the adoption of zoning regulations must do so at public meetings open to all members of the public and pursuant to public notice. This requirement is unquestioned in zoning matters and parallels the constitutional necessity of providing an opportunity for all citizens to be heard prior to the adoption of any zoning ordinance. See §13.4.

In *Town of Palm Beach v. Gradison,* 296 So.2d 473 (Fla. 1974), a novel interpretation of the Sunshine Law resulted in the total invalidation of a community's comprehensive plan and its comprehensive zoning ordinance. The town council of the Town of Palm Beach in that case had employed a professional land planner for the purpose of reviewing its existing comprehensive plan and preparing any recommended amendments that the planner might consider advisable, together with a revision of any of its zoning ordinances that might be required. Following the completion of its study, the planning firm was to make its report to the zoning commission, which would hold public hearings on the planner's recommendations and thereafter report its findings to the town council. Only the town council had the authority to adopt a comprehensive plan and implementing zoning regulations.

To assist the professional land planning firm in gathering information about the community, five citizens were appointed to an ad hoc committee of local residents familiar with the character, historical background and desired future development of the town. As noted in the trial court's opinion, quoted in *IDS Properties, Inc. v. Town of Palm Beach,* 279 So.2d 353 (4th D.C.A. Fla. 1973):

> ... It was the committee's function to transmit to the planner that information and to advise with it so that the eventual plan would be compatible with the known desires of the community. This committee of citizens, while influential in what the planner ultimately produced, was merely advisory as far as the planner, the zoning commission and the town council were concerned. They made no decision which bound either the zoning commission or the town council. Much of what the planning committee did with the planner could have been done by the town manager, or some of the town's staff, or the planner could have sought out citizens on his own initiative for advice and assistance in preparing the plan.

In meeting with the professional land planner, the citizens never gave notice of any of their meetings, nor were their meetings open to the public, nor were minutes taken. Notwithstanding these facts, the record was devoid of any showing that the ad hoc advisory committee had been appointed as a subterfuge to avoid the effect of the statute.

Additionally, the evidence showed that the plan ultimately produced by the professional planners was subjected to full public hearings lasting approximately two weeks, before both the zoning commission and the town council.

In reversing the trial court's dismissal of a property owner's complaint that the Sunshine Law had been violated, the district court of appeal held that the Sunshine Law applied to the activities of the citizens' planning committee that had consulted with the professional land planner; it further held that the zoning plan and ordinance adopted by the town council had its "conception" in the nonpublic meetings of the planner and the advisory group of citizens. In the language of the district court of appeal in *IDS Properties, Inc. v. Town of Palm Beach, supra*:

> . . . The zoning ordinance was, therefore, not conceived eo instanti at the public meetings held by the Town Council and Zoning Commission. It was the product of the deliberations and actions of the Citizens' Planning Committee acting as the alter ego of the Town Council; [t]he action of the Citizens' Planning Committee was an indispensable requisite to and integral part of the "official acts" or "formal action" of the Town Council.

Thus, even though the appellate court found nothing that should be construed as impugning the motives or intentions of the members of the town council in the procedure leading up to the adoption of the zoning ordinance, it held that the comprehensive zoning ordinance covering the entire town was invalid because the professional planner met privately with a citizens' committee in the formulation of his recommendations. The Supreme Court concurred and held that the zoning ordinance so adopted was void ab initio. *Town of Palm Beach v. Gradison, supra*.

The importance of the decision in *IDS* is clear with respect to the enactment of zoning ordinances because all zoning ordinances and the comprehensive plans that they implement must be developed *eo instanti* at the public hearings at which they supposedly are being considered. If the Sunshine Law requires that a professional land planner give notice to the public and also provide the public with an opportunity to be present at any time that he meets with a group of interested citizens to whom he looks for advice, then it also may be argued that the Sunshine Law requires the planner during the course of his studies and investigations, even if conducted solely "inhouse," to give the public the opportunity to observe him in his work and, so to speak, look over his shoulder.

Needless to say, a fertile ground for litigating the validity of any zoning ordinance has been plowed and the attorney for either the governing authority or private landowner will find it necessary to look beyond the notice that was published concerning the ordinance and additionally inquire with respect to the entire proceedings by which the initial idea for a zoning change was conceived.

4. [§13.6] Contract Zoning And Floating Zones

Legislative power cannot be bargained away. Accordingly, courts generally have held that contracts have no place in a zoning plan. If this were not so, each citizen would be governed by an individual rule based upon the best deal that he could make with the governing body, such a notion obviously being repugnant to this country's notion of government by a rule of law that affects everyone alike. Thus, in *Hartnett v. Austin*, 93 So.2d 86 (Fla. 1956), a zoning ordinance was declared invalid when its efficacy was predicated upon the performance of certain contingencies and conditions to be performed by the property owner. Municipalities have no power to enter into private contracts for the enactment of zoning regulations subject to various conditions and restrictions to be executed between the governing authority and property owner. Zoning ordinances instead must be justified by the land uses involved, for to hold otherwise would cause the collapse of the whole scheme and objective of community planning and zoning.

A division of the community into districts is typical of the common zoning ordinance. The uses that are permitted within each district are prescribed and their boundaries are fixed. While these regulations meet the requirement of uniformity, they yield a by-product of rigidity that in some circumstances may be undesirable. The inclusion of "planned unit developments" as more or less "floating" zones has been a technique adopted in many zoning ordinances in an effort to overcome the objection of the traditional rigidity of zoning classifications, while at the same time preserving the certainty and definiteness required for the lawful exercise of the police power.

The planned unit development technique has been approved in a number of out-of-state cases, one of the earliest being *Rodgers v. Tarrytown*, 96 N.E.2d 731 (N.Y. 1951). In the zoning ordinance adopted by that community, the regulations provided for planned unit development districts but no such district appeared on the zoning map of the village. Instead it was provided that a planned unit development district might be established anywhere in the village if the required land were assembled, a plan for development prepared and approved and the zoning map amended by the legislative authority. Notwithstanding the claim that this flexible approach to zoning involved a contracting away of the legislative power, the planned unit development technique has been approved in a number of states.

Although no Florida cases of record have directly challenged the validity of the planned unit development technique, the court in *Hall v. Korth,* 244 So.2d 766 (3d D.C.A. Fla. 1971) approved a trial court's decision directing the local governing authority to approve an application for the rezoning of a property owner's land to a planned unit development district, thus impliedly recognizing the validity of this new zoning technique.

Since the conditions for the establishment of planned unit development districts are the same for all property owners and are established by the zoning ordinance for all to know, the objection of contract zoning as applied to "floating zone" districts appears without real substance.

C.   [§13.7]   Zoning Moratoriums

With the tremendous surge in building development occurring within the past few years, particularly in the metropolitan areas of Florida, many communities have discovered that the zoning ordinances that they previously had enacted are irrelevant to the changing conditions and, in some cases, inadequate to regulate development in accordance with their comprehensive plans. As a result, a number of governing bodies recently have adopted ordinances establishing moratoriums upon the issuance of building permits (or for a particular class of building permit) for a given period of time in order to permit a restudy of their communities and a determination of whether new land use regulations should be adopted.

Although it may be argued that moratorium ordinances are merely amendments to the building code and thus not subject to the requirements of notice and hearing that are a necessary prerequisite to the adoption of zoning regulations, an analysis of their impact clearly demonstrates that in fact they regulate land use by either limiting or prohibiting certain forms of property development. Just as set-back regulations adopted without notice and hearing as purported amendments to a building code were declared invalid in *City of Miami Beach v. State ex rel. Fontainebleau Hotel Corp.*, 108 So.2d 614 (3d D.C.A. Fla. 1959), *app. dism.* and *cert. den.* 111 So.2d 437, land use regulations in the form of moratorium ordinances likewise should be held to the same minimum standards.

The validity of moratorium ordinances is open to more serious question because they are adopted not in accordance with a comprehensive plan (the assumed basis for the enactment of all valid zoning regulations), but rather in express recognition of the absence of such a plan and the necessity to catch up with changed conditions. The question arises whether a property owner should be prohibited from using his land for any period of time due to the failure of a governing body to plan for and anticipate future growth and development properly. The answer to this question remains open in Florida.

In *Jason v. Dade County,* 37 Fla.Supp. 190 (Cir. Ct. Dade 1972), *aff'd* 278 So.2d 311, the trial court held:

> The use of "stop-gap" measures pending a thorough study of community conditions prior to the enactment of a comprehensive zoning ordinance or amendments are [*sic*] generally held to be valid when based on a reasonable period of time to complete the study. . . .

The conclusion of the chancellor in the foregoing case was expressly disavowed by the district court of appeal in its review of his decision. *Dade County v. Jason,* 278 So.2d 311 (3d D.C.A. Fla. 1973). Although the chancellor's judgment was affirmed, the appellate court expressly stated that its opinion "is not to be construed as any ruling on the constitutionality of the moratorium ordinance."

Although no Florida appellate cases of record have yet directly ruled upon the validity of moratorium ordinances, these "stop-gap" emergency measures appear contrary to the fundamental principles upon which the zoning power is predicated, *i.e.,* the *planned* regulation of private land use for the promotion of the public good. As observed by the chancellor in *State v. Lewis* (Circuit Court Case No. 67 C-3937, 15th Judicial Circuit, Palm Beach County):

> . . . The Court finds that the attempt by respondents to create a hiatus or moratorium for a period of ninety (90) days in which no building permits may be issued in

zoning district C-1-A of said municipality and thus halt all construction in said zone by enacting . . . (said moratorium ordinance) is unreasonable, arbitrary and unconstitutional under both the federal and state constitutions, and, accordingly, said ordinance is determined to be void, unenforceable and of no legal effect.

Which of the foregoing competing trial courts' views ultimately will be adopted remains open to question as of this date. Accordingly, careful analysis should be exercised when confronted with such a moratorium situation.

D. [§13.8] Pending Zoning

The validity and effect of "pending zoning" regulations is more easily stated than zoning moratoriums. Generally speaking, a change in the law pending an application for a building permit is operative and is given retroactive application. More simply stated, the law as changed, rather than as it existed at the time the application was filed, determines whether the permit or license should be granted. *City of Boynton Beach v. Carroll,* 272 So.2d 171 (4th D.C.A. Fla. 1973), *cert. den.* 279 So.2d 871. The governing principle applied in cases such as this has been stated succinctly as follows:

. . . A municipality may properly refuse a building permit for a land use repugnant to a pending zoning ordinance, even though application is made when the intended use conforms to existing regulations, and even though the application is made a considerable time before the enactment of the pending ordinance, provided the latter enacted ordinance was legally pending on the date involved. 8 McQUILLIN, MUNICIPAL CORPORATIONS §25.155.

The key to the application of the foregoing rule, which was applied in *Carroll,* is whether the ordinance in question was "legally pending" on the date that the application for building permit was made. In illustration, the city in *Carroll, supra,* published a notice that it was going to conduct a public hearing to consider a proposed zoning change five days *prior* to the property owner making his application for a building permit. The public hearing thus noticed was held six days following the application being received, and at that public hearing the ordinance in question was read for the first time. Approximately two weeks later, the ordinance was adopted on second and final reading.

Recognizing the foregoing general principal, the appellate court correctly held that the zoning ordinance that was adopted following the filing of the building permit application controlled the case, for the permit application was made *after* the publication of the required notice that the proposed ordinance was to be considered. Thus, in *City Co. of City of No. Miami B. v. Trebor Const. Corp.*, 296 So.2d 490 (Fla. 1974) no zoning change was considered legally pending when the proposed amendment to the zoning code was not presented until *after* the action in that case was filed.

By contrast, *Aiken v. Davis,* 106 Fla. 675, 143 So. 658 (1932) involved an application filed *prior* to any action being taken by the municipality relative to the amendment of its ordinances. The Supreme Court affirmed the issuance of a peremptory writ of mandamus compelling the issuance of a building permit based upon the ordinances in effect at the time the application was filed, for the amendment subsequently adopted by the governing body had not been "legally pending" as of the time the application was filed. For an ordinance to be considered "legally pending," at least two circumstances must be shown to exist: (1) a public declaration must be given by the governing body that it proposes to consider the adoption of a proposed change to its ordinances and (2) the governing body must be acting in good faith. As noted by Justice Drew in his dissent in *Broach v. Young,* 100 So.2d 411 (Fla. 1958), quoting from the annotation in 169 A.L.R. 584:

> . . . If, however, action on the application is *unreasonably refused* or *delayed* until after the change has become effective, or the issuing officer arbitrarily fails to perform a ministerial duty to issue the license or permit promptly on an application which conforms to the law at the time of filing, the courts have held that the law at the time of filing of the application controls. [Emphasis supplied by Justice Drew]

The foregoing exception to the general rule that a change in the law pending an application for a permit or a license is operative, was noted in *Dade County v. Jason,* 278 So.2d 311 (3d D.C.A. Fla. 1973). The action of the governing authority in that case clearly demonstrated that it had delayed action on the application for the permit and, as a result of the bad faith conduct, was estopped to deny the issuance of the permit requested.

A careful examination of the chronology of events is essential in determining whether an ordinance adopted subsequent to the application for a building permit will control that application. The attorney for either a governing body or property owner must carefully determine not only the relevant dates, but also the adequacy of the notice that may have been given, the sufficiency of the building permit application and the existence of any facts that may support a claim of bad faith or undue delay.

III. EVALUATION OF ZONING PROBLEM

A.   [§13.9] Testing Of Planning Conclusions

The field of zoning is one in which experts abound, the advice of professional planning and zoning consultants often being relied upon by governing bodies in their adoption of zoning regulations. As is noted in §13.3, zoning regulations are tools used to implement comprehensive plans often developed for a community by planning experts and consultants. Generally speaking, these "master plans" consist of numerous maps, various statistical tables and varying amounts of text that contain general statements of philosophy and the criteria upon which the planners have made their judgments as to the socially desirable use of various land parcels. These planning documents should be carefully examined, for significant inconsistencies and errors may be found that will provide a basis upon which a successful attack can be made upon the implementing regulations. For example, a community in amending its zoning regulations to reduce permitted density in a particular zoning district may be relying on projected population growth patterns developed within the comprehensive plan. In order to determine whether the projected population estimates are reasonable, the basis for the assumed population growth should be examined in light of existing development trends, the amount of remaining undeveloped land and the range of density of existing developments. If the projections are artificially high, such a planning error can be used advantageously to question the reasonableness of the zoning regulation by which it is implemented, for under those circumstances the density reduction may not be necessary for the protection of the public health, safety and welfare.

Similar evaluations, of course, should be made as to planning conclusions relating to traffic congestion, adequacy of public utilities to serve new developments and the character of existing neighborhoods, some or all of which factors may be used as the justification for the zoning regulations.

B. [§13.10] Economic Factors

Planning and zoning consultants often fail to consider fully the economic factors in their development of community plans. The zoning regulations that implement their planning recommendations therefore are often adopted without consideration of the economic impact that will result from their application to specific properties within a zoning district.

A somewhat extreme example of a failure to consider economics in planning is found in *William Murray Builders, Inc. v. City of Jacksonville*, 254 So.2d 364 (1st D.C.A. Fla. 1971), *cert. den.* 261 So.2d 845, in which the zoning regulations applicable to the plaintiff's property restricted its use to single family dwellings. The court noted that the nearest single family development was some distance away and separated from the subject property by vacant marshlands and a sewage disposal plant. A railroad yard, gas station and apartment complex also existed within the immediate neighborhood of the property. The evidence adduced by the plaintiff established that the property was not economically suitable for development with single family residences. Not only had homes in the area sold for less than their land development cost, but a severe buyer resistance to homes previously constructed in the area apparently existed, thus eliminating the availability of financing for single family development within the neighborhood. Based largely upon this demonstration of economic factors and market feasibility, the court granted relief to the property owner, holding that the zoning regulations in question effectively deprived him of the only beneficial use to which his property reasonably could be adapted. Since the continuation of the restrictions could not be shown as necessary to the preservation of the public health, morals, safety or welfare, the regulations limiting the plaintiff's property to single family development were determined invalid.

A mere reduction in the value of land due to rezoning does not render a zoning ordinance void. The fact, therefore, that property may be more valuable for hotels and apartments than for single family residences does not conclude the question of whether the ordinance in question is "fairly debatable." *City of Miami Beach v. Wiesen*, 86 So.2d 442 (Fla. 1956); *City of Jacksonville v. Imler*, 235 So.2d 526 (1st D.C.A. Fla. 1970), *cert. den.* 239 So.2d 829; *City of Miami Beach v. Zorovich*, 195 So.2d 31 (3d D.C.A. Fla. 1967), *cert. den.* 201 So.2d 554; *Neubauer v. Town of Surfside*, 181 So.2d 707 (3d D.C.A. Fla. 1966), *cert. den.* 192 So.2d 488; *Gautier v. Town of Jupiter Island*, 142 So.2d 321 (2d D.C.A. Fla. 1962). Instead, the property owner, in order to sustain his burden of proof, must demonstrate that the regulations have the effect of depriving him of the beneficial use of his property by precluding all uses or the only use to which the property reasonably may be adapted. *William Murray Builders, Inc. v. City of Jacksonville, supra; City of Clearwater v. College Properties, Inc.*, 239 So.2d 515 (2d D.C.A. Fla. 1970); *Watson v. Mayflower Property, Inc.*, 223 So.2d 368 (4th D.C.A. Fla. 1969), *aff'd* 233 So.2d 390; *County of Brevard v. Woodham*, 223 So.2d 344 (4th D.C.A. Fla. 1969), *cert. den.* 229 So.2d 872; *Neubauer v. Town of Surfside, supra.* Market feasibility and saturation studies relative to a permitted zoning use obviously are important and may be critical in sustaining or defeating such a claim.

In evaluating whether a zoning regulation prevents any economically feasible use of a parcel of land, the following factors should be considered:

1. Does a market demand exist for land for the uses permitted by its zoning? If there is no demand or market for the land, a strong argument against the validity of the ordinance exists. *William Murray Builders, Inc. v. City of Jacksonville, supra.*

2. What is the highest and best use of the land? Although this factor will be weighed against the public benefit derived from the zoning regulations, this evidence alone probably will be insufficient to invalidate a zoning ordinance. As noted in *Watson v. Mayflower, Property, Inc., supra*, it is not a prerequisite to the constitutional validity of a zoning regulation that it permit the highest and best use of a particular piece of property. Evidence on this subject, however, may aid support in a conclusion of invalidity when weighed with other additional claims of invalidity.

3. What will be the effect on adjacent properties if the ordinance is set aside? If surrounding properties are devoted to residential uses, the courts generally will not invalidate residential zoning on one piece of property so as to allow its commercial development if it will reduce those residential values. *County of Brevard v. Woodham, supra.* For a broader discussion of this factor, see 1 ANDERSON, AMERICAN LAW OF ZONING §2.25.

4. Has the value of the land been reduced by the zoning ordinance? If so, the reduction in value will be weighed

against the public benefit achieved by the zoning change. Included among the Florida cases that have considered claims of reduced values due to zoning regulations are the following:

City of St. Petersburg v. Aikin, 217 So.2d 315 (Fla. 1968): Ordinance upheld although value for prohibited use ($100,000) was 100% greater than the value of land for the permitted uses under the zoning ordinance ($40,000–$58,000).

City of Miami Beach v. Wiesen, supra: Ordinance upheld that reduced land values to 50% of the value it would have had for business uses.

City of Jacksonville v. Imler, supra: Ordinance upheld although property was purchased for $65,000 and under current zoning had a value between $25,000 and $45,000. If rezoned as requested for business uses, the value of the property was estimated at $150,000.

Neubauer v. Town of Surfside, supra: Ordinance upheld although value as restricted by zoning ordinance was between $60,000 to $80,000. Value of property if devoted to highest and best use was $225,000, a differential of 300 to 400%.

Standard Oil Company v. City of Tallahassee, 87 F.Supp. 145 (N.D. Fla. 1949), *aff'd* 183 F.2d 410, *cert. den.* 340 U.S. 892: Ordinance upheld although property had value of $5,000 as zoned for residential purposes, and a value of $55,000 for commercial use as a filling station.

City of West Palm Beach v. Edward U. Roddy Corp., 43 So.2d 709 (Fla. 1950): Ordinance rezoning property from industrial to residential use set aside because value as industrial property was $60–$75 per front foot and value as residential property was $5–$7 per front foot.

Ehinger v. State ex rel. Gottesman, 147 Fla. 129, 2 So.2d 357 (1941): Ordinance set aside because property as zoned for residential uses had a value of $10,000 and was shown to be unusable for those purposes; property value for desired use as an hotel was $75,000–$100,000 with original land cost to property owner of $40,000.

C. [§13.11] Traffic Studies

That zoning regulations may be used to control land usage so as to prevent excessive traffic congestion on surrounding roads is clearly established as a legitimate exercise of the police power. *Watson v. Mayflower Property, Inc.,* 223 So.2d 368 (4th D.C.A. Fla. 1969), *aff'd* 233 So.2d 390. As with all zoning regulations, however, there must be a reasonable relationship between the restriction imposed and the public benefit achieved. *Stone v. Maitland,* 446 F.2d 83 (5th Cir. 1971). Objection to land development sometimes is made upon the basis that excessive traffic volumes will result, that conclusion often being based on erroneous logic. Traffic volumes depend on a number of factors and cannot be projected reliably without a study of the origin and destination of existing and anticipated traffic, the assignment of that traffic to existing and proposed streets and a determination of the anticipated number of trips per dwelling unit that will be generated by a given population.

In many cases zoning plans and their implementing regulations are predicated on traffic assumptions that are erroneous and not based on factual studies. In preparing a zoning case that includes questions of traffic congestion, therefore, a careful examination should be made of the underlying assumptions. Considerable material often is available from the Department of Transportation that may be useful in determining the validity of the underlying assumptions. Additionally, consideration should be given to employing a traffic engineer to assist in the development of data to determine whether the planning goals and zoning regulations are supported by fact.

D. [§13.12] Changing Neighborhood Conditions

A valid objective of zoning regulations is the protection and preservation of the integrity and character of a given neighborhood. *Stone v. Maitland,* 446 F.2d 83 (5th Cir. 1971); *Watson v. Mayflower Property, Inc.,* 223 So.2d 368 (4th D.C.A. Fla. 1969), *aff'd* 233 So.2d 390; *County of Brevard v. Woodham,* 223 So.2d 344 (4th D.C.A. Fla. 1969), *cert. den.* 229 So.2d 872; *City of Miami Beach v. Zoravich,* 195 So.2d 31 (3d D.C.A. Fla. 1967), *cert. den.* 201 So.2d 554; *Blank v. Town of Lake Clarke Shores,* 161 So.2d 683 (2d D.C.A. Fla. 1964); *Gautier v. Town of Jupiter Island,* 142 So.2d 321 (2d D.C.A. Fla. 1962). Indeed the exclusion of apartment houses from certain areas has been upheld on precisely that basis, their existence being considered inimicable to the continuation of a single family residential community. *Gautier v. Town of Jupiter Island, supra.*

Frequently, however, the neighborhood character identified in the comprehensive zoning plan may vary with the passage of time and the regulations may be attempting to impose a land use no longer in accordance with the pattern of development. For example, the character of a neighborhood originally zoned as a single family residential district, due to changing social and economic patterns, no longer may support that use. Increased traffic on neighborhood streets and the location of apartment or commercial buildings nearby may have had an adverse impact upon the neighborhood, resulting in a change in its character. See *Tollius v. City of Miami,* 96 So.2d 122 (Fla. 1957); *Manilow v. City of Miami Beach,* 213 So.2d 589 (3d D.C.A. Fla. 1968), *cert. den.* 397 U.S. 972. Only a careful field examination will reveal these facts.

In preparing a zoning case, the attorney should carefully inspect the neighborhood to determine its existing conditions. Are the houses and surrounding grounds well maintained? Are the homes owner-occupied? Are the houses being occupied by more than one family unit? Multiple mail boxes on the exterior of the building may provide a quick answer to the latter two inquiries. Building department records also will reveal the dates when the newest homes were constructed, the nature and value of the improvements constructed and the nature and value of repairs and renovations that have been made to neighborhood properties, all of which are relevant factors in determining whether the neighborhood has changed from that which the zoning plan presumes to exist. If the presumption in the zoning plan is found to be erroneous, a change in zoning regulations may be obtained.

E. [§13.13] Aesthetics

The preservation and enhancement of a community's aesthetic appeal and character through zoning and land use regulation is a proper basis for the exercise of the police power. Although this proposition is not universally accepted, the Florida courts have long recognized that aesthetic concerns are a legitimate basis for the exercise of zoning power and have noted the urgent nature of those concerns in an age in which the preservation of the quality of the environment has become a national goal. *Stone v. Maitland,* 446 F.2d 83 (5th Cir. 1971); *City of Miami Beach v. Ocean and Inland Co.,* 147 Fla. 480, 3 So.2d 364 (1941).

The validity of a zoning ordinance based on aesthetic considerations of course is subject to the same test of public good versus private loss as are all other zoning regulations. A zoning ordinance based solely on aesthetic considerations is more susceptible to successful attack for the public benefit to be gained is not as easily measured as reduction of traffic congestion, reduction in population densities and related considerations, all of which are more objective in nature. See *City of Miami Beach v. First Trust Co.*, 45 So.2d 681 (Fla. 1950) and compare the original opinion with the opinion of the court on rehearing.

IV. PREPARATION OF ZONING CASES

A. [§13.14] In General

Zoning litigation differs from personal injury, domestic relations and criminal cases because the fact situations generally tend to be more complicated. In many zoning cases, issues are raised concerning land usage, property valuation, market feasibility, traffic congestion, aesthetics and adequacy of public utilities. Even the environmental impact may be raised. As a result, the lawyer who enjoys marshaling and presenting facts in other types of complicated litigation probably will be successful in handling zoning cases if he is willing to undertake the comprehensive development of his record and the effective dramatization of the most persuasive points in his case.

Because of the complicated nature of most zoning cases, the benefit to the client as a result of the contemplated litigation first should be considered, for considerable expense and fees necessarily will be included in any zoning action.

B. [§13.15] Choice Of Remedy

Various types of action are available to obtain relief from zoning ordinances, including declaratory judgments, injunctions and mandamus. The selection of a particular action therefore depends largely on the form of action that, if successful, will achieve the results the client seeks. Thus, if a client has filed plans and has applied for a building permit that has been denied to him, mandamus is the most appropriate remedy to compel the issuance of the desired permit and to test the validity of any zoning regulation upon which the governmental unit may be relying in refusing to issue the building permit requested. To prevail in such an action, however, it must be clearly established that the applicant has complied with all valid zoning and building regulations and that the building official has a clear legal duty to issue the building permit requested. *State ex rel. Lacedonia v. Harvey,* 68 So.2d 817 (Fla. 1953). See also *Bal Harbour Village v. State ex rel. Giblin,* 299 So.2d 611 (3d D.C.A. Fla. 1974), *cert. den.* 311 So.2d 670. If the applicant fails to file all of the required documents or if his application or plan fails to demonstrate compliance with all valid ordinances and regulations (including zoning regulations "legally pending" as discussed in §13.8), or if his application was for a discretionary permit such as a mere foundation permit, the issuance of which generally is discretionary with the building official), mandamus will not lie and a different action must be selected.

Declaratory judgment proceedings to test the validity of zoning regulations are becoming increasingly common and often include demands for injunctive relief against the enforcement of regulations. To be entitled to maintain such an action, however, the pleadings must establish the existence of a justiciable controversy. *M & E Land Company v. Siegel,* 177 So.2d 769 (1st D.C.A. Fla. 1965). See FLORIDA CIVIL PRACTICE BEFORE TRIAL, Chapter 22, "Declaratory Relief" (CLE 3d ed. 1975); *Colby v. Colby,* 120 So.2d 797 (3d D.C.A. Fla. 1960).

Injunction proceedings may be a useful remedy for the landowner, but only if the court can be persuaded to grant relief in fairly broad terms. Those cases are rare for courts do not have the power to direct that a particular use be permitted, the injunctive power being limited to prohibiting the enforcment of regulations found to be arbitrary and unreasonable as applied to specific properties. *City of St. Petersburg v. Aikin,* 217 So.2d 315 (Fla. 1968); *Village of North Reddington Beach v. Williams,* 220 So.2d 22 (2d D.C.A. Fla. 1969). Instead the jurisdiction of the courts is limited to an examination of the permitted land uses and a determination of whether the regulations involved restrict the use of the property in an arbitrary and unreasonable manner.

An illustration of the dilemma in which a property owner may be placed is found in *City of Miami Beach v. Breitbart,* 280 So.2d 18 (3d D.C.A. Fla. 1973), *cert. den.* 286 So.2d 204. There, the property owner's land was included in a single family residential district that, upon challenge, was found to be an arbitrary and unreasonable classification. The zoning authority thereafter amended its zoning ordinance to include that property in a multiple family district limited to apartment buildings containing not more than four dwelling units. The property owner again challenged this classification and the trial court, in its judgment determining that new classification also was arbitrary and unreasonable, directed the city to rezone the property into a classification so that it might be used for commercial uses consistent with the character of the neighborhood within which it was included.

This judicial rezoning is improper, for as noted in the appellate court's opinion, that type of judicial action invades the legislative field and is prohibited under the doctrine of separation of powers. Although the property owner who wished to erect a commercial building upon his land that was included within a single family zoning district was successful in obtaining an injunction against the enforcement of the single family zoning regulations, that injunction was followed by the adoption of a regulation limiting the land development to apartments, still precluding the property owner's desired commercial development.

To achieve the commercial development, the property owner must obtain an injunction against the enforcement of regulations that prevent that commercial development, a broad grant of relief thus being necessary if the injunctive proceeding is to have any value. To be entitled to such broad relief, the property owner must prove that his property not only is unsuitable for single family development, but also is not reasonably suited for any form of land use permitted by the applicable zoning regulation other than commercial development. That task obviously is difficult.

See also *Watson v. Mayflower Property, Inc.,* 223 So.2d 368 (4th D.C.A. Fla. 1969), *aff'd* 233 So.2d 390 (Fla. 1970).

C. [§13.16] Standing To Maintain Action

The standing of a landowner adversely affected by zoning regulations to contest the validity of those regulations as applied to his land is clearly established. *Renard v. Dade County,* 261 So.2d 832 (Fla. 1972); *Josephson v. Autray,* 96 So.2d 784 (Fla. 1957). Conversely, zoning regulations adopted by a governmental unit may be enforced by it through injunctive or, when provided, criminal process.

The question arises whether a property owner has standing to maintain an action to contest the validity of zoning regulations applicable to adjacent property that will have an adverse effect upon his land. *Renard v. Dade County, supra,* illustrates the problem. The plaintiff and defendant in *Renard* owned adjacent properties, both of which were located in a zoning district permitting only industrial uses. Upon application for rezoning, zoning regulations applicable to the defendant's property were amended to permit multiple family development. Although the industrial use classification of the plaintiff's property apparently remained, the rezoning of the neighboring parcel to multiple family use resulted in an additional set-back restriction on the plaintiff's property. The defendant contended that the plaintiff did not have standing to maintain an action to challenge the validity of the ordinance that rezoned his land to the multiple family use classification. This contention was rejected by the Supreme Court, which held that any person who is aggrieved or adversely affected by an action of the zoning authority has a legally recognizable interest. Implicitly rejecting the rationale expressed in *Florida Palm-Aire Corporation v. Delvin*, 230 So.2d 26 (4th D.C.A. Fla. 1970), *cert. dism.* 234 So.2d 357, the court stated that the interest adversely affected may be shared in common with other members of the community, as when an entire neighborhood is affected. Factors to be considered in determining the sufficiency of the party's interest and "standing" include the proximity of his property to the property to be zoned or rezoned, the character of the neighborhood, the existence of common restrictive covenants and set-back requirements and the type of change proposed.

The *Renard* case *supra* also revisited the question of the standing of a private citizen to maintain an action to enforce a valid zoning ordinance against another person's land, that action being in the nature of a public nuisance. Reaffirming the rule established in *Boucher v. Novotny*, 102 So.2d 132 (Fla. 1958), which required proof of special damages different in kind and degree from those suffered by the community as a whole as a precondition to the right for such an action to be maintained, the Supreme Court noted that a more lenient application of that rule is required due to changed conditions in the 20 years since that case was decided. The requirement of showing unique special damages apparently can now be satisfied merely by proof of proximity to the property upon which the zoning violations exist and a showing that the properties are located in zoning districts in which the same or similar regulations apply.

D. [§13.17] Effect Of Presumptions Of Validity

In enacting zoning ordinances pursuant to their legislative power, governing bodies are presumed to be acting lawfully and the ordinances accordingly are presumed to be valid. The burden of proving that a zoning regulation is unreasonable and not subject to fair debate rests upon the complaining property owner. *City of St. Petersburg v. Aikin*, 217 So.2d 315 (Fla. 1968). This burden of proof has been characterized by the courts as "an extraordinary one." *City of Miami Beach v. Silver,* 67 So.2d 646 (Fla. 1953); *Town of North Reddington Beach v. Williams,* 220 So.2d 22 (2d D.C.A. Fla. 1969).

The presumption of a zoning ordinance's validity applies also to the sufficiency of the allegations in the complaint by which the ordinance is attacked. As noted in *City of Miami Beach v. Silver, supra:*

> One who assails such legislation must carry the burden of both *alleging and proving* that the ... enactment is invalid. ... Allegations in such an attack which are conclusions of the pleader are not enough.

The preparation of the property owner's complaint obviously requires greater care than customarily given in the preparation of other pleadings found in more routine forms of litigation. To state a cause of action for relief against a zoning ordinance that as a matter of law is presumed to be valid, the complaint must allege facts that demonstrate that the ordinance in question is arbitrary and unreasonable in its application to the complainant's property and that the issue is not fairly debatable among reasonable men. *Village of Virginia Gardens v. Johnson,* 143 So.2d 692 (3d D.C.A. Fla. 1962). That burden is extraordinary and obviously requires a careful analysis of the facts of the case at the time the complaint is prepared.

E. [§13.18] Fairly Debatable Rule

Although a person may have sufficient standing to challenge the action of the zoning authority, the burden of proving that the challenged action was not fairly debatable still must be met. *Renard v. Dade County,* 261 So.2d 832 (Fla. 1972).

Because zoning is a legislative function, the discretion that might otherwise be reposed in a reviewing court is somewhat limited. Accordingly, zoning ordinances will be sustained and presumed valid as long as their reasonableness is fairly debatable, the burden of proof in this regard being upon the contestant. *City of St. Petersburg v. Aikin,* 217 So.2d 315 (Fla. 1968); *Watson v. Mayflower Property, Inc.,* 223 So.2d 368 (4th D.C.A. Fla. 1969), *aff'd* 233 So.2d 390; *County of Brevard v. Woodham,* 223 So.2d 344 (4th D.C.A. Fla. 1969), *cert. den.* 229 So.2d 872.

In determining whether a zoning ordinance is fairly debatable, the evidence need not establish the wisdom, propriety or efficacy of the ordinance. Rather, it is only necessary to show that reasonable men might differ as to the reasonableness of the ordinance and, upon such a showing, it must be sustained.

Although the foregoing statement of the "fairly debatable" rule is not difficult, its application to factual disputes is arduous. The mere fact of an evidentiary dispute as to the propriety of an ordinance does not require the application of the fairly debatable rule, for if that were the case, it would be virtually impossible for any property owner to secure judicial relief for his land regardless of the effect of the restrictions imposed. *Davis v. Situs Incorporated,* 275 So.2d 600 (1st D.C.A. Fla. 1973). The difficult question, therefore, is what balance of evidence is required before it can be said that the validity of a zoning ordinance no longer is fairly debatable.

Clearly, mere disputes and conflicts in testimony are insufficient to support a claim that the ordinance is fairly debatable. *Davis v. Situs Incorporated, supra; William Murray Builders, Inc. v. City of Jacksonville,* 254 So.2d 364 (1st D.C.A. Fla. 1971), *cert. den.* 261 So.2d 845. Instead, the emphasis must be on the basic physical facts pertinent to the land to which the zoning regulations apply. Facts relating to permitted land use, land valuation, market feasibility, the physical limitations of the property, neighboring land usage and characteristics, traffic circulation and the like all are among the facts that must be placed in the balance in determining whether the ordinance in question is open to debate on any ground that makes sense and upon which reasonable men might differ. *City of Miami Beach v. Lachman,* 71 So.2d 148 (Fla. 1954); *app. dism.* 348 U.S. 906; *Town of North Reddington Beach v. Williams,* 220 So.2d 22 (2d D.C.A. Fla. 1969).

The attorney handling a zoning case either for the governing body or private landowner therefore must carefully marshal the facts that relate to the particular parcel of property involved. The fairly debatable rule is not applicable to mere words or expressions of opinion of expert witnesses, but instead applies to the basic physical facts that exist as to a particular parcel of land and as to which the ordinance must stand or fall. *Oklahoma City v. Barclay,* 359 P.2d 237 (Okla. 1960).

F. [§13.19] Use Of Exhibits

Graphic demonstration of land use and neighborhood conditions often is essential to the successful handling of a zoning case. Ground level photographs of the properties involved as well as surrounding properties generally should be used. Additionally, aerial photographs showing the property in litigation in the context of the surrounding properties often are useful and are of assistance particularly to expert witnesses and the court when the boundaries of the property in litigation as well as the boundaries of the zoning district in which that property is located are appropriately marked by charting tape or other medium.

An essential exhibit in any zoning case is a certified copy of the official zoning map. Although this map shows the location of the zoning district boundaries, it does not portray the land usage found within each of its respective districts. Whenever possible, a land use map additionally should be prepared, graphically portraying (as specifically as may be feasible) the type of land use found on each parcel. Differing color codes should be used to portray the various densities of multiple family development, commercial development, single family development, public parks and open spaces.

In conjunction with the preparation of a land use map, density graphs often prove helpful in dramatizing the population densities found in certain specific land uses. For instance, two multiple family apartment buildings adjacent to each other may have a significant variation in the number of dwelling units per acre found within each. A bar graph can illustrate this disparity effectively. A similar graphic display can be used to illustrate varying heights of buildings in a situation in which building height is an issue to be considered.

In preparing exhibits in a zoning case, the age and physical condition of buildings within a given zoning district or neighborhood may be of importance. In that situation, a map showing the location of the various buildings within the particular district is of great value when color coded to show the various ages of the buildings and their respective condition.

When traffic congestion is a factor, a street map illustrating the volume of traffic handled by each artery may be used effectively to dramatize the effect of that traffic upon properties abutting the streets. In preparing such a street map, the width of the line depicting the given street is increased proportionately to the volume of traffic it handles, a wide line being used for a high traffic volume street and a narrow line being used to depict a street that handles a limited volume of traffic.

G. [§13.20] Expert Witnesses

The successful handling of a zoning case generally requires the assistance of an expert witness who can testify as to the factors relating to the reasonableness of a given set of land use regulations when considered in light of all relevant factors. Although architects occasionally are used as witnesses due to their general familiarity with building site development and the planning of proposed projects, professional land planners generally can be of greater value due to the broader scope of their professional experience. The following questions used in the examination of a land planner qualified as an expert witness in support of a proposed zoning change illustrate the scope of the testimony that can be presented:

1. Are you familiar with the subject property and the general area where it is located?

2. What is the source of your information?

3. For what is the subject property being used?

4. Describe the character of the adjoining properties, the neighborhood and the general area, including details concerning land use.

5. Have you studied the history of the development of the area? What trends, if any, can you discern?

6. Are you familiar with the zoning in the area? Are there nonconforming uses in the area? Undeveloped property? Please describe and locate.

7. Has a comprehensive plan been developed for the area? When? Are you familiar with the plan?

8. Does the present zoning of the subject property conform to the comprehensive plan?

9. Does the proposed zoning conform to the comprehensive plan?

10. What changes, if any, have occurred in the neighborhood affecting the comprehensive plan?

11. Do you consider the comprehensive plan to be presently valid? On what do you base your opinion?

12. What do you consider the most appropriate present and prospective use for the subject property? Please explain.

13. Do you consider the permitted uses under the present zoning to be practical and appropriate? State whether you consider the present zoning to be a reasonable classification. Please explain.

14. State whether you consider the proposed zoning compatible with the character of the neighborhood as it now exists and as it is developing. What is the basis for your opinion?

15. In your opinion, would the neighborhood benefit from the proposed zoning? Please explain.

When traffic is an issue, the expert land planner also might be asked whether the use of the property for the purpose advocated would lead to the generation of traffic congestion on arterial streets or interfere with the use of those streets by emergency vehicles. When the land planner is being used as a witness in support of zoning regulations, he additionally should be asked whether the zoning regulations applicable to the property implement the principles and objectives of the comprehensive land use plan. The attorney for the property owner at the appropriate time may properly point out that the mere fact that the principles of the comprehensive plan may be implemented does not conclude the question of reasonableness for the reasons set forth in §13.3. Since zoning regulations must be adopted in accordance with a comprehensive plan the foregoing question is relevant to a determination of the validity of the regulation.

Appraisers often are valuable witnesses in a zoning case. If they consider the value of the land for the uses permitted by the zoning ordinance to be as high as its value for other purposes, their opinion will be strong evidence that the planning conclusion resulting in the zoning regulation is sound. On the other hand, if they consider that the value of the land for another use is substantially greater than the value of the land if restricted to the uses permitted by the zoning, the zoning classification may be subject to serious question. The opinion of the land appraiser as to whether the property economically can be used for the purposes permitted by the zoning ordinance also can be of great assistance in many cases. For example, if it can be established that no market exists for single family homes or for apartments or other buildings in the price range that would be required in view of land costs and existing economic and market conditions, the reasonableness of the ordinance will be placed in considerable doubt.

The presentation of the testimony of appraisers in zoning cases is not greatly different from the form of their testimony in other forms of litigation. In addition to the customary testimony of their investigations of comparable land sales, testimony also should be presented as to the unique circumstances of the parcel involved and the neighborhood in which it is located, as well as a knowledge of local sales and market conditions.

V. [§13.21] CONCLUSION

Zoning regulations presently are the principal tool used in urban planning to control and guide population growth in urban development. When enacted to implement a properly considered plan and administered in accordance with that plan, zoning regulations can assist in avoiding many of the urban mistakes of the past.

Because zoning is a relatively new phenomenon as contrasted with other fields of the law [*Village of Euclid v. Ambler Realty Co.,* 272 U.S. 365, 47 S.Ct. 114, 71 L.Ed. 303 (1926), the genesis of zoning law being decided only in 1926], legal research of the issues involved in zoning cases often is more difficult. THE LAW DIGEST and encyclopedias have not kept up with new developments in the law, and their indexes often do not assist in providing an easy access to zoning decisions.

Two multi-volume treatises particularly helpful in researching legal questions relating to zoning and land use are YOKLEY, ZONING LAW AND PRACTICE and ANDERSON, AMERICAN LAW OF ZONING. Written by lawyers particularly familiar with zoning law and land use regulations, they both are kept current through supplements and contain many Florida citations that will be particularly helpful to the Florida practitioner.

J. TRACY BAXTER, JR.[*]

14

SLANDER OF TITLE

I. [§14.1] INTRODUCTION

II. NATURE OF ACTION

    A. [§14.2] In General

    B. [§14.3] Elements Of Action

    C. [§14.4] Damages And Other Relief Available

III. [§14.5] JURISDICTION AND VENUE

IV. [§14.6] SAMPLE COMPLAINT

V. [§14.7] STATUTE OF LIMITATIONS

VI. [§14.8] SAMPLE ANSWER

---

[*]LL.B., 1950, University of Virginia; LL.M., 1956, New York University. Mr. Baxter is a member of the Jacksonville Bar Association and is a sole practitioner in Jacksonville.

I.   [§14.1] INTRODUCTION

Authority for the law of slander of title in Florida is scant. As of the date of this printing there are less than a dozen cases dealing with the subject, and these are seldom exhaustive in nature and often are contradictory and loosely reasoned. It therefore frequently is necessary to resort to the text books (especially the American Law Institute's RESTATEMENT OF THE LAW OF TORTS) for guidance and to develop a large part of the theory of the action.

II. NATURE OF ACTION

A.   [§14.2] In General

The action known as "slander of title" is an action at law, not in equity, based on the tort in the nature of an action on the case for the special damage resulting from the defendant's interference. PROSSER, LAW OF TORTS 915 (4th ed. 1971). It has been said to be more akin to an action for deceit than a branch of the law of libel and slander. 53 C.J.S. *Libel and Slander* §270. A leading authority classes the action as one species of a broader tort called injurious falsehood. PROSSER, LAW OF TORTS, *supra*; Prosser, *Injurious Falsehood: The Basis of Liability*, 59 COL.L.REV. 425 (1959). The action generally covers words or conduct that disparages or brings in question the title or other interest of someone in particular property. A similar tort, sometimes called "slander or disparagement of property," "disparagement of quality" or trade libel, is not discussed in this chapter.

The tort is often treated as a branch of the law of libel and slander or defamation of the person. In Florida it has been held that the words "an action for libel, slander" as set forth in the statute of limitation then in effect [*F.S.* 95.11(3)(o) as of January 1, 1975] includes an action for slander of title. *Old Plantation Corp. v. Maule Industries,* 68 So.2d 180 (Fla. 1953). There are, however, a number of significant differences between an action for defamation of the person and an action for slander of title. In slander of title actions the statements are not actionable unless pecuniary loss results, regardless of how false and malicious; there is no presumption of damage from the falsity of the statements; and the plaintiff has the burden of proving that the statements were made without probable cause or privilege, in addition to proving their falsity and that they caused him pecuniary loss. 50 AM.JUR.2d *Libel and Slander* §540; also see, Introductory Note, Chapter 28, RESTATEMENT OF THE LAW OF TORTS 323.

Although no longer significant in this state because of the broad reach of the survival statute, *F.S.* 46.021, an action for slander of title, being based on pecuniary loss, does not die with the person.

B. [§14.3] Elements Of Action

The minimum requirements constituting a cause of action of slander of title are spelled out in §624 and §625 of the RESTATEMENT OF THE LAW OF TORTS as follows:

§624. General Rule.

One who, without a privilege to do so, publishes matter which is untrue and disparaging to another's property, in land, chattels or intangible things under such circumstances as would lead a reasonable man to foresee that the conduct of a third person as purchaser or lessee thereof might be determined thereby is liable for pecuniary loss resulting to the other from the impairment of vendibility thus caused.

§625. Intention—Scienter—Malice.

One who publishes matter disparaging to another's property in land, chattels or intangible things is subject to liability under the rule stated in §624 although he

(a) did not intend to influence a third person's conduct as purchaser or lessee of the thing in question;

(b) neither knew nor believed the disparaging matter to be false;

(c) did not publish such matter from ill will toward the other or a desire to cause him loss.

The Florida courts have adopted this rule. In *Lehman v. Goldin,* 160 Fla. 710, 36 So.2d 259 (1948) the Supreme Court, in holding that the complaint stated a cause of action, said that the applicable law was set out in §§624–626 of the Restatement and proceeded to quote those sections. In *Glusman v. Lieberman,* 285 So.2d 29 (4th D.C.A. Fla. 1973) the court, relying on *Lehman v. Goldin, supra,* held that §633 was applicable and that attorneys' fees were properly allowable as a measure of damages in a slander of title action asking for cancellation of a recorded document.

The published decisions of the Florida courts give little enlightenment on what constitutes "privilege," so often referred to in the opinions and various texts.

It is noted that the Restatement practically eliminates the requirement of malice except when required to overcome a conditional privilege of the publisher. This aspect of the Restatement rule has been strongly criticized in Prosser, *Injurious Falsehood: The Basis of Liability,* 59 COL.L.REV. 425 (1959):

> Dispassionately considered, the *Restatement* position is startling. According to the *Restatement,* any newspaper, broadcaster, or ordinary citizen who communicates to another any statement, under circumstances which should lead a reasonable man to recognize the possibility that it might cause pecuniary loss to a third person, speaks at his peril.

The article surmises that this Restatement rule has been taken from the law of defamation of the person and incorporated in the law of slander of title because of the association or confusion of the torts brought about by their common name.

In *Gates v. Utsey,* 177 So.2d 486 (1st D.C.A. Fla. 1965) the court made the following statement with respect to malice:

> ... In an action for slander of title, "malice" merely means a lack of legal justification and is said to be "presumed" if the disparagement is false, if it caused damage, and if it is not privileged. If the defendant disparages plaintiff's title under circumstances supporting a privilege, the presumption of malice is rebuted and, as in a case of defamation, the plaintiff must then prove actual or genuine malice in order to recover. *This means that malice, in the ordinary sense of the term, is not important at all except to defeat the defense of privilege or to enhance damages.* [Emphasis supplied]

It is not completely clear that the Florida Supreme Court has eliminated the requirement of malice in slander of title actions. In *Lehman v. Goldin, supra,* the declaration or complaint upheld contained specific allegations of malice in the publication of the matter concerning the plaintiff's title. In *Old Plantation Corp. v. Maule Industries,* 68 So.2d 180 (Fla. 1953) the court made the following statement: "The wrongful and *malicious* filing of the notice of lien by the appellees (as so alleged in the complaint) was the tort which gave rise to the action." [Emphasis supplied]

In *Collier County Publishing Co., Inc. v. Chapman,* 318 So.2d 492 (2d D.C.A. Fla. 1975) "malice" is discussed and apparently the court required its presence to prove a claim of slander. In that case, however, the cause of action, in the words of the court, was "what has variously been called slander of title, disparagement of property, slandered goods, trade libel and injurious falsehood." As noted in §14.2, that is a related tort, not the one with which this chapter is primarily concerned. The degree of relationship obviously is great.

Even if it should be held that malice is not essential to maintain an action of slander of title, it is probable that the point will rise in most cases, either in connection with the necessity of overcoming a conditional privilege of the publisher of the disparaging material or as an element of punitive or exemplary damages. The question arises as to what does constitute "malice" sufficient to overcome a conditional privilege or to serve as a base for punitive or exemplary damages. Certainly it would be sufficient if the publisher acted in anger or had malevolent or vindictive feelings toward the person whose title was slandered, or if the act was committed for the purpose of doing wrong to the owner. Something far less than this will constitute malice, however. As stated in 9A FLA.JUR. *Damages* §127:

> ... It is sufficient if the defendant's conduct shows an entire want of care or attention to duty, or great indifference to the persons, property, or rights of others. A wrongful act without reasonable excuse is malicious within the legal meaning of the term.

A repetition of the disparaging statement or a refusal by the publisher to co-operate voluntarily in clearing up the owner's title is evidence of malice. It would take very little in addition to the commission of a wrongful act to constitute the actual malice necessary to overcome a conditional privilege or to support an award of punitive damages.

C. [§14.4] Damages And Other Relief Available

All appropriate remedies, legal and equitable, are now available in one proceeding. In *Glusman v. Lieberman,* 285 So.2d 29 (4th D.C.A. Fla. 1973) the defendant recorded an affidavit asserting an interest in property owned by the plaintiff. The plaintiff filed an action for slander of title seeking compensatory and punitive damages. He also sought equitable relief in the nature of quieting title, cancellation of the recorded affidavit and injunctive relief against the defendant from claiming any further interest in the property. In holding that the trier of fact in a case involving both legal and equitable claims may award both compensatory and punitive damages as well as any appropriate equitable relief, the court made the following statement:

> ... Granted that under the law of England, as pointed out in Orkin, supra, punitive damages were not assessible by a chancellor in equity, but with the demise of the two sides of the circuit court, equity and law, and the adoption of Rule 1.040 RCP, 30 F.S.A., establishing one form of action, and Rule 1.110(g) RCP, allowing the joinder of legal and equitable claims, the reason for the rule has vanished. . . .

Punitive damages are allowable in an action for slander of title if the complaint contains adequate allegations of actual malice. See RESTATEMENT OF THE LAW OF TORTS §626, Comment on Clause (c). See also *Gates v. Utsey,* 177 So.2d 486 (1st D.C.A. Fla. 1965).

Although appropriate equitable relief will be granted in an action for slander of title, injunctive relief ordinarily will not be granted in the absence of allegations of breach of trust or contract. *Reyes v. Middleton,* 36 Fla. 99, 17 So. 937 (1895). In *Upton House Cooler Corp. v. Alldritt,* 73 So.2d 848 (Fla. 1954) injunctive relief against a trade libel or slander of quality of property was denied in the absence of allegations that the defendant was insolvent, that irreparable damage resulted from the libel publication and that the defendant was attempting to sell a product put out by the petitioner or was attempting to "palm off" on the public a product allegedly manufactured by the petitioner but in fact not manufactured by it.

Compensatory damages in an action for slander of title in which it is sought to remove a cloud cast upon the title includes an allowance for attorneys' fees. *Glusman v. Lieberman, supra.* Consequential damages, however, as distinguished from direct damages, are not allowable. Unfortunately, the decisions of the Florida courts do not make a clear distinction between "direct" and "consequential" damages. *Glusman* refers to "pecuniary" loss as being recoverable and included in the definition of "pecuniary loss" the expense of litigation "to remove the cloud cast upon the title." Paragraph (e) of the Comment to §624 of the RESTATEMENT OF THE LAW OF TORTS gives an example of a would-be mortgagor of property who by reason of a slander of title suffers great harm by losing or missing an opportunity to consumate a mortgage loan that otherwise would have been available to him. Damages as a result of the lost opportunity are not recoverable.

III. [§14.5] JURISDICTION AND VENUE

The action is transitory and in personam and not local, even if the case involves the recording of an instrument disparaging to the title in real property. Thus, the plaintiff must obtain jurisdiction over the publisher by one of the means authorized by statute. See *F.S.* Chapter 48. The general venue statute, *F.S.* 47.011, governs the venue of the action, and the action may be brought in either the county where (a) the defendant resides, (b) the cause of action accrued or (c) the property in litigation is located.

IV. [§14.6] SAMPLE COMPLAINT

(Title of Court)

(Title of Cause)   **COMPLAINT**

    Plaintiff, John Doe, sues defendant, Richard Roe, and alleges:

    1. This is an action for damages that exceed $2,500.

    2. On or about February 1, 1973, defendant recorded a claim of lien in the official records of Duval County, Florida against plaintiff's property described as follows:

    Lot 15, FOXMEADOWS, according to plat thereof recorded in plat book 16, page 34, of the current public records of Duval County, Florida.

    3. The claim of lien is false and untrue, and the claim of lien was wrongfully and maliciously filed by defendant.

4. On or about June 1, 1973, Dan Moe discovered the notice of lien and, as a result, refused to purchase plaintiff's property, which he had agreed to do, all of which defendant could have reasonably foreseen.

5. Because of Moe's refusal to purchase plaintiff's property, plaintiff has suffered a pecuniary loss and been damaged to the extent of $5,000.

6. Plaintiff has engaged the undersigned attorney to cancel the above-described notice of lien and has agreed to pay him a reasonable fee.

WHEREFORE plaintiff demands judgment for damages and cancellation of defendant's notice of lien.

———————————
Attorney

.................(address).................

V. [§14.7] STATUTE OF LIMITATIONS

It is settled in Florida that the statute of limitation [*F.S.* 95.11(3)(o) as of January 1, 1975] applying to actions for libel and slander also applies to the tort of slander of title. *Old Plantation Corp. v. Maule Industries,* 68 So.2d 180 (Fla. 1953). It also has been held in Florida that the disability of insanity existing when the right of action for slander of title accrued and continuing for a period of time does not toll the running of the statute of limitations. *Carey v. Beyer,* 75 So.2d 217 (Fla. 1954).

It is interesting to note exactly when the action is deemed to have accrued. In *Old Plantation Corp. v. Maule Industries, supra,* the court made the following statement:

> ... The wrongful and malicious filing of the notice of lien by the appellees (as so alleged in the complaint) was the tort which gave rise to the action and the date the tort was committed marked the point the statute began to run. Appellee could have instituted suit on any day thereafter. ...

Although the court in that opinion did not disclose sufficient facts to allow the conclusion that the statement was inaccurate, it does seem to be too broad a statement of the applicable law. For instance, if the property owned by the plaintiff was not for sale at the time of the publication, one of the elements of the action was missing, that is, interference with a sale or special damages to the plaintiff as a result of the tort. Also, if no prospective buyer of the plaintiff's property had notice of the lien until some time later, the tort would appear incomplete upon the mere filing or recording in the public records.

In *Old Plantation Corp. v. Maule Industries, supra* it was expressly decided that the action was not a continuing one, that is, did not continue from day to day until the defendant's or publisher's claim to the property was dissolved. The decision in *Gates v. Utsey,* 177 So.2d 486 (1st D.C.A. Fla. 1965) seems irreconcilable on this point, since it was held there that an allegation that the defendant's *retention* of the benefits of a forged deed or conveyance clouding the plaintiff's title to real property, knowingly done, stated a cause of action in slander of title.

VI. [§14.8] SAMPLE ANSWER

(Title of Court)

(Title of Cause)   ANSWER

Defendant, Richard Roe, answers the complaint and alleges:

1. Defendant admits the allegations of paragraphs 1 and 2 of the complaint.

2. Defendant denies the allegations of paragraphs 3, 4 and 5.

3. Defendant is without knowledge of the allegation of paragraph 6.

FIRST DEFENSE

4. Each cause of action, claim and item of damages did not accrue within the time prescribed by law for them before this action was brought.

SECOND DEFENSE

5. At the time of recording the notice of lien defendant honestly believed there was a substantial chance that it would be sustained.

THIRD DEFENSE

6. The value of plaintiff's property has increased beyond the price Dan Moe agreed to pay for it.

———————————————
Attorney

................(address)................

(Certificate of Service)

15

LANDLORD AND TENANT

This chapter has been updated and now appears in the September 1983 supplement, which is located at the end of the original manual.

INDEX TO FLORIDA STATUTES

Statute	Section
2.01	12.3
26.012	1.3, 8.9, 11.25, 15.4, 15.45
26.012(2)(a)	15.4
34.011(1)	15.4, 15.18
34.011(2)	15.4, 15.32, 15.77, 15.81, 15.88
ch. 45	5.73
45.011	3.41
45.031	4.17, 4.25, 4.33, 4.35 4.37, 5.40−.41, 5.47, 6.36
45.031(1)	5.44, 5.46
45.031(2)	5.52
45.031(3)−.031(4)	5.46, 5.52
45.031(5)−.031(6)	5.52
45.031(7)	5.49
46.021	14.2
46.08	3.17
47.011	11.25, 14.5
47.021	11.25
47.122	11.25
ch. 48	5.20, 14.5, 15.88
48.041	1.17
48.041(1)	1.17, 1.23
48.051−.061	1.17
48.111−.121	5.23
48.183	15.88
48.193−.194	1.19
48.23	5.17, 6.13, 8.14
ch. 49	1.16, 1.20, 1.28, 5.24
49.011(2)	1.16
49.011(6)	8.15
49.021	1.16, 1.19
49.031	1.18
49.031(1)	1.21−.22
49.041	1.18, 5.25
49.051−.061	1.18
49.08	1.16
49.08(1)	1.21
49.09	1.16, 5.29
49.10	1.16, 5.29−.30
49.11−.12	1.16
51.011	15.9, 15.32, 15.40−.41, 15.45 15.48−.49, 15.51, 15.82, 15.88, 15.91

51.011(1)	15.41, 15.49
56.021	8.1
56.16	15.24
ch. 64	1.5, 4.1
64.031	4.2
64.041	4.11
64.051	4.15
64.061(1)	4.12, 4.18, 4.24, 4.34
64.061(2)	4.20–.21
64.061(3)	4.23–.24
64.061(4)	4.1, 4.12, 4.17–.18, 4.33–.35
64.071	4.17
64.071(1)	4.21, 4.25, 4.33–.35
64.071(2)	4.17, 4.25
64.071(3)	4.17, 4.25, 4.37
64.081	4.26–.27
64.091	4.1–.2
ch. 65	1.3, 1.16, 1.21, 7.7, 11.11
65.011–.051	1.8
65.061	1.9, 1.20, 2.15
65.061(1)	1.4, 1.9
65.061(2)	1.9, 1.20–.21, 1.23, 1.25
65.061(3)	1.20, 11.34
65.061(4)	1.29
65.071	1.10
65.081	1.11–.12
65.081(2)	1.4
ch. 66	1.4, 2.15, 3.2
66.011	3.9
66.021	3.20
66.021(1)	3.9
66.021(3)	3.29
66.021(4)	3.6, 3.10, 3.14, 3.18
66.021(5)	3.19
66.031(1)	3.24
66.031(2)	3.26
66.041	3.32, 3.34
66.051	3.32, 3.35
66.061	3.32, 3.36–.37
66.071	3.32, 3.38–.39
66.081	3.32, 3.40–.41
66.091–.101	3.32, 3.41
66.28–.47	1.23
69.041(2)	5.15
71.011	8.5, 8.12, 8.14, 8.21, 8.23–.24
71.011(1)	8.4, 8.11
71.011(2)	8.10

71.011(3)	8.3
71.011(4)(a)	8.8, 8.22
71.011(5)	8.8–.9, 8.11
71.021–.031	8.1
71.041	8.5, 8.21, 8.23
71.041(3)	8.23
ch. 82	3.4, 15.1–.3, 15.33, 15.45
82.04	15.45
82.05	3.4, 15.45
82.061	15.48
82.071	15.46, 15.50–.52
82.081	15.51
82.091–.101	15.53
ch. 83	15.1–.3, 15.17, 15.33, 15.43, 15.57
83.001	15.1, 15.65
83.01	15.1, 15.6
83.02	15.1, 15.6, 15.65
83.03	15.1, 15.7, 15.9, 15.64–.65
83.04	15.1, 15.10
83.05	15.1, 15.11
83.06	15.1, 15.9
83.06(1)	15.68
83.07	15.1
83.08	15.1–.2, 15.12, 15.15, 15.18, 15.24
83.08(1)	15.16, 15.82
83.08(2)	15.16, 15.24, 15.82
83.08(3)	15.15
83.09	15.1–.2, 15.15, 15.18
83.10	15.1, 15.14
83.11	15.1–.2, 15.5, 15.17–.19
83.12	15.1–.2, 15.17–.18, 15.21, 15.23
83.13	15.1–.2, 15.17–.18, 15.23
83.14	15.1–.2, 15.17–.18, 15.25, 15.28
83.15	15.1–.2, 15.17–.18, 15.24
83.18	15.1–.2, 15.17–.18, 15.28
83.19	15.1–.2, 15.17–.18, 15.30–.31
83.20	15.1–.2, 15.9, 15.32–.34, 15.37, 15.43, 15.46
83.20(2)	15.34–.35, 15.39
83.21	15.1, 15.4–.5, 15.9–.11, 15.32, 15.39, 15.46
83.22	15.1, 15.4, 15.10–.11, 15.32, 15.40, 15.46
83.231–.251	15.1, 15.4, 15.10–.11, 15.32, 15.46
83.40	15.1, 15.56, 15.69
83.41	15.1, 15.56–.57, 15.69
83.42	15.1, 15.56, 15.69
83.42(1)–.42(5)	15.57
83.43	15.1, 15.56, 15.62, 15.69, 15.71
83.43(2)	15.57

83.43(4)	15.82
83.43(6)	15.71
83.43(9)	15.71
83.43(10)	15.57
83.43(12)	15.71
83.44	15.1, 15.56, 15.69
83.45	15.1, 15.56, 15.60, 15.69
83.45(1)–.45(2)	15.60
83.46	15.1, 15.56, 15.65, 15.69
83.46(1)	15.63, 15.68
83.46(2)	15.64
83.47	15.1, 15.56, 15.61, 15.69, 15.80
83.47(1)(a)	15.75–.76
83.47(1)(b)	15.61
83.47(2)	15.76
83.48	15.1, 15.56, 15.62, 15.69
83.49	15.1, 15.56, 15.69, 15.71
83.49(1)–.49(2)	15.71
83.49(3)(a)	15.72, 15.83
83.49(3)(b)	15.70, 15.72
83.49(3)(c)	15.72
83.49(5)	15.72
83.50	15.1, 15.56, 15.69, 15.71
83.50(1)	15.70, 15.78
83.50(2)	15.70
83.51	15.1, 15.56, 15.58, 15.69
83.51(1)	15.73, 15.75, 15.78–.79, 15.90
83.51(1)(b)	15.73, 15.75
83.51(2)(a)	15.73
83.51(2)(c)	15.73
83.51(4)	15.73
83.52	15.1, 15.56, 15.69, 15.75, 15.83–.84
83.52(2)(d)	15.76
83.53	15.1, 15.56, 15.69
83.53(1)–.53(3)	15.76
83.54	15.1, 15.56, 15.69, 15.75, 15.77, 15.81
83.55	15.1, 15.56, 15.69, 15.70, 15.74, 15.77, 15.81
83.56	15.1, 15.56, 15.69, 15.78
83.56(1)	15.70, 15.78
83.56(1)(a)–.56(1)(b)	15.78
83.56(2)–.56(3)	15.83, 15.85
83.56(4)	15.66, 15.78–.79, 15.83, 15.90
83.56(5)	15.83
83.57	15.1, 15.56, 15.65–.66, 15.69
83.58	15.1, 15.56, 15.68–.69, 15.83, 15.88
83.59	15.1, 15.56, 15.68–.69, 15.88, 15.91
83.59(3)(b)–.59(3)(c)	15.87

83.59(4)	15.88
83.60	15.1, 15.56, 15.69
83.60(1)	15.70, 15.79, 15.90
83.60(2)	15.90
83.61	15.1, 15.56, 15,69, 15.79, 15.90
83.62	15.1, 15.56, 15.69, 15.91, 15.93
83.625	15.91
83.63	15.1, 15.56, 15.69, 15.80
83.68	15.1, 15.56, 15.69, 15.96
83.69	15.1, 15.56, 15.69, 15.93, 15.96—.97
83.69(1)(c)	15.95
83.695	15.96
83.695(2)	15.93, 15.96
83.695(3)	15.96
83.695(4)	15.93
83.70	15.1, 15.56, 15.69, 15.96—97
83.70(1)—.70(2)	15.94
83.70(3)	15.95
83.70(3)(a)	15.94
83.70(3)(c)—.70(7)	15.94
83.71	15.1, 15.56, 15.69, 15.95—.97
83.72—.73	15.1, 15.56, 15.69, 15.96—.97
ch. 85	6.18, 6.21
85.011	6.1, 6.11
85.011(4)	6.11—.12
85.011(5)	15.82
85.011(5)(a)	6.12
85.011(5)(b)	15.82
85.021	6.1, 6.11
85.031	15.82
85.041	6.24
85.051	15.82
ch. 86	1.6, 11.11, 15.55
92.25—.27	8.21
92.29	8.21
92.35	8.21
92.40	15.73
95.031	10.10
95.031(2)	10.10
95.11(2)(b)	8.8, 10.10
95.11(3)(a)	10.10
95.11(3)(c)	10.10
95.11(3)(o)	14.2, 14.7
95.11(3)(p)	8.8
95.11(6)	8.8
95.12	1.30, 2.4, 3.15
95.13	1.30, 3.15

95.14	1.30
95.16	1.21, 1.32, 2.4—.5, 2.11, 3.15
95.16(2)	2.7—.8
95.16(2)(b)	2.12
95.17	1.32
95.18	1.32, 2.4, 2.6, 3.15
95.18(1)	2.12
95.18(2)	2.7, 2.9
95.19	1.32
95.22	1.30
95.231	1.30
95.281	1.30
ch. 163	13.2, 13.4
163.160—.245	13.2
163.250	13.1—.2
163.255—.315	13.2
ch. 166	13.2, 13.4
166.021	13.2
ch. 176	13.2, 13.4
176.04	13.3
193.023(2)	12.4
255.05	6.2
286.011	13.5
472.14	12.9
ch. 475	9.21
475.41	9.21
581.152	12.4
633.08	12.4
672.302	15.60
679.310	15.82
ch. 682	10.5
689.01	2.14
689.07	11.30
689.18	11.15
ch. 694	1.30
695.05	1.30
695.20	1.30
697.01	9.12—.13
702.06	5.65
704.01	12.10
704.04	12.10
ch. 712	1.21, 1.31
ch. 713	6.1, 6.15—.18, 6.21, 6.24, 6.26
713.01	6.1, 6.3
713.01(2)	6.6
713.01(9)	6.6
713.01(11)	6.6
713.01(12)	6.9
713.02	6.1—.2
713.02(5)	6.2
713.02(6)	6.2, 6.21
713.02(7)—(8)	6.2

713.03–.06	6.1–.2, 6.8
713.06(2)	6.4, 6.21, 6.31
713.06(2)(a)	6.6–.7
713.06(2)(b)–.06(2)(c)	6.7
713.06(3)(d)1	6.4
713.06(3)(d)5	6.40
713.06(3)(e)	6.29
713.06(4)	6.29
713.07	6.1, 6.30
713.07(4)	6.29
713.08	6.1, 6.4, 6.7
713.08(3)	6.4
713.08(4)(c)	6.4, 6.7
713.08(5)	6.4
713.09	6.1
713.10	6.1, 6.9
713.11–.12	6.1, 6.38
713.13	6.1, 6.4, 6.9
713.135–.14	6.1
713.15	6.1, 6.37
713.17	6.1, 6.37
713.18	6.1, 6.7
713.19–.21	6.1
713.21(4)	6.10
713.22	6.1
713.22(1)	6.4, 6.10, 6.21
713.22(2)	6.10
713.23	6.1–.2, 6.21, 6.40
713.24	6.1, 6.21
713.24(1)	6.2
713.24(4)	6.21
713.25–.26	6.1
713.27	6.1, 6.27–.28
713.28	6.1, 6.9
713.29	6.1, 6.14
713.30	6.1, 6.39
713.31	6.1
713.31(2)(b)–.31(2)(c)	6.25
713.32–.36	6.1
713.50	15.82
713.691	15.82
713.691(2)	15.15, 15.82
713.691(3)	15.18, 15.46, 15.82
715.06	12.8
ch. 717	5.53
732.401	11.30
744.102(2)	11.30
901.19(1)	12.4

INDEX TO RULES OF CIVIL PROCEDURE

Rule	Section
1.010	1.23, 15.49
1.060(a)	15.26
1.070	5.20
1.070(e)	5.24
1.070(f)	8.15
1.080	5.34
1.090	15.42
1.090(a)	15.49
1.110	11.32
1.110(c)	3.14, 15.26
1.110(d)	15.26
1.110(g)	6.24, 15.49
1.130	5.13
1.130(b)	8.12
1.140(c)	5.34
1.170	15.26, 15.49
1.210(b)	1.23
1.230	6.24
1.260(a)	3.9
1.350	8.18
1.370	8.18
1.430	15.51
1.430(d)	15.27
1.500	1.23, 5.31, 15.23
1.500(a)—(b)	5.31
1.510	5.33
1.510(c)	5.34
1.520	11.39
1.570	7.18
1.580	5.53
1.909	15.23
1.914—.915	3.30
1.916	5.53
1.918	1.20, 5.18, 6.21
1.920	5.30, 8.25
1.938	15.47
1.940	3.6, 3.10, 3.12—.13
1.941	9.11, 9.18
1.944	5.16
1.947	15.39, 15.88
1.960	15.22
1.965	14.8
1.993	1.34, 15.29
1.996	5.40

INDEX TO CASES

                                                                    Section

Adams v. Fielding, 148 Fla. 552, 4 So.2d 678 (1941) 5.26
Adams v. Fryer, 59 Fla. 112, 52 So. 611 (1910)....................... 2.9
Adler v. Schekter, 197 So.2d 46 (3d D.C.A. Fla. 1967) 4.28
Advance Printing and Litho Company, In re, 277 F.Supp.
    101 (W.D. Pa. 1967), *aff'd* 387 F.2d 952 .... 5.80
Aiken v. Davis, 106 Fla. 675, 143 So. 658 (1932) 13.8
Akin v. Godwin, 49 So.2d 604 (Fla. 1951) 2.2
Alkow v. Blocker, 168 So.2d 340 (3d D.C.A. Fla. 1964) 5.65
Allen v. Avondale Co., 135 Fla. 6, 185 So. 137 (1938) 11.12
Allstate Mortgage Corporation of Florida v. Strasser,
    277 So.2d 843 (3d D.C.A. Fla. 1973), *aff'd*
    286 So.2d 201 .... 5.46
Apalachicola Land & Development Co. v. McRae,
    86 Fla. 393, 98 So. 505 (1923) 12.3
Ardell v. Milner, 166 So.2d 714 (3d D.C.A. Fla. 1964) 15.11
Asgrow-Kilgore Co. v. Mulford Hickerson Corp.,
    301 So.2d 441 (Fla. 1974).................................... 10.12
Avery v. Marine Bank & Trust Company, 216 So.2d 251
    (2d D.C.A. Fla. 1968).. 9.10

Babe's Plumbing, Inc. v. Maier, 194 So.2d 666
    (2d D.C.A. Fla. 1967) 6.14
Babsdon Company v. Thrifty Parking Company,
    149 So.2d 566 (3d D.C.A. Fla. 1963) 15.54
Baer v. General Motors Acceptance Corporation,
    101 Fla. 913, 132 So. 817 (1931) 15.13
Baker v. Clifford Mathew Investment Co., 99 Fla. 1229,
    128 So. 827 (1930) 15.37
Baker v. Field, 163 So.2d 42 (2d D.C.A. Fla. 1964) 11.12
Bal Harbour Village v. State ex rel. Giblin,
    299 So.2d 611 (3d D.C.A. Fla. 1974), *cert. den.*
    311 So.2d 670 .... 13.4, 13.15
Baltzell v. Daniel, 111 Fla. 303, 149 So. 639 (1933),
    93 A.L.R. 1259... 4.31
Bank of New Mexico v. Rico, 429 P.2d 368 (N.M. 1967) 10.14
Barber v. Rader, 350 F.Supp. 183 (S.D. Fla. 1972) 15.18, 15.82, 15.87
Barton v. Moline Properties, 121 Fla. 683,
    164 So. 551 (1935) 11.12
Batman v. Creighton, 101 So.2d 587
    (2d D.C.A. Fla. 1958), *cert. den.* 106 So.2d 199 .... 11.9

Bayshore Development Co.v. Bonfoey, 75 Fla. 455,
    78 So. 507 (1918) 10.9
Beebe v. Richardson, 156 Fla. 559, 23 So.2d 718 (1945) 1.11
Benefield v. State, 160 So.2d 706 (Fla. 1964)......................... 12.4
Berwick Corp. v. Kleinginna Investment Corp.,
    143 So.2d 684 (3d D.C.A. Fla. 1962) 15.78
Bigelow v. Summers, 28 Fla. 759, 9 So. 690 (1891) 8.5
Bird v. Bird, 15 Fla. 424 (1875) 4.16, 4.19
Black v. Miller, 219 So.2d 106 (3d D.C.A. Fla. 1969),
    cert. den. 225 So.2d 920 .... 4.6
Blank v. Town of Lake Clarke Shores, 161 So.2d 683
    (2d D.C.A. Fla. 1964) 13.12
Board of Public Instruction v. Town of
    Bay Harbor Islands, 81 So.2d 637 (Fla. 1955).................. 11.6
Boley v. Skinner, 38 Fla. 291, 20 So. 1017 (1896)............ 4.14, 4.16, 4.19
Bossom v. Gillman, 70 Fla. 310, 70 So. 364 (1915).................... 2.10
Boucher v. Novotny, 102 So.2d 132 (Fla. 1958) 13.16
Bowers v. Pearson, 101 Fla. 714, 135 So. 562 (1931) 5.17
Boyles v. Atlantic Federal Savings & Loan Ass'n,
    201 So.2d 909 (4th D.C.A. Fla. 1967)......................... 5.65
Brady v. Scott, 128 Fla. 582, 175 So. 724 (1937)..................... 15.65
Broach v. Young, 100 So.2d 411 (Fla. 1958) 13.8
Brooks v. Taylor, 190 So.2d 205 (1st D.C.A. Fla. 1966) 1.32
Brown v. Sohn, 276 So.2d 501 (1st D.C.A. Fla. 1973)................. 1.21
Brownlee v. Sussman, 238 So.2d 317
    (3d D.C.A. Fla. 1970) 15.79, 15.90
Builders Finance Co., Inc. v. Ridgewood Homesites, Inc.,
    157 So.2d 551 (2d D.C.A. Fla. 1963) 5.65
Burdine v. Sewell, 92 Fla. 375, 109 So. 648 (1926) 11.6
Burney v. Dedge, 56 So.2d 715 (Fla. 1952) 4.5

Cahill v. Chesley, 189 So.2d 818 (2d D.C.A. Fla. 1966)................ 1.32
Camp Phosphate Co. v. Anderson, 48 Fla. 226,
    37 So. 722 (1904) 4.4, 4.6
Campbell v. Skinner Mfg. Co., 53 Fla. 632,
    43 So. 874 (1907) 8.21
Carey v. Beyer, 75 So.2d 217 (Fla. 1954) 14.7
Cathcart v. Turner, 18 Fla. 837 (1882) 15.15
Chasteen v. Chasteen, 213 So.2d 509
    (1st D.C.A. Fla. 1968).. 1.32
Childs v. Dougherty, 73 Fla. 72, 75 So. 783 (1917).................. 12.7
Christy v. Burch, 25 Fla. 942, 2 So. 258 (1887) 8.19
City Co. of City of No. Miami B. v. Trebor Const. Corp.,
    296 So.2d 490 (Fla. 1974) 13.8
City of Boynton Beach v. Carroll, 272 So.2d 171
    (4th D.C.A. Fla. 1973), *cert. den.* 279 So.2d 871 .... 13.8

City of Jacksonville v. Imler, 235 So.2d 526
  (1st D.C.A. Fla. 1970), *cert. den.* 239 So.2d 829 .... 13.10
City of Miami Beach v. Breitbart, 280 So.2d 18
  (3d D.C.A. Fla. 1973), *cert. den.* 286 So.2d 204 .... 13.15
City of Miami Beach v. First Trust Co., 45 So.2d 681
  (Fla. 1950) 13.13
City of Miami Beach v. Lachman, 71 So.2d 148
  (Fla. 1954), *app. dism.* 348 U.S. 906 .... 13.18
City of Miami Beach v. Ocean and Inland Co.,
  147 Fla. 480, 3 So.2d 364 (1941) 12.3, 13.13
City of Miami Beach v. Silver, 67 So.2d 646 (Fla. 1953) 13.77
City of Miami Beach v. State ex rel. Fontainebleau Hotel
  Corp., 108 So.2d 614 (3d D.C.A. Fla. 1959),
  app. dism. and *cert. den.* 111 So.2d 437 .... 13.4, 13.7
City of Miami Beach v. Wiesen, 86 So.2d 442 (Fla. 1956)............. 13.10
City of Miami Beach v. Zorovich, 195 So.2d 31
  (3d D.C.A. Fla. 1967), *cert. den.* 201 So.2d 554 .... 13.10, 13.12
City of St. Petersburg v. Aikin, 217 So.2d 315
  (Fla. 1968) .... 13.10, 13.17—.18
City of West Palm Beach v. Edward U. Roddy Corp.,
  43 So.2d 709 (Fla. 1950).................................... 13.10
Clearwater v. College Properties, Inc., 239 So.2d 515
  (2d D.C.A. Fla. 1970) 13.10
Clements v. Leonard, 70 So.2d 840 (Fla. 1954)...................... 9.10
Coe-Mortimer Co. v. Dusendschon, 113 Fla. 818,
  152 So. 729 (1934) 10.13
Coffrin v. Sayles, 128 Fla. 622, 175 So. 236 (1937)................. 10.13
Coggan v. Coggan, 230 So.2d 34 (2d D.C.A. Fla. 1969),
  quashed in part 239 So.2d 17................................. 4.16
Coggan v. Coggan, 213 So.2d 902 (2d D.C.A. Fla. 1968),
  cert. den. 222 So.2d 25 .... 4.16
Colby v. Colby, 120 So.2d 797 (3d D.C.A. Fla. 1960) 13.15
Coleman v. State, 119 Fla. 653, 161 So. 89 (1935) 15.10
Collier County Publishing Co., Inc. v. Chapman,
  318 So.2d 492 (2d D.C.A. Fla. 1975) 14.3
Colmes v. Hoco, Inc. of Dade County, 152 So.2d 524
  (3d D.C.A. Fla. 1963)... 5.65
Commissioners of Suwanee County v. Commissioners of
  Columbia County, 18 Fla. 78 (Fla. 1881)...................... 8.16
Condrey v. Condrey, 92 So.2d 423 (Fla. 1957) 4.7
Cone Bros. Constr. Co. v. Moore, 141 Fla. 420,
  193 So. 288 (1940).. 5.5
Confederate Point Partnership, Ltd. v. Schatten,
  278 So.2d 661 (1st D.C.A. Fla. 1973) 5.46
Connell v. Mittendorf, 147 So.2d 169
  (2d D.C.A. Fla. 1962) 10.2
Coogler v. Rogers, 25 Fla. 853, 7 So. 391 (1889) 3.9

Cook v. Katiba, 190 So.2d 309 (Fla. 1966) 1.33
County of Brevard v. Woodham, 223 So.2d 344
    (4th D.C.A. Fla. 1969), *cert. den.*
    229 So.2d 872 .... 13.3, 13.10, 13.12, 13.18
Cox v. La Pota, 76 So.2d 662 (Fla. 1955) 9.10
Crane Co. v. Fine, 221 So.2d 145 (Fla. 1969) 6.1, 6.7
Cross v. Aby, 55 Fla. 311, 45 So. 820 (1908) 8.21
Culbertson v. Montanbault, 133 So.2d 772
    (2d D.C.A. Fla. 1961) 1.32

Dade County v. Jason, 278 So.2d 311
    (3d D.C.A. Fla. 1973) .... 13.7—.8
Dade County v. Thompson, 146 Fla. 66, 200 So. 212 (1941) 11.12
Daniels v. Alico Land Development Company,
    189 So.2d 540 (2d D.C.A. Fla. 1966) 1.32
Davis v. Drummond, 68 Fla. 471, 67 So. 99 (1914) 15.50
Davis v. Titus Incorporated, 275 So.2d 600
    (1st D.C.A. Fla. 1973) 13.18
Deltona Corporation v. Kipnis, 194 So.2d 295
    (2d D.C.A. Fla. 1967) 4.26
Deverick v. Bailey, 174 So.2d 440 (2d D.C.A. Fla. 1965),
    cert. den. 183 So.2d 209 .... 1.32
De Vore v. Lee, 158 Fla. 608, 30 So.2d 924 (1947) 15.63
Diversified Enterprises of Florida, Inc. v. Holt,
    188 So.2d 693 (2d D.C.A. Fla. 1966) 5.65
Doddridge v. American Trust & Savings Bank,
    189 N.E. 165 (Ind. 1934) 10.14
Donly v. Metropolitan Realty & Investment Co.,
    71 Fla. 644, 72 So. 178 (1916) 4.2
Doushkess v. Burger Brewing Co., 47 N.Y.S. 312 (1897) 10.14
Downing v. Bird, 100 So.2d 57 (Fla. 1958) 2.4
Doyle v. Wade, 23 Fla. 90, 1 So. 516 (1887) 2.5, 2.8

Easton v. Weir, 125 So.2d 115 (2d D.C.A. Fla. 1960),
    cert. den. 129 So.2d 141 .... 15.73
Edgewater Beach Hotel Corporation v. Bishop,
    120 Fla. 623, 163 So. 214 (1935) 11.13, 11.27
Ehinger v. State ex rel. Gottesman, 147 Fla. 129,
    2 So.2d 357 (1941) 13.10
Eldridge v. E. C. Fitz & Co., 126 Fla. 548,
    171 So. 509 (1936) 5.26
Ellis v. Everett, 79 Fla. 493, 84 So. 617 (1920) 4.5
Ellison v. City of Fort Lauderdale,
    183 So.2d 193 (Fla. 1966) 13.4

Elvins v. Seestedt, 141 Fla. 266, 193 So. 54 (1940),
   126 A.L.R. 1001 .... 4.2, 4.6
Essential Industries Corporation, In re, 150 F.2d 326
   (2d Cir. 1945), 161 A.L.R. 968 .... 5.80

F. B. Collins Inv. Co. v. Sallas,
   260 S.W. 261 (Tex. 1924) 10.14
Famers Bros. Co. v. Huddle Enterprises, Inc.,
   366 F.2d 143 (9th Cir. 1966) 5.82
Farrell v. Forest Inv. Co., 73 Fla. 191, 74 So. 216
   (Fla. 1917), 1 A.L.R. 25 .... 4.15
Filaretou v. Christou, 133 So.2d 652
   (2d D.C.A. Fla. 1961) 15.79
Finchum v. Vogel, 194 So.2d 49 (4th D.C.A. Fla. 1967) 11.7
Firstbrook v. Buzbee, 101 Fla. 876, 132 So. 673 (1931) 9.8
First Federal Savings & Loan Association of Broward
   County v. Consolidated Development Corp.,
   195 So.2d 856 (Fla. 1967) 10.13
Flamingo Ranch Estates, Inc. v. Sunshine Ranches
   Homeowners, Inc., 303 So.2d 665
   (4th D.C.A. Fla. 1974) 11.22
Florida Cent. & W. R. Co. v. Bostwick, 55 Fla. 665,
   45 So. 1033 (1908) 8.16
Florida Palm-Aire Corporation v. Delvin, 230 So.2d 26
   (4th D.C.A. Fla. 1970), *cert. dism.* 234 So.2d 357 .... 13.16
Floro v. Parker, 205 So.2d 363 (2d D.C.A. Fla. 1968) 15.45
Forehand v. Peacock, 77 So.2d 625 (Fla. 1955) 4.7, 4.14
Forman v. Ward, 219 So.2d 68 (1st D.C.A. Fla. 1969) 1.32
Foster v. Thomas, 112 So.2d 33 (1st D.C.A. Fla. 1959) 4.32
Foxbilt Electric, Inc. v. Belefant, 280 So.2d 28
   (4th D.C.A. Fla. 1973) 6.14
Frank v. Maryland, 359 U.S. 360, 79 S.Ct. 804,
   3 L.Ed.2d 877 (1959), *reh. den.* 360 U.S. 914 .... 12.4
Freligh v. Maurer, 111 So.2d 712 (2d D.C.A. Fla. 1959) 5.17
Fuentes v. Shevin, 407 U.S. 67, 92 S.Ct. 1983,
   32 L.Ed.2d 556 (1972) 5.18, 15.82

Gables Lincoln-Mercury, Inc. v. First Bank & Trust Co.,
   219 So.2d 90 (3d D.C.A. Fla. 1969) 15.82
Gancedo Lumber Company, Inc. v. Flagship First National
   Bank of Miami Beach, 340 So.2d 486
   (3d D.C.A. Fla. 1976) 10.12
Gates v. Stucco Corp., 112 So.2d 36
   (3d D.C.A. Fla. 1959) 15.5

Gates v. Utsey, 177 So.2d 486 (1st D.C.A. Fla. 1965) .... 14.3—.4, 14.7
Gautier v. Town of Jupiter Island, 142 So.2d 321
    (2d D.C.A. Fla. 1962) 13.10
Georgia Casualty Co. v. O'Donnell, 109 Fla. 290,
    147 So. 267 (1933) 6.12
Gercas v. Davis, 188 So.2d 9 (2d D.C.A. Fla. 1966)............ 11.20, 11.23
Giovannielli v. Lacedonia, 177 So.2d 506
    (3d D.C.A. Fla. 1965) 1.6
Girtman v. Starbuck, 48 Fla. 265, 37 So. 731 (1904) 4.6, 4.27
Glass v. Layton, 140 Fla. 522, 192 So. 330 (1939)..................... 4.29
Glusman v. Lieberman, 285 So.2d 29
    (4th D.C.A. Fla. 1973) .... 14.3—.4
Gmaz v. King, 238 So.2d 511 (2d D.C.A. Fla. 1970) 1.17, 5.26
Greeley v. Hendricks, 23 Fla. 366, 2 So. 620 (1887) 4.2
Griffith v. Griffith, 59 Fla. 512, 52 So. 609 (1910) 4.4

H & L Land Company v. Warner, 258 So.2d 293
    (2d D.C.A. Fla. 1972) 9.12
Hagan v. Sabal Palms, Inc., 186 So.2d 302
    (2d D.C.A. Fla. 1966), *cert. den.* 192 So.2d 489 .... 11.8, 11.10
Haines Lumber & Millwork Co., In re, 144 F.Supp. 108
    (E.D. Pa. 1956) 5.79
Hall v. Briny Breezes Club, 179 So.2d 128
    (2d D.C.A. Fla. 1965) 11.12
Hall v. Garson, 468 F.2d 845 (5th Cir. 1972)........................ 15.18
Hall v. Korth, 244 So.2d 766 (3d D.C.A. Fla. 1971) 13.6
Hall v. Snavely, 93 Fla. 664, 112 So. 551 (1927) 11.8, 11.10
Hankins v. Smith, 103 Fla. 892, 138 So. 494 (1931) 15.78
Hanna v. American International Land Corporation,
    289 So.2d 756 (2d D.C.A. Fla. 1974) 9.6
Harper v. Green, 99 Fla. 1309, 128 So. 827 (1930) 8.5
Harris v. Sunset Islands Property Owners, Inc.,
    116 So.2d 622 (Fla. 1959).................................. 11.15
Hartnett v. Austin, 93 So.2d 86 (Fla. 1956)......................... 13.6
Harwick v. Indian Creek Country Club, 142 So.2d 128
    (3d D.C.A. Fla. 1962) 11.20, 11.23
Hasle v. Maasbrock, 120 So.2d 794 (3d D.C.A. Fla. 1960)............. 4.17
Heath v. First National Bank in Milton, 213 So.2d 883
    (1st D.C.A. Fla. 1968)...................................... 8.19
Henthorn v. Tri Par Land Development Corporation,
    221 So.2d 465 (2d D.C.A. Fla. 1969), *aff'd*
    on other grounds 241 So.2d 429 .... 11.4
Hickman v. Hickman, 147 So.2d 555 (2d D.C.A. Fla. 1962),
    cert. den. 155 So.2d 150 .... 4.28
Hill v. State ex rel. Watson, 155 Fla. 245,
    19 So.2d 857 (1944), *reversed* 325 U.S. 538 .... 12.4

Hobbs v. Frazier, 56 Fla. 796, 47 So. 929 (1908) 4.2
Hodges v. Cooksey, 33 Fla. 715, 15 So. 549 (1894) 15.15
Hogans v. Carruth, 18 Fla. 587 (1882) 3.18
Holiday Out In America At St. Lucie, Inc. v. Bowes,
    285 So.2d 63 (4th D.C.A. Fla. 1973).................... 11.4, 11.15
Hillsborough City Aviation A. v. Cone Bros. Contr. Co.,
    285 So.2d 619 (2d D.C.A. Fla. 1973) 10.8
Homer v. Dadeland Shopping Center, Inc., 229 So.2d 834
    (Fla. 1970) 11.6
Hopewell Building Co. v. Callan, 193 N.Y.S. 504 (1922).............. 10.14
Horton v. O'Rourke, 321 So.2d 612 (2d D.C.A. Fla. 1975) 9.6
Horton v. Smith-Richardson Inv. Co., 81 Fla. 255,
    87 So. 905 (1921) 2.8
Houdaille-Duval-Wright Co. v. Charldon Const. Co.,
    266 So.2d 106 (3d D.C.A. Fla. 1972) 6.14
Huguley v. Hall, 157 So.2d 417 (Fla. 1963) 9.17
Hunt v. Covington, 145 Fla. 706, 200 So. 76 (1941) 4.2

IDS Properties, Inc. v. Town of Palm Beach,
    279 So.2d 353 (4th D.C.A. Fla. 1973)........................ 13.5
International Kaolin Co. v. Vause, 55 Fla. 641,
    46 So. 3 (1908) 5.13
International Realty Associates v. McAdoo, 87 Fla. 1,
    99 So. 117 (1924) 7.1
Ivey Plants, Inc. v. FMC Corporation, 282 So.2d 205
    (4th D.C.A. Fla. 1973), *cert. den.* 289 So.2d 731 .... 15.61

J. E. DeBelle Co., In re, 286 Fed. 699 (S.D. Fla. 1923) 15.13
Jack Stilson & Co. v. Caloosa Bayview Corporation,
    278 So.2d 282 (Fla. 1973) 6.10
Jason v. Dade County, 37 Fla.Supp. 190
    (Cir. Ct. Dade 1972), *aff'd* 278 So.2d 311 .... 13.7
J. G. Plumbing Service, Inc. v. Coastal Mortgage
    Co., 329 So.2d 393 (2d D.C.A. Fla. 1976),
    cert. dism. 339 So.2d 1169 .... 10.12
John T. Wood Homes, Inc. v. Air Control Products, Inc.,
    177 So.2d 709 (1st D.C.A. Fla. 1965) 6.14
John W. Johnson, Inc. v. J. A. Jones Construction Co.,
    369 F.Supp. 484 (E.D. Va. 1973)........................... 10.14
Johnson v. Three Bays Properties #2, Inc., 159 So.2d
    924 (3d D.C.A. Fla. 1964), 4 A.L.R.3d 565 .... 11.22
Jonas v. Bar-Jam Corp., 170 So.2d 479
    (3d D.C.A. Fla. 1965) 5.65

Jones v. Escambia Land & Mfg. Co., 55 Fla. 783,
    46 So. 290 (1908) 8.5
Jordan v. Sayre, 24 Fla. 1, 3 So. 329 (1888) 5.5
Josephson v. Autrey, 96 So.2d 784 (Fla. 1957) 13.16
Joyner v. Rogers, 182 So.2d 628 (4th D.C.A. Fla. 1966) 4.14

Kanter v. Safran, 68 So.2d 553 (Fla. 1953) 15.54
Katz v. Kenholtz, 147 So.2d 342 (3d D.C.A. Fla. 1963) 15.54
Kennedy v. Kay, 154 So.2d 345 (3d D.C.A. Fla. 1963) 5.65
Kerrigan v. Thomas 281 So.2d 410 (1st D.C.A. Fla. 1973),
    cert. den. 287 So.2d 97 .... 2.13
Kester v. Bostwick, 153 Fla. 437, 15 So.2d 201 (1943) 3.12
Key v. All Persons Claiming Any Estate, Etc.,
    160 Fla. 723, 36 So.2d 366 (1948) 1.15, 1.21, 1.23
Keyes v. Rymer Realty Corporation, 219 So.2d 711
    (3d D.C.A. Fla. 1969) 4.5, 4.8, 4.17
King v. Carden, 237 So.2d 26 (1st D.C.A. Fla. 1970) .... 2.13—.14
Klinger v. Milton Holding Co., 136 Fla. 50,
    186 So. 526 (1939) 5.26
Kollar v. Kollar, 155 Fla. 705, 21 So.2d 356 (1945) 4.2
Kurkjian v. Fish Carburetor Corporation, 145 So.2d 523
    (1st D.C.A. Fla. 1962) 5.65

L. Maxcy, Inc. v. Mayo, 103 Fla. 552,
    139 So. 121 (1932) 12.4
Lambert v. Justus, 313 So.2d 140 (2d D.C.A. Fla. 1975) 1.6
Lamoureux v. Lamoureux, 59 So.2d 9 (Fla. 1952) 4.28
Langford v. Brickell, 103 Fla. 672, 138 So. 75 (1931) 4.2
Larsen v. Allocca, 187 So.2d 903 (3d D.C.A. Fla. 1966),
    cert. den. 195 So.2d 566 .... 5.65
Lehman v. Goldin, 160 Fla. 710, 36 So.2d 259 (1948) 14.3
L'Engle v. Reed, 27 Fla. 345, 9 So. 213 (1891) 3.21
Leonard v. Browne, 134 So.2d 872 (1st D.C.A. Fla. 1961) 4.2
Levene v. Enchanted Lake Homes, Inc., 115 So.2d 89
    (3d D.C.A. Fla. 1959) 10.13
Levering v. City of Tarpon Springs, 92 So.2d 638
    (Fla. 1957) 1.32
Lovett v. Lee, 141 Fla. 395, 193 So. 538 (1940) 15.12
Lovett v. Lovett, 93 Fla. 611, 112 So. 768 (1927) 4.1, 4.4, 4.9
Lovingood v. Butler Const. Co., 100 Fla. 1252,
    131 So. 126 (1930), 74 A.L.R. 513 .... 8.5, 8.16
Lowe v. Turpie, 44 N.E. 25 (Ind. 1896) 10.12, 10.14
Lykes Bros. v. Brautcheck, 106 So.2d 582
    (2d D.C.A. Fla. 1958) 1.32

M & E Land Company v. Siegel, 177 So.2d 769
    (1st D.C.A. Fla. 1965).. 13.15
M. & M. Auto Parts Co. v. Riddle, 102 Fla. 598,
    136 So. 437 (1931) 3.9
MacKay v. Bacon, 155 Fla. 577, 20 So.2d 904 (1945) 5.26
McDaniel v. McElvy, 91 Fla. 770, 108 So. 820 (1926),
    51 A.L.R. 731......................................1.9, 1.20, 5.25
McGee v. City of Cocoa, 168 So.2d 766
    (2d D.C.A. Fla. 1964) 13.4
McKenzie v. Atlantic Manor, Inc., 181 So.2d 554
    (3d D.C.A. Fla. 1966), *cert. den.* 192 So.2d 495 .... 15.73
McQueen v. Forsythe, 55 So.2d 545 (Fla. 1951) 4.26
Mainor v. Hobbie, 218 So.2d 203 (1st D.C.A. Fla. 1969),
    app. dism. 225 So.2d 530 .... 1.9
Manilow v. City of Miami Beach, 213 So.2d 589
    (3d D.C.A. Fla. 1968), *cert. den.* 397 U.S. 972 .... 13.12
Mann v. Thompson, 100 So.2d 634 (1st D.C.A. Fla. 1958)............. 9.10
Markley v. Madill, 259 So.2d 723 (2d D.C.A. Fla. 1972) 1.12
Marshall v. Hollywood, Inc., 236 So.2d 114 (Fla. 1970) 1.31
Marshall v. Scott, 277 So.2d 546 (2d D.C.A. Fla. 1973) 10.12
Matlack v. Owen, 181 So.2d 602 (2d D.C.A. Fla. 1966) 5.65
Matousek v. Cooper, 111 So.2d 65 (2d D.C.A. Fla. 1959) 9.10
Maudo, Inc. v. Stein, 201 So.2d 821 (3d D.C.A. Fla. 1967) 5.65
Maule Industries v. Sheffield Steel Products,
    105 So.2d 798 (3d D.C.A. Fla. 1958), *cert. den.*
    111 So.2d 41... 11.5
Melnick v. Reynolds Metals Company, 230 So.2d 490
    (4th D.C.A. Fla. 1970) 6.29
Merritt v. Unkefer, 223 So.2d 723 (Fla. 1969)...................... 10.12
Meyer v. Law, 287 So.2d 37 (Fla. 1973)............................. 2.12
Mickler v. Reddick, 38 Fla. 341, 21 So. 286 (1896) 9.4
Middleton v. Lomaskin, 266 So.2d 678
    (3d D.C.A. Fla. 1972) 15.61
Mid-State Investment Corporation v. O'Steen,
    133 So.2d 455 (1st D.C.A. Fla. 1961), *cert. den.*
    136 So.2d 349.. 9.16
Miles v. Miles, 117 Fla. 884, 158 So. 520 (1935) .... 4.4—.5
Mills v. Robert W. Gottfried, Inc., 272 So.2d 837
    (4th D.C.A. Fla. 1973) 6.12, 10.4
Moore v. Musa, 198 So.2d 843 (3d D.C.A. Fla. 1967)................. 1.32
Moore v. Price, 98 Fla. 276, 123 So. 768 (1929) 4.2
Moore v. Stevens, 90 Fla. 879, 106 So. 901 (1925),
    43 A.L.R. 1127..11.4, 11.14—.15
Morganthaler v. Holl, 101 Fla. 452, 134 So. 223 (1931).............. 9.4
Morgen-Oswood & Associates, Inc. of Florida v.
    Continental Mortgage Investors, 323 So.2d 684
    (4th D.C.A. Fla. 1976) 10.12

Moskos v. Hand, 247 So.2d 795 (4th D.C.A. Fla. 1971) .... 15.37—.38, 15.61
Mundy v. Carter, 311 So.2d 773 (1st D.C.A. Fla. 1975) 11.9
Munroe v. Birdsey, 102 Fla. 544, 136 So. 886 (1931) 4.23, 4.28

Nahmod v. Nelson, 147 Fla. 564, 3 So.2d 162 (1941) 8.21
Naples Park-Vanderbilt Beach Water District v. Downing,
    244 So.2d 464 (2d D.C.A. Fla. 1971), *cert. den.*
    245 So.2d 257 .... 5.27
Nathanson v. Weston, 163 So.2d 41 (3d D.C.A. Fla. 1964),
    cert. disch. 173 So.2d 451 .... 5.65
Naurison v. Naurison, 132 So.2d 623
    (3d D.C.A. Fla. 1961) 4.2
Nelson v. Haisley, 39 Fla. 145, 22 So. 265 (1897) 4.2
Neubauer v. Town of Surfside, 181 So.2d 707
    (3d D.C.A. Fla. 1966), *cert. den.* 192 So.2d 488 .... 13.10
Nixon v. Temple Terrace Estates, 97 Fla. 392,
    121 So. 475 (1929) 9.8
Norris v. Eikenberry, 103 Fla. 104, 137 So. 128 (1931) 9.8
Norton v. Jones, 83 Fla. 81, 90 So. 854 (1922) 1.33

O'Bryan v. Dr. P. Phillips & Sons, 123 Fla. 302,
    166 So. 820 (1936) 5.17
Ohio ex rel. Eaton v. Price, 364 U.S. 263,
    80 S.Ct. 1463, 4 L.Ed.2d 1708 (1960), *reh. den.*
    369 U.S. 855 .... 12.4
Oklahoma City v. Barclay, 359 P.2d 237 (Okla. 1960) 13.18
Old Plantation Corp. v. Maule Industries, 68 So.2d 180
    (Fla. 1953) .... 14.2—.3, 14.7
Orr v. Peek, 142 Fla. 160, 194 So. 341 (1940) 15.13
Osius v. Barton, 109 Fla. 556, 147 So. 862 (1933),
    88 A.L.R. 394 .... 11.3, 11.12, 11.28

P & N Investment Corp. v. Florida Ranchettes, Inc.,
    220 So.2d 451 (1st D.C.A. Fla. 1969) 12.8
Painter v. Town of Groveland, 79 So.2d 765 (Fla. 1955) 15.9, 15.68
Palm Orange Groves v. Yelvington, 41 So.2d 883
    (Fla. 1949) 2.13
Pan American Bank of Miami v. City of Miami Beach,
    198 So.2d 45 (3d D.C.A. Fla. 1967) 5.5
Paulino v. Hardister, 306 So.2d 125
    (2d D.C.A. Fla. 1975), *cert. den.* 319 So.2d 30 .... 11.31

Phillips Petroleum v. Schun Co., 222 So.2d 491
    (4th D.C.A. Fla. 1969) 10.12
Potter v. Garrett, 52 So.2d 115 (Fla. 1951) 4.16
Potter v. Rowan, 266 So.2d 121 (2d D.C.A. Fla. 1972),
    cert. den. 271 So.2d 143 .... 6.14
Powell v. Lounel, Inc., 173 F.2d 743 (5th Cir. 1949) 15.13
Powell v. New York Life Ins. Co., 141 Fla. 758,
    194 So. 232 (1940) 5.13
Prescott v. Johnson, 8 Fla. 391 (1859) 8.22

R. K. Cooper Construction Company v. Fulton,
    216 So.2d 11 (Fla. 1968) 5.46, 5.49
Ragland v. Clarson, 259 So.2d 757 (1st D.C.A. Fla. 1972) 12.9
Rankin v. Rankin, 258 So.2d 489 (2d D.C.A. Fla. 1972) 4.2
Reed v. Fink, 259 So.2d 729 (3d D.C.A. Fla. 1972) 4.2
Reil v. Myers, 222 So.2d 42 (4th D.C.A. Fla. 1969) 2.14
Renard v. Dade County, 261 So.2d 832 (Fla. 1972) 13.16
Reyes v. Middleton, 36 Fla. 99, 17 So. 937 (1895) 14.4
Reyes v. Perez, 284 So.2d 493 (4th D.C.A. Fla. 1973) 12.10
Richards v. Dodge, 150 So.2d 477 (2d D.C.A. Fla. 1963) 15.78
Richardson v. Holman, 160 Fla. 65, 33 So.2d 641 (1948) 11.7
Roark v. Weldon, 232 So.2d 216 (2d D.C.A. Fla. 1970) 11.17
Roberts v. Lesser, 96 So.2d 222 (Fla. 1957) 6.15
Robinson v. Speer, 185 So.2d 730 (1st D.C.A. Fla. 1966),
    cert. den. 192 So.2d 498 .... 4.3
Rodgers v. Tarrytown, 96 N.E.2d 731 (N.Y. 1951) 13.6
Rountree v. Rountree, 101 So.2d 43 (Fla. 1958) 4.4
Rubin v. Randwest Corporation, 292 So.2d 60 (4th D.C.A.
    Fla. 1974), *cert. den.* 305 So.2d 786 .... 15.58, 15.61
Rudman v. Baine, 133 So.2d 760 (1st D.C.A. Fla. 1961) 4.3
Ruge v. Webb Press Co., 71 Fla. 536, 71 So. 627 (1916) 15.16

Sample v. Ward, 156 Fla. 210, 23 So.2d 81 (1945) 1.23
Schraub v. Charest, 277 So.2d 814 (3d D.C.A. Fla. 1973) 10.12
Seaboard Air Line Ry. Co. v. Atlantic Coast Line R. Co.,
    117 Fla. 830, 158 So. 459 (1935) 1.32
Sea Ledge Properties, Inc. v. Dodge, 283 So.2d 55
    (4th D.C.A. Fla. 1973), *cert. dism.* 285 So.2d 618 ...... 10.6, 10.13
Seaside Properties, Inc. v. State Road Department,
    190 So.2d 391 (3d D.C.A. Fla. 1966), *cert. den.*
    201 So.2d 464, *app. dism.* 389 U.S. 569 .... 1.32
Selective Builders, Inc. v. Hudson City Savings Bank,
    349 A.2d 564 (N.J. 1975) 10.12

Selph v. Purvis, 57 Fla. 188, 49 So. 289 (1909) 8.21
Shaffer v. Pickard, 77 Fla. 697,
    82 So. 232 (1919) .... 4.4, 4.9, 4.14—.15, 4.19
Sharpe v. Ceco Corporation, 242 So.2d 464 (3d D.C.A.
    Fla. 1971), *cert. den.* 247 So.2d 324 .... 6.14
Shaw v. Williams, 50 So.2d 125 (Fla. 1951) 2.10, 2.13
Sheffield v. Carter, 141 So.2d 780 (2d D.C.A. Fla. 1962) 1.17
Shelley v. Kraemer, 334 U.S. 1, 68 S.Ct. 836,
    92 L.Ed. 1161 (1948) 11.15
Silver Blue Lake Apts. v. Silver Blue Lake H. O. Ass'n,
    245 So.2d 609 (Fla. 1971) 11.8
Silver Springs O. & G. R. Co. v. Van Ness, 45 Fla. 559,
    34 So. 884 (1903) 11.7
Simpson v. Lindgren, 133 So.2d 439 (3d D.C.A. Fla. 1961) 1.32
Sloane v. Dixie Gardens, Inc., 278 So.2d 309
    (2d D.C.A. Fla. 1973) 11.4
Smetal Corporation v. West Lake Inv. Co., 126 Fla. 595,
    172 So. 58 (1937) 5.26
Smith v. Continental Insurance Company, 326 So.2d 189
    (2d D.C.A. Fla. 1976) 10.10
Sobel v. Lobel, 168 So.2d 195 (3d D.C.A. Fla. 1964) 7.17
Sohn v. Cominole, 253 So.2d 898 (1st D.C.A. Fla. 1971) 5.65
South Dade Farms, Inc. v. B & L Farms Co.,
    62 So.2d 350 (Fla. 1952) 12.10
Southeastern Fidelity Insurance Co. v. Berman,
    231 So.2d 249 (3d D.C.A. Fla. 1970) 15.45
Southern Realty & Utilities Corp. v. Gettleman,
    197 So.2d 30 (3d D.C.A. Fla. 1967), *cert. den.*
    201 So.2d 560 .... 9.6
Southampton Wholesale Food Terminal v. Providence
    Produce Warehouse Co., 129 F.Supp. 663
    (D. Mass. 1955) 10.12
Speier v. Lane, 254 So.2d 823 (3d D.C.A. Fla. 1971) 8.5
St. Paul at Chase Corp. v. Manufacturer's Life Ins. Co.,
    278 A.2d 12 (Md. App. 1971), *cert. den.*
    404 U.S. 857 .... 10.14
Standard Oil Company v. City of Tallahassee, 87 F.Supp.
    145 (N.D. Fla. 1949), *aff'd* 183 F.2d 410,
    cert. den. 340 U.S. 892 .... 13.10
Staninger v. Jacksonville Expressway Authority, 182
    So.2d 483 (1st D.C.A. Fla. 1966), 22 A.L.R.3d 950 .... 11.17
Stanley v. Powers, 125 Fla. 322, 169 So. 861 (1936) 11.39
Stark v. Frayer, 67 So.2d 237 (Fla. 1953) 1.6, 1.20
State v. Lewis (Circuit Court Q Case No. 67 C-3937,
    15th Judicial Circuit, Palm Beach County) 13.7
State ex rel. Ellis v. Gerbing, 56 Fla. 603,
    47 So. 353 (1908) 12.3

State ex rel. Henry v. City of Miami, 117 Fla. 594,
    158 So. 82 (1934) 13.3
State ex rel. Hillman v. Hutchins, 118 Fla. 220,
    158 So. 716 (1935) 15.43, 15.90
State ex rel. Lacedonia v. Harvey, 68 So.2d 817 (Fla. 1953) 13.15
State Board of Trustees of Internal Improvement Trust
    Fund v. Pineta Company, 287 So.2d 126
    (3d D.C.A. Fla. 1973) 1.6
Stein v. Darby, 126 So.2d 313 (1st D.C.A. Fla. 1961),
    cert. den. 134 So.2d 232 .... 12.10
Stenholm v. Calbeck, 265 So.2d 531 (2d D.C.A. Fla. 1972) 6.4
Stephens v. Stephens, 94 So.2d 366 (Fla. 1957) 1.32
Stewart v. Gadarian, 141 So.2d 289 (1st D.C.A. Fla. 1962) 1.32
Stephl v. Moore, 94 Fla. 313, 114 So. 455 (1927) 11.13
Sterritt v. Baher, 333 So.2d 523 (1st D.C.A. Fla. 1976) 10.12
Steuer v. Glevis, 243 So.2d 453 (4th D.C.A. Fla. 1971) 11.15
Stone v. Maitland, 446 F.2d 83 (5th Cir. 1971) .... 13.3, 13.11—.12
Stovall v. Stokes, 94 Fla. 717, 115 So. 828 (1928) 5.68
Street v. Benner, 20 Fla. 700 (1884) 4.4, 4.15
Stroemer v. Shevin, Case No. 72-1627-Civ.-Wm 5D Fla. ..... 15.2, 15.17—.18
Sudduth v. Hutchison, 42 So.2d 355 (Fla. 1949) 1.12

Tamiami Abstract and Title Company v. Malanka,
    185 So.2d 493 (2d D.C.A. Fla. 1966) 11.26
Tampa Mortgage & Title Company v. Smythe, 109 So.2d 202
    (2d D.C.A. Fla. 1959) 1.32
Taylor v. Taylor, 119 So.2d 811 (2d D.C.A. Fla. 1960) 4.16, 4.26
Thomas v. Greene, 226 So.2d 143 (1st D.C.A. Fla. 1969),
    cert. den. 234 So.2d 117 .... 4.14
Thompson v. Andras—Coggin River Imp. Co.,
    54 N.H. 545 (1874) 12.2
Tilman v. Niemira, 99 Fla. 833, 127 So. 855 (1930) 3.21
Tolar v. Meyer, 96 So.2d 554 (3d D.C.A. Fla. 1957) .. 11.7, 11.9, 11.19, 11.23
Tollius v. City of Miami, 96 So.2d 122 (Fla. 1957) 13.12
Town of North Reddington Beach v. Williams,
    220 So.2d 22 (2d D.C.A. Fla. 1969) .... 13.15, 13.17—.18
Town of Palm Beach v. Gradison, 296 So.2d 473
    (Fla. 1974) 13.5
Town of Surfside v. Abelson, 106 So.2d 108 (3d D.C.A.
    Fla. 1958), cert. den. 111 So.2d 40 .... 13.3
Tropical Attractions, Inc. v. Coppinger, 187 So.2d 395
    (3d D.C.A. Fla. 1966) 15.38
Trowbridge, Inc. v. Hathaway, 233 So.2d 129 (Fla. 1970) 6.7
2765 South Bayshore Drive Corp. v. Fred Howland, Inc.,
    212 So.2d 911 (3d D.C.A. Fla. 1968) 10.10
Twyman v. Roell, 123 Fla. 2, 166 So. 215 (1936) 10.12

United States v. Weissman, 135 So.2d 235
    (2d D.C.A. Fla. 1961) 15.16, 15.82
Upton House Cooler Corp. v. Alldritt, 73 So.2d 848
    (Fla. 1954) 14.4

Van Hoose v. Robbins, 165 So.2d 209 (2d D.C.A.
    Fla. 1964) 15.11, 15.17, 15.82
Van Meter v. Kelsey, 91 So.2d 327 (Fla. 1956) 1.32, 2.13
Vandeventer v. Dale Construction Co., 534 P.2d 183
    (Ore. 1975) 10.12
Vetzel v. Brown, 86 So.2d 138 (Fla. 1956) 11.3
Village of Euclid v. Ambler Realty Co., 272 U.S. 365,
    47 S.Ct. 114, 71 L.Ed. 303 (1926) 13.21
Village of Virginia Gardens v. Johnson, 143 So.2d 692
    (3d D.C.A. Fla. 1962) 13.17
Voight v. Harbour Heights Improvement Association,
    218 So.2d 803 (4th D.C.A. Fla. 1969) 11.14
Volunteer Security Co. v. Dowl, 159 Fla. 767,
    33 So.2d 150 (1948) 11.8

Wade v. Doyle, 17 Fla. 522 (1880) 3.15
Wahrendorff v. Moore, 93 So.2d 720 (Fla. 1957) 11.17
Waller v. First Savings & Trust Co., 103 Fla. 1025,
    138 So. 780 (1931) 12.3
Waln v. Howard, 142 Fla. 736, 196 So. 210 (1940) 15.65
Watkins v. DeAdamich, 187 So.2d 369 (2d D.C.A.
    Fla. 1966) 7.17
Watkins v. Watkins, 123 Fla. 267, 166 So. 577 (1936) 8.8
Watrous v. Morrison, 33 Fla. 261, 14 So. 805 (1894) .... 2.9—.10, 2.14
Watson v. Mayflower Property, Inc., 223 So.2d 368
    (4th D.C.A. Fla. 1969), aff'd
    233 So.2d 390 .... 13.1, 13.3, 13.10—.12, 13.15, 13.18
Weed v. Knox, 157 Fla. 896, 27 So.2d 419 (1946) 4.2, 4.6
Weinstein v. Park Manor Construction Company,
    166 So.2d 842 (2d D.C.A. Fla. 1964) 5.65
Weissenberger v. Central Acceptance Corp., 28 N.E.2d 794
    (Ohio App. 1940) 10.14
Wesley Construction Company v. Yarnell, 268 So.2d 454
    (4th D.C.A. Fla. 1972) 6.10
Whitaker v. Hearnsberger, 233 P.2d 389 (Colo. 1951) 5.7
Whitaker v. Parsons, 80 Fla. 352, 86 So. 247 (1920) 12.4
White v. Crandall, 105 Fla. 70, 143 So. 871 (1932) 9.4
Wicker v. Williams, 137 Fla. 752, 189 So. 30 (1939) 2.9

Wilkes v. Kreutler, 157 So.2d 194 (2d D.C.A. Fla. 1963) 11.12
William Murray Builders, Inc. v. City of Jacksonville,
    254 So.2d 364 (1st D.C.A. Fla. 1971), *cert. den.*
    261 So.2d 845 .... 13.10, 13.18
Williams v. Aeroland Oil Co., 155 Fla. 114,
    20 So.2d 346 (1944) 15.5, 15.54
Williams v. City of North Miami, 213 So.2d 5
    (3d D.C.A. Fla. 1968) 13.4
Williams v. City of St. Petersburg, 57 Fla. 544,
    48 So. 754 (1909) 4.6
Williams v. McFadden, 23 Fla. 143, 1 So. 618 (1887) 9.8
Williams v. Ricou, 143 Fla. 360, 196 So. 667 (1940) 4.5
Willis v. Fowler, 102 Fla. 35, 136 So. 358 (1931) 7.8
Wilmott v. Wilmott, 119 So.2d 54 (1st D.C.A. Fla. 1960) 1.20
Wilton v. St. Johns County, 98 Fla. 26, 123 So. 527
    (1929), 65 A.L.R. 488 .... 12.7
Wismer v. Alyea, 103 Fla. 1102, 138 So. 763 (1932) 3.7
Wolfe v. Hall, 61 Fla. 492, 54 So. 777 (1911) 15.50
Woodruff v. Taylor, 118 So.2d 822 (2d D.C.A. Fla. 1960) 1.20

York v. Pridgen, 141 Fla. 439, 193 So. 433 (1940) 8.5

INDEX TO SUBJECTS *References are to sections*

ABSTRACTS OF TITLE
Mortgage foreclosure prerequisite 5.4

ACCESS TO PROPERTY
Basic concepts 12.2
Duty of tenant to provide landlord with 15.76
Eminent domain 12.7
Generally 12.1
Historical background 12.3
Landlords' right of entry 15.11
Mineral rights 12.8
Police power
    Generally 12.4
    Remedies for excess 12.5
Private rights 12.6
Rights-of-way
    Complaint to establish, form 12.11
    Generally 12.10
Surveyor's right to entry 12.9

ACCOUNTING
Partion action 4.16

ADVERSE POSSESSION *see also* **BOUNDARY LITIGATION**
Ejectment defense 3.15
Quite title action 1.32

AFFIDAVITS
Amounts due in foreclosure action, form 5.37
Attorneys' costs in foreclosure action, form 5.38
Attorneys' fees in foreclosure action, form 5.39
Compliance with 28 U.S.C. §2410, form 5.22
Constructive service, form 5.28
Estoppel and solvency, deed in lieu of foreclosure 5.68
Lien, deed in lieu of foreclosure 5.69
Mechanic's lien foreclosure
    Contractor's, form 6.5
    Generally 6.4
Military service, form 5.10
Record title, foreclosure action, form 5.36
Writ of assistance, form 5.55

ASSISTANCE *see* **WRIT OF ASSISTANCE**

ATTORNEY AD LITEM
Quiet title action
    Generally 1.24
    Motion to appoint, form 1.25
    Order appointing, form 1.26

ATTORNEYS
Affidavits
    Costs in foreclosure action, form 5.38
    Record title in foreclosure action, form 5.36
Certificate of title after foreclosure sale, form 5.60
Fees
    Affidavit, foreclosure action, form 5.39
    Ejectment action 3.31
    Landlord and tenant, lease agreements 15.62
    Mechanic's lien foreclosure 6.14
    Partition action
        Determination of 4.28
        On dismissal 4.29
        Persons entitled 4.27

BANKRUPTCY
Mortgage foreclosure actions
    Action after dissolving stay 5.81
    Alternatives to the stay order 5.82
    Dissolving or modifying stay order 5.80
    Generally 5.78
    Stays of foreclosure 5.79

BETTERMENT *see also* **EJECTMENT**
Generally 3.32
Judgment
    For defendant
        Generally 3.40
        Vesting of title upon plaintiff's failure to pay 3.41
    For plaintiff 3.39
    Generally 3.38
Petition
    Form 3.34
    Generally 3.33
Reply 3.35
Trial 3.36
Verdict 3.37

BOUNDARY LITIGATION
Adverse possession
    Actual, open, continuous, exclusive possession 2.7
    Color of title
        With 2.5, 2.8, 2.11
        Without 2.6, 2.9, 2.12
    Generally 2.4
    Hostility of possession 2.10
    Statutory period 2.5
    Taxes 2.11–.12
Agreement 2.14
Generally 2.1
Recognition and acquiescence 2.13
Remedies 2.15
Settlement 2.3
Survey, role of 2.2

BREACH OF SALE CONTRACT *see* CONTRACTS FOR SALE

BUYER *see* CONTRACTS FOR SALE

CANCELLATION OF INSTRUMENTS
Answer 7.15
Complaint
    Form 7.14
    Generally 7.8
Costs 7.19
Defined 7.4
Determining necessary parties 7.10
Final judgment
    Form 7.22
    Generally 7.18
Generally 7.1
Rescission distinguished 7.7

CHAIN OF TITLE
Ejectment action
    Attached to answer 3.14
    Attached to complaint 3.10
    Form 3.11
    Generally 3.6

CLASS ACTIONS
Restrictive covenants 11.31

CONDITIONS PRECEDENT
Ejectment action 3.7

CONSTRUCTION CONTRACTS, BREACHES OF *see*
subject index to September 1983 supplement

CONTRACTS FOR SALE *see also*
INSTALLMENT LAND SALE CONTRACT
Actions available to real estate broker
  Causes of action available 9.20
  Complaint
    Form 9.22
    Generally 9.21
  Generally 9.19
Action for fraudulently induced purchase, complaint, form 9.9
Alternative remedies available 9.1
Buyer's action for seller's breach
  Complaint, form 9.7
  Purchase fraudulently induced
    Form for complaint 9.9
    Generally 9.8
  When no conveyance
    Damages, measure 9.6
    Generally 9.5
Generally 9.23
Remedies for breach 9.1
Seller's action for buyer's breach
  Answer and defenses 9.4
  Complaint, form 9.3
  Generally 9.2
Specific performance, action for
  Form for complaint 9.11
  Generally 9.10

COSTS
Cancellation of instruments 7.19
Ejectment 3.27
Partition 4.26
Reestablishment of lost instrument 8.7

COUNTERCLAIMS
Ejectment, permissible in 3.17
Partition 4.14

CURATIVE ACTS
Quiet title actions 1.30

DAMAGES
Ejectment 3.12, 3.23

DAMAGES – *Continued*
Landlord and tenant, common-law action 15.54
Slander of title 14.4
Unlawful detainer 15.52

DECLARATORY ACTION
Distinguished from other civil actions 1.6

DEEDS
Special warranty deed following mortgage foreclosure sale
    FHA mortgage
        Form 5.57
        Generally 5.58
        Recording 5.58
    VA mortgage 5.62
Substitute for mortgage foreclosure
    Estoppel and solvency affidavit, form 5.68
    Form 5.67
    Generally 5.66
    Lien affidavit, form 5.69

DEFAULTS
Mortgage foreclosure action 5.31, 5.33
Quiet title, against defendant, proof 1.29
Restrictive covenant 11.37
Summary removal of tenant, waiver 15.28

DEFICIENCY JUDGMENT
Mortgage foreclosure action 5.65

DERAIGNMENT OF TITLE
Ejectment 3.10

DISTRESS FOR RENT *see* **LANDLORD AND TENANT,** Nonresidential relations

EASEMENT
Applicability of ejectment action 3.5
Restrictive covenant distinguished 11.6

EJECTMENT *see also* **BETTERMENT**
Adverse possession, defense 3.15
Answer
    Form 3.16
    Generally 3.14
Attorneys' fees 3.31

EJECTMENT – *Continued*
Burden of proof 3.21
Chain of title
   Attached to answer 3.14
   Attached to complaint 3.10
   Form 3.11
   Relationship with ejectment action 3.6
Complaint
   Form 3.13
   Generally 3.9
Conditions precedent 3.7
Costs 3.27
Counterclaims 3.17
Damages 3.12, 3.23
Defenses, adverse possession and statutes of limitation 3.15
Defined 3.2
Demand for possession as condition precedent
   Form 3.8
   Generally 3.7
Deraignment of title 3.10
Easements 3.5
Evidence, presentation by plaintiff 3.22
Forcible entry distinguished 3.4
Generally 3.1
Judgment
   Enforcement 3.29
   Form for plaintiff 3.28
   Generally 3.26
Mense profits
   Defined 3.12
   Proof of 3.23
Motion to test legal sufficiency of instrument or court proceedings, form 3.20
Parties to action 3.9
Pretrial conference 3.19
Proof, presentation of 3.22
Quiet title distinguished 1.4, 3.3
Requirements for recovery 3.18
Statute of limitation, defense 3.15
Unlawful detainer distinguished 3.4
Verdict
   Form for defendant 3.25
   Generally 3.24
Writ of possession and execution, form 3.30

EMINENT DOMAIN
Access to property 12.7

EQUITIES, SPECIAL
Partition action 4.19

ESTOPPEL AND SOLVENCY AFFIDAVIT, FORM 5.68

EVICTION *see also* **LANDLORD AND TENANT; WRIT OF ASSISTANCE**
Veterans Administration's requirements after foreclosure sale 5.63

EVIDENCE
Ejectment action, presentation by plaintiff 3.22

EXCULPATORY CLAUSE 15.61

EXPERT WITNESS
Restrictive covenant, removal of 11.42
Zoning 13.20

FAIRLY DEBATABLE RULE 13.18

FEDERAL HOUSING ADMINISTRATION *see* **MORTGAGE FORECLOSURE**

FEE SIMPLE DETERMINABLE
Restrictive covenant distinguished 11.7

FEE SIMPLE UPON CONDITION SUBSEQUENT
Restrictive covenant distinguished 11.8

FINAL JUDGMENT
Betterments
   For defendant
      Generally 3.40
      Vesting of title upon plaintiff's failure to pay 3.41
   For plaintiff 3.39
   Generally 3.38
Cancellation of instrument
   Form 7.22
   Generally 7.18
Distress for rent
   Form 15.29
   Generally 15.28
Ejectment actions
   Enforcement 3.29
   Form for judgment for plaintiff 3.28
   Generally 3.26
Eviction, for landlord 15.91
Landlord and tenant 15.53, 15.91

FINAL JUDGMENT – *Continued*
Mechanic's lien foreclosure
    Form 6.36
    Generally 6.35
Mortgage foreclosure action
    After answer 5.34
    After default 5.33
    Federal district court, action in
        Additional paragraphs, form 5.72
        Generally 5.71
    Generally 5.32
    Summary judgment
        Form 5.40
        Motion for, form 5.35
        Order *see* **FORMS**
Partition
    Form 4.33
    Parts to be divided 4.15
Quieting title, form 1.34
Reestablishing lost instrument 8.22
Reestablishing lost promissory note, form 8.26
Reformation, form 7.20
Rescission, form 7.21
Unlawful detainer 15.53

FORCIBLE ENTRY AND UNLAWFUL DETAINER
Ejectment distinquished 3.4

FORMS
Access to property, complaint to establish right-of-way 12.11
Affidavits
    Constructive service
        Foreclosure action 5.28
        Generally 1.18
        Mortgage 5.28
    Military service 5.10
    Mortgage foreclosure action
        Amounts due 5.37
        Attorneys' costs 5.38
        Attorneys' fees 5.39
        Constructive service 5.28
        Estoppel and solvency, when deed accepted in lieu of foreclosure 5.68
        Lien affidavit when deed accepted in lieu of foreclosure 5.69
        Record title 5.36
    United States, service on, compliance 5.22
    Writ of assistance, supporting 5.55
Answers
    Ejectment 3.16

FORMS – *Continued*
    Mechanic's lien foreclosure 6.26
    Rescission 7.16
Assistance, writ of, supporting affidavit 5.55
Attorney's certificate of title after foreclosure 5.60
Attorneys' fees, affidavit in mortgage foreclosure action 5.39
Betterments, petition for compensation 3.34
Cancellation
    Complaint 7.14
    Judgment 7.22
Chain of title in ejectment action 3.11
Complaint
    Cancellation 7.14
    Ejectment 3.13
    Foreclosure
        Mechanic's lien
            Contractor 6.15
            Laborer's summary action 6.18
            Materialman in privity 6.16
            Subcontractor not in privity 6.17
        Mortgage 5.16
    Interplead in mechanic's lien foreclosure 6.28
    Partition 4.13
    Payment bond 6.22
    Quieting title 1.22
    Recission 7.13
    Reestablishment
        Land title destroyed by fire 8.27
        Lost promissory note 8.24
    Reformation 7.12
Constructive service, affidavit
    Generally 1.18
    Mortgage foreclosure 5.28
Contractor's affidavit in mechanic's lien foreclosure 6.5
Contracts for sale
    Action available to real estate broker, complaint 9.22
    Action for fraudulently induced purchase, complaint 9.9
    Buyer's action for seller's breach, complaint 9.7
    Seller's action for buyer's breach, complaint 9.3
Demand for possession in ejectment action 3.8
Ejectment
    Answer 3.16
    Complaint 3.13
    Judgment 3.28
Estoppel and solvency affidavit when deed accepted in lieu
Final judgments
    Cancellation 7.22

FORMS – *Continued*
- Ejectment 3.28
- Mechanic's lien foreclosure 6.36
- Mortgage foreclosure
    - Federal court, additional paragraphs 5.72
    - Summary final
        - Motion 5.35
        - Order 5.40
- Partition 4.33
- Quiet title 1.34
- Rescission 7.21
- Reestablishing lost promissory note 8.26
- Reformation 7.20

Judgments *see* Final judgments
Land title destroyed by fire, complaint to reestablish 8.27
Landlord and tenant
- Nonresidential
    - Distress for rent proceedings
        - Bond 15.22
        - Complaint 15.20
        - Final judgment 15.29
    - Summary removal of tenant, notice 15.36
    - Tenancies at will, notice of termination 15.8
- Residential
    - Periodic tenancies, notice of termination 15.67
    - Recovery of possession by landlord
        - Eviction for failure to pay rent, complaint 15.89
    - Termination for breach by tenant
        - Letter of termination 15.86
        - Notice 15.84
    - Termination for failure to pay rent, notice 15.85

Lien affidavit when deed accepted in lieu of foreclosure 5.69
Lis pendens notice
- Generally 5.18
- Mechanic's lien foreclosure 6.20

Mechanic's lien foreclosure
- Answer 6.26
- Complaint
    - Contractor 6.15
    - Interplead 6.28
    - Laborer's summary action 6.18
    - Materialman in privity 6.16
    - Subcontractor not in privity 6.17
- Judgment 6.36

Military service, affidavit 5.10
Mortgage foreclosure, complaint 5.16

FORMS – *Continued*
Motion
    Attorney ad litem, appointment of 1.25
    Foreclosure sale, for order confirming disbursing funds in federal court 5.76
    Summary final judgment 5.35
Notice
    Foreclosure action 5.30
    Judicial sale
        Additional terms in federal court 5.74
        Generally 5.45
    Reestablish lost promissory note, action to 8.25
Order
    Attorney ad litem, appointment of 1.26
    Foreclosure sale, disbursing funds in federal court, confirming 5.76
    Summary final judgment 5.40
Partition
    Complaint 4.13
    Judgment 4.33
Payment bond, complaint 6.22
Quieting title
    Complaint 1.22
    Judgment 1.34
Recission
    Answer 7.16
    Complaint 7.13
    Judgment 7.21
Reestablishment
    Land title destroyed by fire, complaint 8.27
    Lost promissory note
        Complaint 8.24
        Judgment 8.26
Reformation
    Complaint 7.12
    Judgment 7.20
Restrictive covenants
    Answer, allegations, sample 11.35
    Checklist 11.43
    Complaint
        Allegations, sample 11.33
        Form 11.34
    Release 11.24
Right-of-way, complaint to establish 12.11
Slander of title
    Answer 14.8
    Complaint 14.6
Special warranty deed
    Following foreclosure sale 5.57
    In lieu of foreclosure 5.67

FORMS – *Continued*
Subcontractor's lien transferred to bond 6.23
Substitution of photostatic copies in foreclosure sale, motion and order 5.43
Summons, summary procedure 6.19
United States, service on, affidavit of compliance 5.22
Verdict for defendant in ejectment action 3.25
Writ of assistance
    Generally 5.54
    Supporting affidavit 5.55
Writ of possession and execution in ejectment action 3.30

GUARDIAN AD LITEM
Quiet title action 1.23

IMPROVEMENTS
Liens upon and removal of 6.38

INSTALLMENT LAND SALES CONTRACT
Acceleration 9.14
Conveyance on payment 9.15
Forfeiture 9.16
Generally 9.12
Repossession by seller 9.17
Specific performance 9.18
Time of the essence 9.13

INTERPLEADER
Dispute between lienors
    Complaint, form 6.28
    Generally 6.27

JUDGMENT *see* **FINAL JUDGMENT**

JURISDICTION
Landlord and tenant actions 15.4, 15.88
Mechanic's lien foreclosure 6.12
Partition 4.32
Reestablishment of lost instrument 8.9
Restrictive covenants 11.25
Slander of title 14.5

LACHES 8.8

LANDLORD AND TENANT
Generally 15.1
Nonresidential relations
  Common-law action for damages 15.54
  Distress for rent proceedings
    Bond
      Form 15.22
      Generally 15.21
    Complaint
      Form 15.20
      Generally 15.19
    Final judgment
      Form 15.29
      Generally 15.28
    Generally 15.18
    Tenant's defenses 15.26
    Tenant's right to return of property 15.25
    Third party claims 15.24
    Trial 15.27
  Generally 15.1
  Judicial declaration of termination of leasehold interest 15.55
  Jurisdiction 15.4, 15.88
  Landlord's lien
    Advances 15.14
    Enforcement 15.17
    Exemptions 15.15
    Generally 15.12
    Priority 15.16
    Property kept on premises 15.13
  Right of entry 12.9, 15.11
  Sale of distrained property
    Effect of appeal 15.31
    Generally 15.30
  Self-help 15.11
  Statutory provisions 15.3
  Summary removal of tenant
    Complaint 15.39
    Defenses 15.43
    Generally 15.32
    Grounds for removal 15.33
    Judgment 15.44
    Notice
      Form 15.36
      Generally 15.34
      Service 15.35
      Waiver 15.37

LANDLORD AND TENANT – *Continued*
- Service of process 15.40
- Tenant's response 15.41
- Time for response 15.42
- Trial 15.44
- Waiver of default by landlord 15.28
- Tenancies at will
  - Failure to surrender possession 15.9
  - Generally 15.6
  - Notice of termination, form 15.8
  - Termination 15.7
- Tenancy at sufferance 15.10
- Unlawful detainer
  - Complaint 15.47
  - Damages 15.52
  - Defendant's response 15.49
  - Defenses 15.49
  - Ejectment distinguished 3.4
  - Evidence 15.50
  - Generally 15.45
  - Judgment and execution 15.53
  - Service of process 15.48
  - Summons 15.48
  - Trial 15.51
  - Verdict 15.51
  - When to use 15.45
- Venue 15.5
- Residential landlord tenant act
  - Dwelling unit defined 15.57, 15.92
  - Effective date of act 15.58
  - Generally 15.56
  - Landlord's duties and obligations
    - Advance rent 15.71
    - Deposit money 15.71
    - Duty of disclosure 15.70
    - Generally 15.69
    - Obligation to maintain premises 15.73
    - Security deposits 15.72
  - Lease agreements
    - Attorneys' fees 15.62
    - Exculpatory clauses 15.61
    - Generally 15.59
    - Unconscionable agreements 15.60
    - Waiver of rights 15.61
  - Mobile homes and mobile home lots
    - Deposits 15.94
    - Eviction 15.93

LANDLORD AND TENANT – *Continued*
    Fees 15.94
    Generally 15.92
    Leases 15.96
    Rights and remedies of tenant 15.97
    Rules and regulations of mobile home parks 15.95
  Periodic tenancies
    Failure of tenant to surrender possession 15.68
    Notice of termination
      Form 15.67
      Generally 15.66
    Termination 15.65
    Terms of tenancies without specific duration 15.64
    When rent payable 15.63
  Recovery of possession by landlord
    Eviction for failure to pay rent, form 15.89
    Generally 15.87
    Judgment of eviction 15.91
    Jurisdiction 15.88
    Procedure 15.88
    Tenant's defenses 15.90
  Rights and remedies of landlord
    Generally 15.81
    Lien on personal property 15.82
    Termination for breach by tenant
      Generally 15.83
      Letter of termination, form 15.86
      Notice, form 15.84
    Termination for failure to pay rent, notice, form 15.85
  Tenant's duties and obligations
    Duty to maintain dwelling unit 15.75
    Duty to provide landlord with access 15.76
    Generally 15.74
  Tenant's rights and remedies
    Defense to action for rent or possession 15.79
    Generally 15.77
    Right to terminate lease 15.78, 15.80

LIENS *see also* **MECHANIC'S LIEN FORECLOSURES**
Affidavit with deed in lieu of foreclosure, form 5.69
Improvements, upon 6.38
Landlord's 15.12–.17
Partition action 4.31

LIS PENDENS
Mechanic's lien foreclosure
  Form 6.20
  Generally 6.13

LIS PENDENS – *Continued*
Mortgage foreclosure
    Form 5.18
    Generally 5.17
Reestablishment action 8.14

MARKETABLE RECORD TITLE ACT 1.30

MECHANIC'S LIEN FORECLOSURES
Action on bond
    Complaint, form 6.22
    Generally 6.21
    Subcontractor's lien transferred to bond, form 6.23
Actions at law allowed 6.39
Answer
    Form 6.26
    Generally 6.25
Attorneys' fees 6.14
Complaint
    Contractor, form 6.15
    Generally 6.11
    Laborer's summary action, form 6.18
    Materialman in privity, form 6.16
    Subcontractor not in privity, form 6.17
Consolidation of causes of action 6.24
Cross-claim
    Form 6.26
    Generally 6.25
Early completion problems 6.40
Generally 6.1
Improvements, liens upon and removal of 6.38
Interpleader
    Form 6.28
    Generally 6.27
Intervention in pending actions 6.24
Joinder of lienors 6.24
Judgment
    Form 6.36
    Generally 6.35
Jurisdiction and venue 6.12
Lis pendens, notice filed with complaint
    Form 6.20
    Generally 6.13
Parties
    Determination of 6.9
    Entitled to liens 6.2

MECHANIC'S LIEN FORECLOSURES – *Continued*
Perfection of claim
   Contractor
      Affidavit, form 6.5
      Generally 6.4
   Generally 6.3
   Parties in privity 6.6
   Parties not in privity 6.7
Priorities 6.30
Proof required
   Amount of claim 6.33
   Existence and validity of lien 6.32
   Priority 6.34
Property covered 6.8
Repossession 6.37
Summons, form 6.19
Termination of job before completion 6.29
Time for bringing action 6.10
Venue 6.12

MILITARY STATUS *see also* **SOLIDERS' AND SAILORS' CIVIL RELIEF ACT**
Affidavit, form 5.10
Necessity to determine in foreclosure action
   Generally 5.8
   Procedure as to defendant 5.9
   Procedure as to mortgagor 5.11

MINERAL RIGHTS
Access to property 12.8

MINES AND MINERALS
Partition, rights subject to 4.3

MOBILE HOMES AND MOBILE HOME LOTS *see* **LANDLORD AND TENANT,**
   Residential landlord tenant act

MORTGAGE FORECLOSURE
Abstract of title 5.4
Affidavits
   Amounts due, form 5.37
   Attorney's costs, form 5.38
   Attorney's fee 5.39
   Record title, form 5.36
Bankruptcy proceedings
   Action after dissolving stay 5.81
   Alternatives to stay order 5.82
   Dissolving or modifying stay order 5.80

MORTGAGE FORECLOSURE – *Continued*
    Generally 5.78
    Stays of foreclosure 5.79
Complaint
    Allegations 5.13
    Form 5.16
    Time for filing 5.12
Deed in lieu of
    Estoppel and solvency affidavit, form 5.68
    Form 5.67
    Generally 5.66
    Lien affidavit, form 5.69
Defaults 5.31
Deficiency judgments 5.65
Federal district court, action in
    Final judgment
        Additional paragraphs, form 5.72
        Generally 5.71
    Generally 5.70
Final judgment
    After answer 5.34
    After default 5.33
    Generally 5.32
    Summary judgment
        Form 5.40
        Motion for, form 5.35
Generally 5.1, 5.83
Government insured mortgages 5.2
Letter of instruction 5.3
Lis pendens
    Form 5.18
    Generally 5.17
Military status
    Defendant
        Affidavit, form 5.10
        Necessity to determine 5.8
        Procedure 5.9
    Mortgagor, procedure 5.11
Parties, necessary and proper 5.5
Post sale procedure
    Certificates of sale, title and disbursements 5.52
    FHA mortgages
        Attorney's certificate of title, form 5.60
        Documents required by FHA 5.61
        Evidence of title 5.59
        Execution of instruments by mortgagee 5.56
        Recording of deed 5.58
        Special warranty deed, form 5.57

MORTGAGE FORECLOSURE – *Continued*
    Motion for order confirming sale and disbursing funds, federal court, form 5.76
    Order confirming sale in federal court, form 5.77
    Procedure
        State court 5.47
        United States district court 5.75
    Redemption by defendant 5.46
    Statutory requirements in federal district court 5.75
    Substitution of photostatic copies, motion and order, forms 5.43
    VA mortgages
        Documents required by VA 5.64
        Eviction of mortgagor 5.63
        Notice and execution of deed 5.62
    Writ of assistance
        Generally 5.53
        Motion and order, forms 5.54
        Supporting affidavit, form 5.55
Sale
    Completion and confirmation 5.46
    Generally 5.41
    Mortgagee's bid
        Amount due credited against bid 5.48
        Property worth more than bid 5.49
        Tax considerations 5.50
        VA instructions 5.51
    Notice
        Form, additional terms in federal court 5.74
        Form, state court 5.45
        Generally 5.44
    Notification of FHA and VA 5.42
Service of process
    Constructive service
        Affidavit, form 5.28
        Diligent search and inquiry
            Additional sources 5.27
            Checklist 5.26
            Generally 5.25
        Generally 5.24
        Notice of action
            Form 5.30
            Generally 5.29
    Generally 5.19
    Personal service
        Generally 5.20
        State of Florida 5.23
        United States
            Affidavit of compliance, form 5.22
            Generally 5.21

MORTGAGE FORECLOSURE – *Continued*
Soldiers' and Sailors' Civil Relief Act
    Effect of 5.7
    Generally 5.6
State of Florida as defendant 5.15
United States as defendant 5.14

OWELTY DOCTRINE
Applied in partition action 4.30

PARTIES
Cancellation of instruments, determining 7.10
Ejectment 3.9
Mechanic's lien foreclosure
    Determination of 6.9
    Entitled to lien 6.2
    In privity 6.6
    Not in privity 6.7
Mortgage foreclosure 5.5
Quiet title, defendants 1.14
Reestablishing lost instrument 8.11
Restrictive covenants *see* **RESTRICTIVE COVENANTS,** Party defendants

PARTITION
Accountings 4.16
Attorneys' fees
    Determination of 4.28
    On dismissal 4.29
    Persons entitled 4.27
Commissioners, appointment of
    Generally 4.18
    Powers and duties 4.20
Complaint
    Allegations of necessity of sale 4.12
    Form 4.13
    Statutory requirements 4.11
    Title information 4.10
Costs 4.26
Counterclaims 4.14
Defenses 4.14
Discretion of court 4.8
Equities considered 4.19
Estates subject to 4.2

PARTITION – *Continued*
Generally 4.1
In part only 4.9
Incidental relief 4.5
Interest of plaintiff 4.6
Judgment
    Form 4.33
    Parts to be divided 4.15
Jurisdiction, retention of 4.32
Lienors 4.31
Mines and minerals, rights subject to 4.3
Oil and mineral rights 4.3
Order of sale 4.17
Owelty doctrine 4.30
Property not divisible 4.25
Property subject to 4.2
Quiet title compared 1.5
Reports of commissioners
    Contents 4.21
    Notice of filing 4.23
    Number required to join 4.22
    Objections 4.24
Sale of property
    Approval of court 4.37
    By whom made 4.35
    Distribution of proceeds 4.37
    Persons entitled to bid 4.36
    Public or private 4.34
Waiver 4.7

PERIODIC TENANCY *see* **LANDLORD AND TENANT**, Residential landlord
    tenant act

PERSONAL COVENANT
Restrictive covenant distinguished 11.5

PLEADINGS
Answer
    Ejectment
        Form 3.16
        Generally 3.14
    Mechanic's lien foreclosure
        Form 6.26
        Generally 6.25

PLEADINGS – *Continued*
Complaint
  Mechanic's lien foreclosure
    Contractor, form 6.15
    Generally 6.11
    Laborer's summary action, form 6.18
    Materialman in privity, form 6.16
    Subcontractor not in privity, form 6.17
  Mortgage foreclosure
    Allegations 5.13
    Form 5.16
    Lis pendens
      Form 5.18
      Generally 5.17
    Time for filing 5.12
  Partition
    Allegations of necessity of sale 4.12
    Form 4.13
    Statutory requirements 4.11
    Title information 4.10
  Quieting title
    Drafting 1.21
    Form 1.22
    Generally 1.20
  Reestablishing lost instrument
    Allegation of facts 8.12
    Relief requested 8.13
Cross-claim, mechanic's lien foreclosure
  Form 6.26
  Generally 6.25

POLICE POWER
Access to property 12.4–.5

POSSESSION *see* **EJECTMENT**

QUIET TITLE *see also* **RESTRICTIVE COVENANTS, REMOVAL**
Adverse possession 1.32
Alternative actions 1.3
Attorney ad litem
  Generally 1.24
  Motion to appoint, form 1.25
  Order appointing, form 1.26

QUIET TITLE – *Continued*
Complaint
    Drafting 1.21
    Form 1.22
    Generally 1.20
Constructive service of process
    Affidavit, form 1.18
    Diligent search and inquiry 1.17
    Generally 1.16
    Persons outside state 1.19
Curative statutes 1.30
Declaratory action distinguished 1.6
Defenses 1.33
Ejectment compared 1.4, 3.3
Final judgment, form 1.34
Guardian ad litem 1.23
Initial contact 1.1
Investigation 1.2
Marketable record title act 1.31
Nonjoinder of husband and wife separated more than 30 years 1.10
Nonjudicial remedies 1.7
Partition compared 1.5
Party defendants 1.14
Proof
    Default against defendant 1.29
    Diligent search and inquiry 1.28
    Generally 1.27
Quasi in rem proceeding 1.9, 1.15
Statutes of limitation 1.30
Statutory provisions 1.8–.10
Tax titles
    Complaint 1.12
    Final judgment 1.13
    Generally 1.11

REAL ESTATE BROKER *see* **CONTRACTS FOR SALE**

REESTABLISHING LOST INSTRUMENTS
Admissions 8.18
Answer 8.16
Client interview 8.5
Complaint
    Allegation of facts 8.12
    Relief requested 8.13
Costs 8.7

REESTABLISHING LOST INSTRUMENTS – *Continued*
Fees 8.7
Generally 8.1, 8.3
Interrogatories 8.18
Judgment 8.22
Jurisdiction 8.9
Laches 8.8
Land titles destroyed by fire
    Complaint, form 8.27
    Generally 8.23
    Lis pendens 8.14
Lost instrument, defined 8.2
Notice of action, form 8.25
Parties 8.11
Persons entitled to reestablish 8.4
Process 8.15
Promissory note
    Complaint, form 8.24
    Final judgment, form 8.26
Proof required
    Contents 8.21
    Execution 8.19
    Obtaining 8.6
    Reason for nonproduction of original 8.20
Statute of limitation 8.8
Stipulations 8.18
Trial brief 8.17
Venue 8.10

REFORMATION OF INSTRUMENTS
Answer 7.15
Burden of proof 7.17
Complaint
    Allegation of inadequate remedy at law 7.9
    Form 7.12
    Generally 7.8
Costs 7.19
Defined 7.2
Determining necessary parties 7.10
Final judgment
    Form 7.20
    Generally 7.18
Generally 7.1
Grounds for relief 7.5
Pitfalls in actions 7.11

REMEDIES *see also* **LANDLORD AND TENANT**, Residential landlord tenant act
Boundary litigation 2.15
Contract for sale, breach of 9.1
Quiet title action, nonjudicial 1.7
Restrictive covenant 11.11
Zoning 13.15

REMOVAL OF IMPROVEMENTS 6.38

RENT *see* **LANDLORD AND TENANT**

RESCISSION OF INSTRUMENTS
Answer
   Form 7.16
   Generally 7.15
Burden of proof 7.17
Cancellation distinguished 7.7
Complaint
   Allegation of inadequate remedy at law 7.9
   Form 7.13
   Generally 7.8
Costs 7.19
Determining necessary parties 7.10
Final judgment
   Form 7.21
   Generally 7.18
Generally 7.1
Grounds for relief 7.6
Pitfalls in actions 7.11

RESTRICTIVE COVENANTS, REMOVAL
Actual notice, implied 11.9
Answer, sample allegations 11.35
Checklist 11.43
Class actions 11.31
Complaint
   Allegations, sample 11.33
   Form 11.34
   Generally 11.32
Constructive notice 11.9
Default judgment 11.37
Determining applicability 11.8
Easement distinguished 11.6
Fee simple determinable distinguished 11.7
Fee simple upon condition subsequent distinguished 11.8
Generally 11.1–.2

RESTRICTIVE COVENANTS, REMOVAL – *Continued*
Grounds for removal
    Abandonment 11.13
    Ambiguity 11.14
    Change of conditions 11.12
    Contrary to law, public policy or constitution 11.15
Insufficient grounds for removal
    Decrease in value 11.18
    Generally 11.16
    Release by owner of parcels subject to restrictive covenant 11.20
    Release of retained rights by common grantor or developer 11.19
    Zoning changes 11.17
Jurisdiction 11.25
Nature of 11.3
Oral notice 11.10
Party defendants
    Class actions 11.31
    Common grantor 11.29
    Generally 11.26
    Revealed by title search 11.30
    When no plan of development 11.27
    When uniform plan of development 11.28
Personal covenant distinguished 11.5
Pretrial conference 11.36
Release
    By all parties
        Form 11.24
        Generally 11.21
    By less than all parties 11.23
Remedies 11.11
Reserved right to amend, modify, repeal or alter 11.22
Trial
    Generally 11.38
    View by court 11.39
    Visual aids 11.40
    Witnesses, expert 11.42
    Witnesses, lay 11.41
Types of 11.4
Venue 11.25
Visual notice 11.10

RIGHT OF ENTRY 12.9, 15.11

RIGHT-OF-WAY *see* **ACCESS TO PROPERTY**

SECURITY DEPOSITS 15.72

SELLER *see* **CONTRACTS FOR SALE**

SERVICE OF PROCESS *see* **LANDLORD AND TENANT; MORTGAGE FORECLOSURE; QUIET TITLE**

SLANDER OF TITLE
Answer, form 14.8
Complaint, form 14.6
Damages 14.4
Elements of action 14.3
Generally 14.1
Jurisdiction 14.5
Nature of action 14.2
Statute of limitation 14.7
Venue 14.5

SOLDIERS' AND SAILORS' CIVIL RELIEF ACT
Mortgage foreclosure
    Applicability 5.6
    Effect 5.7

SPECIAL EQUITIES
Partition 4.19

SPECIAL WARRANTY DEED, FORMS 5.57, 5.67

SPECIFIC PERFORMANCE
Breach of sale contract
    Form for complaint 9.11
    Generally 9.10
Installment land sale contract 9.18

STATE OF FLORIDA
Mortgage foreclosure action, service on 5.23

STATUTE OF LIMITATION
Ejectment 3.15
Quieting title 1.30
Reestablishing lost instrument 8.8
Slander of title 14.7

SUNSHINE LAW 13.5

SURVEY
Role of in boundary litigation 2.2

SURVEYOR
Right of entry 12.9

TAX TITLES
Quiet title action
   Complaint 1.12
   Final judgment 1.13
   Generally 1.11

TENANCY AT SUFFERANCE *see* **LANDLORD AND TENANT,** Nonresidential relations

TENANCY AT WILL *see* **LANDLORD AND TENANT,** Nonresidential relations

THIRD PARTY CLAIMS
Distress for rent 15.24

TRAFFIC STUDIES
Zoning 13.11

UNITED STATES
Mortgage foreclosure, service on
   Affidavit of compliance, form 5.22
   Generally 5.21

UNLAWFUL DETAINER
Ejectment distinguished 3.4
Landlord and tenant *see* **LANDLORD AND TENANT,** Nonresidential relations

VENUE
Landlord and tenant, nonresidential relations 15.5
Mechanic's lien foreclosure 6.12
Reestablishing lost instrument actions 8.10
Restrictive covenant, removal of 11.25
Slander of title 14.5

VERDICTS
Betterment proceedings 3.37
Ejectment actions
   For defendant, form 3.25
   Generally 3.24
Landlord and tenant, unlawful detainer 15.51

VETERANS ADMINISTRATION *see* **MORTGAGE FORECLOSURE**

VIEW BY COURT
Restrictive covenant, removal of 11.39

WAIVER
Partition, right to 4.7
Summary removal of tenant
    Default by landlord 15.28
    Notice 15.37

WITNESSES
Restrictive covenant, removal of
    Expert 11.42
    Lay 11.41

WRIT OF ASSISTANCE
Eviction of former mortgagor 5.53
Motion and order, forms 5.54
Supporting affidavit, form 5.55

ZONING
Aesthetics 13.13
Changes, insufficient ground for removal of restrictive covenant 11.17
Changing neighborhood conditions 13.12
Comprehensive plan requirement 13.3
Contract zoning 13.6
Economic factors 13.10
Evaluation of planning documents 13.9
Exhibits 13.19
Expert witnesses 13.20
Fairly debatable rule 13.18
Floating zones 13.6
Generally 13.1, 13.21
Litigation 13.14
Moratoriums 13.7
Notice and hearing requirements 13.4
Pending zoning 13.8
Presumptions of validity 13.17
Remedies 13.15
Source of authority 13.2
Standing 13.16
Sunshine law implications 13.5
Traffic studies 13.11

SEPTEMBER 1983 SUPPLEMENT TO FLORIDA REAL PROPERTY PRACTICE III

SECOND EDITION

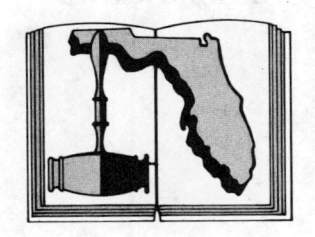

THE FLORIDA BAR

CONTINUING LEGAL EDUCATION

LIBRARY OF CONGRESS CATALOG CARD NO. 72-156745

©1983 by THE FLORIDA BAR
All rights reserved

CONTINUING LEGAL EDUCATION COMMITTEE
1983—1984

Edward F. Koren, Chairman
Davisson F. Dunlap, Jr., Vice Chairman
Leonard E. Ireland, Jr., Vice Chairman
Ronald C. LaFace, Vice Chairman
Robert E. Panoff, Vice Chairman
Ben L. Bryan, Jr., Board Liasion

David F. Albrecht	James W. Head
John E. Alley	Carolyn J. House
Jonathan L. Alpert	Homer H. Humphries, Jr.
Bruce H. Bokor	Lewis Kapner
Edgar C. Booth	Steven B. King
Paul Thomas Boroughs	Peter A. Knocke
James S. Bramnick	Maurice J. Kutner
James C. Burke, Sr.	Tonquin G. Lagrone
William A. Cain	Robb R. Maass
David Earl Cardwell	Deborah J. Miller
Patrick J. Casey	Morton Morris
David M. Chesser	James O. R. Murphy, Jr.
Kenneth F. Claussen	Noel H. Nation
Hume F. Coleman	Bette Ellen Quiat
Kenneth L. Connor	H. Gerald Reynolds
Thomas Corbin	Gerald A. Rosenthal
C. Timothy Corcoran III	Michael S. Rosier
Clinton A. Curtis	Jon A. Sale
William C. Davell	Murray Sams, Jr.
Ella Jane Peebles Davis	Roger W. Sims
Frederick R. Dudley	G. Thomas Smith
Eric C. Eggen	Horace Smith, Jr.
Thomas R. Ewald	Steven J. Uhlfelder
Richard Y. Feder	Roland D. Waller
William H. Green	Donna B. Wolbe
John G. Grimsley	Council Wooten, Jr.
Richard W. Groner	Arthur B. Wroble

1983-1984 COMMITTEE (*Continued*)

Representative Members

Dean Bruce R. Jacob
Dean Ovid C. Lewis
Dean Frank T. Read
Dean L. Orin Slagle
Dean Claude R. Sowle

STEERING COMMITTEE

Robert P. Barnett
Edward J. Kohrs
Robert E. Livingston
Edmund P. Russo

CONTINUING LEGAL EDUCATION PUBLICATIONS STAFF

Preston W. DeMilly, Director
Gerry B. Rose, Associate Director
John M. Knight, Legal Editor
J. Craig Shaw, Legal Editor

PREFACE

This supplement is another in a continuing series of publications designed to aid Florida lawyers to practice more efficiently and effectively. It is the product of teamwork among the Continuing Legal Education Committee, the steering committee, the authors and editors. The Florida Bar is indebted to the authors and steering committee members for their donations of time and talent to the project but has no official view of the contents of this manual. Like other legal publications, it is the work product of the individuals who contributed to it, and The Florida Bar joins them in the confident hope that it will fulfill its purpose of professional and public service.

                                  Preston W. DeMilly, Director
                                  Continuing Legal Education Publications
                                  September 1983

TABLE OF CONTENTS

CHAPTER	Page
1. **Quieting Title** Rollin D. Davis, Jr.	1
2. **Boundary Litigation** Edward J. Kohrs and Robert G. Cochran	9
3. **Ejectment** Roger H. Staley	13
4. **Partition** W. J. Oven, Jr.	17
5. **Mortgage Foreclosures** James F. Durham II and Henry H. Fox	21
6. **Mechanics' Lien Foreclosures** Joseph B. Reisman	35
7. **Reformation, Rescission And Cancellation Of Instruments**	45
8. **Reestablishing Lost Instruments** Robert P. Barnett	47
9. **Breach Of Sale Contract** Sheldon Rosenberg	51
10. **Breach of Construction Contracts And Loan Agreements** Kendall B. Coffey and Rudolph F. Aragon	55
11. **Removal Of Restrictive Covenants** Edward A. Linney	69
12. **Access To Property By Homeowner** James J. Brown	73
13. **Zoning**	81
14. **Slander Of Title** James J. Brown	83
15. **Landlord And Tenant** Malcolm B. Wiseheart, Jr., Gary P. Simon and John J. Boyle	89

INDEXES

Florida Statutes 207

Florida Rules of Civil Procedure 214

United States Code 215

Cases 216

Subjects 224

ROLLIN D. DAVIS, JR.*

1

QUIETING TITLE

I. PRELIMINARY CONSIDERATIONS

    C. Alternatives In Determining The Type Of Action

        4. [§1.6] Declaratory Action Distinguished

II. JURISDICTION

    B. Constructive Service Of Process

        3. [§1.18] Sample Affidavit For Constructive Service

V. ATTORNEY AD LITEM

    B. [§1.25] Sample Motion To Appoint Attorney Ad Litem, Guardian Ad Litem And Administrator Ad Litem (*new title*)

    C. [§1.26] Form For Order Appointing Attorney Ad Litem, Guardian Ad Litem And Administrator Ad Litem (*new title*)

VI. PROOF

    A. [§1.27] In General

    E. [§1.31] Marketable Record Title Act

VIII. [§1.34] SAMPLE FINAL JUDGMENT

---

*J.D., 1956, University of Florida. Mr. Davis is a member of the American and Escambia-Santa Rosa bar associations and is a partner in the firm of Shell, Fleming, Davis & Menge. He practices in Pensacola.

I. PRELIMINARY CONSIDERATIONS

C. Alternatives In Determining The Type Of Action

4. [§1.6] Declaratory Action Distinguished

In *Toombs v. Gil,* 353 So.2d 934 (Fla. 3d DCA 1978) the court stated that an action seeking a declaratory judgment would be a proper remedy to determine boundary lines. In that case, the developers made an error in locating lot line markers, and houses appeared to be encroaching on adjoining neighbors' property.

II. JURISDICTION

B. Constructive Service Of Process

3. [§1.18] Sample Affidavit For Constructive Service

Paragraph 2 of this form must be revised to reflect that *F.S.* 49.041 was amended in 1977 to require that the affidavit set forth whether the defendant is over or under the age of 18 years, rather than 21 years as stated in the manual.

If jurisdiction over unknown parties is desired, the practitioner must follow the procedures set forth in *F.S.* 49.071.

V. ATTORNEY AD LITEM

B. [§1.25] Sample Motion To Appoint Attorney Ad Litem, Guardian Ad Litem And Administrator Ad Litem (*new title*)

IN THE CIRCUIT COURT FOR
.... COUNTY, FLORIDA

Case Number ....

....................,

    Plaintiff,

vs.

.... and ....,

    Defendants.

PLAINTIFF'S MOTION TO APPOINT ATTORNEY AD LITEM, GUARDIAN AD LITEM AND ADMINISTRATOR AD LITEM

Plaintiff, ..., moves for the appointment of an attorney ad litem for defendants, ... and ...., because they are in default for failure to serve any paper on the undersigned or file any paper as required by law, and plaintiff is not able to determine whether any of the defendants are in military service. The affidavit of the undersigned pursuant to 50 U.S.C.App. §520 appears below. Plaintiff further moves for appointment of a guardian ad litem for defendants not sui juris and for appointment of an administrator ad litem for the estates of deceased defendants without an appointed representative.

STATE OF FLORIDA
COUNTY OF ....

Before me, the undersigned authority, personally appeared .... who, being duly sworn, says that he is the attorney for the plaintiff in this action and that plaintiff is not able to determine whether or not defendants are in the military service of the United States.

Attorney for Plaintiff

.........(address and phone number).........

Sworn to before me on ....(date)..........

Notary Public
My Commission Expires:
(Seal)

COMMENT: Regardless of the provisions of *F.S.* 65.061(2), the plaintiff usually requests appointment of a guardian ad litem. Many attorneys also request that an administrator ad litem be appointed. Unless it affirmatively appears that the interests of minors, persons of unsound mind or convicts are involved, appointment of a guardian ad litem is unnecessary unless unknown defendants are parties. If unknown defendants are not parties, the appointment of an administrator ad litem also would appear to be unnecessary.

C. [§1.26] Form For Order Appointing Attorney
Ad Litem, Guardian Ad Litem And
Administrator Ad Litem (*new title*)

(Party Designation)   (Title of Court)

**ORDER APPOINTING ATTORNEY AD LITEM,
GUARDIAN AD LITEM AND ADMINISTRATOR AD LITEM**

THIS ACTION was heard on the plaintiff's motion for the appointment of an attorney ad litem, guardian ad litem and administrator ad litem for defendants. On the evidence presented, it is

ADJUDGED that:

1. .... is appointed attorney ad litem, guardian ad litem and administrator ad litem for the defendants and shall serve written defenses without service of process on him.

2. The attorney ad litem, guardian ad litem and administrator ad litem shall file an oath to discharge his duties faithfully in the several capacities, and upon that filing he shall be qualified to act in each capacity.

ORDERED at ...., Florida on ....(date)..........

                                                            Circuit Judge

Copies furnished to: ....

COMMENT: The requirement of filing an oath for the guardian ad litem and administrator ad litem is found in *Fla.R.P.&G.P.* 5.120, and for convenience, the attorney appointed is ordered to file an oath to discharge his duties faithfully in each capacity. No oath is required by 50 *U.S.C.App.* §520. A bond is not required either by 50 *U.S.C.App.* §520, *Rule* 5.120 or *F.S.* 733.308.

VI. PROOF

A. [§1.27] In General

There is a difference of opinion among attorneys as to whether a lawyer should prove his case in the absence of actual contest. All allegations that are not denied are admitted. If all the defendants are known and are known not to be under 18 or in the military service, then upon default the attorney should immediately seek the entry of a final judgment. Since that knowledge usually is not present, the better practice is for the attorney to prove briefly the grounds for relief at a hearing upon notice to the attorney ad litem, guardian ad litem and administrator ad litem. If nothing else is gained, proof of adverse possession or other ground could dissuade a collateral attack.

E. [§1.31] Marketable Record Title Act

In many cases *F.S.* Chapter 712, the Marketable Record Title Act, makes unnecessary a quiet title action that would have been necessary before its adoption. Other fact situations will remain in which the applicability of the act is not clear enough to cure title without a judicial declaration. It can be expected to be the best ground for a quiet title action.

In *City of Miami v. St. Joe Paper Co.,* 364 So.2d 439 (Fla. 1978), *app. dism.* 441 U.S. 939 the Florida Supreme Court specifically held that the act is constitutional.

In *Kittrell v. Clark,* 363 So.2d 373 (Fla. 1st DCA 1978), *cert. den.* 383 So.2d 909 the court held that it would not construe the term "title transaction" in *F.S.* 712.01(3) to require a description of the land it purports to affect, because to do so would encroach upon the authority of the legislature, which has sole authority to supply statutory terms. In 1981 the legislature attempted to cure the holding in *Kittrell,* which substantially emasculated the act, by amending 712.01(3) to insert in the definition of "title transaction" the words "and which describe the land sufficiently to identify its location and boundaries." Ch. 81-42, §1, Laws of Fla.

Although a full discussion of the act is beyond the scope of this chapter, lawyers should be aware of the latest judicial interpretations of the act because it could greatly affect the need for or basis of proof of a quiet title action.

VIII. [§1.34] SAMPLE FINAL JUDGMENT

The form contained in the manual is more abbreviated than the form used by most practitioners. Most attorneys include an affirmative determination that jurisdiction has been obtained over all the defendants, as well as a brief tracing of the evidence.

EDWARD J. KOHRS*
ROBERT G. COCHRAN**

2

BOUNDARY LITIGATION

III. SETTLEMENT OF BOUNDARY DISPUTES UNDER DOCTRINES OF ADVERSE POSSESSION, BOUNDARY BY RECOGNITION AND ACQUIESCENCE OR BOUNDARY BY AGREEMENT

    B. Boundary By Adverse Possession

        2. Necessary Requirements

            b. Actual, Open And Continuous Exclusive Possession

                (3) [§2.9] Without Color Of Title

    D. [§2.14] Boundary By Agreement

---

*LL.B., 1957, Vanderbilt University. Mr. Kohrs is a member of the American and Hillsborough County bar associations. He is a partner in Macfarlane, Ferguson, Allison & Kelly and practices in Tampa.

**J.D. with honors, 1972, University of Florida. Mr. Cochran is a member of the American and Hillsborough County bar associations. He is a partner in Macfarlane, Ferguson, Allison & Kelly and practices in Tampa.

III. SETTLEMENT OF BOUNDARY DISPUTES UNDER DOCTRINES OF ADVERSE POSSESSION, BOUNDARY BY RECOGNITION AND ACQUIESCENCE OR BOUNDARY BY AGREEMENT

B. Boundary By Adverse Possession

2. Necessary Requirements

b. Actual, Open And Continuous Exclusive Possession

(3) [§2.9] Without Color Of Title

The requirement that the disputed property has been protected by substantial enclosure was discussed thoroughly in the recent case of *Grant v. Strickland,* 385 So.2d 1123 (Fla. 1st DCA 1980), *review den.* 392 So.2d 1374. In that case the land in question was fenced on one side, but the testimony was conflicting as to whether the fence was joined by fences or natural barriers on the other sides. The court stated specifically that the statutory requirement of "substantial enclosure" is not met when the land is fenced on only one of its borders. Natural barriers, such as navigable water, may suffice to provide part of a substantial enclosure.

The court in *Grant* also stated that gaps in a fence "do not dissipate the substantial character of the enclosure so long as 'there was for the full statutory period a conspicuous effort to maintain a fence around the land . . . for the obvious purpose of exercising rights of ownership' to the exclusion of all others."

The question of whether a fence constitutes a substantial enclosure normally is a question for the jury. *Grant, supra.*

D. [§2.14] Boundary By Agreement

In the recent case of *Brooks v. Fletcher,* 393 So.2d 630 (Fla. 4th DCA 1981) the court restated that when a boundary line between contiguous property is disputed, in order to establish the boundary by agreement the respective owners must agree on a certain line as the permanent boundary line and then occupy their respective properties according to that line. The court reaffirmed the necessary elements to be proved as enunciated in *King v. Carden,* 237 So.2d 26 (Fla. 1st DCA 1970).

ROGER H. STALEY*

3

EJECTMENT

II. INTRODUCTION

  D. Demand For Possession As Condition Precedent To Action Of Ejectment

  1. [§3.7] In General

III. THE COMPLAINT

  B. Chain of Title

  1. [§3.10] In General

  C. [§3.12] Claim For Mesne Profits

---

*J.D., 1956, University of Miami. Mr. Staley is a member of the Broward County Bar Association. He is a member of the firm of Saunders, Curtis, Ginestra & Gore, P.A. and practices in Ft. Lauderdale.

II. INTRODUCTION

D. Demand For Possession As Condition Precedent To Action Of Ejectment

1. [§3.7] In General

In *Henry v. Ecker*, 415 So.2d 137 (Fla. 5th DCA 1982), an action for ejectment, the appellate court held that ejectment proceedings would not lie against a defaulting purchaser who entered property under an executory contract for purchase until the seller gave notice of rescission because of the default and allowed the purchaser a reasonable time to perform its obligations under the contract.

III. THE COMPLAINT

B. Chain Of Title

1. [§3.10] In General

To prevail in an action for ejectment a party is required to demonstrate both legal title and a present right to possession of the property. *Byrd v. Culver*, 376 So.2d 41 (Fla. 4th DCA 1979).

C. [§3.12] Claim For Mesne Profits

In *Wilkerson v. Gibbs*, 405 So.2d 1053 (Fla. 1st DCA 1981) the court held that the former common-law action for mesne profits has merged with the statutory action for ejectment, thereby precluding a separate action directed to mesne profits. Mesne profits, therefore, now must be considered in preparing a complaint in ejectment.

Fla.R.Civ.P. Form 1.940 prescribes what should be alleged in a complaint for ejectment. Although the form does not use the words "mesne profits," those words commonly are understood to mean damages. *Wilkerson, supra.*

W. J. OVEN, JR.*

4

PARTITION

I. THE REMEDY

    B. Property And Estate Subject To Partition

        1. [§4.2] In General

II. PROCEDURE

    A. Complaint

        4. [§4.13] Sample Complaint For Partition

    C. Judgment For Partition

        2. [§4.16] Accountings

    E. Final Judgments

        2. Attorneys' Fees

            c. [§4.29] Attorneys' Fees On Dismissal

---

*LL.B. with final honors, 1933, University of Virginia. Mr. Oven is a member of the Tallahassee Bar Association. He is a partner in Oven, Gwynn & Lewis and practices in Tallahassee.

I. THE REMEDY

B. Property And Estate Subject To Partition

1. [§4.2] In General

Article X, §4 of the Florida Constitution allows the partition and forced sale of homestead property upon a lawsuit by one of the owners of that property, if the partition and forced sale is necessary to protect the beneficial enjoyment of the owners in common to the extent of their interests in the property. *Tullis v. Tullis,* 360 So.2d 375 (Fla. 1978). This rule does not apply if the court, in a dissolution proceeding, had granted one of the owners the exclusive possession of the property. *Hoskin v. Hoskin,* 329 So.2d 19 (Fla. 3d DCA 1976).

The court may refuse partition, and may not partition over the objection of the parties benefited, if the property is charged with rights established in a judgment of dissolution of marriage. *Wilisch v. Wilisch,* 335 So.2d 861 (Fla. 3d DCA 1976).

Estates by the entireties are not ordinarily subject to partition, *Hunt v. Covington,* 145 Fla. 706, 200 So. 76 (1941), even though the spouses may have separated, *Naurison v. Naurison,* 132 So.2d 623 (Fla. 3d DCA 1961). If the unity between the parties that forms the basis for the entireties form of ownership has been dissolved by the felonious act of one spouse that causes the other to be incapable of managing his or her own property and to be institutionalized, equitable principles may be invoked to permit partition of property held by the entireties. *Eichman v. Paton,* 393 So.2d 655 (Fla. 1st DCA 1981).

II. PROCEDURE

A. Complaint

4. [§4.13] Sample Complaint For Partition

The complaint for partition need not be verified, but if verified can be used as a basis for constructive service of process.

C. Judgment For Partition

2. [§4.16] Accountings

If, subsequent to a dissolution proceeding, one of the former spouses exclusively occupies the former marital home, not pursuant to court order, the other former spouse is entitled to credit for one half of the reasonable rental value of the premises. *Adkins v. Edwards,* 317 So.2d 770 (Fla. 2d DCA 1975).

E. Final Judgments

2. Attorneys' Fees

c. [§4.29] Attorneys' Fees On Dismissal

If partition is denied, there is no statutory authority for attorneys' fees. *Wilisch v. Wilisch,* 335 So.2d 861 (Fla. 3d DCA 1976). On the other hand, when after much work has been done in a case and one party conveys his interest in the land to the other, the court should proceed to assess costs and attorneys' fees as directed in *F.S.* 64.081. *Greene v. Galloway,* 332 So.2d 52 (Fla. 1st DCA 1976).

It has been held to be error to require the attorney's fee to be paid into the registry of the court before the sale of the property. *Martin v. Estate of Ricks*, 363 So.2d 636 (Fla. 3d DCA 1978).

JAMES F. DURHAM II*
HENRY H. FOX**

5

MORTGAGE FORECLOSURES

II. PREPARATION BEFORE FILING COMPLAINT

    C. Determination Of Parties Defendant

        1. [§5.5] Necessary And Proper Parties

        2. Compliance With Soldiers' And Sailors' Civil Relief Act

           d. [§5.9] Procedure To Determine Military Status

           e. [§5.10] Form For Affidavit As To Military Service

III. THE COMPLAINT AND NOTICE OF LIS PENDENS

    A. [§5.12] Time For Filing Complaint

    B. Allegations Of Complaint

        1. [§5.13] In General

        2. [§5.14] United States As Defendant

    C. [§5.16] Form For Complaint To Foreclose Mortgage

---

*J.D., 1954, Vanderbilt University. Mr. Durham is a member of the Dade County, American and International bar associations and has been admitted to practice in the Commonwealth of Kentucky. He is a partner in the firm of Shutts & Bowen and practices in Miami.

**J.D., 1966, Duke University. Mr. Fox is a member of the Broward County, Dade County and American bar associations. He is a partner in the firm of English, McCaughan & O'Bryan and practices in Ft. Lauderdale.

IV. SERVICE OF PROCESS

    B. Personal Service

        3. [§5.23] Service On State Of Florida

    C. Constructive Service

        1. [§5.24] In General

VI. THE FINAL JUDGMENT

    C. [§5.34] Final Judgment After Defendant Answers

    D. Forms Relating To Final Judgments

        5. [§5.39] Affidavit As To Attorneys' Fees

        5a. [§5.39a] Plaintiff's Affidavit As To Attorneys' Fees (*new*)

        6. [§5.40] Final Judgment

VII. JUDICIAL SALE

    A. [§5.41] In General

    C. Notice Of Sale

        1. [§5.44] In General

        2. [§5.45] Form For Notice Of Sale

    E. The Sale Procedure

        2. Bidding By The Mortgagee

            b. [§5.49] Bids Less Than Value Of Property

VIII. POST SALE PROCEDURE

    B. Writ Of Possession (formerly entitled Writ Of Assistance)

        1. [§5.53] In General

        2. [§5.54] Form For Writ Of Possession

X. THE MORTGAGE IN THE UNITED STATES DISTRICT COURT

    D. Foreclosure Sale In United States District Court

        1. [§5.73] Statutory Requirements

XI. THE MORTGAGEE IN BANKRUPTCY PROCEEDINGS

[§§5.78—.82] **These sections are now obsolete**

XII. [§5.83] CONCLUSION

II. PREPARATION BEFORE FILING COMPLAINT

C. Determination Of Parties Defendant

1. [§5.5] Necessary And Proper Parties

It is a good practice to have the abstract of title continued from the date of its last certification through the date upon which the lis pendens is recorded. This will inform the practitioner immediately whether there have been any subsequent filings of documents that would indicate the necessity for adding additional party defendants to ensure that all inferior lienholders or other possessory interests are eliminated by the foreclosure action.

If a mortgage is being foreclosed against a limited or general partnership, all the general partners should be joined in the action, in addition to joining the partnership in the partnership's name. Until a limited partnership is dissolved, a limited partner need not be joined as a party unless he also is a general partner. A limited partner is not a proper party to a proceeding by or against the partnership except to enforce a limited partner's right against or liability to the partnership. *F.S.* 620.26.

The increased use of foreign and alien corporations in real property transactions has had far-reaching consequences in the mortgage foreclosure field. One example is *F.S.* 692.05(2)(a), which requires that each alien corporation desiring to acquire of record any real property in the state maintain a registered office in the state. *F.S.* 692.05(4) requires that certain disclosure information be filed with the Department of State. Real property is defined by 692.05(1)(b) to include any interest in real property, including a lease or mortgage upon real property. If the alien corporation fails to maintain a registered office or fails to file the required disclosure information, it is not entitled to own, purchase or sell any real property, and is not entitled to sue or defend in the courts of Florida until the requirements have been met. 692.05(7). The disclosure requirements imposed by 692.05 are in addition to the requirements imposed by 607.324, and it is no defense under 692.05 that an alien corporation is registered to do business in Florida. Thus, if an alien corporation purporting to hold a mortgage on real property in Florida fails to maintain a registered office in Florida or fails to file the required disclosure statement, it is arguable that the corporation does not have a valid lien on the property until it complies with the statute. It is very clear, however, that the alien corporation would be unable to maintain an action in Florida to foreclose its mortgage until it reports its registered office and files the required disclosure statement.

Another aspect of mortgage foreclosures by alien and foreign corporations is worth noting. *Batavia, Ltd. v. United States, Department of Treasury, Internal Revenue Service*, 393 So.2d 1207 (Fla. 1st DCA 1981) may be interpreted as requiring a foreign corporation not qualified to do business in Florida to allege in its complaint that it is not otherwise doing business in Florida. In *Batavia* the court reasoned that notwithstanding the fact that *F.S.* 607.304(2)(g) provides that a foreign corporation is deemed not to be doing business in Florida even though it holds a Florida mortgage, the foreign corporation must provide sufficient information to the court to prove that it is not otherwise doing business in Florida. This is so because the foreign corporation must establish to the satisfaction of the court that it is not required to maintain a registered office and registered agent pursuant to 607.034(5). When a foreign or alien corporation not qualified to do business in Florida is suing to foreclose a Florida mortgage, the complaint should contain an allegation that the corporation is not doing business in Florida.

2. Compliance With Soldiers' And Sailors' Civil Relief Act

d. [§5.9] Procedure To Determine Military Status

The certificate referred to on page 5.11 should be revised to read as follows:

> ... This request is made in connection with a loan guaranteed (or insured) under [Title 38 U.S.C. 1801-1828, formerly the Servicemen's Readjustment Act of 1944, as amended] [the National Housing Act]. Any fee imposed and paid for this service will be charged ultimately to [the Veterans Administration] [the Department of Housing and Urban Development], an agency of the federal government.

It is a good practice to document the attorney's file with the source of information that was utilized by the individual signing the affidavit as to military service. If, for example, the practitioner was able to contact the defendant personally, this should be so indicated. Some practitioners feel that it is a better practice to put this information in the affidavit itself, while others feel that this merely is surplusage that may render the affidavit subject to some question as to whether or not appropriate information was obtained.

e. [§5.10] Form For Affidavit As To Military Service

The following paragraph should be added to the form as ¶3:

Defendant is over the age of 21 years and works at ...., or resides at .... This information was obtained by ....

III. THE COMPLAINT AND NOTICE OF LIS PENDENS

A. [§5.12] Time For Filing Complaint

The complaint must be filed within the statutory limitation period applicable to mortgages set out in *F.S.* 95.281. *F.S.* 95.281(1)(b) provides that if the maturity date of the mortgage is not ascertainable from the record, the mortgage terminates 20 years after the date of the mortgage. *F.S.* 95.281(1)(b) was amended in 1983, however, to provide that if the holder of the mortgage prior to the 20-year period re-records the mortgage so that the final maturity date is ascertainable, or records a copy of the obligation, from which the maturity is ascertainable, the lien will terminate five years after the date of maturity. Under 95.11(2)(c) an action to foreclose a mortgage must be commenced within five years of accrual of a cause of action. *F.S.* 95.031(1) provides that a cause of action accrues when the last element constituting the cause of action occurs. The last element constituting a cause of action on a demand note is the first written demand for payment. See *Ruhl v. Perry*, 390 So.2d 353 (Fla. 1980).

B. Allegations Of Complaint

1. [§5.13] In General

In addition to the allegations referred to in the manual the complaint also should allege that the current titleholders are in possession, or that other parties are in possession, with an indication that their possessory interest, if any, is inferior to the rights of the plaintiff. The foreclosure complaint of an unregistered, foreign corporate lender also should contain an allegation that the lender conducts no other business in Florida. See *Batavia, Ltd. v. United States, Department of Treasury, Internal Revenue Service*, 393 So.2d 1207 (Fla. 1st DCA 1981). If appropriate, the plaintiff may wish to allege their compliance with the RICO statutes in order to avoid any allegations or defenses to the contrary. The practitioner should be certain that the plaintiff has fully complied with the provisions of RICO and other corporate statutes as appropriate, to ensure that the complaint is not dismissed because of noncompliance with one of those procedural requirements.

2. [§5.14] United States As Defendant

The United States may waive and release a lien, other than a tax lien, under 28 *U.S.C.* §2410(e). When any person has a lien upon any real or personal property, and the lien has been duly recorded in the jurisdiction in which the property is located, and a junior lien, other than a tax lien, in favor of the United States attaches to the property, the person having the senior lien may make a written request to have the lien of the United States extinguished. See 26 *U.S.C.* §§6325, 7425(c)(2).

C. [§5.16] Form For Complaint To Foreclose Mortgage

The following paragraph should be added to the complaint to allege the ownership of the property and the persons in possession:

The defendants, ... and ...., own and are in possession of the property.

IV. SERVICE OF PROCESS

B. Personal Service

3. [§5.23] Service On State Of Florida

Service on the State of Florida because of a tax lien is made by serving the executive director of the Department of Revenue.

C. Constructive Service

1. [§5.24] In General

In judicial actions involving constructive service, a recurring problem is the failure to comply with the various provisions of the Soldiers' and Sailors' Civil Relief Act of 1940, 50 *U.S.C.* Appx. §§501—591. See §5.6—.11.

VI. THE FINAL JUDGMENT

C. [§5.34] Final Judgment After Defendant Answers

Recent changes in case law require the submission of additional information regarding attorneys' fees and also make it clear that, when requested, an evidential hearing must be held by the trial court. See *Cohen v. Cohen,* 400 So.2d 463 (Fla. 4th DCA 1981); *Trustees of Cameron-Brown Investment Group v. Tavormina,* 385 So.2d 728 (Fla. 3d DCA 1980); *Leader Mortgage Co. v. Rickards Electric Service, Inc.,* 348 So.2d 1202 (Fla. 4th DCA 1977). These cases require not only a change in the format of the affidavits by other attorneys as to the reasonable attorneys' fees in a given case, but also require an affidavit by the plaintiff's attorney as to the reasonableness of the fees and the time and effort involved, and certifying to the fact that the plaintiff is not being awarded an amount for attorneys' fees in excess of that which the plaintiff is obligated to pay. See §5.39a for a suggested form for this new affidavit.

D. Forms Relating To Final Judgments

5. [§5.39] Affidavit As To Attorneys' Fees

The following sentence should be added to the form at the end of the body of the paragraph:

In reaching his opinion, he considered the time required and expended in the handling of the matter, the experience, ability and reputation of the attorneys performing the work, the responsibility involved and the results obtained.

5a. [§5.39a] Plaintiff's Affidavit As To
Attorneys' Fees (*new*)

(Party Designation)   (Title of Court)

ATTORNEY'S AFFIDAVIT OF ACTUAL FEES

STATE OF ....
COUNTY OF ....

Before me, the undersigned authority, personally appeared ...., who after being first duly sworn, says that:

1. I am ...., attorney for the plaintiff, and am the attorney having primary responsibility for representing the plaintiff in the above-captioned action.

2. I am personally familiar with and have personal knowledge of the fees charged and collected, or to be collected, from the plaintiff for services rendered in regard to the above-captioned matter.

3. Our agreement with our client provides that the client will pay us (a) the reasonable fee awarded by the court, (b) the higher of either (i) the reasonable fee awarded by the court or (ii) the fee determined by multiplying the hours worked times the average hourly rate of $..........

4. I have been a practicing attorney licensed in the State of Florida since ....(date).........., and have practiced in .... County, doing primarily commercial litigation since ....(date)..........

5. In the course of handling the above-captioned lawsuit, ... hours of time have been expended in performing the activities required to prosecute this action. I project an additional .... (..........) hours to finalize and file the motion for summary final judgment, affidavits and legal memoranda, conduct settlement discussions and argue at the summary judgment hearing, and complete discovery already scheduled.

(Certificate of Service)

_____
Attorney
......(address and phone number)......

Sworn to before me on ....(date)..........

_____
Notary Public
My Commission Expires:
(Seal)

6. [§5.40] Final Judgment

Paragraph 7 of the form for the final judgment should be deleted and replaced with the following:

The clerk, upon the request of the purchaser at foreclosure sale, shall issue a writ of possession of the property to accomplish possession by purchaser without further order of court. Jurisdiction of this action is retained to enter further orders as are proper, including, without limitation, enforcement of writs of possession and deficiency judgments.

VII. JUDICIAL SALE

A. [§5.41] In General

F.S. 45.031(1) was amended by Chapter 78-68, §1, Laws of Florida and now provides that a judicial sale must be held not less than 20 days rather than ten days after the date of the final judgment. The statute also was amended to provide that the notice of sale must now be published once a week for two consecutive weeks in a newspaper of general circulation, published in the county in which the sale is to take place. The second publication of the notice must be published at least five days before the sale. The statute formerly required only one publication of the notice at least seven days before the sale.

C. Notice of Sale

1. [§5.44] In General

As mentioned in §5.41, the second notice of sale must be published in a local newspaper at least five days before the sale. *F.S.* 45.031(1). In some counties this is done by the clerk. In others, however, the attorney must prepare the notice and send it to the clerk, who then has it published. A form for the notice is set out in §5.45 of the manual. It should be remembered that VA regulations require a copy of the notice of sale to be sent to the VA at least ten days before the sale.

2. [§5.45] Form For Notice Of Sale

At the end of the form where the publication date is given, two dates, rather than one, must be inserted.

E. The Sale Procedure

2. Bidding By The Mortgagee

b. [§5.49] Bids Less Than Value Of Property

There is an additional problem with the bids at the foreclosure sale being for an amount significantly less than the full value of the property involved. There are recent cases that have held that it is possible for a trustee in bankruptcy to set aside a foreclosure sale that takes place within one year of the date of a bankruptcy filed by the title holder when the amount bid at the foreclosure sale is substantially less than the fair market value of the property. The trustee can attack such a sale as being a preferential transfer that may be voided under the bankruptcy code. For a discussion see 14 The Fund Concept 65 (Sept. 1982). See also *Abramson v. Lakewood Bank & Trust Co.,* 649 F.2d 547 (5th Cir. 1981); *Durrett v. Washington National Insurance Co.,* 621 F.2d 201 (5th Cir. 1980).

VIII. POST SALE PROCEDURE

B. Writ Of Possession (formerly entitled Writ Of Assistance)

1. [§5.53] In General

Fla.R.Civ.P. 1.580 was significantly amended in 1980. The amendment eliminated the previous distinction between Writs of Assistance and Writs of Possession. Writs of Assistance were combined with Writs of Possession. *Rule* 1.580(a) now provides that when a judgment has been entered that orders the sale of real property, the judgment, or some other order of court, must direct the clerk to issue a Writ of Possession. The clerk cannot issue the writ without a specific judicial order. The final judgment, as indicated above, should include a provision directing the clerk of the court to issue a Writ of Possession. If this is not done, it will have to be done by appropriate motion and order in accordance with the local practice, either by ex parte motion, or by setting the matter for hearing on the motion calendar.

Throughout the text, and in §5.54, where the form for a writ is set forth, all the references to a "Writ of Assistance" should be changed to a "Writ of Possession."

2. [§5.54] Form For Writ Of Possession

WRIT OF POSSESSION

THE STATE OF FLORIDA:

To the Sheriff of .... County, Florida:

YOU ARE COMMANDED to remove all persons from the following described property in .... County, Florida:

(describe property)

and to put .... in possession of it.

DATED on ...., 19......

(Name of Clerk)
As Clerk of the Court

By _____
As Deputy Clerk

X. THE MORTGAGE IN THE UNITED STATES DISTRICT COURT

D. Foreclosure Sale In United States District Court

1. [§5.73] Statutory Requirements

There are some federal cases that hold that the United States marshal may not be entitled to a strictly statutory percentage fee for the sale of real property in a foreclosure action. See *James T. Barnes & Co. v. United States,* 593 F.2d 352 (8th Cir. 1979); *Federal Land Bank of St. Paul v. Hassler,* 595 F.2d 356 (6th Cir. 1979); *Travelers Insurance Co. v. Lawrence,* 509 F.2d 83 (9th Cir. 1974).

XI. THE MORTGAGEE IN BANKRUPTCY PROCEEDINGS

[§§5.78—.82] **These sections are now obsolete**

The enactment of the Bankruptcy Code has made the discussions in these sections obsolete. These sections should be disregarded since they were written regarding the Bankruptcy Act, which has been superseded by the Bankruptcy Code. The only essential item that must be remembered is that all actions to foreclose a mortgage are *automatically stayed* by the filing of any bankruptcy action. Reference should be made to other current publications for a review of how and under what circumstances a creditor may obtain relief from the automatic stay. An especially good overview is *What Every Real Property Lawyer Should Know About The New Bankruptcy Code,* written by Jules Cohen and found in The New Bankruptcy Code, A Practical Overview And Update (Florida Bar CLE 1981). It has been reprinted and revised in several versions in other publications.

XII. [§5.83] CONCLUSION

In view of the current high rate of foreclosures, it is certain that almost every attorney sooner or later will encounter a foreclosure action either as the representative of a plaintiff or a defendant. The action will occupy the attorney's time for a period that varies from three to six months, depending upon any number of factors that cannot be fully anticipated before the action is filed.

JOSEPH B. REISMAN[*]

6

MECHANICS' LIEN FORECLOSURES

I. [§6.1] INTRODUCTION AND SCOPE

II. PREPARATION PRIOR TO ACTION

    A. [§6.2] Determination Of Existence Of Claim Of Lien

    B. Perfection Of Claim Of Lien

        1. [§6.3] In General

        4. [§6.6] Parties In Privity Other Than The Contractor

        5. [§6.7] Parties Not In Privity

    E. [§6.10] Time For Bringing Action

III. THE COMPLAINT AND NOTICE OF LIS PENDENS — FORECLOSURE

    A. [§6.11] In General

    D. [§6.14] Attorneys' Fees

    E. Forms For Complaint

        3a. [§6.17a] For Sub-Subcontractor (Or Materialman To A Subcontractor Not In Privity (*new*)

---

[*]LL.B., 1951, University of Miami. Mr. Reisman is a member of the American and Dade County bar associations. He is a partner in Rosenberg, Reisman & Glass and practices in Miami.

IV. THE COMPLAINT — ACTION ON BOND

    A. [§6.21] In General

    B. Forms For Complaints On Bonds

        1. [§6.22] On Payment Bond — Materialman To Subcontractor

VI. ANSWER AND CROSS-CLAIM

    A. [§6.25] In General

X. PROOF AT TRIAL

    B. [§6.32] Existence And Validity Of Lien

I. [§6.1] INTRODUCTION AND SCOPE

Although the fundamental purpose of the Mechanics' Lien Law remains as stated in *Crane Co. v. Fine,* 221 So.2d 145 (Fla. 1969), the act was amended by Chapter 77-353, §15, Laws of Florida, adding *F.S.* 713.37, which states that the Mechanics' Lien Law "shall not be subject to a rule of liberal construction in favor of any person."

II. PREPARATION PRIOR TO ACTION

A. [§6.2] Determination Of Existence Of Claim Of Lien

F.S. 713.02(5) was amended by Chapter 78-397, §1, Laws of Florida and now exempts any improvement for which the contract price is $2,500 or less, except for liens of parties in privity with the owner.

B. Perfection Of Claim Of Lien

1. [§6.3] In General

The definition of "lienor" in *F.S.* 713.01(10) was expanded by Chapter 77-353, §1 and Chapter 80-97, §1, Laws of Florida, to include among the claimants entitled to a lien, a sub-subcontractor, a materialman to a sub-subcontractor and a professional lienor under 713.03. *F.S.* 713.08(4)(c) was amended by Chapter 77-353, §6, Laws of Florida, to provide that the failure to serve the claim of lien before recording, or within 15 days after recording, renders the claim of lien voidable to the extent the failure or delay prejudices any person entitled to rely on the service.

4. [§6.6] Parties In Privity Other Than The Contractor

F.S. 713.03(3) has been amended to provide clearly that the affidavit as to unpaid lienors required of a contractor by 713.06(3) is not required of a professional lienor. Ch. 77-353, §3, Laws of Fla.

5. [§6.7] Parties Not In Privity

The class of those not in privity with the owner who may have a lien on the real property improved for money owed for labor, services or materials furnished under their contracts and the direct contracts has been expanded to include sub-subcontractors. See *F.S.* 713.06(1) as amended by Ch. 77-353, §5 and Ch. 80-97, §4, Laws of Fla.

F.S. 713.06(2)(a) has been substantially amended by Chapter 77-353, §5 and Chapter 80-97, §4, Laws of Florida so that a sub-subcontractor or a materialman to a subcontractor must serve the notice to owner on the contractor, as well as on the owner. A materialman to a sub-subcontractor must serve it on the subcontractor and the contractor, as well as the owner. The amendment further provides that failure to serve the notice to the owner is a "complete defense to enforcement of a lien by any person." The amended statute has been strictly construed to bar a claim of lien when the claimant failed to serve the notice to owner within 45 days after commencement of his work. See *Combs v. St. Joe Papermakers Federal Credit Union,* 383 So.2d 298 (Fla. 1st DCA 1980). It should be noted that a lienor who has failed to perfect a mechanic's lien by not serving notice on an owner as required by 713.06(2)(a), thus barring his claim, still may proceed to establish an equitable lien on unpaid or improperly paid funds. See *Crane Co. v. Fine,* 221 So.2d 145 (Fla. 1969); *Combs v. St. Joe Papermakers Federal Credit Union, supra.*

Item (a) of the summary of the matters to be accomplished timely in perfecting the lien of a lienor not in privity with the owner is changed to read: "Service of notice to owner by lienor other than a laborer, person performing professional services or a lienor for subdivision improvements. *F.S.* 713.06(2)(a)." See 713.04, .03(3).

E. [§6.10] Time For Bringing Action

The continuation of a claim of lien effected by the commencement of an action within one year from the date of recording the claim of lien now is qualified so that the continuation of the lien by the commencement of action is not "good against creditors or subsequent purchasers for a valuable consideration and without notice, unless a notice of lis pendens is recorded." *F.S.* 713.22(1) as amended by Ch. 77-353, §9, Laws of Fla. A suggested form for the notice of lis pendens appears at §6.20.

III. THE COMPLAINT AND NOTICE OF LIS PENDENS — FORECLOSURE

A. [§6.11] In General

The statement of classes of lienor in the first sentence of this section should be changed to include sub-subcontractors as one of the classes because of the amendment of *F.S.* 713.01(10) and (19) by Chapter 77-353, §1 and Chapter 80-97, §1, Laws of Florida, respectively, and of

713.06(1) and (2)(a) by Chapter 77-353, §5 and Chapter 80-97, §4, Laws of Florida.

D.   [§6.14]   Attorneys' Fees

The conflict among the decisions of the district courts of appeal on the question of whether attorneys' fees are recoverable for services on appeal in mechanics' lien foreclosures has been resolved by the amendment of *F.S.* 713.29 by Chapter 77-353, §11, Laws of Florida. The statute as amended provides "the prevailing party shall be entitled to recover a reasonable fee for the services of his attorney for trial and appeal."

A lienor recovering less than the amount of his claim has been held to be the prevailing party for award of attorneys' fees under *F.S.* 713.29 when no tender was made by the owner before the lawsuit. *American Insulation of Ft. Walton Beach, Inc. v. Pruitt*, 378 So.2d 839 (Fla. 1st DCA 1980). The court also held in that case that the award of attorneys' fees to the prevailing party was mandatory under the statute.

If a tender is made before the lawsuit of an amount in excess of the recovery by the lienor in his action, the owner, not the lienor, is considered to be the prevailing party and is entitled to be awarded attorneys' fees. *S. C. M. Associates, Inc. v. Rhodes*, 395 So.2d 632 (Fla. 2d DCA 1981). A lienor recovering an amount less than his claim, however, may be considered to be the prevailing party notwithstanding an offer of judgment. *Peter Marich & Associates, Inc. v. Powell*, 365 So.2d 754 (Fla. 2d DCA 1978). If the lien claimant has been denied enforcement of the claimed lien but recovers a judgment on the contract claim, the owner may not be the prevailing party for the award of attorneys' fees under the statutes. *General Development Corp. v. John H. Gossett Construction Co.*, 370 So.2d 380 (Fla. 2d DCA 1979); *First Atlantic Building Corp. v. Neubauer Construction Co.*, 352 So.2d 103 (Fla. 4th DCA 1977).

E.   Forms For Complaint

   3a.   [§6.17a]   For Sub-Subcontractor (Or Materialman
              To A Subcontractor) Not In Privity (*new*)

**IN THE CIRCUIT COURT FOR
.... COUNTY, FLORIDA**

Case Number ....

......................,
Plaintiff,

vs.

......................,
Defendants.

COMPLAINT

Plaintiff, ..., hereafter called "sub-subcontractor," sues defendants, ..., hereafter called "subcontractor," and ...., hereafter called "contractor" and ...., hereafter called "owner," and alleges:

1. This is an action to foreclose a mechanics' lien.

2. On or before ....(date).........., owner and contractor executed and delivered a contract for the construction of improvements by contractor upon the property of owner in .... County, Florida, described as follows:

[legal description]

3. On ....(date).........., owner filed in the Office of the Clerk of the Circuit Court, ... County, Florida, a notice of commencement, which was recorded in Official Records Book ...., at Page ...., of the Public Records of that county.

4. On ....(date).........., contractor executed and delivered a subcontract with subcontractor for the furnishing of the materials and labor necessary for the erection of the structural elements of the improvements. On ....(date).......... subcontractor executed and delivered a sub-subcontract with sub-subcontractor for the furnishing of the materials and labor necessary for the form work in the erection of the structural elements of the improvements, a copy being attached as Exhibit "A".

5. Sub-subcontractor furnished labor and materials under the sub-subcontract and furnished the last of them on ....(date)..........

6. Sub-subcontractor on ....(date).......... served on owner and on contractor a notice to owner.

7. The sub-subcontract was fully performed by sub-subcontractor.

8. There is due to sub-subcontractor under the sub-subcontract $..........., which remains unpaid. A statement of account is attached as Exhibit "B".

COMMENT: See the comment following paragraph 5 in §6.15.

9. Sub-subcontractor filed a claim of lien on ....(date).......... in the Office of the Clerk, which was recorded in Official Records Book ...., at Page ...., of the Public Records of the county. Sub-subcontractor served a copy of the claim of lien on owner on ....(date).......... Sub-subcontractor has complied with all requirements of F.S. Chapter 713.

10. Sub-subcontractor is obligated to pay his attorneys a reasonable fee for their services in this action.

WHEREFORE, sub-subcontractor demands an accounting of the sums due sub-subcontractor under the sub-subcontract, and judgment against subcontractor for the sums determined to be due to sub-subcontractor declaring sub-subcontractor has a lien on the property for all sums due sub-subcontractor, including attorneys' fees, superior to any interest or lien of defendants and ordering a sale of the property to satisfy the lien if the sums shall not be paid within the time set by this court, and that the right, title, interest and lien of defendants and all parties claiming by, through, under or against them since the filing of the notice of lis pendens be foreclosed.

_____
Attorney for Sub-subcontractor
.....(address and phone number).....

IV. THE COMPLAINT — ACTION ON BOND

A. [§6.21] In General

F.S. 713.23 has been amended by Chapter 77-353, §10 and Chapter 80-97, §8, Laws of Florida, to require that either before beginning or within 45 days after beginning to furnish labor, materials or supplies, a lienor not in privity with the contractor, except a laborer, must serve on the contractor a written notice that the lienor will look to the contractor's bond for protection on the work as a prerequisite to an action against the contractor. If a notice of commencement has not been recorded, or a reference to the bond is not given in the notice of commencement, and in either case if the lienor is not otherwise notified in writing of the existence of the bond, the lienor has 45 days from the date of notification of the existence of the bond within which to serve the notice. The form of notice is provided in 713.23(1)(d). The amendment of the statute eliminated the requirement of the giving of notice to the owner under 713.06(2) by parties not in privity with the contractor as a prerequisite to recovery on the bond.

In addition to the notice to contractor, *F.S.* 713.23(1)(e) requires service on the contractor by any lienor not in privity with him of notice of performance and nonpayment within 90 days after performance of the labor or delivery of materials and supplies for which payment is sought. The form of notice is provided in the statute. *F.S.* 713.23(1)(f) provides that no action can be brought against the contractor or surety unless both the notice to contractor and the notice of performance and nonpayment have been given.

B.   Forms For Complaints On Bonds

1. [§6.22] On Payment Bond — Materialman To Subcontractor

Paragraph 9 of the complaint form should be changed to include the requirements for the giving of notice to contractor and notice of nonpayment as contained in the amended statute. The suggested change follows:

9. Within 45 days after beginning to supply materials under the agreement, materialman delivered to contractor written notice that materialman would look to contractor's bond for protection on the work, and within 90 days after complete delivery of the materials delivered to the contractor written notice of delivery of the materials and nonpayment.

VI.   ANSWER AND CROSS-CLAIM

A.   [§6.25] In General

F.S. 713.31(2)(c), as amended by Chapter 77-53, §12, Chapter 79-400, §260 and Chapter 80-97, §9, Laws of Florida, now provides that any contractor, subcontractor or sub-subcontractor who suffers damage as the result of the filing of a fraudulent lien, as well as an owner against whose interest a fraudulent lien is filed, has a right of action against the lienor filing the fraudulent lien for damages including clerk's fees, court costs, attorneys' fees, premium for any bond given to obtain discharge of the lien, interest on money deposited to discharge the lien and punitive damages. The amount of punitive damages is limited to the difference between the amount claimed by the lienor and the amount actually due.

X. PROOF AT TRIAL

B.   [§6.32] Existence And Validity Of Lien

Because of the amendment of *F.S.* 713.23 discussed in §6.21 of this supplement, in actions on payment bonds, the parties not in privity with the contractor will be required to prove service on the contractor of written notice to contractor and notice of performance and nonpayment prescribed in 713.23(1)(d) and (e).

7

REFORMATION, RESCISSION AND CANCELLATION OF INSTRUMENTS

No supplementation of this chapter is needed as of September 1, 1983.

8

REESTABLISHING LOST INSTRUMENTS

IV.   INITIAL CLIENT INTERVIEW

    A. [§8.5] In General

IX.   TRIAL

    A. Order Of Proof

        3. [§8.21] Proof Of Contents

---

[*]J.D., 1968, University of Florida. Mr. Barnett is a member of the American and Dade County bar associations. He is an owner and officer of Barnett & Kress, P.A. and practices in Miami.

IV. INITIAL CLIENT INTERVIEW

A. [§8.5] In General

Previous case law has held that a lost mortgage may not be foreclosed until it and the note have been reestablished. See, *e.g., Harper v. Green*, 99 Fla. 1309, 128 So. 827 (1930). It is the author's opinion, however, that *F.S.* 90.954 may have changed the validity of that holding as binding precedent. *F.S.* 90.954 provides that:

> . . . The original of a writing, recording, or photograph is not required, except as provided in s. 90.953, and other evidence of its contents is admissible when:
>
> (1) All originals are lost or destroyed, unless the proponent lost or destroyed them in bad faith. . . .

The Sponsor's Note to WEST'S F.S.A. 90.954(1) EVIDENCE CODE — 1979 SPECIAL PAMPHLET states that:

> This subsection, in addition to codifying a portion of the common-law "best evidence" rule, provides a litigant the choice of accounting for the loss of the original and introducing secondary evidence *or* of utilizing the procedure of Chapter 71 to reestablish the secondary evidence as an original through the equity proceeding.

It appears, therefore, that there are now two equally appropriate methods for proving a lost instrument.

IX. TRIAL

A. Order Of Proof

3. [§8.21] Proof Of Contents

Former *F.S.* 92.35 referred to in this section was repealed by Chapter 76-237, Laws of Florida. The adoption of the Evidence Code made former 92.35 no longer necessary. *F.S.* 90.951(4)(a) defines a "duplicate" to include a "counterpart produced by the same impression as the original, . . . by means of photography." *F.S.* 90.953, in turn, then provides that when the principal goal of the party offering a duplicate is to place its words or other contents into evidence, a duplicate serves the same purpose as the original. *F.S.* 90.953 applies not only to governmental agencies, but also to businesses and private writings. GARD, FLORIDA EVIDENCE Rule 6:21 (1980).

9

BREACH OF SALE CONTRACT

III. ACTIONS BY BUYER FOR SELLER'S BREACH

    A. Action For Damages When No Conveyance

        2. [§9.6] Measure Of Damages

    C. Action For Damages When Purchase Fraudulently Induced

        1. [§9.8] In General

V. ACTIONS ARISING OUT OF BREACH OF INSTALLMENT LAND SALE CONTRACT

    A. The Installment Land Sale Contract

        3. [§9.14] Acceleration

VI. ACTIONS BY REAL ESTATE BROKERS

    C. The Complaint

        1. [§9.21] In General

---

[*]J.D., 1964, Harvard University. Mr. Rosenberg is a member of the North Dade and American bar associations. He is a partner in Ress, Gomez, Rosenberg & Howland and practices in North Miami.

III. ACTIONS BY BUYER FOR SELLER'S BREACH

A. Action For Damages When No Conveyance

2. [§9.6] Measure Of Damages

In the absence of bad faith on the part of the seller, loss of bargain damages have been considered inappropriate. *Vogel v. Vandiver,* 373 So.2d 366 (Fla. 2d DCA 1979). Bad faith generally implies or involves actual or constructive fraud, or a design to mislead or deceive another. *Bosso v. Neuner,* 426 So.2d 1209 (Fla. 4th DCA 1983).

The case of *Hanna v. American International Land Corp.,* 289 So.2d 756 (Fla. 2d DCA 1974) referred to in this section was reversed in *American International Land Corp. v. Hanna,* 323 So.2d 567 (Fla. 1976), in which the Supreme Court observed that real property cannot be the subject of conversion and that a breach of contract cannot be transformed into a tort merely by general allegations of malice. The court held that there must be specific allegations regarding the malicious conduct, in the absence of which punitive damages are not recoverable in a tort action.

C. Action For Damages When Purchase Fraudulently Induced

1. [§9.8] In General

In *Besett v. Basnett,* 389 So.2d 995 (Fla. 1980) the Florida Supreme Court held that prospective buyers of real property were justified in relying on the sellers' superior knowledge as to the size of the land in question and the business income derived from it, despite the fact that they might have ascertained the falsity of the sellers' representations on these matters had the buyers made an investigation of their own. The court further stated that the buyers' reliance was justified even though the sellers' misrepresentations were not obviously false and even though the buyers did not know the representations were false.

V. ACTIONS ARISING OUT OF BREACH OF INSTALLMENT LAND SALE CONTRACT

A. The Installment Land Sale Contract

3. [§9.14] Acceleration

Unless the installment land sale contract contains a provision for acceleration of the indebtedness upon default in payments due, a buyer's default in making monthly payments does not accelerate the maturity of the entire obligation due. *Adkinson v. Nyberg*, 344 So.2d 614 (Fla. 2d DCA 1977).

VI. ACTIONS BY REAL ESTATE BROKERS

C. The Complaint

1. [§9.21] In General

In *Winter v. Surfview Realty, Inc.*, 400 So.2d 839 (Fla. 5th DCA 1981), an action on a contract for a broker's commission for the sale of real estate, the court held that the contract was unenforceable because the complaint did not allege that the broker was a registered real estate broker, and the broker offered no proof of registration.

KENDALL B. COFFEY*
RUDOLPH F. ARAGON**

10

BREACHES OF CONSTRUCTION CONTRACTS AND CONSTRUCTION LOAN AGREEMENTS

I. [§10.1] INTRODUCTION

II. BREACH OF A CONSTRUCTION CONTRACT

    A. Remedies Available

        2. [§10.3] Remedies Of Contractor Against Owner Who Refuses To Pay

    B. Action By Owner When Contractor Fails To Perform

        1. [§10.5] Investigation And Preparation

        2. [§10.6] Damages

        3. [§10.7] Conditions Precedent

        6. [§10.10] Statute Of Limitations

        7. [§10.11] Sample Complaint

---

*J.D., 1978, University of Florida. Mr. Coffey is a member of the Dade County and American bar associations. He is an associate in the Miami firm of Greenberg, Traurig, Askew, Hoffman, Lipoff, Quentel & Wolff, P.A.

**J.D., 1979, Yale University. Mr. Aragon is a member of the Dade County and American bar associations. He is an associate in the Miami firm of Greenberg, Traurig, Askew, Hoffman, Lipoff, Quentel & Wolff, P.A.

III. REMEDIES FOR BREACH OF CONSTRUCTION LOAN AGREEMENT

   A. [§10.12] In General

   B. [§10.13] Remedies For Breach By Borrower

   C. [§10.14] Remedies For Breach By Lender

   D. [§10.15] Lender Liability To The Borrower (*new*)

I. [§10.1] INTRODUCTION

For a thorough discussion of construction contract litigation see CONSTRUCTION LITIGATION IN FLORIDA (CLE 1983). That manual deals more completely than does this chapter with this particular field of litigation and should be referred to as needed.

II. BREACH OF A CONSTRUCTION CONTRACT

A. Remedies Available

2. [§10.3] Remedies Of Contractor Against Owner Who Refuses To Pay

A contractor is not obligated to sue for damages when the owner has breached the contract. Instead, he can sue in quantum meruit. The contractor may treat the contract as void and sue for his actual expenditures. *United States v. Vehan,* 110 U.S. 338, 4 S.Ct. 81, 28 L.Ed. 168 (1884). In *Mori v. Matsushita Electric Corp. of America,* 380 So.2d 461 (Fla. 3d DCA 1980), *cert. den.* 389 So.2d 1112 the court held that when an owner has repudiated its contract prior to commencement of construction, the proper measure of damages is the contractor's lost profits. While the finder of fact has reasonable discretion in determining lost profits, any such damages nevertheless must be supported by the evidence and cannot be based on mere speculation or conjecture. See *Dade County, Florida v. Palmer & Baker Engineers, Inc.,* 318 F.2d 18 (5th Cir. 1963). In one case, a court held that a contractor's lost profits were sufficiently proved through introduction and use of his bid sheet reflecting quotes from reliable subcontractors. *Edward L. Nezelek, Inc. v. Southern Bell Telephone & Telegraph Co.,* 383 So.2d 979 (Fla. 4th DCA 1980).

B. Action By Owner When Contractor Fails To Perform

1. [§10.5] Investigation And Preparation

An action by the owner against the contractor invariably involves disputes regarding one or more of the following issues: (a) performance by the contractor according to the requirements of the plans and specifications; (b) changes in the plans and specifications; (c) negligent construction; (d) failure of the owner or his agent (an architect or engineer) to provide something upon which the contractor's performance depends; (e) breach of implied and express warranties; and (f) time of completion. It is essential to determine what the plans and specifications called for, what changes have been agreed upon or are claimed to have been agreed upon and the specific failures of performance claimed by each party.

2. [§10.6] Damages

After gathering the factual material and data surrounding the various construction claims, the lawyer must determine the damages potentially available to both sides. This is particularly important, because a lawsuit by an owner often is followed by a counterclaim by the contractor asserting claims for breach of contract by the owner, such as failure to pay "draws" when demanded in accordance with the terms of the contract, quantum meruit and mechanics' lien foreclosure seeking damages as well as attorneys' fees.

An analysis of the measure of damages available to an owner when the contractor breaches a construction contract must begin with *Grossman Holdings Ltd. v. Hourihan,* 414 So.2d 1037 (Fla. 1982). In that case the Hourihans contracted with Grossman to purchase a house to be built in a planned development. Both the model and the office drawings showed the house with a southeast exposure. The contract provided that Grossman would construct the house "substantially the same" as in the plans and specifications at the seller's office or as the seller's model. Grossman, however, built the house in a "mirror image" of what the Hourihans expected and wanted so that the house no longer had a southeast exposure. In all other respects, the house was the same as that which the Hourihans contracted to purchase. The District Court of Appeal, Third District, held that in these circumstances, when Grossman willfully and intentionally failed to perform according to plans and specifications and, therefore, was not in substantial compliance with the contract, the measure of damages was that amount necessary to construct the house to make it conform to the plans and specifications.

The Supreme Court reversed on the issue of damages, holding that to reconstruct the house would result in economic waste and that the proper measure of damages was the difference in value between the house the Hourihans contracted to purchase and the house Grossman actually built, if such a difference existed. Moreover, the Supreme Court adopted the RESTATEMENT, FIRST, CONTRACTS §346(1)(a) (1932) as the law in Florida regarding breaches of construction contracts. That section of the RESTATEMENT provides:

(1) For a breach by one who has contracted to construct a specified product, the other party can get judgment for compensatory damages for all unavoidable harm that the builder had reason to foresee when the contract was made, less such part of the contract price as has not been paid and is not still payable, determined as follows:

(a) For defective or unfinished construction he can get judgment for either

(i) the reasonable cost of construction and completion in accordance with the contract, if this is possible and does not involve unreasonable economic waste; or

(ii) the difference between the value that the product contracted for would have had and the value of the performance that has been received by the plaintiff, if construction and completion in accordance with the contract would involve unreasonable economic waste.

The cost to reconstruct, therefore, is the appropriate measure of damages only if reconstruction is possible and only if reconstruction does not involve unreasonable economic waste. This applies both to commercial structures and to residential dwellings, presumably including condominiums. The difference-in-value rule typically results in a far smaller recovery than the cost-to-reconstruct rule.

The crucial issue for the trier of fact is whether or not reconstruction, if possible, involves economic waste. Factors to be considered in determining if economic waste exists include whether: (a) reconstruction would involve a cost grossly disproportionate to the results to be obtained, *Temple Beth Sholom & Jewish Center, Inc. v. Thyne Construction Corp.,* 399 So.2d 525 (Fla. 2d DCA 1981); (b) defects are curable at a reasonable cost without an entire dismantling of the structure, *Temple Beth Sholom, supra*; (c) to remedy deficiencies would require the undoing of a substantial part of work already done, *Robbins v. C. W. Myers Trading Post, Inc.,* 111 S.E.2d 884 (N.C. 1960); (d) correction of defects and deviations would require expenditures of sums in excess of the value of the structure, *Jim Walter Homes, Inc. v. Castillo,* 616 S.W.2d 630 (Tex. App. 1981), 18 A.L.R.4th 1331; and (e) the cost to make a building conform to contract requirements exceeds the difference, if any, between the market value of the structure as it should have been constructed and its market value as it actually was constructed, *Gray v. Mattingly,* 399 S.W.2d 301 (Ky. 1966).

To be sure, there are recent cases in which condominium associations have been awarded damages in the amount necessary to correct construction defects or complete omissions. See, *e.g., Drexel Properties, Inc. v. Bay Colony Club Condominium, Inc.,* 406 So.2d 515 (Fla. 4th DCA 1981), *review den.* 417 So.2d 328; *B & J Holding Corp. v. Weiss,* 353 So.2d 141 (Fla. 3d DCA 1978). The condominiums in question, however, contained defects that were curable without a dismantling or major reconstruction of the buildings. The issue of economic waste evidently was not raised in these cases. Nevertheless, post-*Grossman* condominium construction cases may present questions of whether damage awards to correct defects involve economic waste, particularly when expensive reconstruction or corrective construction would result in only cosmetic improvements at best. The difference in value rule may be preferable in those cases.

For a further discussion of damages in construction cases see Chapter 7 of CONSTRUCTION LITIGATION IN FLORIDA (CLE 1983).

3. [§10.7] Conditions Precedent

When a contract or subcontract requires a certificate of substantial completion from an architect or engineer the failure to obtain the certificate that the work contracted for has been satisfactorily completed may be a complete defense to an action for breach of a construction contract. The contractor, however, will not be denied recovery when the architect or engineer arbitrarily withholds the certificate of approval. See *Arkin Construction Co. v. Reynolds Metals Co.,* 310 F.2d 11 (5th Cir. 1962); *Poranski v. Millings,* 82 So.2d 675 (Fla. 1955).

6. [§10.10] Statute Of Limitations

An action bottomed on construction disputes generally must be brought within four years whether the action is based on contract or on negligence. *F.S.* 95.11(3)(a), (c). In any event, an action involving a latent construction defect must be commenced within 15 years after the date of actual possession, the date of the issuance of the certificate of occupancy, the date of abandonment of construction or the date of completion or termination of the contract, whichever date is latest. 95.11(3)(c).

The Florida Supreme Court, however, has held *F.S.* 95.11(3)(c), which at the time had a 12-year statute of limitation on an action predicated on a latent defect, to be unconstitutional as violative of the constitutional right of access to the courts. *Overland Construction Co., Inc. v. Sirmons,* 369 So.2d 572 (Fla. 1979). One of the primary bases for the court's decision, in the face of the contrary public policy enshrined in the Florida Constitution guaranteeing litigants access to courts, was that the Florida Legislature had not expressed any public necessity for abolishing a cause of action occurring more than 12 years after the construction was completed.

In response to the Supreme Court's decision in *Overland, supra* the Florida Legislature in 1980 enacted Chapter 80-322, Laws of Florida, which extended to 15 years the period within which an action may be commenced. Moreover, in an attempt to cure what evidently was perceived by the Supreme Court to be a failure to justify the limitation period, the legislature at the same time issued a preamble to *F.S.* 95.11(3)(c) expressing that the best interest of the people in Florida would be served by limiting the period of time an engineer, architect or contractor may be exposed to liability in that: (a) the absence of limitation places a defendant in an unreasonable, if not impossible, position to defend the litigation; (b) such a defendant has no control over an owner who over the 15-year period may negligently maintain the premises or may use or change the premises such that years afterwards unsafe or defective conditions may develop that appear to be part of the original construction; and (c) professional liability insurance may be more difficult to obtain if exposure to liability extends for an indefinite period of time. It is difficult to predict if the reenacted statute, with its longer period of limitation and its expressed rationale, will pass constitutional muster should it come for review before the Supreme Court. Nevertheless, this arena for debate presents an interesting jurisprudential study of conflicting perceptions of the public's interests and, arguably, the judiciary's invasion into the prerogative of the legislature.

7. [§10.11] Sample Complaint

IN THE CIRCUIT COURT FOR LEON COUNTY, FLORIDA

Case Number: XX-300

John Owner,

    Plaintiff,

vs.

Sam Contractor,

    Defendant.

COMPLAINT

Plaintiff, John Owner, sues defendant, Sam Contractor, and alleges:

GENERAL ALLEGATIONS

1. This is an action for damages that exceed $5,000, exclusive of interest and costs.

2. Plaintiff and defendant are both residents of Leon County, Florida.

3. On January 10, 1983, plaintiff and defendant entered into a contract in which defendant agreed to construct a residence for plaintiff in Tallahassee, Leon County, Florida. A copy of the contract and of the plans and specifications referred to in the contract are attached to this complaint and made a part of it.

4. Plaintiff has paid defendant the sum of $70,000 toward the contract price.

COUNT ONE — BREACH OF CONTRACT

5. Defendant breached the contract in that although time was of the essence in the contract, defendant failed to complete the work until June 1, 1983, 31 days after the date specified in the contract. The contract provided for liquidated damages of $100 per day for each day that completion was delayed beyond May 1, 1983.

6. Defendant further breached the contract in the construction of the residence in the following particulars:

[set out the nonconformities with the plans and specifications]

7. All conditions precedent to the bringing of this action have occurred, have been performed or have been excused.

COUNT TWO — NEGLIGENCE

8. Defendant owed plaintiff a duty to use reasonable care in the construction work performed on plaintiff's residence.

9. Defendant breached his duty by failing to use reasonable care in his construction work in the following particulars:

[set out the items of negligent construction]

10. As a direct and proximate result of defendant's failure to use reasonable care in his construction work, plaintiff's residence contained numerous defects outlined above, resulting in damages to plaintiff.

COUNT THREE — IMPLIED WARRANTY

11. Defendant assumed overall responsibility to construct plaintiff's residence so that it would be reasonably fit for habitation and reasonably fit for its intended use and purpose, of which defendant knew or should have known.

12. Due to defendant's failure to construct plaintiff's residence properly, as outlined above, the residence contained numerous defects, and the residence is not reasonably fit for habitation or for its intended use and purpose.

13. These breaches of implied warranties have directly and proximately caused plaintiff damages.

WHEREFORE, plaintiff demands damages from defendant. Plaintiff demands trial by jury of all issues so triable.

/s/ J. S. Martin
Attorney for Plaintiff
123 Broad Street
Tallahassee, Florida 32301
(904) 666-1111

III. REMEDIES FOR BREACH OF CONSTRUCTION LOAN AGREEMENT

A. [§10.12] In General

As with any contract, the enforceability of a lending agreement hinges upon establishing threshold elements such as offer, acceptance, consideration, definiteness and mutuality. The absence of an essential element may make the loan agreement unenforceable. For example, an agreement allowing a lender to withdraw its approval for any reason whatsoever prior to funding would be held unenforceable for its lack of mutuality. Once a lender accepts the borrower's note or mortgage, however, the otherwise voidable agreement becomes a binding contract for both parties. *Financial Federal Savings & Loan Association of Dade County v. Continental Enterprises, Inc.*, 338 So.2d 907 (Fla. 3d DCA 1976). An action for breach of a lending agreement also requires an adequate showing as to both causation and amount of damages.

In addition to actions brought by the borrower, others in the construction process also may make claims against the lender. A general contractor who has not been fully paid by the owner may seek to obtain an equitable lien against undisbursed construction loan funds. *Morgen-Oswood & Associates, Inc. of Florida v. Continental Mortgage Investors*, 323 So.2d 684 (Fla. 4th DCA 1976), *cert. dism.* 342 So.2d 1100. This remedy also exists in favor of subcontractors as long as the undisbursed loan proceeds were targeted for the labor and materials furnished by the unpaid party. *Vista Landscaping, Inc. v. Heck*, 366 So.2d 1264 (Fla. 4th DCA 1979). The mechanism of an equitable lien also may be used by lienors who attempt to obtain a lien position superior to that of the construction lender.

If a lender expressly agrees to guarantee payment to the contractor, the contractor will have a direct contract action at law against the lender on the indebtedness. See *Norin Mortgage Corp. v. Wasco, Inc.*, 343 So.2d 940 (Fla. 2d DCA 1977).

Another avenue that courts have explored concerning lender liability lies in the area of construction defects. As long as a lender acts solely in its lending capacity, it should be free of significant exposure for construction defects. See *Rice v. First Federal Savings & Loan Association of Lake County*, 207 So.2d 22 (Fla. 2d DCA 1968), *cert. den.* 212 So.2d 879, in which the court held that even though the borrower paid the lender as part of the loan costs a fee for "inspection and supervision" of construction, any such services existed only for the lender's benefit in determining progress for funding purposes. The court found that those provisions imposed no duty or liability on the lender to other parties regarding defects that the lender's review of construction failed to disclose.

If a lender subsequently becomes a developer, however, it will share liabilities facing any other builder. In *Chotka v. Fidelco Growth Investors*, 383 So.2d 1169 (Fla. 2d DCA 1980) the court held that a lender who foreclosed a condominium project, completed its construction and sold units to the public was subject to at least three bases of liability. The lender could be sued for patent construction defects existing at the time it acquired the project, for its express warranties to the purchasers, and for any implied warranties applicable to ordinary builders and developers as to those portions of the work undertaken after the lender's acquisition.

B.   [§10.13] Remedies For Breach By Borrower

Deficiency judgments are considered the rule rather than the exception in Florida. *Lloyd v. Cannon*, 399 So.2d 1095 (Fla. 1st DCA

1981), *review den.* 408 So.2d 1092. Unless the market value of the foreclosed property equalled the amount of the judgment or unless particular equitable defenses are sustained, deficiency judgments should be granted. See *Lloyd, supra*; *S/D Enterprises, Inc. v. Chase Manhattan Bank,* 374 So.2d 1121 (Fla. 3d DCA 1979).

C. [§10.14] Remedies For Breach By Lender

If a lender fails to fund pursuant to a construction loan agreement, an action for breach of a contract to loan money may be commenced. The complaint should be similar to Count One of the sample complaint set forth in §10.11. In determining the appropriate remedy, various avenues are possible. Specific performance of a contract to lend money, however, rarely is available. *Southampton Wholesale Food Terminal v. Providence Produce Warehouse Co.,* 129 F.Supp. 663 (D. Mass. 1955). This principle is founded on the law's assumption that money always is available in the money market at the lawful rate of interest. 22 AM.JUR.2d *Damages* §68. An award of money damages, therefore, usually is appropriate to provide an adequate legal remedy. The presumption that money is available may be rebutted with evidence to the contrary. Because an objective standard is applied, it generally is irrelevant that the prospective borrower, because of its individual financial circumstances, is unable to procure an alternate loan. See *Lowe v. Turpie,* 44 N.E. 25 (Ind. 1896). Despite these traditional rules, some courts seem to be leaning toward specific performance as a more realistic remedy due to the difficulties of proving damages. *Vandeventer v. Dale Construction Co.,* 534 P.2d 183 (Ore. 1975), 82 A.L.R.3d 1108; *Selective Builders, Inc. v. Hudson City Savings Bank,* 349 A.2d 564 (N.J. 1975).

In the absence of special circumstances reasonably within the contemplation of the parties when the contract was made, the measure of damages for breach of an agreement to loan money is any difference between the amount of interest that the borrower contracted to pay and the amount it was compelled to pay to procure the money. In determining these damages, a borrower can show that, due to the lender's breach, it was required to obtain financing elsewhere at a higher interest rate. To recover this interest differential, however, it is necessary to take the gross amount of increased interest and other loan costs over the life of the loan and reduce that aggregate sum to its present money value. *Financial Federal Savings & Loan Association of Dade County v. Continental Enterprises, Inc.,* 338 So.2d 907 (Fla. 3d DCA 1976).

Another measure of damages for the lender's breach of a financing commitment allows the borrower to recover sums it expended in commitment fees paid to the lender. For example, in *Plantation Key Developers, Inc. v. Colonial Mortgage Co. of Indiana, Inc.,* 589 F.2d 164 (5th Cir. 1979) the court affirmed a jury verdict awarding the borrower $60,000 of the $90,000 it paid in commitment fees to the defaulting lender.

There may be a number of special circumstances known to both parties that may form an appropriate basis for recovery. Not all such attempts will succeed. In one case, a contractor sought to recover from a lender the attorneys' fees expended in defending actions brought by various subcontractors. Had the lender timely paid, the argument went, the contractor could have paid its subcontractors and avoided the onslaught of litigation against it as well as the accompanying expenses of defending those lawsuits. The court rejected that claim, however, due to a concern that a ruling favorable to the contractor would provoke a multitude of similar claims. *Norin Mortgage Corp. v. Wasco, Inc.,* 343 So.2d 940 (Fla. 2d DCA 1977).

D. [§10.15] Lender Liability To The Borrower (*new*)

Although various sources of exposure touch upon the construction lender, a primary battleground for lender litigation is waged by the borrower after a lender terminates the loan agreement arguing noncompliance with agreed-upon preconditions. The borrower's failure to satisfy a material condition of the lending agreement is a recognized defense in those cases. Moreover, Florida courts strictly construe a lender's obligation to fund as set forth in the construction loan agreement. Before commencing an action, the complete agreement must be read carefully because these agreements often provide escape provisions. *Woodmere North Investment Fund Limited v. Guardian Mortgage Investors,* 393 So.2d 563 (Fla. 3d DCA 1981), *review den.* 402 So.2d 614; *Sterritt v. Baker,* 333 So.2d 523 (Fla. 1st DCA 1976).

A frequent response to the lender's defense of noncompliance is the borrower's claim that the unsatisfied precondition was waived. In *First Prudential Development Corp. v. Hospital Mortgage Group,* 390 So.2d 767 (Fla. 3d DCA 1980), *overruled* on other grounds 411 So.2d 181 the lender extended indefinitely the termination date of its loan commitment and subsequently withdrew its commitment on the basis that the borrower had failed to meet that date. The court found a waiver and held the lender to be in anticipatory breach of its lending contract.

In addition to express waiver, a lender's waiver of a precondition also can be implied by conduct. In *American National Bank of Jacksonville v. Norris,* 368 So.2d 897 (Fla. 1st DCA 1979), *cert. den.* 378

So.2d 342 a bank was found to waive its prerequisite for a 24-month completion date because it continued to meet with and make suggestions to the borrower even after it became evident that the borrower could not complete construction before the deadline.

A lender's cooperation with a struggling borrower need not be a waiver of known failures of compliance, however, if the lender consistently documents its position of nonwaiver. In *United States Life Insurance Co. In The City of New York v. Town & Country Hospital, Inc.,* 390 So.2d 71 (Fla. 2d DCA 1980), *review den.* 399 So.2d 1147, for example, the borrower argued to the jury that the lender's continuing contact after the expiration date of the loan commitment constituted waiver. The lender successfully countered, however, by producing letters written near the time of the alleged waiver, confirming that it was merely considering rather than agreeing to any waiver of the termination date.

In addition to suing for a lender's failure to fund, one borrower claimed a breach based on the lender's failure at the inception of the loan commitment to earmark sufficient money to meet the subsequent duty to fund. *Levenson v. Barnett Bank of Miami,* 330 So.2d 192 (Fla. 3d DCA 1976). Although rejecting any duty to earmark funds, the court concluded that a lender subject to a standby loan commitment owed a duty to be financially capable of meeting its lending obligation through the period of the obligation. As a result, the court ruled that the trial court should have allowed the amendment of the complaint to raise the issue of the financial condition of the lender during the time of its loan commitment.

11

REMOVAL OF RESTRICTIVE COVENANTS

II. PRELIMINARY CONSIDERATIONS

    E. Facts Insufficient To Justify Removal

        2. [§11.17] Zoning Changes

---

[*]LL.B., 1949, Stetson University. Mr. Linney is the Field Attorney for the Attorneys Title Guaranty Fund and is a member of the St. Petersburg Bar Association. He is a partner in Linney & Linney and practices in St. Petersburg.

II. PRELIMINARY CONSIDERATIONS

E. Facts Insufficient To Justify Removal

2. [§11.17] Zoning Changes

If land is taken for a public purpose, for example, a school, the restrictive covenants are not enforceable against the public body and compensation for their violation may not be claimed by beneficiaries of the same covenants owning nearby lands. See *Ryan v. Town of Manalapan*, 414 So.2d 193 (Fla. 1982); *The Board of Public Instruction of Dade County v. Town of Bay Harbor Islands*, 81 So.2d 637 (Fla. 1955).

F.S. 197.281 provides that any covenants and restrictions contained in a deed will survive and will be enforceable after the issuance of a tax deed. *F.S.* 197.281(3) further provides that any right the former owner had to enforce the restrictions will survive to the grantee in the tax deed.

JAMES J. BROWN*

12

ACCESS TO PROPERTY BY NONOWNER

I.   INTRODUCTION

    C. [§12.3] Florida Historical Background

II. ACCESS TO PROPERTY BASED ON POLICE POWER

    A. [§12.4] Public Rights In Private Property

III. ACCESS TO PROPERTY BASED ON PRIVATE RIGHTS

    E. Rights-Of-Way

        1. [§12.10] In General

---

*J.D., 1964; LL.M., 1970, Washington University. Professor Brown is a member of the Ohio State and American bar associations and is a Professor of Law at Stetson University College of Law in St. Petersburg. The author gratefully acknowledges the assistance of Lori M. Lapin in the preparation of this supplement. Ms. Lapin is a member of the New York State Bar Association.

I. INTRODUCTION

C. [§12.3] Florida Historical Background

The philosophical discussion in *City of Miami Beach v. Ocean & Inland Co.,* 147 Fla. 480, 3 So.2d 364 (1941) should be corrected to read as follows:

> It is fundamental that one may not be deprived of his property without due process of law, but it is also well established that he may be restricted in the use of it when that is necessary to the common good. . . . Such restrictions must find their basis in the safety, health, morals or general welfare of the community.

II. ACCESS TO PROPERTY BASED ON POLICE POWER

A. [§12.4] Public Rights In Private Property

Hill v. State ex rel. Watson, 155 Fla. 245, 19 So.2d 857 (1944), which dealt with the reasonableness of regulations asserted under the police power mandate, was reversed at 325 U.S. 538 on other grounds. The concept enunciated about the reasonableness of the assertion of police power controls remains a valid statement of the law. The examples of the valid exercise of police powers listed in this section have changed only slightly since the original publication of this chapter.

1. Chapter 77-102, Laws of Florida amended *F.S.* 193.023, and substituted references to the "property appraiser" for prior references to the "tax assessor."

2. *Benefield v. State,* 160 So.2d 706 (Fla. 1964) has been followed by *State v. Johnson,* 372 So.2d 536 (Fla. 4th DCA 1979), *cert. den.* 385 So.2d 758. These cases refer to peace officers who seek to gain admittance for the purpose of making an arrest.

3. Regarding state fire marshal access right, see *F.S.* 633.081(1).

4. City ordinances dealing with health, safety, fire and sanitation matters remain an area of controversy even though the cases recognize that the enforcement of

standards under these administrative regulations will justify periodic inspection of private premises by public officials. *Frank v. Maryland,* 359 U.S. 360, 79 S.Ct. 804, 3 L.Ed.2d 877 (1959), *reh. den.* 360 U.S. 914 originally had held that as long as the public inspection was reasonably limited to the public health concerns and standards of the ordinance, Fourth Amendment limitations had not been violated. The interpretation in *Frank* was that no probable cause warrant was necessary for a public official to search a person's property, papers and effects under a code-enforcement and safety concern. This was a public purpose objective separate and distinct from the criminal matter objectives to which the Fourth Amendment was addressed.

a. The concepts enunciated in *Frank* were tested in 1967 before the United States Supreme Court in *Camara v. Municipal Court of the City and County of San Francisco,* 387 U.S. 523, 87 S.Ct. 1727, 18 L.Ed.2d 930 (1967). At issue was the right of the municipal housing, fire and health code inspector to obtain a warrantless entry into a ground floor apartment within a larger residential apartment complex. The City of San Francisco had been maintaining, under the authority of *Frank,* an annual inspection of housing and apartment buildings as part of a comprehensive effort to maintain health, safety and housing standards. This annual municipal code housing inspection program was funded under a city bureau that acquired its revenue from annual licenses of apartment house operators. Permits of occupancy were issued once apartment units were found to comply with the ordinance requirements. The repeated refusal of a ground floor tenant to permit the municipal inspectors entry resulted in a local conviction under the code enforcement provisions of the San Francisco ordinance. The Supreme Court reversed the conviction and overruled *Frank v. Maryland, supra.*

The court determined that the Fourth Amendment through the Fourteenth Amendment prevents local prosecution of those who resist warrantless code enforcement inspections of local ordinances. The court applied Fourth Amendment probable cause for reasonable searches of private property in view of the criminal penalty provisions of the local ordinance. This interpretation brings consistency to Fourth Amendment interpretations of official entry when rights of persons, papers, effects and residences are involved.

The court interpreted the reasonableness of a probable cause warrant as the consideration of legislative or administrative standards with respect to particular dwelling units. Those standards, although varying between several municipal programs, should be based on such factors as the passage of time, the nature of the residential unit being inspected or the entire area's condition. The court indicated that as long as these standards were met (any one of which may be sufficient depending on local conditions) and the municipal interests denominated in the ordinance, it was not necessary for the public official to have specific knowledge of the violation of a health, safety or housing condition in the dwelling being inspected. This standard of specific knowledge is a much less stringent standard than that enunciated in criminal law matters. The standard is appropriate for what is now identified as "administrative searches wherein warrants or judicial orders are issued by judges predicated upon municipally defined probable cause standards in the health, safety and housing field." This diminished level of probable cause was enunciated in Florida in *Heinlein v. Metropolitan Dade County,* 239 So.2d 635 (Fla. 3d DCA 1970), an apartment house, housing code case. In *Heinlein* at p. 636 the court stated that the *Camara* case "requires a certain type of 'probable cause' to be demonstrated before the issuance of the search warrant in these types of cases. We hold, therefore, that Section 17-10 of the Code [Code of Metropolitan Dade County] does require 'probable cause' in accordance with the provisions of the *Camara* decision before a search warrant may issue under this provision of the Code." It should be noted that neither the Florida nor the United States supreme courts have preempted municipal officials from making emergency inspections without a warrant. See *Camara, supra* at 539.

The practitioner should note that the court emphasized the reasonableness of the standards to justify probable cause warrants for municipal inspections.

The degree to which *Camara* can be extended is explored in AGO 074-292, in which a careful analysis of precedent in this probable cause area was explored. The opinion clearly identifies that the reasonable standards for health-safety code inspections are not elastic enough to permit municipal officials to use that ordinance process to conduct warrantless searches of property under construction or private occupied buildings for the express purpose of determining whether municipal code inspectors are fulfilling their public functions. The Attorney General's opinion expressly points out a lack of authority for non-code enforcement officials to enter buildings, structures or premises for purposes that are not directly related to code enforcement or the prevention of violation of municipal health or safety standards.

See *Marshall v. Barlow's, Inc.*, 436 U.S. 307, 98 S.Ct. 1816, 56 L.Ed.2d 305 (1978) in which the court analyzed the right of Occupational Safety and Health Act administrators to conduct warrantless inspections of work place conditions. This decision denied federal officials the unlimited power to make nonconsensual warrantless inspections of every type of industry engaged in interstate commerce. The court felt that extension of those powers was unwarranted unless the industries being inspected had a history of being closely regulated at the federal level.

5. *F.S.* 581.031(15) authorizes the Department of Agriculture and Consumer Services to "inspect . . . plants, plant products or other things and substances that may . . . be capable of disseminating or carrying plant pests or noxious weeds, and for this purpose shall have power to enter into or upon any place and to open any bundle, package, or other container . . . thought to contain" the above-mentioned problems.

This statute has not been effectively tested under the same standards noted above but presumably is valid under the state's interest in agricultural pest and weed control.

III. ACCESS TO PROPERTY BASED ON PRIVATE RIGHTS

E. Rights-Of-Way

1. [§12.10] In General

The common-law right-of-way is discussed in 1 THOMPSON ON REAL PROPERTY §6 (1980). Florida's statutory "way of necessity" was discussed in *Ganey v. Byrd,* 383 So.2d 652 (Fla. 1st DCA 1980).

The original chapter pointed out an uncertainty that existed in this area as a result of the decision in *Stein v. Darby,* 126 So.2d 313 (Fla. 1st DCA 1961), *cert. den.* 134 So.2d 232 and the enactment of Article X, §6 of the Florida Constitution. The constitutional change in 1968, which drastically affected the subject matter, was tested and analyzed in *Deseret Ranches of Florida, Inc. v. Bowman,* 349 So.2d 155 (Fla. 1977). *Deseret Ranches* presented a constitutional challenge to the validity of F.S. 704.01(2) in which a landlocked owner was being denied a previously-used way of necessity to reach a public right of way. The Florida Supreme Court upheld the policy reasoning of *Stein v. Darby, supra* and stated that "the statute's purpose is predominantly public and the benefit to the private landholder is incidental to the public purpose." *Deseret Ranches* at 156. The court found "a clear public purpose in providing means of access to such lands" in this state where "sensible utilization of land continues to be one of our most important goals." *Deseret Ranches* at 156. This result recognizes the incidental benefits to private landowners who, as a result of the statute, are able to utilize a public purpose concept to force other private landowners to maintain a servient estate without receiving compensation under 704.04. In a well-written dissent, the significant difference between public purpose and public benefit under the statute and constitutional provision mentioned above are carefully explored. The dissenting opinion strongly relies on the reasoning in *South Dade Farms v. B. & L. Farms Co.,* 62 So.2d 350 (Fla. 1952).

For the most complete statement on the subject in Florida law, the practitioner should refer to the reasoning in *Stein v. Darby, supra,* a case that explores the common-law history on the doctrine of ways of necessity, along with the extensive discussion in *Deseret Ranches, supra.*

13

ZONING

This chapter is not being supplemented. The reader is referred to FLORIDA ZONING AND LAND USE PLANNING (CLE 1980).

JAMES J. BROWN*

14

SLANDER OF TITLE

II. NATURE OF ACTION

    A. [§14.2] In General

    B. [§14.3] Elements Of Action

    C. [§14.4] Damages And Other Relief Available

V. [§14.7] STATUTE OF LIMITATIONS

---

*The biographical sketch for Professor Brown appears on page 73.

II. NATURE OF ACTION

A. [§14.2] In General

The practitioner is referred to Introductory Note, Chapter 28, RESTATEMENT, SECOND, TORTS 333. The evolution of defamation law has tempered the distinctions between injurious falsehood and defamation as noted in that text. The Commentary to the RESTATEMENT suggests that the full extent of the noted differences have yet to be determined by United States Supreme Court Cases. RESTATEMENT, SECOND, TORTS §623A, Comment g.

B. [§14.3] Elements Of Action

The elements and rules that apply to the tort of slander of title are the same as those that apply to disparagement of property, injurious falsehood, slandered goods and trade libel. *Sailboat Key, Inc. v. Gardner,* 378 So.2d 47 (Fla. 3d DCA 1980). The elements for this tort are enumerated and explained in the RESTATEMENT, SECOND, TORTS §§623A and 624 as follows:

> §623A. Liability for Publication of Injurious Falsehood — General Principle
>
> One who publishes a false statement to the interests of another is subject to liability for pecuniary loss resulting to the other if
>
> (a) he intends for publication of the statement to result in harm to interests of the other having a pecuniary value, or either recognizes or should recognize that he is likely to do so, and
>
> (b) he knows that the statement is false or acts in reckless disregard of its truth or falsity.
>
> §624. Disparagement of Property — Slander of Title
>
> The rules on liability for the publication of an injurious falsehood stated in §623A apply to the publication of a false statement disparaging another's property rights in land, chattels or intangible things, that the publisher should recognize as likely to result in pecuniary harm to the other through the conduct of third persons in respect to the other's interest in the property.

The courts in Florida expressly adopted the rule set forth in the RESTATEMENT, FIRST, TORTS §§624 and 625. See *Lehman v. Goldin,* 160 Fla. 710, 36 So.2d 259 (1948). In *Lehman* the court held that the complaint stated a cause of action and quoted the applicable sections of the then existing RESTATEMENT. In 1976 the RESTATEMENT, SECOND was published and seemed to alter the previously published standard of intent. A person now must know of circumstances that would lead a reasonable person to realize that the publication of the falsehood would be likely to cause a pecuniary loss to the other party. This change probably resulted from the criticism that the first RESTATEMENT practically eliminated the requirement of malice, except when it was a required element to overcome a conditional privilege. See Prosser, *Injurious Falsehood: The Basis of Liability,* 59 Col.L.Rev. 425 (1959).

The RESTATEMENT, SECOND, TORTS §§623A and 624 seem to require some type of intent of foreseeability. It imposes a somewhat more stringent standard than noted in previous Florida decisions. Until further litigation results, it is unclear whether Florida will continue its adherence to the RESTATEMENT elements as stated in *Lehman, supra*; *Collier County Publishing Co., Inc. v. Chapman,* 318 So.2d 492 (Fla. 2d DCA 1975), *cert. den.* 333 So.2d 462.

C.   [§14.4] Damages And Other Relief Available

The most significant change in these topical areas involves the decision by a Florida court to apply the defense of privilege in an action for slander of title. *Sailboat Key, Inc. v. Gardner,* 378 So.2d 47 (Fla. 3d DCA 1980). The original litigation in this case involved building construction permits for a project in Biscayne Bay in the city of Miami. Following the settlement of the dispute over permits, the property owner alleged that the original proceedings contained statements of disparagement or slander of its title. Upholding the previous decision of *Gates v. Utsey,* 177 So.2d 486 (Fla. 1st DCA 1965), the court ruled that the same privileges enjoyed in libel actions extend to slander of title and the privileges are absolute. Further support for the holding was excerpted and cited from PROSSER, LAWS OF TORTS §114 at 777—778 and §128 at 924 (4th ed. 1971) and RESTATEMENT, SECOND, TORTS §§587 and 635. Statements in the original complaint that state a cause of action enjoy the absolute privilege. Statements that do not state a cause of action also appear to be privileged, as a result of *Procacci v. Zacco,* 402 So.2d 425 (Fla. 4th DCA 1981). That case involved a slander of title action that arose out of an unsuccessful attempt to establish an easement over the appellee's land. The landowner subsequently filed a slander of title action predicated on the filing of the notice of lis pendens.

The notice of lis pendens had been filed simultaneously with the original easement litigation. He was unsuccessful. In a well-supported decision following majority trends, the court extended the privilege defenses available in actions for personal defamation to actions for slander of title and held that "appellants' filing of a notice of lis pendens was a part of the judicial proceeding to determine the existence of an easement and thus, it is encompassed within the judicial proceedings privilege." *Procacci* at 427. Statements made in the pleadings that are material to the cause at hand are absolutely privileged and cannot serve as the basis for a slander of title claim. See *Sussman v. Damian,* 355 So.2d 809 (Fla. 3d DCA 1977).

Punitive damages are awarded in other jurisdictions when actual malice is established. See 50 AM.JUR.2d *Libel and Slander* §§544, 546, 550, 551. Florida appears to follow this rule. See *Continental Development Corp. of Florida v. Duval Title & Abstract Co.,* 356 So.2d 925 (Fla. 2d DCA 1978) citing *Collier County Publishing Co., Inc. v. Chapman,* 318 So.2d 492 (Fla. 2d DCA 1975), *cert. den.* 333 So.2d 462, which held that a plaintiff must prove actual malice in order to recover punitive damages. The court in *Continental Development Corp.* denied an award of damages because the evidence in a slander of title action involving a mechanics' lien for title services did not adequately prove special damages. The drafters of the RESTATEMENT, FIRST and SECOND, TORTS rendered a publisher of a disparaging comment liable for punitive damages when the existence of personal ill will or knowledge of falsity or a desire to harm constituted the motivation for the action. See RESTATEMENT, FIRST §625, Comment d. This position was further limited to read punitive damages could not be awarded when the publisher of the disparaging comment was merely negligent in ascertaining the truth. See RESTATEMENT, SECOND, TORTS §621, Comment d. While the first RESTATEMENT permitted punitive damages when the complaint contained adequate allegations of actual malice, the RESTATEMENT, SECOND, TORTS §626 is unclear. See also §623A, Comment f.

Compensatory damage rules that previously noted the allowance for attorneys' fees as special damages, *Glusman v. Lieberman,* 285 So.2d 29 (Fla. 4th DCA 1973), have been followed with consistency by additional Florida decisions. See, *e.g., Bloom v. Weiser,* 348 So.2d 651 (Fla. 3d DCA 1977); *Susman v. Schuyler,* 328 So.2d 30 (Fla. 3d DCA 1976).

V. [§14.7] STATUTE OF LIMITATIONS

The law is well settled that *F.S.* 95.11(3)(o), which applies to actions for libel and slander, also is extended to the tort action of slander of title. *Sailboat Key, Inc. v. Gardner*, 378 So.2d 47 (Fla. 3d DCA 1980). This recent decision cites and follows *Carey v. Beyer*, 75 So.2d 217 (Fla. 1954) and *Old Plantation Corp. v. Maule Industries*, 68 So.2d 180 (Fla. 1953).

MALCOLM B. WISEHEART, JR.*
GARY P. SIMON**
JOHN J. BOYLE***

15

LANDLORD AND TENANT

I. [§15.1] INTRODUCTION

II. NONRESIDENTIAL LANDLORD AND TENANT RELATIONS

    A. [§15.2] In General

    B. [§15.3] Bankruptcy

    C. Jurisdiction And Venue

        1. [§15.4] Jurisdiction

        2. [§15.5] Venue

    D. Tenancies At Will

        1. [§15.6] In General

        2. Termination

            a. [§15.7] In General

            b. [§15.8] Form For Notice Of Termination Of Tenancy At Will

---

*J.D., with honors, 1970, University of Florida; M.A. (English Law), 1973, Cambridge University. Mr. Wiseheart is a member of the Dade County and American bar assocations. He practices in Miami under the firm name of Malcolm B. Wiseheart, Jr., P.A.

**J.D., with honors, 1974, Stetson University. Mr. Simon is a member of the Dade County and American bar associations. He is a partner in the firm of Simon & Simon, P.A. and practices in Miami.

***J.D., 1969, University of Miami. Mr. Boyle is a member of the Dade County Bar Association. He is a partner in the firm of Boyle and Boyle and practices in South Miami.

3. [§15.9] Failure Of Tenant To Surrender Possession

E. [§15.10] Tenancy At Sufferance

F. [§15.11] Right Of Entry And Self-Help

G. Landlord's Lien

1. [§15.12] In General

2. [§15.13] Property Usually Kept On Premises

3. [§15.14] Advances

4. [§15.15] Exemptions

5. [§15.16] Priority

6. [§15.17] Enforcement

H. Distress Proceedings To Perfect And Enforce Landlord's Lien

1. [§15.18] In General

2. The Complaint

    a. [§15.19] In General

    b. [§15.20] Form For Distress Complaint

3. Distress Bond

    a. [§15.21] In General

    b. [§15.22] Form For Distress Bond

4. Distress Writ And Levy

    a. [§15.23] In General

    b. [§15.24] Form For Distress Writ

    c. [§15.25] Form For Motion For Final Judgment After Default And For Order Of Levy On Defendant's Distrainable Property

       d. [§15.26] Form For Final Judgment After Default

       e. [§15.27] Claims Of Third Parties To Property Distrained

       f. [§15.28] Tenant's Right To Return Of Distrained Property

       g. [§15.29] Tenant's Defenses

       h. [§15.30] Trial Of Issues

       i. Final Judgment

          (1) [§15.31] In General

          (2) [§15.32] Form For Final Judgment (Nonjury)

       j. Sale Of Distrained Property On Appeal

          (1) [§15.33] In General

          (2) [§15.34] Effect Of Appeal

I. Summary Removal Of Tenant

   1. [§15.35] In General

   2. [§15.36] Grounds For Removal Of Tenants

   3. Notice To Tenant

       a. [§15.37] In General

       b. Service Of Notice

          (1) [§15.38] In General

          (2) [§15.39] Form For Notice To Tenant

       c. [§15.40] Waiver Of Notice

   4. [§15.41] Waiver Of Default By Landlord

   5. [§15.42] The Complaint

   6. [§15.43] Service Of Process

7. Tenant's Response

    a. [§15.44] In General

    b. [§15.45] Time For Response

    c. [§15.46] Defenses

8. [§15.47] Trial And Judgment

J. Unlawful Detainer

1. [§15.48] In General

2. [§15.49] Considerations Determining Whether To Use Unlawful Detainer

3. [§15.50] The Complaint

4. [§15.51] Summons And Service Of Process

5. [§15.52] Defendant's Response And Defenses

6. [§15.53] Evidence

7. [§15.54] Trial And Verdict

8. [§15.55] Damages

9. [§15.56] Judgment And Execution

K. [§15.57] Common-Law Action For Damages

L. [§15.58] Declaration Of Termination Of Leasehold Interest

M. [§15.59] Advance Rent

N. [§15.60] Waste

III. RESIDENTIAL LANDLORD AND TENANT RELATIONS

A. [§15.61] In General

B. Applicability And Scope Of Act

1. [§15.62] Definitions Of "Dwelling Unit" And Exclusions

      2. [§15.63] Effective Date Of Act

  C. Substantive Requirements Or Changes In The Content Of Lease Agreements For "Dwelling Units"

      1. [§15.64] In General

      2. [§15.65] Unenforceability Of Unconscionable Agreements

      3. [§15.66] Exculpatory Clauses And Waivers Of Rights Invalidated

      4. [§15.67] Attorneys' Fees

  D. Duration Of Periodic Tenancies; Rent And Notice Of Termination

      1. [§15.68] When Rent Is Payable

      2. [§15.69] Terms Of Tenancies Without Specific Durations

      3. Termination Of Tenancies Without Specific Durations

         a. [§15.70] In General

         b. Notice Of Termination

            (1) [§15.71] In General

            (2) [§15.72] Form For Notice Of Termination

      4. [§15.73] Failure Of Tenant To Surrender Possession And Holdover Tenancies

  E. Landlord's Duties And Obligations

      1. [§15.74] In General

      2. [§15.75] Duty Of Disclosure

      3. [§15.76] Deposit Money

      4. [§15.77] Retaining Or Claiming Security Deposits

      5. [§15.78] Obligation To Maintain Premises

F. Tenant's Obligations And Duties

    1. [§15.79] In General

    2. [§15.80] Duty To Maintain Dwelling Unit

    3. [§15.81] Duty To Provide Landlord With Access To Dwelling Unit

G. Rights And Remedies Of Tenants

    1. [§15.82] In General

    2. [§15.83] Right To Terminate Rental Agreement For Failure Of Landlord To Perform Duties

    3. [§15.84] Defenses To Action For Rent Or Possession

    4. [§15.85] Right To Terminate Tenancy Because Of Casualty Damage

H. Rights And Remedies Of Landlord

    1. [§15.86] In General

    2. [§15.87] The Landlord's Lien

    3. Termination Of Lease By Landlord For Breach By Tenant

        a. [§15.88] In General

        b. [§15.89] Forms For Notices To Tenant Of Termination; Breach Of Lease

        c. [§15.90] Form For Notice To Tenant Of Termination; Failure To Pay Rent

        d. [§15.91] Form For Letter Of Termination Of Lease

    4. Recovery Of Possession Of Premises By Landlord

        a. [§15.92] In General

        b. [§15.93] Jurisdiction And Procedure For Eviction

        c. [§15.94] Form For Complaint For Eviction Of Tenant For Failure To Pay Rent

        d. [§15.95] Defenses To Action For Eviction

        e. [§15.96] Judgment Of Eviction

I. Rentals Of Mobile Home Lots

    1. [§15.97] In General

    2. [§15.98] Eviction Of Mobile Home Tenants

    3. [§15.99] Deposits And Fees

    4. [§15.100] Rules And Regulations Of Mobile Home Parks

    5. [§15.101] Written Leases

    6. [§15.102] Rights And Remedies Of Mobile Home Owners

    7. [§15.103] State Mobile Home Tenant-Landlord Commission

J. Forms For Mobile Home Tenancies

    1. [§15.104] Three-Day Notice Of Termination For Nonpayment Of Rent For Mobile Home Owner

    2. [§15.105] Complaint For Possession Of Mobile Home Lot For Nonpayment Of Rent

    3. [§15.106] Termination Of Mobile Home Tenancy For Cause

    4. [§15.107] Complaint For Possession Of Mobile Home Lot For Violation Of Rules And Regulations

    5. [§15.108] Notice Of Termination Of Tenancy By Reason Of Change Of Use

    6. [§15.109] Complaint For Possession Of Mobile Home Lot After Change Of Use

    7. [§15.110] Termination Of Tenancy On Twelve Months' Notice And Eviction Of Mobile Home And Mobile Home Owner

8. [§15.111] Termination Of Tenancy On Twelve Months' Notice And Eviction Of Mobile Home Owner

9. [§15.112] Complaint For Possession Of Mobile Home Lot After Twelve Months' Notice (Eviction of Mobile Home And Mobile Home Owner)

10. [§15.113] Complaint For Possession Of Mobile Home Lot After Twelve Months' Notice (Eviction Of Mobile Home Owner)

11. [§15.114] Notice Of Termination Of Tenancy For Conviction Of Violation Of Law Or Ordinance

12. [§15.115] Complaint For Possession Of Mobile Home Lot For Conviction Of Violation Of Law Or Ordinance

13. [§15.116] Final Judgment On Default

14. [§15.117] Final Judgment After Trial

15. [§15.118] Petition For Determination Of Fair Market Value

IV. SELF-STORAGE FACILITY ACT

    A. [§15.119] In General

    B. [§15.120] Liens

    C. [§15.121] Denial Of Access

    D. [§15.122] Enforcement Of Liens

    E. [§15.123] Form For Notice Enforcing Lien

    F. [§15.124] Advertisement

    G. [§15.125] Form For Notice Of Public Sale

    H. [§15.126] Other Matters

V. DISPOSITION OF PERSONAL PROPERTY LANDLORD AND TENANT ACT

    A. [§15.127] In General

    B. [§15.128] Notification Of Tenant And Other Persons

    C. [§15.129] Form For Notice To Former Tenant Of Right To Reclaim Abandoned Property (Value Less Than $250)

    D. [§15.130] Form For Notice To Former Tenant Of Right To Reclaim Abandoned Property (Value $250 Or More)

    E. [§15.131] Form For Notice To Person Other Than Tenant Of Right to Reclaim Abandoned Property (Value Less Than $250)

    F. [§15.132] Form For Notice To Person Other Than Tenant Of Right To Reclaim Abandoned Property (Value $250 Or More)

    G. [§15.133] Storage Of Abandoned Property

    H. [§15.134] Release Of Personal Property

    I. [§15.135] Sale Of Abandoned Property

    J. [§15.136] Nonliability Of Landlord

I.   [§15.1] INTRODUCTION

The subject of this chapter is landlord and tenant litigation. It includes a discussion of the remedies and defenses available to landlords and tenants under Florida law with particular emphasis on the examination and analysis of the provisions of *F.S.* Chapters 82 and 83. Its purpose is to acquaint the practitioner with the substantive and procedural aspects of Florida landlord-tenant law with the object of increasing awareness of the options available to the respective parties.

The relation of landlord and tenant arises from a contract, express or implied, under which the "tenant" occupies land of the "landlord." The landlord usually owns the land in fee simple and the tenant has only a contract or lease permitting him to occupy the property for a period of time at a stipulated rental, but during the life of the lease, the leasehold estate created by it, for all practical purposes, is the equivalent of absolute ownership. *Baker v. Clifford-Mathew Inv. Co.,* 99 Fla. 1229, 128 So. 827 (1930). The rent may be payable in money, services, crops or other chattels. Whether provisions for the payment of insurance premiums and taxes will be considered to be rent depends upon the interpretation of the lease agreement.

The tenancy created by the contract between landlord and tenant may be a tenancy at will, a tenancy at sufferance, a tenancy for years or a periodic tenancy. In addition, it will be a nonresidential tenancy, a residential tenancy (whether for a dwelling or a mobile home park lot) or a tenancy in a self-service storage facility. Because it will determine the applicable law, the type of tenancy should be one of the first determinations made by the attorney when faced with a landlord and tenant dispute.

Landlord and tenant law, like the relation itself, has its origins in antiquity. In Florida, the statutes governing the relation are to be found primarily in *F.S.* Chapter 83. That chapter is divided into five parts. Part I (83.001—.251) governs nonresidential, or commercial, tenancies. Until 1973 those sections comprised the entirety of Chapter 83. But since 1973 changing social conditions have been met with new legislation, in that year, in the form of Part II of Chapter 83, the Florida Residential Landlord and Tenant Act (83.40—.63); in 1976, in the form of Part III of Chapter 83, the Florida Mobile Home Landlord and Tenant Act (83.750—.797); in 1979 and 1982, in the form of Part IV of Chapter 83, which is now known as the Self-Storage Facility Act (83.801—.809); and in 1983, in the form of Part V of Chapter 83, the Disposition of Personal Property Landlord and Tenant Act (83.821—.833). The latter three enactments have made significant changes in the procedural and substantive law applicable to their respective tenancies and each part will receive separate treatment in this chapter.

Due to the substantial differences that now exist between the law governing residential tenancies and that applying to nonresidential tenancies, the following sections attempt to deal with the two subjects separately. Inevitably, there are numerous matters and procedures that tend to overlap both topics and the authors have endeavored to make those apparent when important.

II. NONRESIDENTIAL LANDLORD AND TENANT RELATIONS

A. [§15.2] In General

The statutes governing nonresidential landlord and tenant relations are not new or revolutionary in any sense of the word. The provisions of *F.S.* Chapter 82 and Part I of Chapter 83, and their predecessors, have been an important part of Florida law for many years.

Because of the nature of *F.S.* Chapter 82 and Part I of Chapter 83, the substance of this chapter will deal primarily with the options and remedies available to the landlord under statutory and common law. The protections afforded the tenant under Florida law will be discussed insofar as they relate to various defenses to legal action taken by the landlord.

The provisions of *F.S.* Chapter 82 and Part I of 83 no longer apply to residential tenancies. See Ch. 73-330, Laws of Fla. They govern only nonresidential tenancies. Since their applicability is determined solely by the exclusion of the subject tenancy from those defined as residential by Part II, the reader is referred to §§15.61 and .62 in which the applicability of the Florida Residential Landlord Tenant Act is discussed.

Florida law provides the landlord with a number of options and summary remedies for dealing with tenants who have defaulted under a lease agreement or who have held over after the expiration of their time. For instance, the landlord in certain cases may have the tenant summarily removed. See *F.S.* 83.20. In addition, the landlord may avail himself of the distress proceedings provided by 83.11—.19 and have the tenant's property sold to collect unpaid rent. He also may institute an action for unlawful detainer under Chapter 82, seeking the removal of the tenant and damages. Finally, the landlord always has the option of suing for damages for breach of the lease agreement.

Each of these remedies or options is discussed in the following material and the practitioner is advised to weigh all of the options available before instituting any action against a tenant on behalf of a landlord.

B.   [§15.3]   Bankruptcy

The United States Congress in 1978 enacted a new Bankruptcy Code, which has had, and will have, a significant effect on landlord-tenant matters. See 11 *U.S.C.* §§101—1330 (called Bankruptcy Reform Act of 1978). The new Bankruptcy Code supersedes the old Bankruptcy Act for all cases filed on or after October 1, 1979. A substantial change from previous law is that "ipso facto" clauses in leases that previously created a forfeiture or termination when a tenant became insolvent or bankruptcy proceedings were filed against a tenant are now ineffective with respect to the bankruptcy trustee. Thus, the bankruptcy trustee has the right to assume the lease, to assign it to a third party to operate under the lease, or to reject the lease. 11 *U.S.C.* §363(k)(1).

There also is an automatic stay provision, namely, 11 *U.S.C.* §362, which creates an automatic stay (injunction) with respect to all proceedings and actions against the debtor (tenant). Failure of the landlord to refrain from any action against the tenant could be a contempt of court. Expedited hearings are provided for release from the stay, and release is automatic 30 days after a request has been made, if the court has not acted to continue the stay after notice and hearing.

The trustee is given a limited period of time within which to assume or reject a lease in Chapter 7 proceedings, but the court upon request of either party may set a specific time in Chapter 11 and Chapter 13 proceedings. 11 *U.S.C.* §§365(d)(1), (2).

Although a shopping center lease may be assumed and assigned by the trustee, shopping centers are given special treatment in 11 *U.S.C.* §365(b)(3) which includes adequate assurance of the source of the rent, protection for percentage rent, protection for exclusive use provisions, and protection that assignment will not substantially disrupt any tenant mix. These rights must be written into the shopping center lease to be effective.

Landlords no longer are given a priority claim in bankruptcy proceedings and must file a claim for pre-petition rents due and owing. There is an express limitation on the amount of damages for termination of a lease, 11 *U.S.C.* §502(b)(7). Administrative rent, *i.e.*, rent accruing subsequent to the filing of the petition when the lease is assumed, is calculated on a daily basis and is a priority claim and, accordingly, the landlord should act expeditiously and file a motion to have the trustee pay the administrative rent currently. Rent accruing after the petition is filed when the lease is rejected is treated as part of the pre-petition claim.

Security deposits are treated as a secured claim, with the balance of the claim of the landlord being unsecured.

If there is no equity in the lease, and if this can be shown to the trustee early in the proceedings, the landlord should seek to have the trustee abandon the property directly to the landlord, thus avoiding the necessity of a subsequent eviction. See 11 *U.S.C.* §554.

In order for the trustee to assume a lease, so that a proceeding can continue under Chapter 11 of the Code or so that the trustee can assign the lease under a Chapter 7 proceeding, the trustee must cure the default pursuant to the terms of the lease or provide adequate assurance that the default will be cured. 11 *U.S.C.* §365(b)(1). The amounts necessary to cure the default would include past due rent, sales tax, late charges, if any, as specified in the lease, attorneys' fees for the landlord's attorney involved in the bankruptcy, if specified in the lease, and any other charges called for in the lease that are due and owing as of the date of the filing of the petition in bankruptcy.

Statutory liens under 11 *U.S.C.* §545, such as the landlord's lien for rent, are voidable by the trustee and are inferior to the interests of the trustee. If distress proceedings are completed within the 90 days prior to the filing of the petition in bankruptcy, any sums obtained by the landlord are subject to being voided as a preference by the trustee. See §§545, 547.

Termination of a lease for nonpayment of rent either in accordance with the lease terms or pursuant to a three-day notice may be ineffectual to bar subsequent assumption by a trustee in bankruptcy, even when the petition is filed after the termination of the lease. See, *e.g., In re Belize Airways Ltd.*, BCD 637 (S.D. Fla. 1980).

C. Jurisdiction And Venue

1. [§15.4] Jurisdiction

F.S. 34.011(1) provides that county courts and circuit courts have concurrent jurisdiction to consider landlord and tenant cases involving claims in amounts within the jurisdictional limitations of the respective courts. The county courts have exclusive jurisdiction of all proceedings that relate either to the right of possession of real property or to the unlawful detention of lands and tenements, except as provided in 26.012. *F.S.* 34.011(2).

F.S. 26.012 vests jurisdiction in the circuit court of all "cases in equity" and all "actions involving the title and boundaries of real property." 26.012(2)(c), (g). Actions for removal of tenants involve the right to possession, not title; therefore, 26.012(2)(g) does not deprive the county court of jurisdiction over those actions. The 1974 Florida Legislature modified 26.012(2)(g) by deleting the words "right of possession" from the statute, thus eliminating any possible conflict between 26.012(2)(g) and 34.011.

F.S. 26.012(2)(c) is applicable when the lessor, in addition to seeking removal or damages, seeks equitable relief such as an injunction. Although there is no case law directly on point, it is arguable that if equitable relief is sought in addition to possession of the premises, the complaint should be filed in the circuit court. See *Knight v. Global Contact Lens, Inc.*, 220 So.2d 693 (Fla. 3d DCA 1969), in which the District Court of Appeal, Third District, held that once a court of equity takes jurisdiction of a cause, all the rights and demands of the parties shall be determined by that court.

Accordingly, with the possible exception of those cases in which equitable relief is sought in addition to possession, all removal of tenant actions must be filed in county court pursuant to *F.S.* 34.011(2). See *Kugeares v. Casino, Inc.*, 372 So.2d 1132 (Fla. 2d DCA 1979).

These jurisdictional provisions have consequences that are important to the landlord and that may not be apparent at first glance. For instance, a landlord may desire to commence only one action seeking both the recovery of possession of the leased premises and damages from a defaulting tenant. If the damages claimed exceed $5,000, the action for damages must be filed in the circuit court, while the county court has exclusive jurisdiction of eviction actions. Even if the amount of damages claimed does not exceed the monetary jurisdiction of the county court, the commercial landlord may wish to file a separate action for possession as he will lose his right to the summary removal procedure provided in F.S. 83.21—.251 if the eviction complaint includes a count for damages. See the discussion of the summary removal procedure in §§15.35—.47. See also 83.625, which authorizes a residential landlord to recover possession and rent in the same action. On the other hand, the landlord in the proper case may recover both possession and damages by a single action of unlawful detainer, which is within the exclusive jurisdiction of the county court. See 34.011(2).

As in any case in which legal proceedings are anticipated, the practitioner should give careful consideration to the question of jurisdiction of the county and circuit courts over landlord and tenant actions and the power of each court to grant the relief sought.

2. [§15.5] Venue

The proper venue for landlord and tenant actions or proceedings varies according to the type of action involved. A complaint seeking the summary removal of a tenant must be filed in the proper court of the county where the premises are located. *F.S.* 83.21. Likewise, 83.11 requires that a complaint seeking distress for rent be filed in the county where the land is situated.

Since the action of unlawful detainer is a special statutory proceeding, the proper venue usually is fixed by statute. Former *F.S.* 82.07, requiring the action to be commenced in the county where the land is situated, was repealed in 1967 and no provision has been enacted to take its place. By repealing that statute, the legislature apparently intended to make the venue transitory. Nevertheless, the practitioner may find it advantageous to file the action in the county where the land is to avoid recording certified copies of final orders or judgments in other counties and to avoid having the sheriff of one county serve writs of possession from another.

Not all landlord and tenant proceedings must be commenced in the county where the land is located. For instance, an action seeking a judgment declaring that a lease agreement has been breached and terminated, and seeking an accounting and a return of the security deposit, may be brought in the county where the action accrued or where the defendant resides. See *Gates v. Stucco Corp.*, 112 So.2d 36 (Fla. 3d DCA 1959). *F.S.* 47.011 provides that venue for actions for rent lies in the county in which (a) the property is located, (b) the defendant resides or (c) the cause of action accrues. See *Prahl v. Johnson*, 323 So.2d 682 (Fla. 3d

DCA 1975). The cause of action generally accrues where the act of default occurs. If the alleged default is in the payment of rent and the place of payment has not been determined by agreement of the parties, the rent is payable on the premises and that is the location of the default. See *Williams v. Aeroland Oil Co.,* 155 Fla. 114, 20 So.2d 346 (1944); *Prahl v. Johnson, supra.*

Care should be exercised to file claims for removal of tenants or past due rent in the proper branch court of the county court in those counties in which mandatory branch filing exists. In Dade County, for example, there is a mandatory branch court filing in the county court with respect to all possessory actions. Administrative Order 79-9, *In re Creation of County Court Districts,* Case No. 79-1 (court administration).

D. Tenancies At Will

1. [§15.6] In General

A tenancy at will usually is defined as one in which the tenant has the right to possession of the leased premises for such indefinite period as both the landlord and tenant agree that the possession shall continue. Thus, an essential attribute of a tenancy at will is the ability of either party to terminate the lease "at will."

Under Florida law, a tenancy at will is specifically defined as that estate created by an oral lease agreement or by a written lease in which the term of the tenancy is unlimited. *F.S.* 83.01, .02. A tenancy at will may be from week to week, month to month, quarter to quarter, or year to year, depending upon how the rent is payable. 83.02.

2. Termination

a. [§15.7] In General

Either the landlord or the tenant may terminate a tenancy at will if proper notice of termination is given as provided by *F.S.* 83.03. *F.S.* 83.01 provides that all unwritten tenancies create tenancies at will. Thus, an oral lease may be terminated even though it included an agreement as to a definite time. *Sill v. Smith,* 177 So.2d 265 (Fla. 2d DCA 1965). But see dicta to the contrary in *Eli Einbinder v. Miami Ice Co.*, 317 So.2d 126 (Fla. 3d DCA 1975). Unless both parties agree to the termination, a tenancy at will may be terminated only by giving notice of termination at a specified time before the end of the rental period. The time required for the notice varies in length depending upon the rental period involved. At least three months' notice is required to terminate a year to year tenancy, while only seven days' notice is required to end a week to week tenancy. 83.03.

F.S. 83.03 does not specify either the substance of the notice or the manner in which it is to be given. As a practical matter, the notice should be written and should be served in a manner that facilitates proof of service. Service of the notice may be made by personal delivery or by registered or certified mail with return receipt requested. The particular facts and circumstances of the case may dictate other methods of service, including service by the sheriff.

      b. [§15.8] Form For Notice Of Termination Of Tenancy At Will

To: ....

      Notice is given that ....your/my.......... tenancy at will in the premises located at ....(full address).......... shall be terminated as of ....(date).........., or .... days after service of this notice on you, whichever is later in time.

      Demand is made that you surrender the premises by ....(time).......... on that date.

      The undersigned certifies that a copy hereof has been furnished to .... by .... on ....(date)..........

      ....Landlord/Tenant..........

COMMENT: This form is similar to that in 11 AM.JUR. LEGAL FORMS 2d §§161:1196 and 161:1197. See also 11 AM.JUR. LEGAL FORMS 2d §§161:1198 and 161:1203. An additional form may be found in 2 SAPP, FLORIDA PLEADING, PRACTICE AND LEGAL FORMS §83.03 (2d ed. 1971).

      3. [§15.9] Failure Of Tenant To Surrender Possession

F.S. 83.20 provides that a tenant or lessee at will may be removed from the leased premises if he holds over after the expiration of his time without the permission of his landlord. If a tenant at will fails to surrender possession after receiving proper notice of termination under 83.03, 83.21 permits the landlord to file an action in the county court seeking his removal, and he is entitled to the summary procedure provided in 51.011.

The landlord also may demand double the monthly rent with interest from the time the rent is due if the holding over was willful and without color of title. *F.S.* 83.06. A tenant is not liable for that penalty if he holds over under a bona fide claim of right based on reasonable grounds. The landlord also must give notice to the tenant of his intention to collect double rent. See *Painter v. Town of Groveland,* 79 So.2d 765 (Fla. 1955).

The procedure under *F.S.* 51.011 available for the summary removal of a tenant is not authorized for an action seeking the collection of rent, except with respect to residential tenancies, and this fact should be noted when considering the joinder of a count for double rent with a count for eviction in the same complaint. See 83.625.

E. [§15.10] Tenancy At Sufferance

A tenant at sufferance is one who comes into lawful possession of land and continues to occupy it after his right to occupancy has ceased. See *Coleman v. State, ex rel. Carver,* 119 Fla. 653, 161 So. 89 (1935). When a tenancy with a limited term has been created by a written instrument and that term has expired, the tenant who holds over in possession without renewing the lease by another written instrument is a tenant at sufferance. If, however, the holding over is continued with the written consent of the lessor, the tenancy becomes one at will. *F.S.* 83.04.

A tenant at sufferance has no estate in or title to land, but has only naked possession and may be removed by the landlord under *F.S.* 83.21—.251. The landlord need not give the tenant any notice to surrender possession before commencing an action for his removal, although practicality may dictate that some notice be given to avoid litigation when possible.

F. [§15.11] Right Of Entry And Self-Help

The landlord's right to evict a tenant for breach of the lease technically is termed the "right of reentry." It arises only when there has been a forfeiture of the tenant's leasehold estate. *Baker v. Clifford-Mathew Inv. Co.,* 99 Fla. 1229, 128 So. 827 (1930).

At common law, no forfeiture of the tenant's leasehold estate could be asserted by the landlord for a breach by the tenant of a mere *covenant* in the lease. This included the covenant to pay rent, so the landlord could not evict the tenant for nonpayment of rent. Words of agreement, not contemplating a forfeiture upon the tenant's default, were said to create a covenant only, and the remedy for breach of covenant was an action for damages. On the other hand, if the tenant breached a *condition* of the lease, the landlord could declare a forfeiture of the leasehold estate immediately. A stipulation for a forfeiture drafted into the written lease was considered to frame a condition, even if the stipulation incorporated a mere covenant of the lease. Hence, landlords at common law were careful to insert the stipulation for forfeiture, or a "proviso for reentry," into their leases to allow them the right of reentry upon the tenant's default in the rent. II TIFFANY, LANDLORD AND TENANT §194 (1912).

The Florida Legislature partially changed this common-law rule when, in 1828, it enacted *F.S.* 83.05, providing that the landlord should have an immediate "right of reentry" upon the tenant's default in the rent. Lacking the historical background of this section, some practitioners erroneously interpreted it to authorize the landlord's use of "self-help"; that is, the use of force to retake possession of the leased premises from the tenant. This statute never meant that the landlord had an immediate right to lock the tenant out of the rental premises upon a default in the rent. It meant only that the *covenant* to pay rent was henceforth to be considered a *condition* of the lease, the failure of which condition entitled the landlord to declare an immediate forfeiture of the tenant's leasehold estate. The custom of drafting a proviso for reentry into a lease to take effect upon the tenant's default in the rent was antiquated by 83.05 as enacted in 1828. That statute, however, never was intended to do away with the need for legal process in reacquiring possession from a defaulting tenant. The use of self-help to retake possession of leased premises was never authorized by the common law of Florida, having been outlawed in England since the late fourteenth century. See *Ardell v. Milner,* 166 So.2d 714 (Fla. 3d DCA 1964).

In 1983, the Florida Legislature substantially rewrote *F.S.* 83.05 in such fashion as to eliminate any doubt about the illegality of "self-help" evictions. The revised statute specifically provided that a landlord may recover possession of rental premises only by court order, surrender or abandonment. The statute also provides for a presumption in favor of abandonment when (1) the landlord reasonably believes that the tenant has been absent from the rented premises for 30 consecutive days; (2) the rent is not current; and (3) a notice pursuant to 83.20(2) (a "three-day" notice) has been served and ten days have elapsed. 83.05(3).

How is the authorized forfeiture effected, and how is it enforced? At common law, the remedy was ejectment; under *F.S.* Chapter 83 the landlord is granted the modern, speedy summary procedure. *Ardell v. Milner, supra*; 83.21, 51.011. The landlord must first make a formal demand for payment of the delinquent rent. *Baker v. Clifford-Mathew Inv. Co., supra*. It is not necessary for him to follow up with a formal notice terminating the tenancy. The filing of an action for tenant removal has the effect of a declaration of the forfeiture of the leasehold estate. *6701 Realty, Inc. v. Deauville Enterprises, Inc.*, 84 So.2d 325 (Fla. 1956).

If a tenant actually has abandoned the leased premises, the landlord may reenter and take possession. See *Van Hoose v. Robbins,* 165 So.2d 209 (Fla. 2d DCA 1964). *F.S.* 83.05. If there has been neither abandonment nor voluntary relinquishment of possession, reentry by the landlord and eviction of the tenant by other than legal action may render the landlord liable in damages. See *Ardell v. Milner, supra*. The padlocking of a door to a leased building is tantamount to eviction and the landlord should be advised to avoid such self-help measures. See AGO 071-152. Instead, the landlord should avail himself of the procedure for summary removal of the tenant available under 83.21—.251. See also *Hunt v. Hiland*, 366 So.2d 42 (Fla. 4th DCA 1978); *Vines v. Emerald Equipment Co.*, 342 So.2d 137 (Fla. 1st DCA 1977).

G. Landlord's Lien

1. [§15.12] In General

Under *F.S.* 83.08, a landlord and his heirs, executors, administrators or assigns have a lien for unpaid rent upon the following property:

- a. Agricultural products raised on the leased premises.

- b. All property of the tenant or his subtenant or assignee *usually kept* on the premises. The lien attaches when the tenancy begins or as soon afterwards as the property is brought on the premises. See *Lovett v. Lee,* 141 Fla. 395, 193 So. 538 (1940).

- c. All property belonging to the tenant wherever located. The landlord's lien on property of this category dates from the levy of the distress warrant.

The landlord has a lien upon the above property whether it is found upon or off the leased premises and whether it is in the possession of the tenant or a third party.

2. [§15.13] Property Usually Kept On Premises

It often may prove difficult for the practitioner to determine what property constitutes property "usually kept on the premises." The property first must belong to the tenant before it is subject to a lien at all, and the landlord's lien does not attach to property until its title is in the lessee. *Powell v. Lounel, Inc.,* 173 F.2d 743 (5th Cir. 1949). Therefore, if the tenant has possession of property under a conditional sales contract, no lien exists. *Baer v. General Motors Acceptance Corp.,* 101 Fla. 913, 132 So. 817 (1931). Property "usually kept" on the premises may be removed at occasional intervals as long as it is regularly or habitually kept there. *Orr v. Peek,* 142 Fla. 160, 194 So. 341 (1940). It has been held, however, that property usually kept on the premises means only property kept there during the period for which the landlord makes his claim for unpaid rent and does not include property that was permanently removed from the premises during a period for which the rent was paid in full. *In re J. E. DeBelle Co.,* 286 Fed. 699 (S.D. Fla. 1923). In practice, whenever property is removed from the leased premises, a question of fact may exist as to whether it is property "usually kept" on the premises.

3. [§15.14] Advances

Florida law grants to landlords an additional lien for advances made to their tenants. *F.S.* 83.10. A landlord has a lien on the crop grown on rented land for advances made in money or other things of value to the tenant. The advances to the tenant may be made directly by the landlord or by another person at his request, or the landlord must have assumed a legal responsibility at or before the time when the advances were made. The advances for which the landlord has a lien are those made for the sustenance and well-being of the tenant or his family, or for preparing the ground for cultivation or for cultivating, gathering, saving, handling or preparing the crop for market. In addition to the landlord's lien on the crop, he has a lien for the aggregate value or price of property or articles advanced upon the articles themselves and upon all property purchased with money advanced or property obtained through barter or exchange for articles advanced. The statute declares that the liens thus acquired by the landlord on the crop are of equal dignity with the liens for rent, and the liens upon the articles advanced are superior to all other liens.

4. [§15.15] Exemptions

F.S. 83.09 states that no property of a nonresidential tenant is exempt from distress and sale for unpaid rent other than "beds, bed-clothes and wearing apparel." Furthermore, when the tenant is the head of a family, Article X, §4(a)(2) of the Florida Constitution provides that his homestead and personal property to the value of $1,000 is exempt from forced sale. See also *F.S.* 713.691(2). The personal property exemption ($1,000) has been held not to apply to property grown on the leased premises. *Hodges v. Cooksey,* 33 Fla. 715, 15 So. 549 (1894); *Cathcart v. Turner,* 18 Fla. 837 (1882).

5. [§15.16] Priority

The landlord's lien is superior to all other liens upon agricultural products. *F.S.* 83.08(1). Further, the lien of the landlord for unpaid rent on the tenant's property usually kept on the leased premises is superior to any lien acquired subsequent to the bringing of the property on the premises. 83.08(2). See also *Ruge v. Webb Press Co.,* 71 Fla. 536, 71 So. 627 (1916).

Federal statutes and federal decisions, however, determine whether a federal tax lien has priority over the landlord's lien for unpaid rent under state law. United States v. Weissman, 135 So. 2d 235 (Fla. 2d DCA 1961). Furthermore, the landlord's lien for rent in certain cases may be subordinated to a state tax lien. See AGO 066-111.

The question of priority frequently arises between landlords and parties who have "security interests" under Article IX of the Uniform Commercial Code, *F.S.* Chapter 679. The secured party's interests generally will be superior in priority to those of the landlord when those interests have been perfected prior to the time the goods were brought on the premises. See *U.S. v. S.K.A. Associates, Inc.,* 600 F.2d 513 (5th Cir. 1979); *G. M. C. A. Corp. v. Noni, Inc.,* 227 So.2d 891 (Fla. 3d DCA 1969); *Cabre v. Brown,* 355 So.2d 846 (Fla. 1st DCA 1978).

6. [§15.17] Enforcement

The landlord's lien is not self-executing. To enforce it, he must resort to the statutory procedure of distress for rent described in *F.S.* 83.11—.19. *Van Hoose v. Robbins,* 165 So.2d 209 (Fla. 2d DCA 1964).

H. Distress Proceedings To Perfect And Enforce Landlord's Lien

1. [§15.18] In General

A landlord's lien is enforced by a proceeding known as distress for rent. This remedy has been specifically abolished with regard to residential leases [*F.S.* 713.691(3)], but apparently the legislature intended it to still be available to landlords with respect to nonresidential tenancies.

The Florida Legislature, in 1980, enacted a revised distress for rent statute in order to satisfy the objections concerning constitutionality raised by the Florida Supreme Court in *Phillips v. Guin & Hunt, Inc.,* 344 So.2d 568 (Fla. 1977). *F.S.* 83.11—.19.

2. The Complaint

a. [§15.19] In General

The initial pleading in distress proceedings is a verified complaint filed by the landlord, his agent or attorney. The complaint must allege the amount or quality and the value of the rent due for the land, or the advances, and whether it is payable in money, an agricultural product or thing of value. *F.S.* 83.11. The complaint also must allege the name and relationship of the defendant to the plaintiff and how the obligation for rent arose.

b. [§15.20] Form For Distress Complaint

**IN THE COUNTY COURT FOR
.... COUNTY, FLORIDA**

Case Number ....

...................,
Plaintiff,

vs.

...................,
Defendant.

COMPLAINT FOR DISTRESS

Plaintiff, ..., files this action for distress for rent against defendant, ..., and alleges:

1. This is an action for distress for rent pursuant to F.S. 83.11 et seq.

2. Plaintiff is the ....owner/agent of owner.......... of the premises known as ...., located in .... County, Florida. The property is leased by defendant exclusively for nonresidential purposes and is not a mobile home.

3. Defendant is indebted to plaintiff in the amount of $.......... for rent due and owing for the months of .... and ...., the rent being due on the .... day of each month, payable in ....money/an agricultural product/any other thing of value..........

4. The rent is due pursuant to a ....written/oral.......... lease dated .... A true and exact copy of the lease is attached as Exhibit "B".

5. Plaintiff has retained the undersigned attorney to bring this action and is obligated to pay him a reasonable fee for his services.

WHEREFORE, plaintiff demands that this court issue a distress writ enjoining defendant from damaging and disposing of, secreting or removing any property liable to distress from the rented premises, and further ordering the sheriff of the county in which the property is located to levy on the property and sell it at public sale according to law and to apply the proceeds to the payment of the unpaid rent due and owing plaintiff, plus costs of this action and a reasonable attorneys' fee as permitted by the lease.

_____
Attorney for Plaintiff
..........(address and phone number)..........

By: ....

_____
(Plaintiff's signature)

STATE OF FLORIDA
COUNTY OF ....

Before me, the undersigned authority, personally appeared ...., who was sworn and says that ....he/she/they.......... ....is/are.......... the plaintiff(s) in the above-styled action, that ....he/she/they.......... .... has/have.......... read the foregoing complaint for distress for rent and that each matter in it is true and correct.

Sworn to before me on ....(date)..........

_____
Notary Public
My Commission Expires:
(Seal)

3. Distress Bond

   a. [§15.21] In General

On the filing of a complaint showing a prima facie case, the judge of the court having jurisdiction of the amount claimed, issues a distress writ enjoining the defendant from damaging, disposing of, secreting or removing any property liable to distress from the rented premises after the time of service of the writ and until the sheriff levies on the property or the writ is vacated or the court otherwise orders. A violation of the writ may be punished as a contempt of court. This procedure is a distinct change from prior law.

If the defendant does not move for dissolution of the writ, the sheriff will levy on the property liable to distress. Before the writ may issue, however, a bond must be filed as previously required by law.

   b. [§15.22] Form For Distress Bond

(Party Designation)   **(Title of Court)**

DISTRESS BOND

We, ...(plaintiff)..........., as principal, and ...., as surety, are bound to ....(defendant).......... in the sum of $.......... for the payment of which we bind ourselves, our heirs, personal representatives, successors and assigns, jointly and severally.

THE CONDITION OF THIS BOND is that if plaintiff shall pay all costs and damages that defendant sustains in consequence of plaintiff's improperly suing out the distress writ in this action, then this bond is void, otherwise it remains in force.

Signed and sealed on ....(date)..........

Approved on ....(date)..........

                                                                                (Name of Clerk)
                                                                                As Clerk of the Court
                                                                                By _____
                                                                                    As Deputy Clerk

_____ (Seal)
As Principal

_____
As Surety

COMMENT: See *Fla.R.Civ.P.* Form 1.960.

4. Distress Writ And Levy

a. [§15.23] In General

Once the distress complaint and bond have been filed by the landlord, the court issues a distress writ commanding the sheriff to summon the defendant to answer the complaint. The court also instructs the sheriff either to collect from the defendant the amount claimed by the landlord as advances or unpaid rent or to take custody of a sufficient amount of the tenant's property to satisfy the claim. *F.S.* 83.12. A form for the distress writ appears in *Fla.R.Civ.P.* Form 1.909.

The sheriff may execute the distress writ by either serving the writ on the defendant or by levying on the distrainable property if found within his jurisdiction. If the property is in another jurisdiction, the sheriff must deliver the writ to the proper sheriff in that jurisdiction. The sheriff receiving the writ executes it by levying on the property and delivering it to the sheriff of the county in which the action is pending unless the court issuing the writ instructs him to hold the property and dispose of it in his jurisdiction according to law. *F.S.* 83.13. It is important to remember that if the defendant cannot be found, the statute provides that the levy on the property constitutes service on him.

The distress writ requires the defendant to serve written defenses to the complaint within 20 days after service. The tenant must respond within the given period if he is to avoid the entry of a final judgment by default. *Rule* 1.500. See also Form 1.909.

b. [§15.24] Form For Distress Writ

(Party Designation)   (Title of Court)

DISTRESS WRIT

STATE OF FLORIDA:
TO THE SHERIFF OF .... COUNTY, FLORIDA:

YOU ARE COMMANDED to serve this writ and a copy of the complaint on defendant, ...

This distress writ subjects all property liable to distress for rent on the following property in .... County, Florida:

[property description]

Defendant is enjoined from damaging, disposing of, secreting or removing any property liable to be distrained from the rented real property after the time of service of this writ until the sheriff levies on the property or this writ is vacated, or the court otherwise orders. If defendant does not move for dissolution of the writ, the court may order the sheriff to levy on the property liable to distress after 20 days from the time the complaint in this action is served. The amount claimed in the complaint is the sum of $.......... with interest and costs, and a reasonable attorney's fee.

Dated: ....

..........Circuit/County.......... Court Judge

c. [§15.25] Form For Motion For Final Judgment
After Default And For Order Of Levy
On Defendant's Distrainable Property

(Party Designation) (Title of Court)

**MOTION FOR FINAL JUDGMENT AFTER DEFAULT
AND FOR ORDER OF LEVY ON DEFENDANT'S
DISTRAINABLE PROPERTY**

Plaintiff, ..., moves for the entry of a final judgment after default against defendant, ..., and for the entry of an order directing the sheriff to levy on defendant's property liable to distress, based on defendant's failure to move for dissolution of the distress writ. Plaintiff submits with this motion affidavits showing the amount due from defendant for rent, interest, costs and attorneys' fees.

The undersigned certifies that a copy hereof has been furnished to .... by .... on ....(date)..........

Attorney for Plaintiff
........(address and phone number).........

COMMENT: Counsel should first apply to the clerk for entry of a default in the usual manner by presenting an appropriate affidavit of nonmilitary service and motion for default and default. After default has been entered, counsel may apply to the court for entry of a final judgment by presenting to the court the above motion together with an affidavit of indebtedness, an affidavit of costs and, if appropriate, an affidavit of reasonable attorneys' fees.

d. [§15.26] Form For Final Judgment After Default

(Party Designation)   (Title of Court)

FINAL JUDGMENT AFTER DEFAULT

THIS ACTION was heard by the court. On the evidence presented, it is

ADJUDGED that:

1. Plaintiff, ..., recover from defendant, ..., the sum of $..........., as unpaid rent due on the premises described in the complaint with interest in the sum of $..........., costs assessed at $............, and a reasonable attorneys' fee of $............, making a total of $............, for which let execution issue. Interest shall accrue on this judgment at the rate of ....% per annum.

2. The sheriff is ordered to levy on defendant's property liable to distress and to sell the distrained property pursuant to F.S. 83.19.

3. The court retains jurisdiction of this matter to enter such further orders as may be necessary.

ORDERED at .... County, Florida, on ....(date)..........

             ....Circuit/County.......... Court Judge

Copies furnished to: ....

e. [§15.27] Claims Of Third Parties To Property Distrained

Only the property of the tenant, subtenant or assignee of the tenant's lease is subject to distraint even if the property is "usually kept" on the leased premises. *F.S.* 83.08(2). Property that does belong to the tenant, subtenant or assigns may be subject to distraint even though it is found off the leased premises and in the possession of a third party. 83.08.

Because the ownership of personal property is not always clear, property actually owned by a third party and not subject to levy under the distress writ sometimes may be distrained. Under 83.15, a third party who claims property that has been distrained may interpose in the action and prosecute his claim for it as provided in 56.16. If the third party does interpose, he must post a bond with surety in double the value of the property claimed. The bond must be conditioned to deliver the property to the officer if it is later adjudged to be that of the defendant, and must be conditioned to pay to the plaintiff all damages sustained by him if the claim was interposed only for purposes of delay. 56.16.

f. [§15.28] Tenant's Right To Return Of Distrained Property

F.S. 83.14 provides that distrained property may be restored to the defendant at any time on his giving bond with surety payable to the plaintiff in double the value of the property. The bond must be conditioned upon either the forthcoming of the property in accordance with the final order of the court or the payment to the plaintiff of the amount or value of the rental or advances that may be adjudicated to be payable to the plaintiff.

g. [§15.29] Tenant's Defenses

As in most other legal proceedings, the tenant has the right to file a timely answer to the complaint setting forth any defenses he may have to the landlord's claims. *Fla.R.Civ.P.* 1.110(c). He may answer by alleging that the rent or amount claimed by the landlord is not due, or he may allege any affirmative defenses that he may have, such as payment. *Rule* 1.110(d). His answer also may include any claim that he has against the landlord that could be the subject of a setoff or recoupment. *Rule* 1.170. The tenant, of course, may attack the jurisdiction of the court by showing that no landlord-tenant relationship exists or by showing that the amount of rent claimed by the landlord is not within the court's monetary jurisdiction. The latter attack is primarily a delaying tactic since under *Rule* 1.060(a) the action may be transferred to the court having jurisdiction, or the landlord may file a new action in the proper court.

h. [§15.30] Trial Of Issues

If the defendant avoids a default judgment and if either party manages to overcome any motion for summary judgment filed by the other party, the case when at issue may go to trial. Both parties have the right to demand a jury trial, but only a timely demand will prevent the waiver of this right. *Fla.R.Civ.P.* 1.430(d).

i. Final Judgment

(1) [§15.31] In General

If the court or jury finds for the plaintiff, judgment will be rendered against the defendant for the amount or value of the rental or advances, plus interest and costs. *F.S.* 83.18. If the property had been restored to the defendant under 83.14, the judgment also will be against the surety on the defendant's bond. The landlord may be entitled to reasonable attorneys' fees if provided for in the lease agreement.

On the other hand, if the verdict or finding of the court is for the defendant, the action will be dismissed and the defendant will be entitled to judgment and execution for costs against the plaintiff. *F.S.* 83.18.

(2) [§15.32] Form For Final Judgment (Nonjury)

(Party Designation)   **(Title of Court)**

FINAL JUDGMENT

This action was tried before this court. On the evidence presented

IT IS ADJUDGED that plaintiff recover from defendant the sum of $.......... as unpaid rent and advances due on the premises described in the complaint with interest in the sum of $.........., costs assessed at $.........., and a reasonable attorney's fee of $.........., making a total of $.........., for which let execution issue. Interest on this judgment shall accrue at the rate of ....% per annum.

ORDERED AT .... County, Florida on ....(date)..........

                                                                                                Judge

Copies furnished to: ....

COMMENT: See *Fla. R. Civ. P.* Form 1.993. A form for a final judgment after a jury trial may be found in 2 SAPP, FLORIDA PLEADING, PRACTICE AND LEGAL FORMS §83.18(1) (2d ed. 1971).

j. Sale Of Distrained Property On Appeal

(1) [§15.33] In General

If the judgment is for the landlord, whether by default or otherwise, the property is sold at the leased premises or the courthouse after being advertised two times, the first advertisement being at least ten days before the sale. The proceeds of the sale are applied to the amount due to the landlord under the judgment. If the rent or part of it was due in agricultural products and the property distrained is of a similar kind, the distrained property not exceeding the amount claimed, at his request, may be delivered to the landlord as payment on his execution. If any distrained property is sold to satisfy rent that was payable in agricultural products or things, the amount paid to the landlord will be an amount equal to the value of the rental at the time it becomes due. *F.S.* 83.19.

(2) [§15.34] Effect Of Appeal

The tenant may delay and perhaps prevent the sale by a timely appeal. Upon the filing of a notice of appeal, the payment of all accrued costs and the filing of a supersedeas bond, if required, further proceedings in the lower court including the sale of the distrained property are stayed pending disposition of the appeal. During the period when the stay is effective, the distrained property is returned to the tenant. See *F.S.* 83.19(3).

I. Summary Removal Of Tenant

1. [§15.35] In General

F.S. 83.20—.251 provide the landlord with the summary procedure available under 51.011 for the removal of tenants who no longer are entitled to possession of the leased premises. Under 51.011, the tenant is given five days after service of process within which to serve his answer to the complaint.

The computation of the five days is governed by Florida Rule of Civil Procedure 1.090 and, accordingly, the day of service and intervening Saturdays, Sundays and legal holidays are excluded.

The practitioner should bear in mind that removal of tenant actions are governed by the Florida Rules of Civil Procedure as modified by *F.S.* Chapter 51. See, *e.g., Berry v. Clement,* 346 So.2d 105 (Fla. 2d DCA 1977); *Palm Corp. v. 183rd Street Theatre Corp.,* 344 So.2d 252 (Fla. 3d DCA 1977), *cert. den.* 355 So.2d 516; *Moffett v. MacArthur,* 291 So.2d 134 (Fla. 4th DCA 1974). Such actions are not governed by the entirely different Florida Rules of Summary Procedure which are applicable only to actions for monetary damages for less than $1,500.

There is an unfortunate confusion that has plagued some attorneys (and judges) that arises from the fact that the expedited procedure applicable to actions for removal of tenants and provided for in *F.S.* Chapter 51 also is known as "summary procedure." The "summary procedure" of Chapter 51, however, has nothing to do with the distinct Florida Rules of Summary Procedure.

2. [§15.36] Grounds For Removal Of Tenants

Any tenant or lessee, subtenant or assignee of a lease agreement may be removed from the leased premises under *F.S.* 83.20 for either one of the following two defaults: (a) failure of the tenant to surrender possession after the expiration of this time or (b) failure of the tenant to pay his rent on time. If neither situation exists but the tenant is not entitled to possession to the premises for some other reason, the landlord should consider removal by an unlawful detainer action under Chapter 82.

3. Notice To Tenant

a. [§15.37] In General

Before the landlord is entitled to commence an action for the summary removal of a tenant for failure to pay rent, the landlord is required by *F.S.* 83.20(2) to give the tenant written notice of his default. The notice must give the tenant at least three days in which either to pay the rent or to deliver possession of the premises to the landlord. As a practical matter, the service of the notice often averts the need for litigation by affording the tenant a last chance to pay the rent or quit the premises. In any event, the notice requirement is jurisdictional and the failure to give it will provide the tenant with a good defense to an action for his removal.

Service of the notice on the tenant initiates a type of statutory grace period in which the tenant is permitted to pay the full amount of rent. Upon expiration of the period, the landlord may terminate the rental agreement and, thereafter, need not accept tender even of the full amount of the rent. In order to obtain possession, however, the landlord must file a complaint and seek a writ of possession as provided in *F.S.* 83.21.

If a lease provides a greater "grace period" than specified by *F.S.* 83.20(2), the landlord must observe the greater period before filing the action. *Morris v. Knox Corp.,* 153 Fla. 130, 13 So.2d 914 (1943).

The three-day notice must make demand for payment of the rent or possession of the premises. *F.S.* 83.20(2). A notice that merely states an intention to terminate the rental agreement because the full amount of the rent has not been paid and that fails to demand payment of the rent or possession of the premises is insufficient. *Deauville Corp. v. Garden Suburbs Golf & Country Club,* 164 F.2d 430 (5th Cir. 1947), *cert. den.* 333 U.S. 881.

The notice also should describe the premises, name the parties and specify the date on which the rent demanded became due. Other matters that are desirable to specify in the notice include the amount and date of the next rental payment and the time, date and manner in which the notice is served.

The computation of the three-day period specified in the notice is governed by *Fla.R.Civ.P.* 1.090, which requires exclusion of the day of service and intervening Saturdays, Sundays, and legal holidays. For a listing of legal holidays, see *F.S.* Chapter 683.

A misdescription of the amount of rent owed may not be fatal. See *Masser v. London Operating Co.,* 106 Fla. 474, 145 So. 79 (1932). "The question to be determined in the statutory proceeding to remove a delinquent tenant is not the amount of rent owing, but whether any rent is due, the effect being the same whether the sum is great or small." *Masser* at 85. There is at least some dicta, however, to the effect that the three-day notice should contain the "exact amount" of rent owed. See, *e.g., Baker v. Clifford-Mathew Inv. Co.,* 99 Fla. 1229, 128 So. 827 (1930).

It should be noted that *F.S.* 83.20 does not require a landlord to give any notice to a tenant who is holding over after the expiration of his term. The landlord therefore need not give any notice before filing his complaint for summary removal of the tenant, although practicality again may suggest that the tenant be given a last opportunity to avoid litigation.

    b. Service Of Notice

    (1) [§15.38] In General

The notice to the tenant of his default in the payment of rent must be served by delivering a true copy to the tenant or by leaving a copy at his last or usual place of residence if he is absent from it. *F.S.* 83.20(2) states that the notice must be served "by the person entitled to the rent on the person owing the same." No mention is made of service by the agent or attorney of the landlord, although as a practical matter service by such means probably is sufficient. The landlord in fact may desire that the service be made by the sheriff or a process server to avoid any personal conflict or dispute between the landlord and tenant. If the landlord desires to deliver the notice by mail, it is suggested that registered or certified mail with return receipt requested be used in order to facilitate proof of service.

(2) [§15.39] Form For Notice To Tenant

NOTICE OF DEFAULT

To: ....

YOU ARE NOTIFIED that you are in default in the payment of rent for the premises known as ...., ..., ... County, Florida, which you occupy under an .... oral/written .... agreement to pay rent for the premises from .... to .... at the rate of $.......... due on the .... day of each ....

You have failed to pay the rent that was due on .... for the period of .... to .... in the amount of $.........., and the rent that was due on .... for the period of .... to .... in the amount of $.........., making a total of $...........

Demand is made that you pay the amount due or deliver possession of the premises to the undersigned within three days from the service of this notice on you.

I CERTIFY that I served the foregoing notice by delivering a true copy of it to the person named above or, in his absence from the address set forth above, his usual place of residence, by leaving a copy of the notice at that address on ....(date)..........

                                                                Landlord

c. [§15.40] Waiver Of Notice

The requirement for the three-day notice to the tenant of his delinquency in the payment of rent apparently may be expressly waived by the tenant by provision in a written lease agreement. See *Baker v. Clifford-Mathew Inv. Co.,* 99 Fla. 1229, 128 So. 827 (1930); *Moskos v. Hand,* 247 So.2d 795 (Fla. 4th DCA 1971). It is suggested that the careful landlord or practitioner serve the notice as required by *F.S.* 83.20 even though that requirement apparently has been waived by the tenant, in order to avoid possible delay and expense necessary in litigating the question of waiver.

4. [§15.41] Waiver Of Default By Landlord

The landlord may waive the right to removal of the tenant or be estopped from asserting the tenant's default by the acceptance from him of rent or benefits of the lease after the breach. See *Moskos v. Hand,* 247 So.2d 795 (Fla. 4th DCA 1971); *Tropical Attractions, Inc. v. Coppinger,* 187 So.2d 395 (Fla. 3d DCA 1966). The landlord, of course, would not be estopped by instituting action for the recovery of any past due rent.

5. [§15.42] The Complaint

To remove a tenant, *F.S.* 83.21 requires that the landlord, or his attorney or agent, file a complaint that describes the leased premises and states the facts authorizing the tenant's removal. The complaint must be filed in the county court of the county where the premises are situated. A copy of any written lease agreement and, if the default claimed is the failure of the tenant to pay his rent, a copy of the notice described in 83.20(2) should be attached to the complaint. An approved form for the complaint is found in *Fla.R.Civ.P.* Form 1.947.

6. [§15.43] Service Of Process

The complaint and five-day summons permitted by *F.S.* 51.011 may be served on the defendant or on a member of his family above 15 years of age at his usual place of abode in the county. See 83.22.

F.S. 83.22 also authorizes service of process by posting the premises with a copy of the summons and complaint. This portion of the statute was modified by the Florida Legislature in 1983 to conform with the perceived requirements of the United States Supreme Court case of *Greene v. Lindsey,* 456 U.S. 444, 102 S.Ct. 1874, 72 L.Ed.2d 249 (1982) in which a Kentucky statute similar to 83.22 was held to have been unconstitutionally applied where the tenants did not learn of eviction proceedings until they had been served with writs of possession and after their opportunity for rehearing or appeal had lapsed, where the landlord had made no attempt to notify the tenants of the proceedings other than by posting, and where the record demonstrated that in the particular housing project where the tenants lived, the process servers were aware that posted notices "not infrequently" were removed by children and other tenants before they had their intended effect. The United States Supreme Court suggested in that case that mailing an additional copy of the summons and complaint to the tenant would "surely go a long way" toward providing constitutionally required notice in possessory actions.

Apparently taking its cue from the suggestion contained in *Greene v. Lindsey, supra,* and willing to take a step further in providing notice, the 1983 Florida Legislature modified *F.S.* 83.22 to permit service by posting in commercial evictions only after the sheriff, or process server, has made two attempts at personal service and after the tenant has been mailed two copies of the summons and complaint. One of the sets of suit papers must be sent to the address or location designated by the tenant for receipt of notice in the lease or other agreement, or if none has been designated, to the residence of the tenant, if known. The second set of papers must be sent to the last known business address of the tenant. In order to verify the fact of mailing, the practitioner must submit to the clerk of the court two prestamped, appropriately addressed envelopes, together with the additional copies of the summons and complaint. The clerk is directed by the statute to mail the copies to the indicated addresses, to note the fact of mailing in the docket and to file a certificate in the court file of the fact and date of mailing. 83.22(2).

7. Tenant's Response

a. [§15.44] In General

Under *F.S.* 51.011, the tenant is required to file an answer to the complaint within five days. There is some question as to the effect of the filing of defensive motions. While the statute expressly requires the filing of an answer within five days, it also implicitly authorizes the filing of defensive motions as well. "All defensive motions, including motions to quash, shall be heard by the court prior to trial." 51.011(1).

What happens when the tenant files a defensive motion but does not file an answer within the time required? By virtue of *Fla.R.Civ.P.* 1.010, *F.S.* 51.011, which *requires* the filing of an answer within the "five-day" period, takes precedence over *Rule* 1.140(a), which provides that the filing of certain motions tolls the time for filing an answer. Accordingly, plaintiff's counsel could move for default for failure to file an answer and the trial judge could enter a default final judgment. *Rules* 1.500(b), (e). While this result would be harsh, the only other alternative, *i.e.*, permitting the defendant additional time in which to file an answer, clearly violates the obvious policy of the legislature in providing for summary procedure. *State ex rel. Rich v. Ward*, 135 Fla. 885, 185 So. 846

(1939); *Brownlee v. Sussman*, 238 So.2d 317 (Fla. 3d DCA 1970). Local practice in many counties permits the plaintiff to treat any paper filed by the defendant in a removal of tenant action as an answer for the purpose of setting trial. By permitting the plaintiff to notice the case for trial, the defendant is prevented from delaying the case's progress but is not penalized to the extent of having final judgment entered against him.

F.S. 51.011(1) permits a defendant to incorporate a counterclaim into his answer. See *Avvenire College for Women, Inc. v. G. B. D., Inc.,* 240 So.2d 191 (Fla. 4th DCA 1970). If a counterclaim is filed, the plaintiff must serve an answer within five days after service of the counterclaim. 51.011(1).

The tenant's counsel in defending against actions for possession often will assert a counterclaim in excess of the jurisdiction of the county court and will move for transfer of the cause to circuit court pursuant to *Fla. R. Civ. P.* 1.170(j). The attorney for the landlord will want to resist the transfer principally because of the greater degree of difficulty in scheduling an early trial in circuit court.

The best response for the landlord faced with a motion to transfer to circuit court has been to move the county court to sever the counterclaim, to agree to an order transferring the counterclaim and to ask the county court to retain jurisdiction over the possessory action and to proceed to trial. A strict and literal reading of *Rule* 1.170(j) would appear to render impermissible such a bifurcated handling of the litigation inasmuch as the rule specifically provides "the court to which the action is transferred shall have full power and jurisdiction over the demands of all parties." Nevertheless, the courts have sanctioned the severing of the counterclaim and the retention of jurisdiction over the possessory action by the county court. Thus, in *State ex rel. Attias v. Blanton,* 195 So.2d 870 (Fla. 3d DCA 1967) the court stated:

> Although the rule for transfer, taken literally, appears to command that the entire cause be transferred to the Court of higher jurisdiction upon the filing by the defendant in the civil court of record [a constitutional predecessor of the county court] of a counterclaim for damages in excess of the jurisdiction of that court, the rule should not be given literal application in an anomalous situation where to do so would lead to impracticality. See *City of Miami v. Jafra Steel Corporation,* Fla. 1966, 184 So.2d 178.

In 1977 the Florida Legislature added a provision to *F.S.* 34.011 essentially tracking the language of *Rule* 1.170(j) and specifically providing that in cases transferred to the circuit court pursuant to the rule, "The demands of all parties shall be resolved by the circuit court." Some county courts do not feel the need to apply the statutory language any more literally than the courts have traditionally applied the same language where it appears in the Rules of Civil Procedure, and thus are still willing to grant severance of the action when to do otherwise would lead to "impracticality." Other county courts feel obliged to give a strict and literal interpretation to the new statutory language and will not grant severance.

Alternatively, the landlord's attorney, in appropriate cases, can move the county court to strike the counterclaim sought to be transferred as a sham. It should be noted that the county court has jurisdiction to hear and to rule upon the motion to strike as a sham, even though the "amount in controversy" exceeds the normal monetary jurisdiction of the county court according to the subject counterclaim. *State ex rel. Peters v. Hendry,* 159 Fla. 210, 31 So.2d 254 (1947); *Davis v. Flato,* 210 So.2d 16 (Fla. 4th DCA 1968); *Platt v. Kenco Chemical Co., Inc.,* 132 So.2d 27 (Fla. 3d DCA 1961). See also *Flamingo Blueprint, Inc. v. Monumental Properties of Florida, Inc.,* 358 So.2d 86 (Fla. 3d DCA 1978) in which the appellate court upheld a county court's denial of a motion to transfer to circuit court pursuant to *Rule* 1.170(j) when the underlying counterclaim was clearly improper.

The county court presumably also would be justified in refusing to transfer to the circuit court an action for removal of a tenant solely on the basis of a counterclaim for declaratory judgment that merely reiterates the same matters raised in the answer and adds a prayer for declaratory relief. See, *e.g., Childs v. Eltinge,* 105 Cal.Rptr. 864, 871—872 (4th DCA 1973), in which the court stated:

> ... [W]e think the lessee ought not to have the right to refuse to pay the disputed rent, file and serve an action for declaratory relief and thereby prevent the lessor from employing the summary remedies to which he is entitled under the unlawful detainer statutes. . . . If such were the rule, it would be within the power of the lessee to render nugatory the statutorily prescribed unlawful detainer procedures.

See also *Kugeares v. Casino, Inc.,* 372 So.2d 1132 (Fla. 2d DCA 1979).

Plaintiff's attorney also should be aware of the fact that *Rule* 1.170(j) requires the party seeking transfer to deposit a service charge with the clerk of the court at the time the motion to transfer is filed. The failure of the moving party to deposit the service charge results in a reduction of the claim to an amount within the jurisdiction of the court where the action is pending and a waiver of the claim to the extent it exceeds that court's jurisdiction. *Rule* 1.170(j).

In some counties, including Dade, Broward and Palm Beach counties, the chief judge of the circuit has issued administrative orders automatically appointing and assigning the judges in the civil division of the county court to the circuit court for the purpose of hearing and determining all actions transferred from the county court to the circuit court pursuant to *Rule* 1.170(j). Accordingly, in these counties the plaintiff's counsel no longer faces any significant problem of delay caused by counterclaims that exceed the jurisdiction of the county court.

An attorney for a tenant sometimes will take the initiative by bringing an action in circuit court to enjoin the filing or prosecution in county court of an action for removal of a tenant. Injunctive proceedings commonly were used in the past to provide a forum in which the tenant could assert equitable defenses. See *Nevins Drug Co., Inc. v. Bunch*, 63 So.2d 329 (Fla. 1953); *Rader v. Prather*, 100 Fla. 591, 130 So. 15 (1930); *Masser v. London Operating Co.*, 106 Fla. 474, 145 So. 79 (1932). Now that equitable defenses may be raised in removal of tenant actions in county court, *F.S.* 34.01(1)(c)2, these injunctive proceedings no longer are proper and it is error to deny a motion to dissolve such an injunction. *Palm Corp. v. 183rd Street Theatre Corp.*, 344 So.2d 252 (Fla. 3d DCA 1977), *cert. den.* 355 So.2d 516; *Bowles v. Blue Lake Development Corp.*, 504 F.2d 1094 (5th Cir. 1974).

b. [§15.45] Time For Response

The tenant has five days from the date of service of process on him to serve his answer to the landlord's complaint. *Fla. R. Civ. P.* 1.090 prescribes the method for calculating the return day for the summons. The date of the service will not be included in the five days and, since the period is less than seven days, all Saturdays, Sundays or legal holidays, including intermediate ones, are excluded in the computation.

c. [§15.46] Defenses

The defendant may raise by his answer any defense of law or fact he may have to the allegations of the landlord's complaint. He may answer by alleging that the landlord failed to serve him with the three-day notice to pay rent or deliver possession as required by *F.S.* 83.20. In the absence of waiver, that notice is an absolute prerequisite to maintaining an action for summary removal due to a default in the payment of rent and the failure to give it will result in the dismissal of the action.

Another defense available to the defendant is to show that no landlord and tenant relationship exists between the parties. Since the summary removal proceedings under *F.S.* Chapter 83 are available only where that relationship is present, the failure to prove it will result in dismissal of the action for lack of jurisdiction over the subject matter. See *State ex rel. Hillman v. Hutchins,* 118 Fla. 220, 158 So. 716 (1935).

The defendant also may answer by asserting his own title to the premises, although he is estopped from doing so once the landlord-tenant relationship has been established.

Equitable defenses now may be raised in actions for removal of tenants for nonpayment of rent. See *Palm Corp. v. 183rd Street Theatre Corp.,* 344 So.2d 252 (Fla. 3d DCA 1977), *cert. den.* 355 So.2d 516; *Avvenire College for Women, Inc. v. G. B. D., Inc.,* 240 So.2d 191 (Fla. 4th DCA 1970). See also *Filaretou v. Christou,* 133 So.2d 652 (Fla. 2d DCA 1961); *F.S.* 34.01(1)(c)2. For earlier cases holding to the contrary, see *Nevins Drug Co., Inc. v. Bunch,* 63 So.2d 329 (Fla. 1953); *Brownlee v. Sussman,* 238 So.2d 317 (Fla. 3d DCA 1970).

Other defenses that frequently are raised include a failure to demand rent or possession, *Deauville Corp. v. Garden Suburbs Golf & Country Club,* 164 F.2d 430 (5th Cir. 1947), *cert. den.* 333 U.S. 881; improper service of summons and complaint, *Knight Manor # One, Inc. v. Freeman,* 254 So.2d 375 (Fla. 3d DCA 1971); failure to attach necessary exhibits, *Fla.R.Civ.P.* 1.130; improper plaintiff; failure to register under Fictitious Name Statute, *F.S.* 865.09; payment; tender of payment of full rent within the three-day period, 83.20; and waiver, *Baker v. Clifford-Mathew Inv. Co.,* 99 Fla. 1229, 128 So. 827 (1930); *Tollius v. Dutch Inns of America, Inc.,* 244 So.2d 467 (Fla. 3d DCA 1970), *cert. den.* 247 So.2d 437; *Tropical Attractions, Inc. v. Coppinger,* 187 So.2d 395 (Fla. 3d DCA 1966).

8. [§15.47] Trial And Judgment

Unless a timely demand for jury trial is made, the action when at issue will be tried by the court. The landlord may obtain a judgment for possession and costs only, because no provision is made for recovery of damages in this summary procedure. If the amount claimed is within the monetary jurisdiction of the county court, the attorney may wish to add an additional count for damages for unpaid rent and for attorneys' fees if permitted by the lease. Counsel should be aware, however, that the addition of the count for damages will require the issuance of regular 20-day summons and forfeiture of entitlement to the summary procedure set out in *F.S.* Chapter 51. It may be desirable, therefore, to institute a separate action for damages, especially when the immediate possession of the premises is desired.

J.   Unlawful Detainer

1. [§15.48] In General

Unlawful detainer as provided in *F.S.* Chapter 82 is a civil action for the recovery of possession of real property unlawfully withheld and for the recovery of damages that may have accrued because of the unlawful detention. Although not originally so intended, the action for unlawful detainer has become an important summary remedy for the landlord and should be carefully considered in those instances in which it may be applied.

Unlawful detainer as defined by *F.S.* 82.02 arises when a person who has lawfully and peacefully entered real property continues in possession after the expiration of his time and against the consent of the party entitled to possession. Unlike the common-law action of forcible detainer, unlawful detainer does not require that the wrongful detention be by force. The only questions involved in a detainer proceeding are the present, not ultimate, right to possession and the amount of damages resulting from the wrongful detention. The ultimate right of possession to land is determinable in a separate proceeding at law and is not prejudiced by judgment rendered in any action for unlawful detainer. See *Southeastern Fidelity Insurance Co. v. Berman,* 231 So.2d 249 (Fla. 3d DCA 1970); *Floro v. Parker,* 205 So.2d 363 (Fla. 2d DCA 1968). No question of title to the real property is involved. 82.05.

The action to be timely must be commenced within three years of the date on which the wrongful holding began. *F.S.* 82.04. The county court where the property is located has exclusive jurisdiction of proceedings relating to the unlawful detention of lands and tenements. 34.011(2). Once the action is filed, the landlord is entitled to the summary procedure available under 51.011, including the issuance of a five-day summons. See 82.04.

2. [§15.49] Considerations Determining Whether To Use Unlawful Detainer

When a tenant is either wrongfully holding over after his time has expired or is in default in the payment of rent, the remedies afforded the landlord in *F.S.* 83.20—.251 are entirely adequate and unlawful detainer should not be used. The importance of unlawful detainer arises when a landlord is entitled to possession or a tenant is not so entitled for some other reason. The landlord not only may recover possession of the premises but also may recover damages for the unlawful detainer. If the detention is shown to be willful and knowingly wrongful, the damages may be fixed at double the rental value of the premises from the time that the unlawful holding began. See 82.071.

It is important also to note that Chapter 73-330, §13, Laws of Florida specifically repealed the unlawful detainer provisions with regard to residential tenancies. See *F.S.* 713.691(3). Therefore, the remedy of unlawful detainer is available only in the nonresidential situation.

3. [§15.50] The Complaint

A complaint describing the leased premises and alleging that the plaintiff is entitled to possession and that the defendant has unlawfully withheld possession should be filed to commence the unlawful detainer action. *Fla. R. Civ. P.* Form 1.938 is a form for the complaint.

4. [§15.51] Summons And Service Of Process

The landlord is entitled to issuance of the five-day summons provided for in *F.S.* 51.011. The summons requires the defendant to serve the answer within five days after service of the process.

The process may be served on the defendant personally or by substituted service on a member of his family over 15 years of age at his usual place of residence. If the defendant cannot be found and process cannot be served on his family after at least two attempts to obtain personal service, the summons may be served by posting the process in a conspicuous place on the leased premises described in the complaint. *F.S.* 82.061, 83.22.

5. [§15.52] Defendant's Response And Defenses

Under *F.S.* 51.011, the defendant in an unlawful detainer action must file his answer to the complaint within five days after service of process. The defendant may not file a motion in lieu of his answer within the five-day period, although he may file a motion with the answer and the court will hear it immediately prior to trial. 51.011(1). As noted above, *Fla. R. Civ. P.* 1.090(a) provides for the exclusion of all Saturdays, Sundays and legal holidays in the computation of this time period.

The answer of the defendant must include all defenses of law or fact. It also may include a counterclaim, to which the plaintiff must serve an answer within five days from service. *F.S.* 51.011 makes no provision for other pleadings and, in fact, specifically states that no other pleadings are permitted.

The defendant can attack the jurisdiction of the court or may allege that the wrongful withholding began more than three years before the commencement of the action. He also may defend by asserting that the plaintiff is not entitled to possession or that he is not wrongfully withholding possession against the landlord's consent. There is no specific statutory requirement that the landlord give the tenant any notice to quit or demand for possession, although the making of the demand would be evidence of the fact that the tenant is withholding possession against the landlord's consent.

6. [§15.53] Evidence

The plaintiff must present evidence at the trial that the defendant was in possession of the property at the time the action was commenced. *Wolfe v. Hall,* 61 Fla. 492, 54 So. 777 (1911). The plaintiff also must show that the defendant is withholding possession unlawfully from the plaintiff who is entitled to possession. Because title to the real property is not involved in an unlawful detainer action, but only the right to possession, evidence of title, such as a deed, is both unnecessary and inadmissible. Once possession of part of the lands is shown, however, title documents may be used to show the extent of the possession. See *Davis v. Drummond,* 68 Fla. 471, 67 So. 99 (1914).

If the plaintiff is seeking damages for the unlawful detention, he must present evidence of the monthly rental value of the property wrongfully in possession of the defendant. *F.S.* 82.071.

7. [§15.54] Trial And Verdict

Before 1967, the statutes required the court to empanel a six-man jury automatically for the trial of unlawful detainer cases. The legislature in 1967 repealed the provisions regarding trial by jury and provided that the summary remedy of *F.S.* 51.011 is available in unlawful detainer actions. Under 51.011 and *Fla.R.Civ.P.* 1.430, trial by jury may be demanded, but failure to serve a timely demand waives the right.

The legislature, unfortunately, failed to repeal or amend *F.S.* 82.071 and .081, which specifically refer only to jury verdicts. This area of the law could use some clarification, although the apparent intent of the legislature was to make 51.011 and all of its provisions available in unlawful detainer actions.

F.S. 82.081 provides a specific form for a jury verdict in the case of unlawful detainer.

8. [§15.55] Damages

If the jury or court finds that the detention was unlawful, the plaintiff is entitled to damages. The amount of damages is based on the monthly rental value of the premises, and it is the responsibility of the plaintiff to present evidence of that rental value at the trial. If the court finds that the detention was willful or knowingly wrongful, the damages are fixed at double the rental value of the premises from the date the wrongful withholding began to the date of the judgment. Otherwise, the damages may not exceed the rental value of the premises for that period. *F.S.* 82.071.

9. [§15.56] Judgment And Execution

If the verdict or decision is in favor of the plaintiff, the court will enter judgment entitling the plaintiff to recover possession of the premises and authorizing the issuance of a writ of possession directing the sheriff to put him in possession. *F.S.* 82.091. The plaintiff also is entitled to issuance of execution for damages and costs, if successful.

If the jury or court finds for the defendant, he is entitled to a judgment dismissing the complaint and assessing costs. *F.S.* 82.091.

A judgment rendered for either party will not bar any subsequent action for trespass or injury to the property or ejectment, and no verdict is conclusive evidence of any fact in a subsequent action of ejectment or trespass. *F.S.* 82.101.

K. [§15.57] Common-Law Action For Damages

If either the landlord or the tenant breaches a covenant of the lease on his part to do or refrain from doing a stipulated thing, the other party has an action for damages for breach of contract.

Upon the tenant's breach, abandonment or renunciation of the lease before the expiration of the term, the landlord has the choice of any one of three courses of action:

1. He may treat the lease as terminated and resume possession of the premises, thereafter using the premises exclusively as his own for his own purposes, but refusing to accept a surrender of the leasehold estate, and preserving his immediate right to sue the tenant in damages for anticipatory breach of contract.

2. He may treat the lease as terminated and mitigate his damages by retaking possession of the premises for the account of the tenant, holding the tenant in general damages for the difference between the rentals stipulated to be paid and what, in good faith, he is able to recover from a reletting.

3. He may stand by and do nothing, leaving the premises vacant and treating the lease as still in existence, and hold the tenant to the full terms of the lease, reserving the right to sue the tenant for each installment of rent as it matures or for the whole amount of the delinquent rent when the lease expires. *Hyman v. Cohen,* 73 So.2d 393 (Fla. 1954); *Kanter v. Safran,* 68 So.2d 553 (Fla. 1953); *Williams v. Aeroland Oil Co.,* 155 Fla. 114, 20 So.2d 346 (1944).

In the alternative, the landlord may choose to accept a rescission of the lease and a surrender of the leasehold estate, thereby releasing the tenant from all further liability to him and foregoing any right to damages for the tenant's breach. *Kanter v. Safran, supra.*

The three options set out above are by no means the exclusive remedies available to the landlord. The parties to a lease (especially to a commercial lease) may contract for any remedy they desire, see *Rodeway Inns of America v. Alpaugh,* 390 So.2d 370 (Fla. 2d DCA 1980), but when the lease is silent, or when the agreed remedy violates public policy, the above options are intended to be controlling. *Chandler Leasing Div. v. Florida Vanderbilt Dev. Corp.,* 464 F.2d 267 (5th Cir. 1972). The three remedies, however, are mutually exclusive. For example, the landlord could not choose to seek rent accruing under option number 3 and simultaneously re-enter into possession under option number 1 or option number 2. *Geiger Mutual Agency, Inc. v. Wright,* 233 So.2d 444 (Fla. 4th DCA 1970).

It is a factual question as to which option the landlord has chosen. *Diehl v. Gibbs,* 173 So.2d 719 (Fla. 1st DCA 1965). If he chooses either option number 1 or option number 2, the landlord must declare or accept a termination of the rental agreement in order to seek damages from the tenant. Although the rental agreement is terminated, there is a survival of liability on the part of the tenant because of his breach of contract, *Hyman v. Cohen, supra,* and the rental agreement remains alive for the purpose of measuring the landlord's damages, *Kanter v. Safran, supra.* Option number 3 above is distinguishable from option number 1 and option number 2 in that under option number 3, the landlord seeks the agreed rent and not damages. Under options number 1 and number 2, the landlord's recovery is in the form of damages because future rent cannot accrue after the rental agreement is terminated.

The commercial leasehold often represents an established business that the landlord chooses to rent. The landlord is the entrepreneur, and the tenant is merely somewhat like a plant manager or supervisor, though one that shares in the business profits. If the operator of the business (the tenant) abandons possession, it is perfectly logical for the entrepreneur (the landlord) to step back into the role of plant manager until he can secure a substitute tenant-manager. When the landlord does so, he is choosing option number 1, resuming possession for his own exclusive purposes. In *Hyman v. Cohen, supra* the landlord resumed operation of the hotel upon the tenant's abandonment. In *Robinson v. Loyola Foundation, Inc.,* 236 So.2d 154 (Fla. 1st DCA 1970) the landlord evicted the tenant and resumed control of the apartment house. In *Geiger Mutual Agency, Inc. v. Wright, supra* the landlord took over management of the bakery she had leased to the tenants. In *Wagner v. Rice,* 97 So.2d 267 (Fla. 1957) the landlord resumed operation of the tomato packing plant upon the tenant's eviction. By choosing this option, the landlord may not seek rents that otherwise would have accrued following the lease termination. *Wagner v. Rice, supra.* He may pursue, however, the defaulting tenant for damages for anticipatory breach of contract, measured by the difference between the agreed rental and the then existing rental market value of the premises for the remainder of the term. *Kanter v. Safran, supra.*

The most commercially reasonable choice for the landlord to make following the tenant's default would appear to be option number 2, to retake possession of the premises for the tenant's account. When the landlord resumes possession of the premises, choosing either option number 1 or option number 2, the tenant inevitably will argue that the landlord's actions constituted the acceptance of a rescission of the lease and a surrender of the leasehold estate by operation of law, that is, by implication. When the written lease specifically provides that any retaking of possession by the landlord after the tenant's default will only be for the tenant's account, however, no surrender of the leasehold will be inferred. In that case, the tenant's abandonment of the premises constitutes an implied contract, the terms of which hold the tenant to a continuing liability in damages measured by the terms of the lease. *Kanter v. Safran, supra.* If the landlord wrongfully evicts the tenant, a surrender is effected and the tenant will be released from any further obligation to pay rent. 52 C.J.S. *Landlord & Tenant* §561(2). See *Ruotal Corp. N. W., Inc. v. Ottati,* 391 So.2d 308 (Fla. 4th DCA 1980). In that case the tenant had a written lease and the landlord notified him that his "month to month tenancy" was being terminated. The court held that the tenant's vacating of the premises was wrongfully coerced and constituted a surrender by operation of law of the leasehold estate.

Certain coercive acts on the part of the landlord, however, do not constitute a wrongful eviction. If the tenant is delinquent in the rent, and the landlord serves him with a statutory three-day notice, and the tenant vacates in response to the notice, no surrender of the leasehold estate results. *Katz v. Kenholtz,* 147 So.2d 342 (Fla. 3d DCA 1963). When the landlord sues for a tenant's removal because of the tenant's rent default, and actually obtains a judgment for possession, his lawful eviction of the tenant does not constitute a surrender of the leasehold estate. *Babsdon Co. v. Thrifty Parking Co.,* 149 So.2d 566 (Fla. 3d DCA 1963). Any lawful action of the landlord predicated upon a material breach of the lease covenants by the tenant cannot form the basis for a wrongful eviction. There can be no wrongful eviction from a termination of a lease for a default of the tenant in fulfilling his obligations under the lease. *Sentry Water Systems, Inc. v. ADCA Corp.,* 355 So.2d 1255 (Fla. 2d DCA 1978). This is so because a tenant who defaults in his performance under the lease commits a wrongful act. It is that wrongful act, rather than any wrongful act on the part of the landlord, that sets the eviction process in motion. *McCready v. Booth,* 398 So.2d 1000 (Fla. 5th DCA 1981).

If the landlord chooses to retake possession and re-rent the premises for the tenant's account (option number 2), he acquires two additional duties: (1) he must exercise good faith in attempting to relet the premises; and (2) he must account to the tenant at the end of the term of the lease to determine what amounts, if any, he has received from a reletting of the premises and to credit those amounts against the tenant's liablity under the lease. *Coast Federal Savings & Loan Assoc. v. DeLoach,* 362 So.2d 982 (Fla. 2d DCA 1978); *Jimmy Hall's Morningside, Inc. v. Blackburn & Peck Enterprises, Inc.,* 235 So.2d 344 (Fla. 2d DCA 1970). The credit goes, not to the tenant, but to the tenant's liability under the lease. This requires an initial, informal accounting to determine the amount of the liability. The distinction becomes important when a substantial amount of advance rent has been collected from the defaulting tenant and the tenant claims a credit for the advance rent at the final accounting. The defaulting tenant receives a credit for the advance rent at the "initial" accounting, that is, the amount of the advance rent reduces his potential liability under the lease. He does not receive an additional credit for the advance rent at the final accounting.

Under option number 2, the landlord's damages are measured by the difference between the rentals stipulated to be paid in the terminated lease and whatever sums the landlord is able to recover from a reletting. These are the general damages. *Williams v. Aeroland Oil Co., supra.* The landlord also may recover in special damages for the expenses reasonably necessary to obtain another tenant in mitigation of his general damages under the lease. *Kanter v. Safran, supra.* The landlord is entitled to prejudgment interest on its claim. *Robinson v. Peterson,* 375 So.2d 294 (Fla. 2d DCA 1979). If the landlord succeeds in reletting the premises for a higher rental than that provided in the original lease, the tenant is not entitled to assert a claim for that excess. *Kanter v. Safran, supra.* Inasmuch as the term of the lease is at an end, the landlord need not seek an assignment of the tenant's specific unexpired interest, that is, he need not sell only the remaining term of the original lease. *Kanter v. Safran,* 82 So.2d 508 (Fla. 1955).

The landlord has every right to choose the remedy of option number 3. He may leave the premises vacant, stand by and do nothing and hold the tenant to the full terms of the lease. He has no obligation to declare a termination of the rental agreement, seek damages from the tenant, and mitigate those damages upon the tenant's default. *Coast Federal Savings & Loan Assoc. v. DeLoach, supra.* If the landlord chooses this option, the term of the lease is uncanceled and continuing, and the leasehold estate is unsurrendered. The tenant remains in at least constructive possession of the premises, and has the right to go back into actual occupancy at any time. All the covenants of the lease have continued vigor. This means that the landlord has a cause of action for each installment of rent as it accrues with the passage of time. *Williams v. Aeroland Oil Co., supra.*

If the lease contains an acceleration clause, that is, a clause which at the option of the landlord renders the entire rent for the balance of the lease due and payable upon the tenant's default, the landlord may sue at once for the entire amount of the remaining rents. This clause is valid, and has the same effect as if the entire rental were payable in advance. *Dobbs v. Petko,* 207 So.2d 11 (Fla. 4th DCA 1968). If the tenant tenders the accelerated rents some time in the future (during the term of the lease), the landlord is obligated to accept the payment and to allow the tenant to return to actual occupancy of the premises. See *Major Holding Corp. v. Butler,* 138 Fla. 633, 190 So. 15 (1939).

Even if the landlord chooses option number 3, at any time he may change his mind, reenter the premises and terminate the lease, either for the tenant's account or for his own exclusive purposes. *Williams v. Aeroland Oil Co., supra.* In other words, he may decide at any time to forsake the rent and seek damages from the tenant under option number 1 or option number 2.

The landlord may choose the alternative option of accepting a surrender of the leasehold estate and a rescission of the lease. This choice annihilates the lease so effectively that for legal purposes it never existed. There is no further liability on the part of the tenant, and the landlord cannot recover any damages for the tenant's breach of contract. *Hyman v. Cohen, supra.* The surrender need not be express; it may be implied from the landlord's conduct. If the facts demonstrate that the landlord has been a party to some act incompatible with the continued existence of the landlord and tenant relationship, then there is a surrender "by operation of law." *Kanter v. Safran, supra* at 556.

L.   [§15.58] Declaration Of Termination Of Leasehold Interest

The landlord in certain instances may desire to have a judicial declaration of the cancellation or termination of a lease. When a lease agreement has been made a part of the public records, the recording of a judicial declaration of termination is required before title to the property is clear. The landlord may file an action under *F.S.* Chapter 86 for a declaration of his rights under or the status of the lease. The attorney for the landlord instead may join a count for the cancellation of the lease with an action filed in the circuit court for damages for unpaid rent.

M.   [§15.59] Advance Rent

If the tenant pays the rent in advance, whether for the current rental period or for a future rental period, and then defaults under the lease, he is not entitled to a refund of the advance rent. Upon payment of the advance rent, the right and title to it passes immediately to the landlord, because the advance payment is deemed part of the consideration for the execution of the lease. If the tenant's own misconduct prevents the application of the advance rent to the part of the term for which it is paid, the tenant is not entitled to its refund. See

Annot., 27 A.L.R.2d 656. In *Casino Amusement Co. v. Ocean Beach Amusement Co.,* 101 Fla. 59, 133 So. 559 (1931) the court held that when the parties entered into a 99-year lease and the tenant paid the last year's rent in advance in the amount of $25,000, the tenant was not entitled to a refund of that money upon his default in the current rent payments. See also *Housholder v. Black,* 62 So.2d 50 (Fla. 1952) in which it was held that when the tenant paid the last year's rent in advance under a three-year lease, in the amount of $10,000, and then defaulted, he was not entitled to a refund of the advance rent.

It does not matter whether the tenant abandons possession of the premises voluntarily, or whether he is lawfully evicted by the landlord. Upon his default, the tenant cannot recover any advance rent, *Housholder, supra,* nor is he entitled to a credit for the amount of the advance rent. Under any other view the advance rent would be of no value, since the tenant could merely default and deprive the landlord of the benefit of the advance payment obviously intended by the lease. See *6701 Realty, Inc. v. Deauville Enterprises, Inc.,* 84 So.2d 325 (Fla. 1956). "[T]he landlord is entitled to retain advance rent even though it has not been used. . . . An advance rental is a contractual promise, by the tenant, to pay for the rent to be used in the future and to be obligated to make this payment whether he actually uses the property for that period of time or not." *Paul v. Kanter,* 172 So.2d 26, 28 (Fla. 3d DCA 1965).

On the other hand, if the landlord wrongfully evicts the tenant, the tenant is entitled to a refund of the advance rent or to a credit for the amount of the advance against a default in the current rent. *Trading Post of Naples, Inc. v. Howl,* 371 So.2d 221 (Fla. 2d DCA 1979). The rationale for this principle is that the landlord's wrongful eviction entitles the tenant to declare a rescission of the lease. Upon the rescission, he must be placed back into the position he was in before the contract was made. See *Hyman v. Cohen,* 73 So.2d 393 (Fla. 1954).

It should be observed that the landlord's chief executory duty imposed by law to a tenant in possession of leased premises is to fulfill his covenant of quiet enjoyment. If the landlord does any wrongful act or is guilty of any default or neglect whereby the leased premises are rendered unsafe, unfit or unsuitable for occupancy or for the purposes for which they were leased — and the tenant vacates because of the wrongful act or default — the landlord breaches his covenant of quiet enjoyment. The term for such a default is a "constructive eviction." *Hankins v. Smith,* 103 Fla. 892, 138 So. 494 (1931). Since a wrongful eviction, actual or constructive, entitles the tenant to a refund of advance rent, it is accurate to state that advance rent becomes the property of the landlord upon payment, but his title to it is subject to a condition subsequent, that is, that he fulfill his covenant of quiet enjoyment to the tenant until the expiration of the lease. If he wrongfully evicts the tenant, the condition fails, and he must refund the advance rent. On the other hand, if the tenant is the one who defaults in his obligations to the landlord, the condition is excused, and the landlord becomes the absolute owner of the advance rent.

N. [§15.60] Waste

Waste is a species of tort (34 FLA.JUR. *Waste* §2) and has been defined as the abuse or destructive use of property by one in rightful possession. It is an unlawful act or omission of duty on the part of the tenant that results in permanent injury to the tenement. *Stephenson v. National Bank of Winter Haven,* 92 Fla. 347, 109 So. 424 (1926). The tort of waste often consists of a material alteration of the leased premises and is committed in breach of an express "redelivery covenant" in the lease, that is, a covenant by the tenant to deliver up the premises at the end of the term in the same condition as they were at the beginning of the term, ordinary wear excepted.

Waste, however, need not involve structural changes like the removal of a wall by the tenant. It encompasses cosmetic damage, abuse, neglect or uncleanliness that renders the premises unfit for re-rental. In *Cunningham Drug Stores, Inc. v. Pentland Drug Stores,* 243 So.2d 169 (Fla. 4th DCA 1971) the landlord prevailed in an action for waste when the tenant had left holes in the tile floor and a cracked window, and the interior of the premises was in such an unclean state that it had to be repainted.

The tenant's obligation to refrain from committing waste does not arise only by virtue of an express lease covenant. It also arises by operation of law. "Implicit in the landlord-tenant relationship is the obligation on the part of the tenant not to commit waste to the leased premises." *Stegeman v. Burger Chef Systems, Inc.,* 374 So.2d 1130, 1131 (Fla. 1st DCA 1979).

In an action by the landlord for waste committed to the leased premises, he must show some willful or negligent conduct by the tenant to establish his cause of action for this tort. Since the tenant enjoys the exclusive possession and control of the demised area during the term of the lease, however, the landlord is assisted in his burden of proof by the doctrine of *res ipsa loquitur.* He need only establish that the premises were clean and undamaged when the tenant took possession, and that the premises were surrendered in a dirty, damaged or otherwise unrentable condition. The tenant then must go forward with the evidence to show that the damage resulted from ordinary wear, or the elements, or some other excusable cause. If the tenant fails to do so, the landlord will prevail on his prima facie case. *Powers v. Coates,* 203 A.2d 425 (D.C. App. 1964); *Miller v. Belknap,* 266 P.2d 662 (Idaho 1954); *Case v. Guise,* 6 N.E.2d 469 (Ill. App.Ct. 1937).

Ordinary wear is "the wear which property undergoes when the tenant does nothing more than to come and go and perform the acts usually incident to an ordinary way of life. Stated otherwise, ordinary wear and tear is the depreciation which occurs when the tenant does nothing inconsistent with the usual use and omits no acts which it is usual for a tenant to perform." *Tirrell v. Osborn,* 55 A.2d 725 (D.C. App. 1947). The concept of ordinary wear, therefore, is a two-sided coin: the landlord must allow the tenant ordinary wear, but the tenant must give the landlord ordinary care.

The burden of proving what portion, if any, of the damages and cost of restoration has resulted from normal wear and depreciation, not recoverable by the lessor, is on the tenant. *Stegeman v. Burger Chef Systems, Inc., supra.*

The landlord's measure of damages for waste is not the diminution in market value of the leased premises resulting from the damage; rather it is the cost of restoring the premises to a rentable condition. In *Stegeman, supra* the trial court had entered a pretrial order that one of the issues to be tried was "the damage, if any, done to the demised premises . . . and the *reasonable costs* of repairing any such damage" [emphasis added]. The final judgment appealed from ignored that aspect of the pretrial order, but the appellate court reversed and ordered a new trial held in accordance with the pretrial order. As a measure of damages to real property, the reasonable cost of restoration is especially appropriate as a test of damages when the damage is temporary, is easily repaired at reasonable expense and is inflicted only to improvements, not to the land itself. *Keyes Co. v. Shea,* 372 So.2d 493 (Fla. 4th DCA 1979). Hence, the measure is well suited for waste committed to leased premises.

Landlords who own a substantial number of rental properties often retain a crew of painters, porters and handymen. The landlord's own crew generally can perform repairs more effectively and efficiently than independent contractors. When a landlord sues a tenant for waste to leased premises that the landlord has restored to a rentable condition with his own maintenance crew, the tenant will demand that the landlord disclose the exact wages and materials that he expended in the task. The landlord need not show those figures, even if they are ascertainable and attributable to an individual leased unit. His measure of damages is the reasonable cost of restoring the premises to a rentable condition. *Stegeman v. Burger Chef Systems, Inc., supra.* The landlord must establish the amount of the damages through expert testimony because the reasonable value of personal services is proved by expert witnesses. *Mullane v. Lorenz,* 372 So.2d 168 (Fla. 4th DCA 1979). "The question here of fair compensation for the damage [to leased premises] is not determinable with mathematical accuracy. The Court is compelled to rely to a great extent on the opinion of experts as to the cost of repairs." *New Rawson Corp. v. United States,* 55 F.Supp. 291 (D. Mass. 1943). This expert testimony is not elicited as to the landlord's actual cost of restoring the premises; it is for the purpose of establishing the reasonable value of the services performed that were necessary to the restoration. In *Rakover v. Blum,* 13 N.Y.S.2d 464 (N.Y. App. Div. 1939), the landlord sued the residential tenant for his cost of painting an apartment after the tenant's removal. The landlord's claim was properly dismissed because he failed to prove the reasonable value of the painting service.

The rationale for the above rule is that if the landlord is prodigal in his restoration efforts, he should not be able to penalize the tenant for his own unreasonably high costs of restoration. By the same token, if the landlord is highly efficient in restoring the premises, the tenant should not be able to claim a reduction in damages from the reasonable cost of restoration. If the landlord was prudent enough to have a maintenance crew on hand to repair the damages, the tenant cannot take advantage of that prudence to have his own liability reduced accordingly. This is merely an application of the "collateral source rule."

The "collateral source rule" holds that a wrongdoer is not entitled to have the damages for which he is liable reduced by the fact that his victim has received compensation for the loss from a source independent of the tortfeasor. Because tort damages have the flavor of punishing the tortfeasor, there can be no mitigation of damages on the principle of compensation received for the injury when the compensation comes from a "collateral" source, namely, a source wholly independent of the tortfeasor. The collateral source rule allows an injured plaintiff recovery even when he has suffered no ultimate loss. 25 C.J.S. *Damages* §99(1). When the tortfeasor has contributed to the collateral source, he is entitled to a reduction in damages for the payments received by the victim from the collateral source. In *Publix Theatres Corp. v. Powell,* 71 S.W.2d 237 (Tex. Ct.App. 1934) the landlord sued the tenant for destruction of the leased premises by fire caused by the tenant's negligence. The tenant had kept up the fire insurance policy by paying several of the premiums, and the court allowed him a setoff for the amount of the landlord's insurance recovery. It can be seen that the rule is that the collateral source must be independent of the tortfeasor. There is no requirement, however, that the collateral source be independent of the victim, as when he has exercised foresight in providing himself with insurance or with a maintenance crew.

The collateral source rule was discussed at length in *Paradis v. Thomas,* 150 So.2d 457 (Fla. 2d DCA 1963). That case involved a serviceman injured in an automobile accident caused by the defendant's negligence. The plaintiff received medical services from a government agency completely without charge. The trial court allowed him to introduce testimony concerning the value of those medical services. In affirming, the appellate court stated "The plaintiff is not barred from recovery merely because he suffers no net loss from the injury, as where he is insured or where friends make contributions to him because of the loss." *Paradis* at 459. While the collateral source rule has been abrogated by statute with respect to certain actions, it remains in effect with respect to landlord and tenant relations. See, *e.g., F.S.* 627.736(3), .7372. In *Vaughan v. Mayo Milling Co.,* 102 S.E. 597 (Va. 1920), the plaintiff-landlord leased a four-story brick warehouse to the defendant-tenant for use as a grain warehouse and mill. The defendant overloaded the floors, and the building collapsed. In discussing the landlord's measure of damages, the court said at page 602, "the measure of damages is the cost of putting the premises in the required state of repair, even though the repairs have not been made by the landlord and he does not intend to make them."

Because of previous contractual arrangements made for his own benefit, and not for the tenant's benefit, the landlord may suffer little or no ultimate loss on account of the tenant's negligent waste. This is not to say that the landlord has not been injured. Indeed he has been injured, but because he anticipated the injury and made provision against it, he has suffered little ultimate financial loss. In that case, the damages allowed for the landlord's recovery are measured by the tenant's culpability, not by the landlord's loss.

III. RESIDENTIAL LANDLORD AND TENANT RELATIONS

A. [§15.61] In General

Florida's Residential Landlord and Tenant Act, which was enacted in 1973, appears as Part II of *F.S.* Chapter 83 (83.40—.63), hereafter referred to as the Act.

The Act does not represent a complete or exhaustive codification of all of the law applicable to residential tenancies. For example, it is virtually silent on the landlord's remedies upon the tenant's abandonment prior to the expiration of the lease or the disposition of advance rent in those situations. Moreover, the subject of waste is practically ignored. While the Act creates new procedural requirements for the holding and the imposition of claims against security deposits, it does not address the substantive issues of what constitutes "ordinary wear and tear," nor does the Act even purport to formulate a substantive test or a principle of law governing the ultimate disposition of the security deposit. In all of these areas, the practitioner is required to refer to the pre-1973 case law generally and to the specific case law developments after 1973 with reference to residential tenancies.

Thus, the best view of the Residential Landlord and Tenant Act is that the Act did not entirely *replace* the existing law relating to residential tenancies but, instead, introduced a significant number of specific substantive and procedural changes applicable to "dwelling units" with the result that the general pre-1973 case law, which was previously applicable to all tenancies, retains its efficacy with respect to residential tenancies except to the extent it is specifically modified or abrogated by the Act.

B.   Applicability And Scope Of Act

1. [§15.62] Definitions Of "Dwelling Unit" And Exclusions

The Act applies to the rental of dwelling units and mobile homes rented to tenants. *F.S.* 83.41. Other kinds of rentals are covered by Parts I, III or IV of Chapter 83 or other applicable laws. Excluded from coverage under this Act are occupancies of mobile home lots by mobile home owners and occupancies in a hotel, motel, condominium, rooming house or mobile home park, where the lodging is only transient or temporary. 83.42(3). Whether the occupancy is "transient" will turn on the intent of the parties, and will have to be resolved as a question of fact. 83.43(10). Also excluded from the Act are tenancies when the occupancy is incidental to some other purpose or service, such as medical, geriatric, educational, counseling or religious. 83.42(1). Occupancy by an owner of a condominium unit, a holder of a proprietary lease in a cooperative apartment or by parties to a contract of sale of a dwelling unit also are excluded. 83.42(2), (4), (5). The rental of a condominium unit or cooperative apartment by the owner to a tenant, however, would be within the ambit of the Act.

The Act applies to the rental of a mobile home if both the mobile home and the lot are rented. *F.S.* 83.43(2)(b), .751. When a tenant places his own mobile home upon a rented or leased lot in a mobile home park, however, the tenancy is governed by the Florida Mobile Home Landlord and Tenant Act. 83.750—.797.

The Act defines a "dwelling unit" broadly as "a structure or part of a structure that is rented for use as a home, residence, or sleeping place by one person or by two or more persons who maintain a common household," or a "mobile home rented by a tenant" or "a mobile home lot within a mobile home park that is rented for occupancy by one or more persons who own the mobile home located on the lot." *F.S.* 83.43(2).

In 1981 the legislature added *F.S.* 83.43(2)(c) [formerly 83.43(2)(d)], which defines a "dwelling unit" also as a "structure or part of a structure that is furnished, with or without rent, as an incident of employment for use as a home, residence, or sleeping place by one or more persons." See, in addition, 83.46(3) also added in 1981 and discussed in §15.69. The addition of 83.43(2)(c) and .46(3) generally extends the protection of the Residential Landlord and Tenant Act to persons who receive shelter as an incident of their employment and makes available to them the remedies provided for by the Act.

2. [§15.63] Effective Date Of Act

Most of the substantive provisions of the Act took effect on July 1, 1973. *F.S.* 83.51 (dealing with the duties of the landlord to maintain and furnish utilities and services) and other sections giving the tenant rights against the landlord for failure to comply with 83.51 took effect on January 1, 1974. For dwelling units owned and operated by public housing authorities, 83.51 and related sections took effect on July 1, 1975. Chapter 73-330, §15, Laws of Florida, which provided for these effective dates, is ambiguous as to whether the Act was to operate upon rental agreements for dwelling units entered into before the effective dates. After setting forth the various effective dates, the Act provides that it will apply to "rental agreements entered into, extended, or received after *that date*" [emphasis added]. If not so limited, the enforcement of substantive provisions of the Act would raise constitutional problems, but what effective date is left unclear. The dissenting opinion in *Rubin v. Randwest Corp.,* 292 So.2d 60 (Fla. 4th DCA 1974), *cert. den.* 305 So.2d 786 indicates the Act would be applied to void a provision of a lease entered into before the July 1, 1973 effective date.

C. Substantive Requirements Or Changes In The Content Of Lease Agreements For "Dwelling Units"

1. [§15.64] In General

The Act has empowered the court to refuse to enforce provisions of a rental agreement on the grounds of "unconscionability" and makes "void and unenforceable" certain other provisions. *F.S.* 83.45, .47.

2. [§15.65] Unenforceability Of Unconscionable Agreements

F.S. 83.45 introduces to landlord-tenant law the concept of invalidating "unconscionable" provisions. This concept, borrowed originally from equity practice, recently has been written into the law of contracts and commercial law (see 672.302, part of the Florida Uniform Commercial Code). *F.S.* 83.45(1) provides that if a court "as a matter of law" finds the rental agreement or any provision of it unconscionable at the time it was made, the court may (a) refuse to enforce the whole agreement, (b) enforce the balance of the agreement without the offensive provisions or (c) limit the provision to avoid any "unconscionable result." *F.S.* 83.45(2) obviates any problems with the parol evidence rule by providing that when the claim of unconscionability is raised, the parties may present evidence as to "meaning, relationship of the parties, purpose and effect" of the words in question.

Inherent in the doctrine of court determined unconscionability, of course, is the risk that wholesale and indiscriminate application of the doctrine could easily lead to loss of the parties' ability to bargain with the expectation that their agreement will be enforceable. Fortunately, the courts have shown a considerable amount of judicial restraint. For a general discussion of the elements of unconscionability see *Kohl v. Bay Colony Club Condominium, Inc.*, 398 So.2d 865 (Fla. 4th DCA 1981), *review den.* 408 So.2d 1094. A clause in a rental agreement providing for an increase in rents based upon some appropriate measure of increase in the cost of living is not unconscionable per se. *Sea Tower Apartments, Inc. v. Century National Bank*, 406 So.2d 69 (Fla. 4th DCA 1981). Clearly, the doctrine of unconscionability has no application to rental agreements other than those creating residential tenancies. *Rodeway Inns of America v. Alpaugh*, 390 So.2d 370 (Fla. 2d DCA 1980).

3. [§15.66] Exculpatory Clauses And Waivers Of Rights Invalidated

F.S. 83.47 makes void and unenforceable certain provisions in rental agreements, and gives either party a remedy for actual damages, should any be sustained as a result of the inclusion of a prohibited provision. Made void and unenforceable are any provisions that require a party to waive any right or remedy granted under the Act. Formerly, those waivers were upheld by the courts. See *Moskos v. Hand,* 247 So.2d 795 (Fla. 4th DCA 1971).

F.S. 83.47(1)(b) settles with respect to residential tenancies the argument raised, largely unsuccessfully, that it is contrary to public policy for a landlord to exculpate himself from liability to a tenant for the landlord's breach of duty or negligence. See *Rubin v. Randwest Corp.,* 292 So.2d 60 (Fla. 4th DCA 1974), *cert. den.* 305 So.2d 786; *Middleton v. Lomaskin,* 266 So.2d 678 (Fla. 3d DCA 1972). By legislative fiat, therefore, exculpatory provisions seeking to limit or to preclude the liability of the landlord to the tenant (or vice versa) of any kind, arising under law, are now made void and unenforceable. This prohibition encompasses all kinds of liabilities, including those arising under the law of negligence and torts, as well as the act itself, and it voids any restriction or limitation of liability, such as a purported limitation of liability to the extent there is insurance coverage. See, however, *Mansur v. Eubanks,* 401 So.2d 1328 (Fla. 1981), which contains dicta to the effect that certain of the landlord's duties arising under law can be waived or modified by agreement of the parties.

The landlord's obligation to maintain a "single-family home or duplex" as set out in *F.S.* 83.51(1), however, may be altered or modified in writing. 83.51(1)(b). It should be noted that the additional maintenance obligations of the landlord as set out in 83.51(2) may be altered by written agreement of the landlord and tenant with respect to any rental premises.

4. [§15.67] Attorneys' Fees

F.S. 83.48 provides that in any civil action to enforce the provisions of the rental agreement or Part II of Chapter 83, the party in whose favor a judgment or decree has been rendered may recover court costs, including reasonable attorneys' fees from the nonprevailing party.

F.S. 83.48 has no application to commercial tenancies. See *Dooley v. Culver,* 392 So.2d 575 (Fla. 4th DCA 1980), decided under prior law.

D. Duration Of Periodic Tenancies; Rent And Notice Of Termination

1. [§15.68] When Rent Is Payable

If the parties have not agreed otherwise, either orally or in writing, rent is payable without demand or notice. In the case of a periodic residential tenancy, or a "tenancy without a specific duration," rent is due at the beginning of each rent payment period. *F.S.* 83.46(1). In nonresidential tenancies, rent under the common law is not due until the end of the rental period, absent an agreement otherwise. See *De Vore v. Lee,* 158 Fla. 608, 30 So.2d 924 (1947). *F.S.* 83.46 also changes the common-law rule against apportionment of rent by providing that, unless otherwise agreed by the parties, rent will be uniformly apportionable from day to day. These changes in existing law were made by the Act to conform to usual modern business practices. The first two changes speak for themselves, but the apportionability of residential rent requires some explanation.

"Rent is not, at common law, regarded as accruing from day to day, as interest does, but it is only upon the day fixed for payment that any part of it becomes due. . . . The general rule in this regard is ordinarily expressed by saying that rent cannot be apportioned as to time." I TIFFANY, LANDLORD AND TENANT §176 (1912). The doctrine of the nonapportionability of rent led to many inequitable situations for both the landlord and the tenant. If a tenant with a life estate rented the premises to a tenant for years, and the life tenant died before the expiration of the current rent payment period, the tenant for years owed the rent to the owner of the reversion and not to the estate of the deceased life tenant. This situation was considered to be such a recurrent evil that it was remedied by Statute II, Geo. 2, Ch. 19, §15, which provided that the executor of the deceased life tenant could recover a pro tanto share of rent from the under-tenant. There were many other situations that could arise from the nonapportionability of rent that seem unjust to the modern practitioner. If the landlord sold the premises, the purchaser was entitled to all the rent that accrued on the next rent day after sale; the landlord received none of it. If the landlord wrongfully evicted the tenant between rent payment dates, the landlord could not claim any portion of the rental installment next falling due. If the tenant assigned his leasehold, the assignee was liable for the entire rent that fell due during his occupancy; the tenant-assignor was not obligated to pay any portion of it. If the parties agreed to a surrender of the leasehold estate before the rent payment date, there was no longer any outstanding leasehold estate from which the rent could issue, so no fractional portion of the rent ever came due. I TIFFANY, *supra.*

F.S. 83.46 is in keeping with the modern trend, which is to consider rent, like interest, as accruing from day to day and to be apportioned accordingly.

> The effect . . . is not only to apportion the rent as between persons entitled thereto in succession one after the

other, but also to apportion the liability for rent, as when an assignee of a leasehold re-assigns to another, so as to render him liable for a portion of the installment next becoming payable, calculated from the time of his acquisition of the leasehold to the time of his re-assignment, and to render his assignee liable for the balance.

I TIFFANY, *supra* §176.

The above discussion describes what apportionability of rent means, but it is equally important to understand what apportionability does not mean. The uniform apportionability of residential rent does not mean that a defaulting tenant is entitled to an abatement of his rent. For example, if a residential tenant occupies the premises on an oral month-to-month rental agreement, and he abandons the dwelling unit without notice on the second day of the month and without paying the periodic rent that was due on the previous day, he may argue that he is liable for only one day's rent under the doctrine of "apportionability of rent." This argument ignores the fact that a tenant cannot terminate a periodic tenancy by mere default and abandonment. He must give the prerequisite statutory notice in writing. See *F.S.* 83.57(3).

The doctrine of apportionability of rent or apportionment of rent generally does not limit the liability for rent of a defaulting tenant to the period of actual occupancy of the premises. "Apportionment of rent does not mean abatement of it; in the case of apportionment, the tenant still remains liable to pay the whole rent, but in different parts to different persons." 52 C.J.S. *Landlord and Tenant* §530.

2. [§15.69] Terms Of Tenancies Without Specific Durations

If the rental agreement contains no definite termination date, and it is a periodic tenancy as described in *F.S.* 83.46(2), the duration of the tenancy is determined by the periods for which rent is payable. If rent is payable on a weekly basis, it is a tenancy from week to week; if rent is payable monthly, it is a tenancy from month to month; if payable yearly or quarterly, it is a tenancy from year to year or quarter to quarter. Presumably, the periodic tenancy also could be a payment period not expressly covered by the language of the statute, as, for example, bi-weekly or semiannually.

In 1981 the Florida Legislature added subsection (3) to *F.S.* 83.46, providing that if a dwelling unit is furnished without rent as an incident of employment and there is no agreement as to the duration of the tenancy, the duration is determined by the periods for which wages are payable. If the wages are payable weekly or more frequently, the tenancy is from week to week. If the wages are payable monthly, the tenancy is from month to month. The new subsection, by its terms, is not applicable to a resident manager of an apartment house or an apartment complex when there is a written agreement to the contrary.

3. Termination Of Tenancies Without Specific Durations

a. [§15.70] In General

The establishing of the payment period of the periodic tenancy determines when rent is due and payable (*F.S.* 83.46) and the length of the required notice to terminate the periodic tenancy. If the tenancy is year to year, 60 days' notice before the end of any year is required; if the tenancy is quarter to quarter, the notice period is not less than 30 days; if the tenancy is from month to month, the notice period is not less than 15 days; and if it is weekly, not less than seven days' notice must be given. 83.57. These notice periods are shorter than those required in 83.03 for nonresidential periodic leases from year to year and from quarter to quarter.

If the rent payment period is not one set out in *F.S.* 83.57, as for example, a semiannual tenancy or a biweekly tenancy, there are no required notice periods specified in the statute. *F.S.* 83.02 defines those periodic tenancies as "tenancies at will" and at common law tenancies at will could be terminated at any time, without notice. See *Brady v. Scott,* 128 Fla. 582, 175 So. 724 (1937); 51 C.J.S. *Landlord and Tenant* §167. *F.S.* 83.02, however, is not applicable to residential tenancies and 83.46, which creates residential periodic tenancies, does not categorize them as "tenancies at will." In any event, it is likely that courts will require notice of a "reasonable" duration in order to terminate these periodic tenancies. See *Waln v. Howard,* 142 Fla. 736, 196 So. 210 (1940). The common-law rule with regard to termination of periodic tenancies requires notice in advance of a full periodic payment interval for tenancies of less than one year. 50 AM.JUR.2d *Landlord and Tenant* §1207; 51 C.J.S. *Landlord and Tenant* §§150—154. Thus, notice given at least a full rental payment period in advance of the termination date should satisfy any common-law rule and any requirements of "reasonableness."

b. Notice Of Termination

(1) [§15.71] In General

Notice of termination of a tenancy without a specific duration may be given by either party to the other by written notice, by mail or by delivery to the other party. If the tenant is absent from his last or usual place of business, or usual place of residence, the landlord may notify him by leaving a copy of the notice at his residence. *F.S.* 83.56(4), .57. The notice must be given the full period required for termination, at least, and it should seek to terminate the tenancy for the next or a subsequent rental period. In the computation of time, cases can be found that exclude the day of delivery and the day of termination or quitting, and Sundays and holidays also may be excluded for purposes of computing the day of the termination and time of vacating. See 50 AM.JUR.2d *Landlord and Tenant* §1208. If possible, generous time margins should be allowed to be sure the notice is properly given.

(2) [§15.72] Form For Notice Of Termination

To: ....

YOU ARE NOTIFIED that the undersigned has elected to terminate the tenancy of the premises described as ...., occupied by .... you/me.........., as tenant. This tenancy shall terminate at the end of the .... rental payment period, on ....(date).......... You are directed to .... surrender/retake.......... possession at that time.

Dated: ....

(Certificate of Service)

Landlord/Tenant

COMMENT: This form is similar to that in 12 AM.JUR. LEGAL FORMS 2d §161:1199.

4. [§15.73] Failure Of Tenant To Surrender
Possession And Holdover Tenancies

If the tenant of a tenancy without a specific duration fails to surrender possession of all of the premises after the tenancy has been properly terminated through giving notice as discussed above, and if the tenant continues in possession without consent of the landlord, the landlord may employ the summary removal procedure provided in *F.S.* 83.59.

F.S. 83.58 provides that if the tenant holds over and continues in possession of the dwelling unit after expiration of the rental agreement without the permission of the landlord, the landlord may recover possession of the dwelling unit in a manner provided for in 83.59. *F.S.* 83.58 is the only residential landlord-tenant statute that appears to authorize the filing of a complaint for possession without service of a prelitigation notice. Notice of the landlord's intention not to renew the rental agreement, however, should be served on the tenant as a practical matter, since service of that notice may produce the desired result without court action.

F.S. 83.58 also provides that the landlord may recover from the tenant who holds over after expiration of the rental agreement "double the amount of rent due on the dwelling unit, or any part thereof, for the period during which the tenant refuses to surrender possession." Once again, the statute does not specifically require service of any notice as a precondition to asserting the right. Compare 83.06(1), which is applicable to commercial tenancies and which specifies that the landlord "may demand" and "may recover" double rent from a holdover tenant. This language has been construed to require the commercial landlord to notify the tenant of his intention to demand double rent as a precondition to recovery. *Painter v. Town of Groveland,* 79 So.2d 765 (Fla. 1955). As a practical matter, a landlord seeking to invoke the "double rent" provision of 83.58 should serve the tenant with written notice reasonably in advance.

The "double rent" provisions of *F.S.* 83.58 probably are applicable only when the tenant holds over after the natural expiration date of the rental agreement and not when the tenant holds over after the termination of the tenancy by the landlord under 83.56(2) or (3). Note the word "expiration" rather than "termination" appears in 83.58. For a case reaching the same conclusion in the context of a commercial tenancy, see *Wagner v. Rice,* 97 So.2d 267 (Fla. 1957).

E.   Landlord's Duties And Obligations

1.   [§15.74] In General

The Act imposes on landlords the duty to keep and maintain the premises in a fit and habitable condition. The Act also provides the tenant with remedies to enforce those duties. Also, the landlord is charged with statutory duties regarding disclosures and the handling of security deposits.

2.   [§15.75] Duty Of Disclosure

The landlord, or the rental agent authorized to enter into a rental agreement on his behalf, must disclose in writing to the tenant, before or concurrent with the commencement of the tenancy, the name and address of the landlord or agent authorized to receive notices on the landlord's behalf. *F.S.* 83.50(1). Thereafter, the tenant may give notice or make demands to that person at the given address for all purposes under the Act. If the landlord wishes to change the person or address, it is his obligation to deliver notice of any such changes to the tenant's residence. 83.50(1). Since the exercise of many tenant remedies commences with notifying the landlord, it is important that the name and address be furnished to the tenant and that the address be one calculated to reach the landlord expeditiously. Failure of the landlord to furnish the name and address as is required by 83.50(1) may result in a claim for damages by the tenant. See 83.55. Further, it may excuse the tenant from notifying the landlord, when otherwise the tenant's rights or remedies depend on his notifying the landlord. See, *e.g.*, 83.49(3)(b), .56(1), .60(1).

In addition, under *F.S.* 83.50(2) the landlord or his agent must notify all tenants moving into a newly completed building exceeding three stories in height and containing "dwelling units" whether fire protection is available. As passed by the legislature this is a very limited provision. Tenants in buildings under four stories or old buildings and tenants moving in to replace old tenants or ones who were "initial" occupants of a dwelling unit in a new building would not be included.

3. [§15.76] Deposit Money

In 1973 the Florida Legislature enacted *F.S.* 83.49, which clarified the Florida Security Deposit Law (formerly 83.261). This statute applies to all money deposited or advanced by a tenant on a rental agreement as security for performance of the lease or as advance rent. "Deposit money" includes but is not limited to damage deposits, security deposits, advance rent deposits, pet deposits and any contract deposit. 83.43(11). "Security deposits" are defined as "any moneys held by the landlord as security for the performance of the rental agreement, including but not limited to, monetary damage to the landlord caused by the tenant's breach of the lease prior to the expiration thereof." 83.43(12). The only money that can be safely excluded from the requirements of 83.49 are rent payments or advanced rent payments paid for the current rental payment period. 83.43(6), (9), .49(1).

If any money is held as security for performance of the rental agreement or as advance rent, the landlord or his agent must hold that money in one of the following ways: (a) the landlord may hold the money in a separate noninterest bearing account at a Florida banking institution for the benefit of the tenant or tenants, not commingled with the landlord's funds; (b) the landlord may hold the money in a separate interest-bearing account at a Florida banking institution, in which event he must pay 75% of the interest earned to his tenants or 5% interest, whichever he elects; or (c) he may commingle the money with his own funds and pay his tenants at the rate of 5% simple interest, provided he posts a surety bond with the clerk of the circuit court in the amount of the money held or $50,000, whichever is less. If the landlord opts for either of the last two alternatives, he must pay the interest to the tenants or credit their accounts at least once annually. No interest need be paid to a tenant who wrongfully terminates his tenancy prior to the end of the rental term. *F.S.* 83.49(9).

Regardless of how the deposit money is held, the landlord must disclose in writing to the tenants, within 30 days of receipt of the deposits or advance rent, the manner in which he is holding the money, the rate of interest the tenants will receive (if any) and the time when interest will be paid or credited to them. *F.S.* 83.49(2). This initial disclosure for tenancies should be standardized on printed notice forms, and delivered to the tenants, together with the disclosures required under 83.50, as a matter of standard operating procedure.

4. [§15.77] Retaining Or Claiming Security Deposits

In order for a landlord to retain any portion of a security deposit he must give the tenant written notice by certified mail directed to the tenant's last known mailing address within 15 days after the tenant has vacated the premises of his intent to impose a claim for damages on the deposit. *F.S.* 83.49(3)(a). The result of failing to send the notice within the required time is forfeiture of the landlord's claim upon the security deposit. Thus, the sending of the notice upon termination of a residential tenancy must be implemented as part of the automatic management procedure for the landlord.

This short notice requirement operated unfairly and to the disadvantage of landlords when tenants vacated without notice. For this reason, in 1974 *F.S.* 83.49(5) was added, which now provides that any tenant who vacates or abandons the premises before the expiration date of the rental term or abandons premises subject to a periodic tenancy must give the landlord at least seven days' notice by certified mail before vacating or abandoning. The tenant's failure to notify the landlord excuses the landlord from his duty to notify the tenant under 83.49(3)(a) of his intent to claim against the security deposit.

If a tenant (a) vacates premises subject to a lease according to its terms or a periodic tenancy after giving the required notice of termination as set out in *F.S.* 83.57; (b) vacates or abandons premises subject to a lease before its expiration date but gives the seven-day notice required by 83.49(5); or (c) vacates a periodic tenancy without giving the notice required by 83.57 but does give the seven-day notice specified in 83.49(5), the landlord must notify the tenant of the landlord's intention to claim against the deposit within 15 days of the tenant's vacating the premises.

Since 1982 the notice of intention to claim against the security deposit must set forth the reason for imposing the claim and, accordingly, should be in substantially the following form:

TO: ....(tenant)...................

..........(tenant's address)..........

This is a notice of my intention to impose a claim for damages in the amount of $.......... upon your security deposit, due to ....(reason for claim).......... It is sent to you as required by F.S. 83.49(3). You are hereby notified that you must object in writing to this deduction from your security deposit within fifteen (15) days from the time you receive this notice or I will be authorized to deduct my claim from your security deposit. Your objection must be sent to ....(name and address of landlord or landlord's agent)..........

Name of Landlord

A tenant who receives such a notice must "object" to the landlord's claim within 15 days after receipt of the notice. *F.S.* 83.49(3)(b). If no objection is received, the landlord may deduct the amount of his claim from the deposits, as indicated in the notice to the tenant.

In litigation over security deposits, the prevailing party is entitled to receive court costs plus a reasonable attorney's fee. *F.S.* 83.49(3)(c).

F.S. 83.49(7), which was added in 1982, and amended in 1983, provides that upon sale or transfer of title of the rental property from one owner to another or upon a change in the designated rental agent, all advance rent and security deposits must be transferred to the new owner or agent, together with any earned interest and an accounting showing the amounts to be credited to each tenant.

Under *F.S.* 83.49(8) the Division of Hotels and Restaurants of the Department of Business Regulation is authorized to impose fines or to suspend or revoke the licenses of landlords who fail to comply with 83.49.

5. [§15.78] Obligation To Maintain Premises

The Florida Residential Landlord and Tenant Act imposes on the landlord the duty to maintain the premises and couples this duty with new rights and remedies for the tenant in the event that the landlord defaults. The statutory right of the tenant to raise the landlord's noncompliance with his duty to maintain the premises in an action for possession constitutes a departure from common law. See 51 C.J.S. *Landlord and Tenant* §402 and the former Florida case law as set out in *McKenzie v. Atlantic Manor, Inc.,* 181 So.2d 554 (Fla. 3d DCA 1966), *cert. den.* 192 So.2d 495; *Easton v. Weir,* 125 So.2d 115 (Fla. 2d DCA 1960), *cert. den.* 129 So.2d 141.

F.S. 83.51(1) imposes on landlords a set of minimum duties that cannot be waived or altered by provisions of a rental agreement. These duties are to comply with all requirements of applicable building, housing and health codes. Proof of a violation of building, housing or health code is simplified by 92.40, which makes a certified copy of a report, notice or citation of a violation issued by such an agency admissible as evidence. If there are no applicable codes, the landlord is required to "maintain the roofs, windows, screens, doors, floors, steps, porches, exterior walls, foundations, and all other structural components in good repair and capable of resisting normal forces and loads." In addition, the landlord must keep the plumbing in "reasonable working condition." 83.51(1)(b). If there are applicable codes with less stringent requirements, those codes will control.

Unless the rental agreement provides otherwise or shifts the responsibilities for those duties to the tenant, *F.S.* 83.51(2)(a) imposes a second set of maintenance duties upon the landlord, requiring at all times during the tenancy that he "make reasonable provisions" for:

a. the extermination of rats, mice, roaches, ants, wood-destroying organisms and bedbugs;

b. locks and keys;

c. the clean and safe condition of common areas;

d. garbage removal and outside receptacles; and

e. heat during winter, running water and hot water.

The statute provides that when vacation of the premises is required to carry out extermination, the landlord must abate the rent, but is not otherwise liable for damages. 83.51(2)(a)1.

Excepted entirely from the duties imposed by *F.S.* 83.51(1) and (2)(a) are rentals of mobile homes, when the tenant owns the mobile home. 83.51(2)(c). Also excepted from the duties imposed by 83.51(2)(a) are rentals of single family dwellings and duplexes. In order to alter or modify the basic duties imposed under 83.51(1), however, the landlord of a single family house or duplex must so provide in the written agreement. 83.51(1)(b). Further, if the tenant, a member of his family or another person on the premises with his consent negligently or wrongfully causes a condition to arise that causes the violation of the repair requirements of 83.51(1) and (2)(a), the landlord will be excused from any responsibilities to the tenant. 83.51(4).

In *Mansur v. Eubanks,* 401 So.2d 1328 (Fla. 1981) the Florida Supreme Court overruled the common law doctrine of "caveat lessee" set out in *Brooks v. Peters,* 157 Fla. 141, 25 So.2d 205 (1946), in which it was held that once possession and control of leased premises passed to the tenant, the landlord was not responsible for injuries caused by the condition of the leased premises. In *Mansur, supra* the court held that (a) a landlord has a continuing duty to exercise reasonable care to repair dangerous defective conditions upon notice by the tenant and (b) the landlord has an initial duty to make a reasonable inspection of the premises before allowing the tenant to take possession and to make the repairs necessary to transfer a reasonably safe dwelling unit to the tenant. The court specifically stated, however, that both of these duties could be waived or modified by agreement of the parties. No attempt was made by the court to reconcile its ruling concerning the "waiverability" of the duties it imposed with *F.S.* 83.47, which previously had been thought to prohibit waiver of "duties arising under law" in the residential landlord and tenant context.

F. Tenant's Obligations And Duties

1. [§15.79] In General

The list of obligations and duties of the tenant statutorily imposed by the Act are much fewer than those imposed on the landlord. The drafters of the Act probably contemplated that those duties would be abundantly imposed by the provisions of the rental agreements, which are drafted largely by the landlords. Tenants are required under the Act to comply with all provisions of the rental agreement. *F.S.* 83.55.

2. [§15.80] Duty To Maintain Dwelling Unit

At common law, absent any lease provisions to the contrary, a tenant was obligated only to keep and maintain and use the premises in such a manner as to be consistent with the common-law prohibition against committing waste. If it was a tenancy for years, there was authority that the tenant had a duty to make "fair and reasonable repair." 49 AM.JUR.2d *Landlord and Tenant* §§922—923. These common-law duties were vague and indefinite at best.

The Residential Landlord and Tenant Act in *F.S.* 83.52 thus marks another departure from prior law by specifically imposing upon tenants the duty to:

(1) Comply with all obligations imposed upon tenants by applicable provisions of building, housing, and health codes.

(2) Keep that part of the premises which he occupies and uses clean and sanitary.

(3) Remove from his dwelling unit all garbage in a clean and sanitary manner.

(4) Keep all plumbing fixtures in the dwelling unit or used by the tenant clean and sanitary and in repair.

(5) Use and operate in a reasonable manner all electrical, plumbing, sanitary, heating, ventilating, air-conditioning and other facilities and appliances, including elevators.

(6) Not destroy, deface, damage, impair, or remove any part of the premises or property therein belonging to the landlord nor permit any person to do so.

(7) Conduct himself, and require other persons on the premises with his consent to conduct themselves, in a manner that does not unreasonably disturb his neighbors or constitute a breach of the peace.

The requirement of the tenant to keep the plumbing in good repair duplicates the landlord's duty under *F.S.* 83.51(1)(b). As originally drafted, the tenant's duty with regard to the plumbing was only to keep the fixtures "clean and sanitary." Report and Recommendation on Florida Landlord-Tenant Law, Florida Law Revision Council 18 (March 1973). The Uniform Residential Landlord and Tenant Act, §3.101(4), upon which the Act was based in part, only requires the tenant to keep the plumbing fixtures "as clean as their condition permits." This duplication of duties would appear to require some clarification from the Florida Legislature.

The duties imposed by *F.S.* 83.52 cannot be altered by written agreement. This does not preclude, however, the imposition of more extensive duties of repair on the tenant, as long as those duties do not conflict with, alter or modify the basic maintenance duties imposed on the landlord under 83.51(1).

3. [§15.81] Duty To Provide Landlord With Access To Dwelling Unit

At common law, absent any provision to the contrary in the lease, the landlord had no right to enter upon the premises during the term of the lease, except to prevent waste. 49 AM.JUR.2d *Landlord and Tenant* §277. Thus, leases prepared by landlords generally give the landlord a right of access to the premises for purposes of inspection and repair at any time convenient to the landlord. *F.S.* 83.53(1) allows the landlord reasonable access to the premises for purposes of inspection, repairs, decoration, making alterations, improvements, supplying services or exhibiting the dwelling unit to prospective tenants, purchasers, mortgagees or workers. The landlord, however, is enjoined from abusing the right of access, or using it to harass the tenant. 83.53(3).

The Act imposes on the tenant the duty of giving reasonable consent to the landlord for entry on the premises for the purposes listed above. If the tenant fails to consent reasonably to the landlord's entry, the landlord may enter for the purposes set forth in *F.S.* 83.53(1), without the tenant's consent. Further, he has the right at any time to enter in the case of an emergency or when necessary to preserve the premises, without the tenant's consent. 83.53(2). The tenant's consent also is not necessary when he has been absent from the premises for a period of time equal to half of the time for periodic rental payments without notifying the landlord of his intended absence. 83.53(2)(d).

The statutory duty of the tenant to give reasonable access to the landlord and the landlord's right of entry for the tenant's breach of that duty or in an emergency control over any provisions in the lease to the contrary. *F.S.* 83.47(1)(a).

G. Rights And Remedies Of Tenants

1. [§15.82] In General

The Act gives the tenant a number of effective rights and remedies that are available as defenses as well as causes of action against the landlord. All rights and duties provided by the Act are enforceable by a civil action for damages as well as by an action for an injunction. See *F.S.* 83.54. Either party to a rental agreement may recover damages for noncompliance with that agreement. 83.55. The prevailing party in such litigation now may recover "reasonable attorney's fees" pursuant to the modification of 83.48, enacted in 1983.

Jurisdiction in actions brought by tenants for damages is in the county court or in the circuit court, depending on the amount of damages claimed. In all cases relating to the right of possession of the premises or forcible or unlawful detention of lands, unless the case involves the title or boundary of real estate, the county court has exclusive jurisdiction. *F.S.* 34.011(2).

F.S. 83.535, enacted in 1982, provides that a landlord may not prohibit a tenant from using a "flotation bedding system" (a water bed) in a dwelling unit, provided that the use of such a device does not violate an applicable building code. The new statute provides, however, that the landlord may require the tenant to carry personal injury and property damage insurance in a reasonable amount to protect the landlord's interests. 83.535.

F.S. 83.66, also enacted in 1982, provides that no tenant having a tenancy of one year or more may be unreasonably denied access to any available franchised or licensed cable television service, nor may the tenant or cable television service be required to pay anything of value to obtain or provide that service except those charges normally paid for like services with respect to single family homes within the same area and except for installation charges as agreed between the tenant and provider.

2. [§15.83] Right To Terminate Rental Agreement For Failure Of Landlord To Perform Duties

At common law, in the absence of any provision in the lease so providing, the tenant's right to terminate the lease because of the failure of the landlord to perform a duty imposed on him by law or by the lease agreement turned on the tenant's ability to establish that the landlord's breach was so material and basic as to constitute a "constructive" eviction of the tenant. See *Hankins v. Smith*, 103 Fla. 892, 138 So. 494 (1931); *Berwick Corp. v. Kleinginna Investment Corp.*, 143 So.2d 684 (Fla. 3d DCA 1962); 49 AM.JUR.2d *Landlord and Tenant* §301. The tenant was required to notify the landlord concerning the claims of breach and to abandon the premises within a reasonable time. See *Richards v. Dodge*, 150 So.2d 477 (Fla. 2d DCA 1963); 49 AM.JUR.2d *Landlord and Tenant* §§303—304.

If the landlord "materially" fails to comply with the basic maintenance duties set forth in *F.S.* 83.51(1) or fails to perform a "material provision" of the rental agreement, the tenant may terminate the rental agreement. 83.56. The requirement that there be a breach of a "material provision" of the rental agreement or that the landlord "materially" fail to comply with his duty to repair prevents the tenant from terminating the lease for petty or trifling failures on the part of the landlord.

In order to exercise the tenant's right to terminate, the tenant must deliver to the landlord a written notice specifying the alleged noncompliance of the landlord and indicating the tenant's intention to terminate the rental agreement. *F.S.* 83.56(1). This written notice should be sent by certified or registered mail or be hand-delivered. See 83.56(4). The date of delivery should be noted on the notice for the purpose of establishing the fact of delivery and the date of delivery. If the landlord fails to remedy the noncompliance within seven days of delivery of the notice to him or to his designated agent under 83.50(1), the tenant is authorized to terminate the tenancy. 83.56(1).

The seven-day period within which the landlord may cure his noncompliance is extremely short and as a practical matter the tenant in many cases will easily be able to terminate the rental agreement when the substandard condition of the premises can be attributed to the landlord's negligence, omission or fault.

If the defective condition of the premises is caused by something beyond the control of the landlord, and if the landlord makes and continues to make a reasonable effort to correct the defect, *F.S.* 83.56(1) provides that the rental agreement may be terminated or altered by the parties. If the defect renders the premises "untenantable" and the tenant vacates the premises, the tenant will be excused from any liability for rent during the time the premises remain "uninhabitable." 83.56(1)(a). It is not clear whether the drafters of the statute intended to make a distinction between "untenantable" and "uninhabitable." This statute also is unclear as to whether the tenant could vacate the premises but not terminate the lease, and yet not be liable for any rent. If so, this would put the landlord in a worse position than if the material defect or breach were his fault. If the defect does not make the premises "untenantable," and the tenant remains in possession, rent for the period of noncompliance may be reduced to reflect "loss of value" caused by the noncompliance. 83.56(1)(b).

3. [§15.84] Defenses To Action For Rent Or Possession

Formerly, the tenant could not raise any defense to a landlord's action for possession, other than payment of rent. See *Brownlee v. Sussman*, 238 So.2d 317 (Fla. 3d DCA 1970); *Filaretou v. Christou*, 133 So.2d 652 (Fla. 2d DCA 1961). The Act provides that in an action by the landlord to recover possession of a dwelling unit for nonpayment of rent, or in any other action brought by the landlord for noncompliance with the rental agreement or the duties of the tenant imposed by the Act, the tenant may raise any legal or equitable defense available, including the defense of retaliatory conduct according to *F.S.* 83.64. *F.S.* 83.60(1). If the defense is based on the landlord's failure to perform his basic maintenance duties under 83.51(1), the tenant must have provided the landlord with seven days' written notice specifying the noncompliance and indicating the intent of the tenant not to pay rent. If the landlord fails to make the indicated repairs within the seven-day period, the tenant's withholding of rent is deemed authorized. When properly raised, the defense of the landlord's failure to perform basic maintenance duties under 83.51(1) is a "complete defense" to the landlord's action for possession of the premises based on nonpayment of rent, and the court or jury may reduce the amount of rent to reflect any "diminution in value" of the dwelling unit during the period of noncompliance with 83.51. *F.S.* 83.60(1).

F.S. 83.60(1) does not appear to permit a tenant who is already in default of payment of rent to serve the contemplated notice inasmuch as the statute authorizes only the withholding of rent after seven days have elapsed from the service of the notice. If the tenant was in default of payment of rent at the time that he served his notice, the existing default presumably is neither cured nor authorized by his subsequent service on the landlord of the notice pursuant to 83.60(1).

In order to protect the landlord from economic loss while potentially frivolous defenses are being litigated, *F.S.* 83.60(2) provides that if the tenant raises any defense other than payment in an action for possession of a dwelling unit, the tenant must pay into the registry the "accrued rent as alleged in the complaint" or "as determined by the court" and "the rent which accrues during the pendency of the proceedings."

It should be noted that the statute contemplates that the court could be called upon to fix the amount of the initial deposit if the tenant takes issue with the amount of rent specified in the plaintiff's complaint. Thus, the court and attorneys should be prepared, upon motion, to conduct a preliminary evidentiary hearing immediately prior to trial to determine the amount of rent that should be posted into the registry as a condition precedent to the defendant's proceeding to trial on any defense other than payment. The purpose of the preliminary hearing, if any, is to fix the amount of rent without alleged offsets or abatement, *i.e.*, the gross amount of rent as agreed for the relevant periods less actual payments received. If the required amount of rent so calculated is deposited into the registry, the court is empowered, upon proper proof at trial, to grant possession to the defendant and to award a portion of the funds deposited in the way of rent abatement. See *F.S.* 83.60(1). Alternatively, the court may, after trial, find for the plaintiff and award possession, together with the deposited funds representing accrued rent, to the plaintiff. If the defendant, however, fails to deposit the required funds into the registry in the first place, the defendant's answer may be stricken and default final judgment for possession entered for the plaintiff.

The tenant who raises any defense other than payment must deposit not only "rent as alleged in the complaint" (or as determined by the court) but also "rent which accrues during the pendency of the proceedings, when due." *F.S.* 83.60(2). Thus, supplementary deposits should be made during the pendency of the proceedings and failure to do so also results in "immediate default" according to the statute. For this reason, it may be a good idea to specify in the three-day notice, which is eventually attached to the complaint, the date upon which rent will next be due and the amount of the payment in question.

The practitioner should be aware that if the landlord is "in actual danger of loss of the premises or other personal hardship resulting from the loss of rental income from the premises," the court, upon application, is empowered to release to the landlord pendente lite "all or part of the funds" deposited into the court registry. *F.S.* 83.61.

The United States Supreme Court in *Lindsey v. Normet,* 405 U.S. 56, 92 S.Ct. 862, 3 L.Ed.2d 36 (1972) upheld the constitutionality of Oregon's rent deposit statute against the contention that the statute violated due process of law. The Supreme Court in that case struck down as unconstitutional only certain portions of the Oregon law having no counterparts in the Florida statutory scheme. Indeed, the Supreme Court in *Lindsey* suggested that failure to require deposits in actions for possession might deprive the *landlord* of his property without due process of law. Florida courts generally have recognized that limited and reasonable restrictions may constitutionally be placed on the right of access to the courts. See, *e.g., North Port Bank v. State, Department of Revenue,* 313 So.2d 683 (Fla. 1975). In the majority of cases elsewhere, legislation requiring tenants to pay rent into the court during possessory actions has been upheld specifically as not violative of either state or federal constitutional guarantees. See SCHOSKINSKI, AMERICAN LAW OF LANDLORD AND TENANT 168 (1980). Notwithstanding the foregoing, there is a published county court decision declaring *F.S.* 83.60(2) to be "unconstitutional." *Jones v. Styles,* 46 Fla.Supp. 175 (Palm Beach County 1977). The court in *Jones* purports to rely upon the United States Supreme Court case of *Lindsey v. Normet, supra* (which clearly held the opposite) and apparently misreads its other underlying authorities. The decision generally has not been followed by other courts.

4. [§15.85] Right To Terminate Tenancy Because Of Casualty Damage

At common law, in general, in the absence in a lease of a covenant to repair or rebuild by the landlord, he was under no duty to rebuild or repair. Further, the destruction of the premises, at common law, did not give the tenant the right to terminate the lease but left him liable for rent for the balance of the term. 49 AM.JUR.2d *Landlord and Tenant* §995. This harsh rule was modified by statute in many jurisdictions and by the refusal of courts to apply the common-law rule to rentals of apartments or parts of buildings. 49 AM.JUR.2d *Landlord and Tenant* §§996, 601. The statutory rules were alterable by rental provisions or waivers, however. §601.

On all of the above points, *F.S.* 83.63 created new law. If the premises (defined as the dwelling unit and the structure of which it is a part, or appurtenant facilities in the case of the lease of a mobile home lot) are damaged or destroyed by anything other than a wrongful or negligent act of the tenant so that the enjoyment of the premises is "substantially impaired," the tenant has a right to terminate the lease. If the tenant elects to terminate the lease, he must vacate the premises and his liability for rent accruing after vacating will be excused. If only part of the premises is damaged or destroyed, the tenant may elect to remain in possession and vacate only the unusable portion. In that event, the rent will be proportionately reduced. The tenant presumably also will have the option of terminating the lease when there is a partial destruction of the premises if his enjoyment of the premises is "substantially impaired."

F.S. 83.63 does not require the tenant to send the landlord written notice of his election to terminate the lease. The tenant's mere abandonment or vacation of the premises apparently is sufficient. The landlord, however, is required to comply with the notice requirements regarding asserting a claim against the tenant's security deposit. 83.63.

H. Rights And Remedies Of Landlord

1. [§15.86] In General

The landlord as well as the tenant is empowered to bring a civil action to enforce (by claims for damages or for injunctive relief) any right or duty declared in the Act. *F.S.* 83.54. Jurisdictional limits of the circuit court and the county court will determine the proper court in which to file the damage claim but if the action involves the right to possession of real property, the county court will have exclusive jurisdiction. 34.011(2). In addition, the landlord has other special remedies that will be discussed below.

2. [§15.87] The Landlord's Lien

The landlord has a lien for accrued rent due under the rental agreement on all of the personal property of the tenant located on the premises. *F.S.* 713.691(1). The scope of this lien is narrower than that for commercial leases, as discussed in §§15.12—.17. It does not cover property usually kept on the premises unless in fact it is on the premises, nor does it reach any other property of the tenant. There may be more than one person, however, who can be considered to be a "tenant," defined in 83.43(4). The lien may be modified or waived in whole or in part by the rental agreement. 713.69(1).

Exempted from the landlord's lien when the tenant is a head of the household is personal property owned by that tenant up to the value of $1,000. *F.S.* 713.691(2). This exemption is stated to be no greater than that afforded by Article X, §4 of the Florida Constitution.

The residential landlord's lien is not specifically stated to be superior or prior to other liens acquired and perfected before or after the property is brought on the premises, unlike the statute dealing with commercial leases. Compare *F.S.* 713.691 with 83.08(1) and (2). The general rule stated in 713.50 as to liens on personal property provides that all liens created by Part II of that chapter are "prior in dignity to all others accruing thereafter." Thus, if the personal property is subject to a perfected security interest or lien before it is brought on to the leased property, the landlord's lien will be inferior to that lien but it will be superior to those perfected or accruing after the property is brought on to the premises. See 679.310; *Gables Lincoln-Mercury, Inc. v. First Bank & Trust Co. of Boca Raton*, 219 So.2d 90 (Fla. 3d DCA 1969).

Enforcement of the landlord's lien no longer may be sought through distress for rent proceedings with regard to residential tenancies. *F.S.* 713.691(3). Unless the tenant has vacated the premises and abandoned his property on it, the landlord may not resort to self-help measures to enforce his lien. See *Van Hoose v. Robbins*, 165 So.2d 209 (Fla. 2d DCA 1964). Further, it is clear that any proceeding brought by the landlord to enforce his lien against the tenant's personal property must be through the courts, with due notice and hearing. *Fuentes v. Shevin*, 407 U.S. 67, 92 S.Ct. 1983, 32 L.Ed.2d 556 (1972); *Barber v. Rader*, 350 F.Supp. 183 (S.D. Fla. 1972).

The procedure for enforcement of the landlord's lien is set out in *F.S.* 85.011(5). The landlord may file (in the circuit court or the county court, depending on the jurisdictional amount involved) a complaint describing the property on which the lien is claimed and stating facts giving right to the lien. The landlord filing such an action is entitled to employ the summary procedure set forth in 51.011. See the discussion in §§15.35—.47. If the landlord prevails in the action, he will be entitled to attorneys' fees and costs in the amount of 15% of the recovery. 85.011(5)(b). In addition, if the landlord has reason to believe that the personal property of a tenant subject to a lien for accrued rent is about to be removed from the county, the landlord may seek to attach it, although this procedure will require due notice and a hearing. 85.031.

Any action brought by the landlord seeking to enforce the landlord's lien against a tenant's property must be brought within 12 months from the date of the accrual of the unpaid rent. *F.S.* 83.051.

3. Termination Of Lease By Landlord For Breach By Tenant

a. [§15.88] In General

Prior to 1982, *F.S.* 83.56(2) provided that if the tenant materially failed to comply with the duties imposed upon tenants by 83.52, or any material provision of the rental agreement, other than a failure to pay rent, the landlord could serve a seven-day written notice specifying the noncompliance and indicating the intention of the landlord to terminate the rental agreement. Under the previous noncompliance statute, there was some uncertainty as to the function of the seven-day period. It was thought generally that the period of time was provided to permit the tenant an opportunity to correct his behavior and that upon doing so (*e.g.,* getting rid of his dog) the tenant should be permitted to remain in possession. If the tenant inflicted substantial damage to the premises or posed a substantial threat of injury to persons on the property, however, it also was thought that the landlord should be able to terminate the tenancy, notwithstanding the fact that the acts complained of were of a nonrecurring nature. For example, the landlord could evict a tenant who intentionally burned down one of the buildings in the apartment complex even if the tenant did not continue to set fire to additional buildings during the seven days following service of the notice upon him. The matter, however, was not free from doubt and the wording of the statute provided no particular guidance.

The 1982 Florida Legislature addressed the previous ambiguity by providing the following new language, adding paragraphs (a) and (b) to *F.S.* 83.56(2), which as modified in 1983 provides as follows:

>   (a) If such noncompliance is of a nature that the tenant should not be given an opportunity to cure it or if the noncompliance constitutes a subsequent or continuing noncompliance within 12 months of a written warning by the landlord, of a similar violation, [the landlord may] deliver a written notice to the tenant specifying the noncompliance and the landlord's intent to terminate the rental agreement by reason thereof. Examples of noncompliance which are of a nature that the tenant should not be given an opportunity to cure include, but are not limited to, destruction, damage, or misuse of the landlord's or other tenants' property by intentional act or a subsequent or continued unreasonable disturbance. In such event, the landlord may terminate the rental agreement, and the tenant shall have 7 days from the date that the notice is delivered to vacate the premises. . . .

>   (b) If such noncompliance is of a nature that the tenant should be given an opportunity to cure it, [the landlord may] deliver a written notice to the tenant specifying the noncompliance, including a notice that, if the noncompliance is not corrected within 7 days from the date the written notice is delivered, the landlord shall terminate the rental agreement by reason thereof. Examples of such noncompliance include, but are not limited to, activities in contravention of the lease or this Act such as having or permitting unauthorized pets, guests, or vehicles; parking in an unauthorized manner or permitting such

parking; or failure to keep the premises clean and sanitary. . . .

The landlord waives his right to terminate the lease under *F.S.* 83.56(3) if he accepts the tenant's rental payment or performance of the provisions of the lease by the tenant after actual knowledge of the tenant's breach and default. Acceptance of the tenant's performance of the lease prevents the landlord from terminating the lease or bringing a civil action as to that breach, but not as to a subsequent breach by the tenant. 83.56(5).

If the lease is terminated by the landlord, the landlord must notify the tenant of his claim against the security deposits, or return the deposit to him within 15 days from the date the tenant vacates. *F.S.* 83.56(6).

b. [§15.89] Forms For Notices To Tenant Of Termination; Breach Of Lease

F.S. 83.54(2)(a) and (b) provide the forms for the notices to be served on the tenant as follows:

NOTICE

TO: ....

THIS IS NOTICE OF TERMINATION OF YOUR TENANCY AS AUTHORIZED BY FLORIDA STATUTES 83.56(2)(a)

You are advised that your lease is terminated effective immediately. You shall have seven days from the delivery of this notice to vacate the premises.

This action is taken because of the following:

I certify that I served a true and correct copy of the foregoing notice on the above-named tenant on ....(date).......... in the following manner [check one]:

_____ **By personally serving it on the tenant.**

_____ **By posting it at the above-described premises in the absence of the tenant.**

Dated: ....

Landlord

NOTICE

TO: ....

THIS IS NOTICE OF TERMINATION OF YOUR TENANCY AS AUTHORIZED BY FLORIDA STATUTES 83.56(2)(b)

You are hereby notified that you have failed to comply with the duties imposed upon tenants by law or with a material provision of your lease as follows:

Demand is hereby made that you remedy the noncompliance within seven days of receipt of this notice or your lease shall be deemed terminated, and you shall vacate the premises upon that termination. If this same conduct, or conduct of a similar nature is repeated within 12 months, your tenancy is subject to termination without your being given an opportunity to cure the noncompliance.

I certify that I served a true and correct copy of the foregoing notice on the above-named tenant on ....(date).......... in the following manner [check one]:

_____ By personally serving it on the tenant.

_____ By posting it at the above-described premises in the absence of the tenant.

Dated: ....

                                                                    _____
                                                                            Landlord

COMMENT: Although *F.S.* 83.56(2) does not require a certificate of service on these forms, the authors suggest that the certificate be included as it is useful for evidentiary purposes.

c. [§15.90] Form For Notice To Tenant Of Termination; Failure To Pay Rent

THREE DAY NOTICE

TO: .... and all others in possession of

and located in .... County, Florida.

You are hereby notified that you are indebted to me in the sum of $.......... for the rent and use of the premises described above and now occupied by you.

I demand payment of the rent or possession of the premises within three days (excluding Saturdays, Sundays and legal holidays) from the date of delivery of this notice, on or before ....(date)..........

Your rent is payable from ....week to week/month to month.........., due on the .... of each ....week/month.......... in the amount of $..........

      Landlord: _____
      Address: _____
            _____
      Telephone: _____

_____ This notice was served on the person owing the rent.

_____ The person owing the rent was absent from his last usual place of residence, and this notice was left at that residence by posting.

By: _____ Dated: _____

d. [§15.91] Form For Letter Of Termination Of Lease

TO: ....

This will advise you that because of your failure to remedy the breach of the rental agreement that I set forth in my letter dated ...., ...delivered/mailed.......... to you on ....(date).........., I elect to terminate the rental agreement executed by you and .... on ....(date).........., covering the premises described as .... Termination of the rental agreement is effective on ....(date).......... or upon your receipt of this letter, whichever is earlier. You therefore will quit and surrender the premises on or before ....(date).........., and you are further notified to leave the premises in a clean and good condition.

                _____
                  Landlord

COMMENT: If the attorney is particularly desirous of confirming the fact that the tenancy has been terminated at the expiration of the three-day period, the foregoing form may be used. Most practitioners, however, do not use this "second" notice on the theory that service of notice specified in *F.S.* 83.56(3) is sufficient to effect a termination, unless the default is cured by the tenant, and that no further action is necessary on the part of the landlord who evidences his intention not to reinstate the tenancy by not accepting further rent. The authors are aware of no instances in which the courts have required service of a "second" notice of the variety which appears above.

4. Recovery Of Possession Of Premises By Landlord

a. [§15.92] In General

Under the Act the landlord may reclaim and recover possession of the premises, without resort to court proceedings, only if the tenant surrenders possession to the landlord voluntarily, *F.S.* 83.59(3)(b), or abandons the dwelling unit, 83.59(3)(c). Abandonment will be presumed if the tenant has been absent from the premises for a period equal to one half the time for periodic rent payments. This presumption does not apply if the rent is current or if the tenant has notified the landlord in writing of his intended absence. 83.59(3)(c). Formerly, there was doubt about the legality of self-help evictions. See *Barber v. Rader,* 350 F.Supp. 183 (S.D. Fla. 1972); Barnett, *When the Landlord Resorts to Self-Help: A Plea for Clarification of the Law in Florida,* 19 U.Fla.L.Rev. 238 (1966). The statute clarifies that doubt by prohibiting them except in cases of surrender or abandonment.

It often is difficult, even with the benefit of the statutory presumption of *F.S.* 83.59(3)(c), to be sure that a tenant has abandoned the premises. What may appear to be an "abandonment" may later be determined to be a "wrongful eviction." The safest course for the landlord, when in doubt, has been to seek a court order. For a recent case that illustrates the protection that the landlord receives by procuring a final judgment and permitting the sheriff to remove the tenant's possessions, even in circumstances that, at first blush, might appear somewhat harsh, see *McCready v. Booth,* 398 So.2d 1000 (Fla. 5th DCA 1981). For an alternate procedure for dealing with abandoned personal property, see the Disposition of Personal Property Landlord and Tenant Act, 83.821—.833, which is discussed at §§15.127—.136.

b. [§15.93] Jurisdiction And Procedure For Eviction

An action to evict a tenant may be brought if the lease is terminated, as discussed in §15.73. The action must be filed in the county court where the premises are located. The landlord's complaint should describe the dwelling unit and state the reasons for recovery of possession. The landlord is entitled to employ the summary procedure provided in *F.S.* 51.011 and upon due application the court "shall" advance the cause on the court calendar. 83.59(2). The prevailing party is entitled to judgment for costs. 83.59(4).

Service of process in an action to recover possession of a dwelling unit may be made as provided for all civil actions under *F.S.* Chapter 48. If, however, the tenant or a person residing in the dwelling unit who is over 15 years of age cannot be found at the usual place of residence of the tenant, after at least two attempts to obtain personal service, the summons may be served by attaching a copy to a conspicuous place on the premises described in the complaint. 48.183(1).

In 1982 the United States Supreme Court affirmed a decision from the Circuit Court of Appeals, Sixth Circuit, holding that a Kentucky statute that authorized service or process by posting in landlord and tenant actions had been unconstitutionally applied in the particular circumstances of the case. *Greene v. Lindsey,* 456 U.S. 444, 102 S.Ct. 1874, 72 L.Ed.2d 249 (1982). In its opinion the Supreme Court stopped considerably short of requiring personal service in landlord and tenant actions. The court held that "posting notice on the door of a person's home would, in many or perhaps most instances, constitute not only a constitutionally acceptable means of service, but indeed a singularly appropriate and effective way of ensuring that a person who cannot conveniently be served personally is actually apprised of the proceedings against him."

The court, however, went on to state that the Kentucky statute had been unconstitutionally applied in light of the following particular factual findings that appeared in the record:

1. The defendants-tenants did not actually learn of the eviction proceedings until they were served with writs of possession executed after defaults had been entered against them and after their opportunity for rehearing or appeal had lapsed.

2. The plaintiff-landlord made no attempt to notify the defendants-tenants of the eviction proceedings against them other than by posting copies of the summons and complaint on the premises.

3. In the particular public housing project in which the tenants lived, the process servers were aware that posted notices "not infrequently" were removed by children or other tenants before they could have their intended effect.

In declaring the Kentucky statute unconstitutionally applied, the United States Supreme Court went on to comment that notice by mail "would surely go a long way" to curing the constitutional infirmity. *Greene v. Lindsey, supra*.

Apparently taking its cue from *Greene v. Lindsey, supra*, and willing to take a step further in ensuring that the tenant is likely to receive notice, the 1983 Florida Legislature modified *F.S.* 48.183. The modified statute now provides that in an action for possession of residential premises, if neither the tenant nor a person residing therein who is 15 years of age or older can be found at the usual place of residence of the tenant after at least two attempts to obtain personal service, the summons and complaint may be served by attaching a copy to a conspicuous place on the property described in the complaint or summons. In addition, if the landlord anticipates serving the tenant by posting, the landlord must provide the clerk of the court with an additional copy of the summons and complaint and a prestamped envelope addressed to the defendant at the premises involved in the proceedings. The clerk is directed by the modified statute to mail the copy of the summons and complaint by first class mail, to note the fact of mailing in the docket and to file a certificate in the court file of the fact and date of mailing. Service is deemed effective on the date of mailing and after five days from the date of mailing, final judgment for removal of tenant may be entered.

Revised *F.S.* 48.183, therefore, is similar to revised 83.22, which is applicable to nonresidential tenancies, except that the latter statute requires mailing of two, rather than one, additional copies of the summons and complaint.

c. [15.94] Form For Complaint For Eviction Of Tenant For Failure To Pay Rent

(Party Designation)   (Title of Court)

COMPLAINT FOR REMOVAL OF TENANT FOR NONPAYMENT OF RENT

Plaintiff, ..., sues defendants, ... and ...., and alleges:

1. This is an action for removal of tenant from real property in .... County, Florida, as authorized by F.S. 83.59.

2. Plaintiff is the landlord and the below-named defendants are the tenants in possession of the following-described real property in .... County pursuant to ....a written/an oral........... rental agreement:

[names of defendants and property address]

3. The term of the rental agreement has expired by default in payment of the rent and three days' notice in writing requiring the payment of the rent or the possession of the premises has been duly served but defendants refuse to do either, together with all persons claiming by, through or under the defendants. A copy of the notice showing the date of service, the amount of rent due as of the date of service, the rental rate and period and the time each payment is due is attached to and made a part of this complaint, marked "Plaintiff's Exhibit A." A copy of the rental agreement is attached to and made a part of this complaint, marked "Plaintiff's Exhibit B."

4. Plaintiff is entitled to the summary procedure provided in F.S. Chapter 51.

5. Plaintiff also is entitled to an award of reasonable attorneys' fees pursuant to F.S. 83.48.

WHEREFORE, plaintiff demands judgment for possession of the property and costs against defendants, including reasonable attorneys' fees.

_____
Attorney for Plaintiff
.........(address and phone number).........

COMMENT: Since 1975, *F.S.* 83.625 has authorized the plaintiff to obtain money damages as well as possession in the same action, provided that: (1) no money judgment can be entered without personal service and (2) no money judgment can be entered earlier than the date following the expiration of the time period within which the tenant-defendant would be required to file an answer or otherwise appear if the proceeding was solely an action at law to recover money damages.

Accordingly, it probably is necessary to prepare two different summonses. The defendant is served with one summons prepared pursuant to the summary procedure designated in *F.S.* Chapter 51. In addition, the defendant is served with a regular (20-day) summons or, if the amount of controversy is less than $1,500, with a notice of pretrial conference. Neither the 20-day summons nor the notice of pretrial conference may be served by residential posting.

In effect, *F.S.* 83.625 authorizes a "hybrid action" and contemplates the filing of a complaint consisting of one count for possession and one count for monetary damages. If the tenant-defendant makes no response, default is entered at a two-tier level, once after five days from the service of the summons pursuant to Chapter 51, and again after 20 days from the service of the regular summons or at the time of the pretrial conference. Thus, 83.625 does little more than save the landlord from paying two filing fees.

Consequently, landlords wishing to file for possession and monetary damages probably are best advised to file two separate actions, which counsel will be able to handle more efficiently. Moreover, there are actual disadvantages in attempting to file a "hybrid action" pursuant to *F.S.* 83.625:

1. The sheriff's deputy or other process server often is confused as to whether personal service on the defendant must be obtained, and that confusion tends to result in delay.

2. The clerks of most county courts have separate filing systems for cases to be processed under the Florida Rules of Summary Procedure and for cases to proceed under the Florida Rules of Civil Procedure. When, as usually is the case, the count for monetary damages is less than $1,500 and is combined in the same complaint with a separate count for possession, the personnel of some clerks' offices are uncertain as to which designation or file number to assign to the action.

3. The appellate court in *Freedman v. Geiger*, 314 So.2d 189 (Fla. 3d DCA 1975) held that a landlord who demands both possession and other relief (*i.e.*, monetary damages) in the same complaint forfeits his statutory right to require the tenants to pay the accrued rent and rent as it accrues into the registry of the court.

d. [§15.95] Defenses To Action For Eviction

In an action to recover possession of the dwelling unit after termination of the lease or an action brought by the landlord to recover unpaid rent, the tenant may raise any defense, legal or equitable, that he may have. *F.S.* 83.60(1). The defense of the landlord's material noncompliance with the basic maintenance duties imposed by 83.51(1) (see §15.84) will be a complete defense to an action to recover possession for failure to pay rent. 83.60(1). The court or jury may reduce the amount of rent due to reflect the reduced rental value of the dwelling unit caused by the landlord's failure to perform the basic maintenance duties. To preserve this defense, however, the tenant must send the notice required by 83.60(1). See §15.83.

In order to discourage frivolous defenses from being raised by tenants in eviction actions, *F.S.* 83.60(2) provides that if the tenant raises any defense, other than payment, he must pay into the registry of the court rent as demanded in the complaint or as determined by the court and rent as it accrues during the pendency of the proceedings. Failure of the tenant to pay the rent to the court constitutes a waiver of all of the tenant's defenses other than payment of rent.

The 1983 Florida Legislature enacted *F.S.* 83.64, which is entitled "retaliatory conduct" and which provides that it "shall be unlawful for a landlord to discriminatorily [sic] increase a tenant's rent or decrease a tenant's services, or to bring or threaten to bring an action for possession or other civil action, primarily because the landlord is retaliating against the tenant." The statute provides that the tenant "must have acted in good faith" and provides that examples of conduct for which the landlord may not so retaliate include, but are not limited to, the following:

(a) The tenant has complained to a governmental agency charged with responsibility for enforcement of a building, housing, or health code, of a suspected violation applicable to the premises;

(b) The tenant has organized, encouraged, or participated in a tenants' organization; or

(c) The tenant has complained to the landlord pursuant to s. 83.56(1).

F.S. 83.64(2) provides that retaliatory conduct may be raised as a defense in an action for possession. The statute also provides that the defense is not available when the landlord can show the eviction is for good cause and provides as examples of good cause: nonpayment of rent, violation of the rental agreement or reasonable rules or violation of the terms of Chapter 83.

F.S. 83.64(3) defines "discrimination" to mean that "a tenant is being treated differently [than other tenants residing on the same premises?] as to rent charged, services rendered, or the action being taken by the landlord."

The new statute, as written, does little more than codify the doctrine of retaliatory eviction as first enunciated in *Edwards v. Habib*, 397 F.2d 687 (D.C. Cir. 1968), *cert. den.* 393 U.S. 1016. This doctrine had been recognized previously and adopted as part of the common law of Florida. *Wilkins v. Tebbetts*, 216 So.2d 477 (Fla. 3d DCA 1968), *cert. dism.* 222 So.2d 753; *Kendig v. Kendall Construction Co.*, 317 So.2d 138 (Fla. 4th DCA 1975). An early version of the bill, which was modified and eventually enacted as *F.S.* 83.64, contained a provision that would have provided that evidence of "a complaint or notice of violation or evidence of any other activity protected by subsection (1), within six (6) months prior to the action of the landlord, shall create a rebuttable presumption that the action of the landlord constitutes 'retaliatory conduct'." This proposed provision was omitted from the final enactment and its omission presumably leaves intact the case law in Florida that clearly holds that retaliatory eviction is an affirmative defense that the tenant has the burden of both pleading and proving. *Wilkins v. Tebbetts, supra.*

Now that the Florida Legislature has made its attempt to define and codify the doctrine of retaliatory eviction, it is doubtful that the rules relating to rental housing and mobile home parks, which were promulgated by the Attorney General and which contain provisions on retaliatory conduct that are at odds with the statute, have any continued validity. See Rule 2-11.07, Fla. Admin. Code.

e. [§15.96] Judgment Of Eviction

As in the case of nonresidential leases, the landlord in summary proceedings for eviction may obtain a judgment for possession of the premises, plus costs. *F.S.* 83.625 provides for the recovery of damages and unpaid rent. *F.S.* 83.48 provides for the recovery of reasonable attorneys' fees by the party in whose favor judgment is rendered.

After entry of a judgment by the county court in favor of the landlord declaring that the landlord is entitled to possession of the dwelling unit, the clerk issues a writ of possession to the sheriff describing the premises and commanding him to put the landlord in possession after notice has been conspicuously posted on the premises for a period of 24 hours. *F.S.* 83.62. For the form of the writ of possession, see *Fla. R. Civ. P.* Form 1.915.

Before 1980, if the final judgment for possession did not explicitly state that the writ of possession shall issue "forthwith," the clerk would not issue the writ until five days from the date judgment was rendered.

This delay was occasioned by the interplay between *Rule* 1.550, which generally provides that no execution shall issue until the judgment on which it is based has been recorded and the time for rehearing has expired, and *F.S.* 51.011(4), which provides that motions for new trial in summary procedure cases may be filed and served within five days from the date judgment was rendered. *Rule* 1.550, as modified in 1980, now provides that when "a judgment or order is for the delivery of possession of real property, the judgment or order shall direct the clerk to issue a writ of possession." The rule now also states "The clerk shall issue the writ forthwith and deliver it to the sheriff for execution." Presumably, all final judgments for removal of tenants will now result in the issuance of a writ of possession "forthwith" unless the court specifically provides for a stay of execution. Stays of execution in landlord and tenant cases presumably are governed by *Rule* 1.550(b), which requires both "good cause on motion" and "notice to all adverse parties."

I.   Rentals Of Mobile Home Lots

1. [§15.97] In General

In 1976 the Florida Legislature enacted the Florida Mobile Home Landlord and Tenant Act, Part III, *F.S.* Chapter 83, which governs tenancies created when a mobile home owner rents a mobile home lot from a mobile home park owner for residential purposes. It does not apply when the tenant rents both the mobile home and the mobile home lot from the landlord. Those tenancies are governed by the Florida Residential Landlord and Tenant Act, Part II, *F.S.* Chapter 83. *F.S.* 83.751. An examination of the Florida Mobile Home Landlord and Tenant Act reveals that it incorporates many of the features that were presented in 1973, with respect to residential tenancies, such as the obligation of good faith, the enumeration of duties of the mobile home park owner and of the mobile home owner, the unenforceability of waiver of certain statutory duties and unconscionability. The maintenance duties of both the landlord and the tenant and the procedures established to enforce those obligations are very similar. Because of the shortage of mobile home lots in the state and because of the great expense incurred by a mobile home owner in relocating, the time periods of the Florida Mobile Home Landlord and Tenant Act relating to termination of tenancies and removal of tenants are greater than those of the residential act. See 83.770. Also, because of the nature of living style in a mobile home park community, the mobile home act gives more emphasis to the tenant's use and enjoyment of the appurtenant areas of the leasehold.

2. [§15.98] Eviction Of Mobile Home Tenants

In an action for possession of a mobile home lot, the writ of possession cannot issue any earlier than 30 days from the date the judgment for possession is granted. *F.S.* 83.7597.

The grounds for eviction of mobile home tenants are limited to those set out in *F.S.* 83.759:

a. Nonpayment of rent. *F.S.* 83.759(1)(a).

b. Conviction of a violation of federal or state law, or local ordinance, that may be deemed detrimental to the health, safety or welfare of other dwellers in the mobile home park. *F.S.* 83.759(1)(b).

c. Violation of any reasonable rule or regulation established by the park owner or operator if the mobile home owner received written notice of the grounds for eviction 30 days before the date of eviction and if a copy of the rules and regulations was furnished to the tenant before the lease was created. *F.S.* 83.759(1)(c). The rules also must be posted in a conspicuous place in the mobile home park. In 1982 and 1983 the Florida Legislature amended 83.759(1)(c) to provide that a mobile home park owner may terminate the tenancy of a mobile home owner for a "first violation" of any reasonable rule or regulation that is found by the court to have endangered the safety of the mobile home park or its occupants, the life, health, or property of the occupants, or the peaceful enjoyment of the park by the occupants or for a "second violation" of any reasonable rule or regulation within a 12-month period provided the mobile home park owner has given the mobile home owner written notice within 30 days of the first violation, specifying the actions of the mobile home owner causing the violations. The mobile home owner does not have the right to cure the second violation if committed within 12 months of the first. Violation of the same rule or regulation after the passage of one year, however, does not constitute ground for eviction under the part of the amended statute providing for eviction after a second violation. 83.759(1)(c).

d. Change in the use of land comprising the mobile home park, if all tenants affected are given six months' notice or longer if required by the lease, of the proposed change in use for the land. No zoning body may rezone a mobile home park, however, without first investigating suitable facilities for relocation of the tenants. *F.S.* 83.760(4).

e. *F.S.* 83.759(1)(e), also added in 1982, provides for termination of tenancies and eviction of a mobile home or mobile home owner without cause upon 12 months' written notice and specified procedures.

If tenants of mobile homes or lots on January 1, 1975 have not been offered a written lease, which is a bona fide offer to lease on the same terms and conditions as are offered to the other park tenants, the landlord may not terminate the tenancy. If such a written lease has been offered to the tenant and the tenant has refused or failed to execute it without cause for 60 days, however, the landlord may terminate the tenancy and commence eviction proceedings. *F.S.* 83.760(2).

F.S. 83.7594, enacted in 1982 and amended in 1983, provides specific procedures for termination of a tenancy in the case of nonpayment of rent and in accordance with 83.759(1)(b), (c) or (d).

3. [§15.99] Deposits And Fees

The landlord must fully disclose to a tenant in writing all fees, charges, assessments and rules and regulations before his assumption of occupancy in a mobile home park. These items may not be increased nor the rules changed without more than 30 days' written notice to all tenants. *F.S.* 83.764(3)(a). Failure to disclose in full all the fees, charges or assessments as required will make them uncollectible and unavailable as a cause for eviction. 83.764(4).

The landlord is prohibited from charging any entrance or exit fee except for fees directly incurred by the park owner or operator as the result of placing or removing a mobile home from the park site. *F.S.* 83.764(3)(b). No "entrance fees" may be charged for a move within the same park. 83.764(3)(b). No fee-splitting arrangement between mobile home dealers and mobile home park owners or operators are permitted, and any person entering into such an arrangement may be charged with a misdemeanor of the second degree. 83.764(3)(c).

Indirect charges or profits by mobile home park owners or operators in the form of requiring mobile home owners or residents to purchase equipment from the mobile home park owner or operator is not allowed, although mobile home park owners or operators may specify generally by rule or regulation the style or quality of that equipment. *F.S.* 83.764(1). Similarly, mobile home operators or owners are forbidden from charging tenants fees for the installation of appliances in mobile homes based on the privilege of installation alone. Also forbidden is any restriction on the service, installation or maintenance of appliances, as long as the requirements of applicable building codes are met. 83.764(2).

Indirect fees or charges in the form of required permanent improvements that become part of the real property of the park owner are forbidden. *F.S.* 83.764(5). Also forbidden are any utility charges for electricity or gas by the park owner to the tenants in excess of the public utility's charge to the park owner or operator. 83.764(7).

Entrance fees or the like in the form of "membership" or "initiation" fees may be refundable to the tenant on a proportionate basis. See former *F.S.* 83.68, repealed effective January 1, 1974. If the tenant is not evicted for failure to pay rent or for violation of a federal or state statute or local ordinance, and does not abandon the mobile home or park before the expiration date of the lease, the fee is refundable to the tenant on a prorated basis as set forth in 83.764(6). The refund is due and payable to the tenant within 15 days after the tenant removes the mobile home from the park. 83.764(6)(b).

4. [§15.100] Rules And Regulations Of Mobile Home Parks

In order to be of any effect, all rules and regulations promulgated by park owners or operators must be disclosed in writing to the tenant before his taking occupancy in the park or his signing a lease. *F.S.* 83.764(3)(a). The rules also must be posted in a "conspicuous place" in the park. 83.759(1)(c). The rules and regulations may be changed from time to time, but only after 30 days' written notice is given to all tenants. 83.760(3).

The rules and regulations must be "reasonable." They are presumed to be reasonable if they are "similar" to the rules and regulations customarily found in other mobile home parks in Florida, or if the rule is "not immoderate or excessive." *F.S.* 83.759(1)(c).

Any rule or regulation that denies to a tenant his right to sell his own mobile home within the park, or requires its removal after a sale, is forbidden. Park owners or operators may require their prior approval of a purchaser of a mobile home in a park, but approval cannot be unreasonably withheld if the purchaser otherwise meets all the requirements of a park tenant. They may not charge a fee or commission on the mobile home sale, unless the park owner or operator has acted as a sales agent for the seller pursuant to a written contract. Upon refusal of a park owner to grant permission for a sale to a qualified buyer after three bona fide offers are obtained by the tenant, the next offer may be accepted as a matter of right. *F.S.* 83.765(1).

5. [§15.101] Written Leases

After January 1, 1975 for all mobile home parks with more than ten lots, leases of mobile homes or lots must be in writing in order to be enforceable or terminable by the landlord, unless before occupancy the tenant has been offered a written lease that complies with *F.S.* 83.760. If the tenant does not sign the written lease offered or if he holds over after the expiration of a written lease, the landlord may not terminate the tenancy or evict the tenant except for the reasons set forth in 83.759. See §15.93. Tenants in possession on January 1, 1975 under oral tenancies must be offered bona fide written leases by the landlord, or the landlord thereafter cannot terminate the oral tenancy unless the tenant wrongfully refuses or fails to sign a written lease for more than 60 days. 83.760(2).

All written mobile home lot leases after January 1, 1975 must contain a provision that Part III of *F.S.* Chapter 83 governs the parties' relationship. The leases also must set out the amount of the rent, the security deposit, if any, installation charges, fees, assessments and any other financial obligation of the mobile home owner. *F.S.* 83.760(3).

F.S. 83.7605, added in 1982, provides that each written mobile home lease must contain a description of the type of zoning under which the park operates, the name of the zoning authority and any information available to the mobile home park owner pertaining to future plans for changes in the use of the land comprising the park. The new statute also requires the mobile home park owner to make written disclosure of the foregoing information to any tenant who, after April 2, 1982, fails to enter into a written lease agreement. Finally, the new statute requires the mobile home park owner to provide every owner of a mobile home within the mobile home park notice in writing of any application for a change in zoning of the park within ten days of the filing for the zoning change.

6. [§15.102] Rights And Remedies Of Mobile Home Owners

The tenant may bring a civil action against the park owner or operator who violates any of the provisions of Part III of *F.S.* Chapter 83 in the appropriate court in the county where the violator resides or has his business, or where the violations occur. 83.761(3). The tenant is entitled to obtain damages or equitable relief, and the losing party may be liable for court costs and attorneys' fees. In addition, the state attorneys are authorized to apply to the circuit court in their jurisdictions for an injunction with respect to a violation of the provisions of Part III of Chapter 83 on the basis of a sworn affidavit of any tenant. The circuit court has jurisdiction to grant a permanent or temporary injunction restraining any further violations, whether or not there exists any adequate remedy at law. 83.761(4).

F.S. 83.795, first added in 1980, provides for the right of mobile home owners to peaceably assemble "for any lawful purpose not detrimental to the interests of a majority of the tenants" in the "common areas or recreational area of the mobile home park." The statute, as amended in 1982, provides for the right of mobile home owners "to communicate or assemble among themselves" for the purpose of discussing "any problems relative to the mobile home park." The statute, as amended in 1983, also provides for the right of mobile home owners or tenants to canvass the mobile home owners or tenants who are members of a park association for membership dues.

F.S. 83.796, enacted in 1980, provides for the right of mobile home owners to invite public officers or candidates to appear and speak upon matters of public interest in the common areas or recreational areas of a mobile home park.

The 1983 Florida Legislature provided for what might be called a "statutory right of first refusal" in the hands of tenants of mobile home parks with respect to nonexempt proposed sales of mobile home parks. *F.S.* 83.7730. Certain proposed sales are exempt. 83.7730(5). In order to exercise the rights provided in 83.7730, mobile home owners are authorized to create homeowners associations and provide for the bylaws of those entities. 83.7710, .7720.

7. [§15.103] State Mobile Home Tenant-Landlord Commission

In 1977 the legislature created an administrative agency, the State Mobile Home Tenant-Landlord Commission, to regulate rents and service charges in mobile home parks. The statutory provisions creating the commission, former *F.S.* 83.770—.794, were declared unconstitutional in *Department of Business Regulation v. National Manufactured Housing Federation, Inc.,* 370 So.2d 1132 (Fla. 1979) and subsequently were repealed by the legislature in 1982.

The 1983 Florida Legislature reestablished the Mobile Home Study Commission. The primary function of the recreated commission is to study the mobile home park industry and to make recommendations to the legislature with regard to possible desirability of additional legislation.

J. Forms For Mobile Home Tenancies

1. [§15.104] Three-Day Notice Of Termination For Nonpayment Of Rent For Mobile Home Owner

TO: ....(name of mobile home owner)..........

..........(address and phone number)............

YOU ARE HEREBY notified that you are in default in payment of rent for the premises occupied by you known as Lot ...., ... Mobile Home Park, which is located at ....(address).........., in the sum of $.........., for the period from .... to ....

Demand is hereby made for payment of that sum or possession of the above-described premises within three days after delivery of this demand.

Dated: ....

.... Mobile Home Park

By: _____

2. [§15.105] Complaint For Possession Of Mobile Home Lot For Nonpayment Of Rent

(Party Designation) (Title of Court)

COMPLAINT FOR POSSESSION OF MOBILE HOME LOT FOR NONPAYMENT OF RENT

Plaintiff, ..., sues defendant, ..., and alleges:

1. This is an action for possession of real property in .... County, Florida, pursuant to F.S. 83.7594(4).

2. Plaintiff is the owner of certain real property in .... County, Florida, commonly described as Lot ...., ... Mobile Home Park, which is located at ...., ..., Florida.

3. Plaintiff is a [identify plaintiff].

4. Defendant is a resident of .... County, Florida.

5. Defendant holds possession of the above-described real property pursuant to [describe verbal agreement or attach copy of written agreement].

6. Defendant is in default of its rental agreement with plaintiff by its failure to pay the sum of $............ due on ....(date)..........

7. On ....(date).........., plaintiff furnished to defendant by .... mail/delivery.......... its three-day notice of termination for nonpayment of rent, a true copy of which is attached as Exhibit ....

8. Defendant failed to make payment within three days of delivery of plaintiff's three-day notice of termination and has failed to deliver possession of the subject property.

9. Plaintiff has retained its undersigned attorney and agreed to pay him a reasonable fee for his services in this action.

10. Plaintiff is entitled to the summary procedure of Chapter 51 of the Florida Statutes.

WHEREFORE, plaintiff demands judgment of possession of the real property, costs and attorneys' fees.

        Attorney for Plaintiff
        ....(address and phone number)..........

3. [§15.106] Termination Of Mobile Home Tenancy For Cause

TO: ....(name of mobile home owner)..........

..........(address and phone number)..........

YOU ARE HEREBY notified that on ....(date).......... your tenancy and right of occupancy of Lot ...., ... Mobile Home Park, ..., Florida will terminate.

Your tenancy is being terminated by reason of [describe first violation of the rules and regulations of this mobile home park and state that the violation has endangered the life, health, safety, property or peaceful enjoyment of the mobile home park] as set out below:

OR

Your tenancy is being terminated by reason of [your second violation within a period of 12 months of the rules and regulations of this mobile home park] as set out below:

Dated: ....

.... Mobile Home Park

By: _____

4. [§15.107] Complaint For Possession Of Mobile Home Lot For Violation Of Rules And Regulations

(Party Designation)   (Title of Court)

COMPLAINT FOR POSSESSION OF MOBILE HOME LOT FOR VIOLATION OF RULES AND REGULATIONS

Plaintiff, ..., sues defendant, ..., and alleges:

1. This is an action for possession of real property in .... County, Florida, pursuant to F.S. 83.7594(4).

2. Plaintiff is the owner of certain real property in .... County, Florida, commonly described as Lot ...., ... Mobile Home Park, which is located at ...., ..., Florida.

3. Plaintiff is a [identify plaintiff].

4. Defendant is a resident of .... County, Florida.

5. Defendant holds possession of the above-described real property pursuant to [describe verbal agreement or attach a copy of written agreement].

6. Plaintiff maintains rules and regulations governing the mobile home park, a copy of which were furnished to defendant by plaintiff before entering the rental agreement with defendant and a copy of which was posted conspicuously in the mobile home park, namely, ...

7. Defendant has violated rules and regulations of plaintiff's mobile home park duly enacted and presently and at all relevant times in effect, a copy being attached as Exhibit ...., as follows:

[describe violations and refer to rule and regulation violated]

8. Defendant's violation of the rules and regulations has endangered the life, health, safety, property or peaceful enjoyment of the mobile home park and its occupants.

OR

8. Defendant has violated the rules and regulations on at least two occasions within a 12-month period, the first violation occurring on .... (date).........., and the second violation occurring on .... (date)..........

9. On ....(date).........., defendant was notified of the grounds on which he was to be evicted at least 30 days before the date he was required to vacate, as shown by notice, a copy of which is attached as Exhibit ...., which was furnished to defendant by .... mail/delivery.......... on ....(date).........., but defendant has failed and refused to deliver possession of the subject real estate.

10. Plaintiff is entitled to the summary procedure set out in Chapter 51 of the Florida Statutes.

11. Plaintiff has retained its undersigned attorney and agreed to pay him a reasonable fee for his services in this action.

WHEREFORE, plaintiff demands judgment of possession of the real property, costs and attorneys' fees.

                                                                              _____
                                                                                        Attorney for Plaintiff
                                                                              ....(address and phone number).........

5. [§15.108] Notice Of Termination Of Tenancy
         By Reason Of Change Of Use

TO: ....(name of mobile home owner)..........

           ....(address and phone number)............

YOU ARE HEREBY notified that your tenancy of Lot ...., ... Mobile Home Park, which is located at ....(address).........., will terminate on ....(date).......... by reason of a change in use of the subject property from mobile home lot rentals to ....

You are advised of your need to secure other accommodations as of that date.

.... Mobile Home Park

By: _____

COMMENT: The mobile home park owner must give all tenants at least six months' notice, or longer if provided for in a valid lease, of the projected change of use and of their need to secure other accommodations. *F.S.* 83.759(1)(d).

6. [§15.109] Complaint For Possession Of Mobile Home Lot After Change Of Use

(Party Designation)   **(Title of Court)**

COMPLAINT FOR POSSESSION OF MOBILE HOME LOT AFTER CHANGE OF USE

Plaintiff, ..., sues defendant, ..., and alleges:

1. This is an action for possession of real property in .... County, Florida, pursuant to F.S. 83.7594(4).

2. Plaintiff is the owner of certain real property in .... County, Florida, commonly described as Lot ...., ... Mobile Home Park, which is located at ....(address)...........

3. Plaintiff is a [identify plaintiff].

4. Defendant is a resident of .... County, Florida.

5. Defendant holds possession of the above-described real property pursuant to [describe verbal agreement or attach copy of written agreement].

6. By reason of a change in use of ....the subject mobile home park/a portion of the subject mobile home park..........., affecting the subject real property, plaintiff furnished its notice of termination to defendant on ....(date)..........., by ....mail/delivery..........., a copy being attached as Exhibit ...., but defendant has failed and refused to deliver possession.

7. Plaintiff is entitled to the summary procedure of Chapter 51 of the Florida Statutes.

8. Plaintiff has retained its undersigned attorney and agreed to pay him a reasonable fee for his services in this action.

WHEREFORE, plaintiff demands judgment of possession of the real property, costs and attorneys' fees.

                                   Attorney for Plaintiff
                              ....(address and phone number)..........

7. [§15.110] Termination Of Tenancy On Twelve Months' Notice And Eviction Of Mobile Home And Mobile Home Owner

TO: ....(name of mobile home owners)..........

      ....(address and phone number)..........

YOU ARE HEREBY notified pursuant to F.S. 83.759(1)(e) that your tenancy of Lot ...., ... Mobile Home Park, which is located at ....(address).......... will terminate on [insert date at least one year from date of service].

You will be required as of that date to remove your mobile home and vacate the premises. .... Mobile Home Park will pay the actual cost of relocating your mobile home in a comparable mobile home park within a reasonable distance from your present location. In the event your mobile home cannot be relocated, however, you will be required to place your mobile home for sale on the open market within 20 days of service of this notice as provided in F.S. 83.759(1)(e)2.

Dated: ....

                                      .... **Mobile Home Park**

                                By: _____

COMMENT: The mobile home park owner may elect to evict the mobile home, the mobile home owner or both. If the mobile home park owner elects to evict solely the mobile home owner, he may either elect to purchase the mobile home at its fair market value or force the mobile home owner to place it for sale on the open market.

8. [§15.111] Termination Of Tenancy On Twelve Months' Notice And Eviction Of Mobile Home Owner

TO: ....(name of mobile home owner)..........

............(address and phone number)............

YOU ARE HEREBY notified that pursuant to F.S. 83.759(1)(e) your tenancy of Lot ...., ... Mobile Home Park, which is located at ....(address).........., will terminate on ....(date)..........

You will be required as of that date to vacate the premises.

You are further notified that the .... Mobile Home Park has elected to ....purchase your mobile home for $.......... 60 days after service of this notice, and you are required by law to respond to this offer within ten days/require you to place your mobile home for sale on the open market 20 days after service of this notice..........

Dated: ....

.... Mobile Home Park

By: _____

9. [§15.112] Complaint For Possession Of Mobile Home Lot After Twelve Months' Notice (Eviction Of Mobile Home And Mobile Home Owner)

(Party Designation)   (Title of Court)

COMPLAINT FOR POSSESSION OF MOBILE HOME LOT AFTER TWELVE MONTHS' NOTICE

Plaintiff, ..., sues defendant, ..., and alleges:

1. This is an action for possession of real property in .... County, Florida, pursuant to F.S. 83.7594(4).

2. Plaintiff is the owner of certain real property located in .... County, Florida, commonly described as Lot ...., ... Mobile Home Park, which is located at ....(address)..........

3. Plaintiff is a [identify plaintiff].

4. Defendant is a resident of .... County, Florida.

5. Defendant holds possession of the above-described real property pursuant to [describe verbal agreement or attach copy of written agreement].

6. Plaintiff furnished its notice of termination to defendant on ....(date).......... by ....mail/delivery.........., a copy of which is attached as Exhibit ....

7. Plaintiff offered to pay the actual cost of relocating the defendant's mobile home in a comparable mobile home park within a reasonable distance from .... Mobile Home Park as follows:

[describe offered location]

OR

7. Defendant's mobile home could not be relocated within a comparable mobile home park a reasonable distance from .... Mobile Home Park and plaintiff, therefore, directed defendant to place his mobile home for sale on the open market within 20 days of receipt of the notice set forth in paragraph 6.

8. Notwithstanding defendant's receipt of the notice described in paragraph 6, defendant has failed and refused to deliver possession of the subject real estate.

9. Plaintiff is entitled to the summary procedure of Chapter 51 of the Florida Statutes.

10. Plaintiff has retained its undersigned attorney and agreed to pay him a reasonable fee for his services in this action.

WHEREFORE, plaintiff demands judgment of possession of the real property, costs and attorneys' fees.

_____
Attorney for Plaintiff
..........(address and phone number)..........

10. [§15.113] Complaint For Possession Of Mobile Home Lot After Twelve Months' Notice (Eviction Of Mobile Home Owner)

(Party Designation) (Title of Court)

COMPLAINT FOR POSSESSION OF MOBILE HOME LOT
AFTER TWELVE MONTHS' NOTICE

Plaintiff, ..., sues defendant, ..., and alleges:

1. This is an action for possession of real property in .... County, Florida, pursuant to F.S. 83.7594(4).

2. Plaintiff is the owner of certain real property in .... County, Florida, located at ...., ..., Florida.

3. Plaintiff is a [identify plaintiff].

4. Defendant is a resident of .... County, Florida.

5. Defendant holds possession of the above-described real property pursuant to [describe verbal agreement or attach copy of written agreement].

6. Plaintiff furnished its notice of termination to defendant on ....(date).......... by ....mail/delivery.........., a copy of which is attached as Exhibit ...., directing the defendant to vacate the premises on .... (date).........., and ....notifying the defendant of plaintiff's election to purchase defendant's mobile home for $........../further directing the defendant to place his mobile home for sale on the open market..........

7. Notwithstanding defendant's receipt of the notice described in paragraph 6, defendant has failed and refused to deliver possession of the subject real estate and [describe defendant's failure to sell mobile home or place it for sale on the open market, if appropriate].

8. Plaintiff is entitled to the summary procedure set out in Chapter 51 of the Florida Statutes.

9. Plaintiff has retained its undersigned attorney and agreed to pay him a reasonable fee for his services in this action.

WHEREFORE, plaintiff demands judgment of possession of the real property, costs and attorneys' fees.

Attorney for Plaintiff
..........(address and phone number)..........

11. [§15.114] Notice Of Termination Of Tenancy For Conviction Of Violation Of Law Or Ordinance

TO: ....(name of mobile home owner)..........

..........(address and phone number)............

YOU ARE HEREBY notified that on ....(date).......... your tenancy and right of occupancy of Lot ...., ... Mobile Home Park, located at ...., ..., Florida will terminate.

Your tenancy is terminated by reason of your conviction of the following law or ordinance:

[describe conviction]

Your violation of the described law or ordinance has been deemed detrimental to the health, safety or welfare of other dwellers of .... Mobile Home Park.

Dated: ....

.... Mobile Home Park

By: _____

12. [§15.115] Complaint For Possession Of Mobile Home Lot For Conviction Of Violation Of Law Or Ordinance

(Party Designation)   (Title of Court)

COMPLAINT FOR POSSESSION OF MOBILE HOME LOT FOR CONVICTION OF VIOLATION OF LAW OR ORDINANCE

Plaintiff, ..., sues defendant, ..., and alleges:

1. This is an action for possession of real property in .... County, Florida, pursuant to F.S. 83.7594(4).

2. Plaintiff is the owner of certain real property in .... County, Florida, commonly described as Lot ...., ... Mobile Home Park, which is located at ....(address)..........

3. Plaintiff is a [identify plaintiff].

4. Defendant is a resident of .... County, Florida.

5. Defendant holds possession of the above-described real property pursuant to [describe verbal agreement or attach copy of written agreement].

6. On or about ....(date).........., defendant was convicted of a violation of a federal or state law or local ordinance deemed detrimental to the health, safety or welfare of other dwellers in the subject mobile home park within the meaning of F.S. 83.759 in that [describe conviction].

7. On ....(date).........., plaintiff served on defendant its notice of termination by ....mail/delivery.........., a copy of which is attached as Exhibit ....

8. Plaintiff is entitled to the summary procedure set out in Chapter 51 of the Florida Statutes.

9. Plaintiff has retained its undersigned attorney and has agreed to pay him a reasonable fee for his services in this action.

WHEREFORE, plaintiff demands judgment of possession of the real property, costs and attorneys' fees.

_____
Attorney for Plaintiff
..........(address and phone number)..........

13. [§15.116] Final Judgment On Default

(Party Designation)   (Title of Court)

FINAL DEFAULT JUDGMENT FOR POSSESSION

THIS ACTION was heard by the court and a default having been entered against the defendant and the court being otherwise fully advised, it is

ADJUDGED that

1. Plaintiff recover from defendant the possession of the following-described premises, situated in .... County, Florida:

[description of property]

for which let writ of possession issue 30 days from the date of this judgment.

2. Plaintiff recover from the defendant the costs expended in this action, taxed in the sum of $............ for which let execution issue.

ORDERED at ...., ... County, Florida, on ....(date)..........

County Court Judge

Copies furnished to: ....

14. [§15.117] Final Judgment After Trial

(Party Designation)   (Title of Court)

FINAL JUDGMENT FOR POSSESSION

THIS ACTION was heard by the court. On the evidence presented, it is

ADJUDGED that

1. Plaintiff recover from defendant the possession of the following-described premises, situated in .... County, Florida:

[description of property]

for which let writ of possession issue 30 days from the date of this judgment.

2. Plaintiff recover from defendant the costs expended in this action hereby taxed in the sum of $............, for which let execution issue.

ORDERED at ...., ... County, Florida, on ....(date)..........

County Court Judge

Copies furnished to: ....

15. [§15.118] Petition For Determination Of Fair Market Value

(Party Designation)   (Title of Court)

PETITION FOR DETERMINATION OF FAIR MARKET VALUE

The petition of .... shows:

1. This is an application for determination of the fair market value of a mobile home pursuant to F.S. 83.759(1)(e)3.

2. ....Petitioner/Respondent.......... is [describe].

3. ....Petitioner/Respondent.......... is a resident of .... County, Florida.

4. ....Petitioner/Respondent.......... is a resident of .... Mobile Home Park and the owner of a mobile home more particularly described as follows:

[describe mobile home and provide address]

5. On ....(date).........., ...petitioner/respondent.......... furnished ....respondent/petitioner.......... with a notice of termination and within 60 days offered to purchase ....respondent's/petitioner's.......... mobile home for $..........

6. The offer of purchase was rejected and the petitioner and the respondent cannot agree on the fair market value of the above-described mobile home.

WHEREFORE, petitioner requests that this court take jurisdiction of this cause and determine the fair market value of the above-described mobile home.

                              Attorney for ....Petitioner/Respondent..........
                              ....(address and phone number)................

IV. SELF-STORAGE FACILITY ACT

A. [§15.119] In General

F.S. 83.801—.809 constitutes the "Self-Storage Facility Act" (hereafter referred to as the Act). This brief enactment was originally passed in 1979 as the "Mini-Self-Storage Landlord and Tenant Act" and was renamed and considerably amended in 1982. It applies only to real property "used for the purpose of renting or leasing individual storage space to tenants who are to have access to such space for the purpose of storing and removing personal property." 83.803(1). It does not apply if the owner issues any warehouse receipt, bill of lading or other document of title for the personal property stored.

B.   [§15.120] Liens

The distinctive feature of the Act is the owner's lien for rent, which, unlike the lien of the commercial landlord, *F.S.* 83.08, or the lien of the residential landlord, 713.691, is both possessory and self-effectuating. The lien applies to all personal property, whether or not owned by the tenant, located in a self-storage facility. The priority of the lien is the same as the commercial landlord's lien under 83.08. In the event of default, however, the owner must give notice to persons who hold perfected security interests. 83.805.

C.   [§15.121] Denial Of Access

The Act authorizes an owner to deny access to a tenant of a self-storage facility without notice in the event of default in payment of rent after five days from date the rent is due. *F.S.* 83.8055.

D.   [§15.122] Enforcement Of Liens

The Act contemplates that the lien may be enforced in the following fashion. The tenant must be given written notice, delivered in person or by registered mail to the tenant's last known address and conspicuously posted at the self-storage facility, providing an itemized statement of the owner's claim. The notice also must include a description of the personal property as provided in the rental agreement, a demand for payment within a specified time not less than 14 days after delivery of the notice and a conspicuous statement that unless the claim is paid within the time stated in the notice the personal property will be advertised for sale or other disposition, and will be sold or otherwise disposed of at a specified time and place. The name, street address and telephone number of the owner must be included in addition to the foregoing. *F.S.* 83.806.

E.   [§15.123] Form For Notice Enforcing Lien

TO: ....(name of self-storage facility tenant)..........

......................(last known address)......................

YOU ARE HEREBY notified that you are in default in rent due for the self-storage facility known as and located at Unit ...., ...,

...................., Florida, in the sum of $.........., representing rent for the premises for the months of ....(date).......... through ....(date).........., at the rate of $.......... per month, which is due on the first of each month.

The following personal property is currently stored within the above-referenced premises:

Demand is hereby made for the sum of $.......... within days of the service of this notice upon you. Payment of that sum must be made in full at the office of .... Self-Storage Facility, ..., ..., Florida.

UNLESS THE ABOVE SUM IS PAID WITHIN FOURTEEN DAYS OF THE SERVICE OF THIS NOTICE UPON YOU, ALL PERSONAL PROPERTY LOCATED ON THE DEMISED PREMISES WILL BE ADVERTISED FOR SALE OR OTHER DISPOSITION, AND WILL BE SOLD OR OTHERWISE DISPOSED OF AT .... O'CLOCK, ON ....(date).........., AT ...., ..., FLORIDA.

This notice is given you pursuant to F.S. 83.806.

.... Self-Storage Facility
..........(address and phone number)..........

This notice was served upon the person owing the rent on ....(date).........., by:

_____ Personal delivery.

_____ Registered mail to last known address.

By: _____

Dated: ....

OR

This notice was posted at the self-storage facility on ....(date)..........

By: _____

Dated: ....

F. [§15.124] Advertisement

After expiration of the time given in the notice, an advertisement of the sale or other disposition must be published once a week for two consecutive weeks in a newspaper of general circulation where the self-storage facility is located. *F.S.* 83.806(4). The advertisement must include a brief description of the personal property, the address of the self-storage facility and the name of the tenant, and the time, place and manner of the sale or other disposition. The sale or other disposition cannot take place sooner than 15 days after the first publication.

G. [§15.125] Form For Notice Of Public Sale

NOTICE OF PUBLIC SALE

Notice of public sale or auction of the contents of the following self-storage units located at ...., ..., Florida, will be conducted at ...., ..., Florida, at ....(time)..........

The unit numbers, names of tenants, and general description of the personal property contained in the units are as follows:

UNIT NO.	TENANT NAME	DESCRIPTION
....	....	....
....	....	....
....	....	....

H. [§15.126] Other Matters

The Act provides that before any sale or other disposition of personal property, the tenant may pay the amount necessary to satisfy the lien and the reasonable expenses incurred and thereby redeem the personal property. Upon receipt of the payment, the owner must return the property to the tenant and, in so doing, the owner incurs no liability to any person with respect to the personal property. *F.S.* 83.806(6).

The Act also provides for disposition of the proceeds from the sale. *F.S.* 83.806(8).

V. DISPOSITION OF PERSONAL PROPERTY LANDLORD AND TENANT ACT

A. [§15.127] In General

In 1983, the Florida Legislature enacted the Disposition of Personal Property Landlord and Tenant Act, *F.S.* 83.821—.833. The Act applies to all tenancies to which Parts I and II of Chapter 83 are applicable. 83.822(1). The Act provides for an optional procedure for the disposition of personal property that remains on the premises after a tenancy has been terminated or has expired and the premises have been vacated by the tenant through eviction, surrender, abandonment or otherwise. 83.822(2).

Landlords often are confronted with the problem of what to do with apparently discarded items left behind by tenants who vacate rental premises. While the landlord may obtain lawful possession of the rental premises fairly easily by court order in an action for removal of tenant or by surrender or abandonment (see *F.S.* 83.05, .59), these processes do not vest legal title in the landlord with respect to personal property that may be left behind. Personal property usually is removed by the sheriff in actions for removal of tenants from residential premises and generally placed on the nearest public right-of-way. See, *e.g., McCready v. Booth*, 398 So.2d 1000 (Fla. 5th DCA 1981). Landlords who have had personal property of former tenants removed from their premises pursuant to writs of possession generally have been afforded protection by the court against claims for damages sustained by tenants. *McCready v. Booth, supra.*

The sheriff in most counties usually will not remove personal property from commercial premises and will execute writs of possession with respect to those premises simply by changing the locks on the doors. Commercial landlords particularly, therefore, have had to wrestle with the problem of dealing with personal property left on the rental premises. The methods for dealing with that property have included distress, *F.S.* 83.11—.19, levy after judgment for rent or monetary damages and execution sales, and foreclosure of the landlord's lien. Each of these procedures, however, involves considerable time and expense. Landlords also have sought to deal with the problem of abandoned personal property by means of specific lease provisions. See, *e.g., Jacobs v. Kirk*, 223 So.2d 795 (Fla. 4th DCA 1969). There usually is some considerable degree of uncertainty in relying upon the notion of "abandonment," however, and the issue of whether a given set of facts constitutes an abandonment is one ultimately to be determined by the jury or the trier of fact. See *Rogers v. Parker*, 241 So.2d 428 (Fla. 2d DCA 1970).

The new Act provides for an alternate procedure that is less time consuming and costly than the judicial procedures previously available and provides for a method for dealing with the rights of third parties who generally will not be parties to the lease.

The procedure set out in the Act is optional and, if the procedure is not followed, nothing in the Act affects the rights and liabilities of the landlord, former tenant or any other person. *F.S.* 83.822(2), (4).

B.   [§15.128] Notification Of Tenant And Other Persons

If the personal property remains on the premises after a tenancy has been terminated or has expired and the premises have been vacated by the tenant through eviction or otherwise, the landlord is required to give written notice to the tenant and to any other person the landlord reasonably believes to be the owner of the property. *F.S.* 83.825(1). The term "owner" for the purpose of the Act means "any person other than the landlord who has any right, title, or interest in [the] personal property." 83.823(2). The notice must describe the personal property, must advise the person to be notified that reasonable costs of storage may be charged before the property is returned and must state where the property may be claimed and the date before which the claim must be made. The date specified in the notice must be not less than 10 days after the notice is personally delivered or, if mailed, not less than 15 days after the notice is mailed. 83.825(2). The notice must be personally served or sent by first-class mail to the person to be served at his last known address and, if there is reason to believe that the notice sent to that address will not be received by that person, to such other address, if any, known to the landlord where the person may reasonably be expected to receive the notice. 83.825(3).

C.   [§15.129] Form For Notice To Former Tenant Of Right
       To Reclaim Abandoned Property
       (Value Less Than $250)

NOTICE OF RIGHT TO RECLAIM ABANDONED PROPERTY

TO: ....(name of former tenant)...........

   ....(address of former tenant)..........

   When you vacated the premises at ....(address of premises, including room or apartment number, if any)..........., the following personal property remained: ....(insert description of personal property)..........

You may claim this property ....(address where property may be claimed)..........

Unless you pay the reasonable cost of storage and advertising, if any, for all the above-described property and take possession of the property that you claim, not later than ....(insert date not less than 10 days after notice is personally delivered or, if mailed, not less than 15 days after notice is deposited in the mail).........., this property may be disposed of pursuant to F.S. 83.831.

Because this property is believed to be worth less than $250, it may be kept, sold or destroyed without further notice if you fail to reclaim it within the time indicated above.

Dated: ....

Signature of Landlord
..........(type of print name of landlord)..........
..............(address and phone number)............

D.   [§15.130]   Form For Notice To Former Tenant Of Right To Reclaim Abandoned Property (Value $250 Or More)

NOTICE OF RIGHT TO RECLAIM ABANDONED PROPERTY

TO: ....(name of former tenant)............

..........(address of former tenant)..........

When you vacated the premises at ....(address of premises, including room or apartment number, if any)........., the following personal property remained: ....(insert description of personal property)..........

You may claim this property at ....(address where property may be claimed)..........

Unless you pay the reasonable cost of storage and advertising, if any, for all the above-described property and take possession of the property that you claim, not later than ....(insert date not less than 10 days after notice is personally delivered or, if mailed, not less than 15 days after notice is deposited in the mail).........., this property may be disposed of pursuant to F.S. 83.831.

If you fail to reclaim the property, it will be sold at a public sale after notice of the sale has been given by publication. You have the right to bid on the property at this sale. After the property is sold and the cost of storage, advertising and sale is deducted, the remaining money will be paid over to the county. You may claim the remaining money at any time within one year after the county receives the money.

Dated: ....

Signature Of Landlord
..........(type or print name of landlord)..........
.............(address and phone number).............

E. [§15.131] Form For Notice To Person Other Than Tenant Of Right To Reclaim Abandoned Property (Value Less Than $250)

NOTICE OF RIGHT TO RECLAIM ABANDONED PROPERTY

TO: ....(name)..........

..........(address)........

When ....(name of former tenant).......... vacated the premises at ....(address of premises, including room or apartment number, if any).........., the following personal property remained: ....(insert description of personal property)..........

If you own any of this property, you may claim it at ....(address where property may be claimed).......... Unless you pay the reasonable cost of storage and advertising, if any, and take possession of the property to which you are entitled, not later than ....(insert date not less than 10 days after notice is personally delivered or, if mailed, not less than 15 days after notice is deposited in the mail).........., this property may be disposed of pursuant to F.S. 83.831.

Because this property is believed to be worth less than $250, it may be kept, sold or destroyed without further notice if you fail to reclaim it within the time indicated above.

Dated: ....

Signature of Landlord
.........(type or print name of landlord)..........
............(address and phone number).............

F. [§15.132] Form For Notice To Person Other Than Tenant Of Right To Reclaim Abandoned Property (Value $250 Or More)

NOTICE OF RIGHT TO RECLAIM ABANDONED PROPERTY

TO: ....(name)...........

..........(address)..........

When ....(name of former tenant).......... vacated the premises at ....(address of premises, including room or apartment number, if any).........., the following personal property remained: ....(insert description of personal property)..........

If you own any of this property, you may claim it at ....(address where property may be claimed).......... Unless you pay the reasonable cost of storage and advertising, if any, and take possession of the property to which you are entitled not later than ....(insert date not less than 10 days after notice is personally delivered or, if mailed, not less than 15 days after notice is deposited in the mail).........., this property may be disposed of pursuant to F.S. 83.831.

If you fail to reclaim the property, it will be sold at a public sale after notice of the sale has been given by publication. You have the right to bid on the property at this sale. After the property is sold and the cost of storage, advertising and sale is deducted, the remaining money will be paid over to the county. You may claim the remaining money at any time within one year after the county receives the money.

Dated: ....

_____
Signature of Landlord
..........(type or print name of landlord).........
............(address and phone number).............

G. [§15.133] Storage Of Abandoned Property

The personal property described in the notice may be left on the vacated premises or be stored by the landlord in a place of safekeeping. *F.S.* 83.828. The landlord is required to exercise reasonable care in storing the property, but is not liable to the tenant or other person for any loss unless caused by his deliberate or negligent act. 83.828.

H.   [§15.134] Release Of Personal Property

The personal property described in the notice must be released by the landlord to the former tenant, or at the landlord's option, to any person reasonably believed by the landlord to be its owner, upon payment of reasonable costs of storage and advertising, provided that person takes possession of the property no later than the date specified in the notice. *F.S.* 83.829(1).

When the notice indicates that a public sale will take place, a former tenant may redeem the property at any time prior to the sale as long as he pays the reasonable costs of storage, advertising and sale incurred prior to the time the property is withdrawn from sale. *F.S.* 83.829(2).

I.   [§15.135] Sale Of Abandoned Property

If the personal property is not released pursuant to *F.S.* 83.829, it must be sold at public sale by competitive bidding. If the landlord reasonably believes that the total value of the property not released is less than $250, however, he may retain the property for his own use or dispose of it in any manner he chooses. 83.831(1).

Notice of the time and place of the public sale must be published once a week for two consecutive weeks in a newspaper of general circulation. The sale must be at the nearest suitable location to the place the personal property is held or stored. The advertisement must include a description of the goods, the name of the former tenant, and the time and place of sale. The sale must take place at least ten days after the first publication. The last publication shall be not less than five days before the sale is to be held. *F.S.* 83.831(2).

After deducting the costs of storage, advertising and sale, any balance of the sale proceeds that are not claimed by the former tenant or the owner must be paid into the treasury of the county in which the sale took place not later than 30 days after the sale. *F.S.* 83.831(4).

J.   [§15.136] Nonliability Of Landlord

If the landlord releases the property to the former tenant, the landlord is not liable to any person with respect to the property. *F.S.* 83.832(1). If the landlord releases the property to any person other than the former tenant who the landlord reasonably believes to be the owner of the property, the landlord is not liable to any person to whom he has given notice or to any person to whom notice was not given unless that person proves that, prior to releasing the property, the landlord believed or reasonably should have believed that the person had an interest in the property and also that the landlord knew or should have known the address of that person. 83.832(2). When the property is sold in accordance with 83.831, the landlord is afforded similar immunities. 83.832(3).

INDEX TO FLORIDA STATUTES

Statute	Section
26.012	15.4
26.012(2)(c)	15.4
26.012(2)(g)	15.4
34.01(1)(c)2	15.44, 15.46
34.011	15.4, 15.44
34.011(1)	15.4
34.011(2)	15.4, 15.48, 15.82, 15.86
45.031(1)	5.41, 5.44
47.011	15.5
ch. 48	15.93
48.183	15.93
49.041	1.18
49.071	1.18
ch. 51	15.35, 15.94—.95
51.011	15.9, 15.11, 15.35, 15.43—.44, 15.48, 15.51—.52, 15.54, 15.87, 15.93
51.011(1)	15.44, 15.52
51.011(4)	15.96
56.16	15.27
64.081	4.29
65.061(2)	1.25
ch. 82	15.1—.2, 15.36, 15.48
82.02	15.48
82.04	15.48
82.05	15.48
82.061	15.51
82.071	15.49, 15.53—.55
82.081	15.54
82.091	15.56
82.101	15.56
ch. 83	15.1—.2, 15.11, 15.46, 15.61—.62, 15.97, 15.101—.102
83.001—.251	15.1
83.001	15.70
83.01	15.6—.7
83.02	15.6, 15.70
83.03	15.7, 15.9, 15.70
83.04	15.10
83.05	15.11, 15.127
83.05(3)	15.11
83.051	15.87

83.06	15.9
83.06(1)	15.73
83.08	15.12, 15.15, 15.27, 15.120
83.08(1)	15.16, 15.87
83.08(2)	15.16, 15.27, 15.87
83.09	15.15
83.10	15.14
83.11—.135	15.18
83.11—.19	15.17—.18, 15.127
83.11	15.5, 15.19
83.12	15.23
83.13	15.23
83.14	15.28, 15.31
83.15	15.27
83.18	15.31
83.19	15.33
83.19(3)	15.34
83.20—.251	15.35, 15.49
83.20	15.2, 15.9, 15.36—.37, 15.40, 15.46
83.20(2)	15.11, 15.37—.38, 15.42
83.21—.251	15.4, 15.10—.11
83.21	15.5, 15.9, 15.11, 15.37, 15.42
83.22	15.43, 15.51, 15.93
83.22(2)	15.43
83.40—.63	15.1, 15.61
83.41	15.62
83.42(1)	15.62
83.42(2)	15.62
83.42(3)	15.62
83.42(4)	15.62
83.42(5)	15.62
83.43(2)	15.62
83.43(2)(b)	15.62
83.43(2)(c)	15.62
83.43(4)	15.87
83.43(6)	15.76
83.43(9)	15.76
83.43(10)	15.62
83.43(11)	15.76
83.43(12)	15.76
83.45	15.64—.65
83.45(1)	15.65
83.45(2)	15.65
83.46	15.68, 15.70
83.46(1)	15.68, 15.73
83.46(2)	15.69
83.46(3)	15.62, 15.69

83.47	15.64, 15.66, 15.78
83.47(1)(a)	15.80—.81
83.47(1)(b)	15.66
83.48	15.67, 15.82, 15.96
83.49	15.76
83.49(1)	15.76
83.49(2)	15.76
83.49(3)(a)	15.77, 15.88
83.49(3)(b)	15.75, 15.77
83.49(3)(c)	15.77
83.49(5)	15.77
83.49(7)	15.77
83.49(8)	15.77
83.49(9)	15.76
83.50	15.76
83.50(1)	15.75, 15.83
83.50(2)	15.75
83.51	15.63, 15.84
83.51(1)	15.66, 15.78, 15.80, 15.83—.84, 15.95
83.51(1)(b)	15.66, 15.78, 15.80
83.51(2)	15.66
83.51(2)(a)	15.78
83.51(2)(a)1	15.78
83.51(2)(c)	15.78
83.51(4)	15.78
83.52	15.80, 15.88
83.53(1)	15.81
83.53(2)	15.81
83.53(2)(d)	15.81
83.53(3)	15.81
83.535	15.82
83.54	15.80, 15.82, 15.86
83.54(2)(a)	15.89
83.54(2)(b)	15.89
83.55	15.75, 15.79, 15.82
83.56	15.83
83.56(1)	15.75, 15.83
83.56(1)(a)	15.83
83.56(1)(b)	15.83
83.56(2)	15.73, 15.88—.89, 15.91
83.56(2)(a)	15.88
83.56(2)(b)	15.88
83.56(3)	15.73, 15.88, 15.91
83.56(4)	15.71, 15.83—.84
83.56(5)	15.88
83.56(6)	15.88
83.57	15.70—.71, 15.77

83.57(3)	15.68
83.58	15.73
83.59	15.73, 15.127
83.59(2)	15.93
83.59(3)(b)	15.92
83.59(3)(c)	15.92
83.59(4)	15.93
83.60(1)	15.75, 15.84, 15.95
83.60(2)	15.84, 15.95
83.61	15.84
83.62	15.96
83.625	15.9, 15.94, 15.96
83.63	15.85
83.64	15.84, 15.95
83.64(2)	15.95
83.64(3)	15.95
83.66	15.82
83.750—.797	15.1, 15.62
83.751	15.62, 15.97
83.759	15.98, 15.101
83.759(1)(a)	15.98
83.759(1)(b)	15.98
83.759(1)(c)	15.98, 15.100
83.759(1)(d)	15.98, 15.108
83.759(1)(e)	15.98
83.7594	15.98
83.7597	15.98
83.760	15.101
83.760(2)	15.98, 15.101
83.760(3)	15.100—.101
83.760(4)	15.98
83.7605	15.101
83.761(3)	15.102
83.761(4)	15.102
83.764(1)	15.99
83.764(2)	15.99
83.764(3)(a)	15.99—.100
83.764(3)(b)	15.99
83.764(3)(c)	15.99
83.764(4)	15.99
83.764(5)	15.99
83.764(6)	15.99
83.764(6)(b)	15.99
83.764(7)	15.99
83.765(1)	15.100
83.770	15.97
83.7710	15.102

83.7720	15.102
83.7730	15.102
83.7730(5)	15.102
83.795	15.102
83.796	15.102
83.801—.809	15.1, 15.119
83.803(1)	15.119
83.805	15.120
83.8055	15.121
83.806	15.122
83.806(4)	15.124
83.806(6)	15.126
83.806(8)	15.126
83.821—.833	15.1, 15.92, 15.127
83.822(1)	15.127
83.822(2)	15.127
83.822(4)	15.127
83.823(2)	15.128
83.825(1)	15.128
83.825(2)	15.128
83.825(3)	15.128
83.828	15.133
83.829	15.135
83.829(1)	15.134
83.829(2)	15.134
83.831	15.136
83.831(1)	15.135
83.831(2)	15.135
83.831(4)	15.135
83.832(1)	15.136
83.832(2)	15.136
83.832(3)	15.136
85.011(5)	15.87
85.011(5)(b)	15.87
85.031	15.87
ch. 86	15.58
90.951(4)(a)	8.21
90.953	8.21
90.954	8.5
90.954(1)	8.5
92.40	15.78
95.031(1)	5.12
95.11(2)(c)	5.12
95.11(3)(a)	10.10
95.11(3)(c)	10.10
95.11(3)(o)	14.7
95.281	5.12

95.281(1)(b)	5.12
193.032(2)	12.4
197.281	11.17
197.281(3)	11.17
509.261	15.77
581.031(15)	12.4
607.034(5)	5.5
607.304(2)(g)	5.5
607.324	5.5
620.26	5.5
627.736(3)	15.60
627.7372	15.60
672.302	15.65
ch. 679	15.16
679.310	15.87
ch. 683	15.37
692.05	5.5
692.05(1)(b)	5.5
692.05(2)(a)	5.5
692.05(4)	5.5
692.05(7)	5.5
704.01(2)	12.10
704.04	12.10
ch. 712	1.31
712.01(3)	1.31
713.01(10)	6.3, 6.11
713.01(19)	6.11
713.02(5)	6.2
713.03	6.3
713.03(3)	6.6—.7
713.04	6.7
713.06(1)	6.7, 6.11
713.06(2)	6.7, 6.21
713.06(2)(a)	6.7, 6.11
713.06(3)	6.6
713.08(4)(c)	6.3
713.22(1)	6.10
713.23	6.21, 6.32
713.23(1)(d)	6.21, 6.32
713.23(1)(e)	6.21, 6.32
713.23(1)(f)	6.21
713.29	6.14
713.31(2)(c)	6.25
713.37	6.1
713.50	15.87
713.69(1)	15.87
713.691	15.87, 15.120

713.691(1)	15.87
713.691(2)	15.15, 15.87
713.691(3)	15.18, 15.49, 15.87
733.308	1.26
865.09	15.46

INDEX TO FLORIDA RULES OF CIVIL PROCEDURE

Rule	Section
1.010	15.44
1.060(a)	15.29
1.090	15.35, 15.37, 15.45
1.090(a)	15.52
1.110(c)	15.29
1.110(d)	15.29
1.130	15.46
1.140(a)	15.44
1.170	15.29
1.170(j)	15.44
1.430	15.54
1.430(d)	15.30
1.500	15.23
1.500(b)	15.44
1.500(e)	15.44
1.550	15.96
1.550(b)	15.96
1.580	5.53
1.580(a)	5.53
Form 1.909	15.23
Form 1.915	15.96
Form 1.938	15.50
Form 1.940	3.12
Form 1.947	15.42
Form 1.960	15.22
Form 1.993	15.32

INDEX TO UNITED STATES CODE

Code	Section
7 U.S.C.	15.1—.2
11 U.S.C.	15.1—.2
11 U.S.C. §§101—1330	15.3
11 U.S.C. §362	15.3
11 U.S.C. §363(k)(1)	15.3
11 U.S.C. §365(b)(1)	15.3
11 U.S.C. §365(b)(3)	15.3
11 U.S.C. §365(d)(1)	15.3
11 U.S.C. §365(d)(2)	15.3
11 U.S.C. §502(b)(7)	15.3
11 U.S.C. §545	15.3
11 U.S.C. §547	15.3
11 U.S.C. §554	15.3
13 U.S.C.	15.3
26 U.S.C. §6325	5.14
26 U.S.C. §7425(c)(2)	5.14
28 U.S.C. §2410(e)	5.14
50 U.S.C. §§501—591	5.24
50 U.S.C.App. §520	1.26

INDEX TO CASES

Section

Abramson v. Lakewood Bank & Trust Co., 649 F.2d 547
    (5th Cir. 1981) 5.49
Adkins v. Edwards, 317 So.2d 770 (Fla. 2d DCA 1975) 4.16
Adkinson v. Nyberg, 344 So.2d 614 (Fla. 2d DCA 1977) 9.14
American Insulation of Ft. Walton Beach, Inc. v. Pruitt,
    378 So.2d 839 (Fla. 1st DCA 1980).......................... 6.14
American International Land Corp. v. Hanna,
    323 So.2d 567 (Fla. 1976) 9.6
American National Bank of Jacksonville v. Norris, 368
    So.2d 897 (Fla. 1st DCA 1979), *cert. den.* 378 So.2d 342 .... 10.15
Ardell v. Milner, 166 So.2d 714 (Fla. 3d DCA 1964) 15.11
Arkin Construction Co. v. Reynolds Metals Co.,
    310 F.2d 11 (5th Cir. 1962)................................... 10.7
Avvenire College for Women, Inc. v. G. B. D., Inc.,
    240 So.2d 191 (Fla. 4th DCA 1970) 15.44, 15.46

B & J Holding Corp. v. Weiss, 353 So.2d 141
    (Fla. 3d DCA 1978)... 10.6
Babsdon Co. v. Thrifty Parking Co., 149 So.2d 566
    (Fla. 3d DCA 1963)... 15.57
Baer v. General Motors Acceptance Corp., 101 Fla. 913,
    132 So. 817 (1931) 15.13
Baker v. Clifford-Mathew Inv. Co., 99 Fla. 1229,
    128 So. 827 (1930) 15.1, 15.11, 15.37, 15.40, 15.46
Barber v. Rader, 350 F.Supp. 183 (S.D. Fla. 1972) 15.87, 15.92
Batavia, Ltd. v. United States, Department of Treasury,
    Internal Revenue Service, 393 So.2d 1207
    (Fla. 1st DCA 1981) 5.5, 5.13
Belize Airways Ltd., In re, BCD 637 (S.D. Fla. 1980) 15.3
Benefield v. State, 160 So.2d 706 (Fla. 1964)........................ 12.4
Berry v. Clement, 346 So.2d 105 (Fla. 2d DCA 1977) 15.35
Berwick Corp. v. Kleinginna Investment Corp.,
    143 So.2d 684 (Fla. 3d DCA 1962) 15.83
Besett v. Basnett, 389 So.2d 995 (Fla. 1980) 9.8
Bloom v. Weiser, 348 So.2d 651 (Fla. 3d DCA 1977) 14.4
Bosso v. Neuner, 426 So.2d 1209 (Fla. 4th DCA 1983) 9.6
Bowles v. Blue Lake Development Corp., 504 F.2d 1094
    (5th Cir. 1974) 15.44
Brady v. Scott, 128 Fla. 582, 175 So. 724 (1937)..................... 15.70
Brooks v. Fletcher, 393 So.2d 630 (Fla. 4th DCA 1981) 2.14

Brooks v. Peters, 157 Fla. 141, 25 So.2d 205 (1946),
    overruled 401 So.2d 1329 .... 15.78
Brownlee v. Sussman, 238 So.2d 317
    (Fla. 3d DCA 1970).......................... 15.44, 15.46, 15.84
Byrd v. Culver, 376 So.2d 41 (Fla. 4th DCA 1979) 3.10

Cabre v. Brown, 355 So.2d 846 (Fla. 1st DCA 1978) 15.16
Camara v. Municipal Court of the City and County of
    San Francisco, 387 U.S. 523, 87 S.Ct. 1727,
    18 L.Ed.2d 930 (1967) 12.4
Carey v. Beyer, 75 So.2d 217 (Fla. 1954) 14.7
Case v. Guise, 6 N.E.2d 469 (Ill. App.Ct. 1937) 15.60
Casino Amusement Co. v. Ocean Beach Amusement Co.,
    101 Fla. 59, 133 So. 559 (1931) 15.59
Cathcart v. Turner, 18 Fla. 837 (1882) 15.15
Chandler Leasing Div. v. Florida Vanderbilt Dev. Corp.,
    464 F.2d 267 (5th Cir. 1972)................................. 15.57
Childs v. Eltinge, 105 Cal.Rptr. 864 (4th DCA 1973)................ 15.44
Chotka v. Fidelco Growth Investors, 383 So.2d 1169
    (Fla. 2d DCA 1980)... 10.12
City of Miami v. St. Joe Paper Co., 364 So.2d 439
    (Fla. 1978), *app. dism.* 441 U.S. 939 .... 1.31
City of Miami Beach v. Ocean & Inland Co., 147 Fla. 480,
    3 So.2d 364 (1941)... 12.3
Coast Federal Savings & Loan Assoc. v. DeLoach,
    362 So.2d 982 (Fla. 2d DCA 1978) 15.57
Cohen v. Cohen, 400 So.2d 463 (Fla. 4th DCA 1981) 5.34
Coleman v. State ex rel. Carver, 119 Fla. 653,
    161 So. 89 (1935) 15.10
Collier County Publishing Co., Inc. v. Chapman, 318 So.2d
    492 (Fla. 2d DCA 1975), *cert. den.* 333 So.2d 462 .... 14.3—.4
Combs v. St. Joe Papermakers Federal Credit Union,
    383 So.2d 298 (Fla. 1st DCA 1980)............................ 6.7
Continental Development Corp. of Florida v. Duval Title
    & Abstract Co., 356 So.2d 925 (Fla. 2d DCA 1978)............. 14.4
Crane Co. v. Fine, 221 So.2d 145 (Fla. 1969) 6.1, 6.7
Cunningham Drug Stores, Inc. v. Pentland Drug Stores,
    243 So.2d 169 (Fla. 4th DCA 1971) 15.60

Dade County, Florida v. Palmer & Baker Engineers, Inc.,
    318 F.2d 18 (5th Cir. 1963).................................. 10.3
Davis v. Drummond, 68 Fla. 471, 67 So. 99 (1914) 15.53
Davis v. Flato, 210 So.2d 16 (Fla. 4th DCA 1968) 15.44

Deauville Corp. v. Garden Suburbs Golf & Country Club,
    164 F.2d 430 (5th Cir. 1947), *cert. den.* 333 U.S. 881 ..... 15.37, 1 5.46
Department of Business Regulation v. National Manufactured
    Housing Federation, Inc., 370 So.2d 1132 (Fla. 1979) 15.103
Deseret Ranches of Florida, Inc. v. Bowman, 349 So.2d 155
    (Fla. 1977) 12.10
De Vore v. Lee, 158 Fla. 608, 30 So.2d 924 (1947) 15.68
Diehl v. Gibbs, 173 So.2d 719 (Fla. 1st DCA 1965) 15.57
Dobbs v. Petko, 207 So.2d 11 (Fla. 4th DCA 1968).................. 15.57
Dooley v. Culver, 392 So.2d 575 (Fla. 4th DCA 1980) 15.67
Drexel Properties, Inc. v. Bay Colony Club Condominium,
    Inc., 406 So.2d 515 (Fla. 4th DCA 1981), *review*
    den. 417 So.2d 328 .... 10.6
Durrett v. Washington National Insurance Co.,
    621 F.2d 201 (5th Cir. 1980)................................ 5.49

Easton v. Weir, 125 So.2d 115 (Fla. 2d DCA 1960),
    cert. den. 129 So.2d 141 .... 15.78
Edward L. Nezelek, Inc. v. Southern Bell Telephone &
    Telegraph Co., 383 So.2d 979 (Fla. 4th DCA 1980) 10.3
Edwards v. Habib, 379 F.2d 687 (D.C. Cir. 1968),
    cert. den. 393 U.S. 101 .... 15.95
Eichman v. Paton, 393 So.2d 655 (Fla. 1st DCA 1981) 4.2
Eli Einbinder v. Miami Ice Co., 317 So.2d 126
    (Fla. 3d DCA 1975)... 15.7

Federal Land Bank of St. Paul v. Hassler,
    595 F.2d 356 (6th Cir. 1979)................................ 5.73
Filaretou v. Christou, 133 So.2d 652 (Fla. 2d DCA 1961)....... 15.46, 15.84
Financial Federal Savings & Loan Association of Dade
    County v. Continental Enterprises, Inc., 338 So.2d 907
    (Fla. 3d DCA 1976)................................... 10.12, 10.14
First Atlantic Building Corp. v. Neubauer Construction Co.,
    352 So.2d 103 (Fla. 4th DCA 1977) 6.14
First Prudential Development Corp. v. Hospital Mortgage Group,
    390 So.2d 767 (Fla. 3d DCA 1980),
    overruled 411 So.2d 181 .... 10.15
Flamingo Blueprint, Inc. v. Monumental Properties of Florida,
    Inc., 358 So.2d 86 (Fla. 3d DCA 1978) 15.44
Floro v. Parker, 205 So.2d 363 (Fla. 2d DCA 1968) 15.48
Frank v. Maryland, 359 U.S. 360, 79 S.Ct. 804, 3 L.Ed.2d
    877 (1959), *reh. den.* 360 U.S. 914.......................... 12.4
Freedman v. Geiger, 314 So.2d 189 (Fla. 3d DCA 1975).............. 15.94
Fuentes v. Shevin, 407 U.S. 67, 92 S.Ct. 1983,
    32 L.Ed.2d 556 (1972) 15.87

G. M. C. A. Corp. v. Noni, Inc., 227 So.2d 891
    (Fla. 3d DCA 1969) 15.16
Gables Lincoln-Mercury, Inc. v. First Bank & Trust Co.
    of Boca Raton, 219 So.2d 90 (Fla. 3d DCA 1969) 15.87
Ganey v. Byrd, 383 So.2d 652 (Fla. 1st DCA 1980) 12.10
Gates v. Stucco Corp., 112 So.2d 36 (Fla. 3d DCA 1959) 15.5
Gates v. Utsey, 177 So.2d 486 (Fla. 1st DCA 1965) 14.4
Geiger Mutual Agency, Inc. v. Wright, 233 So.2d 444
    (Fla. 4th DCA 1970) 15.57
General Development Corp. v. John H. Gossett
    Construction Co., 370 So.2d 380 (Fla. 2d DCA 1979) 6.14
Glusman v. Lieberman, 285 So.2d 29 (Fla. 4th DCA 1973) 14.4
Grant v. Strickland, 385 So.2d 1123 (Fla. 1st DCA 1980),
    review den. 392 So.2d 1374 .... 2.9
Gray v. Mattingly, 399 S.W.2d 301 (Ky. 1966) 10.6
Greene v. Galloway, 332 So.2d 52 (Fla. 1st DCA 1976) 4.29
Greene v. Lindsey, 456 U.S. 444, 102 S.Ct. 1874,
    72 L.Ed.2d 249 (1982) 15.43, 15.93
Grossman Holdings Ltd. v. Hourihan, 414 So.2d 1037
    (Fla. 1982) 10.6

Hankins v. Smith, 103 Fla. 892, 138 So. 494 (1931) 15.59, 15.83
Hanna v. American International Land Corp., 289 So.2d 756
    (Fla. 2d DCA 1974), *rev.* 323 So.2d 567 .... 9.6
Harper v. Green, 99 Fla. 1309, 128 So. 827 (1930) 8.5
Heinlein v. Metropolitan Dade County, 239 So.2d 635
    (Fla. 3d DCA 1970) 12.4
Henry v. Ecker, 415 So.2d 137 (Fla. 5th DCA 1982) 3.7
Hill v. State ex rel. Watson, 155 Fla. 245, 19 So.2d 857
    (1944), *rev.* 325 U.S. 538 .... 12.4
Hodges v. Cooksey, 33 Fla. 715, 15 So. 549 (1894) 15.15
Hoskin v. Hoskin, 329 So.2d 19 (Fla. 3d DCA 1976) 4.2
Housholder v. Black, 62 So.2d 50 (Fla. 1952) 15.59
Hunt v. Covington, 145 Fla. 706, 200 So. 76 (1941) 4.2
Hunt v. Hiland, 366 So.2d 42 (Fla. 4th DCA 1978) 15.11
Hyman v. Cohen, 73 So.2d 393 (Fla. 1954) 15.57

J. E. DeBelle Co., 286 Fed. 699 (S.D. Fla. 1923) 15.13
Jacobs v. Kirk, 223 So.2d 795 (Fla. 4th DCA 1969 .... 15.127
James T. Barnes & Co. v. United States, 593 F.2d 352
    (8th Cir. 1979) 5.73
Jimmy Hall's Morningside, Inc. v. Blackburn & Peck
    Enterprises, Inc., 235 So.2d 344 (Fla. 2d DCA 1970) 15.57

Jim Walter Homes, Inc. v. Castillo, 616 S.W.2d 630
    (Tex. App. 1981), 18 A.L.R.4th 1331 .... 10.6
Jones v. Styles, 46 Fla.Supp. 175 (Palm Beach County 1977).......... 15.84

Kanter v. Safran, 82 So.2d 508 (Fla. 1955) 15.57
Kanter v. Safran, 68 So.2d 553 (Fla. 1953) 15.57
Katz v. Kenholtz, 147 So.2d 342 (Fla. 3d DCA 1963) 15.57
Kendig v. Kendall Construction Co., 317 So.2d 138
    (Fla. 4th DCA 1975) 15.95
Keyes Co. v. Shea, 372 So.2d 493 (Fla. 4th DCA 1979) 15.60
King v. Carden, 237 So.2d 26 (Fla. 1st DCA 1970) 2.14
Kittrell v. Clark, 363 So.2d 373 (Fla. 1st DCA 1978),
    cert. den. 383 So.2d 909 .... 1.31
Knight v. Global Contact Lens, Inc., 220 So.2d 693
    (Fla. 3d DCA 1969).. 15.4
Knight Manor # One, Inc. v. Freeman, 254 So.2d 375
    Fla. 3d DCA 1971) 15.46
Kohl v. Bay Colony Club Condominium, Inc., 398 So.2d 865
    (Fla. 4th DCA 1981), *review den.* 408 So.2d 1094 .... 15.65
Kugeares v. Casino, Inc., 372 So.2d 1132 (Fla. 2d DCA 1979).... 15.4, 15.44

Leader Mortgage Co. v. Rickards Electric Service, Inc.,
    348 So.2d 1202 (Fla. 4th DCA 1977) 5.34
Lehman v. Goldin, 160 Fla. 710, 36 So.2d 259 (1948) 14.3
Levenson v. Barnett Bank of Miami, 330 So.2d 192
    (Fla. 3d DCA 1976).. 10.15
Lindsey v. Normet, 405 U.S. 56, 92 S.Ct. 862,
    3 L.Ed.2d 36 (1972) 15.84
Lloyd v. Cannon, 399 So.2d 1095 (Fla. 1st DCA 1981),
    review den. 408 So.2d 1092 .... 10.13
Lovett v. Lee, 141 Fla. 395, 193 So. 538 (1940)...................... 15.12
Lowe v. Turpie, 44 N.E. 25 (Ind. 1896) 10.14

McCready v. Booth, 398 So.2d 1000
    (Fla. 5th DCA 1981) 15.57, 15.92, 15.127
McKenzie v. Atlantic Manor, Inc., 181 So.2d 554
    (Fla. 3d DCA 1966), *cert. den.* 192 So.2d 495 .... 15.78
Major Holding Corp. v. Butler, 138 Fla. 633,
    190 So. 15 (1939) 15.57
Mansur v. Eubanks, 401 So.2d 1328 (Fla. 1981)................ 15.66, 15.78

Marshall v. Barlow's, Inc., 436 U.S. 307, 98 S.Ct. 1816,
    56 L.Ed.2d 305 (1978) 12.4
Martin v. Estate of Ricks, 363 So.2d 636
    (Fla. 3d DCA 1978) 4.29
Masser v. London Operating Co., 106 Fla. 474,
    145 So. 79 (1932) 15.37, 15.44
Middleton v. Lomaskin, 266 So.2d 678 (Fla. 3d DCA 1972) 15.66
Miller v. Belknap, 266 P.2d 662 (Idaho 1954) 15.60
Moffett v. MacArthur, 291 So.2d 134 (Fla. 4th DCA 1974) 15.35
Morgen-Oswood & Associates, Inc. of Florida v. Continental
    Mortgage Investors, 323 So.2d 684 (Fla. 4th DCA 1976),
    cert. dism. 342 So.2d 1100 .... 10.12
Mori v. Matsushita Electric Corp. of America, 380 So.2d 461
    (Fla. 3d DCA 1980), *cert. den.* 389 So.2d 1112 .... 10.3
Morris v. Knox Corp., 153 Fla. 130, 13 So.2d 914 (1943) 15.37
Moskos v. Hand, 247 So.2d 795 (Fla. 4th DCA 1971) ...... 15.40—.41, 15.66
Mullane v. Lorenz, 372 So.2d 168 (Fla. 4th DCA 1979) 15.60

Naurison v. Naurison, 132 So.2d 623 (Fla. 3d DCA 1961) 4.2
Nevins Drug Co., Inc. v. Bunch, 63 So.2d 329 (Fla. 1953) 15.44, 15.46
New Rawson Corp. v. United States, 55 F.Supp. 291
    (D. Mass. 1943) 15.60
Norin Mortgage Corp. v. Wasco, Inc., 343 So.2d 940
    (Fla. 2d DCA 1977) 10.12, 10.14
North Port Bank v. State, Department of Revenue,
    313 So.2d 683 (Fla. 1975) 15.84

Old Plantation Corp. v. Maule Industries, 68 So.2d 180
    (Fla. 1953) 14.7
Orr v. Peek, 142 Fla. 160, 194 So. 341 (1940) 15.13
Overland Construction Co., Inc. v. Sirmons,
    369 So.2d 572 (Fla. 1979) 10.10

Painter v. Town of Groveland, 79 So.2d 765 (Fla. 1955) 15.9, 15.73
Palm Court v. 183rd Street Theatre Corp., 344 So.2d 252
    (Fla. 3d DCA 1977), *cert. den.* 355 So.2d 516 ..... 15.35, 15.44, 15.4 6
Paradis v. Thomas, 150 So.2d 457 (Fla. 2d DCA 1963) 15.60
Paul v. Kanter, 172 So.2d 26 (Fla. 3d DCA 1965) 15.59
Peter Marich & Associates, Inc. v. Powell,
    365 So.2d 754 (Fla. 2d DCA 1978) 6.14
Phillips v. Guin & Hunt, Inc., 344 So.2d 568 (Fla. 1977) 15.18

Plantation Key Developers, Inc. v. Colonial Mortgage Co.
   of Indiana, Inc., 589 F.2d 164 (5th Cir. 1979) 10.14
Platt v. Kenco Chemical Co., Inc., 132 So.2d 27
   (Fla. 3d DCA 1961) 15.44
Poranski v. Millings, 82 So.2d 675 (Fla. 1955) 10.7
Powell v. Lounel, Inc., 173 F.2d 743 (5th Cir. 1949) 15.13
Powers v. Coates, 203 A.2d 425 (D.C. App. 1964) 15.60
Prahl v. Johnson, 323 So.2d 682 (Fla. 3d DCA 1975) 15.5
Procacci v. Zacco, 402 So.2d 425 (Fla. 4th DCA 1981) 14.4
Publix Theatres Corp. v. Powell, 71 S.W.2d 237
   (Tex. Ct.App. 1934) 15.60

Rader v. Prather, 100 Fla. 591, 130 So. 15 (1930).................... 15.44
Rakover v. Blum, 13 N.Y.S.2d 464 (N.Y. App.Div. 1939)............. 15.60
Rice v. First Federal Savings & Loan Association of
   Lake County, 207 So.2d 22 (Fla. 2d DCA 1968),
   cert. den. 212 So.2d 879 .... 10.12
Richards v. Dodge, 150 So.2d 477 (Fla. 2d DCA 1963).............. 15.83
Robbins v. C. W. Myers Trading Post, Inc., 111 S.E.2d 884
   (N.C. 1960) 10.6
Robinson v. Loyola Foundation, Inc., 236 So.2d 154
   (Fla. 1st DCA 1970) 15.57
Robinson v. Peterson, 375 So.2d 294 (Fla. 2d DCA 1979) 15.57
Rodeway Inns of America v. Alpaugh, 390 So.2d 370
   (Fla. 2d DCA 1980)................................... 15.57, 15.65
Rogers v. Parker, 241 So.2d 428 (Fla. 2d DCA 1970) 15.127
Rubin v. Randwest Corp., 292 So.2d 60 (Fla. 4th DCA 1974),
   cert. den. 305 So.2d 786 .... 15.63, 15.66
Ruge v. Webb Press Co., 71 Fla. 536, 71 So. 627 (1916) 15.16
Ruhl v. Perry, 390 So.2d 353 (Fla. 1980) 5.12
Ruotal Corp. N. W., Inc. v. Ottati, 391 So.2d 308
   (Fla. 4th DCA 1980) 15.57
Ryan v. Town of Manalapan, 414 So.2d 193 (Fla. 1982).............. 11.17

Sailboat Key, Inc. v. Gardner, 378 So.2d 47
   (Fla. 3d DCA 1980).............................. 14.3—.4, 14.7
S. C. M. Associates, Inc. v. Rhodes, 395 So.2d 632
   (Fla. 2d DCA 1981) 6.14
S/D Enterprises, Inc. v. Chase Manhattan Bank,
   374 So.2d 1121 (Fla. 3d DCA 1979) 10.13
Sea Tower Apartments, Inc. v. Century National Bank,
   406 So.2d 69 (Fla. 4th DCA 1981) 15.65
Selective Builders, Inc. v. Hudson City Savings Bank,
   349 A.2d 564 (N.J. 1975) 10.14

Sentry Water Systems, Inc. v. ADCA Corp., 355 So.2d 1255
    (Fla. 2d DCA 1978)... 15.57
Sill v. Smith, 177 So.2d 265 (Fla. 2d DCA 1965) 15.7
6701 Realty, Inc. v. Deauville Enterprises, Inc.,
    84 So.2d 325 (Fla. 1956) 15.11, 15.59
South Dade Farms v. B. & L. Farms Co., 62 So.2d 350
    (Fla. 1952) 12.10
Southeastern Fidelity Insurance Co. v. Berman,
    231 So.2d 249 (Fla. 3d DCA 1970) 15.48
Southampton Wholesale Food Terminal v. Providence
    Produce Warehouse Co., 129 F.Supp. 663 (D. Mass. 1955) 10.14
State v. Johnson, 372 So.2d 536 (Fla. 4th DCA 1979),
    cert. den. 385 So.2d 758 .... 12.4
State ex rel. Attias v. Blanton, 195 So.2d 870
    (Fla. 3d DCA 1967)....................................... 15.44
State ex rel. Hillman v. Hutchins, 118 Fla. 220,
    158 So. 716 (1935) 15.46
State ex rel. Peters v. Hendry, 159 Fla. 210,
    31 So.2d 254 (1947) 15.44
State ex rel. Rich v. Ward, 135 Fla. 885,
    185 So. 846 (1939) 15.44
Stegeman v. Burger Chef Systems, Inc., 374 So.2d 1130
    (Fla. 1st DCA 1979) 15.60
Stein v. Darby, 126 So.2d 313 (Fla. 1st DCA 1961),
    cert. den. 134 So.2d 232 .... 12.10
Stephenson v. National Bank of Winter Haven,
    92 Fla. 347, 109 So. 424 (1926) 15.60
Sterritt v. Baker, 333 So.2d 523 (Fla. 1st DCA 1976) 10.15
Susman v. Schuyler, 328 So.2d 30 (Fla. 3d DCA 1976)................ 14.4
Sussman v. Damian, 355 So.2d 809 (Fla. 3d DCA 1977) 14.4

Temple Beth Sholom & Jewish Center, Inc. v. Thyne
    Construction Corp., 399 So.2d 525 (Fla. 2d DCA 1981) 10.6
The Board of Public Instruction of Dade County v. Town
    of Bay Harbor Islands, 81 So.2d 637 (Fla. 1955) 11.17
Tirrell v. Osborn, 55 A.2d 725 (D.C. App. 1947) 15.60
Tollius v. Dutch Inns of America, Inc., 244 So.2d 467
    (Fla. 3d DCA 1970), *cert. den.* 247 So.2d 437 .... 15.46
Toombs v. Gil, 353 So.2d 934 (Fla. 3d DCA 1978) 1.6
Trading Post of Naples, Inc. v. Howl, 371 So.2d 221
    (Fla. 2d DCA 1979)....................................... 15.59
Travelers Insurance Co. v. Lawrence, 509 F.2d 83
    (9th Cir. 1974) 5.73
Tropical Attractions, Inc. v. Coppinger, 187 So.2d 395
    (Fla. 3d DCA 1966)................................. 15.41, 15.46

Trustees of Cameron-Brown Investment Group v.
    Tavormina, 385 So.2d 728 (Fla. 3d DCA 1980) 5.34
Tullis v. Tullis, 360 So.2d 375 (Fla. 1978) 4.2

U.S. v. S.K.A. Associates, Inc., 600 F.2d 513
    (5th Cir. 1979) 15.16
United States v. Vehan, 110 U.S. 338, 4 S.Ct. 81,
    28 L.Ed. 168 (1884) 10.3
United States v. Weissman, 135 So.2d 235
    (Fla. 2d DCA 1961) 15.16
United States Life Insurance Co. in the City of
    New York v. Town & Country Hospital, Inc.,
    390 So.2d 71 (Fla. 2d DCA 1980), *review den.*
    399 So.2d 1147 .... 10.15

Vandeventer v. Dale Construction Co., 534 P.2d 183
    (Ore. 1975), 82 A.L.R.3d 1108 .... 10.14
Van Hoose v. Robbins, 165 So.2d 209
    (Fla. 2d DCA 1964) 15.11, 15.17, 15.87
Vaughan v. Mayo Milling Co., 102 S.E. 597 (Va. 1920) 15.60
Vines v. Emerald Equipment Co., 342 So.2d 137
    (Fla. 1st DCA 1977) 15.11
Vista Landscaping, Inc. v. Heck, 366 So.2d 1264
    (Fla. 4th DCA 1979) 10.12
Vogel v. Vandiver, 373 So.2d 366 (Fla. 2d DCA 1979) 9.6

Wagner v. Rice, 97 So.2d 267 (Fla. 1957) 15.57
Waln v. Howard, 142 Fla. 736, 196 So. 210 (1940) 15.70
Wilisch v. Wilisch, 335 So.2d 861 (Fla. 3d DCA 1976) 4.2, 4.29
Wilkerson v. Gibbs, 405 So.2d 1053 (Fla. 1st DCA 1981) 3.12
Wilkins v. Tebbetts, 216 So.2d 477 (Fla. 3d DCA 1968),
    cert. dism. 222 So.2d 753 .... 15.95
Williams v. Aeroland Oil Co., 155 Fla. 114,
    20 So.2d 346 (1944) 15.5, 15.57
Winter v. Surfview Realty, Inc., 400 So.2d 839
    (Fla. 5th DCA 1981) 9.21
Wolfe v. Hall, 61 Fla. 492, 54 So. 777 (1911) 15.53
Woodmere North Investment Fund Ltd. v. Guardian
    Mortgage Investors, 393 So.2d 563 (Fla. 3d DCA
    1981), *review den.* 402 So.2d 614 .... 10.15

INDEX TO SUBJECTS

References are to sections

ACCESS TO PROPERTY
Public rights in private property 12.4
Rights-of-way
   Landlocked landowner 12.10
Warrantless code enforcement inspections 12.4

BOUNDARY LITIGATION
Adverse possession
   Color of title, without
      Substantial enclosure, requirement of 2.9

CONTRACTS FOR SALE
Buyer's action for seller's breach
   Damages, measure
      Bad faith 9.6

CONSTRUCTION CONTRACTS AND LOAN AGREEMENTS, BREACHES OF
Contracts
  Action by owner when contractor fails to perform
    Complaint, form 10.11
    Conditions precedent 10.7
    Damages
      Generally 10.6
      Mitigation of 10.9
    Economic waste 10.6
    Investigation 10.5
    Penalty provision 10.8
    Reconstruction, cost of 10.6
    Statutes of limitation 10.10
  Remedies available
    Arbitration 10.4
    Contractor against owner 10.3
    Owner against contractor 10.2
Loan agreements
  Lender liability to borrower 10.15
  Remedies
    Borrower, breach by 10.13
    Damages, measure of 10.14
    Equitable liens 10.12
    Lender, breach by 10.14

CONSTRUCTION CONTRACTS AND LOAN AGREEMENTS, BREACHES OF
Loan agreements
  Remedies — *Continued*
    Money damages 10.12, 10.14
    Specific performance 10.12—.14

FORMS
Complaint
  Foreclosure
    Mechanic's lien
      Sub-subcontractor not in privity 6.17a
Landlord and tenant
  Disposition of abandoned personal property
    Right to reclaim, notice to former tenant 15.129—.130
    Right to reclaim, notice to person other than tenant 15.131—.132
  Mobile home lots
    Cause, termination of tenancy for 15.106
    Change of use, complaint for possession after 15.109
    Change of use, notice of termination of tenancy 15.108
    Default, final judgment on 15.116
    Fair market value, petition for determination of 15.118
    Final judgments 15.116—.117
    Nonpayment of rent, complaint for possession of lot for 15.105
    Possession of lot, complaints for
      Change of use 15.109
      Conviction of violation of law or ordinance 15.115
      Nonpayment of rent 15.105
      Rules and regulations, violation of 15.107
      Twelve months' notice 15.112—.113
    Rules and regulations, complaint for possession of lot for violation of 15.107
    Termination of tenancy
      Cause 15.106
      Change of use 15.108
      Conviction of law or ordinance, notice for 15.114
      Twelve months' notice 15.110—.111
  Three-day notice of termination for nonpayment of rent 15.104
Nonresidential tenancies
  Distress bond 15.22
  Distress complaint 15.20
  Distress writ
    Final judgment 15.32
    Final judgment after default 15.26
    Final judgment after default and for order of levy 15.25

FORMS
Landlord and tenant
  Nonresidential tenancies
    Distress writ — *Continued*
      Form for 15.24
    Summary removal, notice to tenant 15.39
    Tenancy at will, notice of termination 15.8
  Residential tenancies
    Failure to pay rent
      Eviction of tenant, complaint for 15.94
      Termination of lease, notice of 15.90
    Letter of termination of lease 15.91
    Mobile home lots *see* Mobile home lots
    Periodic tenancy, notice of termination 15.72
    Termination of lease for breach by tenant, notices of 15.89—.90
Quieting title
  Attorney ad litem, guardian ad litem, and administrator ad litem, appointment of
    Motion 1.25
    Order 1.26

LANDLORD AND TENANT
Administrative rent 15.1
Assumption of lease by bankruptcy trustee 15.1
Attorneys' fees 15.67
Disposition of abandoned personal property
  Forms *see* **FORMS**
  Generally 15.127
  Nonliability of landlord 15.127, 15.136
  Notification of tenant and other persons 15.128
  Release of property 15.134
  Removal of property 15.127
  Sale of property 15.135
  Sheriff, removal of property by 15.127
  Storage of property 15.133
Generally 15.1
Nonresidential relations
  Advance rent 15.59
  Bankruptcy Code, effect of 15.3
  Common-law action for damages 15.57
  Disposition of abandoned personal property *see* Disposition of abandoned personal property
  Distress for rent proceedings
    Bond
      Form 15.22
      Generally 15.21
    Complaint

LANDLORD AND TENANT
Nonresidential relations
  Distress for rent proceedings
    Complaint — *Continued*
      Form 15.20
      Generally 15.19
    Distress writ and levy
      Distrained property
        Sale on appeal 15.33—.34
        Tenant's right to return of 15.28
        Third party claims 15.27
      Final judgment
        Form 15.32
        Generally 15.31
      Final judgment after default and order of levy
        Form 15.26
        Motion for 15.26
      Form 15.24
      Generally 15.23
      Tenant's defenses 15.29
      Trial of issues 15.30
  Judicial declaration of termination of lease 15.58
  Jurisdiction 15.4
  Landlord's lien
    Advances 15.14
    Enforcement 15.17
    Exemptions 15.15
    Generally 15.12
    Priority 15.16
    Property kept on premises 15.13
  Ordinary wear and tear 15.60
  Reentry, right of 15.11
  Sale of distrained property on appeal
    Effect of appeal 15.34
    Generally 15.33
  Security interests, priority 15.16
  Self-help 15.11
  Statutory provisions 15.3
  Summary removal of tenant
    Complaint 15.42
    Counterclaims 15.44
    Defenses 15.46
    Generally 15.35
    Grounds for removal 15.36
    Judgment 15.47
    Notice
      Form 15.39

LANDLORD AND TENANT
Nonresidential relations
  Summary removal of tenant
    Notice — *Continued*
      Generally 15.38
      Service 15.38
      Waiver 15.40
    Rules of Civil Procedure, governed by 15.35
    Service of process 15.43
    Tenant's response
      Defenses 15.46
      Generally 15.44
      Time for 15.45
    Waiver of default by landlord 15.41
  Tenancies at will
    Failure to surrender possession 15.9
    Generally 15.6
    Termination
      Form for notice 15.8
      Generally 15.7
  Tenancy at sufference 15.10
  Unlawful detainer
    Complaint 15.50
    Damages 15.55
    Defendant's response 15.52
    Defenses 15.52
    Evidence 15.53
    Generally 15.48
    Judgment and execution 15.56
    Service of process 15.51
    Summons 15.51
    Trial 15.54
    Verdict 15.54
    When to use 15.49
  Venue 15.5
  Waste 15.60
  Ordinary wear and tear 15.60
Residential relations
  Abandonment 15.61
  Applicability 15.62
  Attorneys' fees 15.67
  Disposition of abandoned personal property *see* Disposition of abandoned personal property
  Dwelling unit defined 15.62, 15.97
  Effective date of Act 15.63
  Generally 15.61
  Landlord's duties and obligations
    Deposit money 15.76
    Duty of disclosure 15.75

LANDLORD AND TENANT
Residential relations
  Landlord's duties and obligations — *Continued*
    Generally 15.74
    Obligation to maintain premises 15.78
    Security deposits 15.77
  Landlord's rights and remedies
    Generally 15.86
    Lien on personal property 15.87
    Termination for breach by tenant
      Generally 15.88
      Letter of termination 15.91
      Notices, forms
        Breach of lease 15.89
        Failure to pay rent 15.90
  Lease agreements
    Attorneys' fees 15.67
    Exculpatory clauses 15.66
    Generally 154.64
    Unconscionable agreements 15.65
    Waiver of rights 15.66
  Mobile home lots
    Deposits 15.99
    Eviction 15.98
    Fees 15.99
    Forms
      Cause, termination of tenancy for 15.106
      Change of use, complaint for possession after 15.109
      Change of use, notice of termination of tenancy by reason of 15.108
      Default, final judgment on 15.116
      Fair market value, petition for determination of 15.118
      Final judgment
        After trial 15.117
        Default 15.116
      Nonpayment of rent, complaint for possession of lot for 15.105
      Possession of lot, complaints for
        Change of use 15.109
        Conviction of violation of law or ordinance 15.115
        Nonpayment of rent 15.105
        Rules and regulations, violation of 15.107
        Twelve months' notice
          Eviction of mobile home and owner 15.112
          Eviction of mobile home owner 15.113
      Rules and regulations, complaint for possession of lot for violation of 15.107
      Termination of tenancy
        Cause 15.106

LANDLORD AND TENANT
Residential Relations
  Mobile home lots
    Forms
      Termination of tenancy — *Continued*
        Change of use 15.108
        Conviction of law or ordinance, notice for 15.114
      Twelve months' notice
        Eviction of mobile home and owner 15.110
        Eviction of mobile home owner 15.111
      Three-day notice of termination for nonpayment of rent 15.104
    Generally 15.97
    Leases 15.101
    Rights and remedies of tenant 15.102
    Rules and regulations of mobile home parks 15.100
    State mobile home tenant-landlord commission 15.103
    Zoning 15.96
  Ordinary wear and tear 15.61
  Periodic tenancies
    Failure of tenant to surrender possession 15.73
    Termination of tenancies without specific duration
      Generally 15.70
      Notice of
        Form 15.72
        Generally 15.71
    Terms of tenancies without specific duration 15.69
    When rent payable 15.68
  Recovery of possession by landlord
    Eviction for failure to pay rent, form 15.94
    Generally 15.92
    Judgment for eviction 15.96
    Jurisdiction 15.93
    Procedure 15.93
    Tenant's defenses 15.95
  Rent, when payable 15.68
  Shelter as incident of employment 15.62
  Tenant's duties and obligations
    Generally 15.79
    Maintenance of dwelling unit 15.80
    Provide access by landlord to unit 15.81
  Tenant's rights and remedies
    Defenses to action for rent or possession 15.84
    Generally 15.82
    Right to terminate lease
      Casualty damage 15.85
      Failure of landlord to perform duties 15.83
  Waste 15.61

LANDLORD AND TENANT — *Continued*
Self-storage facilities
  Access, denial of 15.121
  Advertisement 15.124
  Applicability 15.119
  Generally 15.119
  Liens
    Enforcement 15.122
    Form for notice enforcing 15.123
    Generally 15.120
  Other matters 15.125
  Public sale, form for notice of 15.125
Statutory liens 15.1, 15.12, 15.87, 15.120

LIS PENDENS
Necessary and proper parties 5.5

MECHANIC'S LIEN FORECLOSURE
Prevailing party, who may be considered 6.14
Action on bond
  Notice, service of 6.21
Answer
  Damages, right to 6.25
Complaint
  Sub-subcontractor not in privity 6.17a
Construction, not subject to liberal 6.1
Improvements, exemption of 6.2
Lienor, defined 6.3

MORTGAGE FORECLOSURE
Alien corporation 5.5
Attorneys' fees, plaintiff's affidavit 5.34, 5.39a
Bankruptcy proceedings 5.78—.82
Final judgment
  Attorneys' fees
    Plaintiff's affidavit 5.34, 5.39a
Judicial sale
  Generally 5.41
  Notice 5.44
  Trustee in bankruptcy, setting aside sale 5.49
Partnerships 5.5
Post sale procedure
  Writ of possession
    Form 5.54
    Generally 5.53

MORTGAGE FORECLOSURE — *Continued*
Service of process
  Constructive
    Soldiers' and Sailors' Civil Relief Act, compliance with 5.24

PARTITION
Complaint
  Verification 4.13
  Estate by the entireties, not subject to 4.2

QUIETING TITLE
Attorney ad litem, guardian ad litem and administrator ad litem,
    appointment of
  Motion 1.25
  Order 1.26

REESTABLISHING LOST INSTRUMENTS
Best evidence rule, alternative method 8.1
Duplicate, defined 8.21

RESTRICTIVE COVENANTS, REMOVAL
Zoning changes 11.17

SLANDER OF TITLE
Intent, standard of 14.3
Privilege, defense of 14.4
Punitive damages 14.4